T0210736

Lecture Notes in Computer Science   11336

Commenced Publication in 1973
Founding and Former Series Editors:
Gerhard Goos, Juris Hartmanis, and Jan van Leeuwen

More information about this series at http://www.springer.com/series/7407

Jaideep Vaidya · Jin Li (Eds.)

Algorithms and Architectures for Parallel Processing

18th International Conference, ICA3PP 2018
Guangzhou, China, November 15–17, 2018
Proceedings, Part III

Springer

Editors
Jaideep Vaidya
Rutgers University
Newark, NJ, USA

Jin Li
Guangzhou University
Guangzhou, China

ISSN 0302-9743 ISSN 1611-3349 (electronic)
Lecture Notes in Computer Science
ISBN 978-3-030-05056-6 ISBN 978-3-030-05057-3 (eBook)
https://doi.org/10.1007/978-3-030-05057-3

Library of Congress Control Number: 2018962485

LNCS Sublibrary: SL1 – Theoretical Computer Science and General Issues

This Springer imprint is published by the registered company Springer Nature Switzerland AG
The registered company address is: Gewerbestrasse 11, 6330 Cham, Switzerland

Preface

Welcome to the proceedings of the 18th International Conference on Algorithms and Architectures for Parallel Processing (ICA3PP 2018), which was organized by Guangzhou University and held in Guangzhou, China, during November 15–17, 2018.

ICA3PP 2018 was the 18th event in a series of conferences devoted to research on algorithms and architectures for parallel processing. Previous iterations of the conference include ICA3PP 2017 (Helsinki, Finland, November 2017), ICA3PP 2016 (Granada, Spain, December 2016), ICA3PP 2015 (Zhangjiajie, China, November 2015), ICA3PP 2014 (Dalian, China, August 2014), ICA3PP 2013 (Vietri sul Mare, Italy, December 2013), ICA3PP 2012 (Fukuoka, Japan, September 2012), ICA3PP 2011 (Melbourne, Australia, October 2011), ICA3PP 2010 (Busan, Korea, May 2010), ICA3PP 2009 (Taipei, Taiwan, June 2009), ICA3PP 2008 (Cyprus, June 2008), ICA3PP 2007 (Hangzhou, China, June 2007), ICA3PP 2005 (Melbourne, Australia, October 2005), ICA3PP 2002 (Beijing, China, October 2002), ICA3PP 2000 (Hong Kong, China, December 2000), ICA3PP 1997 (Melbourne, Australia, December 1997), ICA3PP 1996 (Singapore, June 1996), and ICA3PP 1995 (Brisbane, Australia, April 1995).

ICA3PP is now recognized as the main regular event in the area of parallel algorithms and architectures, which covers many dimensions including fundamental theoretical approaches, practical experimental projects, and commercial and industry applications. This conference provides a forum for academics and practitioners from countries and regions around the world to exchange ideas for improving the efficiency, performance, reliability, security, and interoperability of computing systems and applications.

ICA3PP 2018 attracted over 400 high-quality research papers highlighting the foundational work that strives to push beyond the limits of existing technologies, including experimental efforts, innovative systems, and investigations that identify weaknesses in existing parallel processing technology. Each submission was reviewed by at least two experts in the relevant areas, on the basis of their significance, novelty, technical quality, presentation, and practical impact. According to the review results, 141 full papers were selected to be presented at the conference, giving an acceptance rate of 35%. Besides, we also accepted 50 short papers and 24 workshop papers. In addition to the paper presentations, the program of the conference included four keynote speeches and two invited talks from esteemed scholars in the area, namely: Prof. Xuemin (Sherman) Shen, University of Waterloo, Canada; Prof. Wenjing Lou, Virginia Tech, USA; Prof. Witold Pedrycz, University of Alberta, Canada; Prof. Xiaohua Jia, City University of Hong Kong, Hong Kong; Prof. Xiaofeng Chen, Xidian University, China; Prof. Xinyi Huang, Fujian Normal University, China. We were extremely honored to have them as the conference keynote speakers and invited speakers.

ICA3PP 2018 was made possible by the behind-the-scene effort of selfless individuals and organizations who volunteered their time and energy to ensure the success of this conference. We would like to express our special appreciation to Prof. Yang Xiang, Prof. Weijia Jia, Prof. Yi Pan, Prof. Laurence T. Yang, and Prof. Wanlei Zhou, the Steering Committee members, for giving us the opportunity to host this prestigious conference and for their guidance with the conference organization. We would like to emphasize our gratitude to the general chairs, Prof. Albert Zomaya and Prof. Minyi Guo, for their outstanding support in organizing the event. Thanks also to the publicity chairs, Prof. Zheli Liu and Dr Weizhi Meng, for the great job in publicizing this event. We would like to give our thanks to all the members of the Organizing Committee and Program Committee for their efforts and support.

The ICA3PP 2018 program included two workshops, namely, the ICA3PP 2018 Workshop on Intelligent Algorithms for Large-Scale Complex Optimization Problems and the ICA3PP 2018 Workshop on Security and Privacy in Data Processing. We would like to express our sincere appreciation to the workshop chairs: Prof. Ting Hu, Prof. Feng Wang, Prof. Hongwei Li and Prof. Qian Wang.

Last but not least, we would like to thank all the contributing authors and all conference attendees, as well as the great team at Springer that assisted in producing the conference proceedings, and the developers and maintainers of EasyChair.

November 2018   Jaideep Vaidya
                                                                                              Jin Li

Organization

General Chairs

Albert Zomaya — University of Sydney, Australia
Minyi Guo — Shanghai Jiao Tong University, China

Program Chairs

Jaideep Vaidya — Rutgers University, USA
Jin Li — Guangzhou University, China

Publication Chair

Yu Wang — Guangzhou University, China

Publicity Chairs

Zheli Liu — Nankai University, China
Weizhi Meng — Technical University of Denmark, Denmark

Steering Committee

Yang Xiang (Chair) — Swinburne University of Technology, Australia
Weijia Jia — Shanghai Jiaotong University, China
Yi Pan — Georgia State University, USA
Laurence T. Yang — St. Francis Xavier University, Canada
Wanlei Zhou — Deakin University, Australia

Program Committee

Pedro Alonso — Universitat Politècnica de València, Spain
Daniel Andresen — Kansas State University, USA
Cosimo Anglano — Universitá del Piemonte Orientale, Italy
Danilo Ardagna — Politecnico di Milano, Italy
Kapil Arya — Northeastern University, USA
Marcos Assuncao — Inria, France
Joonsang Baek — University of Wollongong, Australia
Anirban Basu — KDDI Research Inc., Japan
Ladjel Bellatreche — LIAS/ENSMA, France
Jorge Bernal Bernabe — University of Murcia, Spain
Thomas Boenisch — High-Performance Computing Center Stuttgart, Germany

Edward Jung	Kennesaw State University, USA
Georgios Kambourakis	University of the Aegean, Greece
Gabor Kecskemeti	Liverpool John Moores University, UK
Muhammad Khurram Khan	King Saud University, Saudi Arabia
Dieter Kranzlmüller	Ludwig Maximilian University of Munich, Germany
Michael Kuhn	University of Hamburg, Germany
Julian Kunkel	German Climate Computing Center, Germany
Algirdas Lančinskas	Vilnius University, Lithuania
Patrick P. C. Lee	The Chinese University of Hong Kong, SAR China
Laurent Lefevre	Inria, France
Hui Li	University of Electronic Science and Technology of China, China
Kenli Li	Hunan University, China
Dan Liao	University of Electronic Science and Technology of China, China
Jingyu Liu	Hebei University of Technology, China
Joseph Liu	Monash University, Australia
Yunan Liu	Jiangxi Normal University, China
Zheli Liu	Nankai University, China
Jay Lofstead	Sandia National Laboratories, USA
Paul Lu	University of Alberta, Canada
Amit Majumdar	University of California San Diego, USA
Tomas Margalef	Universitat Autonoma de Barcelona, Spain
Stefano Markidis	KTH Royal Institute of Technology, Sweden
Alejandro Masrur	Chemnitz University of Technology, Germany
Susumu Matsumae	Saga University, Japan
Raffaele Montella	University of Naples Parthenope, Italy
Francesco Moscato	University of Campania Luigi Vanvitelli, Italy
Bogdan Nicolae	Argonne National Laboratory, Germany
Francesco Palmieri	University of Salerno, Italy, Italy
Swann Perarnau	Argonne National Laboratory, USA
Dana Petcu	West University of Timisoara, Romania
Salvador Petit	Universitat Politècnica de València, Spain
Riccardo Petrolo	Rice University, USA
Florin Pop	University Politehnica of Bucharest, Romania
Radu Prodan	University of Klagenfurt, Austria
Zhang Qikun	Beijing Institute of Technology, China
Thomas Rauber	University Bayreuth, Germany
Khaled Riad	Zagazig University, Egypt
Suzanne Rivoire	Sonoma State University, USA
Ivan Rodero	Rutgers University, USA
Romain Rouvoy	University of Lille, France
Antonio Ruiz-Martínez	University of Murcia, Spain
Françoise Sailhan	CNAM, France
Sherif Sakr	The University of New South Wales, Australia
Giandomenico Spezzano	ICAR-CNR and University of Calabria, Italy

Contents – Part III

Big Data and Information Processing

Internet of Things and Cloud Computing

Big Data and Information Processing

TAMSA: Two-Stage Auction Mechanism for Spectrum Allocation in Cooperative Cognitive Radio Networks

Xinxiang Zhang, Jigang Wu[✉], and Long Chen

Guangdong University of Technology, Guangzhou 510006, China
zxx_0504@163.com, asjgwucn@outlook.com, lonchen@mail.ustc.edu.cn

Abstract. Cooperative cognitive radio networks have been proposed to address spectrum starvation problem and enhance the transmission rate of mobile devices. Most works assume one user could afford the whole spectrum and neglect the selfishness nature, which is not practical. Based on group-buying, a two-stage auction mechanism named TAMSA is proposed to guarantee the quality of service and improve the utilization ratio of spectrum resources. TAMSA is an incentive mechanism involving the primary users (PUs) and relay nodes. TAMSA can also reduce the cost of the secondary users (SUs) and increase utilities for both PUs and relay nodes. In the first stage, SUs submit their budgets, valuations and demands for spectrum resources to relay nodes in group-buying, relay nodes calculate revenues and determine the winning SUs. In the second stage, we execute VCG auction between the relay nodes and PUs, with a maximum-weighted-matching algorithm. TAMSA can effectively allocate spectrum resources to meet the demands of SUs. We show that TAMSA is truthful, individual rational and computational efficient. Extensive simulation results show that TAMSA outperforms random algorithm by 256% in terms of average utility of PUs. TAMSA is able to improve the average utility of SUs and relay nodes significantly up to 213% and 10 times respectively. TAMSA is further improved by 28.33% and 78.65% in terms of average utility of PUs over TASG and TACC, respectively.

Keywords: Spectrum allocation · VCG auction
Incentive mechanism · Cooperative cognitive radio networks

1 Introduction

With the explosive growth of smart phones, wearable devices and Internet of Things (IoT), they are demanding for higher data rates and lower latency. Spectrum resource is one of the most valuable resources for wireless communication devices. However, many spectrum resources have been allocated to licensed users. On one hand, existing un-used spectrum resources have become scarce. On the other hand, some used spectrum resources have not been fully utilized, such as

© Springer Nature Switzerland AG 2018
J. Vaidya and J. Li (Eds.): ICA3PP 2018, LNCS 11336, pp. 3–16, 2018.
https://doi.org/10.1007/978-3-030-05057-3_1

radio and TV-channel, resulting in spectrum cavitation [1–3]. Cognitive radio is proposed to solve the above problems to guarantee of Quality of Service (QoS) for mobile devices and improve the utility ratio of spectrum resources. To enhance the performance of cognitive radio networks (CRNs), cooperative cognitive radio networks (CCRNs) was proposed [4].

In CCRNs, there are two kinds of users, one is the spectrum holder, that is, the primary user (licensed user), denoted as PUs. The other is the secondary user (unlicensed user), represented by SUs [5]. The mobile devices with cognitive function can dynamically detect and utilize the idle spectrum resources. And the CCRNs allows SUs to access the licensed spectrum occupied by PUs to improve spectrum utilization [6,7], but SUs must not cause strong interference to the normal communication of PUs. CCRNs can improve the utilization ratio of spectrum resources by spectrum reuse.

Auction plays an important role in spectrum resources allocation since there have been numerous researches on spectrum allocation using auctions [8–10]. Most prior works design single-seller and multi-buyer auctions with homogeneous channels. In [1] and [4], authors design truthful auction for trading homogeneous channels between a seller and multiple SUs. Besides, a distributed resource allocation algorithm is adopted, and direct or cooperative transmission can be selected with multiple sellers and multiple buyers [5]. Many studies assume that PUs are willing to share their idle spectrum resources, In reality, PUs are usually selfish, hence it is necessary to provide incentives for PUs to participate in. Vickrey-Clarke-Groves (VCG) auction guarantees the truthfulness of the auction process, which provides a new idea for resources allocation and can effectively guarantee the economic returns of the participants. A McAfee based auction mechanism is proposed, which considers the cooperative transmission of relay nodes and ensures the maximum benefit of PUs, but it does not consider the revenues of relay nodes [7]. In existing works [11–13], authors propose VCG-based auction mechanism to maximize the utility of PUs and guarantee the truthfulness. However, the objective is to maximize the amount of PUs neglect the specific demands of SUs for spectrum resources.

In recent years, double auction [10], and combinatorial auction [11] have been considered in spectrum resources allocation. However, most works neglect data transmission cooperatively by relay nodes. Inspired by the popular group buying services on the Internet, authors in [13] and [14] propose auction algorithms based on group buying, which encourages SUs to be voluntarily grouped together to acquire the spectrum resources in spectrum auctions. The group buying algorithm can effectively reduce the payment of the SUs. In [12–14], they equally distribute the spectrum resources to the winning SUs. Besides, In [15], a multiple input and multiple output method is proposed in CRNs with cooperative communication. It allows SUs to help data transmission for PUs and obtain the opportunity to transmit data for themselves, but the mechanism has a higher requirement of hardware configuration. In this work, we reduce the payment of SUs with group buying. We allocate spectrum resources according to the specific demands of the SUs.

In order to effectively allocate spectrum resources and encourage PUs to share spectrum resources in auction we designed, we have to solve the following challenges. (1) Running applications on mobile devices are heterogeneous, so the budget and demand for each SUs are different. Besides, how to reduce the cost of SUs is a challenge. (2) For spectrum holders and relay nodes should be incentivized because of selfishness nature. Therefore, how to provide incentives should be designed for both PUs and relay nodes. (3) Auction should be truthful, budget balance, individual rational and computational efficient. Hence, the auction mechanism should ensure the above properties. Different from the previous works, we focus on investigating an incentive auction mechanism for efficient spectrum resource allocation in CCRN. TAMSA provides an incentive for both PUs and relay nodes to participate in auction. Besides, in the scenario, TAMSA is based on group buying to reduce the payments of SUs, and TAMSA allocates spectrum resources according to the specific demands of SUs.

The main contributions of this work are summarized as follows.

- To reduce the payment of SUs effectively, we propose an auction algorithm based on group buying for the specific demands of spectrum resources. The auction mechanism is applicable to heterogeneous networks. The economic properties, truthfulness, budget balance, individual rationality and computational efficiency are proved.
- We design an incentive mechanism to encourage spectrum holders to share their idle spectrum resources, and encourage relay nodes to transmit data cooperatively.
- Numerous numerical results demonstrate that TAMSA is superior to the algorithm Random by 256% in terms of average utility of PUs. The average utility of relay nodes and SUs in TAMSA outperforms Random by 10 times and 213% respectively. TAMSA is further improved by 28.33% and 78.65% in terms of average utility of PUs over TASG and TACC, respectively.

2   System Model and Problem Formulation

In this section, we not only focus on the system model, but also formulate the problem to be studied. And we introduce the related economic properties that auction scheme should be followed. The basic notations as shown in Table 1.

2.1   System Model

In this paper, we consider a cognitive network with multiple primary users and multiple secondary users. Besides, in order to improve the channel transmission rate, we take the relay node into account. In this scenario, as in [16], we assume all nodes stay static in a given auction period. TAMSA scheme aims to maximize the social welfare in a spectrum auction, which also encourages both PUs and SUs to participate in. To maximize the utilization of spectrum resources, the incentive mechanism should properly assign the matching between the spectrum

Table 1. Notations for system model.

Notations	Meaning
PUs	Set of primary users
SUs	Set of secondary users
R_i	The ith relay node, where $i \in [1, M]$
S_i	The ith group, where $i \in [1, n_i]$
s_i^j	The jth secondary user in the ith group, $1 \leq i \leq M, 1 \leq j \leq n_i$
$d_i^j(k)$	Demand of s_i^j for kth Channel (PU_k), $1 \leq k \leq M$
$b_i^j(k)$	The bid of s_i^j for kth Channel
$v_i^j(k)$	The valuation of s_i^j for kth Channel
A_k	Ask or reserve price of kth Channel
S_i^w	Set of winning secondary users, $1 \leq w \leq n_i$
R_i^w	Set of winning relay nodes
PU_i^w	Set of winning primary users
$p_i^j(k)$	The payment of s_i^j for kth Channel
$p_c(k)$	The clearing price
$F_i(k)$	$S_i(k)'s$ payment for kth relay node
$P_i(k)$	The ith relay node $R_i(k)'s$ payment for PU_k
$B_i(k)$	The bid of the ith relay node $R_i(k)$ for PU_k
u_i^j	The utility of s_i^j
U_{PU_k}	The utility of PU_k
U_{R_k}	The utility of R_k

resources and the demands of SUs. Trading between PUs and SUs should meet certain requirements to benefit both parties, so PUs need to be incentivized to provide resources, and the demands of SUs should be satisfied.

The proposed network model is shown in Fig. 1, which is a hierarchical auction consisting of m PUs and n_i SUs. The PUs possess M heterogeneous channels, and each primary user has a reserved price A_k, where $k \in [1, M]$, which is the lowest price the PU_i is willing to sell the kth channel. The PUs have different reserved prices A_k for spectrum, and we assume each relay node can buy at most one spectrum. In the ith group S_i, where $i \in [1, M]$, there are n SUs and $S_i = s_i^1, s_i^2, \cdots, s_i^n$, $n \in n_i$. Each s_i^j has a bid or budget $b_i^j(k)$ and a valuation $v_i^j(k)$ for the kth channel PU_k. And in order to improve the utilization of spectrum resources, each s_i^j submits the demand for spectrum $d_i^j(k)$ to the PU_k. The spectrum resource is allocated according to the specific demands of the SUs.

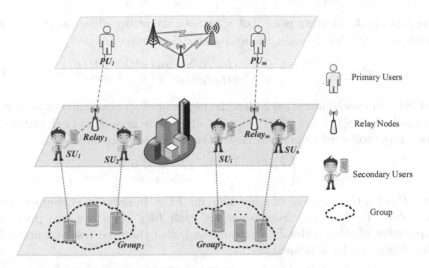

Fig. 1. Auction model.

We design an incentive mechanism to improve the utilities of PUs and relay nodes. TAMSA is a two-stage hierarchical auction, consisting of two-single round sealed bid auctions, called stage I auction and stage II auction respectively. In stage I, auction goes between relay nodes and the group of secondary users S_i, and in stage II, the auction conducts between PUs and relay nodes R_i, and the PUs sell their spectrum resources to relay nodes. The relay node $R_i(k)$ gathers bid and demand from the ith group S_i. Then system model executes the stage II auction. $R_i(k)$ submits the bid $B_i(k)$ to PU_k, and PU_k gives the reserve price A_k, where $k \in [1, M]$, noting that $B_i(k) \geq A_k$. The relay node $R_i(k)$ determines the winners in group $S_i(k)$ after gathering the ith group member's bids, and the set of winning SUs is denoted by $S_i^w(k)$, where $S_i^w(k) \subseteq S_i$, and the gathered bid is $F_i(k)$. We assume that each group pays for at most one relay node at the same time, because one relay node serves for multiple groups might cause transmission delay. If it wins in this auction, relay nodes R_i will allocate spectrum resources to the $S_i^w(k)$.

2.2   Problem Formulation

The system will determine the payment of winners. To achieve fairness, payments of winners should be proportional to the workloads of the demands. The payment of $s_i^j(k)$ is formulated as

$$p_i^j(k) = p_c(k) \cdot d_i^j(k), 1 \leq i \leq M, 1 \leq j \leq n_i \ and \ 1 \leq k \leq M, \tag{1}$$

where $p_c(k)$ is the clearing price. Let u_i^j denote the utility of secondary user s_i^j, for each $s_i^j \in S_i^w$. Accordingly, the utility of s_i^j is defined as

$$u_i^j = \begin{cases} v_i^j(k) - p_i^j(k), & if \ s_i^j \in S_i^w \ and \ p_i^j(k) \leq b_i^j(k) \\ 0, & otherwise. \end{cases} \tag{2}$$

What calls for special attention is that the payment of $s_i^j(k)$ should not be higher than the budget $b_i^j(k)$, $k \in [1, M]$, $s_i^j \in S_i^w$. The relay node $R_i(k)$ calculates the finance $F_i(k)$ collected from SUs. Hence the utility of relay node R_i is

$$U_{R_i} = \begin{cases} F_i(k) - P_i(k), & if \ R_i(k) \in R_i^w \\ 0, & otherwise. \end{cases} \tag{3}$$

Where $P_i(k)$ is the payment of relay node for PUs. In order to encourage spectrum holders to share spectrum resources, each PU_k has a reserved price A_k. The payment of relay nodes $P_i(k)$ should be higher than the reserved price A_k, so the utility of PU_k is defined as

$$U_{PU_k} = \begin{cases} P_i(k) - A_k, & if \ PU_k \in PU_k^w \ and \ R_i \in R_i^w \\ 0, & otherwise. \end{cases} \tag{4}$$

In this auction, the spectrum owners $PU_k s$ allocate spectrum resources to SUs. The speed of channel transmission is increased by the relay nodes cooperatively.

2.3   Economic Properties

In this section, we present several economic properties clearly that we would like to achieve. In an auction, it will not be executed until the economic properties are satisfied.

Definition 1 (Truthfulness). An auction is truthful. If it is a dominant strategy, any participant's utility will be maximized for the bidder's true valuation, and no bidder can improve its utility by misreporting its valuation. In this paper, it implies the auction mechanism designed by us. Each s_i^j submits true valuation to R_i, and each relay node R_i show its true valuation to the kth primary user PU_k.

Definition 2 (Budget Balance). An auction is in budget balance for participators if total payment from buyers are greater than the total revenue of sellers. In our mechanism, the auction is conducted in the form of group in tier I auction. We ensure the utilities of auctioneers are nonnegative. We make sure that the payments that the relay nodes receive from the group are no less than the amount paid to the PUs.

Definition 3 (Individual Rationality). An auction is individual rational. The utility of each participant is nonnegative. In TAMSA scheme, the utilities of SUs, relay nodes R_i and PUs are nonnegative. That is, u_i^j, U_{R_i} and U_{PU_k} are nonnegative.

Definition 4 (Computational Efficiency). An algorithm is computational efficient if the mechanism can terminate in polynomial time. In our auction mechanism, the selection of winning SUs, the matching of PUs and relay nodes, and the clearing price and payment can be completed in polynomial time.

3   Two-Stage Auction Mechanism

In this section, we propose a truthful two-stage auction framework called TAMSA for cognitive radio networks shown in Fig. 1. TAMSA consists of two sub-auctions, which satisfies these properties: truthfulness, budget balance, individual rationality and computational efficiency.

3.1   Stage I Auction

In this stage, the n_i secondary users are randomly divided into multiple groups. The groups submit their bids or budgets to relay nodes separately. Relay nodes will conduct the auction and decide the winning group members virtually. Then relay nodes calculate the payment of each winner and determine the final winners. It will allocate channels to SUs if it gets spectrum resources in tier II auction.

We first introduce the algorithm to buy the spectrum by group and decide the winners (GBDW), the details are as follows. Firstly, relay node R_i collects the bid vector $b_i^1, b_i^2, \cdots, b_i^{n_i}$, demand $d_i^1, d_i^2, \cdots, d_i^{n_i}$ and valuation $v_i^1, v_i^2, \cdots, v_i^{n_i}$ from SUs in S_i as previous mentioned. We design an algorithm to calculate the budget vector $F_i(k)$ for PU_k. Then, relay nodes decide the winner in the best performance ratio way and calculate the optimal unit price for each group. The relay node R_i sells at most $1/2$ time fraction to the S_i for maximizing the revenue. Inspired by the work in [16], we sort the vector of b/d in descending, then we can get the optimal unit price for group S_i, denoted as $OPT(b/d)$,

$$OPT(b/d) = \max_{1 \le i \le |b|} i \frac{b_i}{d_i}, \tag{5}$$

where $|b|$ denotes the length of the array, b_i and d_i denote the ith budget and demand separately. The detail of the algorithm is shown in Algorithm 1.

It should be noted that the clear price is extracted from the group to ensure truthfulness. Relay nodes select the maximum integer m by $OPT(b/d)$, and then eliminate m SUs with smallest budget and lowest valuation. $F_i(k)$ is the gathered bid from those winning SUs, and the PU_k charges $R_i(k)$ less than $F_i(k)$ for trading the kth channel.

In the example, we will show how Algorithm calculates the clearing price and determines the winner. We assume that there are 5 SUs in group i, and their budget and demands vector are as follows: $b = \{2, 3, 7, 6, 8\}$, $d = \{1, 2, 3, 2.5, 4\}$, so $b/d = \{2, 1.5, 2.33, 2.4, 2\}$, which can be obtained by Algorithm 1. We sort b/d in descending and calculate $OPT(b/d)$ to get the maximum m, hence we can get $m = 4$ and the clearing price is $p_c = 8/4 = 2$. S_i participates in the auction need to pay to the ith relay node is $p_i^1 = p_c \times d_i^1 = 2 \times 1 = 2$. In the same way, the payment of the other 4 secondary users can be calculated separately, which is 4, 6, 5 and 8. Therefore, the winners in ith group are s_i^1, s_i^3, s_i^4 and s_i^5, and the amount collected by the ith relay node is 21.

Algorithm 1. GBDW : Group Buying and Decide Winners

Input: Sorted vector of b/d and the valuation.
Output: The revenue of relay nodes, S_i^w and the payment of secondary users.

1: Let $1 \leq m \leq n_i - 1$ be a bid-independent integer.
2: Search for the maximum m in b/d gets the maximum $OPT(b/d)$.
3: $p_c = b_i^m / m$.
4: $S_i^w(k) \leftarrow \emptyset$
5: $F_i(k) \leftarrow \emptyset$
6: **for** $j \leftarrow 1$ to n_i **do**
7:   $p_i^j(k) \leftarrow p_c \cdot d_i^j(k)$, if $p_i^j(k) < b_i^j(k)$ and $p_i^j(k) < v_i^j(k)$
8:   **if** $p_i^j(k) < b_i^j(k)$ and $p_i^j(k) < v_i^j(k)$ **then**
9:       $S_i^w(k) \leftarrow S_i^w(k) \cup s_i^j(k)$
10:       $F_i(k) \leftarrow F_i(k) + p_i^j(k)$
11:   **end if**
12: **end for**
13: **return** $F_i(k), S_i^w(k)$.

3.2 Stage II Auction

In this procedure, auction conducts between PUs and relay nodes, and relay nodes compete for idle spectrum resources of PUs. According to previous research, McAfee auction mechanism cannot be utilized since it only suits for the scenario where there are homogeneous goods to trade [17]. In order to ensure the truthfulness of auction mechanism and apply to heterogeneous networks, we design a spectrum resource allocation algorithm SRA based on VCG auction mechanism.

The detail of SRA is shown in Algorithm 2. We apply VCG-based auction mechanism to maximize the social welfare, that is, the total utility of all the participating bidders. Relay node assigns spectrum resource to the S_i^w when it wins the primary user. Relay node R_i needs to pay for winning PU_k the reward P_i, which is calculated by algorithm SRA.

We use the bid of relay node $B_i(k)$ and the reserve price A_k to construct a weighted complete bipartite graph, and the weight is $(B_i(k) - A_k)$. Maximum-Weighted-Matching (MWM) can optimize all utility of participator in this auction. To ensure the truthfulness of auction, we apply VCG-based auction to calculate payments of relay nodes. The details are as follows.

4   Theoretical Analysis

In this section, we prove that TMASA satisfies the truthfulness, individual rationality, budget balance and computational efficiency.

Theorem 1. *TAMSA is truthful in the network.*

Proof. In the following, we focus on proving the dominant strategy for SUs. For buyer, $s_i^j(k) \in S_i$, it will submit its true bid and demand, because it reflects its true demand for spectrum resource.

Algorithm 2. SRA : Spectrum Resource Allocation

Input: $B_i(k), A_k, for \forall 1 \leq i \leq n_i$ and $1 \leq k \leq M$.
Output: R^w, PU^w, P_i.

1: $W \leftarrow \emptyset, E^* \leftarrow \emptyset, P_i \leftarrow \emptyset //$W is the edge set in the matching graph.
2: Create a weighted complete bipartite graph $G = (R, PU, W, w)$ and the weight of
   $w(R_i, PU_k) = B_i(k) - A_k$ if $B_i(k) \geq A_k$.
3: $E^* \leftarrow Maximum - Weighted - Matching(W)$.
4: **for** each $(R_i, PU_k) \in E^*$ **do**
5:     $R^w \leftarrow R^w \cup \{R_i\}, PU^w \leftarrow PU^w \cup \{PU_k\}$
6:     $W' \leftarrow W \backslash (R_i, PU_k), R' \backslash \leftarrow R \backslash \{R_i\}$
7:     $G_{-i} \leftarrow (R', PU, W', w)$
8:     $E^*_{-i} \leftarrow Maximum - Weighted - Matching(W')$
9:     $P_i \leftarrow w(E^*_{-i}) - (w(E^*) - w(R_i, PU_k)) + A_k$
10: **end for**
11: **return** R^w, PU^w, P_i.

For $s_i^j \in S_i$, it can improve its utility by changing its valuation and budget from the first branch of Eq. (2). Besides, inspired by [18], the clearing price p_c is randomly generated by the optimal price ratio.

For $R_i \in R^w$, it can obtain the maximum utility $max(B_i(k) - A_k)$ if it gets the spectrum resource in this auction. If $R_i \notin R^w$, it will fail during this auction and cannot get the spectrum resource, because $(B_i(k) - A_k) < 0$. If relay node R_i submits untruthful bid, the result will not change, when $B_i(k) < F_i(k)$. When $B_i(k) > F_i(k)$, the utility of relay node $U_{R_i}(k) = F_i(k) - P_i = F_i(k) - B_i(k) \leq 0$, if it submits untruthful bid.

Therefore, both relay nodes and SUs cannot improve their utility by submitting untruthful bids.

Theorem 2. *TAMSA is individual rational and budget balance.*

Proof. For SUs, the utility of $s_i^j(k)$ is calculated by $v_i^j(k) - p_i^j(k) > 0$, for $\forall s_i^j \in S_i^w$, and we have proved the individual rationality of SUs. Then we prove relay nodes are also individual rational. For relay node R_i, the minimum payment price for relay node $R_i(k)$ is A_k for $\forall R_i \in R^w$, $B_i^k \leq F_i(k)$ and $PU_k \in PU^w$. Besides, the utility of primary user $U_{PU_k} = F_i(k) - P_i \geq B_i(k) - A_k > 0$. Therefore, both buyers and sellers are willing to participate in the auction. They can all gain nonnegative utility, and TAMSA mechanism is of individual rationality and budget balance.

Theorem 3. *TAMSA is computational efficient.*

Proof. We now analyze the time complexity of algorithm TAMSA. In Algorithm 1, the time complexity of the sorting process is $O(n_i \log n_i)$. In Algorithm 2, it takes $O(max\{n_i, M\}^3)$ time by applying the algorithm maximum-weighted-matching. The time complexity of computing the payment is $O(n_i max\{n_i, M\}^3)$. Hence, TAMSA is computational efficient.

5   Numerical Results

In this section, we evaluate the performance of TAMSA. In heterogeneous network structure of we designed, this is the first incentive scheme proposed for the specific demands of second users and there are no existing auction schemes to compare with. Instead, We design the upper bound (Upper) and a random algorithm (Random) for TAMSA to compare with. Meanwhile, we also simulate algorithms TASG and TACC to compare with. The algorithm Upper uses the bids of buyers as the payment to maximize the revenue. In TASG and TACC, secondary users are divided into two sets randomly and selected the winning set from other side. TASG is based on VCG mechanism, and TACC sorts the reserve price A_k of primary users in ascending order and the budget $B_i(k)$ of relay nodes in descending order. The experiment tool is MATLAB, and the results are averaged for 100 repetitions.

We consider a heterogeneous network shown in Fig. 1. We assume that the number of PUs is $M = 5$, and there are 5 relay nodes to participate in this auction, and the number of SUs n_i varies from 20 to 120 with an increment of 20. We assume that the valuation of secondary users $v_i^j(k)$ and budget $b_i^j(k)$ are uniform distribution, and their ranges are denote as $U(50, 150)$ and $U(5, 10)$ respectively. The reserve price A_k comply with $U(10, 20)$ following [15–18].

5.1   Simulation Results

We first investigate the running time of TAMSA, and the results are shown in Figs. 2 and 3. From Fig. 2, we can see that the running time is no more than $0.35\,\mathrm{s}$ even if the amount of SUs becomes large, i.e., when there are 120 SUs. For Fig. 3, we can see algorithm Random runs fastest, since the algorithm Random selects winning secondary users S_i^w randomly.

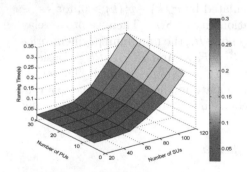
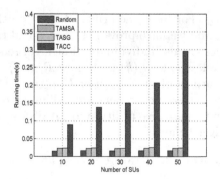

Fig. 2. Running time of TAMSA (a).   **Fig. 3.** Running time of TAMSA (b).

For TACC auction mechanism, the reserve price of primary user A_k is sorted in ascending order, and the budget of relay nodes $B_i(k)$ is in descending order to guarantee the utility of PUs. Besides, TACC needs to match every primary user and relay node, so algorithm runs the slowest. The running time of algorithm TAMSA and algorithm TASG is not large, because they use maximum-weighted-matching algorithm to complete matching between the winning PUs and relay nodes.

Next, to validate Theorem 2 regarding individual rationality and budget balance of TAMSA, we show the truthfulness in Fig. 4. In this auction, the payment of relay nodes $P_i(k)$ is not higher than the collected from SUs $F_i(k)$, and each winning primary user PU_i^w receives a payment not less than its reserve price A_k from the auctioneer.

From the experimental results in Fig. 4, we can see that the utility remains nonnegative when relay nodes submit truthful bids. But when relay node submits an untruthful bid, its utility rapidly reduce and will continue to be negative. Figure 4 depicts the difference of utility. Relay nodes submit truthful bid, when the bid of relay node is less than 50. When the bid is greater than 50, the difference between truthful and untruthful bids is presented. The utility of relay nodes and PUs are nonnegative, because the bid of relay node is less than the collected from SUs, and the bid is greater than the reserve price of PUs, $B_i(k) \leq F_i(k)$ and $B_i(k) \geq A_k$, when relay nodes submit truthful bids. The utility of relay node is negative, that is $B_i(k) > F_i(k)$, if it submits an untruthful bid. In summary, as seen in Fig. 4, the utility of relay nodes cannot be improved by submitting untruthful bid.

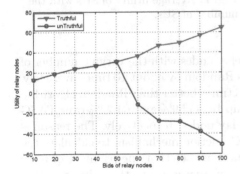
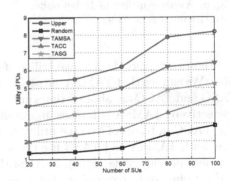

Fig. 4. Truthfulness of TAMSA.   **Fig. 5.** Average utility of PUs with the number of SUs.

Figure 5 shows how the utility of primary users U_{PU_k} varies with the number of SUs. With the increasing number of SUs, the average utility of PUs calculated by the five algorithms is gradually increasing. On average, the proposed algorithm TAMSA in this paper has improved 256% on the utility of PUs compared with the algorithm Random. TASG is about 217% better than algorithm

Random, TACC achieves about 156% utility gains than the algorithm Random on the U_{PU_k}. TAMSA is further improved up by 28.33% and 78.65% over TASG and TACC in terms of average utility of PUs, respectively. That's because both algorithm TAMSA and TASG apply the maximum weighted matching algorithm to match PUs and relay nodes to ensure the maximum benefit. Besides, both TAMSA and TASG use the auction mechanism based on VCG to ensure the truthfulness of algorithm. The difference between TASG and TAMSA is that TAMSA selects the winning set of SUs with the optimal cost performance, and TASG selects the winning set with the subset of SUs's bid by another subset. The optimal cost performance can enhance the revenue of PUs. In TACC, although the utility of PUs can be increase, it cannot guarantee the maximization of its earnings.

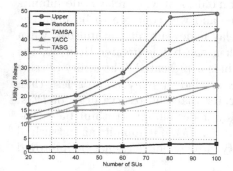

Fig. 6. Average utility of Relay nodes with the number of SUs.

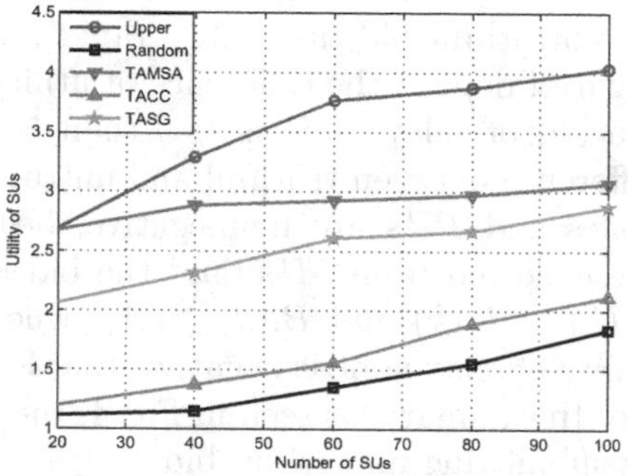

Fig. 7. Average utility of SUs with the number of SUs.

Figure 6 depicts the average utility of relay nodes with the varying number of SUs. We can see that TAMSA outperforms Random by about 10 times averagely, TASG and TACC are about 7 times and 6.6 times better than Random algorithm respectively. TAMSA is further improved up by 44.59% and 64.22% over TASG and TACC in terms of average utility of relay nodes, respectively. The reason is that both TAMSA and TASG use the VCG auction mechanism to calculate the payment of relay nodes $P_i(k)$. In Algorithm 2, we see that the payment of relay node is effectively reduced on the premise of guaranteeing the primary user's revenue, so the utility of relay nodes is improved.

Figure 7 shows the relationship between the average utility of SUs and the number of SUs. The average utility of SUs in TAMSA outperforms Random by 213%, TAMSA is able to improve the average utility of SUs in TASG up to 181%, and TACC achieves about 115% utility gain than the Random algorithm on the utility of SUs. TAMSA is improved up by 16.99% and 85.73% over TASG and TACC in terms of average utility of SUs, respectively. That's because TAMSA selects the winning set S_i^w in optimal cost performance. The payment of SUs is calculated according to their specific demands, so TAMSA effectively improves the utility of SUs. Algorithms TASG and TACC calculate the payment of SUs with the subset of SUs's bid by another subset. TASG adopts the optimal single-price auction to reduce the payment of SUs. In TACC, the payment of SUs is the average value of the winning SUs.

From the above experiments, we can see that TAMSA is suitable for the heterogeneous network where the utility of participants can be maximized at the same time. Algorithm TAMSA can gain higher social welfare than the algorithms Random, TASG and TACC. Hence, TAMSA can be deployed to the real situations, and it can effectively improve the utilization of spectrum resources.

6   Conclusion

In this paper, we have proposed a two-stage truthful auction mechanism for spectrum allocation (TAMSA) in cognitive radio networks with multiple primary users, multiple secondary users and relay nodes. We have investigated an incentive mechanism to encourage the spectrum holders to share their idle spectrum resources and encourage the cooperative transmission of the data to improve the utilization of the spectrum resources. TAMSA is a two-stage auction mechanism. In the first stage, SUs submit budgets and valuations for spectrum resources to relay nodes. Relay nodes calculate the payment of SUs and determine the winning set S_i^w. In the second stage, relay nodes submit bids to PUs to compete for spectrum resources. We have proved that TAMSA satisfies properties such as truthful, individual rational and computational efficient. Extensive simulation results show that TAMSA outperforms random algorithm by 256% in terms of average utility of PUs. TAMSA is able to improve the average utility of SUs and relay nodes significantly up to 213% and 10 times respectively. The performance of TAMSA is further improved by 28.33% and 78.65% in terms of average utility of PUs over TASG and TACC, respectively. Numerical results validated our theoretical analysis and demonstrated improvement in auction mechanism efficiency.

Acknowledgment. This work was supported by the National Natural Science Foundation of China under Grant Nos. 61702115 and 61672171, Natural Science Foundation of Guangdong, China under Grant No. 2018B030311007, and Major R&D Project of Educational Commission of Guangdong under Grant No. 2016KZDXM052. This work was also supported by China Postdoctoral Science Foundation Fund under Grant No. 2017M622632.

References

1. Zheng, Z., Wu, F., Tang, S., et al.: AEGIS: an unknown combinatorial auction mechanism framework for heterogeneous spectrum redistribution in noncooperative wireless networks. IEEE/ACM Trans. Netw. **24**(3), 1919–1932 (2016)
2. Zhu, Y., Li, B., Li, Z., et al.: Truthful spectrum auction design for secondary networks. In: INFOCOM, pp. 873–881. IEEE, Orlando, FL, USA (2012)

3. Chen, L., Huang, L., Xu, H., et al.: Optimal channel allocation for multi-PU and multi-SU pairs in underlay cognitive radio networks. Int. J. Ad Hoc Ubiquitous Comput. **27**(1), 19–33 (2018)
4. Wang, X., Huang, L., Xu, H., et al.: Truthful auction for resource allocation in cooperative cognitive radio networks. In: 24th International Conference on Computer Communication and Networks, pp. 1–8. IEEE, Las Vegas, NV, USA (2015)
5. Wang, X., Huang, L., Xu, H., et al.: Social welfare maximization auction for secondary spectrum markets: a long-term perspective. In: 13th IEEE International Conference on Sensing, Communication, and Networking, Communication, and Networking, pp. 1–9. IEEE, London, UK (2016)
6. Shen, F., Li, D., Lin, P.H., et al.: Auction based spectrum sharing for hybrid access in macro-femtocell networks under QoS requirements. In: IEEE International Conference on Communications, pp. 3335–3340. IEEE, London, UK (2015)
7. Wang, H., Liu, Z., Cheng, Z., et al.: Maximization of link capacity by joint power and spectrum allocation for smart satellite transponder. In: 23rd Asia-Pacific Conference on Communications, pp. 1–6. IEEE, Perth, WA, Australia (2017)
8. Jia, J., Zhang, Q., Zhang, Q., et al.: Revenue generation for truthful spectrum auction in dynamic spectrum access. In: 10th ACM International Symposium on Mobile Ad Hoc Networking and Computing, pp. 3–12. ACM, New Orleans, Louisiana, USA (2009)
9. Liu, Y., Tao, M., Huang, J.: An auction approach to distributed power allocation for multiuser cooperative networks. IEEE Trans. Wirel. Commun. **12**(1), 237–247 (2012)
10. Shi, W., Zhang, L., Wu, C., et al.: An online auction framework for dynamic resource provisioning in cloud computing. IEEE-ACM Trans. Netw. **24**(4), 2060–2073 (2016)
11. Feng, Z., Zhu, Y., Zhang, Q., et al.: TRAC: truthful auction for location-aware collaborative sensing in mobile crowdsourcing. In: INFOCOM, pp. 1231–1239. IEEE, Toronto, ON, Canada (2014)
12. Wu, F., Vaidya, N.: A strategy-proof radio spectrum auction mechanism in non-cooperative wireless networks. IEEE Trans. Mob. Comput. **12**(5), 885–894 (2013)
13. Lee, C., Wang, P., Niyato, D.: A real-time group auction system for efficient allocation of cloud internet applications. IEEE Trans. Serv. Comput. **8**(2), 251–268 (2015)
14. Lin, P., et al.: Groupon in the Air: A three-stage auction framework for Spectrum Group-buying. In: INFOCOM, pp. 2013–2021. IEEE, Turin, Italy (2013)
15. Advaita, A., Gali, M.M., Chu, T.M.C., et al.: Outage probability of MIMO cognitive cooperative radio networks with multiple AF relays using orthogonal space-time block codes. In: Wireless and Mobile Computing, Networking and Communications (WiMob), pp. 84–89. IEEE, Rome, Italy (2017)
16. Yang, D., Xue, G., Zhang, X.: Group buying spectrum auctions in cognitive radio networks. IEEE Trans. Veh. Technol. **66**(1), 810–817 (2017)
17. Yang, D., Fang, X., Xue, G.: Truthful auction for cooperative communications. In: IEEE International Conference on Communications, pp. 1–10. IEEE, Ottawa, ON, Canada (2011)
18. Chen, L., Wu, J., Zhang, X.X., et al.: TARCO: two-stage auction for D2D relay aided computation resource allocation in HetNet. IEEE Trans. Serv. Comput. **PP**(99), 1 (2017)

QoS-Driven Service Matching Algorithm
Based on User Requirements

Mengying Guo[✉] and Xudong Yang

School of Computer Science, Beijing University of Posts
and Telecommunications, Beijing, China
{mengying_1204,xdyang}@bupt.edu.cn

Abstract. Quality of Service (QoS) is an important factor which should be considered in service matching. There are two problems in most existing solutions. Firstly, most QoS models are static model described by determinate values or probability distributions, ignoring the impact of time factor. However, most QoS attributes are time-dependent, such as response time and reliability. Secondly, the service selection criteria of most QoS-driven service matching algorithms are based on service performance, but user requirements and the load of services are not considered. In this paper, we propose a Time-Segmented QoS Model (TSQM) to dynamically model QoS. Based on this model, a Service Matching algorithm based user QoS request and Priority (QPSM) is proposed. The priority of user requests is used to control the load of the services. Simulation results show that the algorithm can achieve a higher response rate and a better effect of load balancing.

Keywords: Service matching · QoS · Dynamic QoS model
Service model · Load balancing

1 Introduction

SOA (Service-Oriented Architecture) has provided a possibility for IoT (Internet of Things) systems to build distributed applications by loosely coupled services [1]. IoT services can be provided for different systems as web services by this way. Selecting services in numerous registered services has become difficult with the number of IoT services increasing rapidly [2]. The characteristics of IoT services determine that service function and service quality must be taken into account simultaneously when performing service matching. QoS (Quality of service) measured in different criterions such as delay, response time, reliability, availability, cost, etc. [3], has been a crucial factor in selecting services from numerous services with the same functions. The results of service matching depend not only on the matching degree to user requirements but also on the QoS attributes of the service itself. QoS-aware service selection is a complex multi-criterion decision problem, which is called NP-hard problem, and it is still a challenging research [4].

ⓒ Springer Nature Switzerland AG 2018
J. Vaidya and J. Li (Eds.): ICA3PP 2018, LNCS 11336, pp. 17–27, 2018.
https://doi.org/10.1007/978-3-030-05057-3_2

There have been many reasonable selection models and effective matching algorithms for QoS-aware service selection. In these models and algorithms, service matching is considered as an optimization problem based on service selecting and the objective is to find the best service. However, the fact that actual requirements of users are not considered is unacceptable for some users, because the matched services may have the best overall performance but cannot satisfy the user requirement for a certain QoS attribute. Another problem of these models is that the QoS attributes are only represented with single-valued model or probabilistic model and the influence of time is not taken into account. Because the service QoS attributes dynamically change with time and user load, the static model cannot accurately represent the QoS values. Thereby the static model will seriously affect the accuracy of matching results.

In this paper, by splitting time and dynamically modeling each time period, we propose a Time-Segmented QoS Model (TSQM) which can represent QoS attributes more accurately. Based on our model, a Service Matching algorithm based user QoS request and Priority (QPSM algorithm) is proposed. In this algorithm, the single QoS performance and comprehensive QoS performance provided by services are considered simultaneously. The load of the service is controlled according priority, so that the purpose of balancing user load on each service can be achieved. The rest of the paper is organized as follows. Section 2 introduces the related work of service matching technology. Section 3 details the TSQM model and the QPSM algorithm. Section 4 shows the simulation results to prove the feasibility and effectiveness of the QPSM algorithm. Section 5 concludes this paper.

2   Related Work

QoS-based service matching can usually be divided into two relatively independent processes, service selection and service ranking [5]. Service selection ensures the most basic functional requirements and QoS requirements of users or systems. Service ranking is a further optimization on this basis. The model and algorithm of service selection can be divided into service-function-based selection and service-quality-based selection according to different selection criteria. In service-function-based model, the concepts such as semantics or ontology are used to build service models [6,7]. The service-quality-based selection can be divided into single QoS performance selection model and comprehensive QoS performance selection model [5]. The service-quality-based selection can also be divided into single value model and probability-based selection model [8–10].

Service function is one of the requirements that should be satisfied in the process of service matching. The fundamental purpose of service matching is to select the most appropriate service for the user based on the service request from the user. More and more models describe and define services based on semantic web and ontology to understand the functional requirements of users more intelligently. A new resource model describing IoT resources in multi-dimensional was proposed in [6]. Based on this model, a resource matching algorithm, that select suitable resource according the similarity between semantic web matching resources, was also proposed. In [7] authors proposed a QoS-based dynamic service composition method in semantic IoT. According to the context-added QoS ontology, after the dynamic semantic annotation of the services in semantic internet of things, the candidate service sets are dynamically selected and combined to provide more accurate services.

Service quality is another requirement that should be satisfied in the process of service matching. The QoS attributes of services will significantly impact on the comprehensive evaluation of services. Therefore, QoS-based service selection is an available scheme of IoT service selection. In most studies, such as [8,9], single-valued model or probabilistic model are usually used to model each dimension of QoS, and the optimal services are selected according to the comparison of service performance. In the process of QoS-aware service matching, not only the overall performance of the service but also each user requirement of QoS should be considered. In [10] authors proposed a service discovery algorithm based on a multi- stage service matching algorithm. In this algorithm, each QoS attribute is assigned a different weight and the QoS constraints are determined according to user requests. Finally, the most suitable service is selected. The QoS of web service dynamically changes with factors such as network condition, user load and time. Static model constructed solely from historical data cannot accurately represent the dynamic changes. Therefore, the time factor must be considered when modeling.

3   Service Model

In a complete process of service matching, the function and quality of service should be taken into consideration. Assume that the virtual service set S is known and all services in the virtual service set S can satisfy the functional requirements requested by the user. Next, the QoS modeling and service matching will be discussed further.

3.1   Time-Segmented QoS Model Definition

The TSQM model is a time-segmented QoS-based model. According to changes of QoS attributes over time, the QoS change period can be divided into some time periods with different intervals and the QoS model can be constructed separately in each time period.

Definition. The TSQM model for a service can be represented as a triple (ET, P, QM), where

- $ET = [T_0, T_0 + T)$ is the effective period of QoS, T_0 is the start time of effective period, T is the time period of QoS attribute updated.
- $P = \{P_1, P_2, \cdots, P_N\}$ is the time period of ET, $P_i = [t_i, t_{i+1})$ and $\bigcup_i P_i = ET$.

- $QM = \langle Q_1, Q_2, \cdots, Q_n \rangle$ is a sequence of QoS models, $Q_i = (f_{DELAY_i},$ $f_{REST_i}, f_{REL_i}, f_{USA_i}, f_{COST_i})$ is the QoS vector of the time period P_i, and $f_{DELAY_i}, f_{REST_i}, f_{REL_i}, f_{USA_i}, f_{COST_i}$ represent the probability distribution function of delay, response time, reliability, availability, and cost.

Given a service, the QoS model of the service can be represented as $Q(t) = (f_{DELAY_t}, f_{REST_t}, f_{REL_t}, f_{USA_t}, f_{COST_t})$, where $t \in [t_i + kT, t_{i+1} + kT)$, $k = 0, 1, \cdots$

The TSQM model shows that the QoS of the service changes with time. The model can be flexibly extended according to different user requirements, and the number of QoS attributes in each time period can be one or more. In this paper, delay, response time, reliability, availability and cost are selected as the QoS attributes.

3.2   Detailed Description of the Model

QoS Model. A QoS model of a service contains k QoS attributes. These attributes can be 5 non-functional attributes defined in the TSQM model, and they can also be extended according to user requirements. The QoS of service S_i corresponds to a set of QoS vectors consisting of a probability distribution function at each time period. In order to compare the QoS performance more easily, the probability distribution function in each time period should be converted into a determined value using the 999 criterion (choose a value that 99.9% of the data satisfies as the QoS value of the current time period), i.e., $f_{QoS_i} \rightarrow q_i$.

For clear expression, the below-mentioned QoS attributes default to QoS attributes within a certain time period. The QoS attributes of service S_i can be represented as a vector, i.e., $Q_i = (q_{i1}, q_{i2}, \cdots, q_{ik})$, where q_{ik} is a value converted from the probability distribution function of the k-th QoS attribute. We assume that the virtual service set consists of n candidate services, $S = \{S_1, S_2, \cdots, S_n\}$, and their corresponding QoS attributes can be represented as an $n \times k$ matrix.

$$M = \begin{bmatrix} q_{11} & q_{12} & \cdots & q_{1k} \\ q_{21} & q_{22} & \cdots & q_{2k} \\ \vdots & \vdots & \ddots & \vdots \\ q_{n1} & q_{n2} & \cdots & q_{nk} \end{bmatrix} \tag{1}$$

Because of the differences in the range of QoS values and the effect on the comprehensive service performance, the QoS values should be normalized by the min-max normalization [11]. According to the impact on the comprehensive performance of the service, QoS attributes can be classified into positive effect attributes and negative effect attributes. The larger value of positive effect attributes (such as reliability, availability, reputation and other attributes) or the smaller value of negative attributes (such as cost, response time, and other attributes), the better overall performance of the service. Assuming that the range of q_i is $[min\,(q_i)\,,max\,(q_i)]$, positive and negative effect attributes should be normalized by formula (2) and (3) respectively.

$$q_i' = \begin{cases} \frac{q_i-min(q_i)}{max(q_i)-min(q_i)}, & max\,(q_i) - min\,(q_i) \neq 0 \\ 1, & max\,(q_i) - min\,(q_i) = 0 \end{cases} \tag{2}$$

$$q_i' = \begin{cases} \frac{max(q_i)-q_i}{max(q_i)-min(q_i)}, & max\,(q_i) - min\,(q_i) \neq 0 \\ 1, & max\,(q_i) - min\,(q_i) = 0 \end{cases} \tag{3}$$

All QoS values are distributed between $[0,1]$ after normalization. The comprehensive performance of the service is enhanced with the increase of each QoS value, that is, the larger the QoS value, the better the service performance.

Service Request. A service request sent from the user to the service platform when the service discovery is performed can be represented as $Req = \{Q_{req}, M_{req}\}$, where $Q_{req} = (\alpha_1, \alpha_2, \cdots, \alpha_k)$ is a QoS request vector and $\alpha_1, \alpha_2, \cdots, \alpha_k$ represent the user's expected values for k attributes $q_{i1}, q_{i2}, \cdots, q_{ik}$. The QoS values in the request vector, $\alpha_1, \alpha_2, \cdots, \alpha_k$, should be normalized by formula (2) or (3), so we can get $\alpha_1', \alpha_2', \cdots, \alpha_k'$. Then Q_{req} is converted to Q_{req}'. The priority vector is $M_{req} = (m_1, m_2, \cdots, m_j)$, $j \in \{1, 2, \cdots, k\}$, and j means the j-th attribute in Q_{req} as the priority attribute of the request Req. M_{req} including one or more priority attributes is defined by the user requirements, which fully reflects the user's preference for the QoS attributes of the target service. The user requirement emphasizes the importance of the j-th attribute q_j' in the target service. And q_j' is expected to satisfy the requirement of α_j' in Q_{req}' as much as possible, i.e., $q_j' \geq \alpha_j'$.

Priority. The priority of the service request depends on α_j' in the QoS request vector Q_{req}'. Suppose h is the user's expected value of a certain QoS attribute, i.e., $h = \alpha_j'$. The priority of the request can be calculated by formula (4).

$$Prior(h) = \begin{cases} 1, & h \in [0, T_1) \\ 2, & h \in [T_1, T_2] \\ 3, & h \in (T_2, 1] \end{cases} \tag{4}$$

T_1 and T_2 are single performance thresholds that is used to determine the priority of the service request. The values of T_1 and T_2 are in the range of $[0, 1]$, and $T_1 \leq T_2$. The priority of the service request Req can be divided into three levels of 1, 2, and 3, which respectively represent the low, medium, and high of the priority. According to the request priority, different matching strategies are selected. The matching strategy set can be represented as $MS = \{MS_H, MS_M, MS_L\}$, where MS_H, MS_M and MS_L respectively indicate the matching strategies of different priority.

QoS Performance Evaluation Value. QoS performance evaluation value is classified to request performance evaluation value QoS_{req} and service performance evaluation value QoS_{ser}. QoS_{req} is selected by the expected QoS value from user and it can be represented as $QoS_{req} = \left|Q'_{req}\right|^2 = \alpha_1'^2 + \alpha_2'^2 + \cdots + \alpha_k'^2 = \sum_{i=1}^{k} \alpha_i'^2$, where $Q'_{req} = \left(\alpha_1', \alpha_2', \cdots, \alpha_k'\right)$ is the QoS request vector after normalization. The QoS_{ser} of service S_i can be represented as $QoS_{ser}(i) = \left|Q_i'\right|^2 = q_{i1}'^2 + q_{i2}'^2 + \cdots + q_{ik}'^2 = \sum_{j=1}^{k} q_{ij}'^2$, where $Q_i' = \left(q_{i1}', q_{i2}', \cdots, q_{ik}'\right)$ is the QoS attribute vector after normalization.

The Utility of Service Matching. $U(i)$ is the utility of the service matching algorithm when the service S_i is selected as the target service satisfying the request Req. It is classified to single performance utility value $U_S(i)$ and comprehensive services utility value $U_C(i)$. $U_S(i)$ is the ratio of a certain QoS attribute of Req to that of S_i, and can be represented as formula (5). $U_C(i)$ is the ratio of the overall performance evaluation value of Req to that of S_i, and can be represented as formula (6). $U(i)$ is the weighted sum of $U_S(i)$ and $U_C(i)$, and it can be represented as formula (7).

$$U_S(i) = \begin{cases} h/q_{ij}', & h < q_{ij}' \\ q_{ij}'/h, & h \geq q_{ij}' \end{cases} \tag{5}$$

$$U_C(i) = \begin{cases} QoS_{req}/QoS_{ser}(i), & QoS_{req} < QoS_{ser}(i) \\ QoS_{ser}(i)/QoS_{req}, & QoS_{req} \geq QoS_{ser}(i) \end{cases} \tag{6}$$

$$U(i) = \mu \times U_S(i) + (1 - \mu) \times U_C(i) \tag{7}$$

The μ is weighted factors in the range of $[0, 1]$. The impact of $U_S(i)$ and $U_C(i)$ on $U(i)$ can be adjusted through μ. In the matching process, the greater utility, the more matched with the user requirements the service is.

4   Service Matching Algorithm

The QoS-based service matching algorithm can be roughly classified to two methods: single-QoS performance matching and overall-QoS performance matching. In the QPSM algorithm, service selection and matching are performed according to user-defined priority attributes and QoS. So the most suitable service to user requirements can be matched.

QPSM algorithm is proposed as Algorithm 1. The main idea of the algorithm is selecting the corresponding matching strategy according to the priority of user request, and selecting the service that is most suitable to the user. The priority of user request is determined by the specified priority attributes, and the different matching strategies are adopted according to the priority. When the request priority is determined as a high priority, the target service must satisfy

---

Algorithm 1. QoS-based service matching algorithm (QPSM)

Input: (1)S // Service Set

      (2)Req // User Requirements

Output: Ser_match // All services that suit for user

1 Initialize Req, S and its corresponding QoS attribute matrix M;

2 Determine the priority of the request;

3 Compose priority service set $Ser\_prior : q'_{ij} \geq h$;

4 Compose the candidate service set $Ser\_wait : QoS_{ser}(i) \geq QoS_{req}$;

5 **while** *Req is not empty* **do**

6   **if** $Prior(h)=3$ **then**

7   **if** $Ser\_prior = \varnothing$ **then**

8 | $Ser\_match \leftarrow null$

9   **else**

10 | $Ser\_match \leftarrow$ the largest $QoS_{ser}(i)$ from Ser_prior

11   **end**

12   **end**

13   **if** $Prior(h)=1$ **then**

14   **if** $Ser\_wait = \varnothing$ **then**

15 | $Ser\_match \leftarrow$ the largest $QoS_{ser}(i)$ from S

16   **else**

17 | $Ser\_match \leftarrow$ the minimum $QoS_{ser}(i)$ from Ser_wait

18   **end**

19   **end**

20   **if** $Prior(h)=2$ **then**

21   **if** $Ser\_prior \neq \varnothing$ *and* $Ser\_wait = \varnothing$ **then**

22 | $Ser\_match \leftarrow$ the largest $QoS_{ser}(i)$ from Ser_prior

23   **end**

24   **if** $Ser\_prior = \varnothing$ *and* $Ser\_wait \neq \varnothing$ **then**

25 | $Ser\_match \leftarrow$ the largest q'_{ij} from Ser_wait

26   **end**

27   **if** $Ser\_prior = \varnothing$ *and* $Ser\_wait = \varnothing$ **then**

28 | $Ser\_match \leftarrow$ the largest $U(i)$ from S

29   **end**

30   **if** $Ser\_prior \neq \varnothing$ *and* $Ser\_wait \neq \varnothing$ **then**

31   **if** $Ser\_inter = Ser\_prior \cap Ser\_wait \neq \varnothing$ **then**

32 | $Ser\_match \leftarrow$ the largest $U(i)$ from Ser_inter

33   **else**

34   **if** $Ser\_union = Ser\_prior \cup Ser\_wait \neq \varnothing$ **then**

35 | $Ser\_match \leftarrow$ the largest $U(i)$ from Ser_union

36   **end**

37   **end**

38   **end**

39   **end**

40 **end**

41 **return** Ser_match;

---

the priority attributes completely with the user requirements. When the request priority is judged as a low priority, a service with the smallest service performance evaluation value which satisfies the user request performance evaluation value is selected. So the load of the entire service system is balanced and the optimized matching of resources is achieved. When the request priority is judged as a medium priority, the user request and service performance are weighed, and the service selection is determined by the utility of service matching.

Ser_match, a matching service set, is composed of services selected by priority attributes. When the number of priority attributes is more than one, a conflict of matching policy selection may occur. The merging of matching services is to merge the services in Ser_match and finally the most suitable service is selected for the user. Algorithm 2 shows the whole procedure of matching service merging.

Algorithm 2. Merge matching service

Input: Ser_match // Matching Service Set
Output: Ser_result // The most suitable service for users
1 Initialize $\alpha' \in \{\alpha'_1, \cdots, \alpha'_k\}, i \in \{1, \cdots, n\}, j \in \{1, \cdots, k\}$;
2 **for** $Ser\_match \neq \varnothing$ **do**
3   **if** $num(Prior(\alpha') = 3) \geq 1$ **then**
4   **if** $num(Ser\_match(q_{ij} \geq \alpha'_j)) \geq 2$ **then**
5 | $Ser\_result \leftarrow$ the largest $U(i)$ from $Ser\_match(q'_{ij} \geq \alpha'_j)$
6   **end**
7   **if** $num(Ser\_match(q'_{ij} \geq \alpha'_j)) = 1$ **then**
8 | $Ser\_result \leftarrow Ser\_match(q'_{ij} \geq \alpha'_j)$
9   **end**
10   **if** $num(Ser\_match(q'_{ij} \geq \alpha'_j)) = 0$ **then**
11 | $Ser\_result \leftarrow$ null
12   **end**
13   **end**
14   **if** $num(Prior(\alpha') = 3) = 0$ **then**
15   **if** $num(Ser\_match) \geq 2$ **then**
16 | $Ser\_result \leftarrow$ the largest $U(i)$ from Ser_match
17   **else**
18 | $Ser\_result \leftarrow Ser\_match$
19   **end**
20   **end**
21 **end**
22 **return** Ser_result;

---

5   Experiment Analysis

The main purpose of the QPSM algorithm is to select the most suitable service for the user according to user-defined QoS request. In order to verify the feasibility and effectiveness of this algorithm, it is compared with the other two QoS-based matching algorithms, Single-QoS and Overall-QoS, in four aspects that is response rate, load, average single performance value and overall performance value. All the experiments were conducted on a computer with a 3.2

GHz Intel Core 2 Duo CPU and 12 GB RAM. The data used for the experiment derived from two sources: a data set containing 1000 actual services and 5 QoS values, and a randomly generated user request data set.

The purpose of the first experiment is to evaluate the response rate of the algorithm, that is the ratio of successfully matched and returned requests to the total requests. In this experiment, 100 services are selected for matching and 1000 service requests are randomly generated. The response rates of this three algorithms are shown in Fig. 1. As the number of user requests increase, the response rate of each algorithm tends to be stable. The QPSM algorithm outperforms other algorithms with the highest response rate at about 96%. However, the response rate of the Single-QoS algorithm [8] is the lowest at about 88%. The reason for this result is that the Single-QoS algorithm will fail to respond when all candidate services do not satisfy the QoS constraints. The Overall-QoS algorithm [10] will fail to respond when the overall performance is lower than user request performance. In QPSM algorithm, the matching results will be found through a comprehensive consideration of user requirement and service performance.

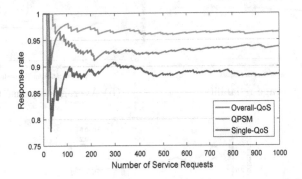

Fig. 1. The response rate of the algorithm with the number of user requests

The second experiment is to evaluate the effect of load balancing, that is indicated by the number of times that services with different QoS performance respond to requests. In this experiment, 5 candidate services with the same function and the different QoS are selected and 1000 service requests are randomly generated. The distributions of service load by using traditional UDDI [5] algorithm and QPSM algorithm are compared. And the load distributions of QPSM algorithm with different single performance thresholds T_1 and T_2 are tested. Figure 2 shows that the QPSM algorithm outperforms the UDDI algorithm in term of load balancing when the number of service requests is the same. The greater difference between T_1 and T_2, the better performance of load balancing. Because the greater difference between T_1 and T_2, the more service requests are judged to be medium priority, and the effect of load balancing is better.

The third experiment is to evaluate the average service single-performance value and the overall-performance value. In this experiment, 1000 services used for matching are selected and 1000 user requests with high demand for response

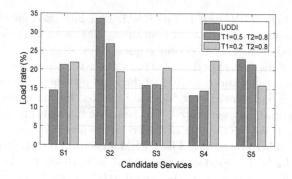

Fig. 2. Distribution of service matching load rate

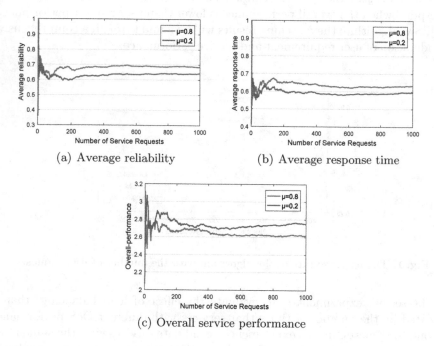

(a) Average reliability   (b) Average response time

(c) Overall service performance

Fig. 3. Service single-performance and overall-performance with the number of user requests

time and reliability are randomly generated. The μ in the service matching utility $U(i)$ is taken as $\mu = 0.2$ and $\mu = 0.8$ respectively. Figure 3 shows that the larger μ, the higher average reliability of the matching service, the shorter response time, and the lower overall service performance value. Because the value of μ determines the proportion of single performance utility value $U_S(i)$ and comprehensive services utility value $U_C(i)$ in the utility of service matching $U(i)$, and affects the final service selection further. The users can select the appropriate μ according to their requirements.

6   Conclusion

Due to the uncertainty caused by the dynamic change of service QoS and the ambiguity of user requirements, there are some limitations in the current service matching algorithms. In order to describe the QoS attributes more accurately, we propose a time-segmented QoS model on the consideration of time. Based on this model, a service matching algorithm based on user QoS request and priority is also proposed. In this algorithm, user requirements and QoS performance preferences is fully considered. And the most suitable service is selected according to user-defined service requests and priorities, which is more suitable for users with specific requirements. Finally, experimental results indicate that the proposed algorithm can achieve a higher response rate and a better effect of load balancing.

References

1. Benslimane, D., Dustdar, S., Sheth, A.: Services mashups: the new generation of web applications. IEEE Internet Comput. **12**(5), 13–15 (2008)
2. He, Q., Yan, J., Jin, H., Yang, Y.: Quality-aware service selection for service-based systems based on iterative multi-attribute combinatorial auction. IEEE Trans. Softw. Eng. **40**, 192–215 (2014)
3. Zhao, S., Wu, G., Zhang, S.: Review of QoS research in SOA. Comput. Sci. **36**(4), 16–20 (2009)
4. Klein, A., Ishikawa, F., Honiden, S.: SanGA: a self-adaptive network-aware approach to service composition. IEEE Trans. Serv. Comput. **7**(3), 452–464 (2014)
5. Guo, D., Ren, Y., Chen, H.: A QoS constrained web service selection and ordering model. J. Shanghai Jiaotong Univ. **41**(6), 870–875 (2007)
6. Zhao, S., Zhang, Y., Yu, L., Cheng, B., Ji, Y., Chen, J.: A multidimensional resource model for dynamic resource matching in internet of things. Concurr. Comput. Pract. Exp. **27**(8), 1819–1843 (2015)
7. Li, L., Liu, N., Li, G.: A QoS-based dynamic service composition method in semantic internet of things. Appl. Res. Comput. **33**(3), 802–805 (2016)
8. Zeng, L., Benatallah, B., Ngu, A.H.H., Dumas, M., Kalagnanam, J., Chang, H.: Qos-aware middleware for web services composition. IEEE Trans. Softw. Eng. **30**(5), 311–327 (2004)
9. Cardoso, J., Sheth, A., Miller, J., Arnold, J., Kochut, K.: Quality of service for workflows and web service processes. Web Semant. Sci. Serv. Agents World Wide Web **1**(3), 281–308 (2004)
10. Jia, B., Li, W., Zhou, T.: A centralized service discovery algorithm via multi-stage semantic service matching in internet of things. In: 2017 IEEE International Conference on Computational Science and Engineering (CSE) and IEEE International Conference on Embedded and Ubiquitous Computing (EUC), pp. 422–427 (2017). https://doi.org/10.1109/CSE-EUC.2017.82
11. Chen, L., Yang, J., Zhang, L.: Time based QoS modeling and prediction for web services. In: Kappel, G., Maamar, Z., Motahari-Nezhad, H.R. (eds.) ICSOC 2011. LNCS, vol. 7084, pp. 532–540. Springer, Heidelberg (2011). https://doi.org/10.1007/978-3-642-25535-9_38

Research on Overload Classification Method for Bus Images Based on Image Processing and SVM

Tingting Li[1] (ID), Yongxiong Sun[2(✉)] (ID), Yanhua Liang[1] (ID), Yujia Zhai[2] (ID), and Xuan Ji[2] (ID)

[1] College of Software, Jilin University, Changchun 130012, China
[2] College of Computer Science and Technology, Jilin University, Changchun 130012, China
sunyx@jlu.edu.cn

Abstract. The speed and efficiency of overloaded artificial screening bus images are relatively low, which results in a large number of human resources waste problems. Therefore, an overload classification method for bus images based on image processing and support vector machine was proposed to intelligently identify the image overload or not. Based on the consideration we have done the following work. Firstly, the bus images were preprocessed, including image enhancement using histogram equalization method and image segmentation using improved Otsu algorithm; Secondly, the features of the segmented images was extracted by Kirsch edge detection operator to establish the image feature sample library; Finally, the appropriate kernel function and parameters were chosen to establish a classifier model based on support vector machine, which can train the sample library to classify the bus images. Theoretical analysis and experimental results show that the average classification accuracy of the polynomial kernel function is better than those of the Gaussian kernel function and the Sigmoid kernel function in the finite range of parameters selection. When the parameter d of the polynomial kernel function is 4, the classification accuracy is 93.68%, and its classification performance is stable and there is no significant increase or fall. And the conclusion was verified in the actual application.

Keywords: Bus overload · Image segmentation · Image feature extraction
Support vector machine · Image classification

1 Introduction

The bus overload refers to the number of passengers in vehicles exceeding the authorized number of passengers. The bus overload is a direct threat to the safety of the passengers. Once a traffic accident occur, it will lead to casualties and have a significant influence on society [1].

In order to prevent vehicles from overloading as much as possible, the public security, transportation, highway and other departments take active measures. On the one hand, they actively propagandize the danger of overload to enhance the safety awareness of passengers. On the other hand, they use different kinds of advanced technology to supervise overload, such as installed the driving recorders, cameras, and other monitoring equipment in the bus [2]. These measures not only reduce the waste of

© Springer Nature Switzerland AG 2018
J. Vaidya and J. Li (Eds.): ICA3PP 2018, LNCS 11336, pp. 28–43, 2018.
https://doi.org/10.1007/978-3-030-05057-3_3

manpower and material resources, but also investigate by evidence and punish the existence of overloaded illegal vehicles.

At present, most provinces and cities in China still use manual recognition method to classify images which are photographed by a camera that is installed in the bus to determine whether the bus is overloaded. Although the accuracy of the manual identification method is high, the efficiency is low. Therefore, the manual identification method cannot meet the current regulatory needs [3]. In order to solve the problem of artificial identification, an overloaded classification method for bus images based on image processing and support vector machine (SVM) is proposed. Compared with existing artificial recognition methods, this method can automatically recognize the overloaded bus images, which saves a lot of human resources and improves the speed and quantity of illegal images recognition [4]. Simultaneously, it has greatly improved the speed and quantity of illegal images identification.

2 Pretreatment of Bus Images

The purpose of this paper is to classify bus images to detect overloaded buses by using image processing and support vector machine. Image preprocessing is the precondition of image classification. It plays an important role in classifying overloaded bus images. The experimental data are derived from the historical data of the transportation department, Jilin City, Jilin Province.

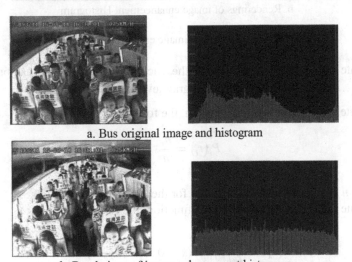

a. Bus original image and histogram

b. Renderings of image enhancement histogram

Fig. 1. First group of bus image enhancement effect graph and contrast histogram

2.1 Histogram Equalization

In this paper, the images were taken by the cameras installed in the bus and the quality is poor. Thus, the image enhancement is necessary before image segmentation. We used histogram equalization to enhance original images, which can make the distribution of whole image gray tend to be uniform. The process is as follows:

a. Bus original image and histogram

b. Renderings of image enhancement Histogram

Fig. 2. Second group of bus image enhancement effect graph

Calculate the number of pixels for the each grayscale of original bus images $n_i, i = 0, 1, \ldots, L - 1$, where L is the total gray level for the image.

1. Calculate the original image histogram, the formula is:

$$P_i(r_i) = \frac{n_i}{n} \tag{1}$$

Where: n is the total number of pixels for the original images.

2. Calculate the cumulative distribution function, the formula is:

$$s_k(r_k) \approx \sum_{i=0}^{k} P_i(r_i) \ (k = 0, 1 \ldots, L - 1) \tag{2}$$

3. Calculate the output gray level, which can be written in the form:

$$g_k = INT\left[(g_{max} - g_{min})s_k(r_k) + g_{min} + 0.5\right]/(L - 1) \tag{3}$$

Where $k = 0, 1 \ldots, L - 1$, $INT[]$ is rounding operator.

In the formula (3), when $g_{min} = 0$, $g_{max} = L - 1$, the formula (4) can be written in the form:

$$g_k = INT\left[(L-1)s_k(r_k) + 0.5\right]/(L-1)\tag{4}$$

4. We can get output images by modifying original images, which is based on the mapping relation between the gray level function (r_k) of original images and output gray level function (g_k).
5. Implementing (Implement) image enhancement to two groups of original bus images, the corresponding results are shown in Figs. 1 and 2.

2.2 Image Segmentation

In order to classify the overloaded bus images by using support vector machine, we need to extract target area from background area to obtain training data. Thus, it is important to segment target area from original image. Threshold Segmentation is one of the first image segmentation methods, which is simple and effective. It includes the maximum between-class variance method, the minimum cross-entropy threshold method, the maximum entropy threshold method and the maximum correlation threshold method [5].

a. Original image

b. Otsu algorithm   c.Minimum cross entropy   d.Maximum entropy   e.The most relevant

Fig. 3. Comparison of image segmentation effects of four segmentation methods

Through analyzed bus images, we regard the aisle in the image as the target area, and surrounding passengers as background area. Then we processing a same image used four traditional segmentation methods mentioned above. The corresponding results are shown in Fig. 3.

As shown in Fig. 3, the four segmentation methods mentioned above all lead to noises and holes, which has greatly effect features extraction. Therefore, in this paper, we first process the bus images used threshold segmentation, and then closed operation is repeatedly used to remove noises and fill holes. Closed operation is a more advanced morphological transformation that combines expansion and corrosion algorithms [6], which expansion operation is firstly used to process segmented images, and then implement corrosion operation to above results. We processed images in Fig. 3 by using three times of closed operations, and the results are shown in Fig. 4.

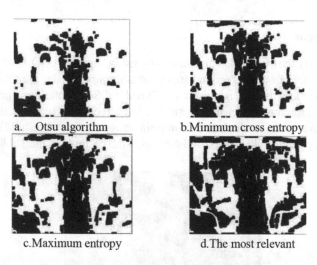

a.   Otsu algorithm   b.Minimum cross entropy

c.Maximum entropy   d.The most relevant

Fig. 4.   Effect graph using threshold segmentation and closed operation

As shown in Fig. 4, the traditional maximum relevant threshold segmentation method has worst results, and the traditional Otsu has the best effects which can effectively separate target areas from background areas, apart from several connecting pixels.

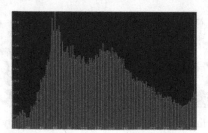

Fig. 5.   Gray histogram of graph a in Fig. 3

In this paper, we select the middle aisle of the bus images as the targets of training samples. Figure 3(a) is a normal bus image in which aisle region accounts for one fifth of original image and non-aisle region accounts for four fifth of original image. Thus, compared with background area, the target area is much small. The gray histogram of graph (a) is shown in Fig. 5.

As shown in Fig. 5, there are less pixels on the left, and the gray distribution of the middle pixels is uniform, and the gray of the rightmost almost reaches peak. That means the pixels of target area focus on left, and the pixels of background focus on middle and right. The gray scale of background area is bigger than the gray scale of target area. Owing to small variance in target area and big variance in background area, the traditional Otsu method makes threshold prefer big variance area, which leads to calculated threshold bigger than ideal threshold and has poor segmentation results. In order to improve the quality of images segmentation and the accuracy of identification over-loaded bus images, in this paper, we try to modify traditional Otsu method. The original formula of Otsu algorithm can be written in the form:

$$\sigma(t) = \omega 0 (\mu 0 - \mu)^2 + \omega 1 (\mu 1 - \mu)^2 = \omega 0 \omega 1 (\mu 1 - \mu 0)^2 \tag{5}$$

Where: $\omega 0$ is the probability of target class, and $\omega 1$ is the probability of background class. It means that the target area and background area are weighted [7].

In this paper, we adjust weighting by descending and ascending the power of $\omega 0$ and $\omega 1$. The improved Otsu formula is:

$$\sigma(t) = \omega 0^\alpha (\mu 0 - \mu)^2 + \omega 1^\beta (\mu 1 - \mu)^2 = \omega 0^\alpha \omega 1^\beta (\mu 1 - \mu 0)^2 \tag{6}$$

Where α represents the proportion of background area in the whole image, and β is the reciprocal of α, which makes the algorithm have no biases to target class. By modifying original formula, we can ensure that the threshold will not be so high when the

a. The first group (b) Otsu algorithm segmentation   b. Improved Otsu algorithm segmentation

c. The second group (b) Otsu algorithm segmentation d. Improved Otsu algorithm segmentation

Fig. 6. Comparison between traditional Otsu algorithm and improved Otsu algorithm

variance of one class is bigger than the other, at the same time, the gray level between two classes is more balanced.

The results from traditional Otsu algorithm and improved Otsu algorithm are shown in Fig. 6.

As shown in Fig. 6, the passengers in the background area are not classified into target area, while the improved Otsu algorithm can effectively separate target area from background area. Therefore, in this paper, we use improved Otsu algorithm and close operation to segment bus images, which resolves the effects of noise and holes, and provides a good base for features extraction.

3   Bus Image Feature Extraction

After image enhancement and segmentation, we select Kirsch operator to extract segmented image features, and build an image features database which is used to classify bus images using support vector machine.

Kirsch operator calculates convolution and derivative for each pixel using eight templates. The eight templates represent eight directions, making the maximal response to the eight specific edge directions of the images. The output of Kirsch operator is the maximum of eight directions. Kirsch is an effective edges detection operator, which can significantly suppress the noise from edge detection [8]. Assuming original image is shown in Fig. 7.

a_3	a_2	a_1
a_4	(i,j)	a_0
a_5	a_6	a_7

Fig. 7. A 3×3 sub-picture of the original image

The gradient of the edge is:

$$G(i,j) = \max\left[1, \max\left(\left|5S_k - 4T_k\right|:k = 1, 2, \ldots 8\right)\right] \tag{7}$$

Where $S_k = x_{k+1} + x_{k+2} + x_{k+3}, T_k = x_{k+4} + x_{k+5} + \ldots + x_{k+8}$, k equals 1 to 8 representing the 8-direction template, as shown in Fig. 8.

The Kirsch operator is based on a fact that the gray scale for the non-edges of image is smaller than threshold and the gray scale for the edges of image is bigger than threshold. When detecting image edges, we first use a lower threshold to binarize the original images, then detect target area and background area. The target area and the background area can be effectively divided by the boundary regions whose gray scale is bigger than the threshold [9]. By using he method mentioned above, we preprocess two groups of original bus images and extract corresponding features. The results are shown in Fig. 9 .

3	5	5	5	5	5
-3	0	5	3	0	-3
-3	-3	-3	-3	-3	3

-3	3	5	-3	-3	-3
-3	0	5	-3	0	5
-3	-3	5	-3	5	5

-3	-3	-3	-3	-3	-3
5	0	3	-3	0	3
5	5	3	5	5	5

5	-3	-3	5	5	3
5	0	3	5	0	3
5	5	3	-3	-3	-3

Fig. 8. Eight directions template

a. The first group   b. The second group

Fig. 9. Two sets of bus original images and features extraction

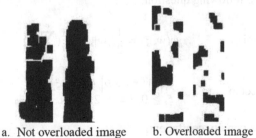

a. Not overloaded image   b. Overloaded image

Fig. 10. Unloaded and overloaded image extraction aisle shape effect

For the classification of bus images, we only concern the target area information. In order to reduce calculation and improve the accuracy of classification, we need to avoid the influence of non-target area after extracting image outlines. In this paper, we process simply process the extracted outline images, and then extract the shape of aisle position as sample data for the image features database. Figure 10 shows extracted aisle shapes.

In this paper, we process 551 bus images. Some results are shown in Fig. 11.

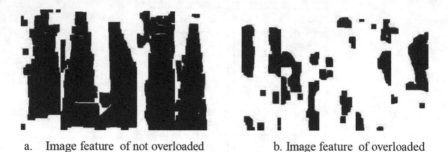

a.   Image feature of not overloaded   b. Image feature of overloaded

Fig. 11.   Part of the bus image feature samples

4   Image Classification Based on Support Vector Machine

Analyzed image features of target area, we can find that the image features of target area that there are passengers in the aisle are significant from the image features of target area that there are no passengers in the aisle. Therefore, we can recognize overloaded bus images by using the shapes of feature images for target area. We can divide training data into two parts, positive training set and negative training set, where positive training set stores outline feature samples from non-overloaded bus images, and negative training set stores outline feature samples from overloaded bus images. We can use support vector machine to classify bus images after constructing two training sets.

Support vector machine is very effective for linear classification problems [10]. For a nonlinear classification problem, we can transform it into a linear problem by nonlinear transformation function, which makes it linearly separable in a high-dimensional space [11]. For a nonlinear classification problem, the solution to the optimal classification surface is equal to the following question:

$$\text{Minimize} \qquad \phi(w, \xi) = \frac{1}{2}\|w\|^2 + C(\sum_{i=1}^{n} \xi_i) \qquad (8)$$

$$\text{Subject to} \qquad \begin{array}{l} y_i\left[(w^T x_i) + b\right] - 1 + \xi_i \geq 0, \\ \xi_i \geq 0, \ i = 1, 2, \dots, n \end{array} \qquad (9)$$

Where: $C > 0$ is a penalty coefficient.

This is a quadratic programming problem that can be solved by the Lagrange method and translated into the following questions:

$$\text{Maximize} \qquad Q(\alpha) = \sum_{i=1}^{n} \alpha_i - \frac{1}{2} \sum_{i,j=1}^{n} \alpha_i \alpha_j y_i y_j (x_i \cdot x_j) \qquad (10)$$

$$\text{Subject to} \qquad \sum_{i=1}^{n} y_i \alpha_i = 0 \qquad (11)$$

$$0 \le \alpha_i \le C, \; i = 1, 2, \ldots, n \qquad (12)$$

The weight coefficient for the optimal classification surface is:

$$w = \sum_{i=1}^{n} \alpha_i y_i x_i \qquad (13)$$

It can be seen that the weight coefficient of the optimal classification surface is the linear combination of training samples. From the formula (12), the smaller the penalty coefficient C is, the smaller the Lagrange multiplier is. Likewise, from formula (13), the smaller α_i is, the smaller $\|w\|$ is, which means that the bigger interval between two classes can improve the generalization performance of SVM. The smaller C is, the bigger the interval between two classes is and the better generalization performance the SVM has, which leads to reduce the accuracy of SVM. On the contrary, the bigger C is, the smaller the interval between two classes is and the poorer generalization performance the SVM has, which leads to improve the accuracy of SVM. Therefore, the penalty coefficient affects the generalization performance and accuracy of SVM. The value of C should select appropriate.

In this paper, we classify bus images based on SVM by choosing an appropriate kernel function. The type of kernel function significantly affects the performance of SVM. Three common kernel functions are used in this paper, including Polynomial kernel function, Gaussian kernel function and Sigmoid kernel function [12]. They can be written in the forms as following:

Polynomial kernel function:

$$K(x_i, x_j) = \left[(x_i \cdot x_j) + 1 \right]^d \qquad (14)$$

Where: d is the degree of the polynomial.
Gaussian kernel function:

$$K(x_i, x_j) = \exp\left(-\sigma \left| x_i - x_j \right|^2 \right) \qquad (15)$$

Sigmoid kernel function:

$$K(x_i, x_j) = \tanh(\sigma(x_i, x_j) + c) \qquad (16)$$

Among them, the polynomial kernel function is related to d, and the gaussian kernel function is related to σ. In the paper, we compare the accuracy of the SVM model with different kernel functions through a large number of testing images. Finally, we choose the optimal classifier.

In this paper, we classify overloaded bus images based on image processing and support vector machine. Firstly, we select training samples from standard samples library, and preprocess the selected images, including histogram equalization, images segmentation and closed operation. Secondly, we extract the edge features of the preprocessed images and build a feature samples training set. Then, we select appropriate kernel function and parameters, and train a model used support vector machine on training set. Finally, we use the trained model to predict the class label of testing set and calculate the accuracy of the model. The whole flow chart is shown in Fig. 12.

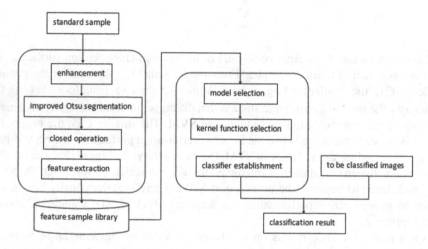

Fig. 12. Image overload and classification based on image processing and SVM

5   Experiments and Results

The purpose of this paper is to divide bus images into non-overloaded images and overloaded images based on images processing and support vector machine. It is difficult for us to determine which type of kernel function is best when features mapping is unknown. Therefore, the performance of model is significantly related to the choice of kernel functions. At present, many researchers make a choice based on the generalization error of the classifier through a great many of experiments [13].

In this paper, 897 bus integral images are used as a sample database which includes 36 obstructed images and 861 normal images. In order to analyze the experimental results, 861 normal images are selected as the standard dataset. The dataset consists of two types of images, of which 669 are non-overloaded and 192 are overloaded. The resolution of each image is 352×288. We divide dataset into training and testing dataset by using "Set aside method" [14]. The so-called "Set aside method" is a popular sampling method, which means that dataset D is divided into two mutually exclusive sets that one of the sets is the training set S, the other is the testing set T. After training a model used the training set S, the testing set T is used to calculate testing error to estimate the generalization error of the model. In this paper, 426 non-overloaded images and 125 overloaded images are selected randomly from the standard 861 images datasets as the training set, and the remaining 310 images (243 non-overloaded images and 67 overloaded images) as the testing set. In order to ensure these testing samples are not used in the training process, in this paper, we select precision as an evaluation indicator, which is the proportion of correct classified samples in the testing set. Each experiment is carried out repeatedly through 5 randomly dividing, and the evaluation result is based on the mean of five times. The result has two digits after the decimal point.

The purpose of this experiment is to observe the classification accuracy of the classifier under different parameters of different kernel functions, and to select the kernel function and parameters that are most suitable for this project. For polynomial kernel function, d value is 1, 2, 3, 4 and 5, respectively. For Gaussian kernel function, σ value is 0.1, 0.5, 1, 2 and 5, respectively. For Sigmoid kernel function, make $\sigma = 1$, c value is 0.5, 0.3, 0.1, 0, −0.1, −0.3 and −0.5. Meanwhile, according to the literature [15], the penalty factor C value is 100. The following is the classification accuracy and the graph of the three kernel functions with different parameters (Table 1).

Table 1. Classification accuracy of polynomial kernel function with different parameters

Group	Parameter d				
	1	2	3	4	5
1	80.65	84.84	89.68	93.23	89.68
2	80.00	85.48	91.61	93.55	89.68
3	81.61	87.10	90.32	94.19	90.00
4	80.97	85.16	90.97	93.87	89.68
5	82.26	86.45	88.71	93.55	89.03
Mean(%)	81.10	85.81	90.26	93.68	89.61

Figure 13 shows the average classification accuracy of polynomial kernel function with different parameters.

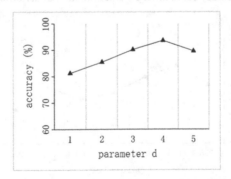

Fig. 13. Mean accuracy curve of polynomial kernel function with different parameters

As can be seen from the trend of the curve in Fig. 13, the classification accuracy of different parameters of the polynomial kernel function is different. With d increasing, the classification accuracy of the model first increases and then decreases. When d is 4, the classification effect is the best, reaching 93.68%. For the experimentally selected parameter d, the average classification accuracy fluctuates within a limited range of 81.10%–93.68%. The performance of the model is relatively stable (Table 2).

Table 2. Classification accuracy of RBF kernel function with different parameters

Group	Parameter d				
	1	2	3	4	5
1	67.74	90.32	85.16	74.19	70.97
2	68.39	89.68	83.87	75.81	70.00
3	70.32	88.71	84.52	74.84	69.35
4	69.35	90.32	84.52	75.81	71.61
5	67.42	90.97	83.23	75.16	70.00
Mean(%)	68.64	90.00	84.26	75.16	70.39

Gaussian kernel function with different parameters of the average classification accuracy curve is shown in Fig. 14 .

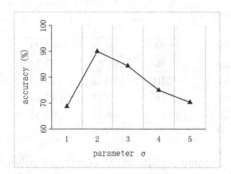

Fig. 14. Mean accuracy curve of RBF kernel function under different parameters

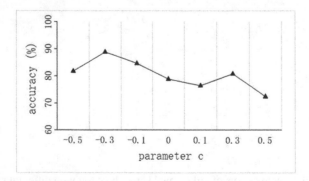

Fig. 15. Mean accuracy curve of Sigmoid kernel function under different parameters

It can be seen from Fig. 14 that the Gaussian kernel function has different classification accuracy with different parameters. For the Gaussian kernel function, its parameters are within a limited range selected, when the value is 0.1, the classification effect is poor. When the value is 0.5, the classification effect is the best; then with the increase of σ, the classification accuracy drops and is not very stable.

The average accuracy curve of Sigmoid kernel under different parameters is shown in Fig. 15.

By analyzing the experimental data of Table 3 and the average precision curve of Fig. 15, the classification accuracy of Sigmoid kernel function fluctuates in the range of 72.32%–88.77%. When c is −0.3, the classification accuracy is the best. Simultaneously, when c takes a negative value, its classification accuracy is better than that of a positive value, which accords with the analysis of Sigmoid kernel in ref. [16].

Table 3. Classification accuracy of Sigmoid kernel function under different parameters

Parameter c	Group					Mean(%)
	1	2	3	4	5	
−0.5	80.65	82.26	81.61	83.87	80.65	81.81
−0.3	88.06	87.10	89.68	90.32	88.71	88.77
−0.1	84.52	85.16	85.48	85.16	83.87	84.84
0	78.06	79.03	78.71	80.00	78.71	78.90
0.1	76.13	75.81	75.81	77.42	76.77	76.39
0.3	80.65	80.65	81.29	80.00	80.97	80.71
0.5	71.94	70.97	72.58	72.58	73.55	72.32

By comprehensively analyzing the three kernel functions selected in this paper, the classification of multiple kernel functions is obviously better than the other two kernel functions. For Gaussian kernel function, only when σ is 0.5, the classification accuracy reaches 90.00%. When the σ takes other values, classification effect is not stable. For the Sigmoid kernel function, it's classification performance is also unstable, and appears the oscillating phenomena. The average classification accuracy among the three of the highest is the polynomial kernel function. The precision is also the highest, up to 93.68%, and the classification performance is relatively stable. In general, it is the best choice to use polynomial kernel function parameter d as 4 in the bus images overload classification in this paper. But it should be noted that it is the best when select kernel function and parameters are only within a limited range.

It can be seen from the above experiments that the average successful rate of bus overload classification using the image classification method based on support vector machines reaches up to 93.68%. And when applying it to the traffic visualization system in Jilin Province, the accuracy rate can still reach about 93%. So the use of image processing and support vector machine technology can achieve bus overload detection.

6 Conclusion

In this paper, based on image enhancement, improved threshold segmentation, and closed operation processing of images of interior passengers photographed inside the bus, feature extraction is performed on these preprocessed image samples to establish a training set, and an appropriate kernel function is then selected. The SVM model is established with the parameters and completes the sample training of the training set. The automatic classification of the imported image is finally completed, and the overloaded image are intelligently identified.

Finally, for the images obtained in this paper, through the comparative analysis of multiple sets of experiments, we notice that when the polynomial kernel function parameter d value is 4, the classification accuracy is the highest. Increasing the recognition speed and efficiency of the overloaded images on buses can save a lot of human resources and increase penalty rates for violations. So, the method of bus image overload classification based on image processing and support vector machines has great values. However, compared with the ideal classification accuracy of 100%, there is a certain distance. How to further improve the classification accuracy is the future work.

References

1. Ding, C.: The effect of overloaded cars and the tire pressure on the stress distribution of the road. Int. J. Intell. Inf. Manag. Sci. 5(3), 264–267 (2016)
2. Wang, W.L., Lu, C.Z., Li, Y.R.: Basic economic measures in long-term effective mechanism for administering overload and oversize of motor vehicles. Int. J. Intell. Inf. Manag. Sci. 24(6), 148–152 (2007)
3. Zhang, Z., Cheng, W., Wu, L., et al.: Study on circular traffic signs recognition method based on invariant moments and SVM. J. Electron. Meas. Instrum. 31(5), 773–779 (2017)
4. Zhao, G.Q., Wang, F.J.: Car train overload signal monitoring system optimization modeling research. Comput. Simul. 33(11), 162–163 (2016)
5. Wu, Y.Q., Meng, T.L., Wu, S.H.: Research progress of image thresholding methods in recent 20 years (1994–2014). J. Data Acquis. Process. 30(1), 1–23 (2015)
6. Yan, J.Z., Lin, S., Sing, B.K.: Change-based image cropping with exclusion and compositional features. Int. J. Comput. Vis. 114(1), 74–87 (2015)
7. A R Correspondng's scientific contributions, Venmathi, Venmathi, A.R., et al.: Kirsch compass kernel edge detection algorithm for micro calcification clusters in mammogram. Middle East J. Sci. Res. 24(4), 1530–1535 (2016)
8. Liu, D.H., Zhang, Y.D., Li, X., et al.: Adaptive thresholding method under the dynamic environment. J. Comput. Appl. 36(S2), 152–156 (2016)
9. A R Correspondng's scientific contributions, Venmathi, A.R., Venmathi, E.N., Ganesh, N.K.: Kirsch Compass kernel edge detection algorithm for micro calcification clusters in mammograms. Middle East J. Sci. Res. 24(4), 1530–1535 (2016)
10. Thang, P.Q., Thuy, N.T., Lam, H.T.: A modification of solution optimization in support vector machine simplification for classification. In: Bhateja, V., Nguyen, B.L., Nguyen, N.G., Satapathy, S.C., Le, D.-N. (eds.) Information Systems Design and Intelligent Applications. AISC, vol. 672, pp. 149–158. Springer, Singapore (2018). https://doi.org/10.1007/978-981-10-7512-4_15

11. Zhi, J., Sun, J., Wang, Z., Ding, W.: Support vector machine classifier for prediction of the metastasis of colorectal cancer. Int. J. Mol. Med. **41**(3), 1419–1426 (2018)
12. Mcdonald, G., Macdonald, C., Ounis, I.: A study of SVM kernel functions for sensitivity classification ensembles with POS sequences. In: SIGIR 2017, pp. 1097–1100 (2017)
13. Yang, L., Wang, Y.: Survey for various cross-validation estimators of generalization error. Appl. Res. Comput. **32**(5), 1287–1290 (2011)
14. Zhou, Z.H.: Machine Learning. 2nd edn. Tsinghua University Press, Beijing (2016)
15. Yu, Z., Wong, H.S., Wen, G.: A modified support vector machine and its application to image segmentation. Image Vis. **29**(1), 29–40 (2016)
16. Hsuan, T.L., Chih, J.L.: A study on Sigmoid Kernels for SVM and the training non-PSD kernels by SMO-type methods. Submitt. Neural Comput. **27**(1), 15–23 (2003)

Accurate Acoustic Based Gesture Classification with Zero Start-Up Cost

Haojun Ai[1,2,3], Liangliang Han[4], Yifeng Wang[1(✉)], and Liang Liao[5,6]

[1] School of Cyber Science and Engineering, Wuhan University, Wuhan, Hubei, China
{aihj,whuyifeng}@whu.edu.cn
[2] Key Laboratory of Aerospace Information Security and Trusted Computing,
Ministry of Education, Beijing, China
[3] Collaborative Innovation Center of Geospatial Technology, Wuhan, China
[4] Aerospace System Engineering Shanghai, Shanghai, People's Republic of China
[5] ChangZhou Municipal Public Security Bureau, Changzhou, China
[6] Key Laboratory of Police Geographic Information Technology,
Ministry of Public Security, Beijing, China

Abstract. Acoustic gesture recognition based on the Doppler effect has garnered much research attention. The accuracy of gesture recognition and potential false positives are the main factors that limit the widespread use of gestures. To this end, we propose a novel gesture classification method based on the acoustic Doppler effect that does not require any custom hardware, simply a speaker and one microphone on a laptop. An effective sound field is built by a high frequency sound wave from the speaker, and the wave reflected by hand motion is captured by the microphone. We design a set with five features, three of them are stable and invariant to different people, so even new users can operate our system with zero start-up cost and no training. The remaining two features are highly correlated with the velocity and the range to computer of the gestures, which can reduce the potential false positives in detection. Besides, a classifier is designed depending on multistage decision rules to identify the 11 kinds of defined gestures. The experiment result about user experience feedback of HCI shows that our system has good usability performance. And the numerical experiments with 10 users show that our system can not only keep less potential false positives, but also achieve a classification accuracy of up to 99.09%.

Keywords: Doppler effect · Gesture classification · Acoustic · HCI

1 Introduction

For years, gesture recognition [2,9,10,17] with a device-free manner has developed rapidly, especially the widely used mobile phones and PCs have audio input and output components composed of speakers and microphones, so a Doppler-based gesture recognition as a new human-machine interface application has attracted the attention of researchers [1,7,8,14,15].

© Springer Nature Switzerland AG 2018
J. Vaidya and J. Li (Eds.): ICA3PP 2018, LNCS 11336, pp. 44–58, 2018.
https://doi.org/10.1007/978-3-030-05057-3_4

Many studies have tried to use machine learning methods [11,13,19–21] to improve the accuracy of gesture recognition. For example, Ai et al. [1] obtained the HMM model of each gesture by training the feature vectors of the samples, finally achieved recognition accuracy of 95% for 18 gestures. Dolphin [16] extracted the effective frequency bins around the peak and normalized them to form a vector feature, and the classifier they chosen was the Liblinear (Large Linear classifier) with 93% accuracy of recognition. In addition, Neural Net [11], Bayes [19] etc. classifiers were also used in some researches. Although the classification accuracy of gestures is significantly improved by adopting machine learning, other problems such as increased computational complexity and time-consuming are caused.

Besides, potential false positives of gesture detection are also a key issue that restricts the widespread use of gestures in HCI. Most acoustic-based hand gesture classification methods show good robustness in an unmanned environment [1, 14,16], but if people walk around, they are prone to false positive performance in detection [1,7,16].

In the paper, we extract three general stable invariant features to characterize one gesture and two other features that reduce the false positives in detecting gestures. Furthermore, we also design a classifier depending on multistage decision rules to categorize the 11 predefined gestures with high accuracy and less false positives.

We have summarized the main contributions in the paper as follows:

- We extract five features from the Doppler shift to characterize a gesture, and design a classifier depending on multistage decision rules to identify all gestures, which keeps a high precision during gesture recognition.
- Two of the features are bandwidth and amplitude of shift, which can significantly reflect the velocity and the range to computer of the gestures. By threshold setting can effectively identify some of the far-range people's walking and slow motions, thereby reducing the potential false positives in detection effectively.
- Remaining three features are direction, count of direction change and distance. They are all stable and invariant property in a gesture so that they generally does not change when a same gesture is performed by different people. Hence the users can operate our system with zero start-up cost and no training.

2   Feature Extraction

The theoretical basis of the gesture identification is a well-known phenomenon: Doppler effect [18]. When a moving object approaches the signal source (the speaker), the frequency of signal perceived by the receiver (the microphone) becomes larger [3], whereas the perceived frequency decreases when the object does an operation far from the wave source.

The Doppler shift f_R caused by a movement can be calculated by the equation:

$$f_R = \left(1 + \frac{\Delta v}{c}\right) \times f \tag{1}$$

$$\Delta f = f_R - f_S \tag{2}$$

Where Δv and c respectively represent the velocity of the object and of the sound in air, and f_S is the pilot tone transmitted from the speaker. Since the speaker and microphone keep stationary and are located on a same laptop, the velocity of receiver and source is out of our consideration.

2.1 Signal Analyze

In this paper, a range of effective sound field is formed by a high-frequency signal of 18 kHz from the speaker. When the operator moves hands in it, the reflected frequency shift is captured by the microphone. According to the characteristics of Doppler frequency shift [6], the whole processing of signal is carried out in the frequency domain.

We set the sampling frequency of the microphone to 44.1 kHz, and then the 2048-point FFT is performed to obtain the frequency-domain characteristic of the sound. In the informal test of SoundWave [8], the fastest gesture can reach 3.9 m/s. Herein, we conservatively estimate the fastest speed as 6 m/s, that is, the maximum frequency shift $\Delta f_{max} = 318$ Hz is calculated according to the Eq. 1, so take the left effective frequency range of the emitted peak is [17682, 18000], the right effective range is [18000, 18318].

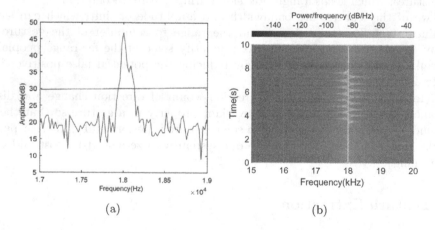

Fig. 1. (a) Positive shift in frequency spectrum generated by a towards-gesture. (b) Time-frequency map caused by a moving hand. The hand moves towards and away from the device alternately from the 4th to 8th s, and no motion in the remaining time.

We set the length of the analysis windows to 50 ms, so the frequency-domain is refreshed every 50 ms. The frequency spectrum is like a micro-image, reflecting the changes in the frequency of gestures in the instantaneous, and contains many tiny details (Fig. 1(a)). A time-frequency graph is generated by adding the time information to the spectrum, as seen in Fig. 1(b), it expresses the direction and distance of gestures at the macro level.

2.2   Feature Extraction

After getting the spectrum of the signal collected by the microphone, we extracted five features, including bandwidth, amplitude of frequency shift, furthermore, the direction and count of direction change, and the moving distance in a gesture, so as to form a feature vector x:

$$x = \left(x^{(1)}, x^{(2)}...x^{(i)}...x^{(n)} \right)^{T} \tag{3}$$

Where $x^{(i)}$ represents the ith feature, and $n = 5$. The overall flow is shown in Fig. 2. Next, we explain each feature of frequency shift in detail.

Bandwidth ($x^{(1)}$). $x^{(1)}$ is the bandwidth of emitted peak by scanning the frequency bins at 30% of the tone amplitude, which is extracted with the same method as SoundWave ([8]). $x^{(1)}$ is a measure of the absolute velocity of gesture movement and divide the hand velocity into different levels (Fig. 3). By setting an appropriate threshold θ_v, false positives caused by unintended slow motions of users can be effectively detected.

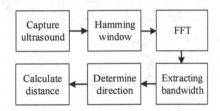

Fig. 2. The processing flow of sound signal.

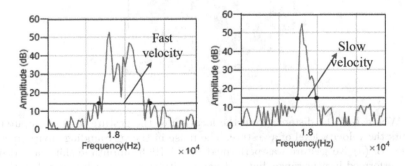

Fig. 3. Bandwidth in frequency spectrum caused by different velocity gestures.

Amplitude of Frequency Shift $(x^{(2)})$. $x^{(2)}$ is the highest amplitude that the frequency shift can reach, which is a percentage-based value relative to the amplitude of tone peak A_{peak}. Shift caused by performing a same gesture at far and near are significantly different, mainly manifested in $x^{(2)}$, as illustrated in Fig. 4. The farther a gesture is performed, the lower $x^{(2)}$ is. Therefore, setting a higher amplitude h_{upper}, gestures can basically divided into two

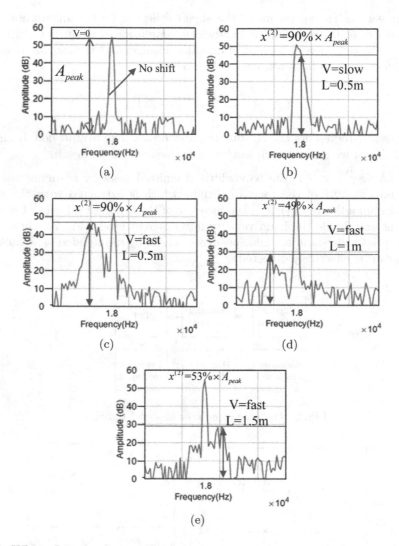

Fig. 4. Where L is the distance from the location of the gesture to the computer, V represents the velocity level of a gesture. The noise in the surrounding environment is about 45 dB. (a) No gesture was performed. (b–c) High amplitude shift caused by a gesture performed in near-range, but $x^{(1)}$ bandwidth in (c) is much larger than that in (b); (d–e) Lower amplitude shift caused by a fast gesture in far-range from computer.

categories: near-range gesture G_{near} and far-range gesture G_{far}. In this paper, we set $h_{upper} = 70\% \times A_{peak}$, it's obvious that $x^{(2)} > h_{upper}$ in the frequency spectrum of G_{near}, but $x^{(2)} < h_{upper}$ of G_{far}.

To summarize, $x^{(1)}$ is the bandwidth covered by the frequency shift on the horizontal axis at a specific amplitude, which reflects a gesture velocity. $x^{(2)}$ is the amplitude that the frequency shift can reach on the vertical axis, so gestures can be simply divided into two categories based on the location of gesture from the computer. Identifying the slow velocity or far-range motion as a false alarm can improve system robustness.

Direction ($x^{(3)}$). $x^{(3)}$ represents the direction of the gesture, which is depending on the energy difference between the right and left side of the peak. When the shift of the frequency shift is positive, the energy on the right of the peak increases, whereas the negative shift causes the energy on the left side to increases.

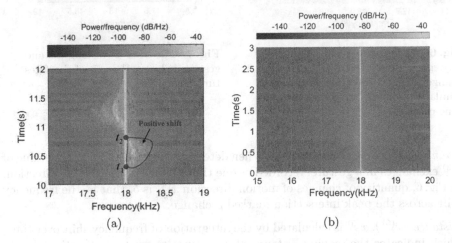

Fig. 5. (a) The red line area shows a positive shift occurs on the right of pilot peak, $x^{(3)} > 0$, meaning a towards-gesture. (b) No movement and no frequency shift, $x^{(3)}$ is near zero. (Color figure online)

Define the energy on the left E_{left} as the integral of the frequency within the effective range

$$E_{left} = \int_{fs-\Delta f_{max}}^{fs} f(x)dx \tag{4}$$

Similarly, define the right energy E_{right}:

$$E_{left} = \int_{fs}^{fs+\Delta f_{max}} f(x)dx \tag{5}$$

Therefore, the difference between the right and left energy $x^{(3)}$:

$$x^{(3)} = E_{right} - E_{left} \tag{6}$$

Where $\Delta f_{max} = 318\,\mathrm{Hz}$, $f(x)$ is the amplitude of the shift at each effective frequency bin. As illustrated in Fig. 5(a), if $x^{(3)}$ is positive, then the hand moves towards the devices, the negative value means away. No movement occurred if $x^{(3)}$ is near zero (Fig. 5(b)).

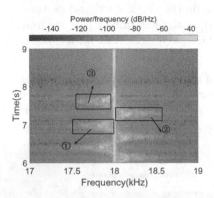

Fig. 6. When the frequency shift property goes from ① to ②, one time change of hand direction is detected. Similarly, from ② to ③ are also one time change.

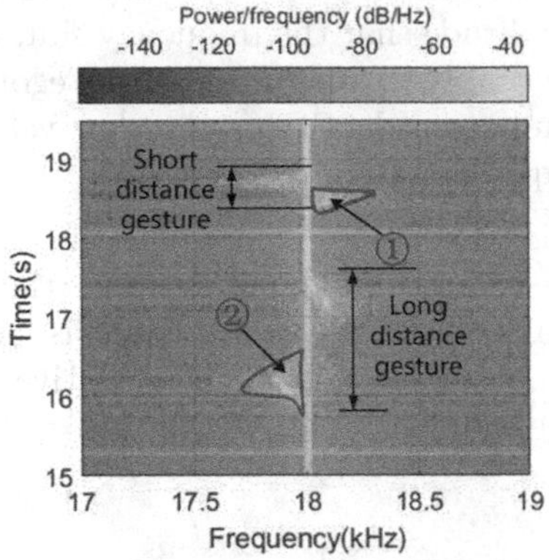

Fig. 7. The area ② of long distance gesture is larger than ① of short gesture obviously.

Count of Direction Change ($x^{(4)}$). When detecting positive and negative value of $x^{(3)}$ exchanges in a gesture, recorded as one time change of the gesture direction. In Fig. 6, quantity of changes of motion direction $x^{(4)}$ is 5, that is, the frequency shift across the peak intersection marked a change.

Distance ($x^{(5)}$). $x^{(5)}$ is calculated by the integration of frequency shift over time, which indicates the moving distance of a gesture in one time direction change to distinguish the long and short distance gesture (Fig. 7). *Distance = time × velocity*, time information can be quickly obtained from the time-frequency map, the key is velocity. There is a proportional relationship between velocity and frequency shift based on Eq. 2. We use the following equation to make a rough calculation of $x^{(5)}$:

$$x^{(5)} = \frac{c}{fs} \times \int_{t_1}^{t_2} \Delta f dt \tag{7}$$

Where t_1 and t_2 respectively represent the start point and the next direction change point of the gesture within once change of the gesture direction.

In Fig. 8, an informal test shows the $x^{(5)}$ distribution of different gestures, where the short and long distance gestures were respectively performed 100 times by 10 participants. The result verified our thoughts that long and short distance gestures have a clear boundary value. So we initially set the threshold $D_{L/S}$ of long and short distance is 500 to make gestures more clearly distinct and make sure a high sensitivity of distinguishing two types gesture.

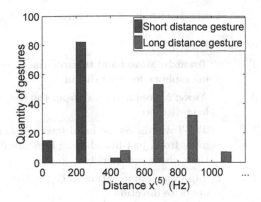

Fig. 8. Histogram of $x^{(5)}$ distribution.

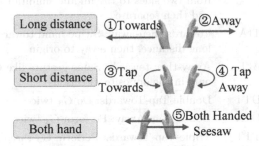

Fig. 9. $G_1 \sim G_5$ graphic representation.

3 Gesture Definition and Classification

The designed gestures are not only the more accessible body language of HCI, but also easily discriminated from each other.

3.1 Gesture Definition

Based on the proposed five features, we can define a simple set that contains 11 gesture actions: $G = \{G_1, G_2...G_j...G_N\}$, where $N = 11$, G_j represents the jth gesture in the set. All gesture descriptions are listed in Table 1. And Fig. 9 shows $G_1 \sim G_5$ motion graphic, where G_1 and G_2 are long distance gestures, while the tap gestures like click mouse, so they are all short distance motions. The remaining gestures $G_6 \sim G_{11}$ are compound gestures. The users need to perform gestures at a certain velocity, without requiring a constant velocity, only need the instantaneous velocity reach the threshold of certain velocity. Users can adjust the velocity threshold according to their own habits.

3.2 Hand Gesture Classification

In this section, we classify gestures step by step based on different features until we categorize each of the gestures. The system first detects G_5 (BHS) because

Table 1. Definition of gestures

Number	Gesture	Description
G_1	T	Towards: Move hand towards the microphone for long distance
G_2	A	Away: Move hand away from the devices for long distance
G_3	TT	Tap-Towards: Swipe hand towards then away from, just like clicking a mouse one time, short and quickly
G_4	TA	Tap-away: Same action as G_3, in the opposite direction
G_5	BHS	Both-Handed-Seesaw: Move both hands from two sides to the middle simultaneously, and then separate
G_6	TtA	Towards-then-away: Swipe hand towards for long distance, then away to origin
G_7	AtT	Away-then-towards: Same gesture like G_6, only in the opposite direction
G_8	DTT	Double-Tap-Towards: Do G_3 twice
G_9	DTA	Double-Tap-Away: Perform G_4 twice
G_{10}	TTT	Triple-Tap-Towards: Perform G_3 three times
G_{11}	TTA	Triple-Tap-Away: Do G_4 three times

it causes significant shifts on both sides of the tone peak simultaneously, a clear distinction from the remaining 10 gestures. Then, we classify the remaining 10 gestures by using a classifier designed depending on multistage decision rules (Fig. 10). Table 2 lists the feature values of the 10 gestures.

4 Evaluation and Results

We evaluated the system performance experimentally. And the system was developed on a laptop PC with Windows 10 and a pair of microphone and speaker without any customized hardware (Fig. 11), so the direction of any gesture performed by the user is same for the microphone and speaker. Note that any gestures within 0.8 m and people walking within 2 m near the computer all can cause significant frequency shifts, the experimental scene has a noise level of 45 dB.

4.1 Numerical Experiment

We conducted a numerical experiment to the robustness of the system through the following three fields: false positive, false negative and classification accuracy.

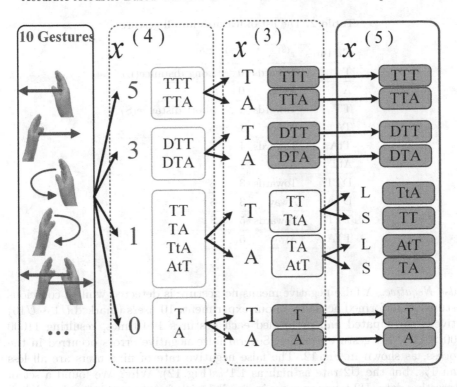

Fig. 10. Identifying gestures using a classifier, when a gesture is detected, the classifier adopts the features $x^{(4)}$, $x^{(3)}$ and $x^{(5)}$ in turn as decision rule for each stage.

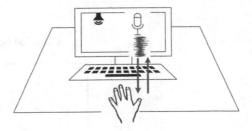

Fig. 11. Devices deployment in experiment environment.

Potential False Positive. A false alarm refers to a gesture is erroneously detected without gestures execution. Experiments were conducted in the following two common living environments, the first is that the user only sat in front of the computer for normal typing and thinking motion, while no one walks around. In half an hour, the number of potential false positives is 6, all of them were single tap actions since these gestures is short and simple. In the second case, the user had no any actions, only three participants were located about 1.5 m from the computer and walked around for half an hour. The system detected 4 false positives finally, and all of them were the result of the participants walking quickly.

Table 2. The list of features for all gestures

Gestures	$x^{(3)}$	$x^{(4)}$	$x^{(5)}$
T	Towards	0	Long distance(L)
A	Away	0	L
TT	Towards	1	Short distance(S)
TA	Away	1	S
TtA	Towards	1	L
AtT	Away	1	L
DTT	Towards	3	S
DTA	Away	3	S
TTT	Towards	5	S
TTA	Away	5	S

False Negative. A false negative means no gesture is detected while a conscious gestures is performed actually. In our experiment, 10 users (marked $U1 \sim U10$) actively participated and performed each gestures 100 times, resulting 11000 ($100 \times 11 \times 10$) gesture samples. Several false negative errors occurred in the process, as shown in Fig. 12. The false negative rate of nine users are all less than 1%, but the U2 rate as high as 1.1% (Fig. 12). Why? We found a set of interesting data, U2 tends to move in parallel with four fingers instead of sliding the palm of hand, resulting in smaller frequency shift. This may be the reason of a high false negative rate.

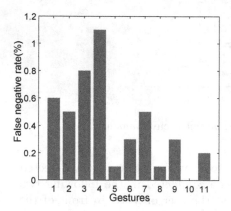

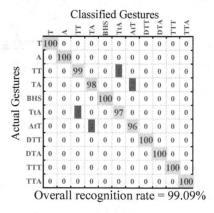

Fig. 12. The rate of false negative during the gesture sample test process.

Fig. 13. The confusion matrix of the gesture classification.

Classification Accuracy. Then the rest of effective gesture successfully detected from above experiment samples were used to measure classification precision. Since the samples were all labeled, so we can easily calculated the final classification accuracy (Fig. 13) up to 99.09%.

There are several samples that have been misidentified, mostly because of the occasional confusion in decision of long or short distance of gestures, as different people have their own preferences to perform hand gestures, so it is very difficult to correctly classify gestures with 100% accuracy by choosing a proper threshold $D_{L/S}$ of long and short distance. However it doesn't mean the evaluation contradicts with the claim, because the experimental result has shown that our method can already identify the different distance gestures with a much high accuracy.

4.2   Gesture Usability Test

Research in gesture usability focus on five main principles [4,5,12]: learnability, efficiency, memorability, errors, and coverage. Among them, the low error rate (99.09% accuracy) and coverage (zero start-up cost and no training) have been basically verified in Sect. 4.1.

Next, we mapped the gesture set to a common remote controller in our life, take MI smart TV remote controller as an example (Fig. 14). Each gesture operates a button, there are 11 buttons on the controller, corresponding to our 11 kinds of gestures. 10 users ($U1 \sim U10$) respectively performed gestures to simulate remote controller to direct MI TV freely.

We collected a total of 151 gesture samples from 10 users, where 2 missed detection and 1 misidentified. We further recorded the user experience to evaluate the usability of the system for gesture classification.

Each participant indicated that the system is particularly efficient, as they can smoothly operate the TV with high precision. Six participants remarked

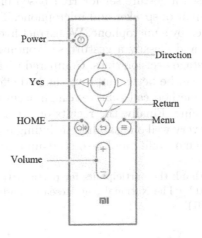

Fig. 14. MI TV remote controller.

specifically on the'learnability', since they were asked to observe the demo and learn gestures for 2–3 min and then operate the TV. Besides, eight participants described the gestures as "memorability" and "learnability", since the meaning of the gestures are easy to understand, so they can remember them (and perform them) easily. However, two participants acknowledged that the gesture action and the function of the menu are not very relevant, increasing the memory burden.

Finally, our method shows better performance in many items (Table 3) by comparison with the state of the art. A computer with one speaker and a microphone can meet our all hardware requirements. In addition, all experiments do not require users to perform gesture samples in advance and no training. Meanwhile, the results of digital experiments have verified that our system is robust. It not only has less potential false positives, but also can keep the false negative rate within 1%, and finally achieve about 99% classification accuracy with the defined 11 gestures.

Table 3. Comparison to the existing sound-based methods

Methods	SoundWave [8]	Dolphin [16]	Multiwave [15]	Our method
Number of speakers	1	1	≥2	1
Needing training?	NO	YES	YES	NO
Improve false positives?	YES	NO	NO	YES (>SoundWave)
Test false negatives?	NO	NO	NO	YES
Accuracy	94.5%	93%	93.9%	99%

5 Conclusion

In this paper, we proposed a gesture set for HCI based on Doppler effect. The sound field consists of a pair of speaker and microphone. The reflected signal by moving gesture is captured by a microphone. We extract five most robust features from the Doppler shift, and classify a gesture set containing 11 gestures by a classifier based-on multistage decision rules. Compared with the state-of-the-art, the features we propose can be better improve the bad effects of potential false positives, especially our method can achieve a high accuracy during classifying all gestures with no training. Finally, the results of experiments illustrate that our gesture set performs very well on usability, including high accuracy, less false positives, learnability, memorability and zero start-up cost.

Acknowledgment. We thank the participants for participating the user study. This work is partially supported by The National Key Research and Development Program of China (2016YFB0502201).

References

1. Ai, H., Men, Y., Han, L., Li, Z., Liu, M.: High precision gesture sensing via quantitative characterization of the doppler effect. In: 2016 23rd International Conference on Pattern Recognition (ICPR), pp. 973–978. IEEE (2016)
2. Asadzadeh, P., Kulik, L., Tanin, E.: Gesture recognition using RFID technology. Pers. Ubiquit. Comput. **16**(3), 225–234 (2012)
3. Aumi, M.T.I., Gupta, S., Goel, M., Larson, E., Patel, S.: Doplink: using the doppler effect for multi-device interaction. In: Proceedings of the 2013 ACM International Joint Conference on Pervasive and Ubiquitous Computing, pp. 583–586. ACM (2013)
4. Bevan, N., Curson, I.: Methods for measuring usability. In: Howard, S., Hammond, J., Lindgaard, G. (eds.) Human-Computer Interaction INTERACT 1997. ITIFIP, pp. 672–673. Springer, Boston, MA (1997). https://doi.org/10.1007/978-0-387-35175-9_126
5. Cabral, M.C., Morimoto, C.H., Zuffo, M.K.: On the usability of gesture interfaces in virtual reality environments. In: Proceedings of the 2005 Latin American Conference on Human-Computer Interaction, pp. 100–108. ACM (2005)
6. Chen, K.Y., Ashbrook, D., Goel, M., Lee, S.H., Patel, S.: Airlink: sharing files between multiple devices using in-air gestures. In: Proceedings of the 2014 ACM International Joint Conference on Pervasive and Ubiquitous Computing, pp. 565–569. ACM (2014)
7. Fu, B., Karolus, J., Grosse-Puppendahl, T., Hermann, J., Kuijper, A.: Opportunities for activity recognition using ultrasound doppler sensing on unmodified mobile phones. In: Proceedings of the 2nd international Workshop on Sensor-based Activity Recognition and Interaction, p. 8. ACM (2015)
8. Gupta, S., Morris, D., Patel, S., Tan, D.: Soundwave: using the doppler effect to sense gestures. In: Proceedings of the SIGCHI Conference on Human Factors in Computing Systems, pp. 1911–1914. ACM (2012)
9. Jeong, J., Jang, Y.: Max-min hand cropping method for robust hand region extraction in the image-based hand gesture recognition. Soft Comput. **19**(4), 815–818 (2015)
10. Kellogg, B., Talla, V., Gollakota, S.: Bringing gesture recognition to all devices. NSDI **14**, 303–316 (2014)
11. Molchanov, P., Gupta, S., Kim, K., Kautz, J.: Hand gesture recognition with 3D convolutional neural networks. In: Proceedings of the IEEE Conference on Computer Vision and Pattern Recognition Workshops, pp. 1–7 (2015)
12. Nielsen, M., Störring, M., Moeslund, T.B., Granum, E.: A procedure for developing intuitive and ergonomic gesture interfaces for HCI. In: Camurri, A., Volpe, G. (eds.) GW 2003. LNCS (LNAI), vol. 2915, pp. 409–420. Springer, Heidelberg (2004). https://doi.org/10.1007/978-3-540-24598-8_38
13. Paramonov, P., Sutula, N.: Simplified scoring methods for HMM-based speech recognition. Soft Comput. **20**(9), 3455–3460 (2016)
14. Pittman, C., Wisniewski, P., Brooks, C., LaViola Jr, J.J.: Multiwave: doppler effect based gesture recognition in multiple dimensions. In: Proceedings of the 2016 CHI Conference Extended Abstracts on Human Factors in Computing Systems, pp. 1729–1736. ACM (2016)
15. Pittman, C.R., LaViola Jr, J.J.: Multiwave: complex hand gesture recognition using the doppler effect. In: Proceedings of the 43rd Graphics Interface Conference, pp. 97–106. Canadian Human-Computer Communications Society (2017)

16. Qifan, Y., Hao, T., Xuebing, Z., Yin, L., Sanfeng, Z.: Dolphin: ultrasonic-based gesture recognition on smartphone platform. In: 2014 IEEE 17th International Conference on Computational Science and Engineering (CSE), pp. 1461–1468. IEEE (2014)
17. Rautaray, S.S., Agrawal, A.: Vision based hand gesture recognition for human computer interaction: a survey. Artif. Intell. Rev. **43**(1), 1–54 (2015)
18. Seddon, N., Bearpark, T.: Observation of the inverse doppler effect. Science **302**(5650), 1537–1540 (2003)
19. Suk, H.I., Sin, B.K., Lee, S.W.: Hand gesture recognition based on dynamic bayesian network framework. Pattern Recogn. **43**(9), 3059–3072 (2010)
20. Xiao, Q., Siqi, L.: Motion retrieval based on dynamic Bayesian network and canonical time warping. Soft Comput. **21**(1), 267–280 (2017)
21. Xiao, Q., Song, R.: Motion retrieval based on motion semantic dictionary and HMM inference. Soft Comput. **21**(1), 255–265 (2017)

An Approach of Collecting Performance Anomaly Dataset for NFV Infrastructure

Qingfeng Du[1,2], Yu He[1,2]($\boxtimes$), Tiandi Xie[1,2], Kanglin Yin[1,2], and Juan Qiu[1,2]

[1] School of Software Engineering, Tongji University, Shanghai, China
{du_cloud,rainlf,xietiandi,14_ykl,Juan_qiu}@tongji.edu.cn
[2] Software Engineering R&D Centre, Tongji University,
Jishi Building, Shanghai, China
https://github.com/XLab-Tongji

Abstract. Network Function Virtualization (NFV) technology is widely used in industry and academia. Meanwhile, it brings a lot of challenges to the NFV applications' reliability, such as anomaly detection, anomaly location, anomaly prediction and so on. All of these studies need a large number of anomaly data information. This paper designs a method for collecting anomaly data from Infrastructure as a Service (IaaS), and constructs an anomaly database for NFV applications. Three types of anomaly datasets are created for anomaly study, including datasets of workload with performance data, fault-load with performance data and violation of Service Level Agreement (SLA) with performance. In order to simulate an anomaly in a production environment better, we use Kubernetes to build a distributed environment, and to accelerate the occurrence of anomalies, a fault injection system is utilized. Our aim is to provide more valuable anomaly data for reliability research in NFV environments.

Keywords: Anomaly database · NFV · Kubernetes · IaaS
Clearwater · Performance monitoring · Fault injection

1 Introduction

Network Function Virtualization (NFV) is becoming more and more popular. Many Communication Service Providers (CSP) have begun to migrate applications to Network Functions Virtualization (NFV) environment [1]. Detection of anomaly and anomaly location is very important for providing better network services. It is necessary to predict anomalies in some special circumstances. It needs to analyze the rules and connections in a large number of anomaly data. But in production environment, the cost of collecting these data is expensive. So it is meaningful to collect these anomaly data for research in the experimental environment.

© Springer Nature Switzerland AG 2018
J. Vaidya and J. Li (Eds.): ICA3PP 2018, LNCS 11336, pp. 59–71, 2018.
https://doi.org/10.1007/978-3-030-05057-3_5

At present, there are many databases for anomaly data, such as KDD CUP 99 dataset[1], NAB dataset[2], Yahoo Webscope S5 dataset[3], and so on. All of these could be a benchmark for evaluating algorithms for anomaly detection. But these datasets also exist some restrictions, like single label, data redundancy and so on. On this basis, we collect anomaly data from three different perspectives.

In NFV environment, the cause of the failure is not single. In order to describe different exceptions more accurately, the multiple types of fault tags are necessary. Our method uses fault injection system to specify fault types of anomaly data, making datasets more suitable to deal with the problem of multiple classification in machine learning [2].

In addition, the malfunction of system resources can also lead to system anomaly happen, the pressure of users on system workload will also lead to system anomaly behavior [3]. In production environment, increase of users may be an important factor leading to anomaly service compared to the occurrence of hardware anomaly events. Our method also collects anomaly data under different workload.

In NFV applications, the typical quality of service index is Service Level Agreement (SLA)[4]. When a violation of SLA occurs, it represents an anomaly service. Our method also collects performance data under different SLA level. It helps researcher to analyze the relationship between a occurrence of SLA violation and performance data of IaaS in a system.

At last, we propose several machine learning models based on supervised learning to detect SLAs of VNFs and anomaly in IaaS. And compare the experimental results of each model. The result of the comparison between the models show that our anomaly database has a certain reference value in the anomaly detection with VNFs Environment.

The paper is organized as follows: Sect. 2 introduces the technical background and our related work in the construction of the anomaly database. Section 3 introduces the architecture of the data collection. Section 4 shows the implementation of our experiment. Section 5 provides a classical case study of Clearwater project[5], gives a detailed description of the building of the anomaly database. And at last, we summarizes the contribution and discuss the future work in Sect. 6.

2   Background and Related Work

With the development of Internet applications and the maturity of hardware virtualization, The emergence of Infrastructure as a Service (IaaS) [4] provides the underlying hardware support for this architecture. It makes network providers do not need care about the details of the underlying hardware devices, and

---

[1] http://kdd.ics.uci.edu/databases/kddcup99/kddcup99.html.
[2] https://github.com/numenta/NAB.
[3] https://webscope.sandbox.yahoo.com/catalog.php?datatype=s.
[4] https://en.wikipedia.org/wiki/Service-level_agreement.
[5] http://www.projectclearwater.org/.

concentrate on providing upper level services. In this context, Virtual Network Functions (VNFs) represent any virtual execution environment configured to provide a given network service. VNFs are often structured in several components each one hosted on single VMs.

The existing anomaly databases collect a lot of anomaly data in different fields. KDD CUP 99 dataset is used for network attack diagnosis. Each of its data records whether or not it has been attacked at the moment. It means that there are only one label in dataset, normal or anomaly.

Even Mahbod Tavallaee and his collaborator further optimized KDD CUP 99 dataset called NSL-KDD, it still has the same limitations [5]. This paper provides a disturbance system to specify the type of fault load to analyze the influence of different fault types on the performance of the tested system.

Markus Thill present a comparative study where several online anomaly detection algorithms are compared on the large Yahoo Webscope S5 anomaly benchmark [6]. But the yahoo Webscope S5 dataset is more suitable for time series analysis. It continues to have some limitations for the classification of different faults. We present a new approach to collecting performance data that with fault label. It has more advantages in the classification problem of anomaly detection.

In this paper, we integrate common single fault time series analysis problems and multiple fault classification problems in complex systems, propose corresponding performance data collection system and disturbance system. Then establish varied dataset in our anomaly database, Provide reference for fault analysis in different scenes. The details is shown in our site[6].

3 Architecture of Data Collection

This section outlines the framework of our performance data collection. In order to accurately collect data that with a fault type label, the framework consists of three systems, target application system (target system), disturbance system and performance monitoring system (monitoring system), as shown in Fig. 1.

3.1 Target System

Target system is a NFV application system, which is software implementations of network functions that can be deployed on a network functions virtualization infrastructure (NFVI). NFVI is the totality of all hardware and software components that build the environment where VNFs are deployed.

3.2 Disturbance System

The core function of the disturbance system is fault injection [7,8], it is used to accelerate the occurrence of anomaly events in the target system, such as

---

[6] https://github.com/XLab-Tongji

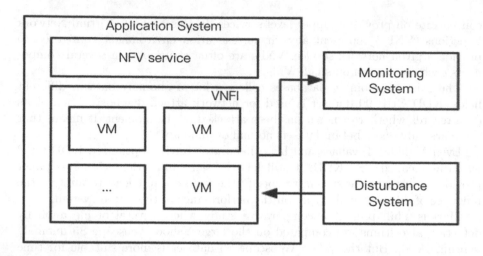

Fig. 1. Architecture of the performance data collection

hardware performance bottlenecks, SLA violation and so on. In this paper, we use linux system stress tool called stress-ng [9] to simulation system pressure to achieve fault injection function.

In order to produce different types of disturbance to the system, we use different types of fault injection in the target system:

- CPU stress fault
- MEMORY stress fault
- IO stress fault

Every type of fault injection will consume the system resources as much as possible to ensure the occurrence of anomaly events.

In most situations, anomaly diagnosis of platforms or systems is often directed against single point failure [10]. So we use a strategy to ensure that only one type of disturbance occurs on only one virtual machine at the same time.

When fault injection occurs, the disturbance system will record the log of the fault injection at the same time, including the start time, the duration, the type of fault and the target virtual machine. After the monitoring system collects performance data, the logs can be used to tag the performance data.

3.3 Monitoring System

There are many kinds of mature IaaS layer monitoring schemes at present, like Zabbix[7], Nagios[8], Cacti[9]. Considering our experimental environment and

---

[7] https://www.zabbix.com/.
[8] https://www.nagios.org/.
[9] https://www.cacti.net/.

monitoring project items, we use Zabbix to monitor the system and collect performance data online.

Zabbix is an enterprise open source monitoring software for networks and applications with C/S model, the zabbix agent is installed in the VMs. The situation shows that agent monitoring is more accurate than agent-less monitoring, and can more accurately describe the performance model of a system [11].

The Table 1 shows the performance model in our approach. Zabbix agents will collect these metrics from VMs, and store them in it's MySQL database. We also offer a JAVA application to download these performance data throw RESTful API from Zabbix server.

Table 1. Zabbix monitoring metrics

Metric name	Description	Metric name	Description
net.if.in[]	Network interface discovery: Incoming network traffic	vfs.fs.inode[/var/lib/docker/aufs,pfree]	Free inodes on /var/lib/docker/aufs (percentage)
net.if.out[]	Network interface discovery: Outgoing network traffic	vfs.fs.inode[/var/lib/kubelet,pfree]	Free inodes on /var/lib/kubelet (percentage)
proc.num[,,run]	Number of running processes	vfs.fs.inode[/var/lib/rancher/volumes,pfree]	Free inodes on /var/lib/rancher/volumes (percentage)
proc.num[]	Number of processes	vfs.fs.size[/,free]	Free disk space on /
system.cpu.intr	Interrupts per second	vfs.fs.size[/,pfree]	Free disk space on / (percentage)
system.cpu.load[percpu,avg1]	Processor load (1 min average per core)	vfs.fs.size[/,total]	Total disk space on /
system.cpu.load[percpu,avg15]	Processor load (15 min average per core)	vfs.fs.size[/,used]	Used disk space on /
system.cpu.load[percpu,avg5]	Processor load (5 min average per core)	vfs.fs.size[/boot,free]	Free disk space on /boot
system.cpu.switches	Context switches per second	vfs.fs.size[/boot,pfree]	Free disk space on /boot (percentage)
system.cpu.util[,idle]	CPU idle time	vfs.fs.size[/boot,total]	Total disk space on /boot
system.cpu.util[,interrupt]	CPU interrupt time	vfs.fs.size[/boot,used]	Used disk space on /boot
system.cpu.util[,iowait]	CPU iowait time	vfs.fs.size[/var/lib/docker/aufs,free]	Free disk space on /var/lib/docker/aufs
system.cpu.util[,nice]	CPU nice time	vfs.fs.size[/var/lib/docker/aufs,pfree]	Free disk space on /var/lib/docker/aufs (percentage)
system.cpu.util[,softirq]	CPU softirq time	vfs.fs.size[/var/lib/docker/aufs,total]	Total disk space on /var/lib/docker/aufs
system.cpu.util[,steal]	CPU steal time	vfs.fs.size[/var/lib/docker/aufs,used]	Used disk space on /var/lib/docker/aufs
system.cpu.util[,system]	CPU system time	vfs.fs.size[/var/lib/kubelet,free]	Free disk space on /var/lib/kubelet
system.cpu.util[,user]	CPU user time	vfs.fs.size[/var/lib/kubelet,pfree]	Free disk space on /var/lib/kubelet (percentage)
system.swap.size[,free]	Free swap space	vfs.fs.size[/var/lib/kubelet,used]	Used disk space on /var/lib/kubelet
system.swap.size[,pfree]	Free swap space in %	vfs.fs.size[/var/lib/rancher/volumes,free]	Free disk space on /var/lib/rancher/volumes
system.swap.size[,total]	Total swap space	vfs.fs.size[/var/lib/rancher/volumes,pfree]	Free disk space on /var/lib/rancher/volumes (percentage)
vfs.fs.inode[/,pfree]	Free inodes on / (percentage)	vfs.fs.size[/var/lib/rancher/volumes,total]	Total disk space on /var/lib/rancher/volumes
vfs.fs.inode[/boot,pfree]	Free inodes on /boot (percentage)	vfs.fs.size[/var/lib/rancher/volumes,used]	Used disk space on /var/lib/rancher/volumes
vfs.fs.inode[/boot,pfree]	Free inodes on /boot (percentage)	vm.memory.size[total]	vm.memory.size[total]
vm.memory.size[available]	Available memory		

4   Implementation

This section presents the implementation of our test bed environment. It includes infrastructure, kubernetes platform, monitoring system, attacker system and the clearwater-docker NFV application running in kubernetes platform, as shown in Fig. 2.

4.1   Infrastructure

The virtualized platform is a VMWare ESXI machine with 64 CPUs, 128 GB memory and 2 TB disk. It can provide multiple virtual machines on a physical machine. In this paper, we create 10 VMs on it. Every VM has 2 CPUs, 8 GB memory and 20 GB disk. VMs are connected through a 1000 Mbps virtualized network. The VMs has the docker environment with version 17.03.2-ce that can deploy most docker container in it.

4.2   Kubernetes

Kubernetes is a powerful container management platform. We use it to deploy the Clearwater project as described below. Here we use the Rancher scheme[10] to deploy kubernetes platform on the VMs. The reason is it can easily deploy the kubernetes platform. The installation steps are described as following:

1. Confirm that the network between the virtual machines just created is working;
2. Select a host as the rancher server host and deploy the latest version of rancher docker image on it;
3. Waiting for the rancher server is running Correctly, access the rancher server page from the 80 port of the host;
4. Create a new environment for test bed based on kubernetes template;
5. Add all other VMs in this environment and wait rancher server add them to kubernetes platform automatically.

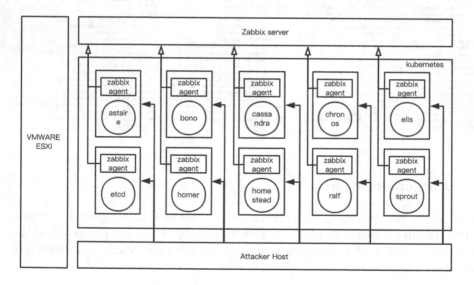

Fig. 2. Deployment of the test bed

4.3   Monitoring and Attack System

The monitoring system consists of zabbix server host and zabbix agents. Zabbix agents were installed on each VM when they were created and connect to zabbix server through the web page configurations. When the connection is set up, the agent will began to collect performance data and report them to the server at a set time interval.

Attacker host is also an independent host. It will execute the attack scripts which we provided to perform fault injection into VMs.

---

[10] https://rancher.com/.

4.4 NFV Application

The NFV application is a distributed computing system running NFV application. Here we utilise the Clearwater project. It is an open source implementation of an IMS for cloud platforms. It provides SIP-based (Session Initiation Protocol) voice and video calling, and messaging applications. It implements key standardized interfaces and functions of an IMS (except a core network) which enable industries to easily deploy, integrate and scale an IMS [3]. Clearwater project is consequently well suited for NFV related studies, it consists of about 10 components, every component plays its own unique functions in the system, and the relationship between components is shown as Fig. 3. Due to the docker deployment scheme, every Clearwater docker container is configured to allow unlimited use of host resources.

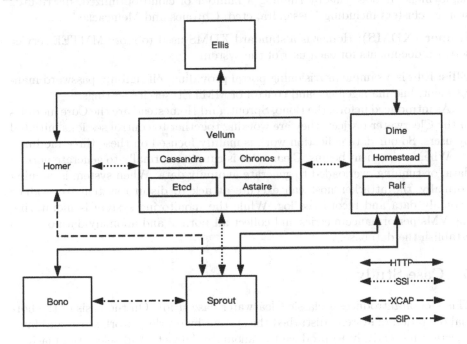

Fig. 3. Architecture of the clearwater project

Bono (Edge Proxy): The Bono nodes form a horizontally scalable SIP edge proxy providing both a SIP IMS Gm compliant interface and a WebRTC interface to clients. Client connections are load balanced across the nodes. The Bono node provides the anchor point for the client's connection to the Clearwater system, including support for various NAT traversal mechanisms. A client is therefore anchored to a particular Bono node for the duration of its registration, but can move to another Bono node if the connection or client fails.

Sprout (SIP Router): The Sprout nodes act as a horizontally scalable, combined SIP registrar and authoritative routing proxy, and handle client authentication and the ISC interface to application servers. The Sprout nodes also contain the in-built MMTEL application server.

Dime (Diameter Gateway): Dime nodes run Clearwater's Homestead and Ralf components. Homestead (HSS Cache) provides a web services interface to Sprout for retrieving authentication credentials and user profile information. It can either master the data (in which case it exposes a web services provisioning interface) or can pull the data from an IMS compliant HSS over the Cx interface; Ralf provides an HTTP API that both Bono and Sprout can use to report billable events that should be passed to the CDF (Charging Data Function) over the Rf billing interface.

Vellum (State Store): Vellum is used to maintain all long-lived state in the deployment. It does this by running a number of cloud optimized, distributed storage clusters including Cassandra, etcd, Chronos and Memcached.

Homer (XDMS): Homer is a standard XDMS used to store MMTEL service settings documents for each user of the system.

Ellis: Ellis is a sample provisioning portal providing self sign-up, password management, line management and control of MMTEL service settings.

As introduced before, the Bono, Sprout, and Homestead are the Core modules in the Clearwater project, they are working together to control sessions initiated by users. So our data collection work is mainly focused on these three modules.

When experiment begins, Clearwater is running normally to generate normal data, or running overloaded to generate anomaly data. When system is running normally, the attacker host can execute attack to disturb system to produce anomaly data and record the log. While the monitoring system is monitoring the VMs performance metrics and collect all normal and anomaly data on it to establish the database.

5   Case Study

This section introduces a classic Clearwater case study. On the basis of the normal operation of system, disturbed the system by overload work stress and fault injection respectively to produce the anomaly dataset. And select the machine learning algorithm with better performance in anomaly detection [12–15] to verify the availability of datasets.

In order to produce a normal workload, use the official recommended tools clearwater-sip-stress-coreonly[11]. It can control the working stress of the system by specifying three parameters as:

- subscriber_count: the number of subscribers to emulate;
- duration: the number of minutes to run stress for;
- multiplier: Optional parameters, multiplier for the VoLTE load profile (e.g. the default is 1 means 1.3 calls and 24 re-registers per sub per hour; passing 2 here will mean 2.6 calls and 4 re-registers per sub per hour).

---

[11] https://clearwater.readthedocs.io/en/stable/Clearwater_stres_testing.html.

We chose 500 subscribers, 60 min and 450 multiplier for experiment, At this point, the system can reach a 100% successful call rate. When the work stress continues to increase, the successful call rate began to decline. So we mark this point as a engineering level point x, it means the system has running in full workload under the current configuration.

5.1 Workload Module

As described above, we use engineering level point x as a standard to produce workload. Test the performance data of the system under 0.8x, 1x, 1.5x, 2x and 2.5x pressure respectively. The structure of collected dataset is shown in the Table 2.

5.2 Faultload Module

In this paper, we forces on the single point fault, it means at the same time, there is only one type of fault be injected into one VM. 0.8x engineering level is chosen to be the normal system running workload to easily observe the anomaly representation generated by fault injection. The process of fault injection is shown in Fig. 4.

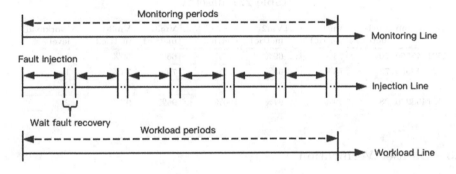

Fig. 4. Fault injection process

Within a specified time period, the fault injecting program will select a Select random fault type, a random target virtual machine, and a random injection period to start a disturbance process. This process will continue until the total of time which fault injection consumed reaches the stipulated time period. As described in Algorithm 1.

The disturbance system also records the injected log while injecting the fault. The key information includes timestamp, fault type, target host and injection duration. As Algorithm 2 described, We use the fault injection log to indicate which fault injection stage each performance data record belongs to, like normal, cpu fault, memory fault or io fault. The result of data process is shown in Table 3.

Algorithm 1. Fault Inject Controller

Input: $vm\_list, inject\_type\_list,$
    $duration\_list, duration$
1: $timer = 0$
2: **while** $timer < duration$ **do**
3:    $inject\_vm = random(vm\_list)$
4:    $inject\_type = random(inject\_type\_list)$
5:    $inject\_duration = random(duration\_list)$
6:    $timer+ = inject\_duration$
7:    $inject(vm, inject\_type, inject\_duration)$
8:    $sleep(pause)$
9: **end while**

In order to collect the anomaly SLA data, the workload module and faultload module work together to disturbance the system. We calculate the SLA level of the system from the percentage of successful requests (PSR). When $PSR \geq 90\%$, means the system is in good condition, marked as level 2. When $50\% \leq PSR \leq 90\%$, means the system is in unhealthy condition, marked as level 1. When $PSR \geq 50\%$, means the system is in bad condition, mark as level 0. The structure of dataset is shown in Table 4.

Table 2. Dataset A

Timestamp	Vm1-metric2	Vm1-metric1	...	Vm2-metric1	Vm2-metric2	...	Vm3-metric1	Vm3-metric2	...	Workload level
1521448560	70%	73%	...	69%	77%	...	66%	69%	...	1
1521448565	73%	73%	...	68%	75%	...	70%	74%	...	1
...										...
1521458230	98%	99%	...	97%	100%	...	95%	97%	...	2

5.3 Dataset Verification

This part introduces four widely used machine learning algorithms, namely, support vector machine, nearest neighbor, naive Bayes and random forests. And use them to locate outliers in the system performance data.

Algorithm 2. Data Labeled Controller

Input: $performance\_data, injection\_log$
1: $labeled\_data = []$
2: **while** $performance\_data.has\_next()! = null$ **do**
3:    $data = performance\_data.next()$
4:    $data\_label = label(data, injection\_log)$
5:    $labeled\_data.append(data\_label)$
6: **end while**

Table 3. Dataset B

Timestamp	Vm1-metric2	Vm1-metric1	...	Vm2-metric1	Vm2-metric2	...	Vm3-metric1	Vm3-metric2	...	Normal	CPU	MEMORY	IO
152263940	70%	73%	...	69%	77%	...	66%	69%	...	1	0	0	0
152263945	73%	73%	...	68%	75%	...	70%	74%	...	1	0	0	0
152263950	73%	100%	...	69%	79%	...	72%	73%	...	0	1	0	0
...												...	
152267680	71%	74%	...	70%	75%	...	99%	72%	...	0	0	0	1

Table 4. Dataset C

Timestamp	Vm1-metric2	Vm1-metric1	...	Vm2-metric1	Vm2-metric2	...	Vm3-metric1	Vm3-metric2	...	SAL level
1521448560	90%	72%	...	92%	74%	...	85%	91%	...	2
1521448565	85%	77%	...	83%	75%	...	73%	88%	...	1
...										...
1521458230	66%	68%	...	92%	89%	...	87%	79%	...	0

Table 5. Validation results of anomaly dataset

Service	Measure	Nearest neighbors	SVM	Naive bayes	Random forset
Dataset A	Precision	0.98	0.89	0.95	0.97
	Recall	0.97	0.88	0.93	0.96
	F1-score	0.97	0.87	0.93	0.98
Dataset B	Precision	0.93	0.90	0.96	0.99
	Recall	0.92	0.91	0.95	0.98
	F1-score	0.93	0.89	0.97	0.99
Dataset C	Precision	0.94	0.87	0.89	0.98
	Recall	0.97	0.93	0.91	0.96
	F1-score	0.96	0.92	0.94	0.97

There are 737 records in dataset A and dataset B, we employed the first 80% of them as the train set, having trained the learning methods, the rest 20% are used as test set to validate the algorithm model. The validation result are shown in Table 5.

The results show that the accuracy, recall rate and F1-score of each model reach a higher value. And because of the multi classification problem of the dataset, the random forest model achieves the best results.

6   Conclusion and Future Work

In this paper, we describe an approach to deploy NFV application Clearwater projects through the Kubernetes platform. On this basis, we use disturbance application system and monitoring system to collect performance data of IaaS layer devices under NFV application scenario to build anomaly database. Three categories of anomaly datasets with specified label are collected, includes workload with performance data, faultload with performance data and SLA level with performance data. The details of the anomaly database can be accessed on our website[12].

Through some widely used machine learning algorithm, we verify these datasets and get high accuracy. This means these datasets have some reference value for anomaly detection. In the future, we will try more anomaly scenes and cause anomaly reasons, and build corresponding anomaly datasets to analyze them. We hope to be of certain guiding significance for the detection of anomaly in different scenes.

References

1. Liu, J., Jiang, Z., Kato, N., Akashi, O., Takahara, A.: Reliability evaluation for NFV deployment of future mobile broadband networks. IEEE Wirel. Commun. **23**(3), 90–96 (2016)
2. Pieters, M., Wiering, M.: Comparison of machine learning techniques for multi-label genre classification. In: Verheij, B., Wiering, M. (eds.) BNAIC 2017. CCIS, vol. 823, pp. 131–144. Springer, Cham (2018). https://doi.org/10.1007/978-3-319-76892-2_10
3. Sauvanaud, C., Lazri, K., Kaâniche, M., Kanoun, K.: Anomaly detection and root cause localization in virtual network functions. In: 2016 IEEE 27th International Symposium on Software Reliability Engineering (ISSRE), pp. 196–206. IEEE (2016)
4. Bhardwaj, S., Jain, L., Jain, S.: Cloud computing: a study of infrastructure as a service (IAAS). Int. J. Eng. Inf. Technol. **2**(1), 60–63 (2010)
5. Tavallaee, M., Bagheri, E., Lu, W., Ghorbani, A.A.: A detailed analysis of the KDD cup 99 data set. In: 2009 IEEE Symposium on Computational Intelligence for Security and Defense Applications, CISDA 2009, pp. 1–6. IEEE (2009)
6. Thill, M., Konen, W., Bäck, T.: Online anomaly detection on the webscope S5 dataset: a comparative study. In: 2017 Evolving and Adaptive Intelligent Systems (EAIS), pp. 1–8, May 2017
7. Natella, R., Cotroneo, D., Madeira, H.S.: Assessing dependability with software fault injection: a survey. ACM Comput. Surv. (CSUR) **48**(3), 44 (2016)
8. Delvaux, J., Verbauwhede, I.: Fault injection modeling attacks on 65 nm arbiter and RO sum PUFs via environmental changes. IEEE Trans. Circuits Syst. I: Regular Papers **61**(6), 1701–1713 (2014)
9. King, C.: Stress-ng (2018)
10. Wang, Y., Li, X.: Achieve high availability about point-single failures in openstack. In: 2015 4th International Conference on Computer Science and Network Technology (ICCSNT), vol. 01, pp. 45–48, December 2015
11. Aversa, R., Panza, N., Tasquier, L.: An agent-based platform for cloud applications performance monitoring. In: 2015 Ninth International Conference on Complex, Intelligent, and Software Intensive Systems, pp. 535–540, July 2015

---

[12] https://github.com/XLab-Tongji/ADNFVI.

12. Buczak, A.L., Guven, E.: A survey of data mining and machine learning methods for cyber security intrusion detection. IEEE Commun. Surv. Tutor. **18**(2), 1153–1176 (2016). Secondquarter
13. Iglesias, F., Zseby, T.: Analysis of network traffic features for anomaly detection. Mach. Learn. **101**(1–3), 59–84 (2015)
14. Kulkarni, A., Pino, Y., French, M., Mohsenin, T.: Real-time anomaly detection framework for many-core router through machine-learning techniques. ACM J. Emerg. Technol. Comput. Syst. (JETC) **13**(1), 10 (2016)
15. Erfani, S.M., Rajasegarar, S., Karunasekera, S., Leckie, C.: High-dimensional and large-scale anomaly detection using a linear one-class SVM with deep learning. Pattern Recogn. **58**, 121–134 (2016)

An Axiomatization for BSP Algorithms

Yoann Marquer and Frédéric Gava[(✉)]

Laboratory of Algorithms, Complexity and Logic (LACL),
University of Paris-East, Créteil, France
yoann.apeiron.marquer@gmail.com, gava@u-pec.fr

Abstract. The Gurevich's thesis stipulates that sequential Abstract State Machines (ASMs) capture the essence of sequential algorithms. On another hand, the Bulk-Synchronous Parallel (BSP) bridging model is a well known model for HPC algorithm design. It provides a conceptual bridge between the physical implementation of the machine and the abstraction available to a programmer of that machine. The assumptions of the BSP model are thus provide portable and scalable performance predictions on most HPC systems. We follow Gurevich's thesis and extend the sequential postulates in order to intuitively and realistically capture BSP algorithms.

Keywords: BSP · ASM · Parallel algorithm · HPC · Postulates
Cost model

1 Introduction

1.1 Context of the Work

Nowadays, HPC (High Performance Computing) is the *norm* in many areas but it remains *more difficult* to have well defined paradigms and a common vocabulary as it is the case in the traditional sequential world. The problem arises from the difficulty to get a *taxonomy* of computer architectures and frameworks: there is a zoo of definitions of systems, languages, paradigms and programming models. Indeed, in the HPC community, several terms could be used to designate the same thing, so that misunderstandings are easy. We can cite parallel patterns [5] versus algorithmic skeletons [8]; shared memory (PRAM) versus thread concurrency and Direct ReMote Access (DRMA); asynchronous send/receive routines (MPI, http://mpi-forum.org/) versus communicating processes (π-calculus).

In the sequential world, it is easier to classify programming languages within their paradigm (functional, object oriented, *etc.*) or by using some properties of the compilers (statically or dynamically typed, abstract machine or native code execution). This is mainly due to the fact that there is an overall consensus on what sequential computing is. For them, *formal semantics* have been often studied and there are now many tools for testing, debugging, cost analyzing, software engineering, *etc.* In this way, programmers can implement sequential algorithms using these languages, which *characterize* properly the sequential algorithms.

© Springer Nature Switzerland AG 2018
J. Vaidya and J. Li (Eds.): ICA3PP 2018, LNCS 11336, pp. 72–88, 2018.
https://doi.org/10.1007/978-3-030-05057-3_6

This consensus is only fair because everyone *informally* agrees to what constitutes a sequential algorithm. And now, half a century later, there is a growing interest in defining *formally* the notion of algorithms [10]. Gurevich introduced an *axiomatic* presentation (largely machine independent) of the sequential algorithms in [10]. The main idea is that there is no language that truly represents all sequential algorithms. In fact, every algorithmic book presents algorithms in its own way and programming languages give too much detail. An axiomatic definition [10] of the algorithms has been mapped to the notion of Abstract State Machine (ASM, a kind of Turing machine with the appropriate level of abstraction): Every sequential algorithm can be captured by an ASM. This allows a common vocabulary about sequential algorithms. This has been studied by the ASM community for several years.

A parallel computer, or a multi-processor system, is a computer composed of more than one processor (or unit of computation). It is common to classify parallel computers (Flynn's taxonomy) by distinguishing them by the way they access the system memory (shared or distributed). Indeed, the memory access scheme influences heavily the programming method of a given system. Distributed memory systems are needed for computations using a large amount of data which does not fit in the memory of a single machine.

The three *postulates* for sequential algorithms are mainly consensual. Nevertheless, to our knowledge, there is not such a work for HPC frameworks. First, due to the zoo of (informal) definitions and second, due to a lack of realistic *cost models* of common HPC architectures. In HPC, the cost measurement is not based on the complexity of an algorithm but is rather on the execution time, measured using empirical *benchmarks*. Programmers are benchmarking load balancing, communication (size of data), *etc.* Using such techniques, it is very difficult to explain why one code is faster than another and which one is more suitable for one architecture or another. This is regrettable because the community is failing to obtain some rigorous characterization of sub-classes of HPC algorithms. There is also a lack of studying algorithmic completeness of HPC languages. This is the basis from which to specify what can or cannot be effectively programmed. Finally, taking into account all the features of all HPC paradigms is a daunting task that is unlikely to be achieved [9]. Instead, a *bottom up strategy* (from the simplest models to the most complex) may be a solution that could serve as a basis for more general HPC models.

1.2   Content of the Work

Using a *bridging model* [20] is a first step to this solution because it simplifies the task of algorithm design, programming and simplifies the reasoning of *cost* and ensures a better *portability* from one system to another. A bridging model is an abstract model of a computer which provides a conceptual bridge between the physical implementation of the machine and the *abstraction* available to a programmer of that machine. We conscientiously limit our work to the Bulk-synchronous Parallel (BSP) bridging model [1,18] because it has the advantage of being endowed with a simple model of execution. We leave more complex models to future work. Moreover, there are many different libraries and languages for programming BSP algorithms, for example, the BSPLIB for C [11] or JAVA [17], BSML [?], PREGEL [12] for big-data, *etc.*

Concurrent ASMs [3] try to capture the more general definition of asynchronous and distributed computations. We promote a rather different "bottom-up" approach consisting of restricting the model under consideration, so as to better highlight the algorithm execution time (which is often too difficult to assess for general models) and more generally to formalize our algorithms of a bridging model at their natural level of abstraction, instead of using a more general model then restrict it with an arbitrary hypothesis.

As a basis to this work, we first give an axiomatic definition of BSP algorithms (ALGO$_{BSP}$) with only 4 postulates. Then we extend the ASM model [10] of computation (ASM$_{BSP}$) for BSP. Our goal is to define a convincing set of parallel algorithms running in a predictable time and construct a model that computes these algorithms only. This can be summarized by ALGO$_{BSP}$=ASM$_{BSP}$. An interesting and novel point of this work is that the BSP cost model is preserved.

1.3   Outline

Many definitions used here are well known to the ASM community. Recalling all of them would be too long but they are available in the online technical report [22].

The remainder of this paper is structured as follows: In Sect. 2 we first recall the BSP model and define its postulates; Secondly, in Sect. 3, we give the operational semantics of ASM$_{BSP}$ and finally, we give the main result. Section 4 concludes, gives some related work and a brief outlook on future work.

2   Characterizing BSP Algorithms

2.1   The BSP Bridging Model of Computation

As the RAM model provides a unifying approach that can *bridge* the worlds of sequential *hardware* and *software*, so Valiant sought [20] for a unifying model that could provide an effective (and universal) bridge between parallel hardware and software. A *bridging* model [20] allows to reduce the gap between an abstract execution (programming an algorithm) and concrete parallel systems (using a compiler and designing/optimizing a physical architecture).

The *direct mode* BSP model [1,18] is a *bridging* model that simplifies the programming of various parallel architectures using a certain level of abstraction. The assumptions of the BSP model are to provide *portable* and *scalable* performance predictions on HPC systems. Without dealing with low-level details of HPC architectures, the programmer can thus focus on algorithm design only. The BSP bridging model describes a parallel architecture, an execution model for the algorithms, and a cost model which allows to predict their performances on a given BSP architecture.

A BSP computer can be specified by **p** *uniform* computing units (**processors**), each capable of performing one elementary operation or accessing a local memory in one time unit. Processors communicate by sending a data to every other processor in **g** time units (gap which reflects network bandwidth inefficiency), and a barrier mechanism is able to synchronise all the processors in **L** time units ("latency" and the ability of the network to deliver messages under a continuous load). Such values, along with the processor's speed (*e.g.* Mflops) can be empirically determined by executing benchmarks.

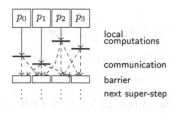

The time **g** is thus for collectively delivering a 1-relation which is a collective exchange where every processor receives/sends at most one word. The network can deliver an h-relation in time $\mathbf{g} \times h$. A BSP computation is organized as a *sequence* of **supersteps** (see Fig. 1). During a superstep, the processors may perform computations on local data or send messages to other processors. Messages are available for processing at their destinations by the next superstep, and each superstep is ended with the *barrier synchronisation* of the processors.

Fig. 1. A BSP super-step.

The execution time (cost) of a super-step s is the sum of the maximal of the local processing, the data delivery and the global synchronisation times. It is expressed by the following formula: $\mathrm{Cost}(s) = w^s + h^s \times \mathbf{g} + \mathbf{L}$ where $w^s = \max_{0 \le i < \mathbf{p}}(w_i^s)$ (where w_i^s is the local processing time on processor i during superstep s), and $h^s = \max_{0 \le i < \mathbf{p}}(h_i^s)$ (where h_i^s is the maximal number of words transmitted or received by the processor i). Some papers rather use the sum of words for h_i^s but modern networks are capable of sending while receiving data. The total cost (execution time) of a BSP algorithm is the sum of its super-step costs.

2.2   Axiomatic Characterization of BSP Algorithms

Postulate 1 (Sequential Time). *A* BSP *algorithm A is given by:*

1. *A set of states $S(A)$;*
2. *A set of initial states $I(A) \subseteq S(A)$;*
3. *A transition function $\tau_A : S(A) \to S(A)$.*

We follow [10] in which states, as first-order structures, are full instantaneous descriptions of an algorithm.

Definition 1 (Structure). *A (first-order) structure X is given by:*

1. *A (potentially infinite) set $\mathcal{U}(X)$ called the **universe** (or domain) of X*
2. *A finite set of function symbols $\mathcal{L}(X)$ called the **signature** (language) of X*
3. *For every symbol $s \in \mathcal{L}(X)$ an **interpretation** $\overline{s}^X$ such that:*
   (a) If c has arity 0 then $\overline{c}^X$ is an element of $\mathcal{U}(X)$
   (b) If f has an arity $\alpha > 0$ then $\overline{f}^X$ is an application: $\mathcal{U}(X)^\alpha \to \mathcal{U}(X)$

In order to have a uniform presentation [10], we considered constant symbols in $\mathcal{L}(X)$ as 0-ary function symbols, and relation symbols R as their indicator function χ_R. Therefore, every symbol in $\mathcal{L}(X)$ is a function. Moreover, partial functions can be implemented with a special symbol **undef**, and we assume in this paper that every $\mathcal{L}(X)$ contains the boolean type ($\neg$, $\wedge$) and the equality. We also distinguish dynamic symbols whose interpretation may change from one state to another, and static symbols which are the elementary operations.

Definition 2 (Term). *A term of $\mathcal{L}(X)$ is defined by induction:*

1. *If c has arity 0, then c is a term*
2. *If f has an arity $\alpha > 0$ and $\theta_1, \ldots, \theta_\alpha$ are terms, then $f(\theta_1, \ldots, \theta_\alpha)$ is a term*

The interpretation $\overline{\theta}^X$ of a term θ in a structure X is defined by induction on θ:

1. *If $\theta = c$ is a constant symbol, then $\overline{\theta}^X \overset{\text{def}}{=} \overline{c}^X$*
2. *If $\theta = f(\theta_1, \ldots, \theta_\alpha)$ where f is a symbol of the language $\mathcal{L}(X)$ with arity $\alpha > 0$ and $\theta_1, \ldots, \theta_\alpha$ are terms, then $\overline{\theta}^X \overset{\text{def}}{=} \overline{f}^X(\overline{\theta_1}^X, \ldots, \overline{\theta_\alpha}^X)$*

A **formula** F is a term with the particular form $\mathbf{true}|\mathbf{false}|R(\theta_1, \ldots, \theta_\alpha)|\neg F$ $|(F_1 \wedge F_2)$ where R is a relation symbol (ie a function with output $\overline{\mathbf{true}}^X$ or $\overline{\mathbf{false}}^X$) and $\theta_1, \ldots, \theta_\alpha$ are terms. We say that a formula is true (resp. false) in X if $\overline{F}^X = \overline{\mathbf{true}}^X$ (resp. $\overline{\mathbf{false}}^X$).

A BSP algorithm works on independent and uniform computing units. Therefore, a state S_t of the algorithm A must be a tuple $(X_t^1, \ldots, X_t^p)$. To simplify, we annotate tuples from 1 to p and not from 0 to $p-1$. Notice that p is not fixed for the algorithm, so A *can have states using different size of "p-tuples"* (informally p, the number of processors). In this paper, we will simply consider that *this number is preserved during a particular execution*. In other words: the size of the p-tuples is fixed for an execution by the initial state of A for such an execution.

If $(X^1, \ldots, X^p)$ is a state of the algorithm A, then the structures $X^1, \ldots, X^p$ will be called **processors** or **local memories**. The set of the *independent* local memories of A will be denoted by $M(A)$. We now define the BSP algorithms as the objects verifying the four presented postulates. The computation for every processor is done in parallel and step by step.

An **execution** of A is a sequence of states $S_0, S_1, S_2, \ldots$ such that S_0 is an initial state and for every $t \in \mathbb{N}$, $S_{t+1} = \tau_A(S_t)$. Instead of defining a set of *final* states for the algorithms, we will say that a state S_t of an execution is **final** if $\tau_A(S_t) = S_t$, that is the execution is: $S_0, S_1, \ldots, S_{t-1}, S_t, S_t, \ldots$ We say that an execution is **terminal** if it contains a final state.

We are interested in the algorithm and not a particular implementation (eg, the variables' names), therefore in the postulate we will consider the states up to multi-isomorphism.

Definition 3 (Multi-isomorphism). $\overrightarrow{\zeta}$ *is a multi-isomorphism between two states $(X^1, \ldots, X^p)$ and $(Y^1, \ldots, Y^q)$ if $p = q$ and $\overrightarrow{\zeta}$ is a p-tuple of applications*

$\zeta_1, \ldots, \zeta_p$ *such that for every* $1 \leq i \leq p$, ζ_i *is an isomorphism between* X^i *and* Y^i.

Postulate 2 (Abstract States). *For every* BSP *algorithm A:*

1. *The states of A are p-tuples of structures with the same finite signature* $\mathcal{L}(A)$;
2. $S(A)$ *and* $I(A)$ *are closed by multi-isomorphism;*
3. *The transition function* τ_A *preserves p, the universes and commutes with multi-isomorphisms.*

For a BSP algorithm A, let X be a local memory of A, $f \in \mathcal{L}(A)$ be a dynamic α-ary function symbol, and $a_1, \ldots, a_\alpha$, b be elements of the universe $\mathcal{U}(X)$. We say that $(f, a_1, \ldots, a_\alpha)$ is a location of X, and that $(f, a_1, \ldots, a_\alpha, b)$ is an **update** on X at the location $(f, a_1, \ldots, a_\alpha)$. For example, if x is a variable then $(x, 42)$ is an update at the location x. But symbols with arity $\alpha > 0$ can be updated too. For example, if f is a one-dimensional array, then $(f, 0, 42)$ is an update at the location $(f, 0)$. If u is an update then $X \oplus u$ is a new structure of signature $\mathcal{L}(A)$ and universe $\mathcal{U}(X)$ such that the interpretation of a function symbol $f \in \mathcal{L}(A)$ is:

$$\overline{f}^{X \oplus u}(\overrightarrow{a}) \overset{\text{def}}{=} \begin{cases} b & \text{if } u = (f, \overrightarrow{a}, b) \\ \overline{f}^{X}(\overrightarrow{a}) & \text{otherwise} \end{cases}$$

where we noted $\overrightarrow{a} = a_1, \ldots, a_\alpha$. For example, in $X \oplus (f, 0, 42)$, every symbol has the same interpretation than in X, except maybe for f because $\overline{f}^{X \oplus (f,0,42)}(0) = 42$ and $\overline{f}^{X \oplus (f,0,42)}(a) = \overline{f}^{X}(a)$ otherwise. We precised "maybe" because it may be possible that $\overline{f}^{X}(0)$ is already 42.

If $\overline{f}^{X}(\overrightarrow{a}) = b$ then the update $(f, \overrightarrow{a}, b)$ is said **trivial** in X, because nothing has changed. Indeed, if $(f, \overrightarrow{a}, b)$ is trivial in X then $X \oplus (f, \overrightarrow{a}, b) = X$.

If Δ is a set of updates then Δ is **consistent** if it does not contain two distinct updates with the same location. Notice that if Δ is inconsistent, then there exists $(f, \overrightarrow{a}, b), (f, \overrightarrow{a}, b') \in \Delta$ with $b \neq b'$ and, in that case, the entire set of updates clashes:

$$\overline{f}^{X \oplus \Delta}(\overrightarrow{a}) \overset{\text{def}}{=} \begin{cases} b & \text{if } (f, \overrightarrow{a}, b) \in \Delta \text{ and } \Delta \text{ is consistent} \\ \overline{f}^{X}(\overrightarrow{a}) & \text{otherwise} \end{cases}$$

If X and Y are two local memories of the same algorithm A then there exists a unique consistent set $\Delta = \{(f, \overrightarrow{a}, b) \mid \overline{f}^{Y}(\overrightarrow{a}) = b \text{ and } \overline{f}^{X}(\overrightarrow{a}) \neq b\}$ of non trivial updates such that $Y = X \oplus \Delta$. This Δ is called the **difference** between the two local memories, and is denoted by $Y \ominus X$.

Let $\overrightarrow{X} = (X^1, \ldots, X^p)$ be a state of A. According to the transition function τ_A, the next state is $\tau_A(\overrightarrow{X})$, which will be denoted by $(\tau_A(\overrightarrow{X})^1, \ldots, \tau_A(\overrightarrow{X})^p)$. We denote by $\Delta^i(A, \overrightarrow{X}) \overset{\text{def}}{=} \tau_A(\overrightarrow{X})^i \ominus X^i$ the set of updates done by the i-th processor of A on the state $\overrightarrow{X}$, and by $\overrightarrow{\Delta}(A, \overrightarrow{X}) \overset{\text{def}}{=} (\Delta^1(A, \overrightarrow{X}), \ldots, \Delta^p(A, \overrightarrow{X}))$

the "multiset" of updates done by A on the state $\overrightarrow{X}$. In particular, if a state $\overrightarrow{X}$ is final, then $\tau_A(\overrightarrow{X}) = \overrightarrow{X}$, so $\overrightarrow{\Delta}(A, \overrightarrow{X}) = \overrightarrow{\emptyset}$.

Let A be a BSP algorithm and T be a set of terms of $\mathcal{L}(A)$. We say that two states $(X^1, \ldots, X^p)$ and $(Y^1, \ldots, Y^q)$ of A **coincide over** T if $p = q$ and for every $1 \leq i \leq p$ and for every $t \in T$ we have $\overrightarrow{t}^{X^i} = \overrightarrow{t}^{Y^i}$.

Postulate 3 (Bounded Exploration for Processors). *For every* BSP *algorithm A there exists a finite set $T(A)$ of terms such that for every state $\overrightarrow{X}$ and $\overrightarrow{Y}$, if they coincide over $T(A)$ then $\overrightarrow{\Delta}(A, \overrightarrow{X}) = \overrightarrow{\Delta}(A, \overrightarrow{Y})$, i.e. for every $1 \leq i \leq p$, we have $\Delta^i(A, \overrightarrow{X}) = \Delta^i(A, \overrightarrow{Y})$.*

$T(A)$ is called the **exploration witness** [10] of A. If a set of terms T is finite then its closure by subterms is finite too. We assume that $T(A)$ is closed by subterms and the symbol **"true"** should always be in the exploration witness [10]. The interpretations of the terms in $T(A)$ are called the **critical elements** and we prove in [22] that every value in an update is a critical element:

Lemma 1 (Critical Elements). *For every state $(X^1, \ldots, X^p)$ of A, $\forall i\ 1 \leq i \leq p$, if $(f, \overrightarrow{a}, b) \in \Delta^i(A, \overrightarrow{X})$ then $\overrightarrow{a}, b$ are interpretations in X^i of terms in $T(A)$.*

That implies that for every step of the computation, for a given processor, only a bounded number of terms are read or written (amount of work).

Lemma 2 (Bounded Set of Updates). *For every state $(X^1, \ldots, X^p)$ of the algorithm A, for every $1 \leq i \leq p$, $|\Delta^i(A, \overrightarrow{X})|$ is bounded.*

Notice that for the moment we make no assumption on the communication between processors. Moreover, these three postulates are a "natural" extension of the ones of [10]. And by "natural", we mean that if we assume that $p = 1$ then our postulates are exactly the same:

Lemma 3 (A Single Processor is Sequential). *A* BSP *algorithm with a unique processor $(p = 1)$ is a sequential algorithm. Therefore* ALGO$_{\text{SEQ}}$ $\subseteq$ ALGO$_{\text{BSP}}$. *We now organize the sequence of states into* **supersteps**. *The communication between local memories occurs only during a communication phase. In order to do so, a* BSP *algorithm A will use two functions $comp_A$ and $comm_A$ indicating if A runs computations or if it runs communications.*

Postulate 4 (Supersteps phases). *For every* BSP *algorithm A there exists two applications $comp_A : M(A) \to M(A)$ commuting with isomorphisms, and $comm_A : S(A) \to S(A)$, such that for every state $(X^1, \ldots, X^p)$:*

$$\tau_A\left(X^1, \ldots, X^p\right) = \begin{cases} \left(comp_A(X^1), \ldots, comp_A(X^p)\right) & \text{if } \exists 1 \leq i \leq p \\ & \text{such that } comp_A(X^i) \neq X^i \\ comm_A\left(X^1, \ldots, X^p\right) & \text{otherwise} \end{cases}$$

A **BSP algorithm** is an object verifying these four postulates, and we denote by ALGO$_\text{BSP}$ the set of the BSP algorithms. A state $(X^1, \ldots, X^p)$ will be said in a **computation phase** if there exists $1 \leq i \leq p$ such that $\text{comp}_A(X^i) \neq X^i$. Otherwise, the state will be said in a **communication phase**.

This requires some remarks. First, at every computation step, every processor which has not terminated performs its local computations. Second, we do not specified the function comm_A in order to be generic about which BSP library is used. We discuss in Sect. 3.3 the difference between comm_A and the usual communication routines in the BSP community.

Remember that a state $\overrightarrow{X}$ is said to be final if $\tau_A(\overrightarrow{X}) = \overrightarrow{X}$. Therefore, according to the fourth postulate, $\overrightarrow{X}$ must be in a communication phase which is like a final phase that would terminate the whole execution as found in MPI.

We prove that the BSP algorithms satisfy, during a computation phase, that every processor computes independently of the state of the other processors:

Lemma 4 (No Communication during Computation Phases). *For every states $(X^1, \ldots, X^p)$ and $(Y^1, \ldots, Y^q)$ in a computing phase, if X^i and Y^j have the same critical elements then $\Delta^i(A, \overrightarrow{X}) = \Delta^j(A, \overrightarrow{Y})$.*

2.3 Questions and Answers

Why not using a BSP-Turing machine to define an algorithm?
It is known that standard Turing machines could simulate every algorithm. But we are here interested in the step-by-step behavior of the algorithms, and not the input-output relation of the functions. In this way, there is not a literal identity between the axiomatic point of view (postulates) of algorithms and the operational point of view of Turing machines. Moreover, simulating algorithms by using a Turing-machine is a low-level approach which does not describe the algorithm at its natural level of abstraction. Every algorithm assumes elementary operations which are not refined down to the assembly language by the algorithm itself. These operations are seen as oracular, which means that they produce the desired output in one step of computation.

But I think there is too much abstractions: When using BSPLIB, messages received at the past superstep are dropped. Your function comm$_A$ does not show this fact.
We want to be as general as possible. Perhaps a future library would allow reading data received n supersteps ago as the BSP+ model of [19]. Moreover, the communication function may realize some computations and is thus not a pure transmission of data. But the exploration witness forbids doing whatever: only a finite set of symbols can be updated. And we provide a realistic example of such a function which mainly correspond to the BSPLIB's primitives [22].

And why is it not just a permutation of values to be exchanged?
The communications can be used to model synchronous interactions with the environment (input/output or error messages, *etc.*) and therefore make appear or disappear values.

And when using BSPLIB *and other* BSP *libraries, I can switch between sequential computations and* BSP *ones. Why not model this kind of feature?*
The sequential parts can be modeled as purely asynchronous computations replicated and performed by all the processors. Or, one processor (typically the first one) is performing these computations while other processors are "waiting" with an empty computation phase.

In [2,3,15,16], the authors give more general postulates about concurrent and/or distributed algorithms? Why not using their works by adding some restrictions to take into account the BSP *model of execution?*
It is another solution. But we think that the restrictions on "more complex" postulates is not a natural characterization of the BSP algorithms. It is better for a model to be expressed at its natural level of abstraction in order to highlight its own properties. For example, there is the problematic of the cost model which is inherent to a bridging model like BSP: It is not clear how such restrictions could highlight the cost model.

Fine. But are you sure about your postulates? I mean, are they completely (and not more) defined BSP *algorithms?*
It is impossible to be sure because we are formalizing a concept that is currently only intuitive. But as they are general and simple, we believe that they correctly capture this intuitive idea. We prove in the next section that a natural operational model for BSP characterizes exactly those postulates.

Would not that be too abstract? The BSP *model is supposed to be a bridging model.*
We treat algorithms at their natural level of abstraction, and not as something to refine to machines: We explicitly assume that our primitives may not be elementary for a typical modern architecture (but could be so in the future) and that they can achieve a potentially complex operation in one step. This makes it possible to get away from a considered hardware model and makes it possible to calculate the costs in time (and in space) in a given framework which can be variable according to what is considered elementary. For example, in an Euclidean algorithm, it is either the Euclidean division that is elementary or the subtraction. If your BSP algorithm uses elementary operations which can not be realized on the BSP machine considered, then you are just not at the right level abstraction. Our work is still valid for *any* level of abstraction.

3   BSP-ASM Captures the BSP Algorithms

The four previous postulates define the BSP algorithms from an axiomatic viewpoint but that does not mean that they have a model, or in, other words, that they are defined from an operational point of view. In the same way that the model of computation ASM captures the set of the sequential algorithms [10], we prove in this section that the ASM$_{BSP}$ model captures the BSP algorithms.

3.1 Definition and Operational Semantics of ASM-BSP

Definition 4 (ASM Program [10])

$$\Pi \overset{\text{def}}{=} f(t_1, \ldots, t_\alpha) := t_0$$
$$\mid \text{if } F \text{ then } \Pi_1 \text{ else } \Pi_2 \text{ endif}$$
$$\mid \text{par } \Pi_1 \| \ldots \| \Pi_n \text{ endpar}$$

where f has arity α; F is a formula; $\theta_1, \ldots, \theta_\alpha, \theta_0$ are terms of $\mathcal{L}(X)$. Notice that if $n = 0$ then par $\Pi_1 \| \ldots \| \Pi_n$ endpar is the empty program. If in if F then Π_1 else Π_2 endif the program Π_2 is empty we will write simply if F then Π_1 endif. An ASM machine [10] is thus a kind of Turing machine using not a tape but an abstract structure X.

Definition 5 (ASM Operational Semantics)

$$\Delta(f(\theta_1, \ldots, \theta_\alpha) := \theta_0, X) \overset{\text{def}}{=} \left\{ (f, \overline{\theta_1}^X, \ldots, \overline{\theta_\alpha}^X, \overline{\theta_0}^X) \right\}$$

$$\Delta(\text{if } F \text{ then } \Pi_1 \text{ else } \Pi_2 \text{ endif}, X) \overset{\text{def}}{=} \Delta(\Pi_i, X)$$
$$where \begin{cases} i = 1 \text{ if } F \text{ is true on } X \\ i = 2 \text{ otherwise} \end{cases}$$
$$\Delta(\text{par } \Pi_1 \| \ldots \| \Pi_n \text{ endpar}, X) \overset{\text{def}}{=} \Delta(\Pi_1, X) \cup \cdots \cup \Delta(\Pi_n, X)$$

Notice that the semantics of the par is a set of updates done simultaneously, which differs from an usual imperative framework. A state of a ASM$_{\text{BSP}}$ machine is a p-tuple of memories $(X^1, \ldots, X^p)$. We assume that the ASM$_{\text{BSP}}$ programs are SPMD (Single Program Multiple Data) which means that at each step of computation, the ASM$_{\text{BSP}}$ program Π is executed individually on each processor. Therefore Π induces a multiset of updates $\overrightarrow{\Delta}$ and a transition function τ_Π:

$$\overrightarrow{\Delta}(\Pi, (X^1, \ldots, X^p)) \overset{\text{def}}{=} (\Delta(\Pi, X^1), \ldots, \Delta(\Pi, X^p))$$
$$\tau_\Pi(X^1, \ldots, X^p) \overset{\text{def}}{=} (X^1 \oplus \Delta(\Pi, X^1), \ldots, X^p \oplus \Delta(\Pi, X^p))$$

If $\tau_\Pi(\overrightarrow{X}) = \overrightarrow{X}$, then every processor has finished its computation steps. In that case we assume that there exists a communication function to ensure the communication between processors.

Definition 6. *An* ASM$_{\text{BSP}}$ *machine M is a triplet $(S(M), I(M), \tau_M)$ such that:*

1. *$S(M)$ is a set of tuples of structures with the same finite signature $\mathcal{L}(M)$; $S(M)$ and $I(M) \subseteq S(M)$ are closed by multi-isomorphism;*
2. *$\tau_M : S(M) \mapsto S(M)$ verifies that there exists a program Π and an application $comm_M : S(M) \mapsto S(M)$ such that:*

$$\tau_M(\overrightarrow{X}) = \begin{cases} \tau_\Pi(\overrightarrow{X}) \text{ if } \tau_\Pi(\overrightarrow{X}) \neq \overrightarrow{X} \\ comm_M(\overrightarrow{X}) \text{ otherwise} \end{cases}$$

3. $comm_M$ *verifies that:*

(1) *For every state* $\overrightarrow{X}$ *such that* $\tau_\Pi(\overrightarrow{X}) = \overrightarrow{X}$, $comm_M$ *preserves the universes and the number of processors, and commutes with multi-isomorphisms*

(2) *There exists a finite set of terms* $T(comm_M)$ *such that for every state* $\overrightarrow{X}$ *and* $\overrightarrow{Y}$ *with* $\tau_\Pi(\overrightarrow{X}) = \overrightarrow{X}$ *and* $\tau_\Pi(\overrightarrow{Y}) = \overrightarrow{Y}$, *if they coincide over* $T(comm_M)$ *then* $\overrightarrow{\Delta}(M, \overrightarrow{X}) = \overrightarrow{\Delta}(M, \overrightarrow{Y})$.

We denote by ASM_{BSP} the set of such machines. As before, a state $\overrightarrow{X}$ is said **final** if $\tau_M(\overrightarrow{X}) = \overrightarrow{X}$. So if $\overrightarrow{X}$ is final then $\tau_\Pi(\overrightarrow{X}) = \overrightarrow{X}$ and $comm_M(\overrightarrow{X}) = \overrightarrow{X}$.

The last conditions about the communication function may seem arbitrary, but they are required to ensure that the communication function is not a kind of magic device. For example, without these conditions, we could imagine that $comm_M$ may compute the output of the algorithm in one step, or solve the halting problem. Moreover, we construct an example of $comm_M$ in [22] (Section D).

3.2   The BSP-ASM Thesis

We prove that ASM_{BSP} captures the computation phases of the BSP algorithms in three steps. First, we prove that during an execution, each set of updates is the interpretation of an ASM program (Lemma 8 p.16 [22]). Then, we prove an equivalence between these potentially infinite number of programs (Lemma 9 p.17). Finally, by using the third postulate, we prove in Lemma 10 p.18 that there is only a bounded number of relevant programs, which can be merged into a single one.

Proposition 1 (BSP-ASMs capture Computations of BSP Algorithms). *For every* BSP *algorithm* A, *there exists an* ASM *program* Π_A *such that for every state* $\overrightarrow{X}$ *in a computation phase:* $\overrightarrow{\Delta}(\Pi_A, \overrightarrow{X}) = \overrightarrow{\Delta}(A, \overrightarrow{X})$.

Theorem 1. $\text{ALGO}_{\text{BSP}} = \text{ASM}_{\text{BSP}}$ *(The proof is available in [22], Section C p.20).*

3.3   Cost Model Property and the Function of Communication

There is two more steps in order to claim that ASM_{BSP} objects are the BSP bridging model algorithms: (1) To ensure that the duration corresponds to the standard cost model and; (2) To solve issues about the communication function.

Cost Model. If the execution begins with a communication, we assume that no computation is done for the first superstep. We remind that a state $\overrightarrow{X_t}$ is in a computation phase if there exists $1 \leq i \leq p$ such that $comp_A(X_t^i) \neq X_t^i$. The computation for every processor is done in parallel, step by step. So, the cost in time of the computation phase is $w \overset{\text{def}}{=} \max_{1 \leq i \leq p}(w_i)$, where w_i is the number of steps done by the processor i (on processor X^i) during the superstep.

Then the state is in a communication phase, when the messages between the processors are sent and received. Notice that $comm_A$ may require several steps in order to communicate the messages, which contrasts with the usual approach in BSP where the communication actions of a superstep are considered as one unit. But this approach would violate the third postulate, so we had to consider a step-by-step communication approach, then consider these actions as one communication phase. ASM$_{\text{BSP}}$ exchanges terms and we show in [22] how formally define the size of terms. But we can imagine a machine that must further decompose the terms in order to transmit them (in bits for example). We just assume that the data are communicable in time **g** for a 1-relation.

So, during the superstep, the communication phase requires $h \times$ **g** steps. It remains to add the cost of the synchronization of the processors, which is assumed in the usual BSP model to be a parameter **L**. Therefore, we obtained a cost property which is sound with the standard BSP cost model.

A Realization of the Communication. An example of a communication function for the standard BSPLIB's primitives `bsp_get`, `bsp_put`, `bsp_send` `bsp_move` is presented in [22] (Section D).

Proposition 2 (Communication). *A function of communication, with routines for distant readings/writings and point-to-point sendings, performing an h-relation and requiring at most h exchanges can be designed using* ASM.

One may argue that the last postulate allows the communication function to do computations. To avoid it, we assume that the terms in the exploration witness $T(M)$ can be separated between $T(\Pi)$ and $T(\text{comm}_M)$ such that $T(\Pi)$ is for the states in a computation phase, and that for every update $(f, \overrightarrow{a}, b)$ of a processor X^i in a communication phase, either there exists a term $t \in T(\text{comm}_M)$ such that $b = \overline{t}^{X^i}$, or there exists a variable $v \in T(\Pi)$ and a processor X^j such that $b = \overline{t_{\overline{v}X^j}}^{X^i}$ (**representation** presented in Section D p.24). To do a computation, a term like $x+1$ is required, so the restriction to a variable prevents the computations of the terms in $T(\Pi)$. Or course, the last communication step should be able to write in $T(\Pi)$, and the final result should be read in $T(\Pi)$.

4 Conclusion and Future Work

4.1 Summary of the Contribution

A bridging model provides a common level of *understanding* between hardware and software engineers. It provides software developers with an attractive escape route from the world of architecture-dependent parallel software [20]. The BSP bridging model allows the design of *"immortal"* (efficient and portable) parallel algorithms using a *realistic* cost model (and without any overspecification requiring the use of a large number of parameters) that can fit most distributed architectures. It has been used with success in many domains [1].

We have given an axiomatic definition of BSP algorithms by adding only one postulate to the sequential ones for sequential algorithms [10] which has been widely accepted by the scientific community. Mainly this postulate is the call of a function of communication. We abstract how communication is performed, not be restricting to a specific BSP library. We finally answer previous criticisms by defining a convincing set of parallel algorithms running in a predictable time.

Our work is relevant because it allows universality (immortal stands for BSP computing): all future BSP algorithms, whatever their specificities, will be captured by our definitions. So, our ASM$_{BSP}$ is not just another model, it is a class model, which contains all BSP algorithms.

This small addition allows a greater *confidence* in this formal definition compared to previous work: Postulates of concurrent ASMs do not provide the same level of intuitive clarity as the postulates for sequential algorithms. But our work is limited to BSP algorithms even if it is still sufficient for many HPC and big-data applications. We have thus revisited the problem of the *"parallel ASM thesis"* *i.e.*, to provide a machine-independent definition of BSP algorithms and a proof that these algorithms are faithfully captured by ASM$_{BSP}$. We also prove that the *cost model* is preserved which is the main novelty and specificity of this work compared to the traditional work about distributed or concurrent ASMs.

4.2   Questions and Answers About this Work

Why do you use a new model of computation ASM$_{BSP}$ *instead of* ASMs*only? Indeed, each processor can be seen as a sequential* ASM. *So, in order to simulate one step of a* BSP*algorithm using several processors, we could use pids to compute sequentially the next step for each processor by using an* ASM.
Even if such a simulation exists between these two models, what you mean, a "sequentialization" (each processor, one after the other) of the BSP model of execution, cannot be exactly the function of transition of the postulates. Moreover, in order to stay bounded, having p exploration witness (one for each sequential ASM) induces p to be a constant for the algorithm. In our work, p is only fixed of each execution, making the approach more general when modeling algorithms.

Is another model possible to characterize the BSP *algorithms?*
Sure. This can be more useful for proving some properties. But that would be the same set, just another way to describe it.

So, reading the work of [3]*, a distributed machine is defined as a set of pairs* (a, Π_a) *where a is the name of the machine and* Π_a *a sequential* ASM. *Reading your definition, I see only one* Π *and not "p" processors as in the* BSP *model. I thus not imagine a* BSP *computer as it is.*
You are absolutely right but we do not model a BSP computer, our work is about BSP algorithms. The ASM$_{BSP}$ program contains the algorithm which is used on each "processor" (a first-order structure as explain before). These are the postulates (axiomatic point of view) that characterize the class of BSP algorithms rather than a set of abstract machines (operational point of view). That is closer to the original approach [10]. We also want to point out that, unlike [3], we are not

limited to a finite (fixed) set of machines: In our model, an algorithm is defined for $p = 1, 2, 1000$, *etc.* And we are not limited to point-to-point communications.

Ok, but with only a single code, you cannot have all the parallel algorithms...
We follow [4] about the difference between a PARallel composition of SEQuential actions (PAR of SEQ) and a SEQuential composition of PARallel actions (SEQ of PAR). Our ASM$_{BSP}$ is SEQ(PAR). This leads to a *macroscopic* point of view[1] which is close to a specification. Being a SEQ(PAR) model allows a high level description of the BSP algorithms.

So, why are you limited to SPMD computations?
Different codes can be run by the processors using conditionals on the "id" of the processors. For example "if pid=0 then code1 else code2" for running "code1" (*e.g.* master part) only on processor 0. Again, we are *not* limited to SPMD computations. The ASM program Π fully contains the BSP algorithm, that is *all* the "actions" that can be performed by *any* processors, not necessarily the same instructions: Each processor picks the needed instruction to execute but there could be completely different. Only the size of Π is finite due to the exploration witness. For example, it is impossible to have a number of conditionals in Π that depends of p. Indeed, according to Lemma 4, during a computation phase, if two processors coincide over the exploration witness, then they will use the same code. And according to Postulate 3, the exploration witness is bounded. So, there exists only a bounded number c of possible subroutines during the computation phase, even if $p \gg c$.

Notice that processors may not know their own ids and there is no order in p-tuples; We never use such a property: Processors are organized like a set and we use tuples only for convenience of notation. We are using p-tuples just to add the BSP execution model in the original postulates of [10].

Ok, but I cannot get the interleavings of the computations as in [3]? Your model seems very synchronous!
The BSP model makes the hypothesis that the processors are uniform. So if one processor can perform one step of the algorithm, there is no reason to lock it just to highlight an interleaving. And if there is nothing to do, it does nothing until the *phase of communication.* Our execution model is thus largely "asynchronous" during the computation phases.

Speaking about communication, why apply several times the function of communication? When designing a BSP algorithm, I use once a collective operation!
An ASM is like a Turing machine. It is not possible to perform all the communications in a single step: The exploration witness forbids doing this. Our function of communication performs some exchanges until there are no more.

---

[1] Take for example a BSP sorting algorithm: First all the processors locally sort there own data, and then, they perform some exchanges in order to have the elements sorted between them. One defines it as a sequence of parallel actions and being also independent to the number of processors.

What happens in case of runtime errors during communications?
Typically, when one processor has a bigger number of super-steps than other processors, or when there is an out-of-bound sending or reading, it leads to a runtime error. The BSP function of communication can return a $\perp$ value. That causes a stop of the operational semantics of the ASM_{BSP}.

4.3 Related Work

As far as we know, some work exists to model distributed programs using ASMs [15] but none to convincingly characterize BSP algorithms. In [6], authors model the P3L set of skeletons. That allows the analyze of P3L programs using standard ASM tools but not a formal characterization of what P3L is and is not.

The first work to extend ASMs for concurrent, distributed, agent-mobile algorithms is [2]. Too many postulates are used making the comprehension hard to follow or worse (loss of confidence). A first attempt to simplify this work has been done in [16] and again simplified in [7] by the use of multiset comprehension terms to maintain a kind of bounded exploration. Then, the authors prove that ASMs captures these postulates. Moreover, we are interested in distributed (HPC) computations more than parallel (threading) ASMs.

We want to clarify one thing. The ASM thesis comes from the fact that sequential algorithms work in small steps, that is steps of bounded complexity. But the number of processors (or computing units) is unbounded for parallel algorithms, which motivated the work of [2] to define parallel algorithms with wide steps, that is steps of unbounded complexity. Hence the technicality of the presentation, and the unconvincing attempts to capture parallel algorithms [3].

Extending the ASMs for distributed computing is not new [3]. We believe that these postulates are more general than ours but we think that our extension still remains simple and natural for BSP algorithms. The authors are also not concerned about the problem of axiomatizing classes of algorithms using a cost model which is the heart of our work and the main advantage of the BSP model.

4.4 Future Work

This work leads to many possible work. First, how to adapt our work to a hierarchical extension of BSP [21] which is closer to modern HPC architectures?

Second, BSP is a bridging model between hardwares and softwares. It could be interesting to study such a link more formally. For example, can we prove that the primitives of a BSP language can truly "be BSP" on a typical cluster architecture?

Thirdly, we are currently working on extending the work of [13] in order to give the BSP algorithmic completeness of a BSP imperative programming language. There are some concrete applications: There are many languages having a BSP-like model of execution, for example PREGEL [12] for writing large-graph algorithms. An interesting application is proving which are BSP algorithmically complete and are not. BSPLIB programs are intuitively BSP. MAPREDUCE is a good candidate to be *not* [14]. Similarly, one can imagine proving which languages are too expressive for BSP. MPI is intuitively one of them. Last, the first author is working on postulates for more general distributed algorithm *à la* MPI.

In any case, studying the BSP-RAM (such as the communication-oblivious of [19]) or MAPREDUCE, would led to define subclasses of BSP algorithms.

References

1. Bisseling, R.H.: Parallel Scientific Computation: A Structured Approach Using BSP and MPI. Oxford University Press, Oxford (2004)
2. Blass, A., Gurevich, Y.: Abstract state machines capture parallel algorithms. ACM Trans. Comput. Log. **4**(4), 578–651 (2003)
3. Börger, E., Schewe, K.-D.: Concurrent abstract state machines. Acta Inf. **53**(5), 469–492 (2016)
4. Bougé, L.: The data parallel programming model: a semantic perspective. In: Perrin, G.-R., Darte, A. (eds.) The Data Parallel Programming Model. LNCS, vol. 1132, pp. 4–26. Springer, Heidelberg (1996). https://doi.org/10.1007/3-540-61736-1_40
5. Cappello, F., Snir, M.: On communication determinism in HPC applications. In: Computer Communications and Networks (ICCCN), pp. 1–8. IEEE (2010)
6. Cavarra, A., Zavanella, A.: A formal model for the parallel semantics of p3l. In: ACM Symposium on Applied Computing (SAC), pp. 804–812 (2000)
7. Ferrarotti, F., Schewe, K.-D., Tec, L., Wang, Q.: A new thesis concerning synchronised parallel computing –simplified parallel ASM thesis. Theor. Comput. Sci. **649**, 25–53 (2016)
8. González-Vélez, H., Leyton, M.: A survey of algorithmic skeleton frameworks. Softw. Pract. Exp. **40**(12), 1135–1160 (2010)
9. Gorlatch, S.: Send-receive considered harmful: myths and realities of message passing. ACM TOPLAS **26**(1), 47–56 (2004)
10. Gurevich, Y.: Sequential abstract-state machines capture sequential algorithms. ACM Trans. Comput. Log. **1**(1), 77–111 (2000)
11. Hill, J.M.D., McColl, B., et al.: BSPLIB: the BSP programming library. Parallel Comput. **24**, 1947–1980 (1998)
12. Malewicz, G., et al.: PREGEL: a system for large-scale graph processing. In: Management of data, pp. 135–146. ACM (2010)
13. Marquer, Y.: Algorithmic completeness of imperative programming languages. Fundamenta Informaticae, pp. 1–27 (2017, accepted)
14. Pace, M.F.: BSP vs MAPREDUCE. Procedia Comput. Sci. **9**, 246–255 (2012)
15. Prinz, A., Sherratt, E.: Distributed ASM- pitfalls and solutions. In: Ait Ameur, Y., Schewe, K.D. (eds.) ABZ 2014. Lecture Notes in Computer Science, vol. 8477, pp. 210–215. Springer, Heidelberg (2014)
16. Schewe, K.-D., Wang, Q.: A simplified parallel ASM thesis. In: Derrick, J., et al. (eds.) ABZ 2012. LNCS, vol. 7316, pp. 341–344. Springer, Heidelberg (2012). https://doi.org/10.1007/978-3-642-30885-7_27
17. Seo, S., et al.: HAMA: an efficient matrix computation with the MAPREDUCE framework. In: Cloud Computing (CloudCom), pp. 721–726. IEEE (2010)
18. Skillicorn, D.B., Hill, J.M.D., McColl, W.F.: Questions and answers about BSP. Sci. Program. **6**(3), 249–274 (1997)

19. Tiskin, A.: The design and analysis of bulk-synchronous parallel algorithms. PhD thesis. Oxford University Computing Laboratory (1998)
20. Valiant, L.G.: A bridging model for parallel computation. Comm. ACM **33**(8), 103–111 (1990)
21. Valiant, L.G.: A bridging model for multi-core computing. J. Comput. Syst. Sci. **77**(1), 154–166 (2011)
22. Marquer, Y., Gava, F.: An ASM thesis for BSP. Technical report (2018). https:// hal.archives-ouvertes.fr/hal-01717647

Efficient and Secure Outsourced Linear Regression

Haomiao Yang[✉], Weichao He[✉], Qixian Zhou[✉], and Hongwei Li

School of Computer Science and Engineering and Center for Cyber Security,
University of Electronic Science and Technology of China, Chengdu, China
{haomyang,hongweili}@uestc.edu.cn, wechaohe@163.com,
qxzhou1010@qq.com

Abstract. The linear regression, as a classical machine learning algorithm, is often used to be a predictor. In the era of big data, the data owner can outsource their linear regression task and data to the cloud server, which has powerful calculation and storage resources. However, outsourcing data may break the privacy of the data. It is a well-known method to encrypt them prior to uploading to the cloud by using the homomorphic encryption (HE). Nevertheless, it is a difficult problem to apply the linear regression protocol in the encrypted domain. With this observation, we propose an efficient and secure linear regression protocol over outsourced encrypted data by using the vector HE, named *ESLR*, and in our protocol, we further present a privacy-preserving gradient descent method. Security analysis shows that our protocol can guarantee the confidentiality of data. And compared to the linear regression over plaintexts, our proposal can achieve almost the same accuracy and efficiency over ciphertexts.

Keywords: Machine learning · Homomorphic encryption
Linear regression · Gradient descent

1 Introduction

Predictive modeling is an essential tool in decision making processes in domains such as policy making, medicine, law enforcement, and finance. Considering a hospital would like to use a cloud service which provide predictive service to analyze the patient's condition so as to improve the quality of care and reduce costs. Due to ethical and legal requirements, the hospital might be restricted to use such service [3,4,12]. Like the hospital, many organizations are collecting ever-increasing data for mining to improve decision-making and productivity. However, they may have no powerful resources to deal with such large-scale data. To solve this problem, an attractive business model is that a service provider, which has powerful platforms and advanced analytic skills, provides such services. Organizations who need the calculation resource can outsource their computational tasks to such powerful service providers. However, because the data

J. Vaidya and J. Li (Eds.): ICA3PP 2018, LNCS 11336, pp. 89–102, 2018.
https://doi.org/10.1007/978-3-030-05057-3_7

may contain sensitive information, outsourcing data to public clouds directly raises privacy concerns.

In current implementations, the learning algorithm must see all user data in the clear in order to build the predictive model. In this paper, we consider whether the learning algorithm can operate in encrypted domains, thereby allowing users to retain control of their data. For medical data, this allows for a model to be built without affecting user privacy. For the book and movie preferences, letting users keep control of their data, can reduce the risk of future unexpected embarrassment in case of a data breach at the service provider.

Roughly speaking, there are three existing approaches to essure the privacy when the server mines the user data. The first lets users split their data among multiple servers by using secure multi-party computation [2,5,9]. These servers, then, run the learning algorithm using a distributed protocol. Privacy is assured as long as a majority of servers do not collude. The second is based on differential privacy protection, where the learning algorithm is executed over data containing noise [6,7,13]. And the third is based on homomorphic encryption, where the learning algorithm is executed over encrypted data [15].

Distributed linear regression is not suitable for outsourced model. In distributed linear regression, every party must take part in computation. Consequently, the secure multi-party computation may be inefficient. In addition, there may be a great loss of accuracy and can not fully guarantee the security of data by using the differential privacy protection. In this work, we choose homomorphic encryption for our privacy-preserving machine learning algorithm. As we know, homomorphic encryption (HE) allows operations on encrypted data, which provides a possible solution for linear regression over ciphertexts. In our work, we propose an efficient and secure linear regression protocol over encrypted data for outsourced environments, namely ESLR, where the cloud performs linear regression processing over encrypted data. The challenge is how to apply the linear regression algorithm over ciphertexts, while maintaining high accuracy and performance. To address these challenges, we exploit the vector HE (VHE) recently presented by Zhou and Wornell [17]. Unlike the fully HE (FHE), VHE only needs to support somewhat homomorphic encryption. As a result, it is much more efficient than many existing FHE schemes. For example, it is orders of magnitude faster than HELib [10], which is a very famous FHE implementation. Especially by designing ingeniously, VHE can be used in the privacy-preserving gradient descent. Different from existed works, our contributions are twofold as follows.

(1) Firstly, ESLR reconstructs linear regression clustering process in the domain of ciphertext by taking advantage of the vector encryption, which allows low computation and communication cost. What's more, we proposed a scheme that can apply privacy-preserving gradient descent method over ciphertext domain efficiently. To our best knowledges, it's very efficient for the optimization algorithm over encrypted data. Experiments shows that ESLR achieves almost the same accuracy compared to the plaintext algorithm.

(2) Secondly, security analysis demonstrates that ESLR achieves the confidentiality of data, ensuring the privacy of the data owner. In addition, we give the definition of loss function, which is needed for optimization over ciphertext domain.

This paper is organized as follows: The problem formulation is described in Sect. 2. The constructions of linear regression protocol are proposed in Sect. 3, followed by further discusses in Sect. 4. Then we give the security analysis and performance evaluation in Sects. 5 and 6, respectively. Finally, the conclusion is presented in Sect. 7.

2   Problem Statement

In this section, we give the problem statement, including system model and threat model, design goals, notations and preliminaries.

2.1   System Model and Threat Model

We give our system model concentrating on how to achieve secure liner regression over encrypted data in outsourced environments. As shown in Fig. 1, we proposed a classical outsourced system model, mainly consisting of two parties. The one is the data owner, and the other is the service provider. We primarily consider the service provider as an "honest-but-curious" server in our model. We assume the public matrix H and encrypted data D' (D' is the encryption of the data D) have been outsourced to the cloud, and the confidentiality of the data

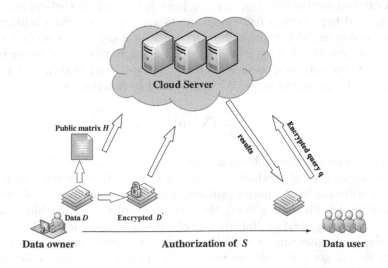

Fig. 1. System model

will be protected by the underlying encryption primitive. After that, the server will implement the regression algorithm based on D'. That is, the data owner outsources his encrypted data D', and the service provider runs the proposed protocol over D'. Finally the service provider returns the predicted results to the data owner.

2.2 Design Goals

The overarching goal is to enable liner regression algorithm to be performed over encrypted data. What's more, for an efficient and secure liner regression protocol, we consider the following requirements to be necessary.

- Accuracy: Enable secure linear regression over encrypted data in outsourced environments and achieve high accuracy.
- Security: Protect privacy of linear regression process.
- Efficiency: Process large amount of data with practical performance.

2.3 Overview of Standard Linear Regression and Gradient Descent

In this section, we give a brief introduction about standard linear regression algorithm [16]. In statistics, linear regression equation is a regression analysis using least square function to find the relationship between one or more independent variables and dependent variables. This function is a linear combination of one or more model parameters called regression coefficients. Linear regression with only one independent variable is called simple regression, and it is called multiple regression with greater than one independent variable. Like all forms of regression analysis, linear regression also focuses on the probability distribution of x and y. Given a random sample $(x_{i1}, x_{i2}, ..., x_{ip}, y_i)$, we have one hypothetical regression output y_i, and hypothetical regression inputs $x_{i1}, x_{i2}, ..., x_{ip}$. So a multivariate linear regression model is expressed as $y_i = w_1 x_1 + w_2 x_2 + \cdots + w_d x_d + b$.

For a data set $D = [(x_1, y_1), (x_2, y_2), \cdots, (x_n, y_n)]$, the goal of linear regression is to get the regression coefficients $\theta = [w_1, w_2, \cdots, w_d, b]$ such that the loss function get the minimum value. We define the loss function as

$$J(\theta) = (\frac{1}{2n}) \sum_{i=1}^{n} (\theta^T x_i' - y_i)^2.$$

Further, we formulate the problem as Algorithm 1.

The gradient descent method [8] is one of the iterative methods, which can be used to solve the least squares problem. Gradient descent is one of the most commonly used methods in solving the model parameters of machine learning algorithm (unconstrained optimization problem). The other method commonly used is the least square method. When solving the minimum value of the loss function, we can get the minimum value of loss function and the model parameters through the gradient descent method.

Algorithm 1. Standard linear regression

Input: data set $D = \{(\boldsymbol{x}_1, y_1), (\boldsymbol{x}_2, y_2), \cdots, (\boldsymbol{x}_n, y_n)\}$ and threshold t
Output: $\theta = [w_1, w_2, \cdots, w_d, b]$
1: Define the loss function $J(\boldsymbol{\theta}) = (\frac{1}{2n}) \sum_{i=1}^{n} (\boldsymbol{\theta}^T \boldsymbol{x}_i - y_i)^2$
2: Generating the $\boldsymbol{\theta}^0$ randomly
3: **repeat**
4:    $\boldsymbol{\theta}^k = \boldsymbol{\theta}^{k-1} - \alpha \frac{\partial J(\boldsymbol{\theta})}{\partial \boldsymbol{\theta}}$, where $\boldsymbol{\theta}^k$ is the value of kth iteration and α is the iteration
      step.
5: **until** $J(\boldsymbol{\theta}^{k+1}) - J(\boldsymbol{\theta}^k) < t$
6: **return** $\boldsymbol{\theta}$

2.4   Notations and Preliminaries

In this section, we review the preliminaries that are necessary for our work. First, we give notations used throughout the paper as illustrated in Table 1.

Table 1. Notations

Notation	Meaning
$\lceil a \rfloor$	To round a to the nearest integer, for $a \in \mathbb{R}$
$\lceil \boldsymbol{a} \rfloor$	To round each entry a_i to the nearest integer, for a vector $\boldsymbol{a} \in \mathbb{R}^n$
a^*	To be a binary representation for a vector $\boldsymbol{a} \in \mathbb{Z}^n$

We outline the VHE scheme as suggested by Zhou and Wornell [17] that encrypts integer vectors to allow computation of arbitrary polynomials in the encrypted domain. For our purpose of ESLR, we only consider the fundamental operations below and more details are referred to [17].

– **VHE.KG(λ):** Input a security parameter λ, choose l, m, n, p, q, $w \in \mathbb{Z}$, and the distribution χ where $l = \lceil \log_2(q-1) \rceil$, $w(p-1) < q$, $q \gg p$, and $m < n$, construct $\boldsymbol{S} = [\boldsymbol{I}, \boldsymbol{T}] \in \mathbb{Z}^{m \times n}$ with $\boldsymbol{I} \in \mathbb{Z}^{m \times m}$ as the identity matrix, and output the secret key $\boldsymbol{S}$ and the public parameters $\boldsymbol{Param} = (l, m, n, p, q, w, \chi)$.
– **VHE.E($\boldsymbol{x}, \boldsymbol{S}$):** Input a secret key $\boldsymbol{S} \in \mathbb{Z}^{m \times n}$ and a plaintext vector $\boldsymbol{x} \in \mathbb{Z}^m$, output a ciphertext $\boldsymbol{c} \in \mathbb{Z}^n$ that satisfies

$$\boldsymbol{S}\boldsymbol{c} = w\boldsymbol{x} + \boldsymbol{e}$$

where w is a large integer, $|\boldsymbol{S}| \ll w$, and $\boldsymbol{e}$ is an error term with $|\boldsymbol{e}| < w/2$.

– **VHE.D($\boldsymbol{c}, \boldsymbol{S}$):** Input a ciphertext vector $\boldsymbol{c} \in \mathbb{Z}^n$ and a secret key $\boldsymbol{S} \in \mathbb{Z}^{m \times n}$, output a plaintext $\boldsymbol{x} \in \mathbb{Z}^m$ that satisfies $\boldsymbol{x} = \lceil \boldsymbol{S}\boldsymbol{c}/w \rfloor$.

For the VHE scheme, the key switching is an important operation in the encrypted domain. Given two secret keys $\boldsymbol{S} \in \mathbb{Z}^{m \times n}$ and $\boldsymbol{S}' \in \mathbb{Z}^{m \times n'}$, and the ciphertext $c \in \mathbb{Z}^n$ which decrypts to the plaintext $x \in \mathbb{Z}^m$ with S, we calculate a matrix $M \in \mathbb{Z}^{n' \times nl}$ producing a new ciphertext $c' \in \mathbb{Z}^{n'}$ so as to decrypt c' to the same x with S'. In specific, this key switching task can be divided two steps: $M \leftarrow VHE.KSM(S, S')$ and $c' \leftarrow VHE.KS(M, c)$.

Furthermore, as inferred by [17], for the plaintext x, the ciphertext c, and the key-switching matrix M, the following equation holds.

$$c = M(wx)^*$$

In addition, it is obvious that VHE supports the operation of the addition in ciphertexts domain as

$$S(c_1 + c_2 + \cdots + c_n) = w(x_1 + x_2 + \cdots + x_n) + e.$$

2.5   Privacy-Preserving Inner Product

In this section, we present a new technique of computing the inner product of two vectors. For simplication, we can assume that there are two vectors x_1 and x_2 which are encrypted to c_1 and c_2 using the vector homomorphic encryption of VHE. The challenge is how to calculate the inner product on ciphertext domain.

To tackle the problem, a matrix H is essential to be calculated. By solving equation $AM = I^*$, we have a matrix A. Then we can get the matrix H from $H = A^T A$. We can prove that

$$c^T H c = w^2 x^T x.$$

Hence, we can calculate the inner product in ciphertex domain, and will later discuss the security of this method.

3   Proposed Protocol

In this section, we will propose the protocol for linear regression over encrypted items in outsourced environments using VHE.

3.1   Reformulating the Problem

In this section, we give a brief introduction about our problem again. We supposed that the data owner owns a database D that can be thought to be a big table of n records $x_1, x_2, \cdots, x_n$. The record $x_i = [x_{i_1} \cdots x_{i_m}]$ includes m attributes. Because the resources of the data owner is limited, so the data owner encrypts his database D record-wise, and then outsources the encrypted database D' to the cloud. After that, the service provider will apply the linear regression over encrypted data sets, and return back the results to the data owner. In this protocol, the service provider know nothing to the plaintext.

3.2   Linear Regression Over VHE

With the preparatory work ahead, we discuss the problem of regression over encrypted data firstly. In order to make our protocol faster and easier, We only consider the security of data properties. Supposed dataset $D = \{(x_1, y_1), (x_2, y_2), \cdots, (x_n, y_n)\}$ which is only known by data owner are encrypted to be $D' = \{(c_1, y_1), (c_2, y_2), \cdots, (c_n, y_n)\}$. The relation between plaintext and ciphertext satisfies $Sc_i = wx_i + e_i$ where $i = 1, 2, \cdots, n$. When the service provider get the encrypted data sets D' from the data owner, he will apply linear regression protocol over D'. The whole process is divided three phases: **Preparation**, **Regression**, and **BackResults**.

- *Preparation*(D, λ). The security parameter λ and the data sets D is taken as the input, and the data owner generates a secret key S and a key-switch Matrix M for every record which satisfies the following equation.

$$c = M(wx)^*,$$

where c is the ciphertext of x. The data owner need to calculate the key-switch matrix M only once and the data owner can use the key-switch M to encrypted data sets x. As we know, the scheme of VHE cost most is key-switch. If we use the same key-switch M to encrypt data, We can save a lot of overhead on encryption. Then, the data owner need to calculate the matrix H, which is used to define the loss function over encrypted data. As we know, the following equation holds.

$$wx = I^*(wx)^*.$$

The data owner solve a matrix equation which satisfies:

$$AM = I^*.$$

Then, the data owner obtains the matrix A from the equation. Finally, the data owner can get the matrix H as

$$H = A^T A$$

Finally, the data owner upload the encrypted data set D' and the matrix H to the service provider.

- *Regression*(D', H). The service provider get the encrypted data set $D' = \{(c_1, y_1), (c_2, y_2), \cdots, (c_n, y_n)\}$ and the matrix H from the data owner and apply the regression algorithm, which includes the steps as below:
  (1) Generate a vector θ' randomly and choose a threshold t.
  (2) Define the loss function over encrypted data as

$$J'(\theta') = (\frac{1}{2n}) \sum_{i=1}^{n} (\frac{1}{w^2} \theta'^T H c_i - y_i)^2.$$

(3) Upload the $\boldsymbol{\theta}'$ based on gradient descent method as below:

$$\boldsymbol{\theta}'^k = \boldsymbol{\theta}'^{k-1} - \alpha \frac{\partial J'(\boldsymbol{\theta}')}{\partial \boldsymbol{\theta}'},$$

where $\boldsymbol{\theta}'^k$ is the value of the kth iteration.

(4) Repeat *step (3)* until the value of the loss function satisfies the condition as below:

$$|J'(\boldsymbol{\theta}'^k) - J'(\boldsymbol{\theta}'^{k-1})| < t.$$

- **BackResults**$(\boldsymbol{\theta}')$. From **Regression** the cloud will get the encrypted parameters. Then, the cloud return it back to the data owner.

4   Discussion

We have shown how to achieve a basic protocol for linear regression over encrypted data in outsourced environment. In this section, we will give the correctness analysis of our protocol and give a brief introduction about how to use the encrypted results.

4.1   Loss Function over Encrypted Data

In this section, we introduce the correctness of loss function over encrypted data, and verify that the following equation holds.

$$
\begin{aligned}
J'(\boldsymbol{\theta}') &= (\frac{1}{2n}) \sum_{i=1}^{n} (\frac{1}{w^2} \boldsymbol{\theta}'^T \boldsymbol{H} \boldsymbol{c}_i - y_i)^2 \\
&= (\frac{1}{2n}) \sum_{i=1}^{n} (\frac{1}{w^2} w^2 \boldsymbol{\theta}^T \boldsymbol{c}_i - y_i)^2 \\
&= (\frac{1}{2n}) \sum_{i=1}^{n} (\boldsymbol{\theta}^T \boldsymbol{c}_i - y_i)^2 \\
&= J(\boldsymbol{\theta})
\end{aligned}
$$

As we can see, the loss function on the encrypted data is equal to the loss function on the plaintext.

4.2   Encrypted Parameters

In this section, we will discuss the relationship between encrypted parameters $\boldsymbol{\theta}'$ and encrypted data. First of all, We analysis loss function of plaintext. The loss function of plaintext is shown as follow:

$$J(\boldsymbol{\theta}) = (\frac{1}{2n}) \sum_{i=1}^{n} (\boldsymbol{\theta}^T \boldsymbol{x}_i - y_i)^2$$

Gradient descent is one of the most commonly used methods in solving the model parameters. When solving the minimum value of the loss function, we can get the minimum value of loss function and the model parameters. $\boldsymbol{\theta} = [\theta_1, \theta_2, \ldots, \theta_d]$ where the iterative equation is given as below:

$$\boldsymbol{\theta} := \boldsymbol{\theta} - \alpha \frac{\partial J(\boldsymbol{\theta})}{\partial \boldsymbol{\theta}}$$

$$\begin{bmatrix} \theta_1 \\ \theta_2 \\ \vdots \\ \theta_d \end{bmatrix} := \begin{bmatrix} \theta_1 \\ \theta_2 \\ \vdots \\ \theta_d \end{bmatrix} - \frac{\alpha}{n} \begin{bmatrix} \sum_{i=1}^{n}(\boldsymbol{\theta}^T \boldsymbol{x}_i - y_i) * x_{i1} \\ \sum_{i=1}^{n}(\boldsymbol{\theta}^T \boldsymbol{x}_i - y_i) * x_{i2} \\ \vdots \\ \sum_{i=1}^{n}(\boldsymbol{\theta}^T \boldsymbol{x}_i - y_i) * x_{id} \end{bmatrix}$$

$$\begin{bmatrix} \theta_1 \\ \theta_2 \\ \vdots \\ \theta_d \end{bmatrix} := \begin{bmatrix} \theta_1 \\ \theta_2 \\ \vdots \\ \theta_d \end{bmatrix} - \frac{\alpha}{n} \sum_{i=1}^{n}(\boldsymbol{\theta}^T \boldsymbol{x}_i - y_i) \begin{bmatrix} x_{i1} \\ x_{i2} \\ \vdots \\ x_{id} \end{bmatrix}$$

$$\boldsymbol{\theta} := \boldsymbol{\theta} - \frac{\alpha}{n} \sum_{i=1}^{n}(\boldsymbol{\theta}^T \boldsymbol{x}_i - y_i)\boldsymbol{x}_i,$$

where α is the iteration step. Note that $\boldsymbol{\theta}$ is a linear combination of $\boldsymbol{x}_i'$ when the initial value is set to the vector $\boldsymbol{0}$. Linear combination is supported by Vector Homomorphic Encryption, and thus we can get the results on the encrypted domain.

5 Security Analysis

In this section, we give the security analysis for ESLR, focusing on the encrypted database $\boldsymbol{D}' = \{c_1, c_2, \cdots, c_n\}$ and the matrix $\boldsymbol{H}$. The honest-but-curious cloud server could not threat the privacy of the data owner, i.e., the cloud could not recover plaintexts database $\boldsymbol{D} = \{\boldsymbol{x}_1, \boldsymbol{x}_2, \cdots, \boldsymbol{x}_n\}$.

First of all, c_i is the ciphertext of $\boldsymbol{x}_i$ by the encryption of VHE, for $i = 1, 2, \cdots, n$. For convenience, we omit the subscripts, denoting as $c = \boldsymbol{VHE}.\boldsymbol{E}(\boldsymbol{x}, \boldsymbol{S})$, where $\boldsymbol{S}$ is the secret key. Therefore, we can ensure the confidentiality of $\boldsymbol{x}$, only if the encryption scheme VHE is secure and the secret key $\boldsymbol{S}$ is not known by the cloud. Of course, we may suppose that the secret key $\boldsymbol{S}$ is stored privately by the data owner, and thus the cloud could not get it. Hence, we would focus on the security of VHE.

As shown in [17], the security of VHE could reduce to the problem of the learning with errors (LWE). It is well known the LWE problem is as hard to solve as several worst-case lattice problems [14]. As a resut, the intracibility of LWE assures the security of VHE.

However, in order to evaluate the distance of two ciphertexts vectors, we introduce a special matrix $\boldsymbol{H}$. It is natural to consider if $\boldsymbol{H}$ may bring certain unknown privacy risk. For example, on one hand, to calculate H, we first solve the equation $I^* = AM$ to obtain A, then compute $H = A^T A$ to get H. On the other hand, according to VHE, for the ciphertext c and the plaintext x, $c = M(w\mathbf{x})^*$ holds. As known, the cloud has H and c. If the cloud combines the equations as follows, it seems that the cloud could recover the plaintext x.

$$\begin{cases} H = A^T \mathbf{A} \\ I^* = AM \\ c = M(w\mathbf{x}) \end{cases}$$

In the following, We would give positive answer about the challenge. The analysis demonstrates that the cloud could not yet recover the plaintext x from the ciphertext c by exploiting H.

As is known, for a random orthogonal matrix Q, satisfying the relation $Q^T Q = I$, where I is an identity matrix, we have

$$\begin{aligned} H &= A^T A \\ &= A^T Q^T Q A \\ &= A^T I A \\ &= H \end{aligned}$$

It is clear that the equation $H = A^T A$ has infinite solutions for A since Q is randomly chosen. Therefore, the cloud could not extract the matrix A from the Norm-matrix H. Futhermore, without knowing A, the cloud could not yet get M. And the cloud could not recover the plaintext x from the ciphertext c. As a result, we achieve the privacy of the database D.

6 Performance Evaluation

In this section, we evaluate the proposed linear regression protocol. Our data sets come from the UCI repository [1], and the experiment environment includes a data owner and a service provider. Python language is used on a Window 10 machine with i3-4130 CPU @1.40 GHz and 4 GB RAM for a user, and the server is a Linux machine with an Intel Xeon E5-2430 v2 CPU @2.5 GHz and 16 GB RAM running Ubuntu 14.04 LTS. The user acts as a data owner and a data user, and the server acts as a service provider. In the following, we will conduct the simulation experiments in terms of the time cost, accuracy, and communication overhead.

6.1 Time Cost and Accuracy

Firstly, we evaluate the time cost by the comparison of running time between plaintext and ciphertext. As illustrated in Fig. 2, we choose 4 data sets to verify our protocol from the UCI repository, and can see that the linear regression

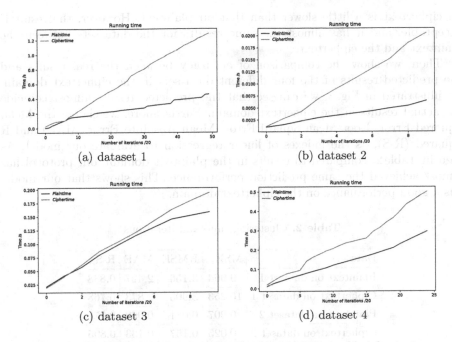

Fig. 2. Comparison of running time between plaintext and ciphertext

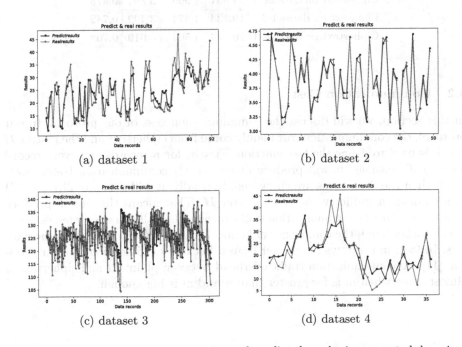

Fig. 3. Comparison between real results and predicted results in encrypted domain

on ciphertext is a little slower than that on plaintext. However, the result is acceptable, and it has almost the same results for the data sets between the plaintext and the ciphertext.

Then, we show the comparison of accuracy between the real results and the predicted results of the four different data sets in the ciphertext domain. As illustrated in Fig. 3, we can see that the predicted results almost coincide the actual results in the ciphertext domain. Furthermore, we choose the Mean Squared Error, Root Mean Squard Error, Mean Absolute Error (MAE) and R Squared (R-S), as the indexes of linear regression to evaluate our model. As seen in Table 2, compared to results in the plaintext domain, our protocol has almost achieved the same prediction performance. This shows that our model has a good performance on the ciphertext domain.

Table 2. Clustering time and iterations

Data	MSE	RMSE	MAE	R-S
Plaintext on dataset 1	9.964	3.156	2.427	0.838
Ciphertext on dataset 1	15.253	3.905	2.873	0.768
Plaintext on dataset 2	0.007	0.081	0.068	0.972
Ciphertext on dataset 2	0.025	0.157	0.133	0.895
Plaintext on dataset 3	23.999	4.899	3.790	0.497
Ciphertext on dataset 3	24.987	4.999	3.897	0.475
Plaintext on dataset 4	19.134	4.374	3.499	0.782
Ciphertext on dataset 4	20.134	4.564	3.619	0.768

6.2 Communication Cost

In this section, we will discuss the communication cost of our protocol. In our protocol, the communication cost mainly come from ciphertext and the matrix H which is used to define the loss function. Firstly, for n records and every record have m dimensions, it will produce $\mathcal{O}(m(n + 1))$ communication traffic overhead when the data items are encrypted. Secondly, it will generate $\mathcal{O}((n + 1)^2)$ communication traffic overhead for matrix H. That means that it will produce $\mathcal{O}(m+n+1)(n+1)$ communication traffic overhead totally on encrypted domain. On the other hand, the complexity of plaintext stage is $\mathcal{O}(mn)$ for the same data sets. In fact, m is always far greater than n because of dimension disaster problem [11]. So communication traffic overhead between plaintext and ciphertext is almost same when m is far greater than n and m is big enough.

7   Conclusion

In this paper we have proposed an efficient and secure linear regression protocol over encrypted data using the vector homomorphic encryption. Especially, we have given a good solution to the challenging problem of privacy-preserving gradient descent method. Performance evaluation shows that it has high accuracy and low computation and communication cost. As we know, many machine learning algorithm base on gradient descent method. In the future, we will use this method on other machine learning algorithms.

Acknowledgement. Our work is supported by of the National Key Research and Development Program of China (2017YFB0802003), the National Natural Science Foundation of China (U1633114) and the Sichuan Science and Technology Program (2018GZ0202).

References

1. Asuncion, A., Newman, D.: UCI machine learning repository (2007)
2. Ben-David, A., Nisan, N., Pinkas, B.: FairplayMP: a system for securemulti-party computation. In: Proceedings of the 15th ACM Conference on Computer and Communications Security, pp. 257–266. ACM (2008)
3. Dankar, F.K., El Emam, K.: The application of differential privacy to healthdata. In: Proceedings of the 2012 Joint EDBT/ICDT Workshops, pp. 158–166. ACM (2012)
4. Centers for Disease Control and Prevention, et al.: HIPAA privacy rule and public health. guidance from CDC and the us department of health and human services. MMWR Morb. Mortal. Wkly. Rep. **52**(Suppl. 1), 1–17 (2003)
5. Du, W., Atallah, M.J.: Secure multi-party computation problems and their applications: a review and open problems. In: Proceedings of the 2001 Workshop on New Security Paradigms, pp. 13–22. ACM (2001)
6. Dwork, C.: Differential privacy: a survey of results. In: Agrawal, M., Du, D., Duan, Z., Li, A. (eds.) TAMC 2008. LNCS, vol. 4978, pp. 1–19. Springer, Heidelberg (2008). https://doi.org/10.1007/978-3-540-79228-4_1
7. Dwork, C., Roth, A., et al.: The algorithmic foundations of differential privacy. Found. Trends® Theor. Comput. Sci. **9**(3–4), 211–407 (2014)
8. Fletcher, R., Powell, M.J.: A rapidly convergent descent method for minimization. Comput. J. **6**(2), 163–168 (1963)
9. Goldreich, O.: Secure multi-party computation. Manuscript. Preliminary version, pp. 86–97 (1998)
10. Halevi, S., Shoup, V.: Helib (2014). Retrieved from HELib: https://github.com. shaih/HElib
11. Huang, Z.: Extensions to the k-means algorithm for clustering large data sets with categorical values. Data Min. Knowl. Discov. **2**(3), 283–304 (1998)
12. Lee, L.M., Gostin, L.O.: Ethical collection, storage, and use of public health data: a proposal for a national privacy protection. Jama **302**(1), 82–84 (2009)
13. McSherry, F., Talwar, K.: Mechanism design via differential privacy. In: 48th Annual IEEE Symposium on Foundations of Computer Science, FOCS 2007, pp. 94–103. IEEE (2007)

14. Regev, O.: On lattices, learning with errors, random linear codes, andcryptography. J. ACM **56**(6), 1–40 (2009)
15. van Dijk, M., Gentry, C., Halevi, S., Vaikuntanathan, V.: Fully homomorphic encryption over the integers. In: Gilbert, H. (ed.) EUROCRYPT 2010. LNCS, vol. 6110, pp. 24–43. Springer, Heidelberg (2010). https://doi.org/10.1007/978-3-642-13190-5_2
16. Wold, S., Ruhe, A., Wold, H., Dunn III, W.: The collinearity problem in linear regression. The partial least squares (PLS) approach to generalized inverses. SIAM J. Sci. Stat. Comput. **5**(3), 735–743 (1984)
17. Zhou, H., Wornell, G.: Efficient homomorphic encryption on integer vectors and its applications. In: Information Theory and Applications Workshop (ITA), 2014, pp. 1–9. IEEE (2014)

New Multi-objectives Scheduling Strategies in Docker SwarmKit

Tarek Menouer, Christophe Cérin[(✉)], and Étienne Leclercq

{tarek.menouer,christophe.cerin,
etienne.leclercq}@lipn.univ-paris13.fr

University of Paris 13, Sorbonne Paris Cité, LIPN/CNRS UMR 7030,
93430 Villetaneuse, France

Abstract. This paper presents new multi-objectives scheduling strategies implemented in Docker SwarmKit. Docker SwarmKit is a container toolkit for orchestrating distributed systems at any scale. Currently, Docker SwarmKit has one scheduling strategy called Spread. Spread is based only on one objective to select from a set of cloud nodes, one node to execute a container. However, the containers submitted by users to be scheduled in Docker SwarmKit are configured according to multi-objectives criteria, as the number of CPUs and the memory size. To better address the multi-objectives configuration problem of containers, we introduce the concept and the implementation of new multi-objectives scheduling strategies adapted for Cloud Computing environments and implemented in Docker SwarmKit. The principle of our multi-objectives strategies consist to select a node which has a good compromise between multi-objectives criteria to execute a container. The proposed scheduling strategies are based on a combinaison of PROMETHEE and Kung multi-objectives decision algorithms in order to place containers. The implementation in Docker SwarmKit and experiments of our new strategies demonstrate the potential of our approach under different scenarios.

Keywords: Systems software · Scheduling and resource management
Container technology · Cloud computing
Application of parallel and distributed algorithms

1 Introduction

Nowadays, cloud computing is the commercial subscription to external services. Its principle is based on pay-for-use model that can affect different elements such as the requested application, data storage capacity, memory processing and number of users. Different forms of cloud computational resources exist such as virtual machines (VMs), containers, or bare-metal resources, having each their own characteristics. Container technology is relatively new in production systems but it is not a new concept. It has increasingly grown up in cloud environment.

J. Vaidya and J. Li (Eds.): ICA3PP 2018, LNCS 11336, pp. 103–117, 2018.
https://doi.org/10.1007/978-3-030-05057-3_8

Docker SwarmKit [25] is a toolkit for orchestrating distributed systems at any scale. It includes primitives for node discovery, raft-based consensus, containers scheduling and more. In the containers context, it selects the first Docker container that must be executed using the classical FIFO (First In First Out) strategy. Then, it chooses the appropriate cloud node from a set of nodes using the Spread scheduling strategy. The principle of Spread is to execute a container on the node having the least number of containers. Spread is a mono-based objective scheduling strategy.

However, the containers scheduled by Docker SwarmKit are configured regarding multi-objectives criteria, like the number of the used CPUs and the size of the used memory. To take into consideration the multi-objectives configuration approach, we present in this paper the idea for new multi-objectives scheduling strategies implemented in Docker SwarmKit. The goal is to address the problem of companies that manage a private infrastructure of nodes i.e. a cloud platform, and would like to optimize the scheduling of several containers submitted online by users. In this paper, for the sake of simplicity, each container is scheduled by taking into consideration two criteria: (i) the number of CPUs and (ii) the memory size.

Indeed, the overall motivation for such multi-objectives scheduling strategies comes from the industrial Fonds Unique Interministériel (FUI-22) Wolphin[1] project, a collaborative industrial project oriented towards the themes of orchestration and optimization of the execution of containers. Ultimately, the project, supervised by Alterway[2], aims to provide an efficient solution for hypervision and invoicing of container-oriented infrastructure. In fact, in the Wolphin project the Alterway company would like to improve the Docker SwarmKit scheduler to optimize the scheduling of containers submitted online by users. AlterWay would like to reduce the cost of the infrastructure by choosing the most appropriate nodes to maximize the number of executed containers during a time period. Each container should be executed in a node with a good compromise between its availability on the number of CPUs cores and its free memory.

This paper demonstrates that we have room for improvements in the Docker SwarmKit toolkit. We propose to particularize two multi-objectives decision algorithms called PROMETHEE and Kung. These algorithms are used to select, for each submitted container, the node that must execute it, according to a "good" compromise between multiple criteria. This is a first step for going on high dimensional decision support for scheduling containers inside the concrete Docker SwarmKit toolkit. The essence of cloud computing is precisely to be able to deal with the challenging problem of multiple objectives in heterogeneous and dynamic environments for the benefit of the user and/or the platform.

The organization of the paper is as follows. Section 2 presents some related works. Section 3 describes our multi-objectives scheduling strategies based on PROMETHEE and Kung algorithms. Section 4 shows a comparative example between the proposed multi-objectives scheduling strategies and the Spread

---

[1] https://www.alterway.fr/wolphin-2-0-laureat-du-fui-22/.
[2] https://www.alterway.fr.

strategy which is the default SwarmKit scheduling strategy. Section 5 introduces exhaustive experiences that allow the validation of our strategies. Finally, a conclusion and some future works are given in Sect. 6.

2   Related Work

In the literature, many problems of resources allocation, or placement of user's containers or requests refer to the same class of scheduling problems. They consist generally in associating a user's container with one or several computing cores to be executed in a particular node. Most of these problems are *NP-difficult* [20]. In this general context, we present in the forthcoming subsection several proposed scheduling systems and computing frameworks. We present also in Subsect. 2.2, some multi-objectives studies proposed in the literature. Subsect. 2.3 discusses quickly about machine learning techniques for large-scale multi-objectives optimization. Then, we conclude this section by a positioning in the Subsect. 2.4.

2.1   Containers Scheduling and Cloud Computing

In the literature, there are some frameworks that have proposed to schedule containers on cloud computing [5,17,23,24]. To give a positioning of our work compared to an industrial point of view, we document, as examples of concrete projects, the schedulers inside Google Kubernetes [24], Docker SwarmKit [25] and Apache Mesos [23].

Google Kubernetes [24] is a scheduler framework which represents an orchestration system for Docker containers based on pods concept. Pods are a group of one or more containers such as Docker containers. They are always co-located, co-scheduled and run in a shared context. Moreover, they will be run on the same physical or virtual machine (node). The principle of the Google Kubernetes scheduling can be summarized in two steps. The first step consists to classify all nodes to remove nodes that do not meet certain requirements of the pod. The second step consists to classify the remaining nodes using priorities to find the best fit to execute a pod. A priority is a key/value representing the name of the priority from the list of existing ones and its weight. For each remaining node, a priority function gives a score which scales from 0 to 10. Each priority function is weighted by a positive number and the final score of each node is calculated by adding up all the weighted scores. When all scores of all nodes are calculated, Google Kubernetes chooses the node with the highest score to run the container.

Docker SwarmKit [25] is an important container scheduler framework developed by Docker. It has two steps to finally choose which node will execute the container. First, it uses filters to select suitable nodes to execute the container according to the number of waiting CPUs cores and the free memory. Then, it uses, according to a Spread scheduling strategy, the most suitable node to execute the selected container. The principle of Spread strategy is to execute a container on the node having the least number of containers. The goal of

Spread is to give a "good" load balancing of containers between all nodes of the infrastructure.

Mesos system [23] for example is delegating control over scheduling to the frameworks because many frameworks already implement sophisticated scheduling [9]. The Apache Mesos [23] framework has a native Docker support which offers many features in terms of scheduling such as constraints, discovery service and load balancing [9]. It is based on four elements to schedule containers on the cluster. *Zookeeper* for example helps *Marathon* to find the address of Mesos master. *Marathon* starts, monitors and scales the containers. The *Mesos master* sends the tasks assigned to a node and informs *Marathon* if there is a node having some free resources. *Mesos slaves* represent the set of nodes used to execute containers.

There exists also some studies related to resource management as studies presented in [5,11,15].

Choi et al. [5] propose a framework which provides useful resource management functions, and more importantly it is possible to apply customized scheduling in local environment. By using this framework, cloud providers or researchers can optimize resources for their purpose.

Jimenez et al. [11] introduce a resource monitoring agent for resource management of containers environment. The advantage of their approach is that it allows the monitor to assign resource of each container through the proposed agent.

Medel et al. [15] inovate with a client-side scheduling approach in Kubernetes that aims to reduce the resource contention phenomenon in container technologies. The principle of the authors approach is to make use of application characterization in terms of the usage of resources, and extends the Kubernetes scheduler so that it can take better allocation decisions on containers based on such characterization. The application characterization consists in dividing applications in two categories, namely high and low usage of resources. The classification process of applications is delegated to the client or developer which provides the category which fits better to the application.

2.2   Short Overview of Multi-objectives Related Problems

Combinatorial and discrete optimization problems such as routing, task allocation, and scheduling are important optimization applications in the real world. Traditionally, the time required to solve a combinatorial problem may increase exponentially in the worst case, thereby making them computationally too costly. Moreover, if the optimization involves multiple objectives, the process becomes more complex and difficult to solve [22].

Xing et al. [21] present a simulation model to solve a multi-objectives Flexible Job-Shop Scheduling Problem (FJSSP). The FJSSP is very important in the fields of combinatorial optimization and production management. Throughout the experiments, authors showed that multi-objectives evolutionary algorithms are very effective for solving the FJSSP.

Knowles et al. [12] propose a Pareto archived evolution strategy to solve multi-objectives optimization problem. The algorithm introduces a Pareto ranking-based selection method and couples it with a partition scheme in objective space. It uses two different archives to save non-dominated solutions.

Chang et al. [4] proposed a new algorithm, called the sub-population genetic algorithm II, to solve multi-objectives combinatorial problems. The algorithm develops a mechanism to exchange information among sub-populations. Once a sub-population reaches a better non-dominated solution, other sub-populations will apply them directly in their search space. In this way, all individuals in the same population will be guided to search toward the true Pareto front.

2.3   Multi-dimensional Search

Machine learning algorithms for large-scale multi-objectives optimization may also be considered as techniques to accelerate the search of solutions in multi-dimensional space. We assume that solving large-scale multi-objectives scheduling problems on large-scale systems remains challenging.

Such general techniques from the field of machine learning are surrogate meta-models, multi-armed bandits [14], landscape analysis [6] and online/offline automatic algorithm selection and configuration [2].

Our work may be considered as a practical work to investigate the limits of known multi-objectives optimization techniques to solve concrete problems inside the popular Docker SwarmKit. Once the limits are isolated and understood we can better choose, in the future, another appropriate technique for multi-dimensional spaces.

2.4   Positioning

To the best of our knowledge, all of the studies proposed previously in the context of scheduling in cloud use a mono-based objective strategy to select a node which executes a container. However, the novelty of this paper is to improve the Docker SwarmKit scheduling system with a new multi-based objectives strategies to select for each submitted container a node that will executes it. Indeed, this paper is an extension of a preliminary paper presented in [3] where the context was a naive scheduling strategy based on a mono-objective scheduling strategy implemented in Docker Swarm.

3   Multi-objectives Scheduling Strategies

In following we start by presenting the PROMETHEE scheduling strategy. Then, we present the Kung scheduling strategy. After the introduction of each multi-objectives scheduling strategy, we give an illustrated example which explains the operation of each strategy.

3.1 PROMETHEE Scheduling Strategy

The first proposed scheduling strategy is based on PROMETHEE II (*Preference Ranking Organization METHod for Enrichment Evaluations*) algorithm [18].

PROMETHEE II is a multi-objectives decision algorithm that permits the building of an outranking between different alternatives [18]. It is used in this step because it allows to provide a node which must execute a container with a "good" compromise between: (i) number of waiting CPUs and (ii) unused memory space.

Indeed, the PROMETHEE II has been used with success to solve many problems [1]. In our case, it is based on a comparison, pair by pair, of possible decisions (nodes) along number of waiting CPUs and the size of the free memory criteria. Each criterion can be evaluated according to two functions (minimization or maximization). The use of the PROMETHEE II algorithm requires for each criterion two informations: a weight and a preference function. In our context, the weight in all criteria is the same and equal to 1. The preference function characterizes the difference for a criterion between the evaluations obtained by two possible nodes into a preference degree ranging from 0 to 1. In [10], six basic preference functions have been proposed. In this work, for the sake of simplicity, we use the usual preference functions. To summarize, the PROMETHEE II algorithm is composed of four steps [19] and it is used as follows:

1. Compute for each pair of possible nodes ($node_a$ and $node_b$) and for each criterion (number of waiting CPUs or free memory size), the value of the preference degree. Let $g_j(node_a)$ be the value of a criterion j for a node $node_a$. We note $d_j(node_a, node_b)$ $(d_j(node_a, node_b) = g_j(node_a) - g_j(node_b))$, the difference of value of a criterion j for $node_a$ and $node_b$. $P_j(node_a, node_b)$ is the value of the preference degree of a criterion j for $node_a$ and $node_b$. The preference function used in this paper to compute these preference degrees is defined such as:

$$P_j(d_j) = \begin{cases} 0 \ d_j \leq 0 \\ 1 \ d_j > 0 \end{cases}$$

2. Compute for each pair of possible nodes, a global preference index. Let C be the set of considered objectives criteria (number of waiting CPUs and free memory size) and w_j the weight associated to the criterion j. The global preference index for a pair of possible $node_a$ and $node_b$ is computed as follows:

$$\pi(node_a, node_b) = \sum_{j \in C} W_j \times P_j(node_a, node_b)$$

3. Compute for each possible node the positive outranking flow $\phi^+(node_a)$ and the negative outranking flow $\phi^-(node_a)$. Let A be the set of nodes with size of n. The positive and negative outranking flow of nodes are computed by the following formula:

$$\phi^+(node_a) = \frac{1}{n-1} \sum_{x \in A} \pi(node_a, x)$$

and

$$\phi^-(node_a) = \frac{1}{n-1} \sum_{x \in A} \pi(x, node_a)$$

4. Compute the outranking flows to establish a complete ranking between nodes. The ranking is based on the net outranking flows $\phi(node_a)$ which is computed as follows: $\phi(node_a) = \phi^+(node_a) - \phi^-(node_a)$. In our work, the first node returned by PROMETHEE II is the node that has the highest value in case of minimization of multi-objectives criteria of the net outranking.

Example of How PROMETHEE Scheduling Strategy Works: Assume that at time t_0, we have a container C_x which need 8 CPUs and 8 GB of memory. We assume also that from all nodes of the infrastructure there are just three nodes ($node_a$, $node_b$ and $node_c$) which can execute C_x. The availability of each node in term of waiting number of CPUs and the size of free memory are presented in Table 1.

Table 1. Nodes configurations in term of waiting CPUs and free memory size

Nodes	Number of waiting CPUs	Memory size
n_a	10	10
n_b	20	40
n_c	30	40
n_d	40	50

As explained before, to select the first node that must execute the container C_x using PROMETHEE scheduling strategy (with a minimization function on all multi-objectives criteria), we start by computing for each pair of nodes a difference value of multi-objectives criteria $d_x(node_i, node_j)$ and the preference degree $P_x(node_i, node_j)$. Then, the system calculates the global preference index $\phi(node_i)$. For example, in Table 2 with the first pair nodes ($node_a$, $node_b$), the difference value of waiting CPUs criterion is $d(node_a, node_b) = 10 - 20 = -10$. In this case the difference value is negative, using our usual preference function, the preference degree equals to 0.

As in our work the weight of all criteria is the same and equal to 1, the global preference index of the first pair nodes ($node_a$, $node_b$) = $1 \times 0 + 1 \times 0 + 1 \times 1 = 1$. Finally, to get the rank of nodes and select the node which can execute a container, our strategy calculates the positive and negative outranking flow and the net outranking flow parameters. Table 3 shows how our strategy calculates these different parameters. For example, for $node_a$, the positive outranking flow (ϕ^+) is $\frac{1}{2}(1 + 1) = 1$. The negative outranking flow (ϕ^-) is $\frac{1}{2}(2 + 1) = 1.5$. The net outranking flow ϕ ($\phi = \phi^+ - \phi^-$) is -0.5 $(1 - 1.5)$.

Using PROMETHEE strategy, the $node_a$ is the first selected node with the minimum net outranking flow.

Table 2. Computing the difference values, preference degree and preference index value for a set of pair nodes

Pair of nodes	Difference values		Preference degree		Weight		Preference index value
	Number of waiting CPUs	Memory size	Number of waiting CPUs	Memory size	Number of waiting CPUs	Memory size	
$d(n_a, n_b)$	−10	−30	0	0	1	1	0
$d(n_a, n_c)$	−20	−30	0	0	1	1	0
$d(n_a, n_d)$	−30	−40	0	0	1	1	0
$d(n_b, n_a)$	10	30	1	1	1	1	2
$d(n_b, n_c)$	−10	0	0	0	1	1	0
$d(n_b, n_d)$	−20	−10	0	0	1	1	0
$d(n_c, n_a)$	20	30	1	1	1	1	2
$d(n_c, n_b)$	10	0	1	0	1	1	1
$d(n_c, n_d)$	−10	−10	0	0	1	1	0
$d(n_d, n_a)$	30	40	1	1	1	1	2
$d(n_d, n_b)$	20	10	1	1	1	1	2
$d(n_d, n_c)$	10	10	1	1	1	1	2

Table 3. Computing of the net outranking flow for each node

Nodes	ϕ^+	ϕ^-	ϕ	Rank
n_a	0	3	−3	1
n_b	1	1.5	−0.5	2
n_c	1.5	1	0.5	3
n_c	3	0	3	4

3.2   Kung Scheduling Strategy

The second multi-objectives scheduling strategy is based on Kung algorithm [13]. It is among the best algorithms used in the multi-objectives criteria context [7]. As presented in [7], Kung algorithm firstly sorts the population (nodes that can execute a container) in descending order according to the first criterion (number of waiting CPUs). Thereafter, the set of nodes are recursively halved as Top half (T) and Bottom half (B) sub set of nodes. As T is better in objectives in comparison to B in first objective (number of waiting CPUs), so we check the B for domination with T. The solution of B which are not dominated by solutions of T are merged with members of T to form merged set of nodes M. In our context, we use a minimization function. That mean a solution x_1 is better that other solution x_2, if the value of x_1 is smaller than the value of x_2. The complete algorithm can be summarized in two steps:

– Sort the nodes according the descending order of importance in the number of waiting CPUs criterion and rename the population as P of size N.

– Front(P): if $|P| = 1$, return P as the output of Front(P). Otherwise, $T = \text{Front}(P^1 - P^{|P/2|})$ and $B = \text{Front}(P^{|P/2|+1} - P^P)$. IF i^{th} non-dominated solution B is not dominated by any non-dominated solution of T, create a merged set M = {T U i}. Finally, return M as output of Front(P).

We say that a solution x_1 dominates an other solution x_2 if two conditions are satisfied:

1. Solution x_1 is no worse than x_2 in all multi-objectives criteria;
2. Solution x_1 is strictly better than x_2 in at least one objective criterion.

If a solution x_1 dominates an other solution $x_2 \Leftrightarrow$ the solution x_2 is dominated by the solution x_1.

In our context, the goal of Kung algorithm is to select a set of nodes with a "good" compromise between the availability of CPUs cores and the free memory. Then, our strategy returns the first node that can execute a container from the set of nodes returned by the Kung strategy.

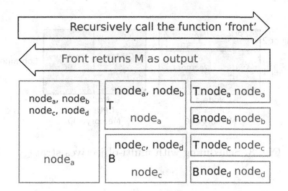

Fig. 1. Example of Kung strategy (Color figure online)

Example of How Kung Scheduling Strategy Works: Assume that at time t_0, we have a container C_x which need 8 CPUs and 8 GB of memory. We assume also that from all nodes of the infrastructure there are just three nodes ($node_a$, $node_b$ and $node_c$) which can execute C_x. The availability of each node in term of number of waiting CPUs and memory size are presented in Table 1 (the same table as the table presented previously in Sect. 3.1). As explained before, to select the first node that must execute the container C_x using Kung strategy, we start by ordering in descending order all nodes according to the value of the waiting CPUs criterion. Then, the set of nodes are recursively halved as Top (T) and Bottom (B) sub set of nodes as it is shown in the Fig. 1 with red color. After applying the second step of the Kung algorithm as presented in the Fig. 1 with blue color, the selected node is the $node_a$. We note that the Kung and PROMETHEE scheduling strategies give the same result and choose the $node_a$ to execute the container C_x.

4   Comparative Example Between Scheduling Strategies

Figures 2 and 3 show a comparison between the scheduling of 3 containers with Spread strategy (Fig. 2) and with multi-objectives strategy (PROMETHEE or Kung) (Fig. 3).

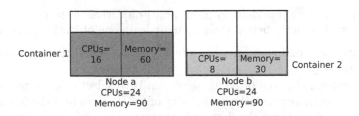

Fig. 2. Scheduling with Spread strategy

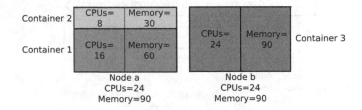

Fig. 3. Scheduling with multi-objectives strategy

The principle of Spread strategy is to execute a container on the node having the least number of containers. For example, with n nodes, Spread selects nodes with the following order: $node_{i\%n}, node_{(i+1)\%n}, node_{(i+2)\%n}, \cdots$.

In this comparison we suppose that we have 2 nodes with the same configuration (24 waiting CPUs and 90 GB of memory). We suppose also that we have 3 containers with the following configurations:

- Container 1: 16 CPUs and 60 GB of memory;
- Container 2: 8 CPUs and 30 GB of memory;
- Container 3: 24 CPUs and 90 GB of memory.

In Fig. 2, the container 1 is executed in $node_a$. The container 2 is executed in $node_b$. When the container 3 is presented, with Spread strategy container 3 can not be executed because there are no node which has enough of resources to execute it.

However, in Fig. 3, the first container is executed on $node_a$. After that, the PROMETHEE and Kung strategies select the $node_a$ to execute the container 2. When the container 3 is presented, it is directly executed in $node_b$.

5   Experimental Evaluation

In this section we introduce experiences with our multi-objectives scheduling strategies implemented in Docker SwarmKit to check if it meets our expectations. For these experimentations, we do experiences inside the Grid5000 platform [8], an experimental large-scale testbed for distributed computing in France. For our experimental evaluation, we reserved an infrastructure composed of a total of 128 computing cores, distributed over 4 nodes (Intel Xeon CPU), each node contains 32 cores and 130 GB of memory.

The following experimental evaluation is performed according to the submission of 18 containers with an execution time equal to 3 minutes. Each container is submitted by one of the following three users, each user has a particular container configuration:

- User 1: for each container, he needs 30 CPUs and 120 GB of memory,
- User 2: for each container, he needs 20 CPUs and 80 GB of memory,
- User 3: for each container, he needs 10 CPUs and 40 GB of memory.

The performance of our multi-objectives scheduling strategies is based on two submitting containers types: (i) containers submitted at the same time, i.e. each user submits 6 containers at the same time; and (ii) containers submitted online with a fixed frequency equal to 1 minute, i.e. each 1 min, 3 containers are submitted by 3 different users. The first type of experiments with submission at the same time stresses the scheduling system. The second type of experiments with submission online represents a "normal" operating mode.

5.1   Distribution of Containers in Different Nodes

In this subsection we present the distribution of containers in our 4 nodes according to the submission type and the three scheduling strategies: (i) Spread; (ii) PROMETHEE; and (iii) Kung.

Containers Submitted at the Same Time: Figures 4, 5 and 6 show the distribution of containers submitted at the same time in 4 nodes using Spread strategy (Fig. 4), PROMETHEE strategy (Fig. 5) and Kung strategy (Fig. 6).

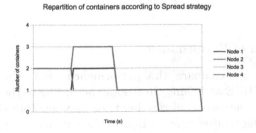

Fig. 4. Distribution of containers submitted at the same time in 4 nodes using Spread strategy

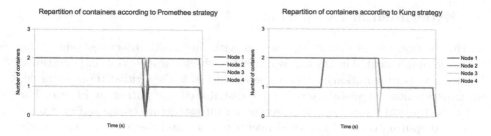

Fig. 5. Distribution of containers submitted at the same time in 4 nodes using PROMETHEE strategy

Fig. 6. Distribution of containers submitted at the same time in 4 nodes using Kung strategy

Using PROMETHEE and Kung strategies, we note that the load of containers in each node is bigger than the load of containers with Spread strategy. This is a good property of our implementation, as expected.

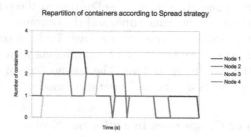

Fig. 7. Distribution of containers submitted online in 4 nodes using Spread strategy

Containers Submitted Online: Figures 7, 8 and 9 show the distribution of containers submitted online in 4 nodes using Spread strategy (Fig. 7), PROMETHEE strategy (Fig. 8) and Kung strategy (Fig. 9). We can emit the same remark as the previous experimentation i.e. the load of containers with PROMETHEE and Kung is bigger than the load of containers with Spread strategy.

5.2   Comparison of Performance

In this subsection we compare the performance of 3 scheduling strategies (Spread, PROMETHEE and Kung) in 4 nodes according to the submission type.

Table 4 shows a comparison of running time between Spread, PROMETHEE and Kung scheduling strategies according to the submission type. We note that the running time obtained with Spread strategy is always the longest. However, the running time of PROMETHEE and Kung strategies is almost the same.

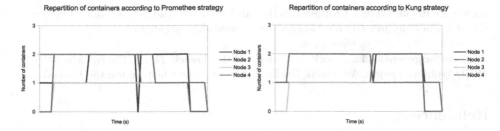

Fig. 8. Distribution of containers submitted online in 4 nodes using PROMETHEE strategy

Fig. 9. Distribution of containers submitted online in 4 nodes using Kung strategy

Table 4. Comparison of performance between 3 scheduling strategies

Scheduling strategies	Submission type	
	At the same time	Online
Spread	747.49 (s)	747.29 (s)
PROMETHEE	**558.62** (s)	622.26 (s)
Kung	559.11 (s)	**621.46** (s)

We note also that sometimes the PROMETHEE running time is better (submission at the same time), and sometimes the Kung running time is better (submission online).

6   Conclusion

We have presented, in this paper, new multi-objectives scheduling strategies for Docker SwarmKit. Our new scheduling strategies are based on PROMETHEE and Kung multi-objectives algorithms. The principle of our strategies is to select from a set of nodes, a node to execute a container by taking into consideration multi-objectives criteria: (i) number of waiting CPUs and (ii) free memory size. The goal is to execute a container in node which has a good compromise between the availability of CPUs cores and the free memory size.

Actually Docker SwarmKit uses a simple FIFO (First In First out) strategy to select the first container that must be executed from a set of containers saved in a queue. As a perspective, we propose to use the same principle as our multi-objectives strategies to select the first container that must be executed from a queue of containers.

We have present previously in [16], a new scheduling and resources management system based on an economic model. To choose the node that must execute a request, the system presented in [16], uses the Bin Packing strategy. As an other perspective, we propose to use our new multi-objectives scheduling strategies in the system proposed in [16] and compare the performance between the Bin Packing and the multi-objectives scheduling strategies.

Acknowledgments. This work is funded by the French *Fonds Unique Ministériel (FUI)* Wolphin Project. We thank Grid5000 team for their help to use the testbed.

References

1. Behzadian, M., Kazemzadeh, R., Albadvi, A., Aghdasi, M.: Promethee: a comprehensive literature review on methodologies and applications. Eur. J. Oper. Res. **200**(1), 198–215 (2010)
2. Cáceres, L.P., Pagnozzi, F., Franzin, A., Stützle, T.: Automatic configuration of GCC using irace. In: Lutton, E., Legrand, P., Parrend, P., Monmarché, N., Schoenauer, M. (eds.) EA 2017. LNCS, vol. 10764, pp. 202–216. Springer, Cham (2018). https://doi.org/10.1007/978-3-319-78133-4_15
3. Cérin, C., Ben-Abdaallah, W., Saad, W., Menouer, T.: A new docker swarm scheduling strategy. In: 7th International Symposium on Cloud and Service Computing, Kanazawa, Japan (2017)
4. Chang, P.-C., Chen, S.-H.: The development of a sub-population genetic algorithm II (SPGA II) for multi-objective combinatorial problems. Appl. Soft Comput. **9**(1), 173–181 (2009)
5. Choi, S., Myung, R., Choi, H., Chung, K., Gil, J., Yu, H.: GPSF: general-purpose scheduling framework for container based on cloud environment. In: IEEE iThings and IEEE GreenCom and IEEE CPSCom and IEEE SmartData (2016)
6. Daolio, F., Liefooghe, A., Vérel, S., Aguirre, H.E., Tanaka, K.: Problem features versus algorithm performance on rugged multiobjective combinatorial fitness landscapes. Evol. Comput. **25**(4), 555–585 (2017)
7. Ding, L., Zeng, S., Kang, L.: A fast algorithm on finding the non-dominated set in multi-objective optimization. In: The 2003 Congress on Evolutionary Computation, CEC 2003, vol. 4, pp. 2565–2571, December 2003
8. Grid5000: https://www.grid5000.fr/
9. Grillet, A.: Comparaison of containers schedulers. Medium (2016)
10. Brans, J.-P., Mareschal, B.: Promethee methods - multiple criteria decision analysis: state of the art surveys. International Series in Operations Research & Management Science, vol. 78 (2005)
11. Jimenez, L.L., Simon, M.G., Schelén, O., Kristiansson, J., Synnes, K., Åhlund, C.: CoMA: resource monitoring of docker containers. In: Proceedings of the 5th International Conference on Cloud Computing and Services Science (CLOSER 2015) (2015)
12. Knowles, J.D., Corne, D.W.: M-PAES: a memetic algorithm for multiobjective optimization. In: Proceedings of the 2000 Congress on Evolutionary Computation. CEC00 (Cat. No.00TH8512), vol. 1, pp. 325–332 (2000)
13. Kung, H.T., Luccio, F., Preparata, F.P.: On finding the maxima of a set of vectors. J. ACM **22**(4), 469–476 (1975)
14. Li, K., Fialho, Á., Kwong, S., Zhang, Q.: Adaptive operator selection with bandits for a multiobjective evolutionary algorithm based on decomposition. IEEE Trans. Evol. Comput. **18**(1), 114–130 (2014)

15. Medel, V., Tolón, C., Arronategui, U., Tolosana-Calasanz, R., Bañares, J.Á., Rana, O.F.: Client-side scheduling based on application characterization on Kubernetes. In: Pham, C., Altmann, J., Bañares, J.Á. (eds.) GECON 2017. LNCS, vol. 10537, pp. 162–176. Springer, Cham (2017). https://doi.org/10.1007/978-3-319-68066-8_13

16. Menouer, T., Cerin, C.: Scheduling and resource management allocation system combined with an economic model. In: The 15th IEEE International Symposium on Parallel and Distributed Processing with Applications (IEEE ISPA 2017) (2017)

17. Peinl, R., Holzschuher, F., Pfitzer, F.: Docker cluster management for the cloud-survey results and own solution. J. Grid Comput. **14**(2), 265–282 (2016)

18. Deshmukh, S.C.: Preference ranking organization method of enrichment evaluation (PROMETHEE). Int. J. Eng. Sci. Inven. **2**, 28–34 (2013)

19. Taillandier, P., Stinckwich, S.: Using the promethee multi-criteria decision making method to define new exploration strategies for rescue robots. In: International Symposium on Safety, Security, and Rescue Robotics (2011)

20. Ullman, J.: NP-complete scheduling problems. J. Comput. Syst. Sci. **10**(3), 384–393 (1975)

21. Xing, L.-N., Chen, Y.-W., Yang, K.-W.: Multi-objective flexible job shop schedule: design and evaluation by simulation modeling. Appl. Soft Comput. **9**(1), 362–376 (2009)

22. Zhou, A., Qu, B.-Y., Li, H., Zhao, S.-Z., Suganthan, P.N., Zhang, Q.: Multiobjective evolutionary algorithms: a survey of the state of the art. Swarm Evol. Comput. **1**(1), 32–49 (2011)

23. The apache software foundation. Mesos, apache. http://mesos.apache.org/

24. Kubernetes scheduler. https://kubernetes.io/

25. Swarm kit. https://github.com/docker/swarmkit/

Internet Performance Prediction Framework Based on PingER Dataset

Wei Zhang, Xiaofei Xing[✉], Saqib Ali, and Guojun Wang

School of Computer Science and Technology, Guangzhou University,
Guangzhou 510006, People's Republic of China
xingxf@gzhu.edu.cn

Abstract. The Internet performance directly affects the scalability, reliability and availability of the online applications. Delay of a few millisecond may cause companies lose millions of dollars. Therefore, Internet measurements are carried out to capture the performance of the Internet links worldwide. Most of the Internet performance monitoring frameworks are active in nature i.e., they can only capture the real-time performance of the Internet links. Thus, these monitoring frameworks are unable to forecast the near future performance of the Internet links in a region. Such estimates are quite critical for the network administrators to carry out bandwidth extensive experiments between different sites, policy makers to suggest future upgrades to the Internet infrastructures or streaming service providers to enhance the quality of service to their customers. Therefore, we analyze different machine learning algorithms including Multiple Linear regression, Random Forest algorithm, Gradient Boosting, and eXtreme Gradient Boosting to predict the performance of the Internet links using PingER (Ping End-to-End Reporting) dataset for the countries like China, India and Japan. Our experimental results show that the Multiple Linear regression has improved Internet performance prediction accuracy compared with the other methods. Our work can be utilized by the Internet service providers, streaming service providers or policymakers for the design, deployment, and evaluation of next-generation Internet infrastructure.

Keywords: Multiple linear regression · Internet performance · Prediction PingER

1 Introduction

Internet traffic is increasing every day. The Internet is used in a wide variety of applications including corporate, education, entertainment, news, games, and social networking. It requires a lot of end-to-end link performance in terms of scalability, reliability, and performance. A delay of several hundred milliseconds may cause companies to lose millions of dollars, which may cause the game industry to lose a large number of users. For example, Singla [1] mentioned that a delay of 100 ms will cause Amazon to lose 1% of sales; in the search response, a 500-ms delay will result in a 1.2% decrease in Bing's revenue and a 250-ms delay in winning competitors, so reducing latency will improve the user experience. On the other hand, the performance of the Internet is also directly related to the country's key economic development

© Springer Nature Switzerland AG 2018
J. Vaidya and J. Li (Eds.): ICA3PP 2018, LNCS 11336, pp. 118–131, 2018.
https://doi.org/10.1007/978-3-030-05057-3_9

indicators. According to the World Bank, a country's economy has grown by 1.3%, while the speed of the Internet has increased by 10%. Therefore, the performance of the Internet plays an important role in our daily lives [2].

The Internet performance directly affect the reliability and availability of the Internet links. Therefore, Internet measurements are carried out to capture the performance of the links worldwide. The key Internet performance metrics includes, throughput, jitter, delay, packet loss, reachability, directivity etc. Many Internet performance monitoring frameworks are offered in literature, for example, SamKnows [3], BIS- mark [4], Dasu [5], Netradar [6], Portolan [7], RIPE Atlas [8], and perfSONAR [9] originally partially based on the PingER architecture [10]. These frameworks use different tools italic i.e., ping, mtr, cron, ntp, dig, netstat, iperf, and traceroute to mine the performance of the Internet links in real time. The findings of these frameworks are really critical for the Internet administrators and mangers to fine tune their infrastructures.

Most of the above Internet performance monitoring platforms are active. They only capture the real-time performance of Internet software or hardware on congestion, bottleneck links, queue overflows, and errors [11]. However, these frameworks do not provide any information on the performance of future Internet links. Information on Internet performance prediction is necessary for optimization of resources for extensive bandwidth experiments conducted between research centers, laboratories, and universities. In addition, this prediction is also crucial for Internet managers, content service providers, and policy makers to make decisions in the future on upgrading the Internet infrastructure in the region.

In this paper, because the Internet performance has more instability and unpredictability, and the traditional Internet performance analysis is only to analyze the current performance parameters, and form a performance log as a basis for analyzing the Internet operating conditions, so we will focus on Internet prediction. We will use historical Internet performance monitoring data in the PingER platform. First, we will preprocess the data. Then, we use machine learning algorithms such as Multiple Linear Regression, Random Forest, Gradient Boost, and XGBoost to build Internet performance prediction model. Finally, we use the Root Mean Square Error (RMSE), Error Rate and other indicators to compare and analyze the prediction accuracy under different models, and finally find a suitable prediction algorithm for PingER Internet performance data.

The remaining paper is organized as follows. The related work is discussed in Sect. 2. Sections 3 and 4 mainly introduce the PingER framework and data. The proposed approach for predicting Internet performance is explained in Sect. 5. Section 6 is mainly about the results and discussion. Finally, Sect. 7 concludes the paper.

2   Related Work

Internet performance prediction is usually based on observation sequence, so the method of Internet traffic prediction can also be used in Internet performance prediction. Currently, common prediction methods are Least Square, Regression, including Auto-Regressive and Moving Average (ARMA), Autoregressive Integrated Moving

Average (ARIMA), Seasonal Autoregressive Integrated Moving Average (SARIMA), Time Series Seasonal Analysis (TSSA), etc. [12–17]. With the maturity of machine learning and data mining algorithms and their strong performance in various fields, many researchers have applied data mining methods to the prediction of Internet traffic in recent years. The study by Zheng [18] proposed an Internet traffic prediction model (ET-SVM) integrating inclusion test and support vector machine. Using some single models are used to prediction the Internet traffic, and the merits of the model are defined by the Root Mean Square Error (RMSE) of the predicting results, then the appropriate single model is selected by surrounding test, finally, the single model prediction results are combined by Support Vector Machine to get the final predicting result of network traffic. The study by Chen [19] proposed an Internet traffic prediction model (ELM-LSSVM) that combines limit learning machine and least squares support vector machine to improve the prediction accuracy of Internet traffic. The study by Hammami [20] give the classification model based on the flow prediction algorithm. The study by Liu [21] applied Back Propagation (BP) neural network to Internet traffic prediction. The study by Cui [22]. Elman neural network was used to replace BP neural network and achieved better results. Elman neural network is compared with BP difference: Elman Internet is the output of the hidden layer will feedback back to the input layer, as the input of the next Internet, based on the characteristics of Elman neural network can better capture the dynamic characteristics of time sequence, thus can better adapt to the prediction of time series.

In this paper, we use four algorithms to building prediction model for the Internet performance data, then use the Root Mean Square Error (RMSE) to judge whether the result is good or bad, and finally select the optimal model to achieve the Internet performance prediction.

2.1 Random Forest Algorithm

The random forest algorithm was first proposed by Breiman and Cutler in 2001 [23]. It use the data sampled from the training set to construct the basic model, and the random forest samples all the attributes and extracts some of the attributes for input. Basic model. In order to reduce the generalization error, random forest algorithm has two layers of sampling, one layer is attribute sampling and the other is training set sampling. The specific algorithm of random forest is used in this paper as follows. This paper deals with a training set of 364 samples of one attribute, and trains K decision trees. The classification result with the most votes will be used as the output of the random forest.

2.2 Gradient Boost Algorithm

Gradient Boosting is a method of implementing Boosting [24, 25]. Its main idea is that each time the model is established, the gradient of the model loss function is established before the gradient is dropped. The loss function describes the degree of failure of the model, and the greater the loss function, the more error-prone the model is. If our model can make the loss function continue to decline, indicating that our model is constantly improving, and the best way is to let the loss function in the direction of gradient. The advantages of this algorithm include no feature normalization, automatic feature selection, model interpretability, and multiple loss functions.

2.3 XGBoost Algorithm

XGBoost Extreme Gradient Rising is a massively parallel Boosted tree, an extension of the Gradient Boosting Algorithm [26]. In the same situation, XGBoost algorithm is more than 10 times faster than similar algorithms [27]. XGBoost can use the CPU multi-threaded parallel tree construction to support yet-another-resource-negotiator (YARN), message-passing-interface (MPI) and other platforms to achieve distributed computing, which can further improve the training speed. It's advantage that efficient and more accurate.

3 The PingER Framework

This paper is based on the PingER framework developed by Stanford University SLAC (Linear Acceleration Center). Originally, it was designed to facilitate the modern High Energy Nuclear and Particle (HENP) physics data-extensive experiments taking place among the SLAC, the Brookhaven National Laboratory (BNL) and the European Center for Particle Physics (CERN). However, for the last fifteen years, the focus of the project is to measure, store and analyze the historical end-to-end performance of the Internet links worldwide [28–30]. PingER consists of more than 50 Monitoring Agents (MAs) active in 20 countries of the world, as shown in Fig. 1. The PingER measurement cycle is activated by the MAs after every half hour. Each MA has a list of remote sites of interest. During each cycle, it sends a set of 100-byte ping requests and 1000-byte ping requests to each target in MA remote site list. The initial 100-byte ping is normally discarded as it is used to prime the routing caches. The cycle for each remote site stops when the MA receives 10 ping responses or it has issued 30 ping requests. The raw data collected for each set of pings consists of an MA name, it's IP addresses followed by the target remote site name and IP address, the payload, time stamp, packets sent, packets received, minimum Round Trip Time (RTT), maximum RTT, average RTT followed by the sequence number of the received packets and the actual RTTs of the received packets. The data is publicly available through a web server (at each monitoring site) running a Common Gateway Interface (CGI) program. The main host at the SLAC works as a central data storage repository. It fetches all the raw data collected by each MA and stores it in a database on a daily basis. The data is analyzed to extract sixteen different Internet performance metrics, e.g., round trip time (average, maximum, and minimum), packet loss, jitter, unreachability, throughput, directivity, unpredictability, and quiescence for each day, month and year. Further, daily, monthly, and yearly summary reports are compiled for each MA and remote site pair. Currently, PingER's data warehouse already has about 60 GB of Internet performance data. The storage method is stored in more than 100,000 text files in a compression ratio of 5:1.

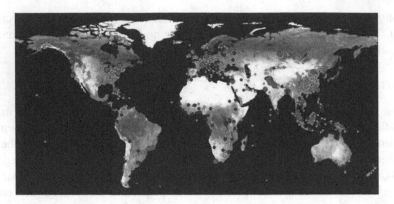

Fig. 1. PingER's MA and remote sites around the world (the red dot in the figure represents the monitoring agents and green represents the remote site). (Color figure online)

4   The PingER Data

As mentioned before, PingER has a long history and data in the field of network performance monitoring, and there is currently no predicting service in the PingER framework. The main advantages of choosing PingER data are as follows: There are many historical data and it is easy to use. The historical data of Internet performance has a very important influence on the prediction of Internet performance. PingER has been operating since 1995 and has continuously monitored the Internet performance of over 700 sites [31]. We can follow hourly, daily, monthly or yearly view historical Internet data from any monitoring host to monitoring site. The data is compressed into a file according to the name of the performance index. At the same time, all Internet performance data is displayed on the PingER visual web page. Users can easily download data and conduct experimental analysis [32]. Furthermore, the PingER monitoring framework still has a large number of users since it's adoption. It helps the development of Internets in various regions. However, the performance of the Internet is not predicted in the PingER platform. Therefore, the performance prediction of the PingER Internet is extremely meaningful.

4.1   Data Sources

As the number of Internet users in Asia is increasing, the total number of Internet users in China, India, and Japan accounted for 66% of the total Asian Internet users, as shown in Table 1 [33]. Therefore, measuring and predicting the Internets of these three countries is extremely important for understanding the Internet conditions in Asia as a whole. Therefore, this paper uses the average round-trip time as the experimental basis. The three selected links are shown in the Table 2.

Table 1. Asia Internet user and population data

Asia	Population	Internet users	Penetration (% Population)	Users (% Asia)
China	1,415,045,928	772,000,000	54.6%	38.1%
India	1,354,051,854	462,124,989	34.1%	22.8%
Japan	127,185,332	118,626,672	93.3%	5.9%

Table 2. Data sources

Monitoring-site	Remote-site	Country
EDU.SLAC.STANFORD.PINGER	CN.EDU.N1	China
EDU.SLAC.STANFORD.PINGER	IN.MITPUNE.WWW	India
EDU.SLAC.STANFORD.PINGER	JP.U-TOKYO.AC	Japan

4.2   Data Pre-processing

The downloaded file is in the format (.tsv), with a total of 1095 records for the three links. It contains the name of the Internet performance metric, monitoring host, remote site, date, and other related information. The missing values in the data are shown as (.) We first convert the source file to a comma-separated (.csv) file, and then replaces the missing value with the average of the link. After the replacement is complete, the original data distribution is shown in Fig. 2.

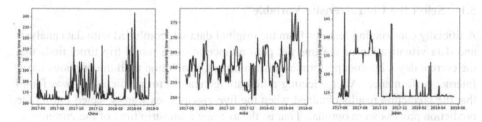

Fig. 2. The raw data distribution of China, India and Japan

5   Proposed Approach

In this paper, the average round-trip time in the PingER monitoring framework is selected as the basic metric for Internet performance prediction for the three countries i.e., China, India, and Japan. Through the data collection, data missing value processing, feature selection, selection algorithm, and the establishment of prediction model, prediction, model evaluation and other steps to achieve the prediction of Internet performance, the specific process shown in Fig. 3.

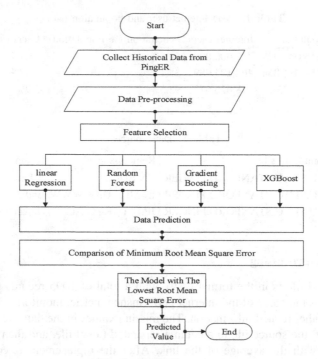

Fig. 3. Predicting process

5.1 Select the Characteristic Variable

Artificially constructing features from the original data set, combined with data analysis and data visualization of the Internet performance average round-trip time, finds that the current day's Internet performance has a certain correlation with the previous days' Internet performance. After selecting different eigenvalues for prediction, it was found that the prediction results obtained when the five eigenvalues were selected during the prediction process were optimal. That is, the average round-trip time of the current day as the dependent variable x1, x2, x3, x4, and x5, and the average round-trip time of the current day as the dependent variable Y. For example, May 19, 2018 was the dependent variable, and May 14, 15, 16, 17, and 18 were independent variables.

5.2 Establish a Multiple-Linear Regression Model

In this paper, we use multiple linear regression, random forest, gradient boost, and XGBoost to build the training model. Then we input the training data into each model and train it. After the training, we build the prediction model, and then input the test data set into the model to predict the results. Finally, the Root Mean Square Error (RMSE) was used to evaluate the performance of the results.

The basic task of multivariate linear regression analysis is to establish a multiple linear regression equation of the dependent variable to multiple independent variables based on the actual observations of the dependent variable and multiple independent variables; to test and analyze the integration of each independent variable on the dependent variable [34, 35]. The significance of the linear effect, choose the independent variables that have the significant linear influence on the dependent variable, establish the optimal multiple linear regression equation, evaluate the relative importance of each independent variable on the dependent variable, and determine the deviation of the optimal multiple linear regression equation. To study the relationship between the variation of two or more independent variables and one dependent variable under the condition of linear correlation, called multiple linear regression analysis, the mathematical equation obtained is a multiple linear regression model. The multiple linear regression model is an extension of the one-dimensional linear regression model.

Let the dependent variable y and the independent variables $x_1, x_2, x_3, \ldots, x_{m-1}$ have n groups of actual observation data, y is an observable random variable, which is subject to m−1 non-random factors $x_1, x_2, x_3, \ldots, x_{m-1}$ and ε effects of random factors. If y and $x_1, x_2, x_3, \ldots, x_{m-1}$ have the following linear relationship as shown in Eq. (1):

$$y = \beta_0 + \beta_1 x_1 + \beta_2 x_2 + \ldots + \beta_{m-1} x_{m-1} + \varepsilon \tag{1}$$

Where y is the dependent variable $x1, x2, x3, \ldots, xm - 1$ is the independent variable, $\beta\_0, \beta\_1, \beta\_2, \ldots, \beta\_{(m-1)}$ are m unknown parameters; ε is the mean 0 and the variance is σ^2 An unobserved random variable of > 0 is called an error term, and it is generally assumed that $\varepsilon \sim N(0, \sigma^2)$. For $n(n \geq p)$ independent observations, n sets of data samples are obtained as show in Eq. (2):

$$\begin{cases} y_1 = \beta_0 + \beta_1 x_{11} + \beta_2 x_{12} + \ldots + \beta_{m-1} x_{m-1} + \varepsilon_1 \\ y_2 = \beta_0 + \beta_1 x_{21} + \beta_2 x_{22} + \ldots + \beta_{m-1} x_{m-1} + \varepsilon_2 \\ \qquad\qquad\qquad \vdots \\ y_2 = \beta_0 + \beta_1 x_{n1} + \beta_2 x_{n2} + \ldots + \beta_{m-1} x_{m-1} + \varepsilon_n \end{cases} \tag{2}$$

Where $\varepsilon_1, \varepsilon_2, \ldots, \varepsilon_n$ are independent of each other, obeying the distribution of $\varepsilon \sim N(0, \sigma^2)$. In order to facilitate mathematical processing, Eq. (2) is represented in a matrix is as follows:

$$\triangleq Y = \begin{pmatrix} y_1 \\ y_2 \\ \vdots \\ y_n \end{pmatrix}_{n \times 1}, \quad X = \begin{pmatrix} 1 & x_{11} & x_{12} & \cdots & x_{1m-1} \\ 1 & x_{21} & x_{22} & \cdots & x_{2m-1} \\ \cdots & \cdots & \cdots & \cdots & \cdots \\ 1 & x_{n1} & x_{n2} & \cdots & x_{nm-1} \end{pmatrix}_{n \times m}$$

$$\beta = \begin{pmatrix} \beta_0 \\ \beta_1 \\ \vdots \\ \beta_{m-1} \end{pmatrix}_{m \times 1}, \quad \varepsilon = \begin{pmatrix} \varepsilon_0 \\ \varepsilon_1 \\ \vdots \\ \varepsilon_n \end{pmatrix}_{n \times 1}$$

Then Eq. (1) is represented by a matrix, to as shown in Eq. 3.

$$\begin{cases} Y = X\beta + \varepsilon \\ \varepsilon \sim N(1, \sigma^2 I_n) \end{cases} \tag{3}$$

5.3 Parameter Calculation

Parameters $\beta_0, \beta_1, \beta_2, \ldots, \beta_{m-1}$ in the regression equation are unknown, When we use sample statistics $\widehat{\beta}_0, \widehat{\beta}_1, \widehat{\beta}_2, \cdots, \widehat{\beta}_{m-1}$ to estimate the parameters $\beta_0, \beta_1, \beta_2, \ldots, \beta_{m-1}$ in the regression equation, Estimated multiple regression equation, as show in Eq. (1):

$$\widehat{y} = \widehat{\beta}_0 + \widehat{\beta}_1 x_1 + \widehat{\beta}_2 x_2 + \cdots + \widehat{\beta}_{m-1} x_{m-1} \tag{4}$$

Then use the least square method to obtain the value of $\widehat{\beta}_0, \widehat{\beta}_1, \widehat{\beta}_2, \cdots, \widehat{\beta}_{m-1}$, That is, the sum of squared residuals is minimized so that the parameters of the regression equation are solved. Show in Table 3:

Table 3. The parameters of the regression equation

	$\widehat{\beta}_0$	$\widehat{\beta}_1$	$\widehat{\beta}_2$	$\widehat{\beta}_3$	$\widehat{\beta}_4$	$\widehat{\beta}_5$
China	31.9188	0.6263	0.069	−0.0823	0.08785	0.1135
India	43.7882	0.8644	0.0965	0.0933	−0.02727	−0.0023
Japan	5.2331	0.813	0.0013	0.07288	−0.1283	0.2002

Therefore, the corresponding regression equations for the above three links as shown in Eqs. (5–7):

$$\text{China: } Y = 31.9188 + 0.6263x_1 + 0.069x_2 - 0.0823x_3 + 0.08785x_4 + 0.1135x_5 \tag{5}$$

$$\text{India: } Y = 43.7882 + 0.8644x_1 - 0.0965x_2 + 0.0933x_3 - 0.02727x_4 - 0.0023x_5 \tag{6}$$

$$\text{Japan: } Y = 5.2331 + 0.813x_1 + 0.0013x_2 + 0.07288x_3 - 0.1283x_4 + 0.2002x_5 \tag{7}$$

Correlation Coefficient Check

Root Mean Square Error (RMSE) is used in this paper to test the pros and cons of the prediction results. RMSE is the sum of the squared error of the predicted value and the real value [36]. It is a quantitative tradeoff method. As shown in Eq. (8):

$$\text{RMSE} = \sqrt{\frac{\sum_{m=1}^{N} (x_{m-1} - \bar{x}_{m-1})^2}{N}} \tag{8}$$

Where x_{m-1} is the real value and $\bar{x}_{m-1}$ is the predicted value. Obviously, the smaller the value of RMSE, the better the prediction effect.

As can be seen from the above Table 4, the multiple linear regression model is superior to the other three algorithms in predicting Internet performance data. Therefore, this paper uses a multiple linear regression to predict Internet performance.

Table 4. RMSE values for the four algorithms

	Liner regression	Random forest	Gradient boosting	XGBoost
JP.U-TOKYO.AC.N1	0.4016	0.627	0.6608	25.4598
IN.MITPUNE.WWW	1.81101	3.1409	5.3875	63.0183
CN.EDU.N1	2.5147	6.6665	6.9849	35.2993

6   Results and Discussion

According to the above theories and methods, the paper finally chooses to use multiple linear regression model to predict the Internet performance. In this paper, the average RTT values of three links from China, India, and Japan are selected. There are a total of 365 data points per links. We select the first 338 data points to be used as the training set input regression model to train and obtain the prediction regression equation. The last 27 data were used as test data. The prediction results of selecting one of the links are as follow in Table 5.

Table 5. Predicted and real values

Date	Real value	Predicted value	Error rate	Date	Real value	Predicted value	Error rate
2018/4/23	163.727	166.200	1.51%	2018/5/7	167.415	169.225	1.08%
2018/4/24	163.216	166.748	2.16%	2018/5/8	164.198	168.036	2.34%
2018/4/25	170.055	170.020	-0.02%	2018/5/9	163.873	166.524	1.62%
2018/4/26	165.683	166.935	0.76%	2018/5/10	164.964	166.817	1.12%
2018/4/27	168.441	168.969	0.31%	2018/5/11	166.781	168.129	0.81%
2018/4/28	168.379	168.875	0.29%	2018/5/12	164.964	166.583	0.98%
2018/4/29	163.766	166.437	1.63%	2018/5/13	163.984	166.054	1.26%
2018/4/30	163.755	166.264	1.53%	2018/5/14	164.408	166.480	1.26%
2018/5/1	164.781	167.080	1.40%	2018/5/15	164.017	166.301	1.39%
2018/5/2	163.775	166.238	1.50%	2018/5/16	163.838	166.006	1.32%
2018/5/3	166.923	167.928	0.60%	2018/5/17	168.782	169.167	0.23%
2018/5/4	183.442	178.659	-2.61%	2018/5/18	187.569	181.341	-3.32%
2018/5/5	169.242	168.890	-0.21%	2018/5/19	174.982	172.483	-1.43%
2018/5/6	164.638	166.801	1.31%				

According to the obtained multiple linear regression equations, the Internet performance prediction and analysis are realized. The real values and predicted values of the three links are shown in Figs. 4, 5, and 6. In addition, using the multiple linear regression to estimate the average error of the predicted and real values of the Internet performance are 0.59%, 0.54%, and 0.12%, respectively, and the prediction accuracy is high. Therefore, the model can be used to predict the Internet performance.

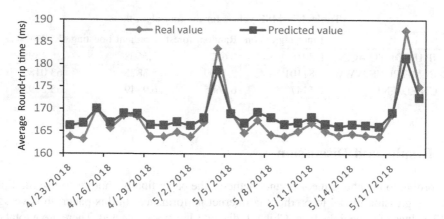

Fig. 4. Comparison of predicted and real values of CN.EDU.N1

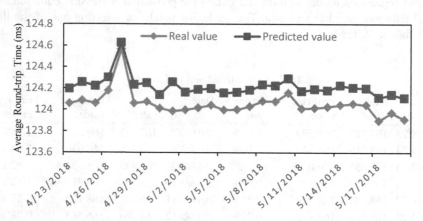

Fig. 5. Comparison of predicted and real values of JP.U-TOKYO.AC.N1

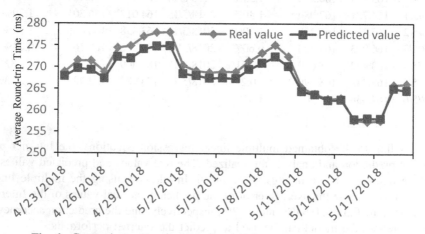

Fig. 6. Comparison of predicted and real Values of IN.MITPUNE.WWW

7 Conclusion

This paper predicts the performance of the Internet links based on the data collected through PingER end-to-end Internet monitoring framework. The main performance indicator is the average round trip time selected from the SLAC monitoring host in USA to the target countries e.g., China, India, and Japan for 365 days. For the first step, we do the pre-processing mainly by replacing the missing values with the average values, file format conversion, and extracting the key features from the data. Afterward, the data set is divided into two parts, with the first 338 days of data as the training set and the last 27 days of data as the test set. Then we use Multiple Linear Regression, Random Forest, Gradient Boost, XGBoost to establish the data prediction model, and use RMSE to evaluate the model. In the end, we found that when we used Multiple Linear Regression to predict the Internet performance of the links data, we got the best results. Therefore, it is expressive to predict the performance of the Internet links using Multiple Linear Regression model. It can help network administrators, policy makers, and network service providers to effectively leverage existing Internet infrastructure. In addition, it will help them to design high-performance next-generation Internet infrastructure.

Acknowledgments. This work is supported in part by CERNET Innovation Project under Grant No. NGII20170102, Natural Science Foundation of China under Grant No. 61772007, 61632009, Guangdong Natural Science Foundation of China under Grant No. 2016A030313540, Guangzhou Science and Technology Program under Grant No. 201707010284.

References

1. Singla, A., Chandrasekaran, B., Godfrey, P.B., Maggs, B.: The Internet at the speed of light. In: Proceedings of the 13th ACM Workshop on Hot Topics in Networks - HotNets-XIII, pp. 1–7 (2014)
2. Ali, S., Cottrell, R.L., Nveed, A.: Pinger Malaysia-internet performance measuring project: A case study (No. SLAC-PUB-16462). SLAC National Accelerator Lab., Menlo Park, CA, United States (2016)
3. Samknows Homepage. https://www.samknows.com/. Accessed 30 May 2018
4. Sundaresan, S., Burnett, S., Feamster, N., de Donato, W.: BISmark: A testbed for deploying measurements and applications in broadband access networks. In: Proceedings 2014 USENIX Annual Technical Conference (USENIX ATC 2014), pp. 383–394 (2014)
5. Sánchez, M., Otto, J.: Dasu: Pushing Experiments to the internet's edge. In: Proceedings of USENIX Association, pp. 487–499 (2013)
6. Sonntag, S., Manner, J., Schulte, L.: Netradar – Measuring the wireless world. In: Wireless Network Measurements, pp. 29–34 (2013)
7. Faggiani, A., Gregori, E., Lenzini, L., Luconi, V., Vecchio, A.: Smartphone-based crowdsourcing for network monitoring: opportunities, challenges, and a case study. IEEE Commun. Mag. **52**, 106–113 (2014)
8. Bajpai, V., Eravuchira, S.J., Schönwälder, J.: Lessons learned from using the RIPE atlas platform for measurement research. ACM SIGCOMM Comput. Commun. Rev. **45**, 35–42 (2015)

9. Hanemann, A., et al.: PerfSONAR: A service oriented architecture for multi-domain network monitoring. In: Benatallah, B., Casati, F., Traverso, P. (eds.) ICSOC 2005. LNCS, vol. 3826, pp. 241–254. Springer, Heidelberg (2005). https://doi.org/10.1007/11596141_19

10. Matthews, W., Coffrell, L.: The PingER project: active Internet performance monitoring for the HENP community. IEEE Commun. Mag. **38**, 130–136 (2000)

11. Paxson, V.: End-to-end Internet packet dynamics. IEEE/ACM Trans. Netw. **7**, 277–292 (1999)

12. Wu, C.L., Chau, K.W., Li, Y.S.: Methods to improve neural network performance in daily flows prediction. J. Hydrol. **372**, 80–93 (2009)

13. Zhou, D., Chen, S., Dong, S.: Network Traffic Prediction Based on ARFIMA Model. arXiv Prepr. arXiv1302.6324, vol. 9, pp. 106–111 (2013)

14. Shang, P., Li, X., Kamae, S.: Nonlinear analysis of traffic time series at different temporal scales. Phys. Lett. Sect. A Gen. At. Solid State Phys. **357**, 314–318 (2006)

15. Nury, A.H., Hasan, K., Alam, M.J.: Bin: Comparative study of wavelet-ARIMA and wavelet-ANN models for temperature time series data in northeastern Bangladesh. J. King Saud Univ. Sci. **29**, 47–61 (2017)

16. Yin, H., Lin, C., Sebastien, B., Li, B., Min, G.: Network traffic prediction based on a new time series model. Int. J. Commun Syst **18**, 711–729 (2005)

17. Karunasinghe, D.S.K., Liong, S.Y.: Chaotic time series prediction with a global model: artificial neural network. J. Hydrol. **323**, 92–105 (2006)

18. Weiyong, Z., Guangli, F.: Network traffic combination forecasting based on encompassing tests and support vector machine. Comput. Eng. Appl. **15**, 84–87 (2013)

19. Hongxing, C.: Network traffic prediction based on extreme learning machine and least square support vector machine. Comput. Eng. Appl. **51**(24), 73–77 (2015)

20. Hammami, C., Jemili, I., Gazdar, A., Belghith, A.: Hybrid live P2P streaming protocol. Procedia Comput. Sci. **32**, 158–165 (2014)

21. Hodge, V.J., Austin, J.: A Survey of outlier detection methodoligies. Artif. Intell. Rev. **22**, 85–126 (2004)

22. Cui, F.: Study of traffic flow prediction based on BP neural network. In: 2010 2nd International Workshop on Intelligent Systems and Applications, pp. 1–4 (2010)

23. Breiman, L.: Random forest. Mach. Learn. **45**, 5–32 (2001)

24. Guelman, L.: Gradient boosting trees for auto insurance loss cost modeling and prediction. Expert Syst. Appl. **39**, 3659–3667 (2012)

25. Parker, C., Fern, A., Tadepalli, P.: Gradient boosting for sequence alignment. In: Proceedings of the National Conference on Artificial Intelligence, vol. 21, no. 1, p. 452. (2006). AAAI Press, Menlo Park. MIT Press, Cambridge, London (1999)

26. Chen, T., He, T.: XGBoost: eXtreme Gradient Boosting. R Packag. version 0.4-2, pp. 1–4 (2015)

27. Chen, T., Guestrin, C.: XGboost: A scalable tree boosting system. In: Proceedings of the 22nd ACM SIGKDD International Conference on Knowledge Discovery and Data Mining, pp. 785–794. ACM (2016)

28. Ali, S., Wang, G., Cottrell, R.L., Masood, S.: Internet performance analysis of south asian countries using end-to-end internet performance measurements. In: 2017 IEEE International Symposium on Parallel and Distributed Processing with Applications, 2017 IEEE International Conference on Ubiquitous Computing and Communications, pp. 1319–1326 (2017)

29. Ali, S., Wang, G., Cottrell, R.L., Anwar, T.: Detecting anomalies from end-to-end internet performance measurements (PingER) using cluster based local outlier factor. In: 2017 IEEE International Symposium on Parallel and Distributed Processing with Applications, 2017 IEEE International Conference on Ubiquitous Computing and Communications, pp. 982–989 (2017)

30. Mal, A., Sabitha, A.S., Bansal, A., White, B., Cottrell, L.: Analysis and clustering of PingER network data. In: Proceedings of 2016 6th International Conference - Cloud System and Big Data Engineering (Confluence), pp. 268–273 (2016)

31. Ali, S., Wang, G., White, B., Cottrell, R.L.: A Blockchain-based decentralized data storage and access framework for PingER. In: 2018 17th IEEE International Conference on Trust, Security and Privacy in Computing and Communications/12th IEEE International Conference on Big Data Science and Engineering (TrustCom/BigDataSE), pp. 1303–1308. IEEE (2018)

32. Ali, S., Wang, G., Xing, X., Cottrell, R.L.: Substituting missing values in end-to-end Internet performance measurements using k-Nearest neighbors. In: 2018 IEEE 16th International Conference on Dependable, Autonomic and Secure Computing, 16th International Conference on Pervasive Intelligence and Computing, 4th International Conference on Big Data Intelligence and Computing and Cyber Science and Technology Congress (DASC/PiCom/DataCom/CyberSciTech), pp. 919–926. IEEE (2018)

33. Internet Word Stats Homepage. https://www.Internetworldstats.com/stats3.htm. Accessed 11 June 2018

34. Guo, H., Wang, X., Gao, Z.: Uncertain linear regression model and it's application. J. Intell. Manuf. 28, 559–564 (2017)

35. Sun, H., Liu, H., Xiao, H., He, R., Ran, B.: Short term traffic forecasting using the local linear regression model. Transp. Res. Rec., 143–150 (2003)

36. Kumar, S., Gangwar, S.S.: Intuitionistic fuzzy time series: an approach for handling nondeterminism in time series forecasting. IEEE Trans. Fuzzy Syst. 24, 1270–1281 (2016)

MS-RAID: An Energy-Saving Data Layout for CDP

Jingyu Liu[1,3], Ziyao Zhang[1,3], Lu Liu[2(✉)], and Xin Chai[1,3]

[1] School of Artificial Intelligence, Hebei University of Technology, Tianjin 300130, China
[2] School of Computer Science and Technology, Beijing Institute of Technology,
Beijing 100081, China
skye66@qq.com
[3] Hebei Province Key Laboratory of Big Data Calculation, Tianjin 300130, China

Abstract. Continuous data protection (CDP) provides unlimited granular recovery point objective (RPO) and nearly instant recovery time objective (RTO). It requires a great fluctuations in the performance of storage system. The system requires higher storage bandwidth when it is active, and lower when inactive. Raid, that is used in storage system normally and provides fixed performance, may face a performance bottleneck or high power consumption. This paper proposes MS-RAID, that bases on S-Raid and can provide multi-level dynamic mapping storage scheme. MS-RAID has vary levels of grouping strategies. MS-RAID can meet the needs of real-time dynamic load by changing the number of parallel disks. When the throughput rises, MS-RAID turns the high-level disk group into running to avoid the bottleneck of system performance. When the throughput falls, MS-RAID turns the low-level disk group into running to save energy consumption. Experiments show that MS-RAID is a more energy-efficient data layout, and can save more energy consumption and improve then performance than S-RAID.

Keywords: RAID · CDP · Energy-saving · Storage · Data layout

1 Introduction

In the era of Big Data, data volume grows exponentially [1, 2]. IDC's analysis predicts that global data volume will double every two years. By 2020, the world's data storage capacity is expected to reach 44 ZB, and China's total data volume will increase to 8.06 ZB, accounting for 18% of the world's total [3]. Data affects every aspect of society, such as government decisions, corporate operations, and personal lives. More and more attention has been paid to the data reliability. Continuous Data Protection (CDP) can backup data automatically, and save any version of data. CDP allows to restore data to any point in time and provide fine granularities of restorable objects.

CDP needs a large amount of storage space. That makes the scale of the data center grow continuously. However, CDP has not fixed requirements on the bandwidth of the storage system, which has certain volatility and obvious time characteristics. When the system is active (usually in the day), high storage bandwidth is required; when the system is inactive (usually at night), low storage bandwidth is required. The current storage systems do not take into account the storage system's responsiveness to dynamic loads.

© Springer Nature Switzerland AG 2018
J. Vaidya and J. Li (Eds.): ICA3PP 2018, LNCS 11336, pp. 132–141, 2018.
https://doi.org/10.1007/978-3-030-05057-3_10

The load characteristics of the CDP system cannot be well adapted. When the load increases, system performance bottlenecks may occur. When the load decreases, additional energy consumption is generated.

Data centers deployed RAID [4] to provide large capacity and high efficiency of the whole storage system. But the energy consumption enlarges dramatically with the data center's expansion, and that cannot be ignored.

Lot of researches are focus on energy-saving of disk storage systems. DRPM [5] (Dynamic Rotations Per Minute) algorithm uses a multistage rotational speed disk according to the real-time change of the workload to save energy consumption. DPPDL [6] (Dynamic Partial-parallel Data Layout) adjusts disks parallelism based on system load dynamically, which reduces energy consumption to a certain extent. But it wastes part of disk space. Xu [7] proposed the SpringFS algorithm that uses an elastic multilevel load allocation method, and assigns different copies among servers according to the changes in the workload to reduce energy consumption.

Study [8, 9] shows that 80% of the total cost of large data centers comes from the energy consumption of disk storage systems. Li [10–12] proposed S-RAID, a storage data layout for continuous data storage, to save the energy consumption of data center.

Energy-saving in storage system can be effective, but its application has not been optimized. According to CDP's throughput characteristics of CDP data, this paper proposes Multiple S-RAID (MS-RAID), a storage space multi-stage mapping data layout for energy-saving, to balance the energy consumption and performance. The contribution of this paper mainly includes:

1. A data layout is proposed: MS-RAID, the disk array is divided into multilevel storage space, which can provide different access performance and dynamic load features suitable for CDP data access;
2. MS-RAID uses Data Increment Algorithm to optimize the number of I/O operations and reduce the writing penalty caused by small-write;
3. A parameter-based disk state control algorithm is proposed, which sets a state parameter for each disk, and adjusts dynamically according to I/O access to achieve the purpose of controlling disk state.

Experiments simulate the 32-way video monitoring system. It is proved that the data layout can not only avoid the overperformance of the system, but also meet the high-performance requirements of the system, and achieve high efficiency and energy saving data transmission.

2   MS-RAID: Multilevel Mapping Data Layout

2.1   MS-RAID Data Layout

RAID5 is a storage solution that can ensure storage performance, data security and storage cost. S-RAID5 groups the data chunks on each stripe and uses parallel access in the group, which is not only conducive to the dormancy of the non-working disk, but also ensures the performance requirements of the system. However, S-RAID5 cannot adapt well to the storage characteristics, because CDP has dynamic requirements for the performance of the system. Based on S-RAID5, MS-RAID5 optimizes the access char-acteristics of CDP data, and uses a multi-level grouping strategy to meet the dynamic demand of the system load and maximize the energy saving effect of CDP.

MS-RAID, as shown in Fig. 1, makes a multilevel grouping of data chunks on the same strip in the storage system. The number of data chunks in the group of different levels is difference. It provides multiple-level performance. Low-level groups, which have less disks, have low performance and energy-consumption. High-level groups, which have more disks, have high performance and energy-consumption. When the system is idle, the performance requirements are lower, low-level group runs, and high-level groups are standby for energy-saving. On the contrary, when the system is busy, the performance requirements are higher, high-level group runs for higher performance, and low-level groups are standby for energy-saving.

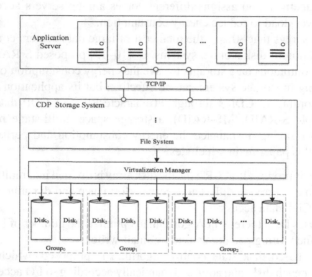

Fig. 1. Schematic of MS-RAID

Because parity disk is the bottleneck of system performance in RAID4, RAID5 is adopted in this paper. MS-RAID5 with N disks ($N \geq 3$) is divided into N stripes. $Stripe_i$ denotes the strip in the array, and $Parity_i$ denotes the parity chunk.

$X(i,j)$ denotes the storage chunk in the array, where i denotes the strip, and j denotes the disk in the array, $0 \leq i, j \leq N-1$. $D(i,j)$ denotes the data chunk in the array. $D(i,j)$ can be expressed as formula (1):

$$D(i,j) = \begin{cases} X(i,j), i+j < N-1 \\ X(i,j+1), i+j \geq N-1 \end{cases}$$

(1)

$Parity_i$ of the same strip can be expressed as formula (2):

$$Parity_i = X(i, N-1-i)$$

(2)

In order to adapt to the dynamic requirement of CDP, multilevel grouping of disk arrays is set. $N-1$ data chunks on each stripe are divided into Q groups, and S_q chunks in each group ($Q \geq 2$, $S_q \geq 1$). The relationship between each group and its chunk allocation satisfies the formula (3):

$$\sum_{q=0}^{Q} Sq = N - 1 \tag{3}$$

Figure 2 is MS-RAID5 with 6 disks that set into two-level groups. Grp_0 includes $Disk_0$ and $Disk_1$, Grp_1 includes $Disk_2$, $Disk_3$ and $Disk_4$. The parity chunk is evenly distributed in all disks shown as Fig. 2. When the system is idle, Grp_1 is set into standby state, and Grp_0 runs to meet requirements. The data is written into the sub-data chunks $D_0 \sim D_7$, $D_{20} \sim D_{27}$... When the system is busy, Grp_1 runs, and Grp_0 is turned into the standby state, and the data is written to the sub-data chunk $D_8 \sim D_{19}$, $D_{28} \sim D_{39}$... More disks running can provide a higher storage bandwidth.

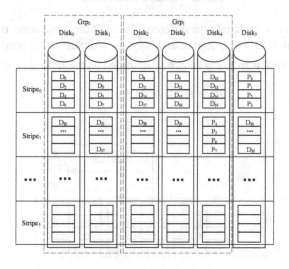

Fig. 2. The 6-disk two-level MS-RAID5 data layout

2.2 Read and Write

MS-RAID calculate parity data using DIP [12] algorithm to avoid the write penalty when writing data into the array. The parity data in the same stripe can no longer read the original data in the data chunk, but only the written data and the original parity data needs XOR operation:

$$P = \oplus Disk_{write} \tag{4}$$

where P denotes the parity data, and $Disk_{write}$ denotes the data to be written.

When each strip begins to write, the parity data is initialized as XOR value with the first chunk and the second chunk, shown in Fig. 3, the initialization of the $Stripe_0$ sub-parity chunk P_0 is:

$$P_0 = D_0 \oplus D_1 \tag{5}$$

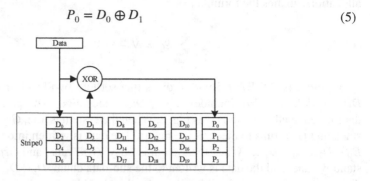

Fig. 3. Initialize parity chunk

When the data is written into the different chunk of the same stipe, the old data need not to be read as in RAID or S-RAID, and only the old parity data need to be read. The new parity P_0' (shown as in Fig. 4) can be calculated as the formula (6):

$$P_0' = D_8 \oplus D_9 \oplus P_0 \tag{6}$$

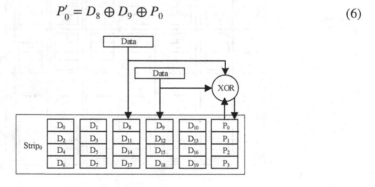

Fig. 4. Calculate new parity data

The DIP algorithm with pre-read strategy can not only avoid waking up inactive disks, but also reduce the writing punishment brought by Read-Modify-Write effectively.

2.3 Disk Scheduling

The purpose disk scheduling is to enable the RAID with multilevel packets to adapt to dynamical requirement of CDP systems for energy-saving.

Because the mapping between the logical block address (LBA) and the physical block address (PBA) is unknown before the data chunk is written, it is necessary to create a mapping table between them and update it in time during the data chunk is written.

Given the logical address *blkno*, its group number: Grp_p is calculated as formula (7):

$$LBA(Grp_p) = \begin{cases} 0 & ,p = 0 \\ N \cdot \sum_{j=0}^{j=p-1} Sj & ,p > 0 \end{cases} \tag{7}$$

The logical address of the data chunk *blkno* is calculated as formula (8):

$$f(blkno) = D(f_{stripei,v}(blkno), f_{Dj}(blkno)) \tag{8}$$

The physical location of the *stripe$_i$* is calculated as formula (9):

$$f_{stripei}(blkno) = \left\lfloor \frac{blkno - LBA(Grp_p)}{m \cdot S_p} \right\rfloor \tag{9}$$

The physical location of the sub-stripe V of the strip group *stripe$_i$* is calculated as formula (10):

$$f_{stripei,v}(blkno) = \lfloor (blkno - S_p \cdot G \cdot m) mod\, S_p \rfloor \tag{10}$$

The disk number of the data chunk is calculated as formula (11):

$$f_{Dj}(blkno) = [blkno - LAB(Grp_p) mod\, S_p + \sum_{k=0}^{k=p-1} S_k] \tag{11}$$

MS-RAID schedule disks according to different system requirements. In order to locate to the data address quickly when disks are started, a write address pointer P_{LBA} is set to record the last chunk which to be written in each group, and it can reduce system addressing delay. The new data is written to the next location of pointer when a new group is started up.

3   Experiment and Analysis

In this section, the performance and energy saving test of MS-RAID is carried out based on CDP of the video monitoring data storage system.

3.1   Performance Testing

The MS-RAID chunk can be adjusted according to the specific requirements of the storage system. Based on the monitoring environment, at least 4.6T data storage space is needed, and the additional 10% storage space for the file system. To meet this environment, a two-level MS-RAID5 consisting of 6 disks(1T) is configured with the Linux 3.1 kernel. G_0 group consists of two disks, and the G_1 group consists of three disks.

IOMeter is a very powerful I/O test software. The IOMeter writes 2 KB–4096 KB, 40%, 60%, 80% and 100% continuous requests to MS-RAID and S-RAID through the Dynamo load generator on the Linux side, respectively.

The performance test results under different load requirements shown as Fig. 5. When the data block is small, the performance of MS-RAID is not much different from that S-RAID. When the size of data block larger than 128 KB, the write performance of MS-RAID is improved significantly. It because that: (1) when the size of the data block is less than 128 KB, the MS-RAID enables the low-level group G_0, the group G_1 is in the standby state, the low-level disk group is as same as the S-RAID5 parallelism, and the writing performance has no obvious gap; (2) when the size of the data block is larger than 128 KB, group G_0 in MS-RAID cannot meet the performance requirements and to adapt to the higher load. In the high-level group G_1, the parallel degree in the group is increased, the stripe size is higher than that S-RAID5. The whole amount of data is increased, the frequency of the parity data writing are less, and the write performance is improved significantly.

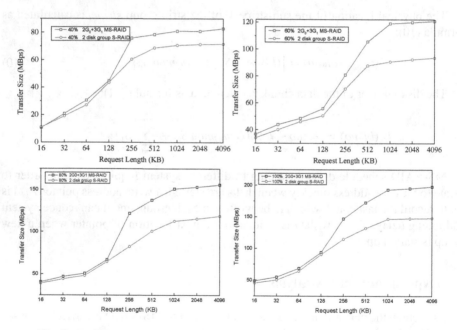

Fig. 5. Performance comparison of 40%, 60%, 80% and 100% sequential write

When the request is smaller than 128 KB, the response time gap between the four schemes is not obvious, shown as Fig. 6, they are in the disk opening process, and the disk group pre-reading is performed. When writing requests is 256 KB, MS-RAID has turned on the G_1 disk group, which has improved parallelism and low response time compared to S-RAID.

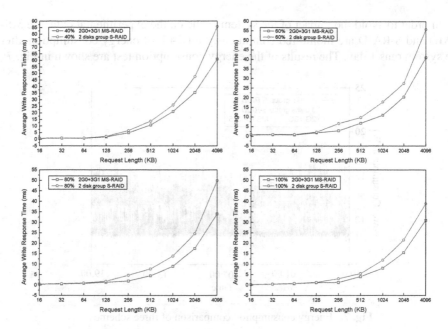

Fig. 6. Comparison of write response time

The performance experiment shows that the multilevel group of MS-RAID can allocate the storage space for writing requests dynamically, adjust the number of disk parallel and open the compatible disk group according to the characteristics of CDP load change. Compared with the more advanced S-RAID, under the demand of low system performance, MS-RAID opens the low-level disk group to reduce disk parallelism and reduce energy consumption. Under the demand of higher system performance, MS-RAID opens a high-level disk group, increases disk parallelism, and ensures the system's demand for performance. MS-RAID can guarantee the performance requirements of the CDP system while opening the appropriate disk group, which effectively balances the contradiction between energy consumption and system performance.

3.2   Energy Consumption Test

In the energy consumption test, the total energy consumption of the disk array is calculated as formula (12):

$$W = \sum_{i=0}^{n} V_i \times I_i \tag{12}$$

where W denotes the total energy consumption of disk array, V_i denotes the real time voltage, and I_i denotes the real time current of disk i.

In order to strengthen the comparison test of different groups' energy consumptions, S-RAID5 with 7 disks is set in the same environment, including two groups of data disks (3 disks per group) and a parity disk.

In order to avoid the impact of the system cache on the experimental data, the MS-RAID and S-RAID are monitored continuously for 24 h of energy consumption after the system runs 1 day. The results of the energy consumption test are shown in Fig. 7:

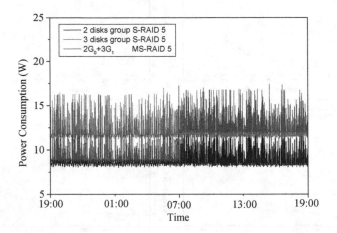

Fig. 7. Energy consumption comparison of three schemes

At the beginning of the test, the difference in energy consumption of MS-RAID5 and S-RAID5 with 2 disks a group is not significant. It because that only 20 cameras are running at first and the load is small. MS-RAID5 only opens the low-level group G_0 on the premise of guaranteeing the performance requirement of the system. The S-RAID5 of the three disks per group opened a disk more than MS-RAID5, and that leads to excessive system performance and greater energy consumption. At this stage, the average energy consumption of MS-RAID is 9.3 W, and the average energy consumption of S-RAID with 3 disks per group is 12.3 W, saving 24.4% energy consumption.

As the experiment goes on to the second stage, 32 cameras work at the same time. The load increases, and the performance requirements of the system increase too. MS-RAID5 has opened a higher performance group G_1, which has increased energy consumption while providing higher performance. Although S-RAID5 with 2 disks per group keeps low energy consumption, it cannot meet the high performance of the system.

The performance test and energy consumption test show that MS-RAID not only reduces the energy consumption when the CDP system is idle, but also ensures the system performance when it is busy. It balances the contradiction between energy consumption and performance.

4   Conclusion

In the paper, a multilevel grouping strategy is proposed for CDP systems, and the data layout of multilevel grouping is designed and implemented: MS-RAID. DIP algorithm is used to optimize the writing performance in MS-RAID. The higher energy efficiency of the storage system is realized by the disk energy saving scheduling. The multiple level division strategy is adopted in the array, and different groups have different amounts of disks. The amounts of disks correspond to the different performance requirements of the CDP system. The experiments show that 6-disk two-level MS-RAID5 performance improves 15.9%, 29.0%, 31.4% and 33.6% than 2-disk group S-RAID5 when the workload is 40%, 60%, 80% and 100% sequential, and saves 34.6% energy consumption than 3-disk S-RAID5. It proves that MS-RAID is a more energy-efficient data layout.

Acknowledgements. The work was supported by the Natural Science Foundation of China (No. 61876019), the Natural Science Foundation of Hebei Province (Grant No. F2016202145), the Youth Foundation of Education Commission of Hebei Province (Grant No. QN2014192), and the Science and Technology Planning Project of Hebei Province of China (grant No. 15210325).

References

1. Yu, X., Tan, Y., Zhang, C., Liang, C., Khaled, A., Zheng, J., Zhang, Q.: A high-performance hierarchical snapshot scheme for hybrid storage systems. Chin. J. Electron. **27**(1), 76–85 (2018)
2. Yan, F., Tan, Y., Zhang, Q., Wu, F., Cheng, Z., Zheng, J.: An effective RAID data layout for object-based de-duplication backup system. Chin. J. Electron. **25**(5), 832–840 (2016)
3. Dong, Y., Liu, J., Yang, J., et al.: HS-RAID 2: optimizing small write performance in HS-RAID. J. Electr. Comput. Eng. **2016**, Article no. 7341735, 8 pages (2016)
4. Patterson, D.: A case for redundant arrays of inexpensive disks. In: Proceedings of ACM SIGMOD Conference (1988)
5. Gurumurthi, S., Sivasubramaniam, A., Kandemir, M., et al.: DRPM: dynamic speed control for power management in server class disks. In: Proceedings of the 30th Annual International Symposium on Computer Architecture, San Diego, pp. 169–179. IEEE (2003)
6. Sun, Z., Zhang, Q., Li, Y., Tan, Y.A., et al.: DPPDL: a dynamic partial-parallel data layout for green video surveillance storage. IEEE Trans. Circuits Syst. Video Technol. **PP**(99), 1 (2016)
7. Xu, L., Cipar, J., Krevat, E., et al.: SpringFS: bridging agility and performance in elastic distributed storage. In: Proceedings of Usenix Conference on File and Storage Technologies, pp. 243–255. USENIX Association (2014)
8. Basmadjian, M., Hermann, M.D., Lent, R., Giovanni, G.: Cloud computing and its interest in saving energy: the use case of aprivate cloud. J. Cloud Comput. Adv. Syst. Appl. **1**(5), 1–11 (2012)
9. Eric, S., Michael, L., Jon, S., et al.: Computational solutions to large-scale data management and analysis. Nat. Rev. Genet. **11**, 647–657 (2010)
10. Li, X., Tan, Y., Sun, Z.: Semi-RAID: a reliable energy-aware RAID data layout for sequential data access. In: Proceedings of IEEE, Symposium on MASS Storage Systems and Technologies, pp. 1–11. IEEE Computer Society (2011)
11. Liu, J., Zhang, J., Li, Y., et al.: Hybrid S-RAID: an energy-efficient data layout for sequential data storage. J. Comput. Res. Dev. **50**(1), 37–48 (2013). (in Chinese)
12. Liu, J., Tan, Y., Xue, J., et al.: Writing optimization strategy in S-RAID based on sequential data characteristics. Chin. J. Comput. **37**(3), 721–734 (2014). (in Chinese)

Incentivizing Multimedia Data Acquisition for Machine Learning System

Yiren Gu[1], Hang Shen[1,2]([✉]), Guangwei Bai[1], Tianjing Wang[1],
Hai Tong[1], and Yujia Hu[1]

[1] College of Computer Science and Technology, Nanjing Tech University,
Nanjing 211816, China
hshen@njtech.edu.cn
[2] Department of Electrical and Computer Engineering, University of Waterloo,
Waterloo N2L3G1, Canada

Abstract. To address restrictions on data collection, incentivizing multimedia data acquisition for machine learning system is proposed. This paper presents an effective QoI (Quality-of-Information)-aware incentive mechanism in multimedia crowdsensing, with the objective of promoting the growth of an initial training model. Firstly, an incentive model is constructed in the form of reverse auction to maximize the social welfare while meeting the requirements in quality, timeliness, correlation and coverage. Then, we discuss how to achieve the optimal social welfare in the presence of an NP-hard winner determination problem. Lastly, a practical incentive mechanism to solve the auction problem is designed, which is shown to be truthful, individually rational and computationally efficient. Extensive simulation results demonstrate the proposed incentive mechanism produces close-to-optimal social welfare noticeably and high-QoI dataset is obtained. In particular, a significant performance improvement for machine learning model growth is achieved with lower complexity.

Keywords: Multimedia crowdsensing · Incentive mechanism
Machine learning · QoI · Auction

1 Introduction

There are two common ways to promote the growth of an initial machine learning model in a short time, i.e., the optimization of algorithm or the improvement of dataset quality. The former (e.g. MobileNets [5, 10]) optimizes model framework by improving algorithm, while the latter provides a large amount of data for continuous training and learning. An immature machine learning model with a large amount of training data can often win a well-designed and high-level model based on only a small amount of training data, such as Automatic Speech Recognition [6] and Image Classification [7]. However, there are strict QoI requirements (including quality, timeliness, correlation, coverage) for datasets with the development of machine learning technology increasingly mature. The model training with large-scale datasets requires a lot of time. Machine learning system hopes receiving high-quality datasets expected before

© Springer Nature Switzerland AG 2018
J. Vaidya and J. Li (Eds.): ICA3PP 2018, LNCS 11336, pp. 142–158, 2018.
https://doi.org/10.1007/978-3-030-05057-3_11

model training which satisfying a certain coverage requirement within the prescribed time and areas at the same time.

Multimedia Crowdsensing (MC) [1, 2], the crowdsourcing of multimedia data, has a huge potential to incentivize many new machine learning assisted multimedia applications expected to capture tremendous benefits in a variety of fields including Google Views [8, 9]. Anyone with a Google account can login into Google Views to share panoramic street view they photograph, which can service for the training of machine learning system. What makes it special is that the homepage of Google Views will recommend some street views users contribute. When you click on an account, the street view album of the user's contribution can be seen. Comparing with traditional data collection methods, MC has made large-scale participatory sensing viable in a speedy manner and with little infrastructure cost by leveraging personal mobile devices as its sensor nodes, which can provide massive datasets for machine learning model training.

In general, the cost occurring to a mobile user participating in MC involves resource consumption and privacy leakage. Mobile users may be reluctant to participate in MC without sufficient incentives, which causes that a large amount of high-QoI [4] datasets are not achieved for model training. Therefore, it is necessary to design an effective incentive mechanism to encourage people to participate.

Recent research has been focused on some game-theoretic incentive mechanisms for MC systems [17–19] and employs user's bidding price as an important metric to give rewards. However, most of the existing mechanisms fail to incorporate QoI requirements which depends on special applications. [12] refers to timeliness and efforts of datasets users collect; effective gathering coverage and time of tasks are defined as QoI in [11]. Nevertheless, these indicators have not been all considered in the existing incentive mechanism works. Moreover, few jobs have been done on combining mechanism designs with machine learning scenarios. The requirement for training data becomes higher with the increasingly maturity of machine learning field.

In this paper, an effective incentive mechanism for multimedia crowdsensing enabled machine learning system is proposed, focusing on obtaining massive high-QoI training datasets for machine learning models to enhance the growth of training model. The main contributions include:

1. To guarantee the utilities of both machine learning system and participating users, an incentive model based on a reserve auction is presented, which maximizes social welfare subjects to the quality requirement of tasks, timeliness of joining task, correlation and coverage of collected pictures.
2. How to achieve the optimal social welfare is discussed in the presence of an NP-hard winner determination problem. Then, a practical incentive mechanism to solve the auction problem is designed, which is shown to be truthful, individually rational and computationally efficient.
3. Extensive simulation results show the proposed mechanism achieves noticeable superiority and produces close-to-optimal solutions. The datasets provided by our mechanism accelerate the growth of machine learning model.

The rest of this paper is organized as follows. Motivation of this work is discussed in Sect. 2. Section 3 describes system model of our mechanism. The optimal solution and auction algorithm are given in Sect. 4. Finally, we present simulation results and performance analysis in Sect. 5 before concluding in Sect. 6.

2 Motivation

To obtain a mature Image Classification Model, a 5-5 layer CNN framework is constructed by us. It is trained with the real Belgian traffic datasets [3]. The training results show classification accuracy of model training approaches to 100% with the number of iteration increasing and the loss value of model indeed is falling to 0 (as illustrated in Fig. 1), which illustrate the model we constructed is becoming relatively mature in later stage. However, no matter what the model framework is optimized, there is not much room for improvement of the classification accuracy at the later period. The results of the accuracy of training classification with different batch sizes are shown in Fig. 2.

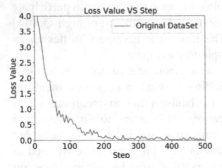

Fig. 1. Variation diagram of loss function

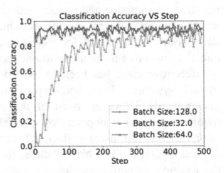

Fig. 2. Training accuracy curve of different samples

In view of this problem, final classification is analyzed by visualization of matplotlib tool. Note that, if the color of forecast and actual category is green, which illustrates classification results are correct; if red, wrong. Part of classification results is shown in Fig. 3. Visual results reveal that misclassified images are almost low-quality, which indicates the datasets quality is also a key factor slowing down the growth of model.

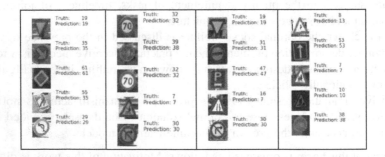

Fig. 3. Comparison of predictions and actual categories under matplotlib visualization

3   System Model

A multimedia crowdsensing system, as shown in Fig. 4, is composed of a machine learning system, a multimedia sensing platform and many smartphone users. For model training needs, the machine learning system announces picture collection tasks ζ directly, which is expected to be accomplished in a period of time $T_1 \sim T_2$. Considering the diversity of training data, machine learning system needs users to collect M types images, a picture type represents a subtask, denoted as $\zeta = \{\tau_1, \cdots, \tau_M\}$.

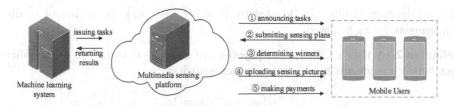

Fig. 4. Interaction model of platform and users in MC

The sensing platform processes requests from the machine learning systems and helps him recruit mobile users. The user set is denoted as $U = \{u_1, \cdots, u_N\}$, where N is the number of users. The interaction between sensing platform and mobile users can be formulated as a reverse auction mechanism design problem, which is described as follows:

1. The platform issues tasks to recruit quality-guaranteed users to participate.
2. Each user submits his sensing plan, which is denoted as a tuple bid_i consisting of the set of tasks he wants to execute $\eta_i \subseteq \zeta$ and his bidding b_i for these tasks.
3. The platform uses an incentive mechanism to select the winners and calculates payments, represented as $\vec{p} = \{p_1, \cdots, p_N\}$.
4. Winners perform sensing tasks and submit results to the platform.
5. The platform checks the results and makes payments for winners. At last, all pictures are sent to machine learning system for model training.

3.1   Auction Framework

Motivated by Sect. 2, low-quality datasets go against enhancing the growth of an initial model. Recruiting a quality crowd to undertake image collection tasks is considered by us.

QoI acts an important index which is integrated into our incentive mechanism. It is calculated by sensing platform, which depends on the sensing application and can be defined according to various factors. For example, in [15], QoI refers to the uploaded photos' quality. Photos with high quality will help the platform better identify the visible problems with medical devices; in [14], QoI refers to the users' estimation accuracy of air quality. The QoI of our paper is defined as the following.

Definition 1 (QoI of image datasets). The QoI of sensing denoted by $\bar{q} = \{q_1, \cdots, q_N\}$ is the clarity of pictures. It often depends on the joining time t_i and task achievements (like correlation α_i and coverage of shooting targets β_i) of users, which are perfectly complimentary factors in the process of executing tasks. The joining time t_i of a user is earlier, he has more time to prepare for collecting images; pictures are often more relevant with the platform's requirements and the coverage of shooting is also wider with sufficient time. If these constraints are changed, image quality will also be changed.

We assume that platform maintains a historical record of users' QoI profile $\bar{q}$ used as inputs for winner and payment determination. Each subtask τ_j needs to be completed with a minimum quality Q_j. Denoted by $\bar{Q} = \{Q_1, \cdots, Q_M\}$ the profile of quality requirements for each subtask.

Definition 2 (A User's Utility). The payoff ψ_i of any $u_i \in U$ is defined as the difference between payments p_i and cost c_i, which satisfies:

$$\psi_i = \begin{cases} p_i - c_i, & x_i = 1; \\ 0, & x_i = 0. \end{cases} \tag{1}$$

There, x_i equals to 1 if u_i wins, and x_i equals to 0 otherwise.

$$x_i = \begin{cases} 1, & \text{if } u_i \text{ is chosen as a winner} \\ 0, & \text{otherwise} \end{cases} \tag{2}$$

If u_i is a winner of our auction, he will be paid p_i for executing the corresponding set of sensing tasks. In contrast, he will not be allocated any sensing task and receive zero payment.

Definition 3 (Platform's Profits). The profit of sensing platform is given as follows:

$$\phi = V(S) - \sum_{i \in S} p_i \tag{3}$$

where the value function $V(S)$ represents the sum of the value v_i contributed by winner set S.

$$V(S) = \sum_{i \in S} v_i = \sum_{i \in S} \lambda q_i |\eta_i| \tag{4}$$

Equation (4) consists of λ, a coefficient that transform the image QoI into monetary reward. $|\eta_i|$ is the number of categories collected by u_i. The value function $V(S)$ is monotonic in q. That is, for any $\vec{q} = \{q_1, \cdots, q_N\}$ and $\vec{q}' = \{q'_1, \cdots, q'_N\}$, we have $V_{\vec{q}}(S) \geq V_{\vec{q}'}(S)$, if $q_i \geq q'_i$ holds $\forall u_i \in U$.

Since the smartphones are owned by different users, which are selfish but with rational behavior. Therefore, mobile users will not participate in the MC without sufficient incentive. To guarantee the utilities of both sensing platform and participating users, the goal of this paper is similar to the traditional VCG mechanism [20, 21], aimed at designing an efficient incentive mechanism that maximize the social welfare. It is formally described in Definition 4.

Definition 4 (Social Welfare). The social welfare of the whole MC is the sum of the users' payoff and sensing platform profits:

$$\gamma = \phi + \sum_{i \in U} \psi_i = V(S) - \sum_{i \in S} c_i \qquad (5)$$

3.2 Desirable Properties

Specifically, a user participating in sensing tasks will incur a cost c_i and his maximum executable task set is η_i', which are private and only known to user himself. As a result, c_i and η_i' could be different from b_i and η_i respectively.

This section describes three desirable properties for our auction mechanism.

- **Truthfulness:** An auction mechanism is *truthful* if and only if for every bidder $u_i \in U$, they all adopt the dominant strategy to bid his true value (η_i', c_i).
- **Individual Rationality:** An auction mechanism is *individually rational* if for any bidder, the payoff is nonnegative when bidder u_i bids his true value (η_i', c_i).
- **Computational Efficiency**: An auction mechanism is *computationally efficient* if the outcome can be computed in polynomial time.

Truthfulness is the most difficult to achieve of the three properties. The bid is two-dimensional that contains two parts: the declared cost b_i and task sets η_i of bidder u_i. Therefore, Myerson's theorem [13] about the properties of one-parameter truthful mechanisms cannot be directly applied. To design a truthful auction mechanism with two dimensions, the following definitions is introduced:

Definition 5 (b-Monotonicity). *if bidder u_i wins by bidding (η_i, b_i), then he also wins by bidding (η_i, b_i') with any $b_i' \leq b_i$.*

Definition 6 (η-Monotonicity). *if bidder u_i wins by bidding (η_i, b_i), then he also wins by bidding (η_i', b_i) with all $\eta_i' \supset \eta_i$.*

Definition 7 (Critical Payment). *the payment p_i for winning bidder u_i is set to the critical value d_i such that bidder u_i wins if $b_i \leq d_i$, and loses if $b_i > d_i$.*

Lemma 1. *A mechanism is truthful if it satisfies b-Monotonicity, η-Monotonicity and critical payment.*

Proof: A truthful bidder will receive positive utility which can be verified easily. If u_i is losing with untruthful sensing plan (η_i, b_i) or $\eta_i \not\subseteq \eta_i'$, his utility will be negative. As a result, the case in which (η_i, b_i) is winning and $\eta_i \subseteq \eta_i'$ requires to be only considered.

Firstly, it can be known that users biding with (η_i', b_i) can win from the property of η- Monotonicity. Suppose that the payment for bid (η_i, b_i) is p and for bid (η_i', b_i) is p'. Any bid (η_i', b_i') with $b_i' \geq p'$ is losing because p' is the critical payment of task η_i'. Similarly, bidding with (η_i, b_i') is also losing from monotonicity. Therefore, the critical payment for (η_i, b_i) is at most that for (η_i', b_i), which means $p \leq p'$; in other words, the user will not increase his utility by bidding (η_i, b_i) instead of (η_i', b_i). Then, the case of true bid with (η_i', c_i) is considered, whose payment is the same as bidding with (η_i', b_i) from the critical payment, i.e.p_i. If bidding (η_i', c_i) loses, then we have $c_i > p' \geq b_i$. Compared with (η_i', c_i), bid with (η_i', b_i) will also not increase his utility.   □

4   QoI-Aware Incentive Mechanism (QoI-RA)

In this section, a QoI-aware based on reverse auction (QoI-RA) is presented. First, we discuss how to achieve approximately maximal social welfare. Then, two Algorithms for the discussion are designed by us. Finally, we present a practical QoI-RA that satisfies three properties.

4.1   Optimal Solution of QoI-RA Auction

The goal of QoI-RA is to maximize the social welfare given in Definition 4 while achieving computational efficiency, individual rationality and truthful. The winner selection (QRA-WS) and pricing determination (QRA-PD) can be decoupled into two separate problems. Solving the maximization problem itself, referred to as the QRA-WS problem, is challenging because QRA-WS is NP-hard (proved by Theorem 1), let alone combining with the other three properties.

QRA-WS Problem: Given the information of a task set ζ and a user set U, the goal of the QRA-WS problem is to find a subset $S \subseteq U$. It can be formulated as the following integer linear program, such that

$$\max_U \sum_{i=1}^{N} w_i x_i \tag{6}$$

Subject to:

$$\sum_{i:\tau_j \in \eta_i, u_i \in U} q_i x_i \geq Q_j, \quad \forall \tau_j \in \zeta \tag{7}$$

$$x_i \in \{0, 1\}, \quad \forall u_i \in U \tag{8}$$

$$\alpha_i(t) \geq \hat{\alpha}, \quad T_1 \leq t \leq T_2 \tag{9}$$

$$\beta_i(t, r) \geq \hat{\beta}, \quad r \leq l \tag{10}$$

Using (4) and (5), we get:

$$\gamma = V(S) - \sum_{u_i \in S} c_i = \sum_{u_i \in U} (\lambda q_i |\eta_i| - b_i) x_i \tag{11}$$

Let $\vec{w} = \{w_1, \cdots, w_N\}$ denote the marginal social welfare profile of all users based on user's bids, where

$$w_i = \lambda q_i |\eta_i| - b_i \tag{12}$$

Hence, maximizing the social welfare is actually maximizing the total marginal social welfare of users.

$$\gamma = \sum_{u_i \in U} w_i x_i \tag{13}$$

4.2   Constraints of Tasks

Definition 8 (Task's Quality). We use $Q_j(S)$ represented by Eq. (14) to denote the total quality that all winners accomplish task $\tau_j \in \zeta$. Therefore, the quality of a subtask is equivalent to guaranteeing that every task is executed by users with sufficient amount of quality in total.

$$Q_j(S) = \sum_{i \in S} q_i, \qquad \forall \tau_j \in \eta_i \tag{14}$$

The platform stipulates that total quality of images users collected must satisfy the requirement of each subtask. Constraint (7) is each subtask's quality requirement.

Definition 9 (Correlation). The correlation of image type between users upload x and tasks require y can be donated as the function $\alpha(\cdot)$:

$$\alpha(t - d) = [2 \cdot \text{sgn}(t - d) \cdot f(d - t) + \text{sgn}(d - t)] \cdot m_{xy} \tag{15}$$

where the relevance of image type collected by users is evaluated from two aspects: objectivity and subjectivity. The former is determined by a function that can satisfy the following properties: (1) it is a monotonically none-increasing of the different between t and d, where t is the joining time of users and d is the deadline of sensing tasks; (2) it returns a value in [0,1]. If users join in tasks earlier than deadline, it always equals to 1. Otherwise, it monotonously decreases from 1 to 0; f(t) is a function of Sigmoid. m_{xy} is decided by platform grades on the image correlation, which ranges from [0,1]. The platform requires that users can meet certain relevance of collecting images, corresponding to (9).

Definition 10 (Coverage). The image coverage $\beta(\cdot)$ is represented by:

$$\beta(r,t) = \begin{cases} (2 - \frac{2}{1+e^{-r}})\frac{d-t}{d-s} & , \quad r > 0, s \leq t \leq d \\ \frac{d-t}{d-s} & , \quad r = 0, s \leq t \leq d \\ 0 & , \quad \text{otherwise} \end{cases} \tag{16}$$

where $\beta(\cdot)$ is decided by two parts. The former is a monotonically decreasing function of r, where r is the distance between the shooting location and the target object. When r is large, the target coverage rate is low. In addition, the joining time of users is different, so they take photos with different numbers. It is assumed that once a user has participated in the task, he always executes tasks and takes the same time on a single picture. As a result, the number of pictures is proportional to joining time t of users, which can be described as the latter. The longer you participate, the more pictures you can collect from different angles under enough time and conditions, so the coverage of target becomes wider. For model training needs, the sensing platform hopes the image coverage can meet the specified standards, which is corresponding to (10).

The optimal QoI-RA problem is achieved as follows:

(1) Winner Selection: Find a subset $S \subseteq U$ by solving QRA-WS problem;
(2) Payment Determination: Determined by the basis of QRA-WS problem. If x_i is equal to 0; p_i is 0; otherwise.

Theorem 1. The QRA-WS problem is NP-hard.

Proof: We prove the NP-hardness of the QRA-WS problem by a polynomial time reduction from the minimum weighted set cover (MWSC) problem, which is NP-hard [23]. The MWSC problem is defined as follows: A universe set, denoted by $E = \{\tau_1, \cdots, \tau_M\}$, consists of M elements, whose subsets can be denoted as a set $\mho = \{\eta_1, \cdots, \eta_N\}$. Every set $\eta_i \in \mho$ has a corresponding non-negative weight $w(\eta_i)$. The MWSC problem is to find the minimum weight subset of $\mho$ whose union is E.

Next, we construct an instance of the QRA-WS problem from an instance of the MWSC problem in polynomial time. Firstly, we transform η_i into η_i' such that for every element in η_i there exist $h_i \in \mathbb{Z}^+$ copies of the same element in η_i'. We require that every element $\tau_j \in E$ is covered for at least $H_i \in \mathbb{Z}^+$ times. After reduction, we obtain an instance of the QRA-WS problem. In such a problem, users' quality profile is denoted as $\vec{q} = \{h_1, \cdots, h_N\}$; users' bidding tasks profile is denoted as $\vec{\eta} = \{\eta_1, \cdots, \eta_N\}$; user's marginal social welfare profile is $\vec{w} = \{-w_1, \cdots, -w_N\}$; user's duration of service profile is $\vec{t} = \{t_1, \cdots, t_N\}$; user's location of service profile is $\vec{r} = \{r_1, \cdots, r_N\}$; tasks' quality requirement profile is $\vec{Q} = \{H_1, \cdots, H_M\}$. It can be seen vividly that the QRA-WS problem represents a richer family of problems in which the quality q_i of any user u_i and any task j's quality requirement Q_j could take any value in $\mathbb{R}^+$. Furthermore, the marginal social welfare can take any value in $\mathbb{R}$. So every instance of the MWSC problem is polynomial-time reducible to an instance of the QRA-WS problem. The QRA-WS problem is NP-hard. □

4.3 Mechanism Design

Because of the NP-Hard nature of QRA-WS problem, it is difficult to find a solution to maximize social welfare in polynomial time. Meanwhile, traditional VCG auction mechanism [20, 21] are not directly tailored because it requires the social welfare is exactly maximized. A natural step is to design a computationally efficient mechanism with close-to-optimal social welfare.

On this basis of the proposed optimal solution, user's bids $\{(\eta_1, b_1), \cdots, (\eta_N, b_N)\}$ are utilized by us to calculate the marginal social welfare of users w, which acts as the input of QRA-WS problem. First, platform excludes the users who don't meet the timeliness, relevance, and coverage of task (lines 2–4). Next, the platform includes the remaining users whose marginal social welfare are non-negative into winner set (lines 5–6). Then the platform will get the user set Ω^- whose marginal social welfare is negative by removing the current winner from user set N^- (line 7). It calculates task's remaining quality requirements profile Q' by subtracting from Q' the quality provided by the currently selected winners (lines 8–9). The main loop is executed until every task's quality is satisfied (lines 10–15).

In the main loop, the minimum marginal social welfare effectiveness is used to select the third batch of users, the formula is defined as follows:

$$\xi = \frac{|w_i|}{\sum_{j:\tau_j \in \eta_i} \min\{Q'_j, q_i\}} \tag{17}$$

where ξ is defined as the ratio between the absolute value of the marginal social welfare $|w_i|$ of u_i and his effective quality contribution $\sum_{j:\tau_j \in \eta_i} \min\{Q'_j, q_i\}$. The user with the minimum ξ among the remaining users in Ω^- is included into S. After that, the platform updates set S(lines 10–13) and the residual quality of subtask $\vec{Q}$ (lines 14–15).

Then, the platform pays for winner set S in Algorithm 1. If a user is not winner, his payoff is zero. Algorithm 2 describes the pricing mechanism, which takes the winner set S as input and outputs the payment profile $\vec{p}$. Firstly, $\vec{p}$ is initialized as a zero vector (line 1). Then, like Algorithm 1, platform excludes users who don't meet the timeliness, relevance, coverage of task and gets set N^+ (lines 2–4). Next, the platform includes all users with non-negative marginal social welfare into Ω^+ (lines 5–6). The main loop (lines 7–14) calculates the platform's payment to every winner. For every winner $u_i \in S$, the winner determination in Algorithm 1 is executed with all users except u_i until the quality requirement of every task in η_i is satisfied (lines 7–8).Then, the platform obtains the current winner set S'(line 9) and calculates differently in the following two case (lines 10–14):

Case 1. Any winner u_i has $w_i \geq 0$ in this case (lines 10–11). As a result, the user's critical payment is his bidding price b'_i, which satisfies $w' = \lambda q_i |\eta_i| - b'_i = 0$. That is:

$$p_i = \lambda q_i |\eta_i| \tag{18}$$

Algorithm 1: QoI-RA Auction Winner Selection	**Algorithm 2:** QoI-RA Auction Winner Pricing
Input : $U, \zeta, \bar{w}, \bar{q}, \bar{\eta}, t, \bar{r}, \bar{Q}$	**Input** : $S, \lambda, \bar{w}, \bar{q}, \bar{\eta}, \bar{t}, \bar{r}, \bar{Q}$
Output: S	**Output:** $\bar{p}$
1: $U^- \leftarrow \varnothing; N^- \leftarrow \varnothing;$ $\Omega^- \leftarrow \varnothing; S \leftarrow \varnothing;$	1: $U^+ \leftarrow \varnothing; N^+ \leftarrow \varnothing; \Omega^+ \leftarrow \varnothing;$ $\bar{p} \leftarrow \{0, \cdots, 0\};$
2: **foreach** i *s.t.* $\alpha_i(t) < \hat{\alpha}$ or $\beta_i(t,r) < \hat{\beta}$ **do**	2: **foreach** i s.t. $\alpha_i(t) < \hat{\alpha}$ or $\beta_i(t,r) < \hat{\beta}$
3: $U^- \leftarrow U^- \cup \{i\};$	3: $U^+ \leftarrow U^+ \cup \{i\};$
4: $N^- \leftarrow U \setminus \{U^-\};$	4: $N^+ \leftarrow U \setminus \{U^+\};$
5: **foreach** $i \in N^-$ *s.t.* $w_i \geq 0$ **do**	5: **foreach** $i \in N^+$ *s.t.* $w_i \geq 0$ **do**
6: $S \leftarrow S \cup \{i\};$	6: $\Omega^+ \leftarrow \Omega^+ \cup \{i\};$
7: $\Omega^- \leftarrow N^- \setminus S;$	7: **foreach** $i \in S$ **do**
8: **foreach** j *s.t.* $\tau_j \in \zeta$ **do**	8: run Algorithm 1 on $N^+ \setminus \{i\}$ until $\sum_{j:\tau_j \in \eta_i} Q'_j = 0$
9: $Q'_j \leftarrow Q_j - \min\{Q_j, \sum_{i:\tau_j \in \eta_i, i \in S} q_i\};$	9: $S' \leftarrow$ the winner set when step 8 stops;
10: **while** $\sum_{j:\tau_j \in \zeta} Q'_j \neq 0$ **do**	10: **if** $|S'| < |\Omega^+|$ **then**
11: $u_i^* = \arg\min_{u_i \in \Omega^-} \dfrac{|w_i|}{\sum_{j:\tau_j \in \eta_i} \min\{Q'_j, q_i\}};$	11: $p_i \leftarrow \lambda q_i |\eta_i|$
12: $S \leftarrow S \cup \{u_i^*\};$	12: **else**
13: $\Omega^- \leftarrow \Omega^- \setminus \{u_i^*\};$	13: **foreach** $k \in S' \setminus \Omega^+$ **do**
14: **foreach** j *s.t.* $\tau_j \in \zeta$ **do**	14:
15: $Q'_j \leftarrow Q'_j - \min\{Q'_j, q_{i^*}\};$	$p_i \leftarrow \max\{p_i, \lambda q_i |\eta_i| - w_k \dfrac{\sum_{j:\tau_j \in \eta_i} \min\{Q'_j, q_i\}}{\sum_{j:\tau_j \in \eta_k} \min\{Q'_j, q_k\}}\}$
16: **return** S;	15: **return** $\bar{p}$;

Case 2. Any winner u_i belonging to case 2 (lines 13–14), we go through every $u_k \in S' \setminus U^+$. Then we calculate the maximum bidding price b'_i of user u_i to be able to replace u_k as the winner, i.e., b'_i satisfies Eq. (19).

$$\frac{|w_k|}{\sum_{j:\tau_j \in \eta_k} \min(Q'_j, q_k)} = \frac{b'_i - \lambda q_i |\eta_i|}{\sum_{j:\tau_j \in \eta_i} \min(Q'_j, q_i)} \tag{19}$$

This can also be expressed as:

$$b'_i = \lambda q_i |\eta_i| - w_k \frac{\sum\limits_{j:\tau_j \in \eta_i} \min\{Q'_j, q_i\}}{\sum\limits_{j:\tau_j \in \eta_k} \min\{Q'_j, q_k\}} \tag{20}$$

At last, the maximum value among all b'_i discussed above is used to pay for u_i.

4.4 Proof of Properties

In this section, we show that QoI-RA auction is truthful, individual rational, computational efficient.

Theorem 2. *The QoI-RA auction is truthful.*

Proof: We consider any other bid (η'_i, b'_i) of u_i, if he wins by bidding (η_i, b_i), where $b'_i < b_i$ or $\eta_i \subset \eta'_i$. It will be analyzed from two cases.

(1) $w_i \geq 0$. When u_i makes a new bid (η'_i, b'_i), $w'_i = \lambda q_i |\eta'_i| - b'_i > \lambda q_i |\eta_i| - b_i \geq 0$.
(2) $w_i \leq 0$. The new marginal social welfare of u_i is not affected by previous bidding. It is the same as case 1, which makes $w'_i \geq 0$.

As a result, u_i can also win by new bid (η'_i, b'_i) from Algorithm 1. QRA-WS satisfies both bidding tasks and price monotonicity. Furthermore, it is easily verifiable that QRA-PD algorithm uses the supremum of bidding price b'_i such that bidding (η_i, b'_i) still wins. Hence, from Lemma 1, we conclude that QoI-RA auction is truthful.   □

Theorem 3. *The QoI-RA auction is individual rational.*

Proof: We prove from two possible cases. First, the payoff of mobile user $u_i \in \{U \backslash S\}$ is 0 if u_i is not a winner according to Algorithm 2. Second, u_i is a winner. We have proved that users bid truthfully in our QoI-RA auction from Theorem 2. As a result, each user bids his true cost c_i. Since QoI-RA preserves the critical payment property as shown in Lemma 1, every winner will be paid the supremum of bidding price. Then, we have $p_i \geq c_i$ for every winner, i.e., $\psi_i = p_i - c_i \geq 0$. Therefore, the utility for every user u_i is always non-negative, i.e. $\psi_i \geq 0$. This completes the proof.   □

Theorem 4. *The computational complexity of the QoI-RA auction is $O(N^3 M)$.*

Proof: QoI-RA auction consists of two algorithms QRA-WS and QRA-PD. The former firstly goes through all users to select someone who meets the requirements of timeliness, correlation, coverage, which needs N iterations. Its computational complexity is embodied in the main loop, which terminates after N iterations in the worst case. In every iteration, it also goes through every task $\tau_j \in \zeta$, i.e., the while-loop runs M times. Hence, the computational complexity of Algorithm 1 is $O(N^2 M)$. Similarly, the problem in Algorithm 2 needs N iterations at first. Then, it chooses users whose marginal social welfare is greater than 0, which iterates N times in the worst case. The third for-loop executes Algorithm 1 for each user $u_i \in S$. So the computational complexity of Algorithm 2 is $O(N^3M)$. Therefore, the overall computational complexity of QoI-RA auction is $O(N^3M)$.   □

5   Performance Evaluation

In this section, we present and discuss simulation results on the real dataset to justify the effectiveness of the proposed mechanism.

5.1   Simulation Settings

All the evaluation results are based on a real datasets of BelgianTS [3]. The dataset consists of two parts: training (4575 images) and testing data (2520 images). Each contains 62 subdirectories. Each subdirectory from 0 to 61 represents a category/label. Each category has different amount of traffic signs images, which are stored as the format of.ppm. In order to compare with previous experiments mentioned in Sect. 2 easily, all the training images of BelgianTS are imported into our simulation environment. Then, each picture is labeled by us. The basic parameter settings are detailed in Table 1.

Table 1. Parameter setting

Parameters	λ	q_i	Q_j	N	M	t_i	r_i
Value	0.1	[1, 2]	[10, 15]	[100,200]	62	[0,40]	[0,7]
Parameters	$\|\eta_i\|$	l	T_1	T_2	c_i	$\hat{\alpha}$	$\hat{\beta}$
Value	[20,30]	5	0	30	[2, 4]	0.6	0.6

For comparison, we choose two well-designed incentive mechanisms. The first baseline is the revised version of greedy auction with our constraints defined in Sect. 4, which is truthful and individual rational. Firstly, the winner determination of it selects user with $w_i \geq 0$ who meets constraint (9) and (10) as the winners. Different from our mechanism, it then selects users who has largest marginal social welfare in remaining users until QoI requirements of tasks are met. The pricing mechanism pays each winner his supremum bidding price. The second baseline method is a modified version of traditional VCG auction [20, 21] based on QoI-Aware (QoI-VCG), which consists of winner determination (VCG-WD) and pricing. The concept of QoI and our constraints are integrated into the VCG-WD problem, which can be solved optimally. The pricing mechanism in [20, 21] is used to pay for winners.

5.2   Simulation Results

Experiment 1 compares our mechanism with two well-designed mechanisms about the social welfare. The parameters are given in Table 1. To evaluate the impact of the number of users on the social welfare, we set the number of tasks to 62 and vary the number of users from 100 to 200 with a step of 20. It can be vividly seen in Fig. 5 that the social welfare of three mechanisms keeps going up when the number of users increases. The social welfare of the QoI-VCG auction equals to the optimal solution of the QRA-WS problem. It can be concluded that the social welfare of QoI-RA auction is close to optimal and far better than the baseline QoI-Greedy auction.

In Experiment 2, one of constraints is chosen by us. The coverage of image is changed among 0.5, 0.6, 0.7 with other parameters fixed. As shown in Fig. 6, the coverage is lower, the value of social welfare is greater. It is due to that, the restrictions of these three indexes are set wider, more mobile users have chances to participate. This is helpful for platform's task accomplished, and thus, the social benefits are relatively high. However, a certain QoI limitation should be set for machine learning model training and it is unsuitable to be set too low.

Experiment 3 looks at the running time. The QoI-VCG auction is compared with it. The parameters are the same as Experiment 1. Simulation results are presented in Table 2. QoI-RA auction executes in significantly less time than the QoI-VCG auction. That is because the QoI-VCG auction calculates actual social welfare maximization. With the increasing of the number of users, its execution time gradually becomes so long, which is infeasible to be used in practice. In contrast, the QoI-RA auction approaches the optimal social welfare, it can keep low execution. In a word, the QoI-RA auction is much more computationally efficient than the QoI-VCG auction.

In Experiment 4, two datasets with the same amounts and different qualities are input into an initial CNN model for its training. One group is a part of the original datasets. The other group is selected by the QoI-RA mechanism. Then, we observe the effects of data quality on model training by comparing the two groups of model training. In Fig. 7, the pictures of QoI-RA collected are input into CNN, the model

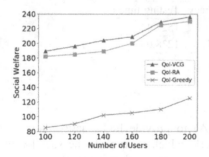 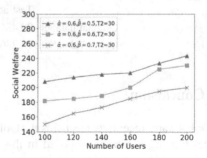

Fig. 5. Impact of number of users   **Fig. 6.** Impact of coverage

Table 2. Comparison of execution time

N	100	150	200	250	300	350	400	450	500
VCG	6.325	8.361	10.574	12.016	65.293	32.786	95.475	60.251	2056
QRA	0.119	0.128	0.132	0.157	0.224	0.195	0.219	0.226	0.230

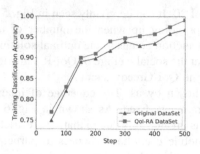

Fig. 7. Comparison of training accuracy   **Fig. 8.** Comparison of loss value

accuracy increases faster. This is because, QoI-RA dataset has the quality constraints. It selects high-quality images in all datasets. In Fig. 8, the loss value of the model trained with QoI-RA datasets falls to 0 more quickly. This indicates that the model trained with high-quality datasets actually has better learning ability. The growth speed of an initial model can be accelerated by the improvement of image quality in some degree. At last, the prepared testing datasets of BelgianTS (2520 images) are used to test the accuracy of trained model, the final classification accuracy can reach 95.7862% and the time spent for classifying is much shorter than before. It shows that our mechanism is helpful for obtaining high-quality data, with which the growth speed of model can be accelerated (Table 3).

Table 3. Testing results

DataSet	Predictive indexes	
	Test accuracy	Testing time (s)
Original dataSet	90.4365%	1527.42
QoI-RA dataSet	95.7862%	1238.04

6   Conclusion

A QoI-Aware incentive mechanism (QoI-RA) to provide high-quality datasets for model training has been proposed in this work, which maximizes the social welfare with the subject of quality requirement of each subtask, timeliness of joining task, correlation and coverage of targets. Through extensive simulation results, we show that the proposed mechanism produces close-to-optimal social welfare noticeably. Datasets acquisition through our mechanism is helpful for machine learning model growth with lower complexity. We believe that our method could lay a foundation of the design of incentive mechanisms for multimedia crowdsensing with QoI constraints over machine learning system.

Acknowledgements. The authors gratefully acknowledge the support and financial assistance provided by the National Natural Science Foundation of China under Grant No. 61502230, 61501224 and 61073197, the Natural Science Foundation of Jiangsu Province under Grant No. BK20150960, the Natural Science Foundation of the Jiangsu Higher Education Institutions of China under Grant No. 15KJB520015, and Nangjing Municipal Science and Technology Plan Project under Grant No. 201608009.

References

1. Guo, B., Han, Q., Chen, H., et al.: The emergence of visual crowdsensing: challenges and opportunities. IEEE Commun. Surv. Tutor. **PP**(99), 1 (2017)
2. Li, Y., Jeong, Y.S., Shin, B.S., et al.: Crowdsensing multimedia data: security and privacy issues. IEEE Multimed. **24**(4), 58–66 (2017)
3. https://btsd.ethz.ch/shareddata/
4. Restuccia, F., Ghosh, N., Bhattacharjee, S., et al.: Quality of information in mobile crowdsensing: survey and research challenges. ACM Trans. Sens. Netw. **13**(4), 34 (2017)
5. Howard, A.G., Zhu, M., Chen, B., et al.: MobileNets: efficient convolutional neural networks for mobile vision applications, arXiv preprint arXiv:1704.04861 (2017)
6. Hsu, W.N., Glass, J.: Extracting domain invariant features by unsupervised learning for robust automatic speech recognition, arXiv preprint arXiv:1803.02551 (2018)
7. Leroux, S., Molchanov, P., Simoens, P., et al.: IamNN: iterative and adaptive mobile neural network for efficient image classification, arXiv preprint arXiv:1804.10123 (2018)
8. Hara, K., Sun, J., Moore, R., et al.: Tohme: detecting curb ramps in google street view using crowdsourcing, computer vision, and machine learning. In: Proceedings of the 27th Annual ACM Symposium on User Interface Software and Technology, pp. 189–204 (2014)
9. Anguelov, D., Dulong, C., Filip, D., et al.: Google street view: capturing the world at street level. Computer **43**(6), 32–38 (2010)
10. Sun, F., Huang, G.B., Wu, Q.M.J., et al.: Efficient and rapid machine learning algorithms for big data and dynamic varying systems. IEEE Trans. Syst. Man Cybern. Syst. **47**(10), 2625–2626 (2017)
11. Man, H.C., Hou, F., Huang, J.: Delay-sensitive mobile crowdsensing: algorithm design and economics. IEEE Trans. Mob. Comput. **PP**(99), 1 (2018)
12. Xu, Y., Zhou, Y., Mao, Y., et al.: Can early joining participants contribute more? - timeliness sensitive incentivization for crowdsensing (2017)
13. Myerson, R.B.: Optimal auction design. Math. Oper. Res. **6**(1), 58–73 (1981)
14. Cheng, Y., Li, X., Li, Z., et al.: AirCloud: a cloud-based air-quality monitoring system for everyone (2014)
15. http://www.fda.gov/MedicalDevices/Safety/ReportaProblem/ucm385880.htm
16. Krontiris, I., Albers, A.: Monetary incentives in participatory sensing using multi-attributive auctions. Parallel Algorithms Appl. **27**(4), 317–336 (2012)
17. Duan, L., Kubo, T., Sugiyama, K., et al.: Incentive mechanisms for smartphone collaboration in data acquisition and distributed computing. In: Proceedings of IEEE INFOCOM, pp. 1701–1709 (2012)
18. Faltings, B., Li, J.J., Jurca, R.: Incentive mechanisms for community sensing. IEEE Trans. Comput. **63**(1), 115–128 (2014)
19. Yang, D., Xue, G., Fang, X., et al.: Incentive mechanisms for crowdsensing: crowdsourcing with smartphones. IEEE/ACM Trans. Netw. **24**(3), 1732–1744 (2016)
20. Clarke, E.H.: Multipart pricing of public goods. Public Choice **11**(1), 17–33 (1971)

21. Groves Jr., T.F.G., Groves, T.: Incentives in Teams[J]. Econometrica **41**(4), 617–631 (1973)
22. Feng, Z., Zhu, Y., Zhang, Q., et al.: TRAC: truthful auction for location-aware collaborative sensing in mobile crowdsourcing. In: Proceedings of IEEE INFOCOM, pp. 1231–1239 (2014)
23. Cormen, T.T., Leiserson, C.E., Rivest, R.L.: Introduction to algorithms. Resonance **1**(9), 14–24 (2009)

Toward Performance Prediction
for Multi-BSP Programs in ML

Victor Allombert[1], Frédéric Gava[2(✉)], and Julien Tesson[2]

[1] Université d'Orléans, LIFO, Orléans, France
[2] Université Paris-Est Créteil, LACL, Créteil, France
gava@u-pec.fr

Abstract. BSML and MULTI-ML are functional parallel programming languages "à la ML" based of the respectively the BSP and MULTI-BSP bridging models. MULTI-BSP extends BSP to take into account hierarchical architectures. For both models, it is possible to predict the performances of algorithms thanks to embedded cost models. To do so, we propose formal operational semantics with cost annotations for the two aforementioned languages. This work has been done in a incremental manner. First we recall the cost semantics of core-ML language. Then, we adapt it to BSML and then to MULTI-ML. It is then possible to evaluate the cost of a program following the annotated semantics. Finally, we compare the theoretical approach with the current implementation on a code example.

Keywords: Semantics · BSP · BSML MULTI-BSP · Cost
Time prediction

1 Introduction

1.1 Context

The Bulk Synchronous Parallelism (BSP) *bridging model* [16] was designed for *flat* parallel architectures. A bridging model is an abstract model of a computer which provides a conceptual bridge between the physical implementation of the machine and the *abstraction* available to a programmer of that machine. But modern High Performance Computing (HPC) architectures are now *hierarchical* and have multiple layers of parallelism, communication between distant nodes cannot be as fast as among the cores of a given processor. We now consider the MULTI-BSP model [17], an extension of BSP. MULTI-ML [1,2] is a MULTI-BSP extension of BSML [8], a functional approach for programming BSP algorithms in ML, BSML being itself an extension of OCAML, a ML language (https://ocaml.org/).

To be compliant with a bridging model eases the way of writing codes that ensures *efficiency* and *portability* from one architecture to another and also avoid deadlocks and non-determinism. The MULTI-BSP bridging model offers a high level of abstraction and takes into account real communications and synchronisation costs on hierarchical architectures. Thanks to the cost model embedded in

© Springer Nature Switzerland AG 2018
J. Vaidya and J. Li (Eds.): ICA3PP 2018, LNCS 11336, pp. 159–174, 2018.
https://doi.org/10.1007/978-3-030-05057-3_12

the (MULTI-)BSP model, it is possible obtain the cost of a given algorithm. Using the (MULTI-)BSP parameters of an architecture allows to predict the execution time of a given code. That can useful for resource bound analysis and find performance bugs thus to provide development-time feedback to HPC programmers.

We chose OCAML (with our own distributed extensions) as the source language "à la ML" for several reasons. For one, OCAML is a widely used language for functional programming which is quite efficient in practice (sophisticated compiler and automatic memory management). Moreover, we wanted to demonstrate that it is possible to define a practical cost semantics for high-level HPC languages; imperative programming is closer to standard assembly codes which already have their cost analysis such as WCET [15]. Even if functional programming is currently not the norm for HPC, it is more and more common that main stream languages (such as JAVA) add functional features. Studying these features in ML, without having to manage others features (such as JAVA's objects), is a classical manner to get them for other languages.

Cost prediction is important for the design of efficient algorithms and is also important in domains where programs are executed with time constraints (such as in physical engines such as aeroplanes *etc.*). In the future, even such domains would benefit of many-cores architectures (at most). Cost prediction of HPC programs is thus an important issue to ensure the safety of such systems.

1.2 Example of the Methodology: The Sequential Case

An important first step to study cost prediction of programs is to define the cost of the construction of the language itself, that is define an operational big-step semantics that assign a parametric cost to a well-formed expression. Having a compositionnal cost semantics is also an important issue in order to get modular and incremental programming: from a software engineering point of view, it makes senses that the cost of a subprogram does not depend (too much) on the context, for example, the cost of an array sorting method should depend only on the size of the input and not when it is called.

The main hypothesis is that the resource consumption of a program is a linear combination of the number of executions of each construct in the program[1]. The semantics models this idea by parameterizing the cost with unknown coefficients that correspond to each ML construct: the number of executions of each of these constructs constitutes the majority of the execution time of most ML codes [10].

Taking the case of the core-ML language. It relies on a minimal set of ML constructions. This set is sufficient enough to express all the behaviour that are used in ML programming. Thus, features such as records, modules, pattern matching, sum types are excluded. The grammar is:

$$e ::= \mathbf{cst} \quad Constants \qquad | \quad \mathbf{let}\ x = e\ \mathbf{in}\ e \quad Binding$$

$e ::=$	**cst**	*Constants*		**let** $x = e$ **in** e	*Binding*
	op	*Operators*		**fun** $x \rightarrow e$	*Function*
	x	*Variables*		**rec** $f\ x \rightarrow e$	*Recursive function*
	$(e\,e)$	*Application*		**if** e **then** e **else** e	*Conditional*

---

[1] But their combination could be not linear as for algorithms with polynomial or exponential complexities.

In this grammar, x and f range over an infinite set of *identifiers*. We also find the typical ML-like constructors such as **let** for bindings and also **fun** and **rec** for, respectively, functions and recursive functions. As expected, the application is denoted (ee). For the sake of readability, we take the liberty to use the familiar infix notation for binary operators, as well as the usual precedence and associativity rules. When the context is clear, we can avoid the usage of parentheses. **op** stands for the standard operators, such as common computations on integers. **cst** stands for constants such as integers, booleans, *etc.* An expression is evaluated into a value v which are defined as:

$$\text{v} ::= \textbf{op} \quad | \quad \textbf{cst} \quad | \quad \overline{(\textbf{fun } x \to e)[\mathcal{E}]} \quad | \quad \overline{(\textbf{rec } f \ x \to e)[\mathcal{E}]}$$

$$\mathcal{E} ::= \{x_1 \mapsto v_1, ... x_n \mapsto x_n\}$$

Values contains constants and closures (a value which stores both a function and its environment). An environment $\mathcal{E}$ is interpreted as a partial mapping with finite domain from identifiers to values. The extension of $\mathcal{E}$ by v in x is written $\mathcal{E} \uplus \{x \mapsto v\}$. An inference rule can be written as following:

$$\frac{\mathcal{P}}{\mathcal{E} \vdash e \Downarrow v \rightsquigarrow C}$$

That is with the premise $\mathcal{P}$, the expression e is evaluated to the value v at cost C. The cost (time and memory) consumed by each construct is averaged out to be a constant. Hence, the execution time of a program C is: $\sum_{c \in \mathcal{C}} n_c \times T_c$ where $\mathcal{C}$ represents the set of constructs and n_c is the count of each construct during the whole program execution, and T_c is the execution time of the respective constructs. Estimating the overall time execution of a program (in "seconds") from the semantics now consists to estimating each T_c (in μs) using microbenchmarking[2] and replacing them into the extracted cost C. The inference rules for core-ML are defined in Fig. 1 and work as follow.

The CSTS and OPS rules do not generate any additional cost. Indeed, we assume that they are static values which are accessible freely. VARS aims to access a value bound in a memory using the *lookup* operator (which returns the corresponding bound value). As this operator access a value stored in a memory, its cost should be proportional to the path trough different caches-memories. However, we chose to set such a constant T_{var} in order to simplify the rules.

The CLOSURE rule mainly models the way the values are enclosed inside a function closure. It is done using the *select* operator which, given an environment $\mathcal{E}$ and a function (code) returns the minimal environment to evaluate such a code. We assume that the cost of building such an environment is proportional to the number of free variables ($\mathcal{F}$, define by trivial induction on expressions) of e. It is an approximation which can be refined by taking into account more OCAML mechanisms. Recursive functions are build in the same way.

The APP, LET and IF rules are straightforward: we simply propagate the cost produced by each expressions. Note the modification of the environment for the application to evaluate the code of the closure. Also, each operator gets a cost noted c_3 in the rule and we note $\overline{\textbf{op } v}$ the new built value. The "s" on the rules

---

[2] This assumption does not truly holds for most of the relevant platforms (*e.g.* the garbage collector and caches-misses) but is still sufficient for our study; We let more subtle analyses to future works and we will focus on parallelism.

$$\text{Csts} \quad \frac{}{\mathcal{E} \vdash^s \textbf{cst} \Downarrow \textbf{cst} \rightsquigarrow^s 0} \quad \text{Ops} \quad \frac{}{\mathcal{E} \vdash^s \textbf{op} \Downarrow \textbf{op} \rightsquigarrow^s 0} \quad \text{Vars} \quad \frac{\{x \mapsto v\} \in lookup(x, \mathcal{E})}{\mathcal{E} \vdash^s x \Downarrow v \rightsquigarrow^s T_{var}}$$

$$\text{Closures} \quad \frac{\mathcal{E}' = select(\mathcal{E}, \mathcal{F}(\textbf{fun } x \to e)) \rightsquigarrow n = |v| \qquad v \equiv \overline{(\textbf{fun } x \to e)[\mathcal{E}']}}{\mathcal{E} \vdash^s \textbf{fun } x \to e \Downarrow v \rightsquigarrow^s T_{def} \oplus n {\times} T_{clo}}$$

$$\text{App1} \quad \frac{\mathcal{E} \vdash^s e_1 \Downarrow \overline{(\textbf{fun } x \to e_3)[\mathcal{E}']} \rightsquigarrow^{s_1} c_1 \quad \mathcal{E} \vdash^{s_1} e_2 \Downarrow v \rightsquigarrow^{s_2} c_2 \quad \mathcal{E}' \uplus \{x \mapsto v\} \vdash^{s_2} e_3 \Downarrow v' \rightsquigarrow^{s_3} c_3}{\mathcal{E} \vdash^s (e_1\ e_2) \Downarrow v' \rightsquigarrow^{s_3} c_1 \oplus c_2 \oplus c_3 \oplus T_{FunApp}}$$

$$\text{App2} \quad \frac{\mathcal{E} \vdash^s e_1 \Downarrow \textbf{op} \rightsquigarrow^{s_1} c_1 \quad \mathcal{E} \vdash^{s_1} e_2 \Downarrow v \rightsquigarrow^{s_2} c_2 \quad v' \equiv \overline{\textbf{op } v} \rightsquigarrow c_3}{\mathcal{E} \vdash^s (e_1\ e_2) \Downarrow v' \rightsquigarrow^{s_2} c_1 \oplus c_2 \oplus c_3}$$

$$\text{Let} \quad \frac{\mathcal{E} \vdash^s e_1 \Downarrow v_1 \rightsquigarrow^{s_1} c_1 \quad \mathcal{E} \uplus \{x \mapsto v\} \vdash^{s_1} e_2 \Downarrow v_2 \rightsquigarrow^{s_2} c_2}{\mathcal{E} \vdash^s \textbf{let } x = e_1 \textbf{ in } e_2 \Downarrow v_2 \rightsquigarrow^{s_2} c_1 \oplus c_2 \oplus T_{let}}$$

$$\text{If1} \quad \frac{\mathcal{E} \vdash^s e_1 \Downarrow \textbf{True} \rightsquigarrow^{s_1} c_1 \quad \mathcal{E} \vdash^{s_1} e_2 \Downarrow v_2 \rightsquigarrow^{s_2} c_2}{\mathcal{E} \vdash^s \textbf{if } e_1 \textbf{then } e_2 \textbf{ else } e_3 \Downarrow v_2 \rightsquigarrow^{s_2} c_1 \oplus c_2 \oplus T_{if}}$$

$$\text{If2} \quad \frac{\mathcal{E} \vdash^s e_1 \Downarrow \textbf{False} \rightsquigarrow^{s_1} c_1 \quad \mathcal{E} \vdash^s e_3 \Downarrow v_3 \rightsquigarrow^{s_3} c_3}{\mathcal{E} \vdash^s \textbf{if } e_1 \textbf{then } e_2 \textbf{ else } e_3 \Downarrow v_3 \rightsquigarrow^{s_3} c_1 \oplus c_3 \oplus T_{if}}$$

Fig. 1. The cost semantics of the sequential core-ML language.

that are unused here but will be necessary for the BSP's supersteps. It is also straightforward to show that $\oplus$ is commutative.

1.3 Outlines

In this article we introduce the formal cost semantics of first the BSML language (Sect. 2) and then we extend it to MULTI-ML (Sect. 3). For both languages, we first present the model of execution, then the cost model and we give the semantics annotated with costs for core languages that describes the syntax of the aforementioned languages. Finally, we compare the predicted execution times with the actual one on a small example (Sect. 4).

2 BSP Programming in ML and Costs Semantics

2.1 The BSP Bridging Model

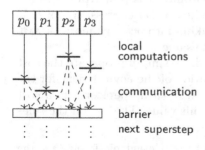

Fig. 2. A BSP superstep.

In the BSP model [16], a computer is a set of **p** *uniform* pairs of processor-memory with a communication network. A BSP program is executed as a *sequence* of *supersteps* (Fig. 2), each one divided into three successive disjointed phases: (1) each processor only uses its local data to perform sequential computations and to request data transfers to other nodes; (2) the network delivers the requested data; (3) a *global synchronisation barrier* occurs, making the transferred data available for the next superstep.

As BSP architecture can be easily mapped on any general purpose parallel architecture. Thanks to the BSP cost model it is possible to accurately *estimate* the execution time of a BSP program with the BSP parameters. The performance of a BSP computer is characterised by four parameters: The local processing speed r; The number of processors **p**; The time **L** required for a barrier; The time **g** for collectively delivering a 1-relation. **g** and **L** can be expressed in FLoating-point Operations (FLOPS) and r in FLOPS per second. To accurately *estimate* the execution time of a BSP program, these 4 parameters can be easily benchmarked [3].

A 1-relation is a collective exchange where every processor receives/sends at most one word. The network can deliver an h-relation in time $\mathbf{g} \times h$. The execution time (cost) of a superstep s is the sum of the maximal local processing time, the data delivery and the global synchronisation times. It is expressed by the following formula: $\text{Cost}(s) = \max_{0 \le i < \mathbf{p}} w_i^s + \max_{0 \le i < \mathbf{p}} h_i^s \times \mathbf{g} + \mathbf{L}$ where w_i^s is the local processing time on processor i during superstep s and h_i^s is the maximal number of words transmitted or received by processor i during superstep s. The total cost of a BSP program is the sum of its superstep's costs.

2.2 The BSML Language

BSML [7] uses a *small set of primitives* and is currently implemented as a library (http://traclifo.univ-orleans.fr/bsml/) for the ML programming language OCAML. An important feature of BSML is its *confluent* semantics: whatever the order of execution of the processors is, the final value will be the same. Confluence is convenient for *debugging* since it allows to get an *interactive loop* (toplevel). That also simplifies programming since the parallelisation can be done *incrementally* from an OCAML program.

A BSML program is built as a ML one but using a specific data structure called *parallel vector*. Its ML type is 'a par. A vector expresses that each of the **p** processors *embeds* a value of any type 'a. Figure 3 resumes the BSML primitives. Informally, they work as follows: let ≪ e≫ be the vector holding e everywhere (on each processor), the ≪ ≫ indicates that we enter into the scope of a vector. Within a vector, the syntax x can be used to read the vector x and get the local value it contains. The *ids* can be accessed with the predefined vector **pid**. When a value is referenced within the scope of a parallel vector, its *locality* is 1 (local); otherwise, the locality is b (BSP).

Primitive	Type	Informal semantics
<< e >>	'a par (if e :'a)	$\langle e, \ldots, e \rangle$, a vector of size **p** the number of processors
pid	int par	A predefined vector: i on processor i
v	'a (if v: 'a par)	v_i on processor i, assumes $\mathtt{v} \equiv \langle v_0, \ldots, v_{\mathbf{p}-1} \rangle$
proj	'a par-> (int->'a)	$(x_0, \ldots, x_{\mathbf{p}-1}) \mapsto (\text{fun } i \to x_i)$
put	(int -> 'a)par-> (int-> 'a)par	$\langle f_0, \ldots, f_{\mathbf{p}-1} \rangle \mapsto \langle (\text{fun } i \to f_i\ 0), \ldots, (\text{fun } i \to f_i\ (\mathbf{p}-1)) \rangle$

Fig. 3. Summary of the BSML primitives.

The **proj** primitive is the only way to *extract* local values from a vector. Given a vector, it returns a function such that applied to the *pid* of a processor, returns the value of the vector at this processor. **proj** performs communication to make local results available globally and ends the current superstep.

The **put** primitive is another communication primitive. It allows any local value to be *transferred* to any other processor. It is also synchronous, and ends the current superstep. The parameter of **put** is a vector that, at each processor, holds a function returning the data to be sent to processor j when applied to j. The result of **put** is another vector of functions: at a processor j the function, when applied to i, yields the value *received from* processor i by processor j.

2.3   Cost Semantics

Extension. To obtain core-BSML, we extends the expressions of core-ML with parallel primitives as follow: $e ::= \cdots \mid$ replicate $(\textbf{fun}\ \_ \rightarrow e) \mid (\text{proj}\ e) \mid (\text{put}\ e)$ $\mid (\text{apply}\ e\ e)$. The distinction made between the syntactic sugar (the $\ll \gg$ and $\$$ notations), used when programming BSML algorithms, and the core parallel primitives (**replicate** and **apply**), available in the semantics only, simplifies the semantics. Indeed, the syntactic sugar eases the way of programming but it is not suitable for the semantics as it introduces implicit assumptions. Thus, we must transform and abstract the syntactic sugar using the *core parallel primitives*. The transformation applied to switch from the syntactic sugar to the core parallel primitives is straightforward and produce and equivalent expression. The parallel vector scope, denoted $\ll e \gg$, is transformed using the **replicate** core primitive. Thus, $\ll e \gg$ is simply transformed into **replicate**$(\textbf{fun}\ \_ \rightarrow e)$. The $\$$ syntax is transformed using the **apply** primitive. The transformation is simple and does not require a complicated expression analysis. To do so, we build a vector of functions that takes, as argument, the dollar's annotated value. Using the **apply** primitive, we can *apply* this vector of functions on the vector of values. For example, the expression $\ll (e\ \$x\$) \gg$ is transformed into apply(replicate($\textbf{fun}\ \_ x \rightarrow ex$))$x$.

Values are also extended with parallel vectors: $v ::= \cdots \mid\ < v_1, \ldots, v_\textbf{p} >$. In the following, to simplify the notations, we indices processors from 1 to $\textbf{p}$ (and not from 0 to $\textbf{p} - 1$ as common in HPC). We make also the hypothesis that there exists a special vector named pid$=< 1, \cdots, \textbf{p} >$ (the ids of the processors).

The main modification is about the costs. During a superstep, the asynchronous costs are counting independently and it is only during the barrier that the maximal of the costs (computation and communication) are to be taken into account. But a same superstep can be in two different parts of an expression (for example **let** x$=\ll$1+1$\gg$ **in** ((**proj** $\ll \$x\$+1\gg$) 2) where the begin of the first superstep is in the first part of the **let**, the next just before the call of the **proj** and the second superstep when apply the result of the **proj** on the constant 2). For this reason, we extends the costs with vector of costs $< c_1, \ldots, c_\textbf{p} >_s$ where each component i describe the current local cost c_i of processor i during the superstep s. This s is modify only by the rules of synchronous primitives. Nevertheless, we add the three following equivalences:

1. $< c_1, \ldots, c_\mathbf{p} >_s \oplus < c_1', \ldots, c_\mathbf{p}' >_s \equiv < c_1 \oplus c_1', \ldots, c_\mathbf{p} \oplus c_\mathbf{p}' >_s$, if c_i and c_i' does not contains vectors
2. $< T_{op} \oplus c_1, \ldots, T_{op} \oplus c_\mathbf{p} >_s \equiv T_{op} \oplus < c_1, \ldots, c_\mathbf{p} >_s$, whatever T_{op}
3. $0 \equiv < 0, \ldots, 0 >_s$, whatever s

These rules aims to keep using the previous rule of the sequential constructions of the languages (let, fun, *etc.*).

Lemma 1. *The costs with parallel vector of costs form a commutative and associative group id where 0 is the neutral element inside or outside cost vectors and where $< 0, \ldots, 0 >_s$ is the neutral element outside vectors only.*

Adding Rules. We must now extend our inference rules in order to take into account the BSP primitives. These rules are given in Fig. 4. They work as follow.

$$\text{RPL} \quad \frac{\forall i \in \{1, \ldots, \mathbf{p}\} \quad \mathcal{E} \vdash^s e \Downarrow v_i \rightsquigarrow^s c_i \quad \text{if } Valid(e, \mathcal{E})}{\mathcal{E} \vdash^s \mathbf{replicate}\,(\mathbf{fun}\, \_ \rightarrow e) \Downarrow < v_1, \ldots, v_p >\rightsquigarrow^s T_{rpl} \oplus < c_1, \ldots, c_\mathbf{p} >_s}$$

$$\text{APPLY} \quad \frac{\begin{cases} \mathcal{E} \vdash^s e_1 \Downarrow < f_1, \ldots, f_p >\rightsquigarrow^{s_1} c_1 \\ \mathcal{E} \vdash^{s_1} e_2 \Downarrow < v_1, \ldots, v_p >\rightsquigarrow^{s_2} c_2 \end{cases} \forall i \in \{1, \ldots, \mathbf{p}\} \quad \mathcal{E} \vdash^{s_2} (f_i\, v_i) \Downarrow v_i' \rightsquigarrow^{s_2} c_i'}{\mathcal{E} \vdash^s (\mathbf{apply}\, e_1\, e_2) \Downarrow < v_1', \ldots, v_\mathbf{p}' >\rightsquigarrow^{s_2} T_{app} \oplus c_1 \oplus c_2 \oplus < c_1', \ldots, c_\mathbf{p}' >_{s_2}}$$

$$\text{PROJ} \quad \frac{\mathcal{E} \vdash^s e \Downarrow < v_1, \ldots, v_\mathbf{p} >\rightsquigarrow^{s'} c \quad f \text{ is such that } \forall i \in \{1, \ldots, \mathbf{p}\} \quad \mathcal{E} \vdash (f\, i) \equiv v_i}{\mathcal{E} \vdash^s (\mathbf{proj}\, e) \Downarrow f \rightsquigarrow^{s'+1} T_{proj} \oplus c \oplus H\,Relation(v_1, \ldots, v_\mathbf{p}) \times \mathbf{g} \oplus \mathbf{L}}$$

Fig. 4. The cost semantics of the core-BSML language.

The RPL rule is for building asynchronously a new parallel vector. The expression e is evaluated for each component, in parallel, making a new vector of cost for the current superstep s. The valid function is used to forbid nested vectors and is fully defined in [1]. A type system has been designed to not be forced to do this check dynamically. Then a construct is linearly add.

The APPLY rule works similarly but for two expressions which thus add two different costs (not necessary vectors and for possibly different supersteps) and we finally built the vector by computing its components in parallel (on each processor) making the linear add of a new costs vector.

The PROJ rule adds a barrier ($\mathbf{L}$) and thus finishes the superstep (updating s). From the exchanged computing values, a h-relation is added: $\mathbf{g}$ and $\mathbf{L}$ are thus special constructs. The PUT cost is quite dense because of the number of communications between all the processors which are done during the evaluation of the primitive. But the rule is close the proj one. For sake of conciseness, we do not show it. The way the data sizes are computed by simple induction on the values ($Hrelation$): it is rather naive but sufficient to an upper born.

To get the overall execution time $\mathcal{E} \vdash^s e \Downarrow v \rightsquigarrow^{s'} c$ then it is $\max(c) \oplus \mathbf{L}$ where the function max first apply the three previous equivalences in order to aggregate (merge) the cost vectors of the same superstep until not merging is possible. Finally, when the cost (time and memory) consumed by each construct is statically known in μs then $\max(< c_1, \ldots, c_{\mathbf{p}} >_s) = c_i$ if $\forall j \neq i, c_j \leq c_i$.

Lemma 2. *max is idempotent that is* $\forall c$ $\max(\max(c)) = \max(c)$.

For example, `let x=<<1+1>> in ((proj <<$x$+1>>) 2)` beginning with whatever environment $\mathcal{E}$ at any superstep s, for a two processors BSP machine, the cost semantics indicates that the adding cost of such expression is: $< T_+, T_+ >_s \oplus T_{rpl} \oplus T_{app} \oplus < T_{var} \oplus T_+, T_{var} \oplus T_+ >_s \oplus 1 \times \mathbf{g} \oplus \mathbf{L} \oplus T_{app}$ (2 vectors constructions both with an addition; a synchronous primitive; and a final application). That is to say, in any context, the expression adds T_+ during the asynchronous phase of the current superstep s, finishes it and begins a new superstep. On it own, the cost of such an expression can be simplify into $2 \times T_+ \oplus \mathbf{g} \oplus \mathbf{L}$.

3   Multi-BSP Programming in ML and Costs Semantics

3.1   The Multi-BSP Bridging Model

MULTI-BSP is a bridging *model* [17] which is adapted to hierarchical architectures, mainly *clusters* of *multi-cores*. It is an extension of the BSP bridging model. The structure and abstraction brought by MULTI-BSP allows to have portable programs with *scalable* performance predictions, without dealing with low-level details of the architectures. This model brings a *tree*-based view of nested components (*sub-machines*) of hierarchical architectures where the lowest stages (*leaves*) are processors and every other stage (*nodes*) contains memory.

Every component can execute code but they have to synchronise in favour of data exchange. Thus, MULTI-BSP does not allow subgroup synchronisation of any group of processors: at a stage i there is only a synchronisation of the sub-components, a synchronisation of each of the computational units that manage the stage $i-1$. So, a node executes some code on its nested components (*aka* "*children*"), then waits for results, does the communication and synchronises the sub-machine. A MULTI-BSP algorithm is thus composed by several supersteps, each step is synchronised for each sub-machine.

An instance of MULTI-BSP is defined by $\mathbf{d}$, the fixed depth of the (balanced and homogeneous) tree architecture, and by 4 parameters for each *stage i* of the tree: $(\mathbf{p_i}, \mathbf{g_i}, \mathbf{L_i}, \mathbf{m_i})$: $\mathbf{p_i}$ is the number of sub-components inside the $i-1$ stage; $\mathbf{g_i}$ is the *bandwidth* between stages i and $i-1$: the ratio of the number of operations to the number of words that can be transmitted in a second; $\mathbf{L_i}$ is the *synchronisation cost* of all sub-components of a component of $i-1$ stage; $\mathbf{m_i}$ is the amount of memory available at stage i for each component of this stage.

Thanks to those parameters, the cost of a MULTI-BSP algorithm can be computed as the sum of the costs of the supersteps of the root node, where the cost of each of these supersteps is the maximal cost of the supersteps of the sub-components (plus communication and synchronisation); And so on.

Let C_j^i be the communication cost of a superstep j at stage i: $C_j^i = h_j \times \mathbf{g_i} + \mathbf{L_i}$ where h_j the maximum size of the exchanged messages at superstep j, $\mathbf{g_i}$ the communication bandwidth with stage i and $\mathbf{L}_i$ the synchronisation cost. We can express the cost T of a MULTI-BSP algorithms as following:

$$T = \sum_{i=0}^{d-1} (\sum_{j=0}^{N_i-1} w_j^i + C_j^i)$$

where $\mathbf{d}$ is the depth of the architecture, N_i is the number of supersteps at stage i, w_j^i is the maximum computational cost of the superstep j within stage i.

It is to notice that the BSP and MULTI-BSP cost models both are a linear combination of costs for the asynchronous computations and costs of communications (separated by barriers).

3.2   The Multi-ML Language

MULTI-ML [1,2] (https://git.lacl.fr/vallombert/Multi-ML) is based on the idea of executing BSML-like codes on every stage of a MULTI-BSP architecture. This approach facilitates *incremental* development from BSML codes to MULTI-ML ones. MULTI-ML follows the MULTI-BSP approach where the hierarchical architecture is composed by *nodes* and *leaves*. On nodes, it is possible to build parallel vectors, as in BSML. This parallel data structure aims to manage values that are stored on the sub-nodes: at stage i, the code **let** v=$\ll$ e$\gg$ evaluates the expression e on each $i - 1$ stages.

Inside a vector, we note #x# to copy the value x stored at stage i to the memory $i - 1$. The (**mkpar** f) primitive is an alternative way to build a vector using a function f. Typed (int $\rightarrow \alpha$) $\rightarrow \alpha$ par, it aims to execute the given function to each processor identifiers (from 0 to $p_i - 1$) of a node locally on it; and then, distribute the results down to its sub-nodes. The main difference with the $\ll$ e$\gg$ notation is that (**mkpar** f) aims to reduce costs when the communication costs of e is high and the execution cost of f and its result is low. As in BSML, we also found the **proj**, **put** primitives and the syntax \$x\$, all of them with the same semantics.

We also introduce the concept of *multi-function* to recursively go through a MULTI-BSP architecture. A *multi-function* is a particular recursive function, defined by the keyword let multi, which is composed by two codes: the node and the leaf codes. The *recursion* is initiated by calling the multi-function (recursively) inside the scope of a parallel vector, that is to say, on the sub-nodes. The evaluation of a multi-function starts (and ends) on the root node. The following code shows how a multi-function is defined.

```
let  multi  mf [args]=
 | where node =
 | |  (* BSML code*)
 | |  ...
 | |  ≪ mf [args] ≫
 | |  ... in v
 | where leaf =
 | |  (* OCaml code *)
 | |  ... in v
```

After the definition of the multi-function mf on line 1 where [args] symbolises a set of arguments, we define the node code (from line 2 to 6). The recursive call of the multi-function is done on line 5, within the scope of a parallel vector. The node code ends with a value v, which is available as a result of the recursive call from the upper node. The leaf code, from lines 7 to 9 consists of sequential computations.

We also propose another parallel data structure called *tree*. A tree is a distributed structure where a value is stored in every nodes and leaves memories. A tree can be built using a multi-tree-function, with the **let multi tree** keyword and can be handled by several primitives of the language. We do not detail this construction here.

Similarly to BSML and its b and l localities, in MULTI-ML we introduce m when a value refers to the MULTI-BSP locality and s on leaves (sequential).

3.3   Cost Semantics

Extension.   To obtain core-MULTI-ML, we extends core-BSML with multi-functions as follow: $e ::= \cdots \mid (\mathbf{down}\, x) \mid \mathbf{multi}\, f x \to e \dagger e$.

The multi-function definition is written with the keyword **multi**. It takes one arguments and two expressions separated by the † symbol; the first argument stands for the node code and the second is for leaf code. The **down** primitive aims to transfer a value to all the sub-nodes. The transformation from the # syntax into the **down** primitive is obvious and work as other syntactic sugars of BSML. For example, the expression $<<\ e\#x\#\ >>$ is transformed into $\mathtt{apply}(\mathtt{replicate}(\mathbf{fun}\_x \to ex))(\mathbf{down}x)$. As the # annotated value is given as argument of the vector of functions, there are no redundant copies. The expression $<<\ \#x\#+\#x\#\ >>$ is transformed into a code that copy x to the sub-nodes, only once. Parallel vectors of values (and costs) now also depend of their deep level n in the MULTI-BSP architecture. Closures of multi-functions are also added. Thus we have $v ::= \cdots \mid <v_1, \ldots, v_{\mathbf{p}_n}> \mid \overline{(\mathbf{multi}\, f x \to e \dagger e)[\mathcal{E}]}$.

Adding Rules.   We must now extend our inference rules in order to take into account the multi-functions and the nested BSML codes. These rules are given in Fig. 5. They work as follow.

$$\text{MultiNode}\quad \frac{\begin{cases} \mathcal{E} \vdash^s e_1 \Downarrow_n^l \overline{(\mathbf{multi}\, f x \to e_1' \dagger e_2')[\mathcal{E}']} \rightsquigarrow^{s1} c_1 \\ \mathcal{E} \vdash^{s1} e_2 \Downarrow_n^l v \rightsquigarrow^{s2} c_2 \end{cases} \quad \mathcal{E}' \vdash^0 e_1' \Downarrow_{n+1}^b v' \rightsquigarrow^{s3} c_3}{\mathcal{E} \vdash^s (e_1\ e_2) \Downarrow_n^l v' \rightsquigarrow^{s3} T_{app} \oplus c_1 \oplus c_2 \oplus \max(c_3) \oplus \mathbf{L}_n)}$$

$$\text{MultiLeaf}\quad \frac{\begin{cases} \mathcal{E} \vdash^s e_1 \Downarrow_n^l \overline{(\mathbf{multi}\, f x \to e_1' \dagger e_2')[\mathcal{E}']} \rightsquigarrow^{s1} c_1 \\ \mathcal{E} \vdash^{s1} e_2 \Downarrow_n^l v \rightsquigarrow^{s2} c_2 \end{cases} \quad \mathcal{E}' \vdash^{s2} e_2' \Downarrow_{n+1} v' \rightsquigarrow^{s2} c_3}{\mathcal{E} \vdash^s (e_1\ e_2) \Downarrow_n^l v' \rightsquigarrow^{s2} T_{app} \oplus c_1 \oplus c_2 \oplus c_3)}$$

$$\text{MultiCall}\quad \frac{\begin{cases} \mathcal{E} \vdash^s e_1 \Downarrow^m \overline{(\mathbf{multi}\, f x \to e_1' \dagger e_2')[\mathcal{E}']} \rightsquigarrow^s c_1 \\ \mathcal{E} \vdash^s e_2 \Downarrow^m v \rightsquigarrow^s c_2 \end{cases} \quad \mathcal{E}' \vdash^0 e_2' \Downarrow_1^b v' \rightsquigarrow^{s3} c_3 \quad Valid(v', \mathcal{E}')}{\mathcal{E} \vdash^s (e_1\ e_2) \Downarrow^m v' \rightsquigarrow^s T_{app} \oplus c_1 \oplus c_2 \oplus \max(\max(c_3)) \oplus SizeOf(v') \times \mathbf{g} \oplus \mathbf{L}}$$

Fig. 5. The cost semantics of the core-MULTI-ML language.

These new rules need some updates of the previous rules. First, the $\Downarrow$ is parameterized by the different levels of execution of MULTI-ML and the stage n (beginning from 1). BSML rules has to be trivially updated with this stage in order to build the right size vectors.

As a node is a particular component where it is possible to express BSP parallelism, we must consider the synchronous costs generated by BSP computations. Those rules, at a stage n, are used to recurse trough the MULTI-BSP architecture using the multi-function. Therefore, the max function now first merge the vectors of the same (sub)superstep and finally we use this following equivalence (for each superstep s): $\max(n_1 \times T_1 \oplus \cdots \oplus n_t \times T_m \oplus < c_1, \ldots, c_{\mathbf{p}_n} >_s) \equiv \max(n_1 T_1 \oplus \cdots \oplus n_t \times T_t, \max_{i=1..\mathbf{p}_n}(c_i))$ that is we take the maximum between the computation of the node parent with the max of its own children.

The MULTICALL rule is for calling the multi-function at the level m. The counter of superstep is initiated to 0 as the stage to 1. The code of the node begins (level b). This rule terminates with a whole and synchronous broadcasting of the final value v where $\mathbf{g} = \mathbf{g}_1 + \mathbf{g}_2 \ldots + \mathbf{g}_d$ (as well for $\mathbf{L}$); This is due to the model of execution of MULTI-ML where the code outside multi-function is run by all the processors in order to manage the whole execution and thus the value must be known by all the processors. The maximum function allow to get the right cost of all child. The rule is possible only if v is valid (as in BSML). Our type system forbids expressions that have not this property [1] and we can assume that all the evaluated expressions are correct.

The MULTILEAF goes to leaf level. The number of supersteps still the same when going throw the leaf level (only sequential codes are allow).

The MULTINODE is for going throw the hierarchical architecture (inside a vector) from one node to another one (the child). Thus the stage is incremented. A final synchronisation is used to finally wait all the child before terminating the node code (the recursive call of the multi-function). This allow to take the maximum of computation of the sub supersteps as wanted in the MULTI-BSP cost model. In MULTI-ML, the building of a vector is an asynchronous operation with a emission of a signal of creation from the node processor to the subnodes (or leaves). It is thus no longer possible using the second equivalence of the $\oplus$ which only becomes commutative between two $\mathbf{L_n}$ (barrier) at a stage n.

It is to notice that the *Lookup* function need also to check the variable at the right memory. Indeed, a variable define in at the stage n is no available on another stages. To do this, one must adding indices in the environment $\mathcal{E}$. More details are available in [1]. Here, only the MULTINODE and MULTILEAF rules can be evaluated. The costs of the multi-function recursive call taking place on both the node and the leaf is simple. We just add the evaluation cost of e_1 and e_2, plus the multi-function call cost, resulting in the recursive call. The MULTINODE rule adds the C_i costs which result from the potential asynchronous computations done on the node. Thus, we collect all the costs engendered by multi-function recursion. As expected, this mechanism is not necessary on the MULTILEAF rule, as there is no parallel computation at this level.

4   Experiments

Thanks to the cost model embedded in the MULTI-BSP model, it is possible to estimate the evaluation cost of a MULTI-ML program. According to the MULTI-BSP parameters standing for a machine specification, it is then possible to predict the execution time of a program.

To verify that the cost estimation retrieved from the MULTI-BSP cost formulae is valid, we are going to compare the computation time of a simple algorithm to the predicted computation cost. To do so, we propose to analyse a matrix vector product algorithm based on the map/reduce skeleton. Using the MULTI-BSP parameters of the targeted architecture able to predict the computation time of various inputs. Our example has been written in a functional style using tail-recursive functions but thanks to the OCAML compiler, these functions are transformed into an efficient imperative version.

4.1 Algorithm Description

We consider a simple algorithm to compute the product of a matrix and a vector. Given a matrix $\mathcal{M}$ of dimension $n \times m$, where n stands for the number of lines and m form the number of columns, and a vector $\mathcal{V}$ of dimension n (number of lines) the computation is the following: $\mathcal{M} \times \mathcal{V} = x$, such as $x = (x_0, ..., x_n)$ where x is composed by m lines and $x_i = \sum_{j=0}^{n} \mathcal{M}_{ij} \times \mathcal{V}_j$. Now, to propose a parallel version of this matrix vector product, we choose to use the map/reduce skeleton [6]. Using map/reduce algorithms is an easy way to propose parallel algorithms using simple associative and commutative operators. A map/reduce algorithms works as following: (1) the data are distributed among the processing units; (2) the *map* operator is applied on each piece of data; (3) the *reduce* operator is used to combine the results; (4) the final result is thus obtained.

To implement the matrix vector multiplication we define: a map operator which compute the product of a matrix and a vector; and a reduce operator which takes i sub-matrices of size (n', m) and assemble them into a $(i \times n', m)$ matrix.

The BSP cost of the BSP algorithm is: $\mathcal{Q}(i) \times T_{map} \oplus \mathcal{Q}(i) \times \mathbf{g} \oplus \mathcal{Q}(i) \times T_{red} \oplus \mathbf{L}$ where $\mathcal{Q}(i)$ stands for the total amount data stored at processor i. The MULTI-BSP cost of the MULTI-BSP algorithm is: $\mathcal{S}(0) \times T_{map} \oplus \sum_{i=1}^{d}(\mathcal{S}(i-1) \times \mathbf{g}_{i-1} \oplus \mathbf{L}_{i-1}) \oplus \mathcal{S}(i) \times T_{red}$ where T_{map} (resp. T_{red}) is the time of the mapping (resp. reducing) and $\mathcal{S}(i)$ stands for the total amount data stored at level i; for example, we have $N \times M/2/2$ elements on each leaf of a dual-core with two thread per core. We assume the following size (quantity of memory) of values such as $SizeOf(\texttt{float}) = 64Bytes$ and $SizeOf(\texttt{floatarray}) = n \times SizeOf(\texttt{float})$ if the array contains n elements. We omit small overheads and alternative costs relative to each level for the sake of simplification. Furthermore, the cost of serialisation of the data is taken into account in the $\mathbf{g}$ parameter.

4.2 Algorithms Implementation

The BSML codes or mapping/reducing and their descriptions are available in [7,8]. In the context of MULTI-BSP functional programming, we must now write the map/reduce matrix vector product algorithm using the MULTI-ML language. As the MULTI-ML language uses a tree based hierarchical way of executing code, the map/reduces algorithms are almost embedded in the syntax of the language. Indeed, the map phase consists in mapping a function toward the leaves of the MULTI-BSP architecture, while the reduce phase is basically the combination of the results toward the root node.

In the map/reduce implementation, we assume that the values were previously distributed such as each leaves already contains the sub-matrices and nodes are empty. Thus, the distribution is handled by a tree data structure of matrices. As in our implementation a matrix is represented by a one dimension array, the input data is typed α array **tree**. The map multi-function is written in Fig. 6 (left). As expected, we call recursively the multi-function map toward the leaves. When reached, the leaves are going to apply the map operator f on their data stored in tda (the tree distributed array of sub-matrices). Then, we build a tree which contains the results on leaves.

```
let m_map f tda =
    let multi tree map tda =
        where node =
            let rc = ≪ map tda ≫ in
            finally (rc ,[])
        where leaf = f (at tda)
    in map tda
```

```
let m_reduce op e tda =
    let multi tree reduce tda =
        where node =
            let rc = ≪ reduce tda ≫ in
            let sub_vals = to_array rc in
            let res = fold_left op e sub_vals in
            finally (rc, res)
        where leaf = at tda
    in reduce tda
```

Fig. 6. Codes of the MULTI-ML mapping (left) and reducing (right).

After reaching the leaves using the recursive calls, the reduce multi-function simply retrieve the sub-results of its sub-nodes from rc. It transform the parallel data structure into a local array using to_array and apply the reduce operator of each sub-matrices. Finally, the resulting matrix is used to propagate the result to the root node (Fig. 6, right).

4.3 Performance Predictions

Benchmarks were performed on the following architecture: MIREV2 8 nodes, each with 2 quad-cores (AMD 2376 at 2.3 Ghz) with 16 GB of memory per node and a 1 Gbit/s network. Based on the computation and communication cost of each phases it is possible to compute the cost of the proposed algorithm. To do so, we use the MULTI-BSP parameters which can be estimated using the probe method [3]. We use the following parameters: $g_0 = \infty$, $g_1 = 6$, $g_2 = 3$ and $g_0 = 1100$, $g_1 = 1800$, $g_2 = 0$ and $L_0 = 149000$, $L_1 = 1100$, $L_2 = 1800$, $L_3 = 0$. For BSP we get $g = 1500$ and $L = 21000$.

Thank to a micro-benchmarking library [13] of OCAML, we have estimated the execution time of the main operators which are used in the map operator: multiplication, get a value from an array *etc.* The timings for each operators are available

Table 1. Operator timings in μs.

$T_{Def} = 2.921$	$T_{Let} = 1.312$	$T_{Get} = 1,324$	$T_{BoolAnd} = 0.184$
$T_{Clo} = 0.167$	$T_{Var} = 0.619$	$T_{FloatAdd} = 0,881$	$T_{IntEq} = 0.284$
$T_{FunApp} = 1.505$	$T_{Set} = 1,778$	$T_{FloatMult} = 1,317$	

in Table 1 where T_{mult}, T_{add}, T_{set} and T_{get} are respectively standing for multiplication, addition, affectation and read in an array. We have neglect the times to build the closures (and apply them) for both multi-functions and the recursive functions since most of the computations come from mapping and reducing.

Thus, we have that $T_{map} = 3 \times T_{get} \oplus T_{set} \oplus 2 \times T_{FloatMult} \oplus 3 \times T_{FloatAdd} \oplus 2 \times T_{BoolAnd} \oplus 2 \times T_{IntEq} + 10 \times T_{Var}$ and $T_{red} = T_{get} \oplus T_{set} \oplus 5 \times T_{var} \oplus T_{IntAdd} \oplus T_{IntEq}$. As the cost of such atomic operations are prone to significant variation because of the compilation optimisation, loops structures and cache mechanisms, we assume that those costs is *"a good approximation"* of the average computation time needed by these operations. A more precise approaches can be found in [10].

The performance prediction compared to the execution time of the matrix vector multiplication can be found in Fig. 7. We perform the tests for both BSML and MULTI-ML. We do not used all the cores since our current MULTI-ML implementation needs specific processes to handle nodes (which is not the case for BSML) and thus we want to be fair for the cost analysis. Note that it is a too small example and BSML is sometime more efficient than MULTI-ML. A comparison between the two languages on bigger examples is available in [1]. The tests has been done for 2 nodes (left) and then for 8 nodes (right).

We can observe that the performance prediction is coherent to the execution time of the algorithm (and its polynomial complexity). The curves slopes are similar even not very accurate. This is mainly due to the fact that the sequential cost of our method is no fine enough. For example, because this is a toy example, we do not use the cache possibilities of the MULTI-BSP model and thus MULTI-ML suffers for some miss-caches that are not currently predicted. The garbage collector of OCAML can also disturb the prediction.

5   Related Work

Close to BSP, the LOGP [5] models are, most of the time, used to study network capabilities and low-level libraries such as MPI. Extensions of BSP such as [14] were proposed to allows sub-synchronisations. Hierarchical approaches were also proposed in [4]. Parallel algorithmic skeleton are often use to proposed a cost prediction based on a structured approach, as in [9]. In [12], a shape analysis techniques developed in the FISH programming language is used to propose language with an accurate, portable cost model.

Resource Aware ML (RAML) [10] allows to automatically and statically computes the resource-use bounds for OCAML programs. A version for parallel (multi-threading) and sequential composition was proposed.

Those models seems not adapted to our approach as they do not provide both simplicity and accuracy for hierarchical architectures with a structured execution scheme.

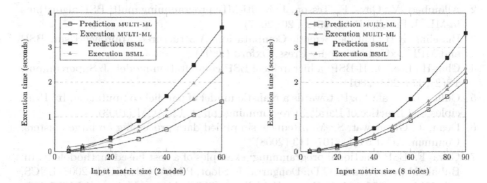

Fig. 7. Performance prediction compared to execution time for BSML and MULTI-ML; For 2 nodes (left) and 8 nodes (right).

6 Conclusion

Overview of the Work. In this article we propose a formal semantic with cost annotations allowing cost prediction of MULTI-BSP algorithms. We propose a set of rules adapted to a (core) version of a sequential and purely functional version of ML. Then, we extend this semantics to allows BSP, and then, MULTI-BSP codes. Thanks to this incremental approach, we propose a restrained set of rules allowing cost prediction of MULTI-BSP algorithms.

To expose the usability of the cost model embedded in the semantics, we compare the performance prediction and actual benchmarks on several parallel architectures. As our approach is simplified and consider abstract BSP and MULTI-BSP parameters and also is based on the estimated execution time of atomic operation, it may suffers to accuracy issue. We show that our cost estimation is close to the execution time on a simple map/reduce algorithm apply to a matrix-vector multiplication.

Future Work. An interesting use of this cost semantic is to propose a analysis able to statically infer a cost of a given algorithm. Such an approach is available for programming imperative BSP algorithm [11] and could be extended to functional MULTI-BSP programming using an approach similar to the one proposed in [10]: It would be possible to give the cost of a program at compile time.

References

1. Allombert, V.: Functional Abstraction for Programming Multi-Level Architectures: Formalisation and Implementation. Ph.D. thesis, UPEC (2017)
2. Allombert, V., Gava, F., Tesson, J.: Multi-ML: programming multi-BSP algorithms in ML. J. Parallel Prog. **45**(2), 20 (2017)
3. Bisseling, R.H.: Parallel Scientic Computation: A Structured Approach Using BSP and MPI. Oxford University Press, Oxford (2004)
4. Cha, H., Lee, D.: H-BSP: a hierarchical BSP computation model. J. Supercomput. **18**(2), 179–200 (2001)
5. Culler, D., et al.: LogP: towards a realistic model of parallel computation. In: Principles and Practice of Parallel Programming, pp. 1–12. ACM (1993)
6. Dean, J., Ghemawat, S.: MapReduce: simplified data processing on large clusters. Commun. ACM **51**(1), 107–113 (2008)
7. Gava, F.: BSP functional programming: examples of a cost based methodology. In: Bubak, M., van Albada, G.D., Dongarra, J., Sloot, P.M.A. (eds.) ICCS 2008. LNCS, vol. 5101, pp. 375–385. Springer, Heidelberg (2008). https://doi.org/10.1007/978-3-540-69384-0_43
8. Gesbert, L., Gava, F., Loulergue, F., Dabrowski, F.: Bulk synchronous parallel ML with exceptions. Future Gener. Comput. Syst. **26**(3), 486–490 (2010)
9. Hayashi, Y., Cole, M.: Static performance prediction of skeletal parallel programs. Parallel Algorithms Appl. **17**(1), 59–84 (2002)
10. Hoffmann, J., Das, A., Weng, S.C.: Towards automatic resource bound analysis for OCaml. In: Principles of Programming Languages. POPL 2017. ACM (2017)
11. Jakobsson, A.: Automatic Cost Analysis for Imperative BSP Programs. Int. J. Parallel Prog. (Feb 2018)
12. Jay, C.: Costing parallel programs as a function of shapes. Sci. Comput. Prog. **37**(1), 207–224 (2000)
13. Roshan, J., et al.: Core_bench: Micro-benchmarking library for OCaml (2014)
14. de la Torre, P., Kruskal, C.P.: Submachine locality in the bulk synchronous setting. In: Bougé, L., Fraigniaud, P., Mignotte, A., Robert, Y. (eds.) Euro-Par 1996. LNCS, vol. 1124, pp. 352–358. Springer, Heidelberg (1996). https://doi.org/10.1007/BFb0024723
15. Abella, J., et al.: wcet analysis methods: pitfalls and challenges on their trustworthiness. In: IEEE Symposium on Industrial Embedded Systems, pp. 39–48 (2015)
16. Valiant, L.G.: A bridging model for parallel computation. Commun. ACM **33**(8), 103–111 (1990)
17. Valiant, L.G.: A bridging model for multi-core computing. J. Comput. Syst. Sci. **77**(1), 154–166 (2011)

Exploiting the Table of Energy and Power Leverages

Issam Raïs[1], Laurent Lefèvre[1(✉)], Anne-Cécile Orgerie[3], and Anne Benoit[1,2]

[1] Laboratoire LIP, École Normale Supérieure de Lyon & Inria, Lyon, France
{issam.rais,laurent.lefevre,anne.benoit}@inria.fr
[2] Georgia Institute of Technology, Atlanta, GA, USA
[3] Univ. Rennes, Inria, CNRS, IRISA, Rennes, France
anne-cecile.orgerie@inria.fr

Abstract. Large scale distributed systems and supercomputers consume huge amounts of energy. To address this issue, a large set of hardware and software capabilities and techniques (leverages) exist to modify power and energy consumption in large scale systems. Discovering, benchmarking and efficiently exploiting such leverages, remains a real challenge for most of the users. In this paper, we define leverages and the *table of leverages*, and we propose algorithms and predicates that ease the reading of the table of leverages and extract knowledge from it.

1 Introduction

Data centers worldwide consumed around 194 terawatt hours (TWh) of electricity in 2014, or about 1% of total demand [2]. This worrying consumption has direct financial and environmental consequences on data center managers, like Cloud providers and supercomputer operators. Several techniques have been developed in order to lower the electrical consumption of data centers. These techniques, that we call leverages, can improve the energy efficiency of data centers at different levels: hardware, middleware, and application. Hardware leverages include Dynamic Voltage and Frequency Scaling (DVFS) [11] and shutdown techniques [10]. At the middleware level, energy-efficient resource allocation policies for job managers are examples of leverages [7]. Finally, leverages at the application level include green programming [1].

While many of these leverages have been independently studied in the literature, few works consider the utilization of several leverages at the same time, and no more than two leverages. Yet, the utilization of a given leverage can impact both the utilization and the efficiency of another leverage. The variety of leverages is added to the data center's complexity, in terms of size and hardware heterogeneity, and makes energy efficiency complex to reach for the users who have access to multiple leverages.

In this work, we aim at extending the current state of the art, which is studying the influence of one or two leverages at maximum at the same time, thus ignoring the impacts incurred by the utilization of more leverages. Thus, we

© Springer Nature Switzerland AG 2018
J. Vaidya and J. Li (Eds.): ICA3PP 2018, LNCS 11336, pp. 175–185, 2018.
https://doi.org/10.1007/978-3-030-05057-3_13

proposed a generic definition, combination and knowledge extraction of multiple leverages in order to fully explore their combined impacts.

We propose a first approach toward a completely automated process to characterize the leverages available on a data center node. The key idea of our contribution consists in providing hints to users about the most suitable solution for their application from a defined score table with a value for each leverage combination and each studied metric. Through these tables could be derived knowledge about leverage combination and effects they incur on each other. From the definition of a table of leverages, a tool to help a user, a developer or an administrator to choose which leverage or leverage combination suits the best his objectives (here with a focus on energy or power metrics), the contribution of this paper consists in the algorithms proposed to extract knowledge about the interaction of leverages and their influence on a given metric.

The remaining of this paper is structured as follows. Section 2 formalizes the concept of leverages, and illustrates this formalism on the leverages under consideration in this paper. Section 3 defines and explains how to build the table of leverages. Section 4 presents the experimental setup and a first full example of table of leverages. Section 5 then shows how to exploit the raw data of the table of leverages and extract useful knowledge. Finally, Sect. 6 concludes this work and gives perspectives.[1]

2   Leverage Definition

In this section, we first propose a formalization of a leverage. Second, we apply this formalism to the leverages that we selected for this paper.

Definition 1. *A leverage L is composed of $S = \{s_0, s_1, \ldots, s_n\}$, the set of available valid states of L, and s_c, the current state of L.*

Thus, an energy or power leverage is a leverage that has a high impact on the energy or power consumption of a device through its various states or through the modification of its current state. Switching from one state to another can have a cost in terms of time and energy. Yet, in the current work, we focus on studying the impacts of leverage combinations over a single intensive application phase [4], and thus we do not study the switching costs between states.

In this paper, we consider multiple leverages available on current hardware, namely multi-thread, computation precision and vectorization. These leverages belong to different categories of leverages: application level with computation precision and vectorization techniques, and middleware level with multithreading. These leverages are described hereafter.

---

[1] This work is supported by the ELCI project, a French FSN project that associates academic and industrial partners to design and provide software environment for very high performance computing. Experiments were carried out using the Grid'5000 testbed, supported by a scientific interest group hosted by Inria and including CNRS, RENATER and several Universities (https://www.grid5000.fr).

Multi-thread Leverage. The first studied leverage is a middleware-level leverage that permits the usage of multiple cores during computation. OpenMP [5], a well-known application programming interface abstraction for multi-threading, can be used to exploit this intra-node parallelism of multi-cores. It consists of a set of directives that modifies the behavior of the executed code, where a master thread forks a specific number of slave threads that run concurrently.

This multi-thread leverage increases the CPU utilization of the node. Consequently, because of the non-power proportionality of current hardware architectures [10], this leverage can improve the energy efficiency of the node. In the rest of the paper, the multi-thread leverage is denoted by $nbThreads$ with the set of states $\{1, \ldots, n_{max}\}$, where 1 means that one OpenMP thread is used, and n_{max} corresponds to the maximum number of threads that could be launched simultaneously on the node. In this work, only the extreme states, 1 and n_{max}, are explored.

Computation Precision Leverage. The second leverage belongs to the application level and exploits the various computation precision options available on actual hardware (i.e., int, float, double). Such a leverage alters the precision of the results computed by the application, but lower precision translates into shorter data representation and so, less computation and less energy consumption. At the application level, the user can specify a desired Quality-of-Service that can be expressed as accessible computation precision states.

This precision leverage is denoted by $Precision$, and the set of states is {int, float, double}, corresponding to the data format for the application. For each of these states, a different code version is provided.

Vectorization Leverage. Finally, the last studied leverage concerns the application level. Current CPUs allow the usage of vectorization capabilities to exploit intra-core parallelism. On Intel architectures, it started with MMX instruction in Pentium P5 architectures in 1997 [9]. It was then extended to SSE [6]. SSE was then extended to SSE2, SSE3, SSSE3 and finally SSE4. AVX [8] then introduces new instructions, followed by AVX2 and finally AVX512 available in XeonPhi architecture. In this paper, we focus on SSE3 and AVX2, which are representative of the SSE and AVX families. These instruction sets permit single instruction on multiple data (SIMD) at application level.

This vectorization leverage is denoted by $Vectorization$. The set of states is {none, SSE3, AVX2}, where $none$ means that no vectorization is used. For each of these states, a different code version is provided using the specific intrinsics and adequate compilation flags for each version.

The proposed leverage formalism described above is used in the rest of the paper to easily describe the state of each considered leverage and the possible combinations of leverages. The three leverages studied here are chosen to be representative examples of available leverages on modern architectures and frequently used during HPC applications. The methodology proposed in this paper is designed to be applied to any number and any type of leverages.

3   The Table of Leverages

We describe the table of leverages, which relies on metrics and benchmarks to characterize the performance and energy impact of each leverage combination on a given node. For each metric and each benchmark, a score is attributed to a given leverage combination. The table is then used to extract knowledge about each leverage and evaluate impacts of leverage combinations in order to help the users to utilize their computing infrastructure in a more energy-efficient way.

Metrics. Leverages may influence the quality of service or performance of an application. For instance, shutdown techniques may induce latency in waking up the required nodes. Consequently, for these leverages, users need to determine their acceptable trade-off between energy-related metrics and performance metrics. The table of leverages relies on three different metrics that represent both energy and performance constraints. These metrics are measured for a given period of time corresponding to the time spent during benchmark execution.

The two first metrics are energy and power related metrics. To define them, we introduce the following notations: $T = \{t_0, \ldots, t_N\}$ is the set of time stamps of energy consumption measurements of a given run; t_0 and t_N represent the starting and ending timestamps (with a distance of one second), respectively; p_j, $j \in [0, N]$, represents the power consumption (in Watt), of the considered node for the timestamp t_j. **Metric 1:** The average power consumption of an executable is denoted $avrgWatt$, and it is defined as $avrgWatt = \sum_{j \in [0,N]} p_j / (N + 1)$. **Metric 2:** The energy consumption of an executable is denoted $Joules$. It represents the energy consumption of the complete node used between t_0 and t_N. It is defined as $Joules = \sum_{j \in [0,N-1]} (t_{j+1} - t_j) \times p_j$. **Metric 3:** The last metric concerns the performance of the run, and is expressed as the execution time, denoted $Time$. It includes whole execution time of an executable, including initialization.

Benchmarks. A benchmark corresponds to a self-contained application that is representative of typical applications or portions of applications. The benchmark is compiled before the run, and once launched, the metrics previously defined are collected during its execution.

Here, for the sake of clarity, we evaluate only one benchmark for a set of embedded leverages. We chose to focus on a well-known CPU intensive code: the line per line matrix multiplication (LpL MM) of dense random large squared matrices (8192 as dimension size). The same algorithm is implemented for the various leverage combinations. The considered leverages are multi-thread, computation precision and vectorization. For the last two leverages, a different state means a different version of code, here generated by hand using dedicated intrinsics and compilation flags (-O3 -msse3 -mavx2). We deactivated the auto vectorization of the compiler (-fno-tree-vectorize) to have a control over the chosen intrinsics and because auto generation of vectorizable code is not one of the focused leverage in this paper.

Formalization of the Table of Leverages. Here, we describe how to compute the score associated to each metric for each leverage. Let X, Y, Z be the sets of available states of three leverages χ, ψ, ω (corresponding to S, the set of states for a given leverage L, from Definition 1): $X = \{x_0, \ldots, x_{n_x}\}$, $Y = \{y_0, \ldots, y_{n_y}\}$, and $Z = \{z_0, \ldots, z_{n_z}\}$. Let $g_1, \ldots, g_m$ be the measured metric functions, as for instance $avrgWatt$, $Joules$, and $Time$. For all u $(1 \leq u \leq m)$, $g_u(x_i, y_j, z_k)$ is the value of metric g_u for the states x_i, y_j, z_k for the leverages χ, ψ, ω.

In the table of leverages, each line corresponds to a combination of states for each leverage and the columns correspond to the measured metrics. We normalize each value on the minimum value for each metric. These normalized values constitute the scores indicated in the table of leverages. Let $h_1, \ldots, h_m$ be the normalized versions of $g_1, \ldots, g_m$. So, we have, for $1 \leq u \leq m$, $h_u(x_i, y_j, z_k) = \dfrac{g_u(x_i, y_j, z_k)}{\min\limits_{x_{i'} \in X, y_{j'} \in Y, z_{k'} \in Z} g_u(x_{i'}, y_{j'}, z_{k'})}$, with $h_u(x_i, y_j, z_k)$ being the value in the table of leverages in column of metric u and corresponding to the line for the states x_i, y_j, z_k respectively for the leverages χ, ψ, ω.

For application-level leverages, here *Precision* and *Vectorization*, the chosen benchmarks correspond to a different combination of application leverage states. Leverage *nbThreads* changes its state through environment variable. When all states are covered, the table of leverages is complete for the considered benchmark. Reducing the creation time of such a table is not the focus of this paper.

4   Building and Analyzing the Table of Leverages

In this section, we present the table of leverages built on a node from our experimental testbed, Grid'5000 [3]. Grid'5000 deploys clusters linked with dedicated high performance networks in several cities in France. As our focus is on energy and performance related metrics, we used the Lyon site, where the energy consumption of every computing node is monitored through a dedicated wattmeter, exposing one power measurement per second with a 0.125 Watts accuracy. The Nova cluster from Lyon is used in the following. This cluster contains Dell PowerEdge R430 with 2 CPU E5-2620 v4 of 8 cores each, 32 GB of memory, 2 HDD disks of 300 GB each.

We applied our previous methodology for the three chosen leverages to the CPU intensive benchmark. This allows us to explore all possible states of chosen leverages, and thus to build a complete table of leverages. The table has the following format: the first three columns present the states of the *nbThreads*, *Precision*, and *Vectorization* leverages respectively, while the last three columns show the normalized results of the three metrics *avrgWatt*, *Joules*, and *Time*, respectively, for every combination of leverage. As can be seen in Table 1 (first six columns), a line represents results of all gathered metrics for the execution of a representative load for a chosen combination of leverages. The results are normalized as explained before. The table of leverages gathers the knowledge of a Nova node, for a given workload done for multiple states of leverages combined.

Table 1. Normalized table of leverage states and ranked impact for line per line matrix multiplication (LpL MM) benchmark on a Nova node.

Leverage states			Table of leverages			Ranked impact		
nbThreads (T)	Prec. (P)	Vector. (V)	avrgWatt	Joules	Time	avrgWatt	Joules	Time
1	int	none	1.05	65.09	61.89	P,T,V	P,T,V	P,T,V
1	int	SSE3	1.06	28.26	26.56	P,V,T	V,P,T	V,P,T
1	int	AVX2	1.06	29.32	27.67	P,V,T	V,P,T	V,P,T
1	float	none	1.05	72.97	69.67	P,V,T	P,T,V	P,T,V
1	float	SSE3	1.06	33.8	31.89	V,P,T	V,P,T	V,P,T
1	float	AVX2	1.05	36.8	34.89	P,V,T	V,P,T	V,P,T
1	double	none	1.06	81.59	76.89	P,T,V	P,T,V	P,T,V
1	double	SSE3	1.07	58.52	54.89	V,P,T	V,P,T	V,P,T
1	double	AVX2	1.06	57.72	54.22	P,V,T	V,P,T	V,P,T
32	int	none	1.43	13.48	9.44	P,T,V	T,P,V	T,P,V
32	int	SSE3	1.4	4.68	3.33	P,V,T	T,V,P	T,V,P
32	int	AVX2	1.0	1.0	1.0	P,V,T	T,V,P	T,V,P
32	float	none	1.45	7.4	5.11	P,T,V	T,P,V	T,P,V
32	float	SSE3	1.41	3.76	2.67	V,P,T	T,P,V	T,P,V
32	float	AVX2	1.56	3.11	2.0	P,V,T	T,V,P	T,V,P
32	double	none	1.53	8.34	5.44	P,T,V	T,P,V	T,P,V
32	double	SSE3	1.53	8.52	5.56	V,T,P	T,P,V	T,P,V
32	double	AVX2	1.54	7.0	4.56	P,T,V	T,V,P	T,V,P

Explanation of the Table: A lot of unexpected results, at first sight, are detected in Table of leverage 1, like the combination with *int* being better than *float* and *double* when *1* and *none* are the chosen state for the *nbThread* and *Vectorization* leverages, with this trend being reversed with *nbThreads=32*.

From the set of combination with *1* as the chosen state for leverage *nbThreads*, it is logic to see that *int* is quicker than *float* then *double* from a cache usage perspective. Indeed, more data can be brought into the cache to compute without the need to fetch new data compared to float or double representation that need more space for the same amount of elements. As for the *SSE* and *AVX* combinations, we have tremendous gain while using it compared to *None*, as it uses vectorial capabilities of the used core. Using a leverage usually comes with a cost. This statement is also true for the *Vectorization* leverage. An operation on vectors has costs, even if it is low. For instance, it is known that loading and saving vectors has a non null cost. With only one active thread, the current architecture, Broadwell here, allows turbo boost, a technology that permits to reach a much higher frequency that the available ones (here it can reach 3.0 GHz, when average frequency is 2.1 GHz). Also, when the OS detects too much load on a core, it context switches the running process and runs it on another core. Hence, the kernel saves the states (stack, registers) of the current process and loads it on another core, implying a storing and loading cost of the given process. This phenomenon can happened several times during a second. Thus, saving and charging states can create a lot of cache misses, which could be dramatical with usage of vectorization, where loading and saving vectors is not free. As *AVX* has longer vectors, its operation costs on vectors can be longer than SSE. Thus, it starts to be beneficial only when comparing *double* combinations for such a *Vectorization* leverage.

When threads are up to 32, data is more likely to be shared between caches of various used cores. Without the previous struggles from caches for one core and because it is also well known that floating points operations(*float* and *doubles* here) are well optimized on current architectures and perform better than integers, {32, float, none} and {32, double, none} perform better than {32, int, none}. All threads are sharing data on separated cache, *SSE* and *AVX* outperforms the none configuration, with *AVX* always outperforming *SSE* for a fixed combination. Due to this data repartition between caches implied by the chosen configuration of the *nbThreads* leverage, there is enough computation to overcome costs of larger vector operations, here *AVX* for all combinations.

Note that the best combination for all metrics used here is always the {32, int, AVX2} combination. This result is the best combination to choose only if we have no constraints about leverage choices. It is expected to see variation, as leverages highly modulate the usage of nodes, either from intensity of usage for example of caches, core usage, availability of specific leverages (like seen with turbo boost with one thread). Results of metrics from combination of leverages is thus complicated to fully understand without a detailed knowledge of the architecture, the underlying used leverages and their influences on a given context. We propose predicates that helps a user underline such interesting points of interest from the table of leverages. For example, this table could help a user to choose a combination taking into account a fixed leverage state. Or to answer the following question: is there a leverage or a state of leverage that is always better for a given metric?

5   Exploiting the Table of Leverages

In this section, we describe the main contribution of this paper: a methodology to exploit the table of leverages and to extract useful knowledge, such as the influence and impact of one or multiple leverages on a given metric or set of metrics. We propose two focuses for extracting a score for each leverage. The first one corresponds to the actual table: it normalizes the results of a given metric for every explored configuration. The second one computes a ratio of contribution for each leverage in order to expose the most relevant leverage (the one with the largest contribution to the considered metric). We define four exploitation predicates that ease the analysis of the table, and answer questions. We illustrate these predicates and the answers of these questions on the selected table (Table 1). These questions target a single metric, h_u.

Question 1: Is a selected combination of leverages states the best one for metric h_u? If a given combination is always the best, it means it should always be applied, if possible, if one wants to optimize h_u. Consider a combination of states x_a, y_b, z_c of leverages χ, ψ, ω for metric h_u. We need to check whether for all $i \in [0, \ldots, n_x] \backslash \{a\}$, $j \in [0, \ldots, n_y] \backslash \{b\}$, and $k \in [0, \ldots, n_z] \backslash \{c\}$, we have $h_u(x_a, y_b, z_c) \leq h_u(x_i, y_j, z_k)$. On Nova nodes and for the three leverages (Table 1), the best combination for all three studied metrics is {32, int, AVX2}.

Question 2: When I fix a state, do I always improve metric h_u? Consider state x_a of leverage χ. We want to check whether for all $i \in [0, \ldots, n_x] \backslash \{a\}$, for all $l, j \in [0, \ldots, n_y]$, and for all $m, k \in [0, \ldots, n_z]$, we have $h_u(x_a, y_l, z_m) \leq h_u(x_i, y_j, z_k)$. On the example of Table 1, for the *Joules* and *Time* metric, only the n_{max} (here, 32) state of *nbThreads* leverage answers this predicate, meaning that using this state will always be beneficial. No specific results can be obtained with this question for the *avrgWatt* metric, meaning that no leverage state is always better for this metric when used.

Question 3: If some states are fixed for a subset of leverages, is a given state for the remaining leverages the best choice to optimize h_u? Consider that the state of leverages ψ, ω is fixed to y_b, z_c. We are asking whether state x_a of leverage χ is the best choice for metric h_u. Therefore, we need to check whether for all $i \in [0, \ldots, n_x] \backslash \{a\}$, we have $h_u(x_a, y_b, z_c) \leq h_u(x_i, y_b, z_c)$, which tells for instance that for the fixed combination {32, SSE3}, the best state for the *Precision* leverage is *float*, when considering the *Joules* or *Time* metric (Table 1). Although, when focusing on *avrgWatt* as the studied metric, for the {32, SSE3} fixed combination, the best state for the *Precision* metric is *int*.

If only state z_c for leverage ω is fixed, and we consider states x_a and y_b of leverages χ and ψ respectively, we check whether for all $i \in [0, \ldots, n_x]$ and for all $j \in [0, \ldots, n_y]$, we have $h_u(x_a, y_b, z_c) \leq h_u(x_i, y_j, z_c)$. Concerning the *Joules* metric (Table 1) for the fixed state *float* of the *Precision* leverage, the best combination for the *nbThreads* and *Vectorization* leverages is {32, AVX2}. However, for the *avrgWatt* metric, fixing again the state *float* of the *Precision* leverage, the best combination is now {32, SSE3}.

Applying this predicate allows us to extract some unexpected results. Concerning the *Joules* and *Time* metrics, for the *Precision* and *Vectorization* leverages, no state emerges as the best one. In fact, it highly depends on the chosen state of other leverages. One could for instance expect *int* to always be the best state, but when comparing the {32, double, none} with {32, int, none}, we see that the *double* combination is more effective than the *int* combination. Similar conclusions can be drawn when the *Vectorization* leverage is used. *AVX2* has larger vectors than *SSE3*, thus we would expect it to be always more efficient. However, when *nbThreads* state is equal to 1, {1, float, SSE3} is more effective than {1, float, AVX2}, leading to a different best choice when combined to the n_{max} state (here, 32), where {32, float, AVX2} is more effective than {32, float, SSE3}. Note that this combination emerges as the best one when *SSE3* is fixed.

Concerning the *avrgWatt* metric, we also get unexpected knowledge. In opposition to the *Joules* and *Time* metrics, no state emerges as the best one for none of the studied leverages. As *AVX2* has larger vectors than *SSE3*, we would expect it to always stress more the CPU, thus always having higher values for this metric. It is the case with the {32, float} and {32, double} combinations. However, it is not observed with other combinations. When *nbThreads=1*, *int* is always the best choice to minimize this metric, whatever the chosen state for *Precision* and *Vectorization* leverages. Moreover, when *Vectorization* and *nbThreads* are set to any studied states, *int* is also always the best choice to minimize the *avrgWatt* metric.

Question 4: Given a combination for all the leverages, how can we rank the states in terms of contribution for metric h_u? To answer this question, we consider a set of states x_a, y_b, z_c of leverages χ, ψ, ω. Then, for each state $w \in \{x_a, y_b, z_c\}$, we compute the contribution score $mc(w)$ for this state on metric h_u as follows. For state x_a of leverage χ, $mc(x_a) = \frac{h_u(x_a, y_b, z_c)}{\max\limits_{i \in [0, \ldots, n_x]} h_u(x_i, y_b, z_c)}$. We define similarly the contribution of states for the other leverages ψ and ω. Then, we rank the contribution scores $mc(x_a)$, $mc(y_b)$, $mc(z_c)$ in ascending order to answer the question.

Table 1 (last three columns) presents the scoring related to the table of leverages. For the best combination {32, int, AVX2}, the ranking goes as follows for the *Joules* metric: "T,V,P" or "*nbThreads, Vectorization, Precision*", meaning that the chosen state for T here is the most contributing state in this combination, followed by the V, and then P states. Thus, for this combination, the precision leverage with the *int* position has the lowest contribution.

This ranking points out unexpected results for the *Joules* metric. We notice a switch between two positions of a given leverage for the fixed combination of other leverage states: {32, double}. In fact, when comparing the scoring of {32, double, SSE3} with {32, double, AVX2}, we get respectively "T,P,V" and "T,V,P". In the first case, *double* and *SSE3* have the same worst possible score, 1.0, meaning that it is the worst state of this leverage for this combination. In the second case, *AVX2* scores better than *SSE3* and thus, it is above *double*. When *nbThreads=1*, we note that combinations including *SSE3* and *AVX2* states always have the *Vectorization* leverage state as the most contributing one, which leads to the conclusion that it is always better to use *SSE3* and *AVX2* states for the *Vectorization* leverage. For the {32, float, SSE3} combination, we get the scoring "T,P,V". *float* gets a better score and thus a better position than *SSE3* because it is the best leverage state for the {32, SSE3} combination, leading to the conclusion that choosing *float* instead of other *Precision* leverage states contributes more than choosing *SSE3* instead of other *Vectorization* leverage states for this combination. For the *avrgWatt* metric, scoring underlines the fact that when choosing *int* as a state of *Precision* leverage, and for a fixed state of the *Vectorization* leverage, the sorting is always the same. In fact, {32, int, none}, {32, int, SSE3} and {32, int, AVX2} get the exact same sorting of contribution that {1, int, none}, {1, int, SSE3} and {1, int, AVX2}, respectively. Moreover, *int* is always the most contributing leverage state, which shows that *int* is always a good choice to improve this metric. This scoring also underlines the fact that in order to minimize the *avrgWatt* metric, a user should better focus on P and V leverages, asT is never the most contributing one. This scoring highlights results that would have been difficult to notice just by looking at the table. It allows a user to quantify how much a leverage position used in a combination contributes to the overall performance for a given metric.

6   Conclusion

Energy efficiency is a growing concern. In the context of HPC and datacenters where the size of infrastructures grows drastically, energy consumption has to be taken into account as a high expense. There is a wide range of techniques, that we formally define as leverages, that permits to modulate the computing capabilities and/or the energy/power used by a device. We propose a generic solution to extract fine grain knowledge and hints from the table of leverages, thanks to the defined predicates. Our solution underlines new knowledge about leverages alone and about combinations of leverages. Thus, it allows us to extract influences of leverages on each other and understandable knowledge by the user.

Knowledge could be extracted from a table on CPU-intensive workload. For example, our solution underlines the fact that if *Precision* is set to the *double* state, it is always better to use it with *AVX2* state for the *Vectorization* leverage to minimize the *Joules* metric. Also, for *Vectorization* fixed to the *SSE3* state, our solution tells us that *float* is the best state to minimize the *Joules* metric. We also underline the fact that some unexpected behavior can be seen when combining leverages. For example, we underline the fact that changing *float* or *int* to *double* for *Precision*, and keeping the *SSE3* state activated for *Vectorization* state, turns out to be counterproductive for the *Joules* metric.

The first short term future work is the parallelization of the creation of the table of leverages in order to improve the time needed to build it. Then, we plan to apply this methodology on other non CPU-intensive phases, such as IO, HDD, and RAM-intensive phases with appropriate leverages for every phase. Finally, a future working direction would be to extend this methodology to costly transition leverage states, as for instance shutdown policies. Also, we would like to investigate how to reduce the completion time for building such a table. In fact, the time to solution here could be greatly reduced, for example by predicting which run is not needed to know values of relevant metrics using learning or prediction techniques.

References

1. Acar, H., Alptekin, G.I., Gelas, J.-P., Ghodous, P.: Towards a green and sustainable software. In: Concurrent Engineering, pp. 471–480 (2015)
2. International Energy Agency. Digitalization & Energy. White paper (2017)
3. Balouek, D., et al.: Adding virtualization capabilities to the Grid'5000 testbed. In: Ivanov, I.I., van Sinderen, M., Leymann, F., Shan, T. (eds.) CLOSER 2012. CCIS, vol. 367, pp. 3–20. Springer, Cham (2013). https://doi.org/10.1007/978-3-319-04519-1_1

4. Chetsa, G.L.T.E.A.: A user friendly phase detection methodology for hpc systems' analysis. In: IEEE International Conference on and IEEE Cyber, Physical and Social Computing (2013)
5. Dagum, L., Menon, R.: OpenMP: an industry standard API for shared-memory programming. IEEE Comput. Sci. Eng. **5**, 46–55 (1998)
6. Gallas, B., Verma, V.: Embedded Pentium (R) processor system design for Windows CE, Wescon/98, pp. 114–123. IEEE (1998)
7. Georgiou, Y., Glesser, D., Rzadca, K., Trystram, D.: A scheduler-level incentive mechanism for energy efficiency in HPC. In: CCGrid, pp. 617–626 (2015)
8. Lomont, C.: Introduction to intel advanced vector extensions. Intel White Paper, pp. 1–21 (2011)
9. Peleg, A., Weiser, U.: MMX technology extension to the Intel architecture. IEEE Micro **16**(4), 42–50 (1996)
10. Raïs, I., Orgerie, A.-C., Quinson, M.: Impact of shutdown techniques for energy-efficient cloud data centers. In: Carretero, J., Garcia-Blas, J., Ko, R.K.L., Mueller, P., Nakano, K. (eds.) ICA3PP 2016. LNCS, vol. 10048, pp. 203–210. Springer, Cham (2016). https://doi.org/10.1007/978-3-319-49583-5_15
11. Suleiman, D., Ibrahim, M., Hamarash, I.: Dynamic voltage frequency scaling (DVFS) for microprocessors power and energy reduction. In: International Conference on Electrical and Electronics Engineering (2005)

A Semantic Web Based Intelligent IoT Model

Chao Qu(iD), Ming Tao(✉)(iD), Jie Zhang(iD), Xiaoyu Hong(iD), and Ruifen Yuan(iD)

School of Computer Science and Network Security,
Dongguan University of Technology, Dongguan 523808, China
{quc,zhangjie,hongxy,yuanrf}@dgut.edu.cn,
ming.tao@mail.scut.edu.cn

Abstract. Different from the sensor network, the devices in the intelligent Internet of Things (IoT) should be able to organize and coordinate spontaneously to accomplish specific tasks. By taking advantage of various intelligent technologies, we proposed an intelligent IoT model based on the Semantic Web. The framework consists of top ontology, entity link layer, semantic label layer, service register center, transaction construction layer, and transaction execution control layer. For the sake of constructing and executing the transactions automatically in the intelligent IoT, entity functions are represented by Semantic Web Services. Additionally, the framework also acts as a manager during the execution of a transaction and makes effective management and control to the entities. We demonstrated the effectiveness and superiority of the proposed model with a case study of the comprehensive rescue service for transportation accidents.

Keywords: Intelligent IoT · Semantic Web · IoT framework

1 Introduction

The ultimate purpose of IoT is to realize the smart interconnection between objects and many applications have applied [1]. The logic expression ability, knowledge discovery and reasoning capabilities of the Semantic Web ingratiate with the needs of further development of the Internet of Things. The Semantic Web has become an important technology for promoting the Internet of Things. In the past few decades, semantic techniques have provided means for description, information sharing, and integration of heterogeneous objects. Moreover, the artificial intelligence and knowledge engineering are combined in the field of the Semantic Web to represent and process data and knowledge.

2 Related Work

The corresponding research results of the Intelligent IoT include the Smart-M3 system which aims to merge the Semantic Web and IoT domain. The system

© Springer Nature Switzerland AG 2018
J. Vaidya and J. Li (Eds.): ICA3PP 2018, LNCS 11336, pp. 186–195, 2018.
https://doi.org/10.1007/978-3-030-05057-3_14

provides a semantic publishing and subscription software architecture [2]. Tao et al. [3] used semantic ontology to manage devices in smart home. Wu et al. [4] proposed a unified knowledge framework to improve the Semantic Web of Things (SWoT) for interoperability between IoT applications in specific areas. Jahan et al. [5] discussed a ubiquitous knowledge base, CoAP-based framework and intelligent gateway for SWoT framework. Gyrard et al. [6] proposed the SEG3.0 as a joint, unified approach to semantic interoperability and applied it to smart city systems. Poslad et al. [7] proposed a new IoT EWS system framework, a semantic information organization model, which aims to explore the scalability of the IoT [8]. Singh et al. [9] proposed a new IoT architecture model using Semantic Fusion Model (SFM), which uses intelligent semantic framework to encapsulate information gathered from sensor networks. The most representative ones are the Semantic Web of Things model proposed by Floriano [10].

3 Problem Statement

The purpose of the Intelligent IoT is to realize the direct correlation between the information space and the physical world and achieve complete intelligent interaction. Since the specific process is completed without the involvement of human activities, the problems are more complex and diverse. The intelligent interaction between the human society, information space and physical world "Fig. 1" is different from the IoT and also different from the Semantic Web. The complexity is increasing geometrically and the system will face more unprecedented problems and challenges. The problems include the following four aspects: The existing frameworks of Intelligent IoT mainly focused on the information processing and do not substantially involve the driving and control of entities. In essence, the existing framework still research on information field. There are still many issues about device connection are not mentioned. The existing frameworks of Intelligent IoT do not completely separate from manual control to achieve true intelligence. The ultimate purpose of the Intelligent IoT is to hand over all information processing to the machine or entity. People only act as perceivers of the end result and do not need to participate in the query, composition and processing. The existing frameworks cannot provide solutions for such intelligent

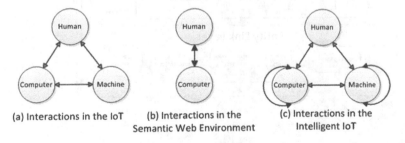

(a) Interactions in the IoT   (b) Interactions in the Semantic Web Environment   (c) Interactions in the Intelligent IoT

Fig. 1. Interactions in IoT, SW and SWoT.

development. The existing frameworks of Intelligent IoT cannot provide support for complex process construction. Although the existing frameworks can settle the problems of service composition, it did not provide support for service composition which coupled with dynamic entity information. The existing frameworks of Intelligent IoT cannot manage and control the execution of complex processes. Physical world entities need an effective scheduling mechanism and a mechanism to resolve errors is also needed. In some conditions system must resolve errors immediately and eliminate the expected impact of errors.

4   Semantic Web Based Intelligent IoT Model

To settle the problems in Sect. 3, we proposed a Semantic Web based intelligent IoT model (ISWM). And in this section we will explain it in detail.

4.1   Framework

Based on previous research, We proposed a more reasonable Intelligent IoT model, as shown in "Fig. 2".

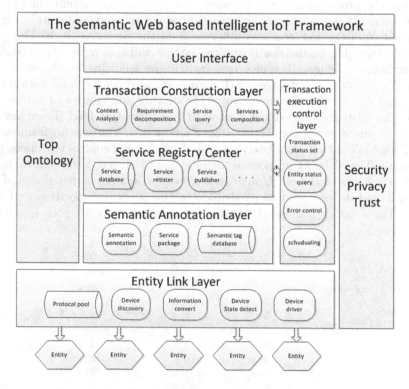

Fig. 2. Framework of Semantic Web based intelligent IoT model.

Top Ontology. The top ontology used to represent the concepts and relationships involved in the IoT. It is the basis of the framework and provides logical reasoning for the whole architecture [11].

Entity Link Layer. The entity link layer implements functions such as information transfer and drive control for various entities, and is an intermediate layer between the logic part and the entity. This layer should not only discover the added physical devices, convert various types of device communication protocols and drive devices, but also acquire the devices status information in real time to provide the basis for the establishment and execution of transactions.

Semantic Annotation Layer. The semantic annotation layer implements the semantic annotation of the original data in order to provide semantic support for the upper application. This layer also packages the semantic information of entities into Semantic Web Services. This layer is mainly divided into three functional modules: The semantic tag database is a set of semantic representation tags for existing entities, similar to the DTD in XML. The semantic annotation module labels the functions and features of the underlying entities with the normalization tags, providing a basis for selection during transaction construction. The function of the service package module is to encapsulate semantically labeled entity functions into Web services.

Service Registry Center. In the semantic annotation layer, the entity information is converted into machine-readable semantic format. The content of this information includes two parts: static attributes, such as state and external environment description, and the functional attributes, which is packaged as a Web Service. Using a similar approach to the Web service, this information is stored on a registry or cloud platform and can be updated using periodic queries or transaction triggers. The service register can use the existing technologies in SOA to store and manage the services provided by the IoT entity. The service registry center can adopt a centralized management mode and a distributed management mode. Its working principle and implementation technology can also directly draw on UDDI.

Transaction Construction Layer. This layer regards the Web Service as dynamically configurable resources for management and scheduling. The main function of this layer is to build the service chain to meet user requirements. There are two steps for transaction construction: semantic decomposition of user requires and service discovery and composition. The function module includes the following four: The context analysis module analyzes the requirements of semantic information delivered by the user interface through ontology reasoning and a priori rules, and then makes a definitive judgment on the requirement according to the corresponding context. The requirement decomposition module uses the ontology and its inference rules to decompose the request into sequential calls of several entities, which is translated into Web services. The function of the service query module is to find the Web service that satisfies the conditions in the registration center according to the result of requirement decomposition.

The function of the service composition module is to organize the queried services and build a transaction that meets the requirements of users.

Transaction Execution Control Layer. The main function of this layer is to manage and control the execution of IoT transactions. Including: state information, the definition of entities states in the transaction; State awareness of subsequent entities during execution; Dynamic replace entity or terminate the transaction when error occurs; Synergistic scheduling or process consolidation between synergistic IoT transactions. The function module includes the following four: The transaction status set is a predefined rule set, which defines a set of states, environment requirements et., which should be fulfilled during the execution of the IoT transaction. The transaction status set must be determined in advance by using the ontology reasoning rules based on the semantic information while constructing the IoT transaction. The entity status query module is directly associated with the device state module in the entity link layer, and obtains the state information of the entities in real time. When the error control module encounters a service failure that represents an entity's function during the execution of the IoT transaction, it determines whether or not the pre-driver result is retained and how the successor sequence is handled according to the semantic environment. The scheduling module controls the concurrently, cooperatively or mutually exclusive IoT transactions, and scheduling non-concurrent entities according to the actual environment.

4.2   Working Mechanism

The workflow of ISWM includes the following three aspects:

Entity Functions are Registered as Web Service. First, the entities connected to the IoT are captured by the device discovery module at the entity link layer. Second, the entities are matched with its driver, which is configured by the device driver module. And then the entities information is passed to the semantic annotation layer for semantic encapsulation. After that, the semantic annotation module represents the entities according to the metadata in the semantic tag database. The service package module expresses the entity functions as Web Services. Finally, the services are registered in service registry center and published by the service publisher module. The process is shown in "Fig. 3".

Construct IoT Transaction to Meet the Users Requirement. User requirement is provided to the system in natural language and passed to the transaction construction layer. The requirement is analyzed by the context analysis module and translated into semantic information which is machine-readable. The semantic information decomposed into a combination of simple requirements by the demand decomposition module. The format of these simple requirements is the same with Web Services. The service query module finds and matches the entity services in the service registry center. The service combination module organizes them to construct the transaction and establishes the transaction status set. The process is shown in "Fig. 4".

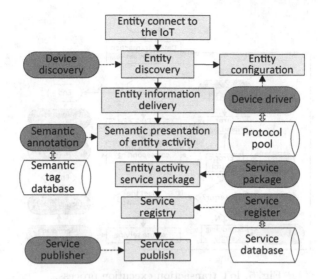

Fig. 3. The process of entities registered as web services.

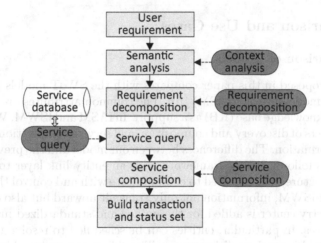

Fig. 4. IoT transaction construction process.

Control the Execution of IoT Transaction. After the construction of the IoT transaction, services are called in turn according to its logical sequence under the control of the transaction execution control layer. In the service invocation process, the entity status query module detects the state of the entity, which provides the service, in real time through the device state module in the entity link layer, and updates the transaction state set. At the same time, the semantic parameters in the requirements are transferred as driver parameters to the corresponding entities by the information convert module. During the entire transaction execution process, the error control module and the scheduling module in the transaction execution control layer are responsible for the processing and management of errors. The process is shown in "Fig. 5".

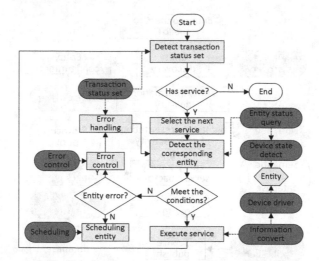

Fig. 5. IoT transaction execution process.

5   Comparison and Use Cases

5.1   Comparison of Models

The ISWM proposed in this paper compares with the SWoT models [9] and the active service model for IoT (IASM) [10]. The common attributes are as follows: They all need knowledge base (KB) as a support. In IASM and ISWM, Web Service is used as objects of discovery and composition and service composition is used for managing information. The differences between our model and the previous architectures are as follows: ISWM framework adds an entity link layer to the aforementioned structure, which is used to communicate with and control the underlying entities. In ISWM, information not only transmit upward but also downward. A service registry center is added for the unified and standardized management of entity services. In particular, entities can be scheduled to resolve unexpected problems when abnormal conditions occur. The differences are listed in "Table 1".

Table 1. Comparison of SWoT, IASM and ISWM

	KB support	Service discovery	Entity composition	Entity status feedback	Entity control and schedule
SWoT	Yes	No	No	No	No
IASM	Yes	Yes	Yes	No	No

Table 2. The implementation of transport rescue process in different environments

	Manual operation	SWoT	ISWM
Information collection	Rescuers	Sensor network	Sensor network
Accident determination	Traffic police	KB	KB and ontology
Decision making	Emergency rescue department	Decision Support Systems	Decision Support Systems
Organization	Emergency rescue department and rescuers	Emergency rescue department and rescuers	Transaction execution and control system and rescuers
Information publication	Emergency rescue department	Emergency rescue department	Emergency rescue department or KB

Table 3. Executioner and method in rescue process in different environments

	SWoT		ISWM	
	Executioner	Method	Executioner	Method
Information report	Emergency rescue department	By phone	Transaction construction system	Message trigger
Wrecker dispatch	Emergency rescue department	Query and scheduling manually	Transaction execution control system	Policy scheduling message triggering
Ambulance dispatch	Emergency rescue department	Query and scheduling manually	Transaction execution control system	Policy scheduling message triggering
Fire truck dispatch	Emergency rescue department	Query and scheduling manually	Transaction execution control system	Policy scheduling message triggering
Traffic control	Traffic police	Command by traffic police	Transaction execution control system	IoT entities such as traffic light and indicator,traffic police if needed
Material dispatch	Emergency rescue department	Preparation and transportation manually	Transaction construction system and transaction execution control system	Intelligent storage and intelligent logistics system scheduling

5.2   Case Study of Traffic Rescue

The Intelligent Transportation System (ITS) utilizes the IoT technology to equip the road network to real-time monitoring and exact management. Its most important function is to detect and deal with traffic accidents in time. The model proposed in this paper is compared with the manual operation and SWoT model in the implementation of the comprehensive rescue process for traffic accidents as shown in "Table 2". We can see that in the comprehensive rescue process of traffic accidents, the proposed model in this paper is as effective as the manual operation and the SWoT structure. The biggest difference in the model compare with the other two structures is the executioners in the integrated rescue procedure as shown in "Table 3". It can be seen from "Tables 2 and 3", that in the comprehensive rescue process, the SWoT model can use the sensor network and knowledge system to discover, determine, and formulate rescue strategies for accidents, but it is ineffective for the organization of subsequent rescue work.

6   Conclusion

In order to achieve the intelligent objectives, this paper proposed an intelligent IoT model based on the Semantic Web. We described the framework and working mechanism of the model. The framework uses the ontology as the logical reasoning basis and is divided into several parts: the entity link layer, the semantic annotation layer, the service registry center, the transaction construction layer, and the transaction execution control layer. Semantic technology is used to describe the IoT entity as a dynamic Web Service. In the model, the technologies of service discovery, service composition are used to build IoT transactions that meet users requirements and control the transaction processes. Due to the addition of physical feedback, entity control and scheduling, the advances of our model are shown in the use case of traffic accident rescue. In another work we study the security of the model [12].

Acknowledgment. This work was supported in part by the Natural Science Foundation of Guangdong Province, China (Grant No. 2018A030313014); Guangdong University Scientific Innovation Project (Grant No. 2017KTSCX178); the outstanding young teacher training program of the Education Department of Guangdong Province (Grant No. YQ2015158); Guangdong Provincial Science & Technology Plan Projects (Grant Nos. 2016A010101035 & 2016A010101034); and National Natural Science Fund, China (Grant Nos. 61300198 & 61772233).

References

1. Tao, M., Zuo, J., Liu, Z., Castiglione, A., Palmieri, F.: Multi-layer cloud architectural model and ontology-based security service framework for IoT-based smart homes. Futur. Gener. Comput. Syst. **78**, 1040–1051 (2016)
2. D'elia, A., Viola, F., Roffia, L., Azzoni, P., Cinotti, T.S.: Enabling interoperability in the Internet of Things: a OSGi semantic information broker implementation. Int. J. Semant. Web Inf. Syst. **13**(1), 147–167 (2017)

3. Tao, M., Ota, K., Dong, M.: Ontology-based data semantic management and application in IoT- and cloud-enabled smart homes. Futur. Gener. Comput. Syst. **76**, 528–539 (2016)

4. Wu, Z., Xu, Y., Zhang, C., Yang, Y., Ji, Y.: Towards semantic web of things: from manual to semi-automatic semantic annotation on web of things. In: Wang, Y., Yu, G., Zhang, Y., Han, Z., Wang, G. (eds.) BigCom 2016. LNCS, vol. 9784, pp. 295–308. Springer, Cham (2016). https://doi.org/10.1007/978-3-319-42553-5_25

5. Jahan, F., Fruitwala, P., Vyas, T.: Towards the next generation of web of things: a survey on semantic web of things' framework. In: Satapathy, S.C.C., Das, S. (eds.) Proceedings of First International Conference on Information and Communication Technology for Intelligent Systems: Volume 1. SIST, vol. 50, pp. 31–39. Springer, Cham (2016). https://doi.org/10.1007/978-3-319-30933-0_4

6. Gyrard, A., Serrano, M.: Connected smart cities: interoperability with SEG 3.0 for the Internet of Things. In: IEEE 30th International Conference on Advanced Information Networking and Applications Workshops, pp. 796–802 (2016)

7. Poslad, S., Middleton, S.E., Chaves, F., et al.: A semantic IoT early warning system for natural environment crisis management. IEEE Trans. Emerg. Top. Comput. **3**(2), 246–257 (2015)

8. Sun, Y., Jara, A.J.: An extensible and active semantic model of information organizing for the Internet of Things. Pers. Ubiquitous Comput. **18**(8), 1821–1833 (2014)

9. Singh, D., Tripathi, G., Jara, A.J., et al.: A survey of Internet-of-Things: future vision, architecture, challenges and services. In: 2014 IEEE World Forum on Internet of Things, pp. 287–292 (2014)

10. Scioscia, F., Ruta, M.: Building a semantic Web of things: issues and perspectives in information compression. Proceedings of the 2009 IEEE International Conference on Semantic Computing (ICSC), pp. 589–594 (2009)

11. Qu, C., Liu, F., Tao, M.: Ontologies for the transactions on IoT. Int. J. Distrib. Sens. Netw. **11**, 1–12 (2015)

12. Qu, C., Tao, M., Zhang, J., Hong, X.Y., Yuan, R.F.: Blockchain based credibility verification method for IoT entities. 2018, Secur. Commun. Netw. **2018**, 1–11 (2018)

Accelerating CNNs Using Optimized Scheduling Strategy

Rui Xu[1], Sheng Ma[2(✉)], Wenwu Li[1], and Yang Guo[1]

[1] College of Computer, National University of Defense Technology,
Changsha 410073, Hunan, China
[2] The State Key Laboratory of High Performance Computing, National
University of Defense Technology, Changsha 410073, Hunan, China
masheng@nudt.edu.cn

Abstract. Convolutional neural networks (CNNs) have a wide range of applications in image and video recognition, recommender systems and natural language processing. But CNNs are computationally intensive, and its computational cost is hard to accept. In order to speed up the calculations, people focus on optimizing convolution that account for most of the proportion of CNNs' operation. So, many algorithms have been proposed to accelerate the operation of convolution layers. However, each algorithm has its advantages and disadvantages, and there is no one algorithm that can handle all situations. In this paper, we examine the performance of various algorithms in GPU environment. By building a customized CNN model, we have fully explored the impact of the neural structure on the performance of algorithms, including inference/training speed, and memory consumption. In addition to the algorithms, we also focus on how their implementations in GPU environment affect their performance. Finally, we summarize the characteristics of each algorithm., and design a strategy to assigns the appropriate implementation for different convolutional layers in CNNs. With our strategy, we can make AlexNet run 1.2x to 2.8x faster than other strategies in GPU environment. This work has very important meaning for understanding these algorithms and may provide insights for further optimizations of the architecture of GPUs and accelerators.

Keywords: Artificial intelligence · Convolutional neural networks
Scheduling strategy · GPU framework

1 Introduction

Since deep learning [1] was proposed, it has rapidly become a hot topic. Especially, deep neural networks (DNNs) have made significant progress in image classification, target recognition, speech recognition, language translation, etc. [2]. In some cases, the accuracy of neural network even exceeds the accuracy of human identification [3].

This work is supported by the National Natural Science Foundation of China (No. 61672526) and Research Project of NUDT (ZK17-03-06).

J. Vaidya and J. Li (Eds.): ICA3PP 2018, LNCS 11336, pp. 196–208, 2018.
https://doi.org/10.1007/978-3-030-05057-3_15

A series of successful and mature network models have also been proposed, including Convolutional Neural Networks (CNNs), Long Short-Term Memory (LSTM) and Recurrent Neural Networks (RNNs) [2], etc. In this paper, we focus on CNNs, which play a key role in image and video recognition, recommender systems and natural language processing [3].

However, the training/inference time of CNNs is long and sometimes unbearable. Due to the complexity of convolution operations, CNNs will bring a huge workload to the device. Meanwhile, CNNs is becoming more and more complicated, since the number of convolutional layers is continually increasing. These changes can bring improvement in the accuracy, but will result in a huge increase in training or inference time.

There are many ways to solve this problem, one of which is using acceleration algorithm. At present, there are three popular convolutional acceleration algorithms, Matrix multiplication (GEMM) [5], Fast Fourier Transform (FFT) [6], and Winograd's minimal filtering algorithm (Winograd algorithm) [7]. GEMM converts convolution operations into more efficient matrix operations, while FFT and Winograd algorithms reduce computational complexity of CNNs.

People usually implement CNNs in GPU environment, because GPU uses many-core architectures and have massively parallel processing power [2]. Moreover, NVIDIA has developed a deep learning library called cuDNN, which is a GPU-accelerated library of primitives for deep neural networks [8]. It can provide highly tuned implementations for convolution to accelerate the execution of CNNs in GPU environment. Therefore, more and more users choose GPUs to speed up the execution of CNN. And, cuDNN is also being used more and more widely.

Currently, users can choose an appropriate framework to build CNNs model. But they rarely understand the implementations or algorithms of convolution used by these frameworks. Few studies have really shown the differences between these convolution algorithms. In this paper, we show the detailed comparisons on the characteristics between these algorithms. We choose GPUs as the main hardware platform for convolution operation and compare seven most popular implementations of convolution.

We choose a customized CNN model as the workload to obtain performance characteristics of these implementations. The customized CNN model was built and trained using the same framework, Caffe [9]. Our work shows that each implementation has pros and cons, and no algorithm can perform best in all situations. The actual performance of these algorithms or implementations will be heavily dependent on the configuration of convolutional layer. Moreover, in the same configuration, the GPU implementation will further affect the performance of these algorithms. This work has very important meaning for understanding these algorithms and may provide insights for further optimizations of the architecture of GPUs and accelerators.

Based on the characteristics of algorithm, we provide optimization techniques to implement efficient CNN models using the algorithm libraries. We design an Optimized Algorithm Scheduling Strategy, which assign the appropriate convolution algorithm for each convolutional layer of CNNs. We also designed an experiment to verify the superiority of our strategy. We compare our design with several existing solutions, such as Caffe+CUDA and Caffe+cuDNN. Our experimental show that our strategy can increase the execution speed up to 2.8x compared to Caffe+CUDA and 1.2x compared to Caffe+cuDNN.

2 Background and Related Work

2.1 Convolutional Neural Networks

A Convolutional Neural Networks (CNN) is the feedforward neural network [2]. It has an excellent performance for large-scale image processing and identification. In a CNN, multiple convolutional layers are connected. Such structure allows CNN to abstract the features of the image as much as possible.

The main purpose of the convolution layers is to extract the features in the image. They use well-trained filters that are highly responsive to specific good patterns. However, the type of features extracted by different convolutional layers are not the same. In AlexNet, the first layer of convolution is used to detect low-order features such as edges, corners, curves, etc. As the number of convolutional layer increase, the features detected by filters are more complex [10].

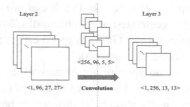

Fig. 1. The description of the part of AlexNet, which is from Layer 2 to Layer 3, by using the 4D-tensor.

In a CNN, feature data is stored as tensors. In the traditional method, feature images or maps is processed in two dimensions, <H, W>, where H represents the height of images and W represents the width of images. But there are a lot of images that need to be processed in the same layer, we can treat the feature map data as four dimensions tensor, <N, C, W, H>, where N and C means the number of images in a batch, and the number of channels, respectively. In this way, we can easily describe CNNs' network structure (see Fig. 1) Similarly, we can also use 4D-tensor to describe the kernels, <K, C, R, S>, where K represents the number of kernels, R represents the height of the kernel, and S represents the width of the kernel.

2.2 Convolution Algorithms

Convolution is the key operation of CNNs. How to carry out these operations efficiently has become a hot research topic. Many algorithms have been proposed and most of them have different implementations in GPU environment.

The formulation of convolution operation is Eq. (1) [5]. Where N means the mini-batch size, C means the number of channels, K means the number of filters, R and S mean the filter size, P and Q mean the output size, U means the stride size, F means filters of CNNs, and D means input maps.

The traditional method of calculating convolution is based on Eq. (1). We called it the direct convolution algorithm. It completes the multiplication between elements and accumulate their results according to Eq. (1) [11]. It is the most straightforward way to perform convolution. Cuda-convnet2 [11] is a widely used direct convolution library.

$$O[n,k,p,q] = \sum_{c=0}^{C-1}\sum_{r=0}^{R-1}\sum_{s=0}^{S-1} F[k,c,r,s] \cdot D[n,c,p \times U + r, q \times U + s],$$

$$n \in [0,N), k \in [0,K), p \in [0,P), q \in [0,Q). \tag{1}$$

Another algorithm is matrix multiplication (GEMM). It transforms the matrix convolution operation into a matrix multiplication operation as shown in Fig. 2 [5]. Because matrix multiplication has efficient computational libraries in GPU environment, this simpler approach has gained considerable efficiency.

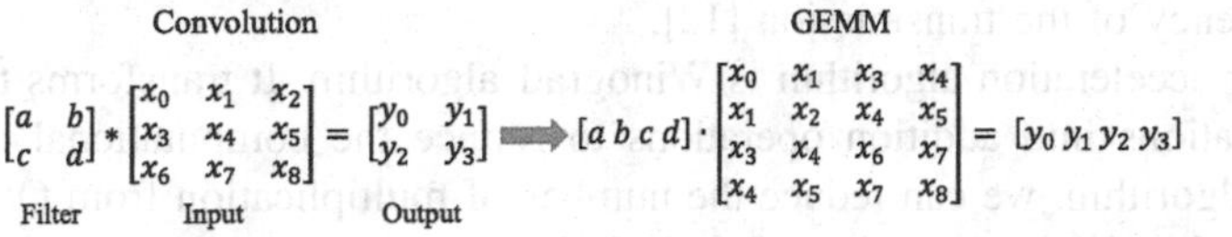

Convolution   GEMM

$$\begin{bmatrix} a & b \\ c & d \end{bmatrix} * \begin{bmatrix} x_0 & x_1 & x_2 \\ x_3 & x_4 & x_5 \\ x_6 & x_7 & x_8 \end{bmatrix} = \begin{bmatrix} y_0 & y_1 \\ y_2 & y_3 \end{bmatrix} \implies [a\,b\,c\,d] \cdot \begin{bmatrix} x_0 & x_1 & x_3 & x_4 \\ x_1 & x_2 & x_4 & x_5 \\ x_3 & x_4 & x_6 & x_7 \\ x_4 & x_5 & x_7 & x_8 \end{bmatrix} = [y_0\,y_1\,y_2\,y_3]$$

Filter   Input   Output

Fig. 2. Transforming the matrix convolution into a matrix multiplication [2]. This process produces redundant data, which marked in red in this figure.

One of the implementations of GEMM in GPU environment is called explicit GEMM. This implementation directly calculates the convolution according to GEMM algorithm flow. But it has the disadvantage that there is redundant data in the input matrix, and they will take up extra memory space. Therefore, implicit GEMM [12] was proposed. It divides these matrixes into small pieces and uses the index to guide the calculation. Small amount of data can be loaded into the on-chip memory directly without taking up extra GPU memory. But this method requires additional calculation of the index and sufficient bandwidth.

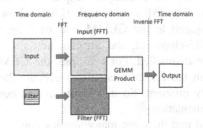

Fig. 3. Use FFT to calculate convolution. In the frequency domain space, it can be seen that the small-size filter becomes the same size as the input image, which takes up extra space.

Another implementation of GEMM is implicit-precomp GEMM. It is based on implicit GEMM. But unlike implicit GEMM, it does not require index calculation during the operation of convolution. It obtains the index in advance by calculating the parameters of CNNs structure and block size. It can further speed up the calculation, However, it takes up some memory space to store the index.

In order to further speed up the operation, Fast Fourier Transform (FFT) is also implemented. It transforms the input and filter data into the frequency domain space and completes these matrices product [6]. Then, the result is transformed back into the time domain space to get the final convolution result (see Fig. 3).

FFT speeds up computation by reducing computational complexity of convolution. The number of multiplication of convolution is $O(P^2 \times R^2)$ in direct algorithm, whereas the FFT algorithm can reduce the number to $O(P^2 \times logP)$ [2].

The disadvantage of FFT algorithm is that it needs to store a large amount of intermediate data. The transformation of FFT also expands the filter to the size of the input maps [5]. Due to the above reasons, the algorithm needs to take up significant memory space, especially when facing small-size kernels and large-size inputs.

To solve these problems, FFT-tiling was proposed, which is another implementation of the FFT algorithm in the GPU. Similar to implicit GEMM, it divides input maps into small tiles. It uses block transmission and calculation to reduce memory usage and hide the latency of the transmission [12].

Another acceleration algorithm is Winograd algorithm. It transforms the multiplication operations into addition operations to reduce the computational cost [7]. By using this algorithm, we can reduce the number of multiplication from $O(P^2 \times R^2)$ to $O((P + R - 1)^2)$ in the operation of convolution.

However, the disadvantage of this algorithm is the lack of good flexibility. When the size of filters changes in CNNs, the parameter matrices used for transformation has to be changed. In addition, the process also generates intermediate data that needs to be stored [12].

2.3   Related Work

Since convolutional neural networks were introduced to public, few studies focus on the comparison between the convolutional algorithms. At present, the best way to evaluate the convolution algorithms is to refer to experimental data provided by several algorithm developers. Mathieu, et al. (2013) show the performance of the FFT algorithm [13, 19]. Chetlur, et al. (2014) compare implicit GEMM, explicit GEMM and Direct algorithms in their work [5]. Lavin et al. (2015) show the advantages of the Winograd algorithm compared to the GEMM and FFT algorithms [14]. However, through these years of development, the implementations of algorithms in GPU environment have become diversified. For example, the GEMM algorithm has three implementations. Although these implementations execute the same algorithm, their performance is completely different. So it is necessary to conduct a comprehensive evaluation of these implementations.

It also should be noted that there are many studies comparing the performance of different DNN frameworks, like [20, 21]. But our work wants to show the characteristics of different convolution algorithms in the same framework. When the user selects the appropriate framework, we will give our optimization suggestions for reference. Meanwhile, based our experiments' result, we design an Optimized Algorithm Scheduling Strategy. Through this strategy we can improve the computational efficiency of CNNs.

3   Experimental Methodology

We conduct two experiments in our work. In the first experiment, we compare the characteristics between different implementations. we measure the execution time and memory usage of these implementations to compare their characteristics. In order to identify the performance limit factors for each algorithm, we select the customized convolutional neural network as the workload, because it is representative and flexible enough to simulate many conditions. The default structure parameters of the custom network structure are as follows, N = 64 (mini-batch), C = 64 (channel), H = 56 (input-size), R = 5 (kernel-size), K = 128 (filter-number), U = 1 (stride-size). The choice of these parameters is reference to GoogLeNet [4, 8]. After that, we adjust the network parameters (N, H, R, K, U) and use variable-controlling approach to change one of them and keep the others constant. In this way, we can observe the performance changes with this parameter.

Table 1.   System configuration

CPU	Intel Core i7-6700k (4.00 Ghz)
GPU	NVIDIA GeForce GTX1080
Main memory	8 GB
GPU memory	8 GB
Operating system	Ubuntu 16.04 LTS
Framework	Caffe V1.0.0
Libraries	CUDA 8.0; cuDNN 6.0; cuda-convnet2;

In the second experiment, we measure the execution speed of AlexNet in GPU environment using different algorithm scheduling strategy. Based on our previous experiments, we suggest possible optimization techniques to improve the speed of CNNs. We also design an optimized algorithm scheduling strategy, which assign the best suited implementations for AlexNet's convolutional layers. We verify our strategy by comparing with Caffe+CUDA or cuDNN's strategy.

Our experiments are performed with a system described in Table 1, including the versions of the deep learning frameworks and libraries used. We use Caffe to build our CNNs model. Since cuDNN does not support direct convolution, we implement the direct convolution algorithm with cuda-convnet2.

4   Comparison of Algorithms

The characteristics of the algorithm are reflected by the execution efficiency under different conditions. In this section, we characterize the seven implementations (implicit GEMM, implicit-precomp GEMM, explicit GEMM, FFT, FFT-tiling, Winograd) of convolution algorithms in GPU environment. We measure the runtime and memory usage to compare the performance of seven implementations with respect to different size of input image, kernel size and stride-size. In this way, we show the influence of the network structure on the performance of the implementations.

For convenience, we use GEMM1 as implicit GEMM, GEMM2 as implicit-precomp GEMM, GEMM3 as explicit GEMM, FFT1 as traditional FFT, and FFT2 as FFT-tiling.

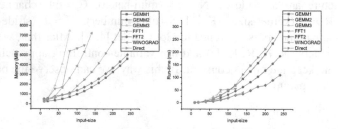

Fig. 4. The impact of the input size on performance

4.1   Input Size

Figure 4 shows the performance of all algorithms with different input sizes. For a small input size (<20), GEMM2, FFT1 and Winograd algorithm result in better performance than others. For example, the speed of FFT1 is 2.77 times faster than the FFT2 when the input size is equal to 10. But with the increase of the input size (>20), the performance advantage of FFT2 is becoming more obvious. Winograd algorithm has similar runtime as FFT2, but it experiences an out of memory error when the input size is equal to 160.

The runtime of FFT1 is fluctuant when the input size is around 64. The reason is that, for different input sizes, FFT1 will call different functions or libraries to calculate the Fourier transform, and one of the thresholds is 64. So FFT1 results in the worst performance in our experiment when the input size is 80.

GEMM1 and GEMM2 still consume the least memory. GEMM3, FFT1 and Winograd algorithm experience the out of memory error when input sizes are equal to 100, 140 and 160 respectively. Interestingly, the memory usage of FFT2 is less than the direct algorithm when input size is greater than 80. The main reason is that these two algorithms use different acceleration libraries.

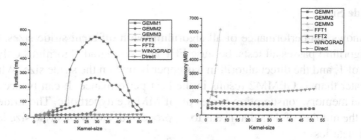

Fig. 5. The impact of the kernel size on performance

4.2 Kernel Size

Figure 5 shows the performance of all algorithms with different kernel sizes. It is noted that Winograd algorithm only supports 3×3 and 5×5 kernels, so its runtime is reported with two dots in Fig. 5. In addition, the direct algorithm cannot support all given filter numbers in our experiment.

For a small kernel size (kernel size < 5), the speed of GEMM2 is faster than FFT2, and Winograd algorithm has the similar runtime to GEMM2. But when the kernel size is greater than 5, FFT2 results in the best performance, and FFT1 is a bit slower than FFT2. Moreover, their runtime tends to be a constant value when the kernel size is smaller than 32. The reason is that the FFT algorithm need to do Fourier transform on the kernel, and the size of kernel is adjusted to the same as the input size. So, the kernel size basically has no effect on the calculation of FFT algorithm. Since FFT2 divides the input into 32×32 tiles [12], it experiences an error when kernel size is equal to 32.

Interestingly, for GEMM algorithm, the trend of GEMM1 and GEMM2 runtime is arched. By calculating the number of multiplication ($O(P2 \times R2)$, $R = (H - P)/S + 1$) of GEMM, a quadratic function is obtained, which is the same as the trend of GEMM runtime in Fig. 5.

In memory usage, GEMM3 has the highest consumption, and it even experiences an out of memory error when kernel size is equal to 9. However, the memory usage of other algorithms is not affected by the kernel size, so their memory consumption is basically unchanged.

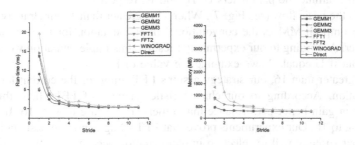

Fig. 6. The impact of Stride on performance

4.3   Stride Size

Figure 6 shows the performance of all algorithms with different stride sizes. Only the GEMM algorithm passes all tests, because FFT and Winograd algorithms only support stride size of 1, and the direct algorithm has upper bound on the stride size. When stride size is greater than 1, GEMM2 results in the best performance. It can be seen that the runtime and memory consumption curves of GEMM are hyperbolic. The stride size has impact on the number of data that needs to be processed, and with stride size larger, the amount of data less.

In conclusion, FFT2 is the fastest implementation to train a CNN model with large kernel sizes (large than 20 in our experiment) and large input sizes (large than 5 in our experiment), due to its low arithmetic complexity and block operation. Winograd algorithm also has a similar performance, but considering the memory usage, we prefer to the FFT2. FFT1 is a bit slower than FFT2 when computing convolution with a large input size. But for a small input size (smaller than 20), FFT2 is slower than FFT1.

For small kernel sizes and input sizes, Winograd algorithm and GEMM2 would be a good choice. But GEMM2 is more flexible than Winograd algorithm or FFT2, because Winograd algorithm only supports 3×3 and 5×5 kernels, and FFT2 or Winograd algorithm can only support the stride size as 1. Moreover, GEMM2 always occupy the minimum memory space, it is well suitable for cases when the memory is limited.

5   Optimized Scheduling Strategy

As we have mentioned earlier, with same neural network structure, different implementations of convolution algorithms often have different performance. So, the diversity of DCNN's layer sizes and the different performance of implementations demand an efficient scheduling strategy to assign the appropriate implementation for each convolutional layer. In this way, we can optimize both power efficiency and performance.

By analyzing our experimental data, we propose an optimized algorithm scheduling strategy. The strategy completes the algorithm selection according to the structure parameters of the current convolutional layer of neural networks. For each layer, the strategy read the model parameter file to obtain the input mapping data structure <N, C, H, W>, the weight data structure <K, C, R, S> , and the stride-size U. After that, the strategy will examine the parameters U, H, and R, respectively.

So that's the basic flow (see Fig. 7): When U is greater than 1, our strategy arranges implicit-precomp GEMM as the convolutional implementation for the current convolutional layer. According to our experimental results, this implementation works best in this case. But if U equals 1, we examine the value of H.

If H is greater than 16, our strategy assigns FFT-tiling for the current layer as the implementation. According to our characteristic analysis of FFT-tiling, this implementation can gain better performance than others in the case of H > 16. If H is less than or equal to 16, Our experiments prove that FFT-tiling is not the best choice at this time, and our strategy will re-select an implementation according to the value of R.

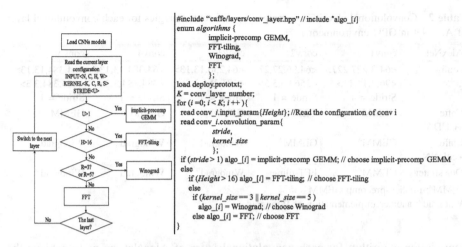

Fig. 7. The workflow and pseudocode of Optimized Algorithm Scheduling Strategy

When R is equal to 3 or 5, our strategy will arrange the Winograd as the implementation for the current layer. But if R is not equal to 3 or 5, according to our experimental results, the FFT implementation is the best choice.

With this strategy, we can obtain the best implementation for each convolutional layer with the optimal performance in GPU environment. By reducing the execution time, we also reduce energy consumption. The workflow also shows that our strategy involves only the structural parameters of the network and does not care about the operation data or the process during execution of CNNs. This feature allows us that we can execute our strategy in advance, so that the operation process of CNNs will not be affected.

In order to verify our strategy, we compare it with two scheduling of Caffe+CUDA and Caffe+cuDNN. The Caffe+CUDA solution is rely on the GEMM algorithm and uses CUDA library to accelerate the convolution operation in the GPU environment. There is no algorithm scheduling in this solution. The Caffe+cuDNN solution uses multiple algorithms to accelerate CNNs. It uses cudnnGetConvolutionAlgorithm(), which serves as a heuristic for seeking the suitable algorithm for cuDNN-convolution for the given layer specifications.

In our experiments, we use these three strategies to accelerate the AlexNet network and measure their execution time respectively. The experimental results are shown in Fig. 8.

From the experimental data, it can be seen that the speed of Caffe+CUDA is the slowest. Because Caffe+CUDA only uses GEMM algorithm, which is inefficient to execute AlexNet with different layer structure. In contrast to Caffe+CUDA, Caffe+cuDNN has a variety of convolutional algorithms. It chooses the appropriate algorithm or implementation to accelerate each convolutional layer of AlexNet. In this way, it further improves the computational efficiency of CNNs. In experiments, Caffe+cuDNN increases the speed by 2.3× than Caffe+CUDA. According to the data structure parameters of the neural networks, our solution arranges the most suitable

Table 2. Convolutional algorithms arranged by different strategies for each convolutional layer of AlexNet in GPU environment.

AlexNet	conv1	conv2	conv3	conv4	conv5
config	<64,3,227,227> <96,3,11,11> Stride = 4	<64,96,27,27> <256,96,5,5> Stride = 1	<64,256,13,13> <384,256,3,3> Stride = 1	<64,384,13,13> <384,384,3,3> Stride = 1	<64,384,13,13> <256,384,3,3> Stride = 1
Caffe +CUDA	GEMM	GEMM	GEMM	GEMM	GEMM
Caffe +cuDNN	GEMM[a]	GEMM[a]	Winograd	Winograd	Winograd
Our strategy	GEMM[a]	FFT-tiling	Winograd[b]	Winograd	Winograd

GEMM[a]: implicit-precomp GEMM
Winograd[b]: another implementation of Winograd

convolution algorithm for each convolutional layer of AlexNet, so as to achieve the maximum acceleration effect. Our strategy increases the speed by 2.3× than Caffe +CUDA. Meanwhile, it is 1.2x faster than the Caffe+cuDNN.

In order to further explore the differences between these strategies, we record the algorithms, respectively, that they choose for each layer of AlexNet (Table 2).

In conv1, conv4 and conv5, both our strategy and the Caffe+cuDNN chooses the same implementation to speed up convolutional operations. But in conv2, Caffe +cuDNN chooses precomp-implicit GEMM, and our strategy chose FFT-tiling. In comparison, our strategy, which increases the speed of convolutional operations by 40% than Caffe+cuDNN, is more efficient. Similarly, in conv3, our strategy chooses another implementation of the Winograd algorithm, making it 10% faster than Caffe +cuDNN.

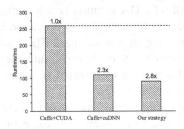

Fig. 8. The execution time of AlexNet using different strategies in GPU environment

Our experiments show that our strategy is better than Caffe+CUDA or Caffe +cuDNN. It should be noted that our strategy only needs to read the structural parameters of the current layer of the CNNs network, and it has nothing to do with the data actually participating in the calculation. In this way, we can use our strategy in advance to rationalize the calculations for each convolutional layer in the CNNs network. Our strategy does not affect the actual execution time of CNNs.

6 Conclusion

The convolutional neural network has become a hot topic in current research. Our work is aimed at comparing the performance of popular convolution algorithms in the GPU environment with the same framework. Based on our experiment, we find that choosing convolution algorithms carefully can make a CNN model faster in executing convolution layers. For this reason, we propose an optimized algorithm scheduling strategy, which can assign the best implementation for each convolutional layer. This strategy is simple and does not affect the implementation of CNNs. Experiments show that using our strategy can speed up the execution of the CNNs model from 1.2x to 2.8x.

References

1. Lecun, Y., Bengio, Y., Hinton, G.: Deep learning. Nature **521**(7553), 436 (2015)
2. Sze, V., et al.: Efficient processing of deep neural networks: a tutorial and survey. Proc. IEEE **105**(12), 2295–2329 (2017)
3. Krizhevsky, A., Sutskever, I., Hinton, G.E.: ImageNet classification with deep convolutional neural networks. Commun. ACM **60**(2), 84 (2012)
4. Simard, P., Lecun, Y., Denker, J.S.: Efficient pattern recognition using a new transformation distance. In: Advances in Neural Information Processing Systems (NIPS 1992), pp. 50–58 (1992)
5. Chetlur, S., et al.: cuDNN: efficient primitives for deep learning. Computer Science (2014)
6. Mathieu, M., Henaff, M., Lecun, Y.: Fast training of convolutional networks through FFTs. Eprint Arxiv (2013)
7. Lavin, A., Gray, S.: Fast algorithms for convolutional neural networks, pp. 4013–4021. Computer Science (2015)
8. Cheng, J., Grossman, M., Mckercher, T.: Professional CUDA C Programming. Wiley, New York (2014)
9. Jia, Y., et al.: Caffe: Convolutional Architecture for Fast Feature Embedding, pp. 675–678 (2014)
10. Zeiler, M.D., Fergus, R.: Visualizing and understanding convolutional networks. In: Fleet, D., Pajdla, T., Schiele, B., Tuytelaars, T. (eds.) ECCV 2014. LNCS, vol. 8689, pp. 818–833. Springer, Cham (2014). https://doi.org/10.1007/978-3-319-10590-1_53
11. Krizhevsky, A.: cuda-convnet2 (2014). https://github.com/akrizhevsky/cuda-convnet2/
12. NVIDIA: CUDNN User Guide (2017). https://developer.nvidia.com
13. Chen, T., et al.: MXNet: a flexible and efficient machine learning library for heterogeneous distributed systems. Statistics (2015)
14. Collobert, R., Kavukcuoglu, K., Farabet, C.: Torch7: a Matlab-like environment for machine learning. In: BigLearn, NIPS Workshop (2011)
15. Szegedy, C., et al.: Going deeper with convolutions. In: Computer Vision and Pattern Recognition, pp. 1–9. IEEE (2015)
16. Lecun, Y., et al.: Backpropagation applied to handwritten zip code recognition. Neural Comput. **1**(4), 541–551 (2014)
17. Simonyan, K., Zisserman, A.: Very deep convolutional networks for large-scale image recognition. Computer Science (2014)
18. He, K., et al.: Deep residual learning for image recognition. In: Computer Vision and Pattern Recognition, pp. 770–778. IEEE (2016)

19. Vasilache, N., Johnson, J., Mathieu, M., et al.: Fast convolutional nets with FBFFT: a GPU performance evaluation (2014)
20. Li, X., et al.: Performance analysis of GPU-based convolutional neural networks. In: International Conference on Parallel Processing, pp. 67–76. IEEE (2016)
21. Kim, H., et al.: Performance analysis of CNN frameworks for GPUs. In: IEEE International Symposium on PERFORMANCE Analysis of Systems and Software, pp. 55–64. IEEE (2017)

Data Analysis of Blended Learning
in Python Programming

Qian Chu[1,2], Xiaomei Yu[1,2(✉)], Yuli Jiang[1,2], and Hong Wang[1,2]

[1] Institute of Information and Engineer, Shandong Normal University, Jinan, China
yxm0708@126.com
[2] Shandong Provincial Key Laboratory for Distributed Computer Software
Novel Technology, Jinan 250014, Shandong, China

Abstract. The rapid emergence of blended learning has sparked a great deal of research interest in the field of educational data mining. We apply the novel educational form of blended learning in the undergraduate curriculum of python programming. With the questionnaire before curriculum is obtained to capture the basic information of undergraduate students, we design educational resources and activities for online studying and face-to-face teaching. Since the learning process of each student is captured continuously, we make teaching and learning evaluations weekly to improve current teaching methods hence arouse students' interest of continuous learning. With analyzing data and mining knowledge received in the process of blended learning, some beneficial results are gained to promote the quality of blended learning in the undergraduate curriculum of python programming, and benefit the undergraduate students as well as higher education in the long run.

Keywords: Blended learning · Education · Python · Data analysis

1 Introduction

Blended learning is an effective teaching approach where learning occurs both online and face-to-face, with the purpose to capture educational strengths both on the internet and in the classrooms. This novel teaching form has opened up a new era of education by pushing the so-called "forced-feeding method of teaching" to a blended learning form with both online video learning and flipped classroom. On one hand, offloading lecture time to video makes it possible for the teachers to spend more time interacting with students in class. On the other hand, the flipped classroom actually enhances the oversight, and promotes the students to taking part in class activities. Therefore, we introduce blended learning into the undergraduate curriculum of python programming.

Supported by the National Nature Science Foundation of China (No. 61672329, No. 61773246), Shandong Normal University's Educational Project for Blended Learning (No. 2016KG79, No. 2016JG54).

J. Vaidya and J. Li (Eds.): ICA3PP 2018, LNCS 11336, pp. 209–217, 2018.
https://doi.org/10.1007/978-3-030-05057-3_16

In fact, most first year students in the university are required to take a semester course on computer science, a large portion of which is based on their interests and background with computer science. The purpose of the course is twofold: (1) to introduce the programming language of python to freshmen and show them common data analysis and machine learning libraries in python as well as their uses; (2) to teach them the basics of programming and introduce the engineering problem-solving methodology. Considering that the students enrolled are from diverse majors and show sharp difference in their motive intensity and their study attitude, we carry out a simple questionnaire before curriculum to capture the basic information of undergraduate students. Then we design educational resources and activities for online studying and face-to-face teaching as well as for selective and personalized study. Since the learning process of each student is captured continuously, we make teaching and learning evaluations weekly to improve current teaching methods hence arouse students' interest of continuous learning. Finally, data preprocess such as pretreatment and standardization is done on data collected in the process of blended learning, with the purpose to promote quality of blended learning in the undergraduate curriculum of python programming.

The main contributions of this paper are outlined as follows:

- The questionnaire before and after curriculum is designed to capture the basic information of the undergraduate students and further improve the blended learning in the follow weeks.
- Creative work including personalized teaching video and educational resources is produced to benefit the whole blended learning process.
- With analyzing data and mining knowledge received in the process of blended learning, some beneficial results are gained to promote quality of blended learning in the next semester.

The remainder of this paper is organized as follows. In Sect. 2, we review related work on blended learning. After address some relevant problem, we present our blended learning process in Sect. 3. With analyzing data and mining knowledge in blended learning, Sect. 4 describes the methods of teaching and learning evaluations. Finally, some conclusions are outlined and future work is presented in Sect. 5.

2   Related Work

Blended learning is a learning approach that retains the values of traditional education while incorporates advanced educational technologies. In 2008, Garrison and Vaughan introduced three cases of mixed learning. In a small class of politics, blended learning enables students to gain more meaningful experience. In a large class of chemistry, blended learning is used to increase teacher-student interaction and improve problem-solving skills [1]. Graham et al. put forward a framework for adoption and implementation of blended learning based on the investigation in six American universities. They are divided into three categories:

awareness or exploration, adoption early implementation and mature implementation growth [2]. In general, blended teaching can be understood in such a way: the students acquire knowledge not only in the classroom, but also have online courses in extracurricular time, so they have the freedom to control the progress of learning themselves. With the two study phases connected as a whole, the students' individual learning needs are met.

In 2003, professor He proposed the concept of blended learning in China firstly. Combining the advantages of traditional learning and e-learning, blended learning further emphasizes the role of teachers' leading guidance as well as the dominant position of student's studying abilities. The theory of blended learning causes a revolution in the education sectors [3]. In 2006, Huang et al. addressed the way of using appropriate technology and means to impart knowledge to students, so as to optimize the effect of learning [4]. Professor Li Kedong believe that blended learning can be applied on the appropriate teaching platform and media, so as to benefit the effect of learning [5]. The theory of blended learning has been continuously improving and developing.

3   Practice of Blended Learning in Python Programming

In order to follow the idea of "Internet + education" and improve the quality of teaching, we choose the "python programming" as a practical object in the elective course at colleges, then introduce the blended learning to explore the effect of teaching in practical courses.

3.1   Analysis Before Class

Before implementing the form of blended learning, we design the questionnaire, with the aim to fully know student's basic information, such as learning ability, cognition, and so on. There are 98 copies are issued, and all of the copies are actually received, so the effective rate is 100%.

Basic Information About Students. The objects are four-year undergraduate students from different grades and schools, and the course of python programming is organized for a mixed class. The student's cognitive style, computer knowledge and learning habits are different, that is to say, the basic information of students should not only conducive to their aptitude, but also conducive to a reasonable teaching plan in content. The students in the class come from 12 different colleges in this university, including the school of Information Science and Engineering, the school of Music, the school of Physics and Electronic Sciences, etc. The analysis of the basic information of students is shown in Table 1.

As the proportion of boys and girls is close to 1:1, the teachers have to take the logical differences between boys and girls into account. In fact, the boys have some advantages in practical abilities, while the girls have more advantages on careful thinking, which make it possible for the teachers to strengthen unity and cooperation among students, so as to promote the advantages of complementarity. Based on the actual situation, the curriculum designed for python programming is as follows: the content of the course emphasizes basic theoretical knowledge and important technical practice; the face to face teaching adopts the form of case-driven teaching and group collaboration methods; the online teaching content adopts the task learning list which is driven by the combination of a variety of learning forms, including online video, knowledge point testing, projects and so on.

Table 1. Basic information about students.

Grade	Gender	School		
		Computer	Management	Others
Freshman	Male	13	3	12
	Female	2	15	27
Sophomore	Male	13	0	3
	Female	0	0	9

Students' Level of Basic Knowledge. There are differences in the basis of students' computer knowledge. For example, Question-Whether you have ever studied a programming course? It can be seen that the proportion of those who studied programming and those who have never studied programming is close to 1:1, which means that nearly half of the students have blank knowledge or have a very weak foundation for programming.

Continuing with Question-What do you think of your ability to program now? The results are shown in Fig. 1, from level 1 to level 5, the ability is decreasing. Accounting to about 50% of the total, the proportion of the students with poor programming ability is about 33%. Nearly 90% of the students have poor programming skills. Maybe they consider that this course is too hard to understand. Therefore, teachers may explain to them that the purpose of this course is to teach basic application, so as to enhance the self-confidence learning in studying such a course.

Students' Attitude to Blended Learning. Blended learning differs from traditional teaching. Prior to class, teachers should be aware of students' attitudes about blended learning. For Question-Which teaching method do you prefer? The result is shown that more than half of the students tend to blended learning model, what' more, for Question-Do you support learning the course in a blended learning fashion? 82% of the students support the method of blended learning, only a few students hesitant or hold opposition attitude, indicating that most students have a positive attitude towards mixed-type courses, which is important in the process of mixed teaching.

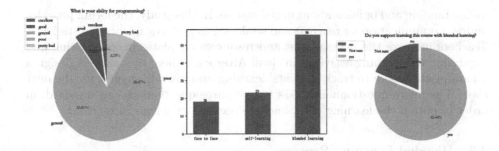

Fig. 1. The feedback students' ability for blended learning

From the above it can be seen that there is much differences in the basis in students' abilities in programming, but students have a strong motivation to learn and most students are willing to try this new approach in the curriculum.

3.2 Resources and Activities Design

Selecting the appropriate learning platform helps teachers control the entire teaching process better. From the studies of Xu [6], the online learning platform for blended learning is increasingly being transformed from the formal platform to the informal platform where the informal platform is more personalized according to the truly customized teaching situation. In the course of python programming, we select Superstar online as our blended learning platform.

Teaching resources design is essential to rich the learning resources in online platform. Teachers add modules and upload learning resources to Superstar learning platform, which meets the individual teaching needs of teachers, while the Micro lesson videos are recorded. Compared with the existing open class or excellent courses on the internet, 8 to 10 min of high efficiency micro-class is benefit to make a deep impression on students. Moreover, homemade microclasses can satisfy the needs of students more accurately, and flexibly adjust the learning content by students themselves. The python programming resources online includes general introduction to python, python basic operation, python data structure, python data reading and analysis data, project practice, and etc. Weekly course is equipped with a sheet on autonomy learning task to give guidance in learning. Other modules such as the homework module and QA module are set to meet our needs. In the course of blended learning, information technology is regards as a means of teaching, and the teachers would not be replaced by technical means [7].

In teaching activities, learning activities for students mainly include collaborative learning, self-learning, physical learning, practical learning and so on. In addition, interaction among students and teachers are also included. Such a learning style is an indispensable part, though it is more informal, for online forums play an important role in necessary communication. Moreover, the teachers obtain a large amount of information from the forums. For example, students' understanding and opinion about mixed course. In this study, the forum provides online communication for teachers and students, as well as students and students. Teachers improve the management and resources on platform, monitoring and regulating the learning activities in class. After each class, the teachers design a micro-questionnaire to track students' learning and provide suggest for the next class. The micro-questionnaire takes two or three questions as the standard, in order to obtain the learning effect and the possible problems in teaching.

3.3   Blended Learning Process

With the development of Internet and educational technologies, blended learning is better to meet the study needs of students. Before the class, the teachers place recorded video which is necessary on the teaching platform; students can control the learning process by themselves. When difficult points are met, students can watch the video repeatedly. In the face-to-face teaching, teachers in the class-room focus on the key point in learning. On problems that arise in practice, the students communicate with their classmates or ask teachers in their class time. In this way, the students' abilities of hands-on in practice are strength-ened. Compared with traditional teaching, the students' passive acceptance of the rigid knowledge in the book is changed so as to achieve the skills and abilities of being practical.

For each session in python programming, students autonomously study on the teaching platform, refer to the autonomous learning quiz, watching instructional videos, etc. As to the questionable points of knowledge, they discuss with class-mates or teachers in the discussion form. Generally speaking, a group consists of five or six students, and the members of the group work together. Moreover, they would communicate with each other among different groups. The form of group learning enables everyone to participate in the learning activities, which greatly stimulates students' enthusiasm in learning. The teachers guide the students to focus on the memory of knowledge points and solve the students' doubts, using a task-driven approach to enable students to "do" the theory and practice linked. As a result, A project or some small exercises are selective to encourage students to demonstrate their learning results in the classroom, and the classroom is left to demonstrate their experiments and experience in using python if necessary.

4   The Analysis of Evaluation Results

In modern education, the public pay more attention to the performance of stu-dents in practice and prefer multiple evaluations. Therefore, the goal of teaching is changed to "promote the all-round development of students".

4.1   Subjective Teaching Effectiveness Survey

After the course, questionnaires and interviews are applied to have an insight on students' thinking about blended learning. From the students' evaluation for the course, it can be seen that the improvement of students' learning ability, as well as the outstanding scores of students' participating in competitions are achieved. Moveover, the blended learning bring advantages in learning habits for both teachers and students.

Using the novel form of blended learning, the cooperative ability of students is improved. About 89% of the students think that their abilities are improved. Then the teachers communicate with the rest part of students to find out possible reasons that affect their ability to enhance. These factors are the key points for improving blended learning.

As to the question of whether or not to support blended learning, 49% of the students chose strong supporting and 47% of them just support blended learning, while only 4% of them oppose it. Compared with the premixed questionnaire survey, 35% of the students strongly support it, and 45% of them just support it, while 20% of them oppose it. It can be seen that the overall number of students who support it rising markedly and the number of students who oppose it is remarkably decreased. From Question-with blended learning, what are you most benefits from the course? 40% of the students gain knowledge about python and improve their ability to programming, 22% of them increase their ability to collaborate, and 24% increase their ability to discover problem and the ability to solve problems, 14% of the students get more interest in learning. In all, these factors promote the improvement of the overall abilities of the students. In Question-whether the blended learning activities boost your learning in the python class? 53% of the students think it very helpful, 38% consider it helpful, which shows that blended teaching helps student learn better. The results are shown in Fig. 2.

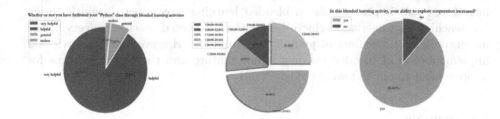

Fig. 2. The analysis of evaluation results

Can you finish the learning tasks easily and in time? As to this question, about 30% of the students delay the completion of the task, or can't complete the task of learning on time, which indicates that the learning efficiency of students is not high. On the main factors that affect students' completing the task of learning, 31% of the students think it is inconvenient to complete the task, while 17% of students think it inconvenient to use computer network, and 30% of the students think that they lack of good learning habits. In order to enhance the responsibility of the students in the course, the teachers should adjust the learning tasks to a reasonable level and make a more humanized arrangement to ensure that the students have enough time to complete the task. In fact, about 54% of the students believe that the blended learning put forward higher requirements to teaching and learning, which requires the cooperation in teachers and students to coordinate learning activities and improve their adaptability to blended learning.

4.2   Objective Teaching Effect Survey

After a semester of blended learning activities, the teaching platform recorded the students' performance of learning activities in detail, and obtained the data such as the number of visiting, students' scores, the duration of the videos, the number of discussions, the chapter tests and so on. With the data obtained, data process such as pretreatment and standardization is applied to obtain valuable information on blended learning.

As for the interview period, 73.44% of the students visited the learning platform from 16.00 pm to 24.00 pm. Thus, most of the students took advantage of the one-day course after completing their daytime course, and used free time in evening to study. They visit the learning platform in dormitory or study room to review or preview the course, which means the students' online learning are achieved mainly by computers. Therefore, the next improvement is to extend a more flexible fashion of mobile terminals for blended learning.

5   Summary

In this study, a semester' teaching with the novel form of blended learning is introduced and improvements on blended learning is conducted, which enrich the teaching methods and achieve better-than-expected teaching effects in the undergraduate curriculum of python programming. However, the research and implementation of blended learning is not mature and there is still rooms for improvement in our following study.

References

1. Garrison, D.R., Vaughan, N.D.: Blended Learning in Higher Education: Framework, Principles, and Guidelines. Wiley, New York (2008)
2. Graham, C.R., Woodfield, W., Harrison, J.B.: A framework for institutional adoption and implementation of blended learning in higher education. Internet High. Educ. **18**, 4–14 (2013)
3. Kukang, H.: From blending learning to see the new development of educational technology theory (Part Two). China Electrochem. Educ. **3**, 5–10 (2004)
4. Ronghuai, H.: The Theory and Practice of Blended Learning, pp. 33–35. Higher Education Press, Beijing (2006)
5. Li, K., Zhao, J.: The principle and application of hybrid learning. Electr. Educ. Res. **2**(7), 1–6 (2004)

6. Meidan, X.: Study and Design of Mixed Learning Based on WeChat Public Platform. Normal University, Nanjing (2016)
7. Cheng, G., Chau, J.: Exploring the relationships between learning styles, online participation, learning achievement and course satisfaction: an empirical study of a blended learning course. Br. J. Educ. Technol. 47(2), 257–278 (2016)

APs Deployment Optimization for Indoor Fingerprint Positioning with Adaptive Particle Swarm Algorithm

Jianhui Zhao[1], Jun Li[1], Haojun Ai[1,2], and Bo Cai[1(✉)]

[1] School of Computer Science, Wuhan University,
Wuhan 430072, Hubei, China
bo_cai@yeah.net
[2] Collaborative Innovation Center of Geospatial Technology,
Wuhan 430079, Hubei, China

Abstract. Indoor positioning service gives people much better convenience, but its efficiency is affected by the spatial deployment of access points, APs. We propose an algorithm from adaptive particle swarm, APS, and then apply it in APs deployment optimization for fingerprint based indoor positioning. In our method, solutions of APs placement are taken as individuals of one population. Particle swarm method is improved with adaptive technology to ensure the population diversity and also avoid large number of inferior particles. After evolutions, the optimal result is obtained, corresponding to the best solution of APs deployment. The algorithm works well for both single-objective and multi-objective optimizations. Experiments with deployments of 107 iBeacons have been tested in an underground parking lot. Compared with the existing APs placement methods, our APS algorithm can obtain the least indoor positioning error with fixed APs number, while receive the best integrated evaluation considering both positioning error and APs cost with unfixed APs number. The proposed algorithm is easily popularized to the other kinds of indoor spaces and different types of signal sources.

Keywords: Indoor positioning · APs deployment · Optimization algorithm
Adaptive particle swarm

1 Introduction

Positioning technology can be used in outdoor and indoor environments. Outdoor positioning technology includes GPS, Galileo, Beidou navigation satellite system, etc. However, satellite signal attenuates seriously when it penetrates building, while the complex indoor environment causes further signal attenuation, thus it is impossible to achieve indoor positioning with satellite signal. Currently, there is an increasing demand for indoor positioning, e.g., locating one person in a building, floor, or even room; finding certain good in the warehouse; positioning your wallet, key in an office; and so on. Indoor positioning can greatly facilitate people's work and life, and it has received more attentions from users and researchers [1, 2].

© Springer Nature Switzerland AG 2018
J. Vaidya and J. Li (Eds.): ICA3PP 2018, LNCS 11336, pp. 218–228, 2018.
https://doi.org/10.1007/978-3-030-05057-3_17

The indoor positioning system may use different types of signal sources [3], such as WiFi, Bluetooth, UWB, LED, Ultrasonic, RFID, Infrared, ZigBee, etc. According to the positioning algorithm, indoor positioning mainly includes cell-ID positioning, triangle positioning, multilateral positioning and fingerprint positioning methods [4]. Cell-ID positioning and triangle positioning methods cannot guarantee the accuracy of positioning. Multilateral positioning method has theoretically high positioning accuracy, but it is difficult to obtain time and angle parameters from the ordinary equipment. Fingerprint based positioning collects signal characteristic parameters of different positions in space, and establishes the fingerprint database, then the target position is determined by comparing the received signals with signal characteristic parameters in database. Therefore, fingerprinting method is usually used for indoor positioning. Ma et al. [5] presented an indoor positioning system based on intelligent fingerprint assisted method to calculate the reliable reference point data and develop a learning mechanism through wireless network connection. Xia et al. [6] developed a method of processing the off-line data and an improved KNN positioning method to improve the positioning precision based on fingerprint. Raspopoulos [7] studied the use of deterministic channel modeling through 3D Ray Tracing for constructing the device independent radio maps for WiFi RSSI-based fingerprinting indoor positioning system, which is applicable to different devices.

Deploying the signal sources (access points, APs) properly in advance is very important for indoor positioning technology. There are two types of APs deployment approaches: non-optimal and optimization methods, while the non-optimal method mainly refers to uniform deployment. Traditional APs deployment usually adopts the uniform method, i.e., signal sources are evenly distributed in one space. But there may be less accurate positioning result with too few APs, or unnecessary waste with too many APs. In order to achieve both precise indoor positioning and low cost, APs deployment should be optimized. Maximum and Minimum Coverage (MMC) method proposed by Dhillon and Chakrabarty [8] uses the polynomial-time algorithms to determine the number of sensors and their placement to help address the coverage optimization under constraints of imprecise detections and terrain properties. Based on Cramer-Rao Lower Bound (CRLB) and Simulated Annealing (SA), Zhou et al. [9] presented an optimization method for APs placement, which focuses on the error bound analysis of indoor WiFi fingerprint based positioning for intelligent APs placement using Fisher Information Matrix (FIM) to characterize the relationship between positioning errors and signal distributions. Besides, there are other kinds of complex optimization methods [10, 11], e.g., genetic algorithm, artificial immune algorithm, particle swarm optimization, etc., and they can also be used for APs deployment optimization of indoor positioning.

Particle Swarm Optimization (PSO) has been widely utilized in the fields of neural network training, function optimization and fuzzy system control. For optimization, PSO has good search depth, but its search breadth is insufficient [12]. Therefore, an adaptive particle swarm algorithm, APS, is proposed to optimize APs deployment for indoor fingerprint positioning. The APS can improve the breadth searching ability of traditional PSO, and can generate better global optimization. Compared with existing optimization algorithms, our proposed method can obtain more optimal indoor APs placement, including both single-objective (e.g., indoor positioning error) and multi-objective (e.g., positioning error and APs cost) evolutions.

2 Our Algorithm for Indoor APs Deployment

In our work, fingerprint based positioning method is used for indoor location, while positioning error and APs cost are mainly considered in defining the objective function. The adaptive PSO, APS, is implemented for spatial optimization of APs.

2.1 Objective Function and Fingerprint Positioning

To test the efficiency of different optimization algorithms for APs deployment, APs are initially placed on the reference points in indoor space. Then some of the APs are chosen as one possible solution of deployment optimization, and their locations are estimated with fingerprint positioning method. The differences between reference points and estimated points are calculated, and taken as positioning error for the selected APs. Considering the positioning error, or considering both the positioning error and the cost of APs, the objective function value can be computed, and then used to evaluate the spatial deployment of APs. With the help of optimization algorithm, the optimal APs deployment is obtained after iterations of searching. Given indoor space and APs parameters, the optimization algorithm can provide installing suggestion for signal sources.

Suppose there are n APs in indoor place, and m of them are selected as one deployment. The chosen APs are evaluated as follows.

1. Place all the n APs evenly in the building for indoor positioning, i.e., their row spacing and column spacing are both k meters, and coordinates of all the APs are recorded as reference points in a database.
2. For the selected m APs, their coordinates or the corresponding m reference points are retrieved from the database.
3. Signal values from APs are received at each reference point, and are recorded by mobile phone as fingerprints in a 2D array, i.e., data in the jth column and the ith row is the signal value of the jth AP collected at the ith reference point.
4. Coordinates are estimated for each of the selected m APs, and then are recorded as their estimated points.
5. As one solution of APs spatial deployment, the selected m APs are evaluated by the unified objective function:

$$OF = \alpha * APE + \beta * COA \tag{1}$$

$$APE = \frac{\sum_{i=1}^{m} \sqrt{(x_{ei} - x_{ri})^2 + (y_{ei} - y_{ri})^2}}{m} \tag{2}$$

where *OF* is the objective function, while *APE* is the averaged positioning error and *COA* is the cost of APs, α and β are their weighting parameters, (x_{ri}, y_{ri}) is coordinates of the ith reference point, (x_{ei}, y_{ei}) is coordinates of the ith estimated point.

Obviously, the smaller value of objective function means the better APs placement, i.e., the deployment with less positioning error and APs cost. The average positioning error is obtained through fingerprint positioning, and the method for obtaining the estimated coordinates of the ith reference point is described as follows.

1. For each of the *m* APs, compare its fingerprint with every fingerprint already recorded in the database, i.e., calculate the Euclidean distance between two fingerprints.
2. Find the 3 fingerprints with the smaller Euclidean distances w1, w2 and w3 from database, then obtain coordinates of the 3 corresponding reference points (x1, y1), (x2, y2), (x3, y3).
3. The estimated coordinates of the ith reference point is computed as:

$$x_{ei} = ((x1/w1) + (x2/w2) + (x3/w3))/((1/w1) + (1/w2) + (1/w3)) \qquad (3)$$

$$y_{ei} = ((y1/w1) + (y2/w2) + (y3/w3))/((1/w1) + (1/w2) + (1/w3)) \qquad (4)$$

where coordinates of the ith estimated point are calculated from 3 reference points with similar fingerprints, and the more similar reference point has the bigger effect by using the reciprocal of Euclidean distance as weighting parameter.

For the application of indoor positioning, position of mobile phone is estimated in the same way. In our work, the mobile phone is supposed to be placed at each location of APs one by one. Thus the reference points and their estimated points can be used to define the positioning error of the related deployment.

2.2 Implementation of Adaptive PSO

PSO algorithm is easy to fall into the local optimum, so we improve the optimization algorithm to increase its breadth searching ability. The improved PSO is named as Adaptive Particle Swarm (APS) algorithm, which can ensure the population diversity and avoid the introduction of large number of inferior particles.

The basic idea of APS is: (1) set up a threshold; (2) take one particle as an excellent particle if its objective function value is no more than the threshold, otherwise take it as an inferior particle; (3) increase the threshold adaptively if the number of excellent particles is too small, or reduce the threshold adaptively if the number of them is too big. The proposed APS is used for the problem of indoor positioning APs placement optimization, and the procedure is as follows.

1. Initialize the population of particles, and calculate the objective function value of each particle, the specific process is described in Pseudocode 1.
2. Initialize the history optimal value "pbest" for each particle, and initialize the population optimal value "gbest" for all particles, i.e., "gbest" is the least value of all "pbest" in the same generation.
3. Adaptively adjust the particles to obtain better optimization result, and the specific process is described in Pseudocode 2.
4. Update the individual history optimal value "pbest" with the least objective function value for each particle, and the population optimal value "gbest" with the least objective function value for all particles.
5. Take "gbest" as result if the maximum number of iterations is reached or if "gbest" satisfies the requirement, and take the corresponding particle with "gbest" as the optimal solution of APs deployment; otherwise, go to Step (3).

Pseudocode 1:

---

01 **for** i:=0 **to** sizepop-1
02   num[i] = random(n); // Number of APs randomly generated for the ith particle
03   **for** j:=0 **to** num[i]-1
04   Randomly generate the x-coordinate x_{ij} in the range of [Xmin, Xmax];
05   Randomly generate the y-coordinate y_{ij} in the range of [Ymin, Ymax];
06   Randomly generate the velocity in x direction and the velocity in y direction in the range of [Vmin, Vmax];
07   Obtain AP number tmp[j] corresponding to the coordinates (x_{ij} , y_{ij});
08   **repeat**
09   Remove the duplicated APs in tmp array due to the random generation;
10   Randomly generate new APs if the number of APs is less than num[i];
11   **until** there is no duplicated APs in tmp array;
12   fitness[i] = Calculate(num[i], tmp); // Calculate the objective function value of the ith particle

---

For each particle, sizepop is the population size, num[i] is the number of APs in the ith particle, and fitness[i] is the objective function value of the ith particle. [Xmin, Xmax] is the x coordinate range of indoor space, [Ymin, Ymax] is the y coordinate range of indoor space, and [Vmin, Vmax] is the velocity range of particles. Based on the coordinates, the corresponding AP is determined, thus our method can deal with randomly labeled APs in indoor space.

Pseudocode 2:

---

01 **repeat**
02   goodnum = 0; // Number of good particles is initialized
03   **for** i:=0 **to** sizepop-1
04   if fitness[i] <= Tgood
05   goodnum++;
06   **if** goodnum > Nmax
07   Tgood = Tgood-v1;
08   **else if** goodnum < Nmin
09   Tgood = Tgood+v2;
10 **until** goodnum >= Nmin;
11 Sort all particles according to their objective function values from small to large;
12 Eliminate all the inferior particles;
13 **if** number of excellent particles <= half of population size
14   Increase a copy of all the excellent particles;
15 **else**
16   Increase a copy of some excellent particles according to their objective function
values from small to large, until the number of particles is the size of population;
17 Update speed and location of excellent particles except for the copied particles;
18 Calculate objective function values for the updated particles;
19 **if** number of particles < population size
20   Use the same method as Pseudocode 1 to generate particles randomly;
21   Calculate the objective function values of the supplementary particles;

The threshold Tgood is predefined to decide one particle as an excellent or inferior particle. The number of excellent particles is goodnum, while Nmax is the maximum number of excellent particles and Nmin is the minimum number of excellent particles. Values v1/v2 are defined to decrease/increase the threshold Tgood, and we set v1 > v2 to avoid the large number of inferior particles.

3   Experimental Results and Analysis

Based on experiments of APs deployment for fingerprint based indoor positioning, efficiency of our APS algorithm is analyzed. Our approach is also compared with the existing optimization methods, including Maximum and Minimum Coverage (MMC) based method, Cramer-Rao Lower Bound (CRLB) based method, Genetic Algorithm (GA) and Artificial Immune Algorithm (AIA).

3.1   Testing Environment

In our work, all the algorithms are tested in the positioning space of one underground parking lot, as shown in Fig. 1. Taking iBeasons as APs, there are 107 signal sources.

The APs are evenly deployed in the indoor parking lot, with row spacing and column spacing about 4.5 m.

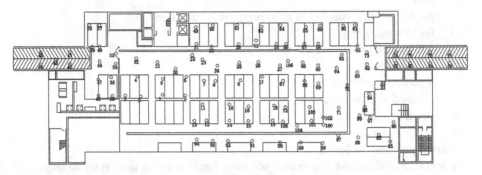

Fig. 1. Positioning space of underground parking lot with 107 iBeacons

Fingerprint database is acquired as follows: take the 107 APs locations as reference points; at each reference point use an Android mobile phone orientated to the same direction to collect the received signal strength from each AP; obtain 600 sets of data from each reference point within 1 min with once collection every 100 ms; store the collected data of each reference point as one XML file; calculate the average value of 600 sets of data, and take it as fingerprint of the reference point.

Our experiments are executed in a computer with Inter (R) Core i5-6400 processor, 2.70 GHz CPU, 8 GB memory, NVIDIA GeForce GTX 1050 Ti graphics card, Win7 64-bit operating system, and VS2015.

3.2 Parameters of Each Algorithm

Based on the positioning space of underground parking lot, the parameters of our APS algorithm are set as: Xmin is 4832, Xmax is 4863, Ymin is 5353, Ymax is 5449, Vmin is -30 (speed in the negative direction), Vmax is 30 (speed in the positive direction), the initial Tgood is 7.1, Nmin is 5, Nmax is 20, v1 is 0.05, v2 is 0.03, c_1 and c_2 are 2.0, s_{min} is 0, s_{max} is 10, σ_{xinit} is 15.0, σ_{xfinal} is 5.0, σ_{yinit} is 45.0, σ_{yfinal} is 5.0.

The parameters of MMC based algorithm are the same as Reference [8].

The parameters of CRLB based algorithm are the same as Reference [9].

The parameters of GA algorithm are set as: the occurrence probability of the cross operations is 0.5, the occurrence probability of the mutation operations is 0.2.

The parameters of AIA algorithm are set as: the cross mutation rate is 0.85, the mutation rate of a single gene is 0.65, the parameter of diversity evaluation is 0.95.

For all the above optimization algorithms, the population size is 50, the maximum number of iterations is 80, the maximum number of APs is 107.

When number of APs is fixed, the objective function only considers the average positioning error, which is:

$$OF = 1.0 * APE + 0.0 * COA \tag{5}$$

When number of signal sources is unfixed, the objective function considers both the average positioning error and the cost of APs, i.e., the number of APs since they are all iBeasons in our experiments, which is:

$$OF = 1.0 * APE + 0.075 * COA \tag{6}$$

3.3 Performances with Fixed APs Number

When the number of APs is fixed, all algorithms are compared only considering the average indoor positioning error for the deployment optimization. There are 88 tests performed for each algorithm, corresponding to the number of APs from 20 to 107. As illustrated in Fig. 2, our combined algorithm obtains the minimum location error with the same number of APs as other methods, and thus gives the best deployment of APs. From the experiment result, performances of all related algorithms are ordered ascendingly as: CRLB, MMC, GA, AIA, APS.

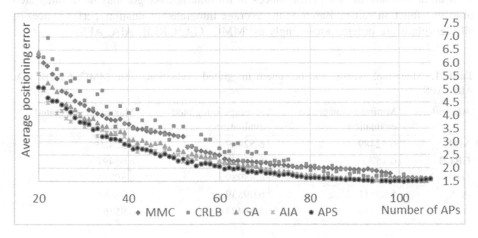

Fig. 2. Positioning errors from MMC, CRLB, GA, AIA, APS

3.4 Performances with Unfixed APs Number

When the number of APs is unfixed, all algorithms are compared considering both the average positioning error and the cost of APs (i.e., the number of iBeasons) for deployment optimization. There are 10 tests for each algorithm, and the results are shown in Fig. 3. Obviously, APS algorithm obtains the minimum objective function value or the best integrated evaluation of positioning error and APs cost, and thus gives the best deployment of iBeasons.

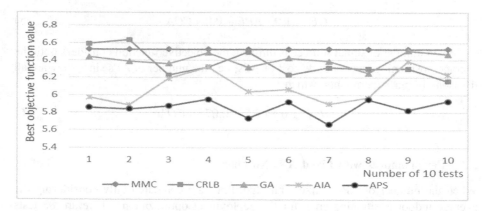

Fig. 3. Integrated evaluations of positioning error and APs cost from MMC, CRLB, GA, AIA, APS

Then the minimum, average and maximum integrated objective function values of the 10 tests are listed in Table 1 for all the methods. It can be found that the proposed APS algorithm has all best performances in minimum, average, maximum integrated objective function values. Based on the average integrated evaluation, performances of all algorithms are ordered ascendingly as: MMC, GA, CRLB, AIA, APS.

Table 1. Minimum, average and maximum integrated evaluations from MMC, CRLB, GA, AIA, APS

Algorithms	Minimum integrated evaluation	Average integrated evaluation	Maximum integrated evaluation
MMC	6.52489	6.52489	6.52489
CRLB	6.15706	6.35707	6.63497
GA	6.25092	6.38989	6.50733
AIA	5.88511	6.09539	6.38688
APS	5.73439	5.85493	5.95164

According to the above experiments in the underground parking lot, our APS algorithm has been proven to be the best optimization method of APs spatial deployment for fingerprint based indoor positioning. From the tests with fixed or unfixed APs number, the proposed combination algorithm can generate the best optimal result, including both single-objective (indoor positioning error) evolution and multi-objective (positioning error and APs cost) evolution.

4 Conclusion

The indoor positioning technology is becoming more and more important, since it can bring much convenience to people. With the development of various signal sources, a lot of indoor positioning approaches have been designed. Among existing algorithms, the fingerprint positioning is usually used with established fingerprint database. The efficiency of indoor positioning is affected by the spatial deployment of access points, which should be considered before APs installing. There are already some algorithms for APs deployment, such as uniform placement, linear programming and nonlinear optimization. Some complex optimization methods have been used for deployment of APs, such as GA, AIA, etc.

To help overcome the disadvantage of PSO such as insufficient searching breadth, we propose a new algorithm, APS. The breadth searching ability of PSO is improved with an adaptive method, which can maintain the population diversity and avoid more inferior particles. The APS method has better depth and breadth searching abilities, and works well for APs deployment with single or multiple objectives. Based on a series of experiments with 107 iBeacons in an underground parking lot, our algorithm is tested and compared with the other optimization methods. It has been proven that the proposed APS achieves the best APs deployment with the least indoor positioning error, or the least integrated evaluation considering both positioning error and APs cost. All the algorithms are tested with fingerprint indoor positioning in underground parking lot, taking iBeacons as signal sources. In the future, APS will be tested in more positioning spaces, with more types of APs. The optimization algorithm will consider affects and constraints of different indoor environments, and complementary advantages from various kinds of APs. Our ultimate aim is to provide a very popular optimization method for APs spatial deployment, and help implement precise indoor positioning in complex spaces with multiple types of APs.

Acknowledgments. This work was supported by the National Key Research and Development Program of China (Project No. 2016YFB0502201).

References

1. Li, C.C., Su, J., Chu, T.H., Liu, J.W.S.: Building/environment data/information enabled location specificity and indoor positioning. IEEE Internet Things J. **4**, 2116–2128 (2017)
2. Zou, H., Wang, H., Xie, L., Jia, Q.S.: An RFID indoor positioning system by using weighted path loss and extreme learning machine. In: IEEE International Conference on Cyber-physical Systems, Taipei, Taiwan, pp. 66–71 (2013)
3. Khalajmehrabadi, A., Gatsis, N., Akopian, D.: Modern WLAN fingerprinting indoor positioning methods and deployment challenges. IEEE Commun. Surv. Tutor. **19**, 1974–2002 (2017)
4. Chen, K., Wang, C., Yin, Z., Jiang, H., Tan, G.: Slide: towards fast and accurate mobile fingerprinting for wi-fi indoor positioning systems. IEEE Sens. J. **18**, 1213–1223 (2018)
5. Ma, Y.W., Chen, J.L., Liao, J.J., Tang, C.L.: Intelligent fingerprint-assisted for indoor positioning system. In: IEEE International Workshop on Electromagnetics, vol. 85, pp. 108–109 (2014)

6. Xia, M., Chen, J., Song, C., Li, N., Chen, K.: The indoor positioning algorithm research based on improved location fingerprinting. In: 27th Chinese Control and Decision Conference, Qingdao, China, pp. 5736–5739 (2015)
7. Raspopoulos, M.: Multidevice map-constrained fingerprint-based indoor positioning using 3-D ray tracing. IEEE Trans. Instrum. Meas. **67**, 466–476 (2018)
8. Dhillon, S.S., Chakrabarty, K.: Sensor placement for effective coverage and surveillance in distributed sensor networks. In: Wireless Communications and Networking, WCNC, vol. 3, pp. 1609–1614 (2003)
9. Zhou, M., Qiu, F., Xu, K., Tian, Z., Wu, H.: Error bound analysis of indoor wi-fi location fingerprint based positioning for intelligent access point optimization via fisher information. Comput. Commun. **86**, 57–74 (2016)
10. Du, X., Yang, K.: A map-assisted wifi AP placement algorithm enabling mobile device's indoor positioning. IEEE Syst. J. **11**, 1467–1475 (2017)
11. Chen, X., Zou, S.: Improved wi-fi indoor positioning based on particle swarm optimization. IEEE Sens. J. **17**, 7143–7148 (2017)
12. Cai, Y., Guan, W., Wu, Y., Xie, C., Chen, Y., Fang, L.: Indoor high precision three-dimensional positioning system based on visible light communication using particle swarm optimization. IEEE Photonics J. **9**, 1–20 (2017)

Deployment Optimization of Indoor Positioning Signal Sources with Fireworks Algorithm

Jianhui Zhao[1], Shiqi Wen[1], Haojun Ai[1,2], and Bo Cai[1(✉)]

[1] School of Computer Science, Wuhan University, Wuhan 430072, Hubei , China
bo_cai@yeah.net
[2] Collaborative Innovation Center of Geospatial Technology, Wuhan 430079, Hubei , China

Abstract. Spatial deployment of signal sources affects performance of indoor positioning systems, thus has received more attentions in recent years. This paper presents a FWA method from fireworks algorithm, to provide the optimal deployment solution. Taking fine chromosomes as fireworks, the explosion factors are set including the number of explosion sparks and the radius of all explosion sparks. The supplemented individuals are produced from explosion and random generation, which helps increase the diversity of population and guarantee the qualities of individuals. After crossover and mutation, population evolves to the next generation. The optimal result from evolutions refers to a deployment solution, i.e., certain number of signal sources with their locations. The FWA algorithm has been tested to have good convergence ability by a series of experiments, with iBeacons based indoor positioning system in an underground parking lot and the fingerprint based indoor location method. Compared with the usually used optimization algorithms, FWA has the best searching ability in single-objective and multi-objective cases, and it obtains the best optimization result considering only positioning error, or both positioning error and the cost of iBeacons. Therefore, the proposed FWA provides optimal deployment of signal sources for indoor positioning systems.

Keywords: Spatial deploying · Fireworks method · Indoor position Fingerprint

1 Introduction

Positioning technology can be divided into outdoor positioning and indoor positioning. GPS is the most famous outdoor positioning system, which implement locating by transmitting signal source, receiving signal intensity and calculating distances. Due to the irregularity of building structure and the complexity of indoor materials in certain complicated interiors such as shopping malls, there are different influences on the attenuation of satellite signal intensity. Therefore, people are trying to install sensors such as Wi-Fi, Bluetooth and LED for indoor positioning.

Multiple signal sources, or even different types of them have been used for indoor locating. Jung and Han presented a WRMs calibration system that automates the initial construction and maintenance of Wi-Fi maps for crowdsourcing based indoor

© Springer Nature Switzerland AG 2018
J. Vaidya and J. Li (Eds.): ICA3PP 2018, LNCS 11336, pp. 229–238, 2018.
https://doi.org/10.1007/978-3-030-05057-3_18

positioning, it uses crowdsourced fingerprints collected from numerous smartphones and incorporates an unsupervised learning algorithm [1]. Chen et al. used both a commodity flashlight and a smartphone to achieve linear positioning, which allows automatic mapping from received signal strength to the position on a line, serving as a building block for fingerprinting in general environments [2]. Popoola and Sinanović designed a low complex indoor positioning system, and the accuracy is improved using overlap between LED beams, while collision handling algorithms are designed for LED packets in the overlap region [3]. Zheng et al. proposed an optical indoor positioning scheme using a single LED as beacon and a camera as receiver, where the joint measured angle of arrival and received light strength are utilized as fingerprint to determine the position of receiver [4]. There are other kinds of sensors used as signal sources for indoor positioning, such as ultrasonic [5], ZigBee [6], radio maps [7], etc. Based on the properties of different kinds of sensors, they can also be utilized together to combine their advantages together. Zou et al. implemented an indoor localization and tracking system, using smartphone built-in Inertial Measurement Unit (IMU) sensors, WiFi received signal strength measurements and the opportunistic iBeacon corrections based on particle filter [8].

In case that the number of signal sources is fixed, optimal spatial deployment can improve the positioning accuracy effectively. Besides, the optimization technology can help reduce the number of signal sources while maintains the level of positioning accuracy. How to balance multiple factors such as precision, cost and so on, is the main problem of deployment optimization. The initially used spatial deployment is non-optimization method, i.e., the uniform coverage of signal sources whose core technique is to divide a space evenly. There are many ways for space dividing [9], e.g., triangulation, trilateration, hyperbolic localization, etc. Uniform coverage is simple, and works well for indoor environments with regular layout and less obstacles. However, most indoor environments are irregular and complex, thus are not suitable for uniform coverage. Maximum and minimum coverage [10] is an optimization method, which uses polynomial-time algorithms to determine the number of sensors and their placement to address the coverage optimization under the constraints of imprecise detection and terrain properties. Compared with non-optimization methods, this scheme can achieve a relatively reasonable deployment of signal sources in complicated indoor spaces. Based on Cramer-Rao Lower Bound (CRLB) and Simulated Annealing (SA), Zhou et al. designed a method for APs placement, which focuses on the error bound analysis of indoor Wi-Fi fingerprint based positioning for intelligent APs placement optimization by using Fisher Information Matrix (FIM) to characterize the relationship between positioning errors and signal distributions [11].

There are complex optimization methods, e.g., Particle Swarm Optimization (PSO), Artificial Immune Optimization (AIO), Genetic Algorithm Optimization (GAO), etc., and some of them have been adopted in spatial location optimization. Chen and Zou presented a Wi-Fi indoor positioning method using an improved unscented Kalman filter, and PSO is proposed to reduce the ranging error and improve the positioning accuracy [12]. Chen et al. predicted the next location of a mobile object based on AIO, taking into account the characteristics of short moving time and an elusive moving tendency [13]. Eldeeb et al. gave a GAO based framework to solve APs placement problem, which finds APs setup with unique fingerprints at each signal test point while maximizing diversity among these fingerprints [14]. The Fireworks Algorithm (FWA) simulates the explosion process of fireworks, thus it can increase the diversity of fireworks, meanwhile maintain the quality of fireworks. Till now, there is only a few FWA based references [15] for spatial optimization, but no report for the indoor positioning applications. The advantage of FWA makes it have possible applications in spatial deployment of indoor signal sources, thus the FWA based algorithm is proposed for indoor positioning in this paper.

2 The iBeacons Based Indoor Positioning System

2.1 The iBeacons Based Testing Environment

The testing environment is an underground parking lot, which is an indoor space with 2,800 m². As shown in Fig. 1(a), each dot means an iBeacon in the space, while red dots represent an example of deployment with certain number of signal sources and their locations. The target of our work is to find an optimal deployment with less number of iBeacons and better locating accuracy. As shown in Fig. 1(b), the installed iBeacons are labeled with red circles. There are 107 iBeacon signal sources, and they are uniformly arranged in the space. For each iBeacon, the distances between it and its adjacent signal sources are about 4.5 m. The iBeacons are taken as reference points, and they are used to locate any position in the underground parking lot.

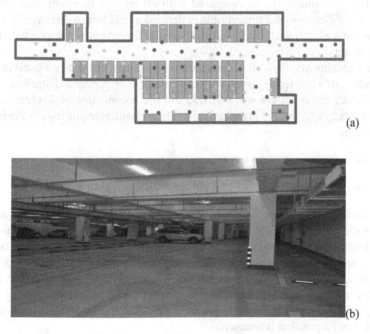

Fig. 1. The iBeacons based testing environment, (a) the layout of indoor positioning space, (b) the installed iBeacons (Color figure online)

2.2 Fingerprint Based Indoor Location Method

In our work, the fingerprint based positioning approach is adopted, which includes fingerprint database establishment and fingerprint matching. For each reference point, Received Signal Strength Indicator (RSSI) from every signal source is collected to set up the fingerprint database. During fingerprint matching, the RSSIs of one observing point (any position to be located) is compared with fingerprints in database, and location of the observing point is computed from the most similar reference points.

(1) Fingerprint database establishment

The fingerprint database for n reference points is consisted of n records, and each record is consisted of n RSSIs from all signal sources. Thus, there is an n * n matrix in database, while each record is a fingerprint. If no signal strength can be received, the RSSI is set as zero for the related row and column in matrix.

In our experiments, a mobile phone with android 5.5 is used to collect RSSIs from all iBeacons. For each reference point, the collecting time is 1 min. The acquisition frequency is once per 100 ms, so a total of 600 sets of 107 RSSIs are obtained. Then, the average values are calculated for the 600 sets, and the averaged 107 RSSIs are taken as the fingerprint for one reference point. Fingerprints for all reference points are stored into a XML file, which is the fingerprint database.

(2) Fingerprint matching

To locate an observing point, fingerprint is collected with n RSSIs from all signal sources. Then the fingerprint is compared with all records in established fingerprint database. The difference of 2 fingerprints is defined as Euclidean distance between the related 2 n-dimensional vectors. So the most similar fingerprint is the one with the least Euclidean distance.

In our experiments, 3 similar fingerprints are found for every observing point, corresponding to 3 reference points with the smallest 3 Euclidean distances. Suppose the 3 Euclidean distances are w1, w2, w3, and the coordinates of 3 reference points are (x1, y1), (x2, y2), (x3, y3) respectively. Then coordinates of the observing point is estimated by:

$$x = ((x(1)/w(1)) + (x(2)/w(2)) + (x(3)/w(3)))/((1/w(1)) + (1/w(2)) + (1/w(3))) \tag{1}$$

$$y = ((y(1)/w(1)) + (y(2)/w(2)) + (y(3)/w(3)))/((1/w(1)) + (1/w(2)) + (1/w(3))) \tag{2}$$

The coordinates (x, y) obtained from the above formula are regarded as the measured location of the observing point. Positioning error of the observing point is evaluated by the Euclidean distance between its measured location and true location. Obviously, the longer distance means the larger error. After measurements of all observing points, the averaged positioning error can be computed for them. Since the coordinates of all reference points are known in our experiments, the reference points are directly used as observing points. That is, the mobile phone is placed in the location of each reference point, and then its position is measured.

(3) Fitness function

To evaluate the located results, fitness function is defined, which may consider only the positioning precision, or consider multiple factors simultaneously. In our system, two factors are mainly considered, i.e., positioning error and cost of signal sources. Because only iBeacons are employed, cost of signal sources is the number of iBeacons being used for indoor positioning.

With the increasing of the number of signal sources, the whole positioning error decreases, while the cost of system increases. How to combine these two factors to achieve a relatively optimal result is the problem to be solved in our system. To represent and evaluate the combination, we adopt the following fitness function:

$$FFV = a * PE + b * NS \qquad (3)$$

where FFV is fitness function value, PE is the whole position error, NS is the number of signal sources, while a and b are weighting parameters.

3   Fireworks Algorithm for Indoor Positioning

Fireworks algorithm (FWA) is used for deployment optimization of signal sources, which is the first application of FWA in indoor positioning to our knowledge. The optimization procedure is shown in Fig. 2, and its main steps are described as follows.

(1) Initialization of fireworks

In FWA method, there are many fireworks, and each firework is consisted of some sparks. One firework means a set of randomly generated spatial deployment of signal sources, while each spark of firework means a signal source. The initialization procedure of FWA is the same as that of Genetic Algorithm, i.e., firework refers to chromosome, and spark refers to gene.

(2) Selection of fine fireworks

For each firework, its fitness function value is calculated. In evolution procedure of FWA, fine fireworks should increase generation after generation to obtain the more optimal results. Therefore, a constant threshold is set for fitness function value to make sure the convergence of FWA. The values of all fireworks are compared with the fitness function threshold, and the fireworks with less values than threshold are selected as fine fireworks. For the fine fireworks, they are ordered with their fitness function values from small to large.

(3) Set of explosion factors

For every fine firework, its explosion factors include the number of explosion sparks and the radius of all explosion sparks. The number of explosion sparks of fine firework x_i is computed by:

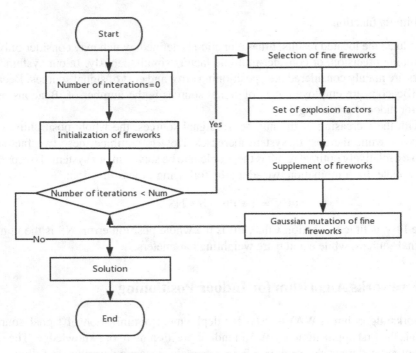

Fig. 2. Flowchart of FWA for indoor positioning

$$s_i = m * \frac{y_{max} - f(x_i) + a}{\sum_{i=1}^{n} (y_{max} - f(x_i)) + a} \tag{4}$$

where m represents the total number of sparks of the x_i firework, $f(x_i)$ represents the fitness function value of the x_i firework, y_{max} represents the maximum fitness function value of all m fireworks of current generation, the constant a is used to avoid the denominator from becoming zero.

The radius of all explosion sparks in fine firework x_i is computed as:

$$A_i = A * \frac{f(x_i) - y_{min} + a}{\sum_{i=1}^{n} (f(x_i) - y_{min}) + a} \tag{5}$$

where A represents the maximum explosion radius value set in advance, y_{min} represents the minimum fitness function value of all m fireworks of the current generation, the other parameters are the same as Eq. (4).

When a firework is exploded, the new sparks with the number from Eq. (4) are randomly selected within the range of radius from Eq. (5), while the new sparks should be different from the old ones.

(4) Supplement of fireworks

Except for the mf fine fireworks, the other mi ones of current generation are discarded since their fitness function values are too large. To make the population size m unchanged, fireworks need to be supplemented. There are two cases: mi > mf and mi <=mf. When mi > mf, the fine fireworks explode using explosion factors to generate mf new fireworks, then the (mi-mf) fireworks are randomly generated the same as initialization procedure. When mi <=mf, a ratio of mi (e.g., 0.8 * mi) number of fine fireworks with lower fitness function values are selected and explode to generate new fireworks, then the other fireworks are randomly generated.

(5) Gaussian mutation of fine fireworks

In order to increase the diversity of the population, some fine fireworks should be mutated. The number of mutation fireworks is determined with the help of Gaussian distribution, i.e., mf multiplied by a random value from Gaussian distribution. The mutation fireworks are selected randomly from mf fine fireworks, and each of them is mutated: a ratio of its sparks (e.g., 10%) are mutated, i.e., every mutation spark is replaced by another signal source with different location.

One iteration includes the above steps of selection, setting of explosion factors, supplement and Gaussian mutation. The FWA performs a certain number (Num) of such iterations (e.g., 100 times), to obtain the optimal result.

4 Experimental Results and Analysis

For the irregular underground parking lot, 6 optimization algorithms are used in our experiments for spatial deployment of signal sources. The implemented algorithms include: Maximum and Minimum Coverage (MMC), Cramer-Rao Lower Bound (CRLB), Particle Swarm Optimization (PSO), Artificial Immune Optimization (AIO), Genetic Algorithm Optimization (GAO) and our Fireworks Algorithm (FWA). All algorithms are tested with the iBeacons based indoor positioning system, and their optimization performances are compared and analyzed considering the positioning error and the cost of signal sources.

4.1 Parameters of Related Algorithms

For all the optimization algorithms, the maximum iteration number is set as 80 generations, while the population size is 50. For each optimization algorithm, the other parameters are the selected best parameters through experiments, and they are introduced as follows.

The parameters of MMC based algorithm are the same as Reference [16].

The parameters of CRLB based algorithm are the same as Reference [17].

In PSO, the particle positional range includes X coordinate range of [4832, 4863] and Y coordinate range of [5353, 5449] (corresponding to the size of underground parking lot), the particle velocity range is [−30, 30], the learning factor for particle velocity updating is 2.0.

In AIO, the crossover rate is 0.85, the mutation rate is 0.65, the weighting parameter of individual fitness is 0.95.

In GAO, the crossover rate is calculated, and the mutation rate is 0.70.

In the proposed FWA, the number of explosion sparks is calculated by Eq. (4), the radius of all explosion sparks is calculated by Eq. (5), and the Gaussian mutation rate is set as 0.4.

Our experiments are executed in a computer with Inter (R) Core i5-6400 processor, 2.70 GHz CPU, 8 GB memory, NVIDIA GeForce GTX 1050 Ti graphics card, Win7 64-bit operating system, and VS2015.

4.2   Results and Analysis

(1)   Optimization performances of positioning error

To compare the optimization performances of positioning error from all algorithms, a series of experiments are performed with different number of signal sources, i.e., 87 tests of 6 algorithms on iBeacons with the number of 20, 21,......, 106. As shown in Fig. 3, the X axis represents the 87 tests, while the Y axis represents the positioning error, i.e., PE of Eq. (3). From the experimental results, it can be found that our FWA obtains the optimal deployment with the least positioning error. From Fig. 3, performances of all related algorithms are ordered ascendingly as: CRLB, MMC, GAO, AIO, PSO, FWA.

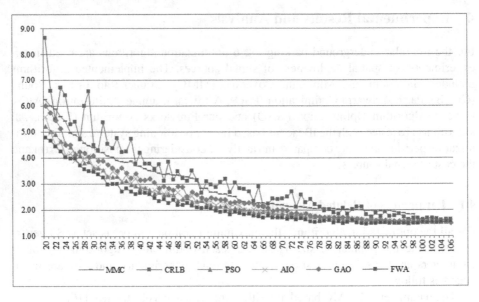

Fig. 3. Optimization comparison of positioning error

(2)   Optimization performances of positioning error and cost

Considering both positioning error and cost of signal sources, the fitness function value is the FFV of Eq. (3), with $a = 1.0$ and $b = 0.075$ in our experiments. To compare the performances of multi-objective optimization, 10 tests are executed for the 6 algorithms. As shown in Fig. 4, the X axis represents the 10 tests, while the Y axis represents the fitness function value. From the experimental results, it can be found that our proposed FWA algorithm obtains the optimal deployment with the least fitness function value.

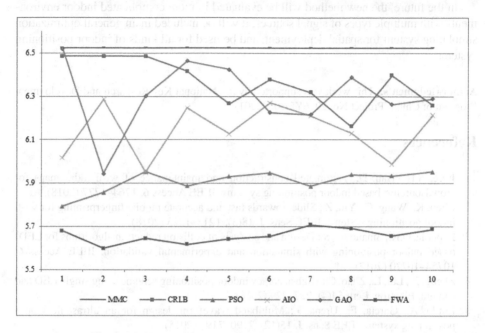

Fig. 4. Optimization comparison of positioning error and cost

From the 10 tests, the averaged fitness function values are computed, and they are: 6.5250 (MMC), 6.3650 (CRLB), 5.9087 (PSO), 6.1444 (AIO), 6.3040 (GAO), 5.6584 (FWA). Thus performances of all the algorithms are ordered ascendingly as: MMC, CRLB, GAO, AIO, PSO, FWA. Obviously, the FWA algorithm also has the best performance for indoor spatial deployment.

5 Conclusion

Indoor positioning technology is very closely related with the daily life of people. The problem of positioning precision has been studied using multiple sensors or with the fusion of different types of sensors. Recently, spatial deployment of signal sources has received more attentions from researchers, since the optimal deployment can bring higher location accuracy or lower cost. In our paper, a new optimization method, FWA, is proposed from Fireworks Algorithm. The novel algorithm presents a better technology for spatial deployment of signal sources in indoor positioning system.

The proposed FWA algorithm has been tested with experiments of iBeacons based indoor positioning in an underground parking lot. In summary, the FWA algorithm has the better convergence ability, i.e., has the best search ability than the other methods considering only positioning error, or both positioning error and cost of signal sources. Based on experiments, FWA can converge to the best optimization result in single-objective and multi-objective cases. Therefore, the proposed algorithm can provide the optimal solution of spatial deployment.

In the future, the new method will be evaluated in more complicated indoor environments with multiple types of signal sources. It will be included in an general optimization simulating system for spatial deployment, and be used for all kinds of indoor positioning systems.

Acknowledgments. This work was supported by the National Key Research and Development Program of China (Project No. 2016YFB0502201).

References

1. Jung, S.H., Han, D.: Automated construction and maintenance of wi-fi radio maps for crowdsourcing-based indoor positioning systems. IEEE Access **6**, 1764–1777 (2018)
2. Chen, K., Wang, C., Yin, Z.: Slide: towards fast and accurate mobile fingerprinting for wi-fi indoor positioning systems. IEEE Sens. J. **18**(3), 1213–1223 (2018)
3. Popoola, O.R., Sinanovic, S.: Design and analysis of collision reduction algorithms for LED-based indoor positioning with simulation and experimental validation. IEEE Access **6**, 10754–10770 (2017)
4. Zheng, Z., Liu, L., Zhao, C.: High accuracy indoor positioning scheme using single LED and camera. Electron. Lett. **54**(4), 227–229 (2018)
5. Lindo, A., García, E., Ureña, J.: Multiband waveform design for an ultrasonic indoor positioning system. IEEE Sens. J. **15**(12), 7190–7199 (2015)
6. Alvarez, Y., Heras, F.L.: ZigBee-based sensor network for indoor location and tracking applications. IEEE Lat. Am. Trans. **14**(7), 3208–3214 (2016)
7. Zhang, X., Wong, K.S., Lea, C.T.: Unambiguous association of crowd-sourced radio maps to floor plans for indoor localization. IEEE Trans. Mobile Comput. **17**, 488–502 (2017)
8. Zou, H., Chen, Z., Jiang, H.: Accurate indoor localization and tracking using mobile phone inertial sensors, WiFi and iBeacon. In: IEEE International Symposium on Inertial Sensors and Systems, pp. 1–4. IEEE (2017)
9. Menzies, T., Greenwald, J., Frank, A.: Data mining static code attributes to learn defect predictors. IEEE Trans. Softw. Eng. **33**(1), 2–13 (2016)
10. Dhillon, S.S., Chakrabarty, K.: Sensor placement for effective coverage and surveillance in distributed sensor networks. In: Wireless Communications and Networking, 2003. WCNC 2003, pp. 1609–1614. IEEE (2003)
11. Zhou, M., Xu, K.: Error bound analysis of indoor wi-fi location fingerprint based positioning for intelligent Access Point optimization via Fisher information. Comput. Commun. **86**(C), 57–74 (2016)
12. Chen, X., Zou, S.: Improved wi-fi indoor positioning based on particle swarm optimization. IEEE Sens. J. **99**, 1 (2017)
13. Chen, C.M., Pi, D.C., Fang, Z.R.: Artificial immune algorithm applied to short-term prediction for mobile object location. Electron. Lett. **48**(17), 1061–1062 (2012)
14. Eldeeb, H., Arafa, M., Saidahmed, M.T.F.: Optimal placement of access points for indoor positioning using a genetic algorithm. In: Computer Engineering and Systems, pp. 306–313 (2017)
15. Kim, D.W., Park, G.J., Lee, J.H.: Hybridization algorithm of fireworks optimization and generating set search for optimal design of IPMSM. IEEE Trans. Magn. **53**(6), 1–4 (2017)

A Study of Sleep Stages Threshold Based on Multiscale Fuzzy Entropy

Xuexiao Shao[1,2], Bin Hu[1,2(✉)], Yalin Li[1,3], and Xiangwei Zheng[1,2]

[1] School of Information Science and Engineering,
Shandong Normal University, Jinan 250014, China
binhu@sdnu.edu.cn
[2] Shandong Provincial Key Laboratory for Distributed Computer Software
Novel Technology, Jinan 250014, China
[3] School of Information Engineering, Shandong Management University,
Jinan 250357, China

Abstract. The classification of sleep stages based on EEG signals has become a prerequisite for monitoring sleep quality and diagnosing sleep-related diseases. Many researchers have conducted related research work. But, they often overlook the effect of the extracted characteristics on actual sleep staging results and the interpretation in psychology and clinical medicine. Therefore, this study calculates the value of multiscale fuzzy entropy as evaluation criteria and measures the threshold range of sleep stage based on CEEMDAN algorithm and psychophysics method. The experimental results show that the proposed method can effectively distinguish between different sleep stages by using fuzzy entropy as a measure of sleep staging thresholds. In addition, we designed a set of comparative experiments based on the single-channel EEG sample data and studied the gender factor on sleep stages by comparing sleep entropy thresholds of different genders. It was found that the sleep threshold of female was significantly greater than male.

Keywords: CEEMDAN · Sleep stages · Multiscale fuzzy entropy
Threshold

1 Introduction

Sleep is an unconscious state characterized by the loss of consciousness and external stimuli. At present, sleep-related diseases become important causes of diseases which seriously affect the quality of patients' life. Therefore, effective sleep quality monitoring and analysis can help improve poor sleep state. Electroencephalograph (EEG) is a record which reflects regular electric action of brain cells groups, which contains a large number of physiological and pathological information. And it can be used to improve the reliability and accuracy of diagnosis and detection of neurological injury in the brain. On the other hand, it provides an effective means for the detection of brain diseases by conducting a series of studies [1]. In 1937, the American scholar Loomis [2] first proposed to use EEG instead of behavior as a standard for judging sleep depth.

© Springer Nature Switzerland AG 2018
J. Vaidya and J. Li (Eds.): ICA3PP 2018, LNCS 11336, pp. 239–248, 2018.
https://doi.org/10.1007/978-3-030-05057-3_19

Currently, the classification of sleep stages based on EEG signals has become a prerequisite for monitoring sleep quality and diagnosing sleep-related diseases.

The sleep staging method is to analyze and calculate the different characteristics of EEG signals. We have detailed the characteristics of its different stages in the literature [3]. Traditionally, experts use the whole night PSG records to perform visual scoring according to the guidelines developed by the American Academy of Sleep Medicine (AASM). In this article, we divide the sleep staging into W, S1, S2, SS and REM stages. However, the selection of eigenvectors is a major difficulty, experts and scholars have done a lot of work on them, but they did not conduct further analysis of the characteristics. Therefore, it is necessary and meaningful to study the thresholds and impact factors of sleep stages.

Most researchers focus on the study of automatic sleep stage classification to further improve the accuracy and efficiency by improving feature extraction methods and classifier algorithms. However, they often overlook the effect of extracted sample characteristics on actual sleep staging results and the interpretation in psychology and clinical medicine. Various algorithms for automatic sleep stages classification have been introduced [4, 5] and they demonstrate good experimental results. Among them, the calculation of various entropy values is particularly prominent. It is worth mentioning that Hassan et al. [6] first applied the complete ensemble empirical mode decomposition with adaptive noise (CEEMDAN) to automatic sleep stages classification.

In order to find a more appropriate method and standard for measuring threshold, this study calculates the value of fuzzy entropy as evaluation criteria and measures the threshold range of sleep stage by CEEMDAN based on the single-channel EEG signal, which provides valuable reference data for automatic sleep stage classification. Firstly, the EEG signal segment is decomposed into an intrinsic mode function (IMF) by using CEEMDAN. Secondly, we select an appropriate number of IMF components from the intrinsic mode function and reconstruct it as a new high-precision signal. Thirdly, the entropy of the reconstructed EEG signal is calculated by using the multiscale fuzzy entropy (MFE). Finally, we compare the fuzzy entropy values with others between the different stages to determine a feature standard based on the fuzzy entropy, and apply this criterion to the specific analysis of EEG data, such as the influence of gender and age [7].

2 A Study of Sleep Stages Threshold Based on MFE

The proposed method calculates fuzzy entropy values of five sleep stages (W, S1, S2, SS, REM) based on CEEMDAN and MFE. On the one hand, the CEEMDAN is used to decompose EEG data which effectively reduces the temporal dimension. On the other hand, we use MFE as a feature to analyze the different sleep stages. Especially, the reconstructed EEG signals are calculated by using the fuzzy entropy as shown in Fig. 1. The sleep staging threshold is determined by fuzzy entropy.

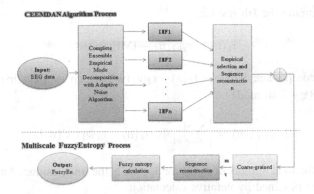

Fig. 1. Flow chart based on CEEMDAN and MFE

2.1 CEEMDAN

The CEEMDAN is improved from original empirical mode decomposition (EMD) and ensemble empirical mode decomposition (EEMD). The added Gaussian white noise is subjected to EMD decomposition to obtain the IMF component based on the bootstrap aggregation method. The CEEMDAN steps are as follows:

Step 1: Calculate $\Phi_j(.) = x(n) + \epsilon_0 w^i(n)$ to produce the jth mode of EMD.

Where $w^i(n)$ with $i = 1, 2, \ldots, I$ represents different realizations of white Gaussian noise, ϵ_0 is the standard deviation of white Gaussian noise.

Step 2: Decompose the mixed signals by EMD and the first modes $\widetilde{IMF}_1$ can be obtained. Compute $\widetilde{IMF}_1$ of CEEMDAN:

$$\widetilde{IMF}_1(n) = \frac{1}{I} \sum_{i=1}^{I} IMF_k^i(n) = \overline{IMF}_k(n) \tag{1}$$

Step 3: Find the first residue.

$$r_1(n) = x(n) - \widetilde{IMF}_1(n) \tag{2}$$

Step 4: Decompose realizations $r_1(n) + \epsilon_1 \Phi_1(w^i(n))$ up to their first EMD mode. ϵ_k ($k = 1$ in this step) is the standard deviation of white Gaussian noise of the kth stage. And compute the second modes $\widetilde{IMF}_2(n)$.

$$\widetilde{IMF}_2(n) = \frac{1}{I} \sum_{i=1}^{I} \Phi_1 r_1(n) + \epsilon_1 \Phi_1(w^i(n)) \tag{3}$$

Step 5: Compute the kth residue.

$$r_k(n) = r_{k-1}(n) - \widetilde{IMF}_k(n) \tag{4}$$

Step 6: Decompose realizations $r_1(n) + \epsilon_1 \Phi_1(w^i(n))$ up to their first EMD mode and define the $(k + 1)$th mode.

$$\widetilde{IMF}_{k+1}(n) = \frac{1}{I}\sum_{i=1}^{I} \Phi_1\left(r_k(n) + \epsilon_1 \Phi_1(w^i(n))\right) \tag{5}$$

Where k is the total number of modes and $r_k(n)$ is the final residue. And then, $k + 1$ EMD modes are obtained by iterative calculation.

Step 7: Go to step (5) for next k.

Repeat steps (5) to (7) until the residual becomes a monotonic function, and further extraction of an IMF is not possible. As shown in Formula (5). At this point, we have multiple intrinsic modal functions (IMFs), that is: $IMF_1, IMF_2, \ldots, IMF_k$.

Step 8: The input $x(n)$ can be reconstructed from all the $IMFs$.

$$x(n) = \sum_{k=1}^{k} \widetilde{IMF}_k(n) + r_k(n) \tag{6}$$

The number of CEEMDAN $\widetilde{IMF}s$ is 7 (where IMF_k with $k = 7$).

2.2 Multiscale Fuzzy Entropy

MFE is defined to measure the complexity and self-similarity of time series under different scale factors according to the definition of fuzzy entropy. This paper uses the idea to calculate the fuzzy entropy values.

(1) For the original sequence of length N, $X_i = \{x_1, x_2, \ldots, x_N\}$, the embedding dimension m and the similar tolerance r are predefined, and a new coarse-grained vector is established.

$$y_j(\tau) = \frac{1}{\tau}\sum_{i=(j-1)\tau+1}^{j\tau} x_i, 1 \leq j \leq \frac{N}{\tau} \tag{7}$$

Where $\tau = 1, 2, \ldots, N$, τ is the scale factor.

(2) The fuzzy entropy for each coarse-grained sequence is calculated and plotted as a function of the scale factor. The m-dimensional vector is set up sequentially for the N-point time series $\{ui : 1 \leq i \leq N\}$. The steps of fuzzy entropy are defined [8].

2.3   Algorithm Description

The algorithm process is described as follows:

Algorithm: The Calculation of Sleep Stages Threshold Based on MFE

Input:

The original EEG signal.

Initialization:

Define $x(n)$, an N-point EEG epoch X.

Noise standard deviation (Nstd=0.2); Number of realization (NR=500);

Maximum number of sifting iterations allowed (MaxIter=3000);

The steps of EMD decomposition are shown as Formula (1-3).

For $k = 1,2,...,K$ **do**

1. Calculate the kth IMF component and residual component.
2. Keep decomposing to achieve the $K+1$ mode.

End For

The new $x(n) = \sum_{k=1}^{k} \widehat{IMF}_k(n) + r_k(n)$ is reconstructed. The calculation of MFE is performed on the reconstructed $x(n)$.

Embedding dimension m=3; Similar tolerance r=0.2; Scale factor $\tau = 2$;

The data length is N;

Define X_i^m, the value of consecutive u from the ith point.

Define the maximum distance $d[X_i^m, X_j^m]$.

Create a new coarse grain vector $y_j(\tau)$. Reconstruct coarse-grained time series.

For $n = 1,2,...,N$ **do**

1. Build m-dimensional vectors sequentially for N-point time series.
2. Define the maximum difference between distances between vectors d_{ij}^m.

$$d_{ij}^m = d[X_i^m, X_j^m] = \max_{k\in(0,m-1)}\{|(u(i+k) - u_0(i)) - (u(j+k) - u_0(j))|\}$$

3. The similarity D_{ij}^m of the vector X_i^m and X_j^m is defined by the fuzzy function.

$$D_{ij}^m = \mu(d_{ij}^m, n, r) = e^{-(d_{ij}^m/r)^n}$$

4. Define functions: $\phi^m(n,r) = \frac{1}{N-m}\sum_{i=1}^{N-m}(\frac{1}{N-m-1}\sum_{\substack{j=1 \\ j\neq i}}^{N-m}D_{ij}^m)$.

End For

Output:

The fuzzy entropy: FuzzyEn(m, n, r, N) = $\lim_{N\to\infty}[\ln\phi^m(n,r) - \ln\phi^{m+1}(n,r)]$.

---

3   Experiments and Discussion

3.1   Evaluation Criteria

The Student's test (T-test) uses the t-distribution theory to deduce the probability of occurrence in differences. It is generally used to test whether the mean difference between the two populations is significant. Therefore, we use the T-test to illustrate the authenticity and accuracy of the experiment in a statistical sense. The T-test can be expressed mathematically as:

$$t = \frac{\bar{x} - \mu}{S/\sqrt{n}} \sim t(n-1) \tag{8}$$

Where, $\bar{x}$ is the sample average, μ is the ensemble average, S is the sample standard deviation, and n is the sample size. The t statistic follows the t-distribution with $n-1$ degrees of freedom. In our experiment, the values of MFE were introduced into the SPSS software.

3.2   Datasets

Experimental data can be obtained from the Physionet Data Bank's Sleep-EDF database [expanded]. The experimental samples were from Caucasian men and women (21–35 years old) who did not take any medication. Our experimental sample selected the sleep data from ten healthy volunteers (The subjects currently included 5 males and 5 females, and were 25–34 years old at the time of the recordings). According to the AASM guidelines, we defined sleep stages as five categories (S3 and S4 were combined into SS periods), and calculated by using MATLAB2014b. Each of samples contains the level of EOG, Fpz-Cz and Pz-Oz EEG data, and each sampled at 100 Hz. Pz-Oz channel was chosen for our study by comparing with the literature [5].

3.3   Results

We studied the sleep stage thresholds based on the computational model of CEEM-DAN and MFE. First of all, EMD is decomposed on the EEG data labeled by stages. We can get the IMF components (Let $K = 7$) by using the CEEMDAN algorithm (Fig. 2). At the same time, we perform the calculation of multiscale fuzzy entropy on the IMF1 component of each sample to observe the threshold characteristics from different sleep stages (Fig. 3). Experimental results show that the calculation of fuzzy entropy can effectively distinguish different sleep stages, and it provides a basis for

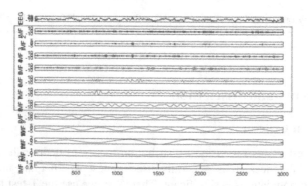

Fig. 2. The IMF components in the time-domain are decomposed by CEEMDAN

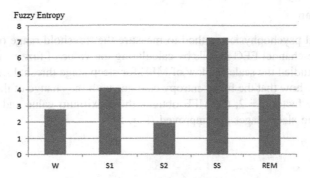

Fig. 3. MFE values of IMF1.

feature extraction of automatic sleep stage classification. At this point, we get a new EEG signal with higher accuracy compared to the original EEG signal.

Then, we calculated the fuzzy entropy values of sleep stages (W, S1, S2, SS, REM) for 10 samples (Fig. 4). Through the comparison and analysis of data, we found that it can effectively distinguish different sleep stages and further determined the threshold between them.

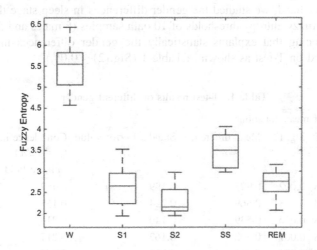

Fig. 4. Box-whisker plots of the fuzzy entropy values from 10 samples

The experimental results show that there are obvious thresholds of fuzzy entropy between different sleep stages, and the W stage has a higher threshold of fuzzy entropy (MFE > 4.5), which is obviously different from other stages. Moreover, the SS stage can also be better differentiated from other sleep stages based on the entropy value. However, the difference between the S1 stage and the REM stage is less obvious, and it requires to further study.

3.4   Discussion

This study used psychophysics method to measure the threshold range of sleep stages based on single-channel EEG signals by calculating the value of fuzzy entropy. On the one hand, we studied the scale shadow of MFE for sleep stage thresholds. The effect of the experiment show that the fuzzy entropy changes with the change of the scale factor. When the scale factor $\tau = 2$, the MFE obtains the maximum value and the threshold resolution of the sleep stages are improved (Fig. 5).

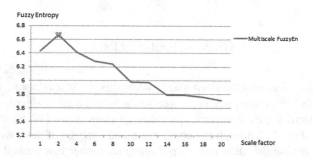

Fig. 5. Influence of different scale factors on fuzzy entropy

On the other hand, we studied the gender differences in sleep stage thresholds by comparing the fuzzy entropy thresholds of 10 data samples (5 males and 5 females). It is more convincing that explains statistically the gender differences in sleep stage thresholds based on T-test as shown in Table 1 (Sig.(2) ≤ 0.05,).

Table 1. T-test results of different gender

	T-test of mean equation						
	t	f	Sig. (2)	Mean difference	Standard error value	Confidence interval ($\rho = 95\%$)	
						Subthreshold	Threshold
W	4.619	8	0.002	0.923	0.199	0.462	1.384
S1	2.983	8	0.018	0.669	0.224	0.151	1.186
S2	3.833	8	0.016	0.539	0.140	0.214	0.863
SS	3.645	8	0.007	0.592	0.162	0.217	0.966
REM	4.559	8	0.004	0.761	0.166	0.376	1.146

The experimental results show that there are significant differences in the entropy threshold of sleep stages between different gender, and the sleep threshold of female is significantly higher than that of male. It may be related to the active areas of the brain in both male and female [9], and we find the explanations in psychophysiology. Gur et al. [10] used fMRI to find that in the unit volume of the brain, female have higher gray matter than male, and the male have higher white matter than female. In addition, one of the reasons for the threshold difference is the social differences between male and female. Of course, it needs a further research.

4 Conclusion

In this paper, The CEEMDAN and MFE method were used to study the threshold of sleep stages based on single-channel EEG signals. First, the adaptive EMD decomposition of the EEG data is performed. We can get a new high-precision EEG data. Then, the MFE of each new data is calculated and used as the feature of sleep stage threshold which provides a reference for the study of the automatic sleep stages classification. Finally, the influence of the fuzzy entropy scale factor and different gender samples on the sleep stage threshold was studied. The experimental results showed that the sleep threshold of female was significantly higher than male's. We will continue our research in the future. On the one hand, our experimental sample size is too small to be universal and representative. On the other hand, the experimental results show that the sleep stage thresholds in S1 and REM stages cannot be accurately measured by using fuzzy entropy. This requires us to further study to better understand the meaning of sleep.

Acknowledgments. National Natural Science Foundation of China (61373149) and the Taishan Scholars Program of Shandong Province, China.

References

1. Chen, X.: Automatic sleep staging based on EEG. Nanjing University of Posts and Telecommunications (2014)
2. Loomis, W.E., Shull, C.A., Snedecor, G.W.: Methods in Plant Physiology: A Laboratory Manual and Research Handbook. McGraw-Hill, New York City (1937)
3. Shao, X., Hu, B., Zheng, X.: A study on automatic sleep stage classification based on clustering algorithm. In: Zeng, Y., et al. (eds.) BI 2017. LNCS (LNAI), vol. 10654, pp. 139–148. Springer, Cham (2017). https://doi.org/10.1007/978-3-319-70772-3_13
4. Tang, Q.: Automatic sleep staging based on EEG signals. Guangdong University of Technology (2016)
5. Cheng, J.: Sleep stage analysis based on EEG signals. Beijing Institute of Technology (2015)
6. Hassan, A.R., Bhuiyan, M.I.H.: Computer-aided sleep staging using complete ensemble empirical mode decomposition with adaptive noise and bootstrap aggregating. Biomed. Signal Process. Control **24**, 1–10 (2016)
7. Tiantian, L., Yong, L.: Measurement of thresholds in facial expressions and their age and gender differences. Psychol. Behav. Res. **13**(6), 771–777 (2015)
8. Jinde, Z., Minjun, C., Junsheng, C., et al.: Multi-scale fuzzy entropy and its application in fault diagnosis of rolling bearings. J. Vib. Eng. **27**(1), 145–151 (2014)

9. Lee, T.M., Liu, H.L., Hoosain, R., et al.: Gender differences in neural correlates of recognition of happy and sad faces in humans assessed by functional magnetic resonance imaging. Neurosci. Lett. **333**(1), 13–16 (2002)
10. Gur, R.C., Gunningdixon, F., Bilker, W.B., et al.: Sex differences in temporo-limbic and frontal brain volumes of healthy adults. Cereb. Cortex **12**(9), 998–1003 (2002)

Blind Estimation Algorithm Over Fast-Fading Multipath OFDM Channels

Jing Liu[1], Kun Han[1], Wenhua Wu[1], Shu Wang[2], and Xiao Yu[3(✉)] 🆔

[1] School of Information and Communication, National University of Defense Technology,
Xian 710106, China
[2] Institute of Systems Engineering, Academy of Military Sciences, Beijing 100039, China
[3] School of Computer Science and Technology, Shandong University of Technology,
Shandong Zibo 255000, China
yuxiao8907118@163.com

Abstract. The Maximum likelihood (ML) estimation algorithm of timing deviation and carrier frequency offset in orthogonal frequency division multiplexing (OFDM) system is studied, and the ML algorithm is extended to the fast fading multipath wireless channel environment using the multi-symbol Joint estimation technique. This method is based on the autocorrelation of cyclic prefixes (CP) in OFDM blocks without training data, the spectral efficiency and throughput of the system are improved. Meanwhile, in the case of the extremum of signal-to-noise ratio, two algorithms are deduced, which are suboptimal but less computational complexity and more adaptable to channel. Simulation results indicate that this scheme can effectively improve the estimation performance of symbol timing deviation and carrier frequency offset in fast fading multipath channel.

Keywords: OFDM · ML estimation · Synchronization · Multipath fading

1 Introduction

OFDM have advantages of higher spectral efficiency and eliminating interference within cells has been recently received great attention, which is widely applied to the digital audio and video broadcasting system, indoor broadband wireless system, etc. [1, 2]. Because of separating one subcarrier from other subcarriers by utilizing the orthogonal characteristics, symbol timing offset and carrier frequency offset have made great effects on system performance, such as FFT window offset and inter-carrier interference. By inserting pilot symbol and training serial, the existing synchronization algorithm is a simple technology which is always used to the time-varying multipath system. The technology decreases spectral efficiency and throughput. To improve system performance, blind synchronization technology based on slow-varying channel models is widely studied, which needs a large quantity of OFDM data block and including cycle prefix [3, 4] and cyclostationarity [5–7]. The paper proposes a blind synchronization algorithm based on ML which does not need the pilot symbol and is suitable for fast-fading multipath OFDM system.

© Springer Nature Switzerland AG 2018
J. Vaidya and J. Li (Eds.): ICA3PP 2018, LNCS 11336, pp. 249–256, 2018.
https://doi.org/10.1007/978-3-030-05057-3_20

2   Signal Model

2.1   OFDM System Model

The baseband model of OFDM system is shown in Fig. 1 [8, 9]. Assume that there are N subcarriers and transmitted symbols are defined as $X(0)$, $X(1)$, ..., $X(N-1)$. After fast Fourier transforming, spectral signals can be transformed into time signals $x(0)$, $x(1)$, ..., $x(N-1)$. Cycle prefix with the length of D which is copied from the last D data of time domain data block is added to the front of each data block, i.e. $x(k) = x(k+N)$, $k \in [-D; -1]$ [10, 11]. Time domain discrete signal to transmit can be expressed as [12–14]:

$$x(k) = x(k+N), k \in [-D, -1] \tag{1}$$

where σ_s^2 denotes transmitted energy per symbol, $X(n)$ denotes the signal with mean of 0 and variance of 1, and $x(k)$; $k \in [0, N-1]$ denotes the signal with mean of 0 and variance of σ_s^2.

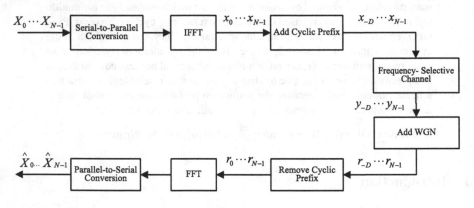

Fig. 1. OFDM system model

The signal received from the fast-fading multipath channel can be written as:

$$y(k) = \sum_{l=0}^{L} h(k, l)x(k - l), \tag{2}$$

Where $L+1$ denotes channel length and is lower than the length of cycle prefix D, and $h(k, l)$, $l = 0, \ldots, L$ is impulse response of the channel. The correction of $h(k, l)$ can be expressed as:

$$E\{h(k_1, l_1), h^*(k_2, l_2)\} = \gamma J_0(2\pi f_D T |k_1 - k_2|/N)e^{-l/D}|_{l_1=l_2}, \tag{3}$$

Where γ is normalized constant, $J_0(.)$ is the first kind Bessel function, f_D denotes the max Doppler shift, and T is the valid symbol time. The received signal can be expressed as:

$$r(k) = y(k - \theta)e^{j2\pi k\varepsilon/N} + w(k), \tag{4}$$

Where θ denotes discrete delay during signal transmitting, ε is the normalized carrier offset and $w(k)$ is AWGN with a variance of σ_w^2.

2.2 Signal Correction

Cycle prefix in the symbol of OFDM to send is the data block which is the copy of the last D data. We define the set I as the cycle prefix corresponding to received data and I^* as the original data which is copied to cycle prefix where the data in I correspond to those in I^*. For $k \in I$ we have

$$E\{r(k)r^*(k+m)\} = \begin{cases} \gamma \sum_{l=0}^{L} J_0(0)e^{-l/D}\sigma_s^2 + \sigma_w^2 = \beta_0\sigma_s^2 + \sigma_w^2, & m = 0, \\ \gamma \sum_{l=0}^{L} J_0(2\pi f_D T)e^{-l/D}\sigma_s^2 e^{j2\pi\varepsilon}\sigma_s^2 = \beta_1 e^{j2\pi\varepsilon}\sigma_s^2, & m = N, \\ 0, & \text{otherwise}, \end{cases} \tag{5}$$

Where $\beta_0 = \gamma \sum_{l=0}^{L} J_0(0)e^{-l/D}$, $\beta_1 = \gamma \sum_{l=0}^{L} J_0(2\pi f_D T)e^{-l/D}$. For $k \notin I$ and $m \notin 0$,

$E\{r(k)r^*(k+m)\} = 0$. SNR is defined as $\dfrac{\beta_0\sigma_s^2}{\sigma_w^2}$.

3 Optimal Estimated Value Based on ML

In the last section, the symbol to send and channel noise is assumed to be a complex Gaussian signal. For $k \in I$, the joint probability density function (pdf) of the received signal can be expressed as:

$$f(r(k), r(k+N)|\theta, \varepsilon) = \frac{\exp\left(-\dfrac{|r(k)|^2 + |r(k+N)|^2 - 2\rho\mathrm{Re}\{e^{j2\pi\varepsilon}r(k)r^*(k+N)\}}{(1-\rho^2)(\beta_0\sigma_s^2 + \sigma_w^2)}\right)}{\pi^2(1-\rho^2)(\beta_0\sigma_s^2 + \sigma_w^2)^2} \tag{6}$$

Where weighting coefficient ρ is defined as:

$$\rho = \frac{|E\{r(k)r^*(k+N)\}|}{\sqrt{E\{|r(k)|^2\}}\sqrt{E\{|r(k+N)|^2\}}} = \frac{\beta_1\sigma_s^2}{\beta_0\sigma_s^2 + \sigma_w^2} \tag{7}$$

For all k, pdf of the received signal can be written as:

$$f(r(k)|\theta, \varepsilon) = \frac{\exp\left(-\dfrac{|r(k)|^2}{(\beta_0 \sigma_s^2 + \sigma_w^2)}\right)}{\pi(\beta_0 \sigma_s^2 + \sigma_w^2)}. \tag{8}$$

By using the vector form of received signal, logarithm likelihood function can be written as:

$$\log f(r|\theta, \varepsilon)$$

$$= \log\left(\prod_{k\in I} f(r(k), r(k+N)|\theta, \varepsilon) \prod_{k\notin I \cup I^*} f(r(k)|\theta, \varepsilon)\right) \tag{9}$$

$$= \log\left(\prod_{k\in I} \frac{f(r(k), r(k+N)|\theta, \varepsilon)}{f(r(k)|\theta, \varepsilon) f(r(k+N)|\theta, \varepsilon)} \prod_k f(r(k)|\theta, \varepsilon)\right),$$

Where $f(.)$ is pdf of random variable margin. From (8), we can find that $f(r(k)|\theta, \varepsilon)$ does not correspond to θ or ε. Assuming that the number of received data blocks is M, we have

$$I = \{\theta, \ldots, \theta + D - 1, \theta + K, \ldots, \theta + K + D - 1, \ldots, \theta + (M-1)K, \ldots, \theta + (M-1)K + D - 1\}, \tag{10}$$

Where $K = N + D$ the total length of one OFDM data block. By substituting (9), (10) and (12) into (11), we have

$$\log f(r|\theta, \varepsilon) = C_1 + C_2 \sum_{i=0}^{M-1} \sum_{k=\theta}^{\theta+D-1} \left[\mathrm{Re}\{e^{j2\pi\varepsilon} r(k+iK) r^*(k+iK+N)\}\right.$$

$$\left. \frac{-\rho}{2} \sum_{k=\theta}^{\theta+D-1} \left(|r(k+iK)|^2 + |r(k+iK+N)|^2\right)\right], \tag{11}$$

where

$$C_1 = \sum_{k=\theta}^{\theta+D-1} \log(1 - \rho^2),$$

$$C_2 = \frac{2\rho}{(1-\rho^2)(\beta_0\sigma_s^2 + \sigma_w^2)}. \tag{12}$$

By transforming (11), we have

$$\log f(r|\theta, \varepsilon) = |T_1(\theta)| \cos(2\pi + \angle T_1(\theta)) - \frac{\rho}{2} T_2(\theta), \tag{13}$$

Where $\angle$ denotes the plural phase.

$$T_1(\theta) = \sum_{i=0}^{M-1} \sum_{k=\theta}^{\theta+D-1} r(k + iK)r^*(k + iK + N),$$ (14)

$$T_2(\theta) = \sum_{i=0}^{M-1} \sum_{k=\theta}^{\theta+D-1} \left(|r(k + iK)|^2 + |r(k + iK + N)|^2 \right).$$ (15)

$T_1(\theta)$ can be seen as self-correction of signal and $T_2(\theta)$ is accumulating energy function [15]. The ML estimated value of θ and that of ε can be computed by maximizing (13). We can compute these values in two steps as following:

$$\max_{\theta, \varepsilon} \log f(r|\theta, \varepsilon)$$

$$= \max_\theta \max_\varepsilon \log f(r|\theta, \varepsilon)$$ (16)

$$= \max_\theta \log f(r|\theta, \varepsilon_{ML}(\theta)).$$

Where ε is between $[0, 2\pi]$. The ML estimated value of ε is:

$$\varepsilon_{ML}(\theta) = \frac{1}{2\pi} \angle T_1(\theta).$$ (17)

By substituting (16) and (18) into (13), the ML estimated value of θ is

$$\theta_{ML} = \arg \max_\theta |T_1(\theta)| - \frac{\rho}{2} T_2(\theta).$$ (18)

From (17) and (18), we can find that the value of the variance to estimate depends on the length of OFDM data block M, the length of cycle prefix D and weighting coefficient ρ. Meanwhile the variance to estimate $T_1(\theta)$ determines the performance of estimate algorithm. When $\theta_{ML} = \theta$, we have the largest value of $T_1(\theta)$'s altitude.

From (18), we weighting coefficient ρ is computed according to existing station of the channel. When the SNR is very large, $\beta_0 \sigma_s^2 \gg \sigma_w^2$. After substituting it into (10), we have $\rho \to 1$. We substitute it into (18) and get the value of θ, which is the result from the MMSE-likely algorithm. It can be written as:

$$\theta_{MMSE} = \arg \max_\theta |T_1(\theta)| - \frac{1}{2} T_2(\theta).$$ (19)

When the value of signal to noise ratio (SNR) is very low, $\beta_0 \sigma_s^2 \gg \sigma_w^2$. After substituting it into (10), we have $\rho \to 0$. We substitute it into (18) and get the value of θ, which is the result from the MC-likely algorithm. It can be written as:

$$\theta_{MC} = \arg \max_\theta |T_1(\theta)|.$$ (20)

From (19) and (20), we can find that the computation complexity of these two algorithms is very little and they both adapt well to the channel. For different value of SNR, we can get estimate algorithm of ε, which is shown in (17). Note that the performance of ε is related to estimate result of θ.

4   Results and Analysis

The performance of proposed algorithm based on ML algorithm is estimated by Monte Carlo method in this section. The parameters is set as [16]: 20 symbols are transmitted in OFDM system, $N = 128$, $T = 224$ us, $L = 20$, $M = 20$, $D/N = 1/4$, and $f_D = 1$ kHz. The gain for each channel follows the same Gaussian distribution and independently. Timing deviation $\theta = 50$ and frequency offset $\varepsilon = 0.1$.

The variance curve of Timing deviation estimation VS SNR and multipath length of traditional Maximum mean square error, that of MC, and that of the proposed algorithm based on ML algorithm are shown in Figs. 2 and 3. From Fig. 2 we can find that the performance of these three algorithms increases as SNR increases. From Fig. 3 we can find that when the length of multipath increase, the estimation performance of these three algorithms decreases with the decrease of channel quality. In these three algorithms, the performance is the worst with the lowest computation complexity.

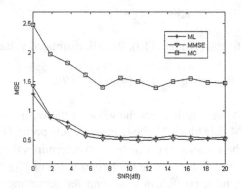

Fig. 2. Timing deviation estimation VS SNR

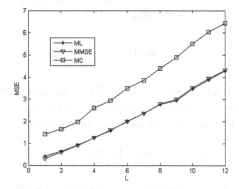

Fig. 3. Timing deviation estimation VS the length of multipath increase

The variance curve of frequency offset estimation VS SNR and multipath length of traditional Maximum mean square error, that of MC, and that of the proposed algorithm based on ML algorithm are shown in Figs. 2 and 3. From Fig. 4 we can find that the performance of these three algorithms increase as SNR increases and this performance of these three algorithms is the same adaptability to SNR. From Fig. 5 we find that the performance of these three algorithms decrease with the increase of multipath length and the performance of MC is the worst. From Fig. 2 to Fig. 5, we find the performance of the presented algorithm can meet with the requirement of real system under some condition. Compared with other blind estimation algorithms, these three algorithms base on ML algorithm get much better performance.

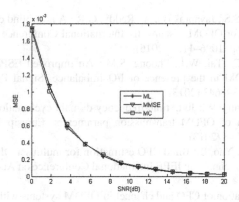

Fig. 4. Frequency offset estimation VS SNR

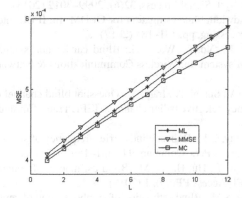

Fig. 5. Frequency offset estimation VS multipath length

5   Conclusions

Estimation algorithm based on ML algorithm is proposed to resolve the problem of blind synchronization over fast-fading multipath channels. Two suboptimal estimation algorithms with low computation complexity are conducted under different SNR. The presented algorithms without training data can increase spectral efficiency throughput. Results of simulation indicate that the presented algorithms can improve the performance of estimating symbol timing deviation and carrier offset.

References

1. Lin, T.C., Phoong, S.M., New, A.: Cyclic-prefix based algorithm for blind CFO estimation in OFDM systems. IEEE Trans. Wireless Commun. 15(6), 3995–4008 (2016)
2. Fang, C., Gong, X., Huang, M.: On sequential blind channel estimation for time-varying OFDM system. In: IEEE International Conference on Ubiquitous Wireless Broadband, pp. 1–4 (2016)
3. Prakash, D., Pillai, S.S., Jayaprakash, A., Reddy, G.R.: A new blind carrier frequency offset estimation scheme for OFDM systems. In: International Conference on Communication & Signal Processing, pp. 1096–1100 (2016)
4. Lin, T.C., Pan, Y.C., Tai, W.J., Phoong, S.M.: An improved ESPRIT-based blind CFO estimation for OFDM in the presence of I/Q imbalance. Signal Process. Adv. Wireless Commun. 395(6), 639–643 (2013)
5. Sun, Z., Liu, R., Wang, W.: Joint time-frequency domain cyclostationarity-based approach to blind estimation of OFDM transmission parameters. Eurasip J. Wireless Commun. Network. 2013(1), 1–8 (2013)
6. Zhang, W., Gao, F., Yao, B.: Blind CFO estimation for multiuser OFDM uplink with large number of receive antennas. In: IEEE International Conference on Acoustics, vol. 64 (9), pp. 2255–2268 (2016)
7. Lim, J.: Joint estimation of CFO and channel in OFDM systems with blind noise statistics. IETE Tech. Rev., 1–13 (2016)
8. Liu, M., Li, B., Yang, Q., Tang, N.: Blind joint estimation for OFDM time-frequency parameters. Circuits Syst. Signal Process. 32(6), 2999–3012 (2013)
9. Liu, M., Li, B.: Bandwidth blind estimation for OFDM. In: IEEE International Conference on Digital Signal Processing, pp. 181–184 (2017)
10. Li, X., Hu, J., Wei, H., Yu, F., Wang, G.: Blind carrier and sampling frequency offsets estimation in OFDM system. In: Wireless Communications & Networking Conference, pp. 1–6 (2017)
11. Saci, A., Al-Dweik, A., Shami, A., Iraqi, Y.: One-shot blind channel estimation for OFDM systems over frequency-selective fading channels. IEEE Trans. Commun. 65(12), 5445–5458 (2017)
12. Jayaprakash, A., Reddy, G.R.: Robust blind carrier frequency offset estimation algorithm for OFDM systems. Wireless Pers. Commun. 94(3), 1–15 (2017)
13. Tian, J., Zhou, T., Xu, T., Hu, H., Li, M.: Blind estimation of channel order and SNR for OFDM systems. IEEE Access PP(99), 1 (2018)
14. Wang, Y.C., Phoong, S.M.: Blind estimation of symbol timing offset in OFDM systems. In: IEEE International Workshop on Signal Processing Advances in Wireless Communications, pp. 1–5 (2017)
15. Ramadhan, M., Bouzidi, D.A., Iyad, D.: A low complexity joint semi-blind estimation of CFO and channel for OFDM systems. In: International Conference on Electrical Engineering-boumerdes, pp. 1–6 (2017)
16. Lin, T.C., Phoong, S.M.: MSE-optimized CP-based CFO estimation in OFDM systems over multipath channels. In: Asia-pacific Signal & Information Processing Association Summit & Conference, pp. 818–822 (2018)

Facial Shape and Expression Transfer via Non-rigid Image Deformation

Huabing Zhou[1], Shiqiang Ren[1], Yong Zhou[2]([✉]), Yuyu Kuang[1],
Yanduo Zhang[1], Wei Zhang[1], Tao Lu[1], Hanwen Chen[1], and Deng Chen[1]

[1] Hubei Key Laboratory of Intelligent Robot, Wuhan Institute of Technology,
Wuhan 430205, China
[2] Yangtze University College of Technology and Engineering, Jingzhou 434100, China
clarkzydsy@126.com

Abstract. In this paper, we present a novel approach for transferring
shape and expression of a face in image to that of another, regardless of
variance between the two faces in illumination, color, texture, resolution
and even some mild occlusion. We first use a face alignment algorithm to
locate accurate facial landmark points for both original face and target
face, then align them with a global similarity transformation to eliminate their inconsistency in pose, size and position. Finally, we use our
non-rigid image deformation method to deform the original face by fitting a map function for each of its pixel point according to the two sets
of facial landmark points. Our method can be full-automatic or semi-
automatic for conveniently tuning a better result by combining a face
alignment algorithm and a non-rigid image deformation method. Experiment results show that our method can produce realistic, natural and
artifact-less facial shape and expression transfer. We also discuss the
limitation and potential of our proposed method.

Keywords: Non-rigid image deformation · Face editing
Expression transfer

1 Introduction

Image deformation, which refers to deforming objects into desired shapes or
poses, has long been an active research area in image processing. Specially, face
deformation aims at deforming faces to obtain new face images with expected
shape or expression, It has a number of useful applications ranging from face
image beautify, medical imaging and facial animation in the entertainment industries. However, due to the fact that human face has extremely complex geometric
form and movement mechanism, as well as subtle variations in color and texture.

The authors gratefully acknowledge the financial supports from the National Natural
Science Foundation of China under Grant Nos. 41501505, 61502354 and the Scien-
tific Research Project of Education Department of Hubei Province under Grant No.
Q20181508.

© Springer Nature Switzerland AG 2018
J. Vaidya and J. Li (Eds.): ICA3PP 2018, LNCS 11336, pp. 257–269, 2018.
https://doi.org/10.1007/978-3-030-05057-3_21

Lots of works tried to challenge this problem in different ways. In image blending based methods [6,9,18], to transfer the expression from one face to that of another, the target face with expected expression is cut and pasted to the original face following with a seamless blending [5]. These methods can create quite realistic expression transfer when the two faces have similar color and texture, but they may change the identity of original face and are not robust to in-consistencies in illumination, color, texture, resolution or occlusion. Morph-based approaches [3,19] synthesize new expressions which are between two different facial expressions through interpolation, one limitation of these methods is not capable of transferring facial expression between different people.

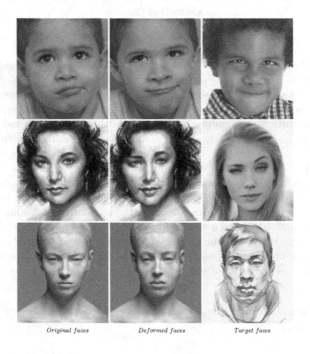

Original faces   *Deformed faces*   *Target faces*

Fig. 1. Three example of face shape and expression transfer with our face deformation method. The left column shows original faces, namely to be deformed faces; the middle column shows results of facial expression and shape transfer from target faces to original faces with our method; the right column shows target faces which contain expected facial expression and shape.

Image deformation methods are one of the common ways of dealing with these troubles. Shen *et al.* [22] achieve face smilization by using image deformation method to deform a normal face to smile one. Deformation methods view face deformation as a mapping from original face to deformed face and solving of the mapping function only rely on face counter information, which means deformation methods can achieve facial shape and expression transfer between different people regardless of variances in illumination, color, texture, resolution and even occlusion [25,27].

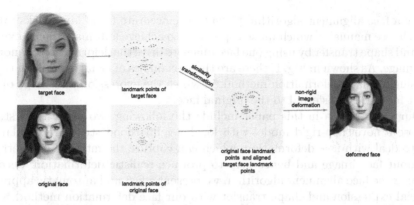

Fig. 2. Framework of our method. Firstly, landmark points are extracted from the original and target face, then landmark points of target face are align to that of original face with a global similarity transformation, finally the original face are deformed according to original face landmark points and aligned target face landmark points with our nonrigid image deformation method.

Many image deformation methods have been proposed to satisfy the requirements such as intuitive user interaction, realistic deformation results. Among them, the methods that avoid unnatural local scaling and shearing are of special interest. To produce such deformations, Schaefer [21] proposed Moving Least Squares (MLS) [8] using linear functions such as rigid transformation. The use of MLS and rigid formations makes the deformation as-rigid-as-possible. [1] However, the deformation methods mentioned above are modeled for deformation of general objects, the special geometrical structure features of face are not taken into account. These geometrical structure features can provide intrinsic structure information of the original face, which is beneficial to the face deformation estimation. Therefore, we need to develop a non-rigid model.

To address these issues and produce more realistic and natural face deformation, we propose a new algorithm based on MLS and a non-rigid transformation modeled [10–13,15] by specifying it in a reproducing kernel Hilbert space (RKHS) [2,14]. Furthermore, taking the special geometrical structure features of face into account, we introduce the local neighborhood structure constraint into our model as a regularization term. Benefiting from the combination of these factors, our algorithm can avoid superfluous global or local deformation, and lead to more natural and realistic face deformation. Specifying the transformation in an RKHS leads to a simple closed-form solution which is computationally efficient.

In general, image deformation methods are typically controlled with a set of distinct handles, including points [4], lines [3], and even polygon grids [17], which are usually chosen by users manually. In our face deformation method, we use the facial landmark points as handles. Benefiting from the impressive progress in real-time face detection and facial landmark alignment in recent years [7,20,23,24], we use a face alignment algorithm [7] to locate accurate facial landmarks rather than choose manually, which make it possible to achieve automatic facial expression and shape transfer by using one face image to drive the deformation of another face image. As shown in Fig. 1, there are three examples of facial expression transfer using our face deformation method, in which the expression and shape of the target faces are transferred to the original face.

Our contribution in this paper include the following two aspects. First, we propose a novel non-rigid model with local neighborhood structure regularization to deal with face deformation, which can capture the intrinsic geometry of the input face image and hence help to produce realistic deformation. Second, combing the face alignment algorithm, we present a fast and automatic approach of facial expression and shape transfer with our face deformation method.

2 Facial Expression and Shape Transfer

The framework of our method is showed in Fig. 2. To achieve automatic facial expression and shape transfer between two faces, we first utilize a cascade regression tree based face alignment algorithm [7] to extract 68 accurate face landmark points from the two face images. This algorithm is quite robust to face images of sculpture, sketch, comic and painting. Then, to eliminate the inconsistencies between the two faces in position, size and rotation, we align the target landmarks to original landmarks with a similar transformation which can be solved with an ordinary Procrustes analysis. After the transformation, the target face landmarks have a similar size, pose and location to the source face, and in the same time, it retains the contour details which are of fatal importance for the face deformation. Finally, we transfer facial expression and shape from target face to original face by deforming the original face to the shape of target face with our non-rigid face deformation method.

Let $X = \{x_i\}_{i=1}^{n}$ be the original face landmark points and $Y = \{y_i\}_{i=1}^{n}$ be the aligned target face landmark points, where x_i and y_i are column vectors and present coordinate of the i-th landmark point, n is the numbers of points in the two sets. The deformation can be viewed as a map f from original image to deformed image, each pixel point p in original image have a unique map function f_p:

$$f_p(p) = p + g_p(p) \tag{1}$$

where g_p is the displacement function which is solved through the interpolation of X and Y, and $f_p(p)$ is coordinate in deformed image where p is mapped to. More details of the deformation will be discussed in the following sections.

We can see that all the color and texture features of the deformed image are mapped from the original image and only landmark features are from the target face image; this lead to a fact that our method can avoid artifacts caused by inconsistency of the two faces in illumination, color, texture and resolution.

3   Local Feature Guided Non-rigid Image Deformation

In this section, we describe the detail of our non-rigid face deformation algorithm. As mentioned above, the deformation is built according to two sets of distinct points. Let X be a set of control points(original face landmarks), and Y be the corresponding target points(aligned target face landmarks). We view the deformation as a function f that maps the points in the original image to those in the deformed image, and formulate the function estimation as a vector-field interpolation that should satisfy the following three properties [21]: (i) Interpolation: the points $\{x_i\}_{i=1}^n$ should map directly to $\{y_i\}_{i=1}^n$ under deformation; (ii) Smoothness: f should produce smooth deformations; (iii) Identity: f should be the identity function if the deformed handles $\{y_i\}_{i=1}^n$ are the same as $\{x_i\}_{i=1}^n$ (i.e., $\forall i, x_i = y_i \Rightarrow f(x) = x$ with x being an arbitrary point in the image). These properties are very similar to those used in scattered data interpolation. Thus, we construct a non-rigid deformation function f satisfying these three properties with a closed-form solution.

3.1   Problem Formulation

The mathematical formulation of the deformation problem is based on Moving Least Squares (MLS) [21]. For each point p in the image, MLS is used to solve for a rigid-body transformation $f_p(x)$ that minimizes a weighted least squares error functional:

$$\sum_{i=1}^n w_i(p)\|f_p(x_i) - y_i\|^2 \tag{2}$$

where $w_i(p)$ is a non-negative weight function defined as

$$w_i(p) = \|p - x_i\|^{-2\alpha} \tag{3}$$

where α controlling the weight of each control point and $\|\cdot\|$ being the Euclidean distance. The global deformation function f is obtained from a set of local functions, and is defined as $f(p) = f_p(p)$, which is continuously differentiable.

As traditional MLS method model the deformation with rigid transformation for general objects, to specialize in face deformation, we consider to generalize the formulation to the non-rigid case and take the special geometrical structure features of face into account.

To generalize this formulation to the non-rigid case, we first replace the deformation function in MLS method with a non-rigid one. As mentioned in Eq. (1), we model the non-rigid displacement function $g_p(p)$ by requiring it to lie within a specific functional space, namely a reproducing kernel Hilbert space (RKHS). We define an RKHS by a positive definite matrix-valued kernel $\varGamma \colon \mathbb{R}^2 \times \mathbb{R}^2 \to \mathbb{R}^{2\times 2}$ [16] and here we choose a diagonal decomposable kernel:

$$\varGamma(x_i, x_j) = e^{-\|x_i - x_j\|^2/\beta^2} I \tag{4}$$

with β determining the width of the range of interaction between points and I is an identity matrix.

The optimal displacement function $g_p(p)$ then takes the form:

$$g_p(x) = \sum_{i=1}^{n} \Gamma(x, x_i)c_i \tag{5}$$

where the coefficient c_i is 2×1 vector (to be determined).

To take advantage of geometrical structure features of face, we introduce the local neighborhood structure regularization, for the local structures among neighboring feature points are very strong and stable. This is particularly beneficial to the non-rigid facial movement. Therefore, we preserve the local neighborhood structure with a local geometrical constraint during deformation.

In our deformation problem, we hope that the local structures in Y could be preserved after the displacement of X, which could be achieved by the following three steps [26]. First, search the k nearest neighbors for each point in X, and enforce the weight $M_{ij} = 0$ if x_j does not belong to the set of neighbors of x_i, where M is an $n \times n$ neighboring weight matrix with M_{ij} summarizing the contribution of x_j to x_i for reconstruction. Second, minimize the reconstruction errors measured by the cost function:

$$E(M) = \sum_{i=1}^{n} \left\| x_i - \sum_{j=1}^{n} M_{ij}x_j \right\|^2 \tag{6}$$

under a constraint that the rows of the weight matrix sum to one: $\sum_{j=1}^{n} M_{ij} = 1$ The optimal neighboring weights M_{ij} can be obtained by solving a least squares problem. Third, the local geometry of each control point after the transformation f is preserved by minimizing the cost function:

$$\sum_{i=1}^{n} w_i(p) \left\| x_i + g_p(x_i) - \sum_{j=1}^{n} M_{ij}(x_j + g_p(x_j)) \right\|^2 \tag{7}$$

Combining the moving last square error term in Eq. (2) and the local regularization term in Eq. (7), the optimal displacement function g_p can be solved by minimizing:

$$\sum_{i=1}^{n} w_i(p) \| x_i + g_p(x_i) - y_i \|^2$$
$$+ \eta \sum_{i=1}^{n} w_i(p) \left\| x_i + g_p(x_i) - \sum_{j=1}^{n} M_{ij}(x_j + g_p(x_j)) \right\|^2 \tag{8}$$

where the positive real numbers η control the tradeoff between the two terms. With a close form solution of the coefficient set C, we define our deformation function as the initial position plus the displacement function:

$$f(p) = p + (\Gamma_p C)^T \tag{9}$$

where kernel vector $\Gamma_p = (\Gamma(p, x_1), \dots, \Gamma(p, x_n))$ with size $1 \times n$ and the coefficient matrix $C = (c_1, c_2, \dots, c_n)^T$ with size $n \times 2$.

Note that this deformation function f is smooth, and as p approaches x_i, $w_i(p)$ approaches infinity, and then the function interpolates, i.e., $f(x_i) = y_i$. Moreover, if $\forall i$, $x_i = y_i$, then $g_p(p) \equiv 0$, therefore, f is the identity transformation, i.e., $f(p) = p$.

3.2 Close-Form Solution

By substituting Eq. (5) into Eq. (8), it can be rewrite in the following matrix form:

$$E(C) = \left\| W^{1/2}(X + \Gamma C - Y) \right\|_F^2$$
$$+ \eta \left\| W^{1/2}(X + \Gamma C - M(X + \Gamma C)) \right\|_F^2 \tag{10}$$

where the kernel matrix $\Gamma \in \mathbb{R}^{n \times n}$ is called the Gram matrix with $\Gamma_{ij} = e^{-\|x_i - x_j\|^2 / \beta^2}$, the weight matrix W is a diagonal matrix with the i-th entry determined by Eq. (3), X are the control points and Y are target points respectively, in which the i-th rows represent x_i and y_i, C is the coefficient matrix with size $n \times 2$, and $\| \cdot \|_F$ denotes the Frobenius norm. Equation (10) is quadratic in C. Taking the derivative of it with respect to C and setting it to zero, we obtain a closed-form solution:

$$C = (I + \eta Q W^{-1})^{-1} \Gamma^{-1} Y - \Gamma^{-1} X \tag{11}$$

where I is the identity matrix, and $Q = (I - M)^T W(I - M)$. With this closed-form solution for C, we can write a simple expression for the deformation function:

$$f(p) = p + [\Gamma_p[(I + \eta Q W^{-1})^{-1} \Gamma^{-1} Y - \Gamma^{-1} X]]^T \tag{12}$$

where Γ_p is an row vector with the i-th entry $\Gamma_{p,i} = e^{-\|p - x_i\|^2 / \beta^2}$. To deform a new face image more efficiently, we approximate the original face image with a grid and apply the deformation function (12) to each vertex, then use a bilinear interpolation in each quad of the grid. We summarize our approach in Algorithm 1.

3.3 Computational Complexity and Fast Implementation

According to solution Eq. (12), the computation complexity is mainly determined by time complexity of solving the weight matrix M, Gram matrix Γ and the inversion of a matrix of size $n \times n$. To search the k nearest neighbors for each point in X, the time complexity should be close to $O((k + n) \log n)$ by using the kd tree [20]. According to Eq. (6), the time complexity of obtaining the weight matrix M is $O(k^3 n)$ because each row of M can be solved separately with $O(k^3)$ time complexity. Due to the Gram matrix being of size $n \times n$, the time complexity of solving the Γ is $O(n^2)$. Since weight matrix M and Gram matrix Γ share for deformation function of each point, namely they only need to be computed once, while inversion

---

Algorithm 1. The Proposed Algorithm

Input: original and target face, kernel Γ, parameters k, α, β, η
Output: Deformed face
1 Extract face landmark points and get the correspondences $\{x_i, y_i\}_{i=1}^n$;
2 Construct the Gram matrix Γ based on $\{x_i\}_{i=1}^n$;
3 Search the k nearest neighbor for each point in X;
4 Compute M by minimizing the cost function (6);
5 Approximate the original face image with a grid;
6 **repeat**
7 | Choose a vertex p on the grid;
8 | Compute the weight W by Eq. (3);
9 | Compute the vector Γ_p;
10 | Compute f at vertex p by using Eq. (12);
11 **until** *all the vertexes are computed*;
12 The deformed face is generated by a bilinear interpolation of $\{f(p)\}$.

---

of a matrix of size $n \times n$ in solution (13) are different for each point in the image, the total complexity of our method is $O(k^3 n + n^2 + n^3 l)$. Since $k \ll n \ll l$, and it can be written as $O(n^3 l)$, where l is the number of vertex in the grid which is used for approximating the image. Moreover, users in general creates the deformations by manipulating the target point set, and the control points are fixed. Therefore, much of Eq. (12) can be precomputed. In particular, we can rewrite Eq. (12) in the form:

$$f(p) = S + (VY)^T \tag{13}$$

where $V = \Gamma_p (I + \eta Q W^{-1})^{-1} \Gamma^{-1}$ and $S = p - (\Gamma_p \Gamma^{-1} X)^T$ can be precomputed leading to fast implementation. In this case, the time complexity of our algorithm is reduced to $O(nl)$.

Parameter Setting: There are mainly four parameters in our method: k, α, β and η. Parameter k controls the number of nearest neighbors for local neighborhood structure regularization. Parameter α controls the weight of each control points. Parameter β and η affect the amount of the local structure constraint, β determines how wide the range of interaction between points, η determines the trade-off between the MLS error term and the local structure regularization term. We finally set $k = 15$, $\alpha = 2$, $\beta = 2$ and $\eta = 10$ according to the parameter tuning experiments.

4 Experiment

In this section, we test our method on different types of face images. We use the dlib library to implement the cascade regression tree based face alignment algorithm [7], and extract the landmark points for both original and target face images. To demonstrate our method, we conduct the experiment based on a self-organized dataset which include various kind and style of face images. More exactly, the dataset include face image of men, women, children and the style range from image of nature face, sculpture, sketch, comic and painting. The face images vary in factors such as illumination, color, texture, resolution and occlusion. Here, we present some representative types of face deformation.

In Fig. 3, we show 4 representative facial expression and shape transfer results obtained with our method. To evaluate the performance of our method, we also report the results of MLS [21] and blending based face swap(face blending) [9] method as comparison. In the figure, the first row presents original faces and the fifth row presents target faces, while the second, third and fourth rows are the corresponding facial expression and shape transfer (from target faces to original faces) results of our method, MLS and face swap method.

Fig. 3. Face expression and shape transfer results of our method, MLS [21] and face blending method [9]. the first row: original face, the second row: results of our method, the third row: results of MLS, the fourth row: results of face blending method, the fifth row: target faces

First column shows facial expression and shape transfer between two head sculpture images, we can see that both deformation method (our method and MLS) and face swap method have their advantages and produce natural and smooth results. The result of face swap method shows more significant facial expression and shape transfer since more counter detail of target face are transferred, but it tend to change the identity of result face in the same time; our method retains most counter detail of original face and achieve transfer with smooth deformation; MLS method performs similar to our method but slightly poor in some details, e.g. unnatural curving in jaw and mouth.

In the second column, we consider transfer facial expression and shape from an image of natural face to a face painting. We can see that the result of face swap method occurs obvious blur; the blur is caused by its blending operation which aim at eliminating the inconsistent in color, texture and revolution, while our method are not affected by these inconsistence and produce natural, smooth and clear deformation result, and for MLS method, the unexpected zigzag again appear on the lips. To further explore the performance of the three method, we consider facial expression and shape transfer between two face image with more significant difference in expression and factors such as illumination, color, texture and occlusion.

As shown in the third and fourth column, both MLS and face swap method degenerate. From the third column of the figure, we can see that all the three method can transfer facial expression and shape in a large degree, but face swap method yield relatively poor results due to the obvious artifacts caused by the inconsistence of the two face images in color and collusion of glasses in the target face. For the result of MLS, there are some imperfections such as unnatural curving in the jaw and defects in the right brow, while result of our method are smooth and natural.

From the fourth column of the figure, we can see that there are lots of flaw in the result of face swap method due to the inconsistence of the two face in color and texture; in the result of MLS, there are unnatural curving in jaw, mouth and brow; moreover, fold-over, another unexpected property of MLS, appears between left eye and brow. Our method is not troubled by the above problems which show that our method can achieve more natural and smooth face deformation and it's quite robust to the inconsistence of original face and target face.

In previous examples, we deform the entire face, namely transfer facial shape and expression at same time; however, our proposed method can only deform part of face according to your needs. Figure 4 shows two examples of transfer external face shape and internal facial expression separately by choosing different landmark points. The first column presents original faces and the fourth column presents target faces, the second column shows the results of internal expression transfer and the third column shows the results of external shape transfer.

Figure 5 shows two example of generating facial animation with our method by using different face to drive a static face image deformation. Images in the left are original face images, in the top are target face images and in the bottom are deformed face image. The results show that the deformation is smooth, natural and artifact-less despite the significant variances between original face image and target face images.

original faces   *expression deform*   *shape deform*   *target faces*

Fig. 4. Two example of transfer external face shape and internal facial expression separately. The first column: original faces, the second column: the results of internal expression transfer, the third column: the results of external shape transfer, the fourth column: target faces

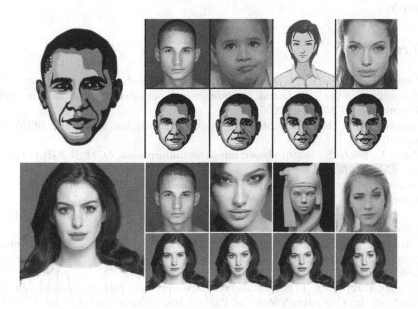

Fig. 5. Tow example of facial animation generate by our method. left: original faces, top: target faces, bottom facial animation.

5   Discussion and Future Work

As mentioned above, our method completely rely on original and target face land-marks points for both the accuracy and amount. As a result, inaccurate face land-mark localization will lead to deadly affecting to our results and too few landmark points will cause the losing of detail counter information of target face, which far-ther lead to an insignificant deformation effect. Another limitation of our method is the deformation of mouth and eyes, e, g. if we try to deform a mouth or eye from close statement to open, there will be a hole since there is no information of these region in original image. We consider to use a generative model to solve this problem in the future work. A potential breakthrough of our non-rigid deforma-tion method is that it is available for the deformation of 3D point cloud objects. We will try to generalize our method to 3D case in the future work.

6   Conclusion

Within this paper, we present a novel approach that transfers the appearance and expression of a face in image to that of another regardless of variance between the two faces in factors such as illumination, color, texture, resolution and even some mild occlusion. Our method can be full-automatic or semi-automatic for con-veniently tuning a better result by combining a face alignment algorithm and a non-rigid image deformation method. The final results are realistic, natural and artifact-less.

References

1. Alexa, M., Cohen-Or, D., Levin, D.: As-rigid-as-possible shape interpolation. In: Proceedings of the 27th Annual Conference on Computer Graphics and Interactive Techniques, pp. 157–164 (2000)
2. Aronszajn, N.: Theory of reproducing kernels. Trans. Am. Math. Soc. **68**(3), 337–404 (1950)
3. Beier, T., Neely, S.: Feature-based image metamorphosis. ACM SIGGRAPH Comput. Graph. **26**(2), 35–42 (1992)
4. Bookstein, F.L.: Principal warps: thin-plate splines and the decomposition of defor-mations. IEEE Trans. Pattern Anal. Mach. Intell. **11**(6), 567–585 (2002)
5. Gangnet, M., Blake, A.: Poisson image editing. In: ACM SIGGRAPH, pp. 313–318 (2003)
6. Garrido, P., Valgaerts, L., Rehmsen, O., Thormaehlen, T., Perez, P., Theobalt, C.: Automatic face reenactment. In: IEEE Conference on Computer Vision and Pattern Recognition, pp. 4217–4224 (2014)
7. Kazemi, V., Sullivan, J.: One millisecond face alignment with an ensemble of regres-sion trees. In: Computer Vision and Pattern Recognition. pp. 1867–1874 (2014)
8. Levin, D.: The approximation power of moving least-squares. Math. Comput. **67**(224), 1517–1531 (1998)
9. Liu, L., Liu, L., Nie, X., Feng, J., Yan, S., Yan, S.: A live face swapper. In: ACM on Multimedia Conference, pp. 691–692 (2016)

10. Ma, J., Zhao, J., Tian, J., Bai, X., Tu, Z.: Regularized vector field learning with sparse approximation for mismatch removal. Pattern Recognit. **46**(12), 3519–3532 (2013)
11. Ma, J., Zhao, J., Tian, J., Yuille, A.L., Tu, Z.: Robust point matching via vector field consensus. IEEE Trans. Image Process. **23**(4), 1706–1721 (2014)
12. Ma, J., Zhao, J., Guo, H., Jiang, J., Zhou, H., Gao, Y.: Locality preserving matching. In: Proceedings of the 26th International Joint Conference on Artificial Intelligence, pp. 4492–4498. AAAI Press (2017)
13. Ma, J., Zhao, J., Jiang, J., Zhou, H.: Non-rigid point set registration with robust transformation estimation under manifold regularization. In: Proceedings of the AAAI Conference on Artificial Intelligence, pp. 4218–4224 (2017)
14. Ma, J., Zhao, J., Tian, J.: Nonrigid image deformation using moving regularized least squares. IEEE Signal Process. Lett. **20**(10), 988–991 (2013)
15. Ma, J., Zhao, J., Tian, J., Tu, Z., Yuille, A.L.: Robust estimation of nonrigid transformation for point set registration. In: Proceedings IEEE Conference Computer Vision Pattern Recognition, pp. 2147–2154 (2013)
16. Ma, J., Zhao, J., Tian, J., Yuille, A.L., Tu, Z.: Robust point matching via vector field consensus. IEEE Trans. Image Process. **23**(4), 1706–1721 (2014)
17. Maccracken, R., Joy, K.I.: Free-form deformations with lattices of arbitrary topology. In: Conference on Computer Graphics and Interactive Techniques, pp. 181–188 (1996)
18. Min, F., Sang, N., Wang, Z.: Automatic face replacement in video based on 2D morphable model. In: International Conference on Pattern Recognition, pp. 2250–2253 (2010)
19. Pighin, F., Hecker, J., Lischinski, D., Szeliski, R., Salesin, D.H.: Synthesizing realistic facial expressions from photographs (1998)
20. Ren, S., Cao, X., Wei, Y., Sun, J.: Face alignment at 3000 fps via regressing local binary features. In: IEEE Conference on Computer Vision and Pattern Recognition, pp. 1685–1692 (2014)
21. Schaefer, S., Mcphail, T., Warren, J.: Image deformation using moving least squares. ACM Trans. Graph. **25**(3), 533–540 (2006)
22. Shen, S., Yamasaki, T., Aizawa, K., Sugahara, T.: Data-driven geometric face image smilization featuring moving least square based deformation. In: IEEE Third International Conference on Multimedia Big Data, pp. 220–225 (2017)
23. Xiao, S., Yan, S., Kassim, A.A.: Facial landmark detection via progressive initialization. In: IEEE International Conference on Computer Vision Workshop, pp. 986–993 (2015)
24. Zhang, Z., Luo, P., Loy, C.C., Tang, X.: Facial landmark detection by deep multi-task learning. In: Fleet, D., Pajdla, T., Schiele, B., Tuytelaars, T. (eds.) ECCV 2014. LNCS, vol. 8694, pp. 94–108. Springer, Cham (2014). https://doi.org/10.1007/978-3-319-10599-4_7
25. Zhou, H., Kuang, Y., Yu, Z., Ren, S., Dai, A., Zhang, Y., Lu, T., Ma, J.: Non-rigid image deformation algorithm based on MRLS-TPS. In: 2017 IEEE International Conference on Image Processing (ICIP), pp. 2269–2273. IEEE (2017)
26. Zhou, H., Ma, J., Yang, C., Sun, S., Liu, R., Zhao, J.: Nonrigid feature matching for remote sensing images via probabilistic inference with global and local regularizations. IEEE Geosci. Remote Sens. Lett. **13**(3), 374–378 (2016)
27. Zhou, H., Ma, J., Zhang, Y., Yu, Z., Ren, S., Chen, D.: Feature guided non-rigid image/surface deformation via moving least squares with manifold regularization. In: 2017 IEEE International Conference on Multimedia and Expo (ICME), pp. 1063–1068. IEEE (2017)

P-Schedule: Erasure Coding Schedule Strategy in Big Data Storage System

Chao Yin, Haitao Lv$^{(\boxtimes)}$, Tongfang Li, Yan Liu, Xiaoping Qu,
and Sihao Yuan

Jiujiang University, Jiujiang 332005, China
lvhaitao0301@gmail.com

Abstract. Erasure coding technology is one of the key technologies in big data storage system. A well designed erasure coding can not only improve the reliability of the big data storage system, but also greatly improve the performance. Most of the existing big data storage systems use replica strategy, which can provide good availability and real-time, but it has caused a lot of data redundancy and waste of storage space. A large part of the data stored in the storage system exists in the form of cold data. In this paper, we aim at the cold data which doesn't require highly on data availability and real-time in the big data storage system. We have proposed a scheme to support both replica strategy and coding strategy, and designed the node scheduling and data addressing scheme. We selected Liberation code which is excellent in writing operation, and developed P-Schedule scheme to optimize the decoding speed. Through a series of designs, we can effectively improve the disk utilization and write speed of the cold data in the big data system. The test results show that the sequential write performance of erasure coding is better than that of the replica strategy. The larger the data block is, the better the performance is.

Keywords: Big data · Erasure coding · Liberation · P-Schedule

1 Introduction

Since the birth of the Internet, the data grows in an explosive way [1]. Especially in recent years, the development of mobile terminals, networking, cloud computing, which make the speed of data growth faster and faster. "China Mobile Phone Market Research Report in 2016–2017" shows that internet users in China have reached 668 million until June 2016, and mobile phone users are 593 million. According to the results report released by Tencent Inc. in 2017, active users have reached 549 million in WeChat monthly. The more data there is, the more important they are. The popularity of deep learning [2] and big data [3, 4] is a very good description in recent years.

While the traditional centralized storage can't afford such a large amount of data, the big data storage comes into being in such a context [5]. Combining with the advantages of storage systems and network systems, big data storage can provide more reliability, security and scalability. In order to guarantee the reliability of the data, the big data system needs to use some kind of backup scheme to avoid data loss when one node is damaged [6]. The existing big data system always adopts replica scheme [7], which will cause a lot of waste of storage space.

© Springer Nature Switzerland AG 2018
J. Vaidya and J. Li (Eds.): ICA3PP 2018, LNCS 11336, pp. 270–279, 2018.
https://doi.org/10.1007/978-3-030-05057-3_22

The traditional RAID [8] has used erasure coding to store, especially RAID6 uses erasure coding to control the data redundancy in a very low level at the same backup situation. There are many erasure codes similar RAID6, RDP [9, 10], EVENODD [11], STAR [12] and so on. However, because of the complexity and data availability, and a large amount of network bandwidth occupied by erasure codes in the encoding and decoding process, large-scale erasure codes scheme has not been introduced to big data system.

We have proposed an erasure coding scheme to solve the storage pressure and data availability in cold data storage. This scheme can greatly reduce the data redundancy. Considering that cold data usually occupies a large proportion in the system, this scheme has focused on optimizing the sequential write operations of cold data and greatly improves the writing performance.

The contributions of this paper are described as follows:

1. After comparing and analyzing the advantages and disadvantages of big data storage system in replica strategy and erasure code strategy, we have proposed to solve the problem that cold data causing a lot of waste of storage space by the application of erasure code.
2. We have proposed to improve cold data storage capacity of big data storage system by using Liberation code scheme, and we have successfully designed and implemented erasure codes in a fault tolerance big data storage system.
3. Through detailed comparative experiments, it verifies the feasibility and great practicability of erasure code to store cold data in the big data storage system. It also can greatly reduce the data redundancy without affecting the availability of data.

The rest of this paper is organized as follows. Section 2 is related works. Section 3 introduces the theory of P-Schedule algorithm and Sect. 4 introduces the implement. The experimental result and evaluation are described in Sect. 5. Section 6 is the conclusion.

2 Related Works

2.1 Coding Based on Matrix

Matrix is the key component of erasure coding. Both array codes and RS codes need to be encoded and decoded in the form of matrix.

Coding based on matrix is essentially a dot product operation of matrices and vectors. Suppose there are k data blocks and m check blocks, and each block contains w bits. The matrix contains k + m rows and K columns. The element of the matrix is an integer in the finite field $GF(2^W)$ [13]. The matrix is called distribution matrix (DM in short).

Different codes have different coding matrices. The distribution matrix and the vectors containing the data block are multiplied to a vector containing the data block and the check block. When encoding, the erasure matrix and the data vector are dot product, and then the check block can be obtained.

We know that each data block corresponds to a row inside the distribution matrix. When decoding, we only need to find the corresponding rows of K data blocks which are not damaged in the distribution matrix to form an erasure matrix. The matrix is transposed and multiplied by a vector composed of data blocks without damage, and the damaged data blocks can be computed and fixed up.

2.2 Coding Based on Bit-Matrix

If we launch the big data matrix $(k + m) * k$ in row and column direction by w in the finite field $GF(2^W)$, we can get a matrix with $w * (k + m)$ rows and $w * k$ columns. We call this matrix BDM (Binary Distribution Matrix), and the $m * (w * w)$ matrix at the bottom is called CDM (Coding Distribution Matrix). We extend the vector mentioned in the previous section to wk elements.

Since each element is a bit in the matrix and the vector, we can use XOR operations instead of dot product operations [15]. We set the data vectors corresponding to the bit of 1 in BDM to XOR operations. By replacing the original dot product operations with XOR operations, the speed of encoding and decoding operations can be greatly improved. Moreover, we can see that the number of XOR operations is directly related to the number of 1 in the BDM, so that we can determine the performance of the encoding by the number of 1 in BDM.

3 P-Schedule Scheme

3.1 The Principle of P-Schedule Scheme

Figure 1 shows a Bit-matrix encoding procedure for $k = 3$ and $w = 5$. Let's analyze the calculation steps in the coding process of the matrix. The most direct way is to do 5 dot product operations, and then we convert these dot product operations into XOR operations.

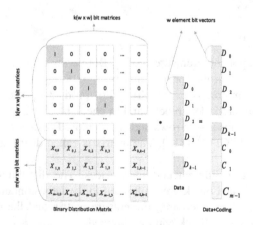

Fig. 1. The encoding process based on Bit-matrix.

However, we can see that the bit-matrix is a sparse matrix. Compared with doing encoding operation directly, it is more efficient for us to preprocess the encoding operations. We use five tuples to represent the encoding process in Eq. 1:

$$<op, sd, sb, dd, db> \tag{1}$$

We can use XOR operations instead of dot product operations and set the data vectors corresponding to the bit of 1 in BDM to XOR operations. By replacing the original dot product operations with XOR operations, the speed of encoding and decoding operations can be greatly improved. The performance of the encoding will be determined by the number of 1 in BDM.

Op represents operation type, 0 is copy operation, and 1 is XOR operation. Sd is the device number of the source data. Sb is the bit number of source data. Dd and db represent the device numbers and digits of the destination data, respectively. For convenience, we unify the device number from 0 to k + m − 1. When ID i < k, it indicates the data device Di. When ID i > k, it represents the check device Ci-k.

The validation process of bit-matrix in Fig. 2, which we can express in schedule, as shown in Table 1.

It can be seen that schedule algorithm can effectively reduce the number of XOR operation. When we encode and decode in any bit-matrix encoding system, we should convert them into schedule to improve the efficiency of encoding and decoding.

Fig. 2. An example of bit-matrix encoding for k = 3 and w = 5.

Table 1. Schedule for bit matrix operation.

Schedule	Dot product
<0,0,0,3,0>,<1,1,1,3,0>,<1,2,2,3,0>	$C0,0 = d0,0 \oplus d1,1 \oplus d2,2$
<0,0,1,3,1>,<1,1,2,3,1>,<1,2,3,3,1>	$C0,1 = d0,1 \oplus d1,2 \oplus d2,3$
<0,0,2,3,2>,<1,1,2,3,2>,<1,1,3,3,2>,<1,2,4,3,2>	$C0,2 = d0,2 \oplus d1,2 \oplus d1,3 \oplus d2,4$
<0,0,3,3,3>,<1,1,4,3,3>,<1,2,0,3,3>	$C0,3 = d0,3 \oplus d1,4 \oplus d2,0$
<0,0,4,3,4>,<1,1,0,3,4>,<1,2,0,3,4>,<1,2,1,3,4>	$C4,1 = d0,4 \oplus d1,0 \oplus d2,0 \oplus d2,1$

3.2   Encoding

In the coding system, there are k data devices and m checkout devices, each of which has w bits word length. Usually, there is a matrix with w * (k + m) * wk in the finite field $GF(2^W)$ used as the erasure matrix. We select several representative erasure coding to check the performance of erasure matrix, such as Liberation, Evenodd, RDP and Cauchy Reed-Solomon.

For any given w and k, the number of 1 in parity matrix of Liberation code is $kw + k - 1$ and that in in the unit matrix of the head of the BDM matrix is kw. The total numbers of 1 in the erasure matrix are $2kw + k - 1$. We know that if the number of 1 is x in an erasure matrix contains, the XOR operation number in the encoding process is $X - 1$. In order to obtain a parity bit, the number of XOR operations required in Liberation code is shown as Eq. 2:

$$\frac{2kw + k - 1 - 2w}{2w} = k - 1 + \frac{k - 1}{2w} \tag{2}$$

The optimal value of Eq. 2 is $k - 1$.

While to get a check bit, the number of XOR operations in EVENODD code is shown as Eq. 3:

$$\frac{kw + (w - 1)(k - 1) + kw - 2w}{2w} = \frac{3}{2}(k - 1) + \frac{k - 1}{2w} \tag{3}$$

As we can see, the number of XOR operations in EVENODD code is almost one and a half times than that of Liberation code.

In addition, we can use the ratio of 1 in the parity matrix to compare the various codes. The proportion of 1 of Liberation code is 16%, while that of RDP code is 28% and CRS code is 21%.

From the above comparison, we can see that the number of 1 in erasure matrix of Liberation code is the least, which means that we can achieve the purpose of coding through less XOR operations in the actual coding process. Therefore, the coding scheme used in this paper is based on Liberation code.

3.3 Decoding

Suppose that the data on the data node D_0 and D_1 is missing while $k = 5$, $w = 5$. In order to recover the missing data, we take the first ten rows of the parity matrix and transpose them. We can get the data on D_0 and D_1 from the transposed matrix and the remaining data nodes.

The number of 1 is 134 in the ten row of the transposed matrix, so that the number of XOR operations is $134 - 10 = 124$. Now, let's check the number of 1 in the zeroth and fifth lines that are used to calculate $d_{0,0}$ and $d_{1,0}$, respectively. The number of 1 in the first line is 16 while that in the fifth lines 14. This means that 28 XOR operations are required through the above matrix operations. We have found that there are thirteen columns in which both of the two lines are 1. If we calculate $d_{1,0}$ first, it only needs 13 XOR operations, and then we'll calculate the $d_{0,0}$ by $d_{1,0}$:

$$d_{0,0} = d_{1,0} \oplus d_{2,0} \oplus d_{3,0} \oplus d_{4,0} \oplus p_0 \tag{4}$$

Equation 4 requires only 4 XOR operations. The number of XOR operations is reduced from 28 to 17 times in this way.

4 Implement

4.1 Architecture

Our system is based on Linux system, and the original backup strategy is replica. In this paper, we add erasure code to the basis of multiple replicas. The specific system framework is as Fig. 3.

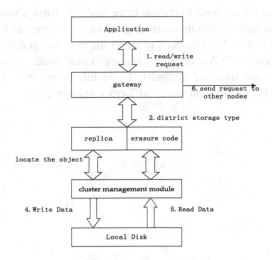

Fig. 3. The architecture of the system.

Cluster management module manages the system nodes and maintains the membership among the nodes. For example, when the system nodes fail or there are new nodes added to the system, it will inform upper level and manage operations to maintain consistency information among nodes.

When the application initiates the read/write request, the native gateway receives the request and positions the server node where the data block is located through the consistent hash algorithm. If it is on another server node, the request is forwarded to another node. If it is on the local node, the requested data is classified in the form of replication or in the form of erasure code.

The node management module receives the request from the gateway and performs the read/write operation according to the request type.

4.2   Node Schedule

In order to avoid the bottleneck, our system adopts symmetric and decentralized ring architecture. A consistent hash algorithm is used to locate in the file of the storage node. There is no longer a super node or a metadata server, and all nodes have equal status.

The virtual nodes are evenly distributed on the ring after the consistency of hash algorithm of IP and port number. When we select the storage group, we can carry out the hash algorithm according to the user names of the client. We can select the first virtual node and the next N nodes according to the hash value. If a node and a selected node are on the same physical node, the node will be given up and the next will be chosen. Continue the selection to select the N nodes.

As Fig. 4 shows, we suppose to choose three nodes to form a storage group. After we can carry out the hash algorithm according to the user names of the client, the first node to be obtained is A-1. We turn back to select the next two nodes, B-1 and A-2. We find that node A-2 and node A-1 are in the same physical node, so we have to give up A-2, then go backward traversal to find C-1. At this point, A-1, B-1, and C-1 are located on three different physical nodes to form a storage group.

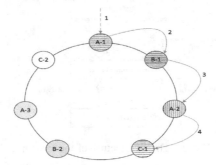

Fig. 4. The relationship among data blocks, nodes, and hash space.

This scheme avoids the possibility of multiple faults in the scenario one, and still fails to find the appropriate storage group.

5   Evaluation

5.1   Experimental Setup

The test environment consists of three hardware servers on which a big data storage cluster are built up by virtual machines to test. The hardware configuration of each server is shown in Table 2.

The most commonly used indicators to measure the reading and writing performance of a storage system are IOPS. All of the tests are based on these two indicators as test standards in this paper. In addition, we have fixed gradient values for the size of data blocks, 4 K, 64 K, 512 k and 1028 k respectively. In the reading and writing performance test, we test a big data storage system in different backup mode, triple replication and different erasure codes. In order to ensure the same effect between fault tolerance model and replication, we set the ratio of k and m 4:2 in erasure code model.

Table 2. The parameters of test server

Name	Parameter
CPU	Intel(R) Xeon(R) CPU X5650 @ 2.67 GHz × 2
Memory	Qimonda 1333 MHz 4 GB × 2
System Disk	WDC WD1003FBYX-0 1 TB 7200 rpm
Data Disk	ST1000DM003-9YN1 1 TB × 4 7200 rpm
SSD	Seagate 600 SSD 120G MLC

5.2 Read Performance Tests

The read operation can be divided into sequential reading and random reading according to the location of each reading. Sequential reading begins at a certain location and reads backwards until the end of a position. Random reading randomly selects a location to read a small amount of data, and jumps to a random location to continue read. In theory, the speed of sequential reading is much better than that of random reading, especially in the systems using disks as storage medium.

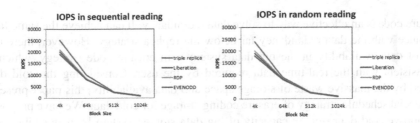

Fig. 5. IOPS in reading.

In Fig. 5, the horizontal axis represents the size of the data block, and the vertical axis represents the sum of the IOPS values of the nodes. As we can see, IOPS is decreasing on the whole with the data block increases. This is because the time reading each block increases as the block size increases, so that the overall IOPS of the system decreases. In addition, for the same block size, the IOPS of sequential reading in the erasure code strategy is lower than that of the replication mode. The smaller the data block, the greater the IOPS gap between the two modes. When the block is larger than 4 K, the value of the erasure pattern is about 25% lower than that of the replica mode. When the block size is 1024 k, It is only about 10.4% lower than the other's.

5.3   Write Performance Tests

Figure 6 shows the sequential write of the IOPS. We can see that in the overall trend, the IOPS value becomes smaller with the data block becomes larger. However, unlike reading operations, the IOPS in erasure code strategy is larger than the IOPS value of replica strategy in writing operations. Moreover, with the data block becomes larger, the IOPS in erasure code strategy almost becomes two times that in the replica mode. This is because the amount of data written in the replica strategy is much higher than that in the erasure code strategy for the same data write request. For each data write request with 1 K, the replica strategy is written 3 K data and consumes 2 K of the network bandwidth, while the erasure code strategy only needs 1.5 k to write data and consume 1.25 k network bandwidth.

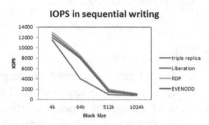

Fig. 6. IOPS in writing.

6   Conclusion

Erasure code is an effective way to solve data redundancy. It can achieve the same fault tolerance with the data redundancy far below the replica strategy. However, there is a lack of data availability in the big data system with erasure code strategy, which is inconsistent with the real-time data required by the user. Considering the cold data caused by the massive waste of storage space and data availability, this paper presents the special schedule strategy of erasure coding storage for cold data. We have proposed to improve cold data storage capacity of big data storage system by using Liberation code. The experiments show that erasure code can greatly reduce the data redundancy without affecting the availability of data.

Decoding in the erasure code system will consume a large amount of network bandwidth, which is also a factor restricting the use of erasure codes in big data storage systems. Although regenerative codes have been proposed to solve the problem of network bandwidth to some extent, this is achieved by sacrificing storage efficiency. How to optimize the decoding bandwidth without sacrificing the storage efficiency is also a research direction.

Acknowledgements. This work was supported by National Natural Science Foundation of China (No. 61662038), Science and technology project of Jiangxi Provincial Department of Education (No. GJJ151081), the Visiting Scholar Funds by China Scholarship Council, the JiangXi Association for Science and Technology.

References

1. Morris, R.J.T., Truskowski, B.J.: The evolution of storage systems. IBM Syst. J. **42**(2), 205–217 (2003)
2. Najafabadi, M.M., Villanustre, F., Khoshgoftaar, T.M., Seliya, N., Wald, R., Muharemagic, E.: Deep learning applications and challenges in big data analytics. J. Big Data **2**(1), 1–21 (2015)
3. Schermann, M., Hemsen, H., Buchmüller, C., Bitter, T., Krcmar, H., Markl, V., Hoeren, T.: Big data. Bus. Inf. Syst. Eng. **6**(5), 261–266 (2014)
4. Chen, Y., Chen, H., Gorkhali, A., Lu, Y., Ma, Y., Li, L.: Big data analytics and big data science: a survey. J. Manag. Anal. **3**(1), 1–42 (2016)
5. Li, S., Cao, Q., Wan, S., Qian, L., Xie, C.: HRSPC: a hybrid redundancy scheme via exploring computational locality to support fast recovery and high reliability in distributed storage systems. J. Netw. Comput. Appl. (2015)
6. Calder, B., Wang, J., Ogus, A., et al.: Windows Azure storage: a highly available cloud storage service with strong consistency. In: Proceeding of the Twenty-Third ACM Symposium on Operating Systems Principles, pp. 143–157 (2011)
7. Chun, B.G., Dabek, F., Haeberlen, A., et al.: Efficient replica maintenance for distributed storage systems. In: Proceedings of NSDI, pp. 225–264 (2006)
8. Chen, P.M., Lee, E.K., Gibson, G.A., et al.: RAID: high-performance, reliable secondary storage. ACM Comput. Surv.–CSUR **26**(2), 145–185 (1994)
9. Corbett, P., English, B., Goel, A., et al.: Row-diagonal parity for double disk failure correction. In: FAST 2004: Proceedings of the 3rd USENIX Conference on File and Storage Technologies, pp. 1–14 (2004)
10. Xiang, L., Xu, Y., Lui, J., et al.: Optimal recovery of single disk failure in RDP code storage systems. In: SIGMETRICS 2010 Proceedings of the ACM SIGMETRICS International Conference on Measurement and Modeling of Computer Systems, pp. 119–130 (2010)
11. Blaum, M., Brady, J., Bruck, J., et al.: EVENODD: an efficient scheme for tolerating double disk failures in RAID architectures. IEEE Trans. Comput. **44**(2), 192–202 (1995)
12. Huang, C., Xu, L.: STAR: an efficient coding scheme for correcting triple storage node failures. IEEE Trans. Comput. **57**(7), 889–901 (2008)
13. Reed, I.S., Solomon, G.: Polynomial codes over certain finite fields. J. Soc. Ind. Appl. Math. **8**(2), 300–304 (1996)
14. Rodrigues, R., Liskov, B.: High availability in DHTs: erasure coding vs. replication. In: Castro, M., van Renesse, R. (eds.) IPTPS 2005. LNCS, vol. 3640, pp. 226–239. Springer, Heidelberg (2005). https://doi.org/10.1007/11558989_21
15. Luo, J., Bowers, K.D., Oprea, A., Xu, L.: Efficient software implementations of large finite fields GF(2n) for secure storage applications. ACM Trans. Storage **8**(2) (2012)

Answer Aggregation of Crowdsourcing Employing an Improved EM-Based Approach

Ran Zhang[✉], Lei Liu, Lizhen Cui, Wei He, and Hui Li

Shandong University, Jinan, Shandong, China
632378963@qq.com, l.liu@sdu.edu.cn

Abstract. Crowdsourcing platforms are frequently employed to collect answers from numerous participants on the Internet, e.g., Amazon Mechanical Turk. Different participants may have different answers for the same question. This cause unexpected aggregated answers. The accuracy of aggregated answers depends on answer quality. Answer quality varies by skill level of participants. In crowdsourcing, participants are defined as workers. Existing studies always characterize worker quality with their skills. However, the personality features of individual persons may have significant impact on the quality of their answers, e.g. worker emotion and worker intent. To this end, aggregating answers without taking into account the personality characteristics of persons may lead to unexpected results. To fill the gap this paper employs an improved EM-based approach for answer aggregation based on the answer data of workers and considering personality characteristics. The approach not only aggregates answers but also simultaneously estimates the skill level of each worker, worker emotion, worker intent and the difficulty of the task. Last but not least, the verification is conducted on real-world datasets Affect Text and simulation datasets.

Keywords: Crowdsourcing · Worker skill · Task difficulty · Worker quality
Personality characteristics · EM-based approach · Answer aggregation

1 Introduction

Crowdsourcing is a distributed problem-solving solution, which aids computers in completing tasks that computers cannot solve on their own [1]. There are many crowdsourcing platforms e.g., Amazon Mechanical Turk, Crowd Flower, www.zbj.com, and www.weichaishi.com. Crowdsourcing platform publishes tasks e.g., sentiment labeling task [17] form requesters and collect answers from workers. Hundreds of workers on such platforms can accept tasks and send back the corresponding answers. Based on the collected answers, aggregated answers can be obtained through some aggregation algorithm. The accuracy of the aggregated answers depends on answer quality. Answer quality varies due to the difference of skill level, intent and emotion of workers. Existing works always study the influence of skill level and worker intent on the answer quality and ignores the personality characteristics of persons e.g., worker emotion. Therefore, in order to obtain the aggregated answers, this paper takes worker skill, worker emotion and worker intent into consideration. Besides, difficulty of the task is also taken into account.

© Springer Nature Switzerland AG 2018
J. Vaidya and J. Li (Eds.): ICA3PP 2018, LNCS 11336, pp. 280–290, 2018.
https://doi.org/10.1007/978-3-030-05057-3_23

Personality characteristics of persons are important for model worker quality. There are factors that have impact on answers of workers. For tasks, each task has its own difficulty level, which has impact on the judgment of workers. Due to different characters of workers, they have different worker skill and worker intent. In addition, emotion as the personality characteristics of persons will also have impact on the accuracy of answers of workers [11]. Some researchers [8] find that workers who are in positive emotion are more productive than workers who are in negative emotion. Although there have been many studies that have considered worker quality, it hardly find studies which takes into account worker emotion. In this paper, in order to aggregating answers from workers, worker emotion is taken into consideration.

The improved answer aggregation approach is based on the EM algorithm in this paper. In this method, the influence of worker intent, worker emotion, worker skill and task difficulty on answers of workers is considered, and according to this method, aggregated answers are obtained. The EM-based method in this paper is called the four-parameter EM approach. In this model, workers with different emotions and different intent are formulated based on workers' behavior. This paper defines three types of workers: workers who are non-malicious and are in positive emotion, workers who are non-malicious but are in negative emotion, and workers who are malicious that answer only for money.

A generalized Expectation-Maximization algorithm [9, 10] is used to perform parameter estimation in this paper. The improved EM-based approach is divided into two steps which performs iteratively until convergence of the parameter set: (1) Expectation step: use the existing estimates for worker skill, worker emotion, worker intent and task difficulty of the parametric probabilistic model for aggregated answers to calculate the expectation of aggregated answers; (2) Maximization step: find the worker skill, worker intent, worker emotion and task difficulty that make the expected log likelihood maximize. When the parameters are converged, the probability distribution of the aggregated answers is also constant, so the aggregated answers of the task can be obtained, as well as the worker skill, worker intent, worker emotion and task difficulty at that time. Experiments show that this method is effective.

Contributions of this paper are as follows:

- This paper aggregates answers considering personality characteristics of persons e.g., worker emotion. It hardly finds works that takes into account it. And it is challenging to evaluate it. To this end, a method for evaluate personality characteristics of persons can be provide, which considers the influence of worker emotion;
- This paper develops an improved EM algorithm with four parameters, which are worker emotion, worker intent, worker skill and task difficulty, respectively. The method combines these four parameters to evaluate the worker quality, and meanwhile obtains the aggregated answers.

This rest of the paper is organized as follows. Section 2 is related work on answering aggregation and quality control. In Sect. 3, the paper will describe in detail the improved EM-based method, which is a method with four parameters. Section 4 is validation and the verification result of the improved method on the simulated dataset and real-world dataset. The real-world dataset is a sub-dataset of Affect Text. Section 5 concludes this paper.

2   Related Work

Collecting answers from numerous workers through crowdsourcing platforms has been widely accepted. To obtain aggregated answers, answer aggregation approach is often used. Majority voting [5, 6] is a simple approach to obtain the aggregated answer. However, majority voting has the assumption that all workers have same accuracy. In fact, workers have different individual accuracy, since they have different characters, e.g., worker skill, worker intent, worker emotion.

To fill the gap, methods considering different characters of workers arise. In [3], Cao et al. utilize weighted majority voting to aggregate answers of workers, which considers accuracy of workers based on the history information of workers answers. In [7], Demartini et al. propose a probabilistic model which is based on factor graph considering answers of workers and accuracy of answers. Both [3] and [7] use historical answers of workers to analyze individual accuracy of workers. In [13], Koulougli et al. propose accumulative weighted voting method which takes into account both uncertainty and skill levels. In [12], Sun et al. propose a probabilistic model for quantitative crowd-sourcing problem by considering the changing of worker ability so as to achieve better quality control. Both [13] and [12] consider worker skills in analyzing accuracy of answers of workers. In addition, worker intention also has impact on answers of workers. For example, spammers in crowdsourcing system may choose answers randomly for the financial reward. To distinguish spammers and non-spammers, Kurve et al. [2] add the worker intention as a parameter into the EM-based algorithm for identifying malicious workers. Kurve thinks malicious workers will choose the wrong answers when they know the correct one or they will choose answers randomly. In [14], Moayedikia et al. propose a reliability estimation algorithm which relies on Gaussian process model, based on bee colony algorithm to distinguish spammers and non-spammers. Both [2] and [14] consider worker intention in analyzing answers of workers.

In addition to the factors mentioned above that have impact on the accuracy of answers of workers, there are other factors. In [15], Wu et al. propose a novel ground truth inference algorithm which is based on EM algorithm and aggregates answers. Wu considers the reliability of each worker and the difficulty of each instance. Algorithm GLAD [16] takes the difficulty of instances into consideration and adopts a logistic regression model for inference. [15] and [16] considers the influence of task difficulty on the answer accuracy of workers. In [11] Yu et al. leverage the relationship between worker emotion and their productivity to schedule work time of workers for high answer quality. Yu considers personality characteristics of persons of workers. Some researchers [8] find that workers who are in positive emotion are more productive than workers who are in negative emotion. In this paper, factors such as worker skill, task difficulty, worker intent and worker emotion are all taken into account to aggregate answers.

3   Crowdsourcing EM-Based Approach with Four Parameters

3.1   Four Parameters in the Improved EM-Based Approach

Four parameters in the algorithm will be mentioned here. Worker skill, task difficulty, worker intent and worker emotion are taken into account here. Continuous parameters are used to describe worker skill and task difficulty. $k_j \in (-\infty, +\infty)$ represents worker skill of worker j; $d_j \in (-\infty, +\infty)$ represents the difficulty level of task i. Binary parameters are used to denote workers emotion and worker intent. $(m_j, w_j) \in \{(1, 1), (0, 1), (1, 0), (0, 0)\}$, where m_j indicates the emotion of the worker j, and w_j indicates the intent of the worker j. As can be seen in Table 1, there are types of workers based on combination of worker emotion and worker intent. $(1, 1)$ denotes that workers are in positive emotion and have non-malicious intent. They are called PN workers. $(0, 1)$ denotes workers are in negative emotion but have malicious intent. They are called NN workers. $(1, 0)$ and $(0, 0)$ indicate that the worker is malicious. Whether the worker emotion is positive or negative, they are all called MM workers. PN workers tend to answer questions correctly at the best level of ability. NN workers tend to answer as accurately as possible, but negative emotion will reduce their accuracy to answer questions. The influence factor q is used to indicate the extent of the effect of emotion of workers. MM workers tend to answer at random, regardless of their emotion.

Table 1. Types of workers

Worker emotion	Worker intent	
	Non-malicious: 1	Malicious: 0
Positive: 1	PN	MM
Negative: 0	NN	MM

3.2   Expectation Step of the Improved EM-Based Approach

Suppose there are a group of workers to answer T_n non-probe tasks. Each worker answers at least one task and each task receives at least one answer from workers. The probe task is a task with known ground truth. Let M_i denote the number of workers answering the task i. There are T_p tasks that are also published to workers, but workers do not know that these are probe tasks. Therefore, workers with low accuracy cannot escape detection of the system. Take $\{1, 2, 3 \dots, T_p\}$ as the index of probe tasks, $\{T_p + 1, T_p + 2, T_p + 3 \dots, T_p + T_n\}$ is the index of non-probe tasks. Answers for task i is chosen from the set of options $O_i \equiv \{1, 2, 3, \dots, C_i\}$. Let $z_i \in O_i$ be ground truth answer to task i. Let $r_{ij} \in O_i$ be answer for the task i from the worker j. Referring to stochastic generative model for generating answers of workers based on worker behavior [2], the parameter set of four-parameter model is defined as: $\Omega = \{\{(w_j, m_j, k_j, q_j) \forall j\}, \{d_i\} \forall i\}$.

In order to define the probability model of ground truth, this paper gives the probability distribution of answers of workers based on answering behaviors of workers of different types. Based on the difference between the worker skill and the difficulty of the task, use the sigmoid function to model the probability that the workers will answer the tasks correctly: $\dfrac{1}{1+e^{-(k_j-d_i)}}$. $q_j \in (0,1)$ is indicates the probability that negative emotion has impact on accuracy of workers.

PN Workers

Probability mass function φ is defined as (1). It expresses the probability that the answer of the worker is r_{ij} when the emotion of the worker is positive and the intent is non-malicious. In this scenario, the possibility for workers to answer correctly is only decided by the difference between the worker skill and task difficulty. The greater the value of $(k_j - d_i)$ is, greater the probability to answer correctly, the value of the φ will tend to $\dfrac{1}{C_i}$.

$$\varphi\left(r_{ij} = l \mid \Omega_{ij}, (m_j, w_j) = (1,1), z_i\right)$$

$$= \begin{cases} \dfrac{1}{1+e^{-(k_j-d_i)}} + \left(\dfrac{1}{C_i}\right)\left(\dfrac{e^{-(k_j-d_i)}}{1+e^{-(k_j-d_i)}}\right) & for\ l = z_i \\ \left(\dfrac{1}{C_i}\right)\left(\dfrac{e^{-(k_j-d_i)}}{1+e^{-(k_j-d_i)}}\right) & otherwise \end{cases} \tag{1}$$

NN Workers

Probability mass function φ is defined as (2).

$$\varphi\left(r_{ij} = l \mid \Omega_{ij}, (m_j, w_j) = (0,1), z_i\right)$$

$$= \begin{cases} \dfrac{1}{1+e^{-(k_j-d_i)}} + \left(\dfrac{1}{C_i}\right)\left(\dfrac{e^{-(k_j-d_i)}}{1+e^{-(k_j-d_i)}}\right) & for\ l = z_i \\ \dfrac{q_j}{1+e^{-(k_j-d_i)}} + \left(\dfrac{1}{C_i}\right)\left(\dfrac{e^{-(k_j-d_i)}}{1+e^{-(k_j-d_i)}}\right) & otherwise \end{cases} \tag{2}$$

When a worker is in negative emotion but has non-malicious intent to answer the question, his ability to answer correctly will be reduced partly. Symbol q is used to denote the influence probability.

MM Workers

When a worker has malicious intent, no matter he is in positive emotion or in negative emotion, he tends to choose the answer randomly. Probability mass function φ is defined as:

$$\varphi\left(r_{ij} = l | \Omega_{ij}, w_j = 0, z_i\right)$$

$$= \begin{cases} \dfrac{q_j}{1 + e^{-(k_j - d_i)}} + \left(\dfrac{1}{C_i}\right)\left(\dfrac{e^{-(k_j - d_i)}}{1 + e^{-(k_j - d_i)}}\right) & for\ l = z_i \\[4mm] \dfrac{e^{-(k_j - d_i)}}{1 + e^{-(k_j - d_i)}} + \left(\dfrac{1}{C_i - 1}\right)\left(\dfrac{1}{1 + e^{-(k_j - d_i)}}\right) & otherwise \end{cases} \qquad (3)$$

Based on the generation model above and Bayes rule, the posterior probability mass function is denoted as (4), which can also be called as probability distribution of

$$P_i\left(Z_i = c | X, \Omega^t\right) = \frac{\prod_{j=1}^{M_i} \varphi\left(r_{ij} | \Omega_{ij}^t, z_i = c\right)}{\sum_{l=1}^{C_i} \prod_{j=1}^{M_i} \varphi\left(r_{ij} | \Omega_{ij}^t, z_i = c\right)} \qquad (4)$$

$$\forall c, \forall i \in \left\{T_p + 1, \ldots, T_n + T_p\right\}$$

the ground truth of non-probe tasks, where Ω^t is current parameter set, $c \in \{1, 2, 3 \ldots, C_i\}$ and X denotes the observed data containing workers answers to every tasks and the ground truth answer of probe tasks. This paper treats ground truth of non-probe tasks $\left(Z_n\right)$ as latent variables in our EM model.

3.3 Maximization Step of the Improved EM Algorithm

There are observed data and unobserved data here, observed data is denoted as X above, the ground truths of non-probe tasks $\left(Z_n\right)$. X and $\left(X, Z_n\right)$ is called incomplete data and complete data respectively. To estimate the parameter set Ω, the incomplete data log-likelihood should be calculated. The incomplete log-likelihood is obtained by iteratively maximizing the expectation of the complete log-likelihood $Q(\Omega | \Omega')$. Based on generation model above and $P(Z_i = c | X, \Omega^t)$ obtained in expectation step, the expected complete data log-likelihood $Q(\Omega | \Omega')$ can be written as (5).

$$Q(\Omega|\Omega^t) = E[logL_C|X, Z_n, \Omega^t]$$

$$\propto \sum_{i=1}^{T_p} \sum_{j=1}^{M_i} \log \varphi\left(r_{ij}|\Omega_{ij}^t, z_i\right) + \sum_{i=T_p+1}^{T_p+T_n} \sum_{j=1}^{M_i} \log \sum_{c=1}^{C_i} \varphi\left(r_{ij}|\Omega_{ij}^t, z_i = c\right)$$

$$= \sum_{i=1}^{T_p} \sum_{j:r_{ij}=z_i} \{w_j[m_j log\varphi(r_{ij}|\Omega_{ij}^t, (m_j, w_j) = (1,1), z_i = r_{ij})$$

$$+ (1-m_j) \; log\varphi(r_{ij}|\Omega_{ij}^t, (m_j, w_j) = (0,1), z_i = r_{ij})]$$

$$+ (1-w_j) \; log\varphi(r_{ij}|\Omega_{ij}^t, (m_j, w_j) \in \{(0,0), (1,0)\}, z_i = r_{ij})\}$$

$$+ \sum_{i=1}^{T_p} \sum_{j:r_{ij}\neq z_i} \{w_j[m_j log\varphi(r_{ij}|\Omega_{ij}^t, (m_j, w_j) = (1,1), z_i \neq r_{ij})$$

$$+ (1-m_j) \; log\varphi(r_{ij}|\Omega_{ij}^t, (m_j, w_j) = (0,1), z_i \neq r_{ij})]$$

$$+ (1-w_j) \; log\varphi(r_{ij}|\Omega_{ij}^t, (m_j, w_j) \in \{(0,0), (1,0)\}, z_i \neq r_{ij})\} \tag{5}$$

$$+ \sum_{i=T_p+1}^{T_p+T_n} \sum_{c=1}^{C_i} \sum_{j:r_{ij}=c} P(z_i = c)\{w_j[m_j log\varphi\left(r_{ij}|\Omega_{ij}^t, (m_j, w_j) = (1,1), z_i = c\right)$$

$$+ (1-m_j) \; log\varphi(r_{ij}|\Omega_{ij}^t, (m_j, w_j) = (0,1), z_i = c)]$$

$$+ (1-w_j) \; log\varphi(r_{ij}|\Omega_{ij}^t, (m_j, w_j) \in \{(0,0), (1,0)\}, z_i = c)\}$$

$$+ \sum_{i=T_p+1}^{T_p+T_n} \sum_{c=1}^{C_i} \sum_{j:r_{ij}\neq c} P(z_i = c)\{w_j[m_j log\varphi\left(r_{ij}|\Omega_{ij}^t, (m_j, w_j) = (1,1), z_i \neq c\right)$$

$$+ (1-m_j) \; log\varphi(r_{ij}|\Omega_{ij}^t, (m_j, w_j) = (0,1), z_i \neq c)]$$

$$+ (1-w_j) \; log\varphi(r_{ij}|\Omega_{ij}^t, (m_j, w_j) \in \{(0,0), (1,0)\}, z_i \neq c)\}.$$

$k_j \forall j$ and $d_i \forall i$ are continuous parameters, $(m_j, w_j) \forall j$ are discrete parameters, and there are 3^M (three types of workers) crowd configurations, it is infeasible to find a closed solution for $\Omega^{t+1} = \arg\max_\Omega Q(\Omega|\Omega^t)$. Therefore, the maximization step of this improved EM algorithm is divided into two steps: continuous parameters calculation and discrete parameters calculation, and maximize these two steps iteratively.

Discrete Parameters Calculation

In this sub-step, a closed solution for $(m_j, w_j) \forall j$ will be found with $k_j \forall j, q_j \forall j$ and $d_i \forall i$ fixed. $(\tilde{m}_j, \tilde{w}_j)$ denotes the result of the worker emotion and worker intent in these discrete parameters calculation sub-step. $\tilde{\Omega}$ denotes the result of previous continuous parameters calculation sub-step. Genetic algorithm is used here.

Continuous Parameters Calculation

The expectation of the complete log-likelihood $E[logL_C \backslash \{(m_j, w_j)\}|X_j, \{(m_j, w_j)\}]$ is calculate in this sub-step to find $k_j \forall j, q_j \forall j$ and $d_i \forall i$ that can maximize it, with $(m_j, w_j) \forall j$ fixed. The value of $(m_j, w_j) \forall j$ is from previous concrete parameters calculation sub-step. There is a gradient ascent being used to find a local maximum for $k_j \forall j, q_j \forall j$ and $d_i \forall i$, which is performed until the change of likelihood between the two gradient steps falls below a certain threshold. Two sub-steps are performed iteratively until the convergence of the parameters in Ω. Then the results of maximization step are stored in Ω^{t+1}.

Expectation step and maximization step are performed iteratively until the change of the expectation of the likelihood between the two steps falls below a certain threshold. The EM algorithm with four parameters is guaranteed to find a local solution.

4 Validation

Validation on Simulated Dataset

Simulated data generated by the above generation model is used. Firstly, a group of 10 workers are generated with $k_j \sim N(1, 1000)$; 10% of workers have malicious intent, and 10% of workers with non-malicious intent are in negative emotion. This paper only considers the effect of negative emotion on non-malicious workers. The tasks are generated with $d_i \sim N(20, 500)$. The emotion influence factor $q_j \in (0, 1)$ follows normal random distribution. The ground truth for each task is chosen randomly from $\{1, 2, 3\}$. To make the result more clearly to observe, the results of worker skill and task difficulty are fitted by the least squares fitting method respectively. In this paper, based on the above probability distribution of worker skill and task difficulty, comparison values of the worker skill and task difficulty are separately generated. They are actual values which are used to generate simulated data. Four-parameter algorithm and Three-parameter algorithm (EM-based algorithm of Kurve) are utilized respectively to obtain the estimated values for worker skill and task difficulty.

Figure 1 shows the comparison of estimated values of worker skill with actual value. Figure 2 shows the comparison of estimated values of task difficulty with actual value. The solid line in the figure denotes values estimated through Four-parameter algorithm. The dotted line with dot denotes values estimated through Three-parameter algorithm. The last line denotes actual value. Figures 1 and 2 show highly consistent trends between the estimated value of worker skill and task difficulty and the actual value.

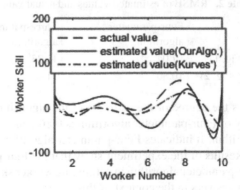

Fig. 1. The comparison of estimated values of worker skill with actual values

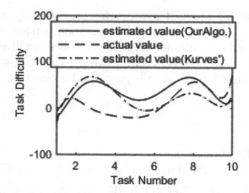

Fig. 2. The comparison of estimated values of task difficulty with actual values

For better explanation of two figures, two indicators are used: NSE and RMSE. NSE (Nash-Sutcliffe efficiency coefficient) measures the fitting degree of values estimated through Four-parameter algorithm with actual values. As long as the value of the NSE is between 0 and 1, the fitting effect of the model is credible. For worker skill, the NSE value of Four-parameter algorithm is 0.49. For task difficulty, its NSE is 0.58. It indicates Four-parameter algorithm is credible for estimating task difficulty and worker skill. Credible estimated worker skill and task difficulty can be obtained through Four-parameter algorithm.

As shown in Table 2, RMSE (root-mean-square error) of Four-parameter algorithm for workers skill is 7.04, RMSE of Three-parameter algorithm is 11.33, which indicates the fitting effect between worker skill estimated through Four-parameter and actual values is well. For task difficulty, MSE of Four-parameter algorithm is 10.08, and RMSE of Three-parameter algorithm is 11.40. It also indicates the fitting effect between task difficulty estimated through Four-parameter and actual values is well.

Table 2. RMSE of estimated values and actual values

Parameters	Four-parameter algorithm	Three-parameter algorithm
Worker skill (Fig. 1)	7.04	11.33
Task difficulty (Fig. 2)	10.80	11.40

Accuracy measures the degree of the estimate of the algorithm for the aggregated answers. The accuracy of Four-parameter algorithm is 0.86 which is as good as that of Three-parameter algorithm. It indicates Four-parameter algorithm can obtain accurate aggregated answers. Results of the experiment show that the four parameter algorithm is not worse than three-parameter algorithm in estimating worker skill and task difficulty as well as aggregating answers in the context of this paper.

Validation on Real-World Dataset

Affect Text Dataset. The Affective Text dataset is collected as a sentiment labeling task proposed by Strapparava et al. [17]. They employ workers to rate the title of a piece of news for a few types of emotions and a comprehensive score (Valence) to indicate the entire emotion of this news. Snow et al. [18] select a set of 100 samples from the SemEval set and obtain 1000 scores for each emotion and Valence scores. For each emotion, workers provide a score in a range of [0, 100]. For the score Valence, workers provide a score in a range of [−100, 100]. This paper maps the Valence score to two classes, three classes, four classes and five classes respectively. We obtain four sub-datasets: Two classes dataset, Three classes dataset, Four class dataset and Five classes dataset.

Figure 3 shows the comparisons between the developed method and ZenCrowd [7], KOS [4] as well as the base line Majority voting (MV). The dataset used is sub-dataset Valence of Affect Text dataset. As mentioned, the sub-dataset Valence is divided into four sub-datasets based on the number of the class. In Fig. 3, the four- parameter algorithm performs well on three classes, four classes and five classes. The experimental comparisons show that the four-parameter algorithm performs well on multiple category sentiment labeling tasks.

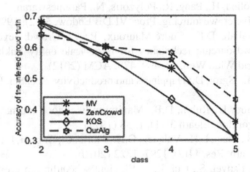

Fig. 3. The comparison of accuracy of the aggregated answers between MV, ZenCrowd, KOS and OurAlgo.

5   Conclusions

Answer aggregation considering worker quality is a useful tool for aggregating answers of workers. The aggregated answers depend on quality of answers. Answer quality varies through worker skill, worker intent and worker emotion. In this paper, an improved method of answer aggregation is utilized to obtain the aggregated answers. The approach is based on EM algorithm. The improved EM-based method not only can obtain aggregated answers considering worker quality but also can simultaneously estimate the worker skill, worker emotion, worker intent and the difficulty of each task. Taking into account the three factors that have impact on the answers of workers, more accurate analysis of the possibility of workers answering correctly is achieved, so as to obtain aggregated answers considering worker quality. Verification is performed on the simulated dataset and real-world dataset. Compared to other method, the improved method is efficient on multiple category sentiment labelling tasks. It can obtain more accurate result in that scenario.

Acknowledgment. This work is partially supported by National Key R&D Program No. 2017YFB1400100, SDNFSC No. ZR2018MF014.

References

1. Feng, J.H., Li, G.L., Feng, J.H.: A survey on crowdsourcing. Chin. J. Comput. **38**(9), 1713–1726 (2015)
2. Kurve, A., Miller, D., Kesidis, G.: Multicategory crowdsourcing accounting for variable task difficulty, worker skill, and worker intention. IEEE Trans. Knowl. Data Eng. **27**(3), 794–809 (2014)
3. Cao, C.C., She, J., Tong, Y., Chen, L.: Whom to ask? Proc. VLDB Endow. **5**(11), 1495–1506 (2012)
4. Karger, D.R., Oh, S., Shah, D.: Iterative learning for reliable crowdsourcing systems (2011)
5. Lee, J., Cho, H., Park, J.W., Cha, Y.R., Hwang, S.W., Nie, Z., Wen, J.R.: Hybrid entity clustering using crowds and data. VLDB J. **22**(5), 711–726 (2013)
6. Park, H., Garcia-Molina, H., Pang, R., Polyzotis, N., Parameswaran, A., Widom, J.: Deco: a system for declarative crowdsourcing. Proc. VLDB Endow. **5**(12), 1990–1993 (2012)
7. Demartini, G., Difallah, D.E., Cudré-Mauroux, P.: ZenCrowd: leveraging probabilistic reasoning and crowdsourcing techniques for large-scale entity linking. In: International Conference on World Wide Web, pp. 469–478. ACM (2012)
8. Oswald, A., Proto, E., Sgroi, D.: Happiness and productivity. Soc. Sci. Electron. Publ. **33**(4), 789–822 (2008)
9. Dempster, A.P., Laird, L., Rubin, D.B.: Maximum likelihood estimation from incomplete data via the EM algorithm. Elearn **39**(1), 1–38 (1977)
10. Raykar, V.C., Yu, S., Zhao, L.H., Valadez, G.H., Florin, C., Bogoni, L., et al.: Learning from crowds. J. Mach. Learn. Res. **11**(2), 1297–1322 (2010)
11. Yu, H., Shen, Z.J., Fauvel, S., Cui, L.Z.: Efficient scheduling in crowdsourcing based on workers' emotion. In: IEEE International Conference on Agents IEEE Computer Society, pp. 121–126 (2017)
12. Sun, H., Hu, K., Fang, Y., Song, Y.: Adaptive result inference for collecting quantitative data with crowdsourcing. IEEE Internet Things J. **4**(5), 1389–1398 (2017)
13. Koulougli, D., Hadjali, A., Rassoul, I.: Leveraging human factors to enhance query answering in crowdsourcing systems. In: IEEE Tenth International Conference on Research Challenges in Information Science, pp. 1–6. IEEE (2016)
14. Moayedikia, A., Ong, K.L., Boo, Y.L., Yeoh, W.: Bee colony based worker reliability estimation algorithm in microtask crowdsourcing. In: IEEE International Conference on Machine Learning and Applications, pp. 713–717. IEEE (2017)
15. Wu, M., Li, Q., Zhang, J., Cui, S., Li, D., Qi, Y.: A robust inference algorithm for crowd sourced categorization. In: International Conference on Intelligent Systems and Knowledge Engineering, pp. 1–6 (2017)
16. Whitehill, J., Ruvolo, P., Wu, T., Bergsma, J., Movellan, J.: Whose vote should count more: optimal integration of labels from labelers of unknown expertise. In: International Conference on Neural Information Processing Systems, vol. 46, pp. 2035–2043. Curran Associates Inc. (2009)
17. Strapparava, C., Mihalcea, R.: SemEval-2007 task 14: affective text. In: International Workshop on Semantic Evaluations, pp. 70–74. Association for Computational Linguistics
18. Snow, R., O'Connor, B., Jurafsky, D., Ng, A.Y.: Cheap and fast—but is it good?: evaluating non-expert annotations for natural language tasks. In: Conference on Empirical Methods in Natural Language Processing 2008 (2008)

Internet of Things and Cloud Computing

A Parallel Fast Fourier Transform Algorithm for Large-Scale Signal Data Using Apache Spark in Cloud

Cheng Yang[1], Weidong Bao[1], Xiaomin Zhu[1,2]([✉]), Ji Wang[1],
and Wenhua Xiao[1,3]

[1] National University of Defense Technology, Changsha, China
xmzhu@nudt.edu.cn
[2] State Key Laboratory of High Performance Computing, Changsha, China
[3] Academy of Military Sciences, Beijing, China

Abstract. In the field of signal process, Fast Fourier Transform (FFT) is a widely used algorithm to transform signal data from time to frequency. Unfortunately, with the exponential growth of data, traditional methods cannot meet the demand of large-scale computation on these big data because of three main challenges of large-scale FFT, i.e., big data size, real-time data processing and high utilization of compute resources. To satisfy these requirements, an optimized FFT algorithm in Cloud is deadly needed. In this paper, we introduce a new method to conduct FFT in Cloud with the following contributions: first, we design a parallel FFT algorithm for large-scaled signal data in Cloud; second, we propose a MapReduce-based mechanism to distribute data to compute nodes using big data processing framework; third, an optimal method of distributing compute resources is implemented to accelerate the algorithm by avoiding redundant data exchange between compute nodes. The algorithm is designed in MapReduce computation framework which contains three steps: data preprocessing, local data transform and parallel data transform to integrate processing results. The parallel FFT is implemented in a 16-node Cloud to process real signal data The experimental results reveal an obvious improvement in the algorithm speed. Our parallel FFT is approximately five times faster than FFT in Matlab in when the data size reaches 10 GB.

Keywords: Fast fourier transform · Cloud computing
Apache spark · Parallel algorithm

1 Introduction

Target detection usually employs some traditional methods such as radar detection to detect aerial targets [14,28]. However these methods are not available when the signal from aerial aircrafts is weak. Fortunately, utilizing spatial electric signal from satellites to detect targets is a feasible developing approach to

© Springer Nature Switzerland AG 2018
J. Vaidya and J. Li (Eds.): ICA3PP 2018, LNCS 11336, pp. 293–310, 2018.
https://doi.org/10.1007/978-3-030-05057-3_24

detect aerial targets [10,13]. Since aircrafts would reflect the signal from satellites, the ground receiving station gets two different signals (the pure signal from satellites directly and the reflect signal reflected by aircrafts). By making analysis and comparison between pure-signal and reflect-signal, the position information about aerial targets can be obtained. It should be noted that the process of comparison, a huge quantity of data (3 TB) need to be processed in one hour in real-time, which requires the data processing systems in the back to have the capability to perform computations for large-scale signal data in time.

Specifically in signal comparison, numerous data are needed to be processed ,which generates tremendous intermediate data at the same time. In this process, Fourier transform plays a significant and indispensable role [18]. Fourier transform decompose a function of time into frequency [15,26]. Discrete Fourier Transform, as one algorithm in the series of Fourier transforms, is widely used to detect the features of received signals. From these features, the target's information can be obtained. However, Discrete Fourier Transform has a great amount of calculation which results in low efficiency. Fast Fourier Transform (FFT) algorithm, proposed by Cooley and Turkey, simplifies and accelerates the Discrete Fourier Transform effectively. [6] It successfully reduces the complexity of Discrete Fourier Transform from $N*N$ to $N*logN$. Although Fast Fourier Transform is more efficient than Discrete Fourier Transform, when the data scale becomes giant, this conventional algorithms cannot solve the signal processing problem effectively. The FFT algorithm is not only used for signal processing but also applied to many other field, i.e., image processing [20,22], spectral analysis [23], data compression [12], and so on. Improving the efficiency of FFT algorithm on big data can be beneficial to many research field.

Due to the importance of processing such big-scale data, a wide variety of approaches are designed to optimize the performance of signal processing [31]. Among these methods, parallel Fast Fourier Transform is a unique approach since it enables the algorithm implemented on multi-machines. Furthermore, with the fast improvement of Cloud computing technology [1,2], the thought of parallel FFT can be implemented in big data processing frameworks. To the best of our knowledge, there is little work to conduct parallel FFT with big data processing frameworks in Cloud. We use Apache Spark to optimize the real-time FFT job. Apache Spark is an efficient parallel big data processing framework [21,30]. It derived from the conventional Cloud computing framework, MapReduce that repeatedly read and write data from an external stable storage system [32]. Nonetheless, when an application needs to frequently reuse the intermediate data, MapReduce becomes inefficient. Apache Spark presents a new strategy to avoid such futile read or write operations on disks. It introduces Resilient Distributed Dataset (RDD), an unique distributed memory abstraction that enables data to be stored in memory. By this way, the speed of cyclic computation work is greatly improved.

There is a close correlation between Fast Fourier Transform and Apache Spark. Iteration and Parallelization are two main properties of FFT, which makes Apache Spark suitable for FFT. First, as FFT intensely generates and reuses the intermediate data, immense read and write operations are unavoidable in conventional method. To solve this problem, Apache stores intermediate data in memory so that it performs such iterative computation efficiently [29]. Second, inside each step of FFT, the Discrete Fourier Transform conducts computation separately on data, which makes it feasible to parallelize FFT on Apache Spark.

Simply using Apache Spark to implement parallel FFT algorithm is not sufficient for big data processing. The background computing system is also needed to be suitable. In order to improve the utilization of resources, a strategy to optimally allocate compute resources to each node is proposed. We design two resource allocation strategies for parallel FFT. The equally-split strategy provides a simple method to make full use of compute resources. The optimized-split strategy is designed to improve the efficiency by reducing the data exchange between compute nodes, which further improves the resource utilization.

The major contributions of this paper are as follows:

- A MapReduce-based mechanism to efficiently distribute signal data to compute nodes. The MapReduce process contains three steps: data preprocessing (map data to compute nodes), local data transform and parallel data transform to integrate processing results (collect results).
- A parallel approach to implement Fast Fourier Transform based on Apache Spark. The parallel approach of FFT provides an effective method to utilize more compute resources.
- Optimized strategies to allocate compute resources in the Cloud for parallel FFT for high speed computation. During the process of parallel FFT, there are many redundant data exchanges between compute nodes. Our allocation strategies provide methods to reduce the data exchanges.

The remainder of the paper is organized as follows. The next section reviews related work in the literature. Section 3 formally describes the system model of computation Cloud we designed. This is followed by Sect. 4, the framework of parallel Fast Fourier Transform algorithm. The allocation strategy of computation resource is given in Sect. 5. Section 6 depicts the performance development of the algorithm. Section 7 concludes the paper with a summary and future work.

2 Related Work

Since Cooley and Tukey [6] firstly introduced Fast Fourier Transform, FFT has had a substantial influence on the area of signal processing. FFT algorithm provides an efficient method for the Fourier analysis to produce spectrograms. Unfortunately, with the exponential growth of data, the original FFT algorithm cloud not meet the computation demand gradually. Therefore, many approaches had been proposed to improve the speed of FFT. Interests were arisen both in finding efficient implementation of FFT and in improving the algorithm itself.

On the one hand, a variety of study focused on faster algorithms to improve the inner computation process of FFT. Preuss [19] proposed a radix-2 Fast

Table 1. Summary of the Main Notation used throughout the paper

Symbol	Description
N	Total number of signal points in input data
p	Number of compute nodes
D_k^l	The lth data set in stage k
C_k	The lth compute node in a Cloud
x_k	Input data array in a Fourier Transform
E_k	Even number part of input data array
O_k	Odd number part of input data array
X_k	Result data array in a Fourier Transform
e	Natural base
T_k	Time of the kth stage in the algorithm
T_{total}	Total time of the algorithm
n	Number of cores in the Cloud
m	Cache size(GB) of the Cloud

Fourier Transform algorithm which reduces the number of multiplications to two-thirds of the effort required by most radix-2 algorithms. Frigo et al. [8] proposed a FFT program that tunes the computation automatically for any particular hardware which performs significantly better than other softwares. Mullin [16] employed the use of monolithic array analysis as a way to remove the constraints imposed on performance by a machine's underlying hardware to accelerate FFT algorithm. In our study, we choose to parallelize the radix-2 Fast Fourier Transform algorithm, which is widely used in most signal-processing area.

On the other hand, many approaches were proposed to parallelize the computation of the FFT algorithm. Githens et al. proposed a framework called Parallel Element Processing Ensemble to conduct signal processing [9]. Based on this framework, Bergland introduced a parallel implementation of Fast Fourier Transform that segments the algorithm into groups of identical parallel operations [4]. Wold devised a method to implement parallel FFT in VLSI [27]. Since Google introduced Hadoop [3], many efficient efforts have been proposed to process the data on the efficient Cloud Computing architecture. Hassen et al. [11] distributed the FFT feature extraction techniques using the MapReduce programming model in Cloud Computing environment. Vincke et al. [24] concluded several parallel software design patterns to calculate Fast Fourier Transform, such as MapReduce, Divide-and-Conquer, Fork/Join, and so on.

Besides FFT, a variety of researches have been conducted to improve the performance of Cloud computing. Dean et al. [7] introduced the MapReduce programming model to separate large-scale data into partitions and parallelize the computation across large-scale Clouds. Wang et al. [25] proposed a system to combine long-running VM service with typical batch workload like MapReduce.

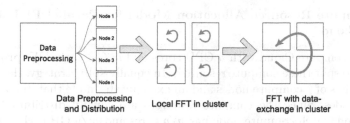

Data Preprocessing and Distribution   Local FFT in cluster   FFT with data-exchange in cluster

Fig. 1. The process of parallel FFT in Cloud

Palanisamy [17] proposed a MapReduce resource allocation system aimed at enhancing the performance of MapReduce jobs in the Cloud. Zaharia et al. [29] designed the resilient distributed datasets and Apache Spark that uses cache memory to conduct computations. Zadeh et al. [5] proposed feasible matrix computation methods on Apache Spark. Recently Apache Spark has been used in many application fields like machine learning and graph calculation. To the best of our knowledge, there is little work to conduct parallel FFT with Spark in Cloud.

3   System Model

In this section, we introduce the strategies, algorithms and terminologies used in this paper. For reference, we summarize the main notation used in this paper in Table 1.

3.1   Data Processing Model

We consider the data processing model as follows. To conduct FFT in parallel, the data need to be processed in the model of MapReduce. Consider a N points signal data, in which each point has 16-bit data. The data are divided into p data sets $D_{0,0}, D_{0,1}, ...D_{0,p-1}$. These data sets are mapped to a compute Cloud which is formed by p compute nodes $C_1, C_2, ..., C_p$. The data sets are processed in the butterfly algorithm from stage 0 to stage $log_2(N/p)$. In the lth stage, each even numbered data set $D_{l,2k}$ combines with each odd numbered data set $D_{l,2k+1}$ to execute Fourier Transform to get result as $D_{l+1,k}$. Finally, two last data sets combine to the final result $D_{log_2(N/p-1,0)}$. Inside a compute node, the data are stored in an array X_k. The data are separated into even numbered parts E_k and odd numbered parts O_k. In order to test the effectiveness, we let T_k denote the time consumed in the kth stage and $T_{total} = \sum T_k$, the total time of the algorithm. Figure 1 reveals the process of the parallel FFT based on Apache Spark in Cloud environment.

3.2   Compute Resource Allocation Model for Parallel FFT Job in Cloud

Consider a compute Cloud with n CPU cores and m GB cache. We propose two strategies to split these compute resources. In equally-split strategy, the compute Cloud consists of p compute nodes and an extra master node that manages these compute nodes. Since the compute resources are equally distributed to each compute node, each compute node has n/p cores and m/p GB cache. All of the compute nodes participate in the process of data processing from beginning to the end.

In optimized-split strategy, the compute resources are distributed into compute nodes with different sizes. In order to execute different stages of FFT, the compute Cloud is separated to several sections $s_1, s_2, ..., s_n$. Different compute sections conduct different stages of FFT. Inside each section s_i, the resource is equally divided to r_i compute nodes C_i^k. The size of compute nodes vary in different sections. To increase the efficiency of data processing, we search the optimal portion of each section by defining the size θ_k of each section and size ω_k of each node in sections.

For different strategies, the data processing methods are different, which will be discussed in later parts.

4   Framework of Parallel FFT Algorithms

In this section, we discuss the framework of the parallel FFT in this paper.

4.1   Parallel FFT Algorithms in Distributed Compute Cloud

The overall methodology of the Parallel Fast Fourier Transform Algorithm is breaking down the input data and distributing the small data sets to compute nodes in a Cloud. Then each compute node executes FFT algorithm independently and collaboratively. At last, the results are collected by the master node of the Cloud.

During the whole process, Apache Spark takes the role of distributing the input data and collecting the result. This big data processing framework provides an efficient approach to storing and computing data in the form of RDD. Each RDD is mapped to each compute node to conduct FFT computation. The compute node is organized in two ways according to different resource allocation strategies which will be discussed in Sect. 5. After the FFT computation, the results are collected by the master node.

4.2   Fast Fourier Transform Algorithm

Fast Fourier Transform is a widely used numerical algorithm in signal processing field. Fast Fourier Transform re-expresses the Discrete Fourier Transform of an arbitrary composite size $N = N_1, N_2$ in terms of N_1 smaller DFTs of sizes N_2,

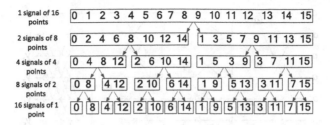

Fig. 2. Data Preprocessing: Bit reverse

recursively, to reduce the computation time to $O(NlogN)$ for highly composite N. The Discrete Fourier Transform is expressed as follows:

$$X_k = \sum_{n=1}^{N-1} x_n e^{-i2\pi k \frac{n}{N}}, \tag{1}$$

where x_n is a time signal array with period N and $k = 0, ..., N-1$. Among all the Fourier Transform algorithms, the radix-2 Cooley-Tukey algorithm is the most popular FFT algorithm. Using the thought of divide-and-conquer, the time of DFT is largely shortened. FFT separates the vector into even and odd numbered parts and reduces the length from N to $N/2$. FFT recursively executes the separate-operation to attain smaller data sets. After small data sets are generated, FFT combines these data sets and calculates the results:

$$X_k = \sum_{m=0}^{\frac{N}{2}-1} x_{2m} e^{-i2\pi k \frac{2m}{N}} + \sum_{m=0}^{\frac{N}{2}-1} x_{2m+1} e^{-i2\pi k \frac{2m+1}{N}}. \tag{2}$$

The formula above consists of two summations. The left summation contains the even number part of the original formula and the right contains the odd number part. By defining a twiddle factor $W_N^k = e^{-i2\pi k \frac{1}{N}}$, the former formula implies:

$$X_k = \sum_{m=0}^{\frac{N}{2}-1} x_{2m} W_N^{2km} + W_N^k \sum_{m=0}^{\frac{N}{2}-1} x_{2m+1} W_N^{2km}. \tag{3}$$

Further, It can be found that the twiddle factor $W_N^{2km} = W_{\frac{N}{2}}^{km}$. The equation can be simplified to:

$$X_k = \sum_{m=0}^{\frac{N}{2}-1} x_{2m} W_{\frac{N}{2}}^{km} + W_N^k \sum_{m=0}^{\frac{N}{2}-1} x_{2m+1} W_{\frac{N}{2}}^{km}. \tag{4}$$

Let E_k be the even part of the vector and O_k be the odd part. The N/2-potint DFT outputs can be written as:

$$E_k = \sum_{m=0}^{\frac{N}{2}-1} x_{2m} W_{\frac{N}{2}}^{km} \quad O_k = \sum_{m=0}^{\frac{N}{2}-1} x_{2m+1} W_{\frac{N}{2}}^{km}. \tag{5}$$

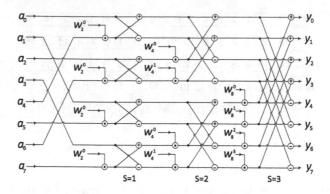

Fig. 3. 8 points Butterfly Diagram

Consequently, the complete DFT can be expressed as:

$$X_k = \begin{cases} E_k + W_N^k O_k & 0 \leq k \leq N/2 \\ E_{k-N/2} - W_N^{k-N/2} O_{k-N/2} & N > k \geq N/2 \end{cases}. \qquad (6)$$

By using the divide-and-conquer concept, FFT reduces the complexity of the algorithm from $O(N^2)$ to $O(N\log_2(N))$. Rather than computing the complete data, it is easier to compute a number of smaller data sets. As a result, the number of Fourier Transform calculations needed to be executed decreases dramatically. Before the decompose operation, the initial data need to be rearranged in bit-reverse order, as shown in Fig. 2.

Next, the rearranged data are combined so that the DFT can be calculated. The DFT process and combine process are represented in a so called "butterfly diagram" as is illustrated in Fig. 3.

In the first stage, a pair of data sets forms the input of the first DFT calculation. Then, the output data sets of the first stage become the input of the DFT calculation in second stage. Since this process is repeated time after time, data sets combine together and become larger ones. As a new data set is formed by two smaller data sets, the number of calculation stages is determined by $\log_2 N$ operations.

4.3   Parallel FFT Algorithm

Although the FFT algorithm effectively decreases the amount of calculations in DFT, however, when data size becomes immensely large and data processing faces the real time demand, FFT in single compute device cannot fulfill the requirements in practice. Fortunately, we can parallelize the algorithm in a compute Cloud to further accelerate the computing process.

Our Parallel Fast Fourier Transform Algorithm consists of three steps: Data Pre-processing, individual Butterfly computation, and collaborative Butterfly computation.

The first step is preprocessing the data for later computation. In this step, data are rearranged in bit-reverse order and divided into m blocks so that N/m data items can be separately stored into RDDs (Resilient Distributed Dataset, the data structure in Spark), where N is the number of sampling points in the signal data and m is the number of compute nodes.

The second step is to execute the butterfly computation within each compute node. In the first $log_2(N/p)$ data processing stages, no data exchange between compute nodes is required. So after the data are rearranged in bit reverse order and stored in each compute node, the N/p-point FFT is performed to obtain the result separately. However, in the rest $log_2(N/p)$ stages of FFT, data exchange is necessary because the data length is larger than N/p.

In the last step, the compute nodes cooperate to calculate the result.

Data Preprocessing. As shown in Fig. 2, before the calculation is performed, the data need to be rearranged in bit-reverse sequence. The algorithm of bit-reverse is shown in Algorithm 1. This job is finished in the master node of the Cloud. Then, the reordered data are sequentially separated into p data sets. These data sets are stored in Resilient Distributed Datasets in Apache Spark. Then these data sets are sent to the compute nodes to complete the rest calculation.

Algorithm 1. Preprocessing

Require:
 $a = (a_0, a_1, ..., a_{n-1})$
Ensure:
 $b = (b_0, b_1, ..., b_{n-1})$
 $b = \text{bitReverse}(a)$
 for $i \leftarrow 0$ to $p - 1$ **do**
  for $k \leftarrow 0$ to $N/p - 1$ **do**
   $P[i].c[k] \leftarrow b[i * N/p + k]$
  end for
 end for

Local FFT Inside Each Compute Node. Once N/p data are received by each compute node, N/p-point FFT will be executed on these data sets. Since there is no data exchange between compute nodes, each compute node performs original FFT on its local data, as shown in Algorithm 2.

FFT with Data Exchange. After the former half $log_2 p$ FFT, each data set needs to be combined to complete the rest calculations. Therefore the data exchange is required. The computation is performed from the $log_2(N/p)$-th stage to the $(log_2 N - 1)$-th stage where the compute nodes need communication. The algorithm is shown in Algorithm 3.

Algorithm 2. Local $N/p - point$ FFT on each compute node

Require:
　$c = (c_0, c_1, ..., c_{N/p-1})$
Ensure:
　$c = (c_0, c_1, ..., c_{N/p-1})$
　for $i \leftarrow 0$ **to** $p - 1$ **do**
　　for $k \leftarrow 0$ **to** $N/p - 1$ **do**
　　　$P[i].c[k] \leftarrow b[i * N/p + k]$
　　　;
　　　if $((i * N/p + k) \bmod l = (i * N/p + k) \bmod 2l)$ **then**
　　　　$c[k] = c[k] + c[k + l * z^m]$
　　　　$; c[k + 1] = c[k] - c[k + l * z^m]$
　　　　;
　　　end if
　　end for
　end for

Algorithm 3. FFT with data exchange

Require:
　$c = (c_0, c_1, ..., c_{N/p-1})$
Ensure:
　$c = (c_0, c_1, ..., c_{N/p-1})$ $j = log_2(p) + 1$
　;
　for $e \leftarrow 0$ **to** $log_2(p) - 1$ **do**
　　$t = 2e, l = 2^{(e+log_2(N/p))}, q = n/2l, z = w^q$
　　$; j = j - 1, v = 2^j$
　　;
　　for $i \leftarrow 0$ **to** $p - 1$ **do**
　　　if $(i \bmod t = i \bmod 2t)$ **then**
　　　　Receive data block from $(i + p/v)$th compute node and store into $c[N/v] - c[N/v + N/p - 1]$
　　　　;
　　　　for $k \leftarrow 0$ **to** $N/p - 1$ **do**
　　　　　$m = (i * N/p + k) \bmod l$
　　　　　$; c[k] = c[k] + c[k + N/v] * z^m$
　　　　　$; c[k + N/v] = c[k] - c[k + N/v] * z^m$
　　　　　;
　　　　end for Send transformed data in $c[N/v] - c[N/v + N/p - 1]$ to the $(i + p/v)$th compute node
　　　　;
　　　else
　　　　Send the data of this compute node to the $(i - p/v)$th compute node
　　　　; After the transformation, Receive data from the $(i - p/v)$th compute node and store them into c.
　　　　;
　　　end if
　　end for
　end for

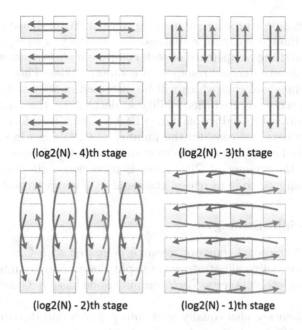

(log2(N) - 4)th stage   (log2(N) - 3)th stage

(log2(N) - 2)th stage   (log2(N) - 1)th stage

Fig. 4. Data exchange in a 16-compute-node Cloud

As shown in Algorithm 3, N/p-pair butterfly computation is performed in one compute node while the other paired compute node just sends whole N/p data to the corresponding compute node and waits until transformed data return. For communication overhead, $2N/p$ data are exchanged at every stage where two N/p data transfers are needed for sending and receiving on an idle compute node.

5 Compute Resource Allocation Strategy

As discussed above, the parallel FFT performs butterfly calculation on a compute Cloud. The input data are mapped to each compute node and the results are sent to the master node at last. During this process, the speed of computing is determined by the performance of the compute Cloud. In our experiments to process large amount of signal data, we found that the data exchange results in a great amount of I/O time between compute nodes when data size becomes large, as shown in Fig. 4. This is because in the last $log_2p - log_2(n/p)$ stages, the sizes of data to be calculated is larger than the size of local data in each compute node. As a result, the performance of parallel FFT algorithm is limited to a low level. In order to increase the speed and make full use of the compute resources in a Cloud, we propose two strategies, i.e., equally-split strategy and optimized-split strategy to allocate them.

In a compute Cloud, the compute resource is fixed in common sense. We assume that the compute resources are fully used by the compute Cloud because in this way the compute process can be more efficient. We designed two strategies to allocate the limited compute resources. One strategy is to equally split the total resources and the competence of each compute node is equal while another strategy is to allocate unequal resource to compute nodes. These two methods have their own pros and cons which will be discussed in later sections.

In common sense, computation ability is decided by the number of CPU cores, the size of cache, and so on. Since Fast Fourier Transform mainly uses CPU to process data, we consider the number of CPU cores in each compute node as the main factor to decide the computation ability. In a certain compute Cloud, because the amount of CPU cores is fixed, when the number of CPU cores in each compute node increases, the number of compute nodes decreases.

5.1   Equally-Split Strategy

We assume that the total compute resource is limited to n CPU cores and m GB caches. The equally-split strategy is to split these resources into p (p should be 2^t where t is a integer) pieces. Each compute node has k/p G caches and m/p GB cache.

The input data are also equally split into p pieces and distributed to each compute node. After each compute node completes its calculation on its local data, data exchange between compute nodes is required to finish the rest computing work.

Assume the input data size is N. There are $log_2(l)$ steps in a whole butterfly computing process. Between every two steps, data need to be exchanged once. Hence, the total size of data to be exchanged is

$$N * (log_2(l) - 1).$$

5.2   Optimized-Split Strategy

The core idea of optimized-split strategy is to make data flow as stream in the Cloud. This method can avoid data exchange. Although equally-split strategy is a simple way to conduct parallel FFT Algorithm, unfortunately, too many data exchanges result in low speed. To better use the compute resources, we design optimized-split strategy to redistribute the compute resources.

Like in equally-split strategy, we also set the total compute resources in the Cloud as n CPU cores and m GB caches. In our experiments, we found that the CPU and cache both have important impact on the FFT algorithm altogether. Therefore, we bind 1 core and 2 GB together as a computing unit. Every compute node can have 1 or n (n is an integer) computing units only.

In order to execute different stages of FFT, the compute Cloud is separated to sections $s_1, s_2, ..., s_n$. Different compute sections conduct different stages of FFT. Inside each section s_i, the resource is equally divided into compute nodes C_i^k to complete parallel calculations. Because the workload in each stage varies, we set different size θ_k for nodes and different size ω_k for sections.

For example, there are 48 CPU cores and 96 GB cache in a compute cloud. These resources can be divided into 3 sections s_1, s_2, s_3. The first section s_1 has 16 compute nodes $C_1^i, C_1^2, ..., C_1^{16}$, each of which has 1 core and 2 GB cache. The second section s_2 has 4 compute nodes $C_2^i, C_2^2, ..., C_2^4$, each of which has 4 cores and 8 GB cache. The third section s_3 has 1 compute node C_3^1 which has 16 cores and 32 GB cache.

When data come to this Cloud, they are divided to 16 parts $D_1^i, D_1^2, ..., D_1^{16}$ and sent to each compute $C_1^i, C_1^2, ..., C_1^{16}$ in the first section. Then these compute nodes conduct FFT on their local data and send the results to compute nodes $D_2^i, D_2^2, ..., D_2^4$ in the second section. $D_2^i, D_2^2, ..., D_2^4$ also execute the later stages of FFT on their local data and send results to D_3^1. D_3^1 completes the rest computations and obtains the final result.

It should be mentioned that the data come as a stream. Hence, the data stream is constantly flowing in the Cloud from section 1 to section n. Therefore, there is no idle resource in our system.

The main goal of this distribution method is to find an optimal way to balance the portion of sections. Compute node's size determines its performance. More CPU cores and larger cache means faster speed on computation. When former stage of FFT is too slow, the later stage will not be executed and the next section will be idle. When compute nodes take too much resources, they may wait former computations.

6   Experiment Results

In this section, we present experimental results to illustrate the previous theoretical improvements. The ASFFT (parallel FFT algorithm is implemented in Apache Spark) and comparison with the MFFT algorithm (FFT in Matlab) is given.

The data used in the experiments are signal data from satellites. Since the satellites constantly send data to data center, the data arrive in stream. When an amount of 64 MB data arrive, the data become a data block. Hence, a requirement of the system is to finish data processing job before the next data block comes or the data are accumulated and the computation is delayed.

The compute Cloud we used has the resource of 48 CPU cores and 96 GB cache. Apache Spark is installed in the virtual machines to send data and execute computation. Different distribution strategies are implemented to the Cloud.

In Figs. 5 and 6, we show the comparison between our parallel FFT in Apache Spark and the FFT in Matlab. We use 10MB data unit and 2MB data unit to conduct our experiments. The results show that when data scale is small (shown in the left-side columns in Figs. 5 and 6), MFFT takes less time than ASFFT algorithm. The reason is that Apache Spark is designed to conduct computation for big data. When data scale is small, the initialization of Spark engine takes a big portion of total time. When data scale rise up, the initialization of Spark takes smaller portion so the parallel FFT performs better.

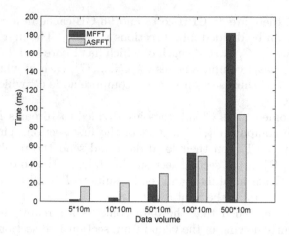

Fig. 5. 10 MB data unit comparison

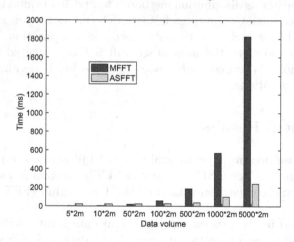

Fig. 6. 2 MB data unit comparison

However, with increase in data scale, the time spent in computation increases drastically. By comparison, although ASFFT spends more time than MFFT when data scale is small, the ASFFT shows its advantage when data scale is large.

By comparison between Figs. 5 and 6, we can observe that the ASFFT shows more obvious advantage when the data unit is smaller (2MB). This is because when the data unit's size is smaller, the FFT algorithm is easier to be conducted.

From Figs. 7 and 8, we can see that the parallelization of FFT effectively reduces the algorithm time. With more CPU cores, the speed of algorithm increases. When there is 1 CPU core in the Cloud, the FFT is not parallelized and the speed is low. When there are 2 cores, the time spent by the algorithm reduces greatly to nearly a half. With more and more cores, the increase of the algorithm becomes more and more unobvious.

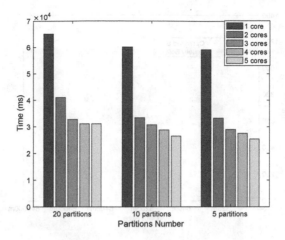

Fig. 7. Parallel effectiveness comparison of 10 MB data

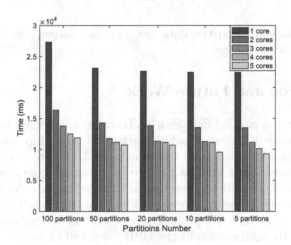

Fig. 8. Parallel effectiveness comparison of 2 MB data

In addition, the partition number also affects the algorithm speed. Too many partitions cause low efficiency. This result is because more data partitions mean more data RDDs formed in Spark. Spark divides the original data into more data partitions, which takes redundant time. Therefore, finding a smaller number of data partitions can be significantly efficient.

Figure 9 reveals the comparison between the two split strategies. The experiment was conducted in a Cloud with 16 CPU cores and 32G cache. In the equally-split strategy, there are 8 workers with 2 CPU cores and 4G cache. In the optimized-split strategy, there are 4 small workers with 2 CPU cores and 4G cache and 1 large worker with 8 CPU cores and 16G cache. When data size is small, the equally-split strategy performs better than the optimized-split

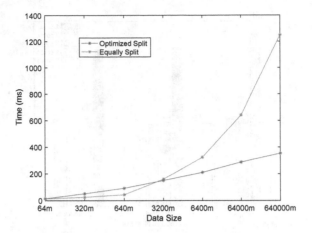

Fig. 9. Comparison between split strategy

strategy. Nonetheless, when the data size becomes larger, the optimized-split strategy shows its advantage.

7   Conclusion and Future Work

We have presented a parallel Fast Fourier Transform algorithm in Cloud. Using a big data framework called Apache Spark, this algorithm stores intermediate data in cache which decreases the time in FFT. A three-step parallel FFT method is proposed, which enables FFT to be computed concurrently in different compute nodes. The existing parallel FFT algorithm has the problem of too many data exchange between compute nodes. This problem results in the low efficiency of the algorithm. We propose a new strategy to reallocate the computation resource. By optimized-split the CPU cores and cache into each compute node, data exchange decreases. We have validated our algorithm through comparisons and implementation in a Cloud.

To improvement the performance of parallel FFT algorithm, there are many other works could be done. In this paper, we propose some strategies to allocate the computation resources. However, they can be further developed by considering more attributes of computation resources. We also noticed that some researches study the performance of FFT algorithm on GPU cluster, which could be another direction of our future work.

Acknowledgements. The authors would like to thank the anonymous referees for their helpful comments from which the preparation for this version of the paper has benefited. Thanks for Johann Sebastian Bach for his inspiring music accompanying the authors to complete the research. This work was supported in part by the National Natural Science Foundation of China under Grant 61572511 and Grant 91648204 and Grant 61872378, in part by the Scientific Research Project of National University of

Defense Technology under Grant ZK16-03-57, in part by the China Postdoctoral Science Foundation under Grant 2016M602960 and Grant 2017T100796, in part by Science Fund for Distinguished Young Scholars in Hunan Province under Grant 2018JJ1032. Xiaomin Zhu is the corresponding author.

References

1. Armbrust, M., et al.: A view of cloud computing. Commun. ACM **53**(4), 50–58 (2010)
2. Armbrust, M., et al.: Above the clouds: A Berkeley View of Cloud Computing. Tech. rep., Technical ReportD UCB/EECS-2009-28, EECS Department, University of California, Berkeley (2009)
3. Baker, S.: Google and the wisdom of clouds. Business Week 14 (2007)
4. Bergland, G.D.: A parallel implementation of the fast fourier transform algorithm. IEEE Trans. Comput. **100**(4), 366–370 (1972)
5. Bosagh Zadeh, R., et al.: Matrix computations and optimization in apache spark. In: Proceedings of the 22nd ACM SIGKDD International Conference on Knowledge Discovery and Data Mining, pp. 31–38. ACM (2016)
6. Cooley, J.W., Tukey, J.W.: An algorithm for the machine calculation of complex fourier series. Math. Comput. **19**(90), 297–301 (1965)
7. Dean, J., Ghemawat, S.: Mapreduce: simplified data processing on large clusters. Commun. ACM **51**(1), 107–113 (2008)
8. Frigo, M., Johnson, S.G.: FFTW: An adaptive software architecture for the FFT. In: Proceedings of the 1998 IEEE International Conference on Acoustics, Speech and Signal Processing, vol. 3, pp. 1381–1384. IEEE (1998)
9. Githens, J.: A fully parallel computer for radar data processing. In: IEEE Transactions on Aerospace and Electronic Systems, p. 736. No. 5 (1970)
10. Hassanieh, H., Adib, F., Katabi, D., Indyk, P.: Faster gps via the sparse fourier transform. In: International Conference on Mobile Computing and Networking, pp. 353–364 (2012)
11. Hassen, H., Khemakhem, M.: Arabic islamic manuscripts digitization based on hybrid K-NN/SVM approach and cloud computing technologies. In: Taibah University International Conference on Advances in Information Technology for the Holy Quran and Its Sciences (32519), pp. 366–371. IEEE (2013)
12. Kulkarni, P., Kumar, V., Verma, H.: Diagnostic acceptability of FFT-based ECG data compression. J. Med. Eng. Technol. **21**(5), 185–189 (1997)
13. Li, F., Xu, J., Zhouhong, J., Miao, W.: Aerial target detection via GPS satellite broadcast signal. J. Chin. Inert. Technol. **22**(6), 788–793 (2014)
14. Marcum, J.: A statistical theory of target detection by pulsed radar. IRE Trans. Inf. Theory **6**(2), 59–267 (1960)
15. Marple, L.: Computing the discrete-time "analytic" signal via FFT. IEEE Trans. Signal Process. **47**(9), 2600–2603 (1999)
16. Mullin, L.R., Small, S.G.: Four easy ways to a faster FFT. J. Math. Model. Algorithms **1**(3), 193–214 (2002)
17. Palanisamy, B.: Purlieus: locality-aware resource allocation for MapReduce in a cloud. In: High Performance Computing, Networking, Storage and Analysis, pp. 1–11 (2011)
18. Prasad, N., Shameem, V., Desai, U., Merchant, S.: Improvement in target detection performance of pulse coded doppler radar based on multicarrier modulation with fast fourier transform (fft). IEE Proc. Radar, Sonar Navig. **151**(1), 11–17 (2004)

19. Preuss, R.: Very fast computation of the radix-2 discrete fourier transform. IEEE Trans. Acoustics, Speech, Signal Process. **30**(4), 595–607 (1982)

20. Reddy, B.S., Chatterji, B.N.: An FFT-based technique for translation, rotation, and scale-invariant image registration. IEEE Trans. Image Process. **5**(8), 1266–1271 (1996)

21. Spark, A.: Lightning-fast cluster computing (2016)

22. Tang, G., Peng, L., Baldwin, P.R., Mann, D.S., Jiang, W., Rees, I., Ludtke, S.J.: Eman2: an extensible image processing suite for electron microscopy. J. Struct. Biol. **157**(1), 38–46 (2007)

23. Ubeyli, E., Güler, I.: Spectral analysis of internal carotid arterial doppler signals using FFT, AR, MA, and ARMA methods. Comput. Biol. Med. **34**(4), 293 (2004)

24. Vincke, R., Landschoot, S.V., Cordemans, P., Peuteman, J., Steegmans, E., Boydens, J.: Algorithm parallelization using software design patterns, an embedded case study approach. In: Eighth International Conference on P2P, Parallel, Grid, Cloud and Internet Computing, pp. 470–473 (2013)

25. Wang, Y., Yang, R., Wo, T., Jiang, W., Hu, C.: Improving utilization through dynamic VM resource allocation in hybrid cloud environment. In: IEEE International Conference on Parallel and Distributed Systems, pp. 241–248 (2015)

26. Welch, P.: The use of fast fourier transform for the estimation of power spectra: a method based on time averaging over short, modified periodograms. IEEE Trans. Audio Electroacoust. **15**(2), 70–73 (1967)

27. Wold, E., Despain, A.: Pipeline and parallel-pipeline FFT processors for VLSI implementations. IEEE Trans. Comput. **C–33**(5), 414–426 (1984)

28. Xu, L., Li, J., Stoica, P.: Target detection and parameter estimation for mimo radar systems. IEEE Trans. Aerosp. Electron. Syst. **44**(3), 927–939 (2008)

29. Zaharia, M., Chowdhury, M., Franklin, M.J., Shenker, S., Stoica, I.: Spark: cluster computing with working sets. HotCloud **10**(10–10), 95 (2010)

30. Zaharia, M., et al.: Apache spark: a unified engine for big data processing. Commun. ACM **59**(11), 56–65 (2016)

31. Zhu, X., Mong Sim, K., Jiang, J., Wang, J., Chen, C.: Agent-based dynamic scheduling for earth-observing tasks on multiple airships in emergency. IEEE Syst. J. **10**(2), 661–672 (2016)

32. Zhu, X., Wang, J., Guo, H., Zhu, D., Yang, L.T., Liu, L.: Fault-tolerant scheduling for real-time scientific workflows with elastic resource provisioning in virtualized clouds. IEEE Trans. Parallel Distrib. Syst. **27**(12), 3501–3517 (2016)

Task Offloading in Edge-Clouds
with Budget Constraint

Lei He[1], Hongli Xu[1(✉)], Haibo Wang[1], Liusheng Huang[1], and Jingyi Ma[2]

[1] Department of Computer Science and Technology, University of Science
and Technology of China (USTC), Hefei, China
{hl1994,wanghaib}@mail.ustc.edu.cn, {xuhongli,lshuang}@ustc.edu.cn
[2] TianPing College of SuZhou University of Science and Technology,
SuZhou 215011, Jiangsu, China
tpxyjw@usts.edu.cn

Abstract. Edge computing is an emerging computing model that extends the cloud and its services to the edge of network. In edge-cloud computing, a set of servers are deployed near the mobile devices such that these devices can offload tasks to the servers with low latency. Most existing works usually focus on offloading tasks under the premise that sufficient resources are owned by edge servers while ignoring budget constraint of user. If failed to consider about this, the existing offloading schemes may cause user to overspend, this is unacceptable to user. Thus, in this paper, we investigate the task offloading problem in edge-cloud computing aiming to minimize the task duration while tasks are generated by user with constrainted budget. Besides edge servers are equipped with limited computation and storage resources. Specifically, the problem we formulate is an NP-hard problem. In order to solve it, we propose a heuristic strategy. The simulation results prove that the proposed scheme can improve the success ratio and reduce the task duration, compared to random and greedy offloading schemes.

Keywords: Edge computing · Task offloading · Budget constraint

1 Introduction

Mobile devices are commonly used in people's life everyday. It is predicted that by 2020 the total quantity of devices would be 75 billion, while the volume of mobile traffic would exceed 24.3 exabytes/month [1]. Furthermore, mobile devices will be more and more intelligent while the applications in mobile devices become increasingly resource-hungry. These applications include wearable virtual reality (VR) [2] streaming, augmented reality (AR) [3] and vehicular system [4], etc. However, the gap between required resources and those available in mobile devices widens. To bridge this gap, mobile applications can offload their computation-intensive tasks to remote clouds [5]. However, an evident weakness of public cloud based mobile cloud computing is that mobile users may experience long latency for data exchange with the public cloud through the wide area

© Springer Nature Switzerland AG 2018
J. Vaidya and J. Li (Eds.): ICA3PP 2018, LNCS 11336, pp. 311–326, 2018.
https://doi.org/10.1007/978-3-030-05057-3_25

network. Long latency would hurt the interactive response, since humans are acutely sensitive to delay and jitter. Moreover, it is very difficult to reduce the latency in the wide area network. To deal with long latency of remote clouds, edge computing [6,7] has been proposed, which extends the cloud computing by placing a number of small scale servers at the edge of network. In this way, users can offload their tasks to edge servers and receive computing results with low network latency. However, compared to cloud computing, the scale of edge servers is rather small. The development of tasks is restricted by both the resource and computation capacity. Any particular edge server might not be able to support large scale computing tasks. Therefore, the tension between resource-hungry tasks and resource-constrained edge servers hence poses a significant challenge for the future mobile platform development.

In recent years, researchers have been pay more attention to the performance of edge-cloud network, especially for the task offloading problems. In summary, those works focus on two main aspects of task offloading. (i) Minimizing the task duration(e.g. [8,9]). When mobile devices create tasks, those works first decide whether the tasks should offload to edge-cloud or not. Then choose between the remote and nearby edge servers to offload tasks, which is based on the amount of computation resources required. (ii) Considering saving the network energy cost, the energy efficient resource allocation scheme is studied for mobile edge computing in [10,11].

However, when we consider more about this, the effective of the offloading strategy faces the following challenges: (i) The limited resources of edge servers. These resources include the computation resources and storage resources. In the big data era, most tasks are created to train a general model from big data. Those tasks need appropriate edge servers to generate models and store data set. So, how to control these computing resources is a challenge problem. (ii) The budget constraint of user. As an extension of cloud computing, edge servers charge for the services from user, the price of service depends on the resources asked from tasks. Thus, the existing works may not useful at this, because those works may leading the overspend of user. For example, when a user plays VR game on mobile device, the user needs to pay for the game. So when the game application decides to offload tasks to edge-clouds, the cost of the offloading should not exceed the amount of payment, and the user desires the low delay of tasks and high success ratio of task offloading. Thus how to conduct an effective task offloading according to the budget constraint is challenging. Under this context, to get low latency of task offloading, we should consider how to match the desired resources of users to the limited resources of edge servers.

In this paper, we study the offloading problem in edge-cloud network. To be specific, the edge servers are equipped with limited computation and storage resources, while the user who decides to offload tasks to edge servers with constrainted budget. Furthermore, the task offloading problem we formulate is an NP-hardness problem. To solve the problem, we propose a budget constraint task offloading scheme (BCTO). Our proposed strategy of task offloading aims to minimize task duration. In detail, our task offloading scheme includes two parts: (i) Computing cost of the computation. When a task offloading to an edge server, the edge server gives the cost of the computation of this task based on the computation and storage resources required by the task. (ii) According to the cost of computation task on every edge server and the user budget, our scheme calculates the effective of the cost and decides which of the server should be allocated to the task. In this paper we assume the task duration is the execution time of the tasks on edge servers, the budget is set by the user who decides to offload tasks. When user creates many tasks, we assume these tasks are independent. Which means for any two tasks, the result of one task has no impact on another task, so tasks can be executed concurrently.

When user decides to offload tasks to edge servers. User acts as a buyer with constrainted budget, while the computation and storage resources are regarded as the commodities. To ensure the cost of the computing and store of tasks does not exceed the budget. The BCTO scheme chooses the appropriate edge server for offloading tasks. The main contributions of this paper are summarized as follows:

1. We propose a price model of the edge servers, which measures the price of computation tasks based on the computation and storage resources required by tasks. By using this model, the cost of each task on each edge server can be obtained, and thus enabling the optimal task offloading.
2. We present an efficient budget constraint task offloading scheme. Based on the budget, the cost of every task and the execution time on edge servers, the scheme chooses an appropriate edge server for every task. Our scheme can not only improve the success ratio of offloading but also reduce the task duration.
3. We conduct extensive experiments to evaluate the performance of BCTO scheme. The experimental results validate that our proposed algorithm can improve 5%~10% success ratio and reduce at least 30% of the task duration compared to random and greedy offloading schemes.

The rest of this paper is organized as follows. In Sect. 2, we present the related works. In Sect. 3 the system model is described. In Sect. 4 we give the problem formulation. We propose the efficient task offloading algorithm in Sect. 5. Our simulation results and discussions are given in Sect. 6. Finally, Sect. 7 concludes this paper.

2 Related Works

2.1 Mobile Edge Computing

At present, mobile devices become more and more powerful and intelligent. However, the development of mobile devices does not catch up with the demand of resource of applications. So it is difficult to handle all application tasks directly in mobile devices. Mobile cloud computing has proposed as a solution, and offloading heavy computation tasks to the remote cloud data centers has been studied for over a decade. CloneCloud [12] was proposed to use cloned virtual machine images in the cloud for mobile job offloading. Follow me cloud [13] was proposed for offloading computation-intensive tasks to the cloud for processing. COMET [14] migrates the application threads between mobile device and the cloud by using a distributed shared memory model.

However, since the locations of cloud servers are far away from mobile devices, offloading tasks to cloud may get a long delay. To overcome this challenge, mobile edge computing was proposed to provide nearby rich computing resources to mobile users [15], and there have been quite a lot of studies on the resource allocation problem. [16,17] offload the tasks to the nearest edge servers since it is easy to apply, but it may lead a severe competing for the limited resources of edge server, To solve this problem, a hierarchical architecture has been proposed [9]. The architecture divides the edge-clouds into different levels according to the distance to the edge, and presents heuristic algorithm to minimize the task duration.

Most existing works consider a single edge server in task offloading. The work in [18] proposed that the cooperation of edge clouds can not only reduce the processing delay of user tasks, but also reduce the energy consumption. In a word, mobile edge computing can improve the quality of service and energy efficiency by optimizing task offloading and resource allocation policies. [19] pointed out that it is much better to processing the tasks in edge-clouds than processing at the edge-clouds in isolation. Some of the works above assumed that the releases of tasks follow some known stochastic. So in [8] an online algorithm without any assumption of the task release distribution has been proposed.

2.2   Task Offloading with Limited Budget

There are many works on task scheduling with budget constraint, such as in the grid or cloud environments, [20] developed scheduling approaches, LOSS and GAIN, to adjust a schedule which is generated by a time optimized heuristic and a cost optimized heuristic to meet users budget constraints respectively. But this strategy should be supported by other scheduling algorithm. BaTS [21], a budget and time-constrained scheduler, can schedule large bags of independent tasks onto multiple Clouds. Zhu et al. [22] proposed a dynamic scheduling for fixed time-limit and resource budget constraint tasks. Reference [23] focuses on using genetic algorithms to solve the scheduling problems considering the budget and deadline of entire network. Recently, HCOC [24] discusses workflow execution in a cloud context. HCOC reduces monetary cost while achieving the established desired execution time by deciding which resources should be leased from the public cloud or be used in the private cloud. Byun et al. [25] provided PBTS (Partitioned Balanced Time Scheduling) which estimates the minimum number of computing hosts required to execute a workflow within a user-specified finish time. However, the computing hosts are used as the same monetary cost per time unit. For large graph processing in Cloud, Li et al. [26] designed a cost-conscious scheduling algorithm (CCSH) which is an extension of HEFT.

In this paper, we construct analytical models to quantify independent tasks execution performance in edge computing, and we incorporate the price model into cost calculation.

3   System Model

3.1   Network Model

We consider an edge computing scenario with M heterogenous edge servers, $\mathcal{M} = \{s_1, s_2, ..., s_M\}$ each of which is equipped with limited computation and storage resources. For each of the edge server, we assume the resource status of edge server s_i be the 2-tuple (R_i^c, R_i^m), where R_i^c and R_i^m are the computation resource and storage resource owned by edge server s_i. The computation resource is described in terms of CPU cycles while the storage resource is quantified by the size of GB. There is a set $\mathcal{T} = \{t_1, t_2, ..., t_N\}$ of indivisible tasks, those tasks are offloaded by user with the constrained budget B. We adopt a widely used task model (see [7,27,28]) to describe task $t_j = (a_j, c_j)$, i.e., where a_j stands for computation amount of task, i.e., the CPU cycles needed in total to compute task, and b_j stands for the size of computation task, i.e., the amount of data contents (e.g, the data input and associated processing code) to be delivered toward the edge servers. In our model, a mobile device will dispatch tasks to an edge server immediately after its release. We do not allow the servers to migrate a task to other servers after the offloading to avoid migration overhead, and we assume a server can execute at most one task at a time preemptively.

3.2   Price Model

When an edge server equips with limited computation and storage resources, the price of those resources refers to the cost of offloaded tasks to be executed in the server. It is more reasonable to value the resources according to edge servers' performance when utilizing these resources. Let $P_i^C(q)$ denotes the price of computation for q units of CPU cycles per second of edge server s_i, and $P_i^S(e)$ stands for the price of e units size of storage of edge server s_i. In our price model of computation price, we adopt a nonlinear model. The function can be denoted as:

$$\frac{x}{y} \leq \frac{P_i^C(x)}{P_i^C(y)} \quad i \in M, x, y \in \{1, 2, ..., R_i^c\}. \tag{1}$$

where $P_i^C(x)$ and $P_i^C(y)$ denote the price of x and y units of CPU cycles on edge server s_i, R_i^c denotes the computation resource limitation on edge server s_i.

For the storage price, we define a linear function to the size of storage. The function can be denoted as following:

$$\frac{x}{y} = \frac{P_i^S(x)}{P_i^S(y)} \quad i \in M, x, y \in \{1, 2, ..., R_i^m\}. \tag{2}$$

where $P_i^S(x)$ and $P_i^S(y)$ denote the price of x and y units of storage size on edge server s_i, R_i^m denotes the storage resource limitation on edge server s_i.

3.3   Task Offloading Model

In this section, we will introduce the computation task offloading model in detail. As we describe above, the task t_j can be described $t_j = (a_j, c_j)$, considering the difference of computation resources of edge server, we denote the computation resources (CPU cycles per second) of edge server s_i as R_i^c, according to the network model, the task duration on edge server s_i is the time when task is executed on the edge server. Therefore, the task duration of task t_j on edge server s_i can be obtained as follow:

$$t_{ij} = \frac{a_j}{R_i^c} \quad i \in M, j \in N. \tag{3}$$

Similar to the study [29], we ignore the transmission delay for edge servers to send data from user or to user. This is because the edge servers are deployed very close to the mobile devices. The processing time of tasks on edge servers are the main part compared to the transmission time of tasks.

4   Problem Formulation

In this paper, in terms of limited computation and storage resources of edge servers, we consider the following problem: how to select the appropriate edge servers for tasks while achieving the minimum task duration under the constraint budget of user.

Define the matching matrix as $X = \{x_{ij}\}_{M*N}$, where x_{ij} is the indicator revealing whether edge server s_i can serve task t_j. If task t_j is offloaded to the edge server s_i, then we have $x_{ij} = 1$, otherwise $x_{ij} = 0$, the matching matrix must satisfy the following constraint:

$$\sum_{i=1}^{M} x_{ij} \leqq 1 \quad i \in M, j \in N. \tag{4}$$

which ensures that one task can only be served by at most one edge server.

If task t_j is allowed to be served by edge server s_i, then the cost of computation of task t_j on edge server s_i is:

$$p_{ij} = P_i^C(a_j) + P_i^S(c_j) \quad i \in M, j \in N. \tag{5}$$

For each edge server s_i, the total cost for the tasks executed on the server is:

$$p_i = \sum_{j=1}^{N} x_{ij} p_{ij} \quad i \in M, j \in N. \tag{6}$$

When task t_j is offloaded to edge server s_i, the time of the execution of task t_j on edge server s_i is t_{ij} as we describe in the task offloading model. Thus, the overall time of task execution on edge server s_i can be expressed as follows:

$$T_i = \sum_{j=1}^{N} x_{ij} t_{ij} \quad i \in M, j \in N. \tag{7}$$

According to the analysis above, the problem we need to solve can be formulated as the following:

$$min \quad max(T_i) \quad i \in M, j \in N \tag{8}$$

$$subject \quad to: \quad \sum_{i=1}^{M} p_i \leqq B \quad i \in M, \tag{9}$$

$$\sum_{i=1}^{M} x_{ij} c_j \leqq R_i^m \quad i \in M, j \in N, \tag{10}$$

$$\sum_{i=1}^{M} x_{ij} \leqq 1 \quad i \in M, j \in N, \tag{11}$$

$$x_{ij} \in [0,1] \quad i \in M, j \in N. \tag{12}$$

Table 1. Notation Table

Parameter	Definition
M	Set of edge server
T	Set of computation task
s_i	Edge server
t_j	Computation task
R_i^c	Total number of CPU cycles owned by edge server s_i
R_i^m	Total number of storage size owned by edge server s_i
a_j	The CPU cycles need of task t_j
c_j	The size of storage amount need of task t_j
$P_i^C(q)$	The price of q units of CPU cycles and per time unit on edge server s_i
$P_i^S(e)$	The price of e unit size of storage on edge server s_i
t_{ij}	The task duration of task t_j executed on edge server s_i
x_{ij}	The indicator revealing whether edge server s_i can serve the task t_j
T_i	The overall time of edge server s_i
T_{exe}	The minimum execution time of all the tasks
p_{ij}^r	The price ratio
p_{ij}^s	The effective of price
p_{all}	The cost of all offloaded tasks
p^s	The set of effective of price of all tasks on edge servers edge servers

The objective function (8) is to minimize the maximum execute time of tasks on edge server. The first constraint (9) indicates for all the tasks execute on edge servers, the cost of the computation and storage should not exceed the constraint budget B. The second constraint (10) states for any edge server s_i, the storage resource asked of any tasks execute on this edge server is no more than the edge server's storage resource. The third constraint (11) means that one task can only be served by at most one edge server. The last condition (12) indicates whether a task t_j is served by edge server s_i or not. The problem we formulate is a NP-hard problem [30], therefore, we focus on design of a heuristic approach to this optimization problem (Table 1).

5   Task Offloading Scheme in Edge Computing

Our work targets computation-intensive tasks in edge-cloud, where the data transfer time is assumed negligible since: (i) the time for data transfers in most computation-intensive tasks constitutes less than 10 of the overall task execution time [21]. (ii) the edge servers are deployed very close to the mobile devices.

Algorithm 1. BCTO($\mathcal{M}$, $\mathcal{T}$, B).

Input:
>   A set of edge servers $\mathcal{M}$ equipped with computation and storage resource.
>   A set of tasks $\mathcal{T}$ with required computation and storage resource.
>   A fixed budget B.

Output:
>   The minimum execution time T_{exe} of tasks.

1: **for all** s_i in $\mathcal{M}$ **do**
2:     Set the overall time on edge server s_i $T_i = 0$.
3:     **for all** t_j in $\mathcal{T}$ **do**
4:         **if** $c_j \leqq R_i^s$ **then**
5:             Calculate the execution time t_{ij} and the price p_{ij} according the equation (3) and (5).
6:             **if** $p_{ij} > B$ **then**
7:                 Exit the program with an error.
8:             **end if**
9:             Calculate the price ratio as $p_{ij}^r = \frac{p_{ij}}{B}$.
10:            Calculate the effective of price p_{ij}, $p_{ij}^s = p_{ij}^r \times \frac{p_{ij}}{t_{ij}}$.
11:        **else**
12:            Set $t_{ij} = 0$, $p_{ij} = 0$ and $p_{ij}^r = 0$.
13:        **end if**
14:    **end for**
15: **end for**
16: T_{exe} = Offload(p^s, $\mathcal{T}$, B).
17: **return** T_{exe}.

We propose the BCTO algorithm as shown in Algorithm 1. The Algorithm 1 first estimates the cost and time of every task based on the resources required by every task and the computation and storage resources owned by edge servers. If the cost of any task is greater than the budget then we finish the offloading. Then Algorithm 1 gives the price ratio of the task on every edge server. According to the price ratio of task on every edge server, we give the effective of the price on each edge server.

In Algorithm 1, the effective of price is part of the offloading strategy in Algorithm 2. Based on the effective of price on each edge server, Algorithm 2 sorts the value of cost of effective. After the sort of the effective of price of a task on each servers, we drop out some of the edge servers that with much lower price effective. From the start index to the end index indicate the edge servers we keep for offloading, in this paper, we drop out two lower price effective edge servers. After the drop out, we will offload the task on the edge server with minimizing increase on the time of edge servers. It is obviously the cost of all the computation tasks will not exceed the budget in Algorithm 2. The time complexity of Algorithm 1 is $O(M \times N)$, where M is the number of edge servers, and N is the number of computation tasks.

Algorithm 2. Offload(p^s, $\mathcal{T}$, B)

Input:
   The set of effective of price of all tasks on edge servers edge servers p^s.
   The set of tasks $\mathcal{T}$ with the price p_{ij} and t_{ij}.
   A fixed budget B.

Output:
   The minimum execution time T_{exe} of those tasks.

1: Set the cost of all offloaded tasks $p_{all} = 0$.
2: Set M is the number of edge server, start = 1, and end = M-2.
3: Set the overall time on every edge server $T_i = 0$.
4: **for all** t_j in $\mathcal{T}$ & $p_{ij} \neq 0$ & $t_{ij} \neq 0$ **do**
5:    **if** $p_{all} \leq B$ **then**
6:       Sort the p_{ij}^s for every i in ascending order.
7:       **for** i from start to end **do**
8:          Offloading the task t_j to the edge server s_i and $s_i = \arg \min_{s_i \in \mathcal{M}} T_i + t_{ij}$.
9:       **end for**
10:       $T_i = T_i + t_{ij}$, $p_{all} = p_{all} + p_{ij}$.
11:    **end if**
12: **end for**
13: Set $T_{exe} = \arg \max_{i \in M} T_i$.
14: **return** T_{exe}.

---

6   Simulation and Performance Evaluation

In this section, a simulation experiment is provided concerning task offloading for edge computing. The experiment is divided into three parts: (i) We implement task offloading algorithm and evaluate the impact of offloading performance in comparison with two other task offloading schemes in terms of budget number, the number of edge server and the number of task. (ii) We study the impact of the computation amount on the performance of task offloading in comparison with random offloading and greedy offloading schemes. (iii) We investigate the impact of task data size on the performance of task offloading in comparison with random offloading and greedy offloading schemes.

6.1   Simulation Settings

For task t_j, we assume the resources required, namely the CPU cycles a_j and data size b_j are generated by a probability distribution. Similar to the work [11], we set the computation resources owned by edge servers are range from 20 to 50 GHZ, while the storage resources owned by edge servers are range from 1 GB to 16 GB.

6.2   Comparison to Other Methods

We set the comparison of our algorithm to other two different task offloading strategies: random offloading scheme and greedy offloading scheme.

1. Random offloading scheme: the computation tasks are offloaded to edge servers for processing randomly. We first set up a random generator that can generate a M-tuple, the value in the tuple ranges from 0 to 1 and is generated with equal probability, the sum of value in the tuple is 1, where M is the number of edge server. Then, we get the index which value is maximum in the tuple, finally we offload computation task to the edge server according to the index we get.
2. Greedy offloading scheme: the greedy offloading scheme offloads the tasks to the most powerful edge server to get the minimum task duration. Most of the works (e.g., [16,31]) on edge servers adopted the greedy strategy as the task offloading policy.

For the three methods above, the offloading performance we evaluate refers to the task duration and the success ratio of task offloading. The task duration in our work refers to task execution time on edge server, while the success ratio means that the number of successful offloading tasks to the total number of tasks. The CPU cycles of each task are generated by the normal distribution with mean value of 2 GHZ, and the data size of each task is generated by the normal distribution with mean value of 2 GB.

When we evaluate the impact of user budget, we set the number of task is 10000, and the number of edge servers is 20. Figure 1 shows the impact of user budget. When compared with random offloading scheme, our proposed scheme can improve 6% success ratio and reduce about 30% of task duration of task offloading. Compared with greedy offloading scheme, our proposed scheme can improve about 30% success ratio while reduce 45% task duration of task offloading.

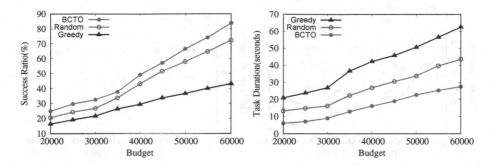

Fig. 1. Impact of user budget

Figure 2 shows the impact of the number of edge servers, we set the number of tasks is 10000, while the user budget is 60000. We can know that when compared with random offloading scheme, our proposed scheme can improve 8% success ratio and reduce about 30% of task duration of task offloading. Compared with greedy offloading scheme, our proposed scheme can improve about 35% success ratio while reduce 45% task duration of task offloading.

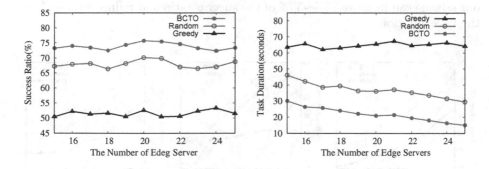

Fig. 2. Impact of edge server number

Figure 3 shows the impact of the number of tasks, we set user budget is 100000, while the number of edge servers is 20. When compared with random offloading scheme, our proposed scheme can improve 5% success ratio and reduce about 35% of task duration of task offloading. Compared with greedy offloading scheme, our proposed scheme can improve about 20% success ratio while reduce 40% task duration of task offloading.

6.3 Impact of Computation Amount of Task Offloading

In this section, we consider the impact of computation amount on task offloading performance. The data size of task follows a normal distribution with mean value

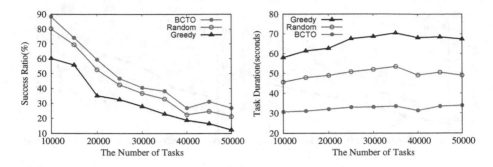

Fig. 3. Impact of task number

of 2 GB. The user budget we set is 70000. The number of tasks is 10000 and the number of edge servers is 20. For the computation amount, three kinds of distribution are utilized, i.e., uniform distribution, normal distribution and pareto distribution.

In the first figure of Fig. 4 and first figure of Fig. 5, when the computation amount follows uniform distribution. Compared with random offloading scheme, it is shown that our proposed BCTO scheme can improve 5% success ratio while reduce about 30% task duration. And compared with greedy offloading scheme, our scheme can improve 25%~30% of the success ratio and reduce 40%~50% of the task duration.

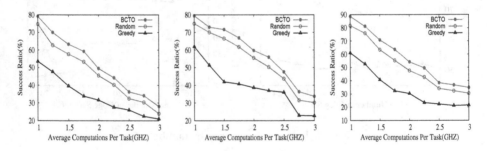

Fig. 4. Impact of computation amount: success ratio under uniform distribution, normal distribution and pareto distribution

As shown in the second figure of Fig. 4 and second figure of Fig. 5, when the computation amount follows normal distribution. We can get that our scheme can improve 5% success ratio and reduce 35% task duration when compared with random offloading scheme. Compared with the greedy offloading scheme, our scheme can improve 25% of success ratio, while reduce 45% of task duration.

In the third figure of Fig. 4 and third figure of Fig. 5, when the computation amount follows pareto distribution. When compared with the random offloading scheme, our scheme can improve 5% of success ratio, while reduce more than

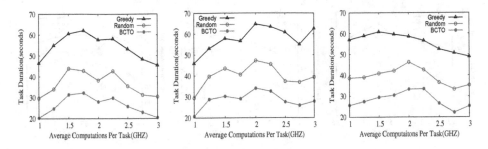

Fig. 5. Impact of computation amount: time duration under uniform distribution, normal distribution and pareto distribution

30% task duration. Compared with greedy offloading scheme, our scheme can improve 20%~25% success ratio, while reduce 40% task duration.

6.4   Impact of Data Size of Task Offloading

In this section, we consider the impact of data size on task offloading performance. The computation amount follows a normal distribution with mean value of 2 GHZ. The user budget is 40000. The number of tasks we set is 10000, and the number of edge servers is 20. For the data size, three kinds of distribution are utilized, i.e., normal distribution, uniform distribution and pareto distribution.

As shown in Figs. 6 and 7, we can conclude that our proposed offloading scheme exhibits higher success ratio of task offloading and shorter task duration than random offloading scheme and greedy offloading scheme. In first figures of Fig. 6 and first figure of Fig. 7, when computation amount follows uniform distribution. Compared with random offloading scheme, it is shown that our proposed offloading scheme can improve 5% of the success ratio and reduce 30% of the task duration on average of task offloading. And compared with greedy offloading scheme, our scheme can improve 30% of the success ratio and reduce 40% of the task duration on average of task offloading.

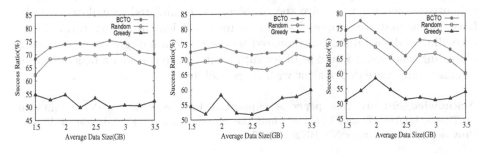

Fig. 6. Impact of data size: success ratio under uniform distribution, normal distribution and pareto distribution

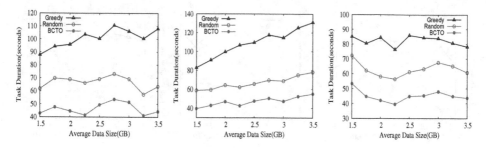

Fig. 7. Impact of data size: time duration under uniform distribution, normal distribution and pareto distribution

As shown in second figure of Fig. 6 and second figure of Fig. 7, when computation amount follows normal distribution. Compared with random offloading scheme, it is shown that our proposed offloading scheme can improve 5%~10% of the success ratio and reduce 30% of the task duration on average of task offloading. And compared with greedy offloading scheme, our scheme can improve 25% of the success ratio and reduce 45% of the task duration on average of task offloading.

In the third figure of Fig. 6 and third figure of Fig. 7, when computation amount follows pareto distribution. When compared with random offloading scheme, it is shown that our proposed offloading scheme can improve 5%~10% of the success ratio and reduce 35% of the task duration on average of task offloading. And compared with greedy offloading scheme, our scheme can improve 25% of the success ratio and reduce 45% of the task duration on average of task offloading.

7 Conclusion

In this paper. We first formulate a budget-constraint task offloading problem for delay minimization in edge computing environments, where the edge servers are equipped with limited computation and storage resources. Then we proposed a heuristic algorithm to solve the problem we formulated. Simulation results have shown that our proposed scheme is more efficient in success ratio of task offloading and task duration compared to the random and greedy computation offloading schemes. It would be of our future interest to consider a task offloading in more complicate deployment with users mobility.

Acknowledgement. This paper is supported by the NSFC under Grant No. 61472383, U1709217, and 61472385, and the Natural Science Foundation of Jiangsu Province in China under No. BK20161257.

References

1. Networking, V.: Cisco visual networking index: Global mobile data traffic forecast update, 2014-2019 white paper
2. Chen, Z., et al.: An empirical study of latency in an emerging class of edge computing applications for wearable cognitive assistance. In: SEC, p. 14 (2017)
3. Hu, Y.C., Patel, M., Sabella, D., Sprecher, N., Young, V.: Mobile edge computing–a key technology towards 5G. ETSI White Pap. 11(11), 1–16 (2015)
4. Truong, N.B., Lee, G.M., Ghamri-Doudane, Y.: Software defined networking-based vehicular adhoc network with fog computing. In: IFIP/IEEE International Symposium on Integrated Network Management (IM), pp. 1202–1207 (2015)
5. Barbera, M.V., Kosta, S., Mei, A., Stefa, J.: To offload or not to offload? the bandwidth and energy costs of mobile cloud computing. In: Proceedings IEEE INFOCOM, pp. 1285–1293, April 2013
6. Taleb, T., Samdanis, K., Mada, B., Flinck, H., Dutta, S., Sabella, D.: On multi-access edge computing: a survey of the emerging 5G network edge cloud architecture and orchestration. IEEE Commun. Surv. Tutor. 19(3), 1657–1681 (2017)
7. Zhang, S., Zhang, N., Zhou, S., Gong, J., Niu, Z., Shen, X.: Energy-aware traffic offloading for green heterogeneous networks. IEEE J. Sel. Areas Commun. 34(5), 1116–1129 (2016)
8. Tan, H., Han, Z., Li, X.Y., Lau, F.C.M.: Online job dispatching and scheduling in edge-clouds. In: IEEE INFOCOM 2017 - IEEE Conference on Computer Communications, pp. 1–9, May 2017
9. Tong, L., Li, Y., Gao, W.: A hierarchical edge cloud architecture for mobile computing. In: IEEE INFOCOM 2016 - The 35th Annual IEEE International Conference on Computer Communications, pp. 1–9, April 2016
10. You, C., Huang, K., Chae, H., Kim, B.H.: Energy-efficient resource allocation for mobile-edge computation offloading. IEEE Trans. Wirel. Commun. 16(3), 1397–1411 (2017)
11. Chen, M., Hao, Y.: Task offloading for mobile edge computing in software defined ultra-dense network. IEEE J. Sel. Areas Commun. 36(3), 587–597 (2018)
12. Chun, B.G., Ihm, S., Maniatis, P., Naik, M., Patti, A.: Clonecloud: elastic execution between mobile device and cloud. In: Proceedings of the Sixth Conference on Computer systems, pp. 301–314. ACM (2011)
13. Claffy, K.C., Polyzos, G.C., Braun, H.W.: Application of sampling methodologies to network traffic characterization. In: ACM SIGCOMM Computer Communication Review, vol. 23, pp. 194–203. ACM (1993)
14. Gordon, M.S., Jamshidi, D.A., Mahlke, S.A., Mao, Z.M., Chen, X.: Comet: code offload by migrating execution transparently. OSDI 12, 93–106 (2012)
15. Taleb, T., Dutta, S., Ksentini, A., Iqbal, M., Flinck, H.: Mobile edge computing potential in making cities smarter. IEEE Commun. Mag. 55(3), 38–43 (2017)
16. Jia, M., Cao, J., Liang, W.: Optimal cloudlet placement and user to cloudlet allocation in wireless metropolitan area networks. IEEE Trans. Cloud Comput. 5(4), 725–737 (2017)
17. Urgaonkar, R., Wang, S., He, T., Zafer, M., Chan, K., Leung, K.K.: Dynamic service migration and workload scheduling in edge-clouds. Perform. Eval. 91, 205–228 (2015)
18. Xiao, Y., Krunz, M.: Qoe and power efficiency tradeoff for fog computing networks with fog node cooperation. In: IEEE INFOCOM 2017 - IEEE Conference on Computer Communications, pp. 1–9, May 2017

19. Tran, T.X., Pompili, D.: Joint task offloading and resource allocation for multi-server mobile-edge computing networks (2017). arXiv preprint arXiv:1705.00704
20. Sakellariou, R., Zhao, H., Tsiakkouri, E., Dikaiakos, M.D.: Scheduling workflows with budget constraints. Integrated Research in GRID Computing, pp. 189–202. Springer, Boston (2007). https://doi.org/10.1007/978-0-387-47658-2_14
21. Oprescu, A.M., Kielmann, T.: Bag-of-tasks scheduling under budget constraints. In: 2010 IEEE Second International Conference on Cloud Computing Technology and Science, pp. 351–359, November 2010
22. Zhu, Q., Agrawal, G.: Resource provisioning with budget constraints for adaptive applications in cloud environments. In: Proceedings of the 19th ACM International Symposium on High Performance Distributed Computing, HPDC 2010, pp. 304–307. ACM, New York (2010)
23. Gharooni-fard, G., Moein-darbari, F., Deldari, H., Morvaridi, A.: Scheduling of scientific workflows using a chaos-genetic algorithm. Procedia Comput. Sci. $1(1)$, 1445–1454 (2010)
24. Bittencourt, L.F., Madeira, E.R.M.: Hcoc: a cost optimization algorithm for workflow scheduling in hybrid clouds. J. Internet Serv. Appl. $2(3)$, 207–227 (2011)
25. Byun, E.K., Kee, Y.S., Kim, J.S., Maeng, S.: Cost optimized provisioning of elastic resources for application workflows. Futur. Gener. Comput. Syst. $27(8)$, 1011–1026 (2011)
26. Li, J., Su, S., Cheng, X., Huang, Q., Zhang, Z.: Cost-conscious scheduling for large graph processing in the cloud. In: IEEE International Conference on High Performance Computing and Communications, pp. 808–813, September 2011
27. Chen, X., Jiao, L., Li, W., Fu, X.: Efficient multi-user computation offloading for mobile-edge cloud computing. IEEE/ACM Trans. Netw. $24(5)$, 2795–2808 (2016)
28. Mao, Y., You, C., Zhang, J., Huang, K., Letaief, K.B.: A survey on mobile edge computing: the communication perspective. IEEE Commun. Surv. Tutor. $19(4)$, 2322–2358 (2017)
29. Sun, Y., Zhou, S., Xu, J.: EMM: Energy-aware mobility management for mobile edge computing in ultra dense networks. IEEE J. Sel. Areas Commun. $35(11)$, 2637–2646 (2017)
30. Wu, C.Q., Lin, X., Yu, D., Xu, W., Li, L.: End-to-end delay minimization for scientific workflows in clouds under budget constraint. IEEE Trans. Cloud Comput. $3(2)$, 169–181 (2015)
31. Tawalbeh, L.A., Jararweh, Y., Ababneh, F., Dosari, F.: Large scale cloudlets deployment for efficient mobile cloud computing. JNW 10, 70–76 (2015)

Motion Trajectory Sequence-Based Map Matching Assisted Indoor Autonomous Mobile Robot Positioning

Wenping Yu[1], Jianzhong Zhang[1(✉)], Jingdong Xu[2], and Yuwei Xu[1]

[1] College of Cyberspace Security, Nankai University, Tianjin, China
yuwenping@mail.nankai.edu.cn,
{zhangjz,xuyw}@nankai.edu.cn
[2] College of Computer Science, Nankai University, Tianjin, China
xujd@nankai.edu.cn

Abstract. Position information is one of basic elements for context awareness of autonomous mobile robots. This paper studies the positioning algorithm of autonomous mobile robots suitable for search and rescue in dark building corridors and underground mine tunnels when an emergency occurs, and proposes a novel map matching aided positioning algorithm based on a Hidden Markov Model. This algorithm does not rely on a camera, and only uses the inertial sensors installed in mobile robot and the indoor map to realize the fusion of dead reckoning and map matching. Firstly, it detects the position-related motion postures during the motion process, and then the motion trajectory is divided into a sub-trajectory sequence. By matching the sub-trajectory sequence with the indoor map, the proposed algorithm achieves tracking and positioning of the mobile robot. In order to verify the effectiveness of the proposed algorithm, this paper adopts four-wheel differentially driven robot to conduct experimental analysis in an actual indoor scenario. The experimental results show that compared with the traditional dead reckoning technology, this algorithm can distinctly reduce the average positioning error of mobile robot, and it is robust to heading angle noises within a certain error range.

Keywords: Mobile robot · Indoor positioning
Hidden Markov Model · Posture pattern detection

1 Introduction

With the advancement of artificial intelligence, network and sensor technologies, the research and application of autonomous mobile robots have made remarkable progress in recent years. Indoor autonomous mobile robots are increasingly integrated into people's daily lives [1]. Autonomous mobile robots can be extensively used not only in modern intelligent warehouses, home services and many other aspects, but also in corridors of complex buildings, tunnels of subway

© Springer Nature Switzerland AG 2018
J. Vaidya and J. Li (Eds.): ICA3PP 2018, LNCS 11336, pp. 327–341, 2018.
https://doi.org/10.1007/978-3-030-05057-3_26

and underground mines when accidents occur. Therefore, the research of indoor autonomous mobile robot technology has gradually become a hot topic, and many domestic research institutes such as Tsinghua University, Harbin Institute of Technology, Nankai University and South China University of Technology are committed to the research and development of indoor autonomous mobile robots [2–6]. The autonomous positioning of the mobile robot is a process in which the robot autonomously determines its position in the working environment, and is one of the most basic problems in improving the autonomous capabilities of the mobile robot.

In terms of outdoor positioning, the Global Positioning System (GPS) has become a widely used positioning technology for mobile robots. However, in terms of indoor positioning, due to the blocking and interference of GPS signals by the external walls of buildings and indoor complex electromagnetic environment, there is no universal solution to the positioning problem of indoor mobile robots [7,8]. Currently, researchers have proposed a variety of positioning methods for indoor autonomous mobile robots, including navigation beacon-based positioning [9], computer vision-based positioning [10,11], dead reckoning positioning [12], map matching positioning [13,14] and simultaneous localization and mapping (SLAM) [15,16], and so on. Positioning techniques based on navigation beacons rely on a series of deployed feature signals to provide the stable and accurate location information, but require high deployment and maintenance costs. Dead reckoning technique uses inertial sensors or encoders to provide relatively accurate positions over short distances, but exists cumulative error that gradually increases as the distance travels, and the robot's starting point needs to be known in advance. Map matching positioning uses known indoor maps to construct topological maps, feature maps, and other abstract maps, and then the position of the mobile robot is obtained by matching the robot motion trajectory with the indoor maps. The real-time performance of map matching is relatively poor according to its realization principle. The SLAM technology has unique advantages in the face of unknown environments and can provide indoor floor plans or 3D maps while providing positioning [17]. However, this method requires mobile robots equipped with more complex sensor devices, such as infrared, ultrasonic radar and RGB-D vision systems. Therefore, it has higher implementation cost.

Corridors of buildings, subway station tunnels and underground mines often have complex passageways, similar to "mazes". In the event of an accident such as a fire, the power supply is damaged, the communication infrastructure becomes unusable and smoke and dust cause the lack of indoor lighting, and so on. All these situations pose challenges for the positioning of indoor autonomous mobile robots. Due to limitations in working environment or deployment conditions, it is difficult to establish visual or wireless navigation beacons in advance. Therefore, positioning technology based on navigation beacons is not suitable; the influence of high temperature and smoke on the indoor environment makes it difficult for cameras to provide image information, visual positioning technology fails; the timeliness of SLAM technology can not meet the urgent need for time factors in the above scenarios. In response to these problems, this paper introduces a hidden Markov model (HMM) based map matching algorithm that does not rely on a camera, only uses inertial sensors (accelerometer, gyroscope, and magnetometer) installed in autonomous mobile robots and known indoor maps to effectively track and position mobile robots.

2   Robot Motion Model and Positioning Method

In the field of indoor autonomous mobile robot positioning, dead reckoning technology and map matching technology have a good complementarity. This paper proposes a map matching-assisted positioning method based on motion trajectory sequence of mobile robot to realize the fusion of the above two technologies. The positioning algorithm uses stairs and corridor corners in the indoor environment as virtual landmarks. When the mobile robot passes through these landmarks, the inertial sensor data will show a specific pattern. Therefore, in this paper, the above landmarks are called posture-related positions. When the robot's movement distance is short, the dead reckoning technology can give the real-time position of the robot. When the robot's movement distance is long, the robot's motion trajectory can be divided into multiple sub-trajectories according to the landmarks, consecutive sub-trajectories form sub-trajectory sequence. With the help of HMM model, the above sub-trajectory sequence can be matched to the corresponding road in the indoor map, and then the position estimation of the mobile robot is given. Further, when the robot's motion trajectory is long enough, the absolute position of the mobile robot can still be estimated even without knowing the robot's starting point.

2.1   Robot Motion Model and Its Dead Reckoning Algorithm

In this paper, a four-wheel differential-driven mobile robot is used to study the positioning problem of autonomous mobile robots in indoor environment. The driving motor is a direct-current (DC) motor. The two driving motors on one side are connected in reverse parallel and use the *L298N* motor driving module to control the DC motor, and the mobile robot adopts the Raspberry Pi *B.V1.2* as the main control chip. According to the driving mode of the mobile robot, the motion models of the two wheels on each side of the wheeled robot are the same. Therefore, the motion model of the mobile robot can be simplified to a left and right two-wheel differential driving mode. Figure 1(a) shows the simplified motion model of the mobile robot, where (x, y) is the position coordinate of the mobile robot in the global coordinate system, Θ is the angle between heading direction of the mobile robot and the true north direction.

The autonomous mobile robot used in this paper has built-in digital compass, three-axis accelerometer and gyroscope. The digital compass gives the initial attitude of the mobile robot. The accelerometer and the gyroscope can measure the movement acceleration and rotation angular velocity of the mobile robot.

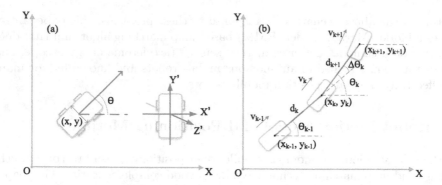

Fig. 1. Simplified motion model and its dead reckoning principle for four-wheel differentially driven robot. (a) Motion model and self coordinate system. (b) Dead reckoning in the global coordinate system.

The distance and heading direction change of the mobile robot can be obtained by integration, then we can derive the latest position and posture of the mobile robot.

In order to determine the position and posture of the mobile robot in the plane, we establish the global coordinate system OXY. Assuming that the starting point (x_0, y_0) is the origin of the coordinates and the starting attitude is the positive direction of the X-axis, then the position and posture of mobile robot at the k time can be expressed by vector $(v_k, \theta_k, x_k, y_k)^T$, where v_k denotes the instantaneous velocity of the mobile robot, θ_k denotes heading direction of the mobile robot and x_k, y_k denote the coordinates of the mobile robot in the global coordinate system, as shown in Fig. 1(b). When the update cycle of sensor data is very small, such as 5 ms in this paper, in one cycle, the trajectory of mobile robot can be approximated to a straight line, then the position of mobile robot at the k time can be recursively obtained by the Eq. 1.

$$\begin{pmatrix} v_k \\ \theta_k \\ x_k \\ y_k \end{pmatrix} = \begin{pmatrix} v_{k-1} \\ \theta_{k-1} \\ x_{k-1} \\ y_{k-1} \end{pmatrix} + \begin{pmatrix} 0.5(a_{k-1} + a_k)\Delta t \\ 0.5(\omega_{k-1} + \omega_k)\Delta t \\ d_k \cos \theta_{k-1} \\ d_k \sin \theta_{k-1} \end{pmatrix}, k \geq 1 \tag{1}$$

where, Δt is the time interval from the k-1 time to the k time, if the sensor fixes the data update period, Δt also represents the update period, a_k indicates the instantaneous acceleration in the direction of the mobile robot at the k time, which can be measured by the Y-axis component of the accelerometer, ω_k indicates the angular velocity of the heading direction at the k time, which can be measured by the Z-axis of the gyroscope, and d_k indicates the movement distance of the mobile robot from $k - 1$ to k, which can be drawn from the following Equation:

$$d_k = \frac{v_{k-1} + v_k}{2}\Delta t \tag{2}$$

2.2   Architecture Overview

The overall architecture of mobile robot positioning algorithm presented in this paper is shown in Fig. 2. The sensor data and the indoor floor plan are used as the input of the positioning algorithm. The sensor data is collected by the inertial sensors of the mobile robot and the indoor floor plan is obtained by manually input or the indoor electronic map construction algorithm such as SLAM technology. The indoor floor plan abstraction module translates the indoor floor plan into a directed graph, and the dead reckoning module and the motion posture detection module use the sensor data to give the relative displacement and position-related postures of the mobile robot respectively. The goal of map matching module is to match the motion trajectory of the mobile robot with the sequence of nodes in the directed graph, and then estimate the real time position of the mobile robot. First, the road segments are selected according to the heading direction estimation and the connection of road segments. Secondly, this algorithm updates the related parameters in the hidden Markov model according to the latest candidate road segments. Finally, it estimates the possibilities of all the alternative roads through the Viterbi decoder. When the proposed algorithm is in the convergence stage, the most possible alternative road is the optimal estimation. The final output of the algorithm proposed in this paper is the real-time position and heading direction of mobile robot.

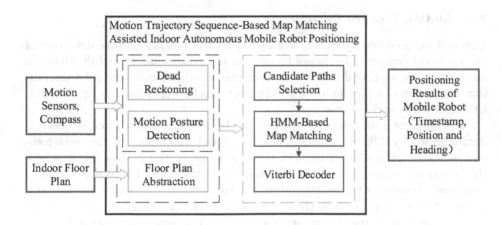

Fig. 2. System architecture of mobile robot positioning algorithm.

2.3   Indoor Floor Plan Abstraction

The posture-related positions divide the indoor roads into road segments. Taking the road segment as a node, the posture change pattern from one road segment to another as a directed edge, the indoor floor plan can be abstracted as a directed graph. Figure 3 shows an example of indoor floor plan and its corresponding directed graph. In this paper, a node is represented by the tuple

$(id, x_1, y_1, x_2, y_2, \varphi_1, \varphi_2)$, where $x_i, y_i, i = 1, 2$ represent coordinates of the two endpoints of the road segment, φ_1, φ_2 represent the heading direction when the mobile robot moves on the road segment and reaches the corresponding endpoint. A tuple $(id_1, id_2, x, y, change\ of\ motion\ attitude(MA))$ represents a directed edge between nodes, where, id_1 denotes the identity of the starting node, id_2 denotes the identity of the end node and x, y, MA represent the coordiantes of position and the change of motion attitude from the starting node to the end node, respectively.

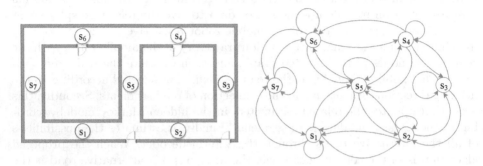

Fig. 3. Indoor floor plan example and its corresponding directed graph.

2.4   Motion Posture Detection

This section presents a decision tree model for the motion posture detection of indoor mobile robots. This paper focuses on the positioning of mobile robots in indoor 2D plane. Therefore, our decision tree considers only the relevant postures detection of a mobile robot on the plane, including stationary, go straight, left/right turns and U-turns.

The horizontal movement posture of the indoor autonomous mobile robot is distinguished by different modes of the horizontal component of the accelerometer and the vertical component of the gyroscope in the mobile robot, where the horizontal component of the accelerometer is the data of Y-axis in the local coordinate system of the mobile robot and the vertical component of the gyroscope is the data of Z-axis in the robot's local coordinate system. Furthermore, by extracting the vertical component of the accelerometer, this method can be easily extended to three-dimensional indoor positioning scenes.

Figure 4 shows a decision tree for the motion posture detection of an indoor autonomous mobile robot. The decision tree uses the signal characteristics of built-in acceleration and gyroscope to identify different motion posture patterns of the mobile robot. Considering that the linear velocity of the mobile robot is obtained from the integration of the acceleration horizontal component in time, the instantaneous velocity has an accumulated error at a certain moment. Therefore, the top layer of the decision tree uses the variance of the acceleration horizontal component to separate the stationary and going straight; the second level of the decision tree uses the rotation rate measured on the Z-axis of the

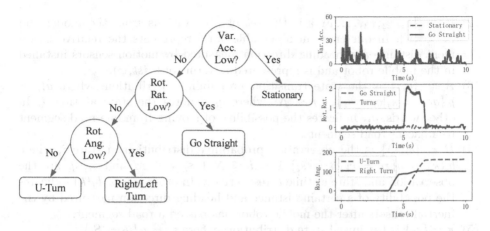

Fig. 4. Decision tree for motion posture detection.

gyroscope to separate turns and going straight; finally, the third level of the decision tree uses the rotation angle to separate the U-turn from the left or right turn.

3 HMM Based Map Matching Algorithm

With the help of the motion posture detection based on inertial sensor data, the motion trajectory of the mobile robot can be divided into sub-trajectory segments by position-related postures, such as left or right turn and U-turn, and these sub-trajectory segments form a sub-trajectory sequence in the time dimension. This section gives a detailed description of Hidden Markov Models for matching sub-trajectory sequence to indoor abstract graph.

3.1 Hidden Markov Model

A Hidden Markov Model is a time-series probability model that describes the state of a process using discrete random variables. A basic HMM can be represented as $\lambda = (S, V, A, B, \pi)$, where:

(1) $S = \{s_1, s_2, s_3, \ldots, s_N\}$ is the set of possible hidden states and $N = |S|$. In our case, each state represents an indoor road segment, that is, a node of the directed graph. Therefore, a state s is represented by the tuple in the form of $(id, x_1, y_1, \varphi_1, x_2, y_2, \varphi_2)$, where id is the identification of road segment, x_1, y_1, φ_1, x_2, y_2 and φ_2 are different attributes of node of the directed graph, respectively. It should be noted that if the mobile robot can reach another road segment by going straight from one road segment, these two road segments can be merged into a new road segment, also a new hidden state. The road segments s_4, s_6 can be combined into new road segments as shown in Fig. 5.

(2) $V = \{v_1, v_2, v_3, \ldots, v_M\}$ is the set of observations from the model and $M = |V|$. In our case, an observable state represents the relative movement distance and heading direction measured by motion sensors installed in the mobile robot and is represented in terms of $(dist, \varphi)$.

(3) $A = \{a_{ij}\}$ is the state transition probability distribution, where $a_{ij} = p\{q_{t+1} = s_j | q_t = s_i\}, i, j \leq N$, where q_t denotes the state at time t. In other words, a_{ij} indicates the possibility of moving from one road segment to adjacent road segments.

(4) $B = \{b_i(k)\}$ is the observation probability distribution in state i, where $b_i(k) = p\{z_t = v_k | q_t = s_i\}, 1 \leq i \leq N, 1 \leq k \leq M$ and z_t, q_t are the observation and state at time t, respectively. In other words, $b_i(k)$ indicates the possibility of a certain distance and heading direction measured by the inertial sensors after the mobile robot has passed a road segment.

(5) $\pi = \{\pi_i\}$ is the initial state distribution, where $\pi_i = p\{q_1 = S_i\}$.

3.2 Transition Probability Distribution (A)

The transition probability distribution refers to the possibility of moving from a hidden state to the next hidden state. In this paper, it also means the possibility of moving from one road segment to the adjacent road segment. The adjacent road segments are divided by posture-related positions. Each posture-related position has a corresponding motion posture. The higher the degree of matching between the mobile robot's motion posture and position-related posture is, the greater the probability that the mobile robot moves from one road segment to another road segment through this posture-related position is, and vice versa. Therefore, we use the degree of matching between the motion posture of the mobile robot and position-related posture to represent the transition probabilities between adjacent road segments. Let e^{ij} denote the edge of the directed graph from s_i to s_j, the corresponding position-related posture can be represented by $e^{ij}.MA$ according to definition in Sect. 2.3. Given the motion posture of the mobile robot $Rob_{MA}(t)$ at time t. The probability from s_i to s_j is shown in Eq. 3, where $p(Rob_{MA}(t)|e^{ij}.MA)$ can be obtained from the motion posture confusion matrix in Sect. 2.4.

$$p(s_{j,t}|s_{i,t-1}) = p(s_j|s_i, Rob_{MA}(t)) = p(Rob_{MA}(t)|e^{ij}.MA) \tag{3}$$

3.3 Observation Probability Distribution (B)

In this paper, an observable state consists of the relative displacement of the mobile robot and the heading direction, and the two are independent of each other. Therefore, the observable probability distribution can be defined as:

$$P(v_{k,t}|s_{j,t}) = P(\varphi(t)|s_{j,t}) \cdot P(dist(t)|s_{j,t}) \tag{4}$$

where, $P(\varphi(t)|s_{j,t})$ represents the observable probability of the mobile robot's heading direction at time t, and $P(dist(t)|s_{j,t})$ denotes the observable probability determined by the relative displacement of the mobile robot.

The higher the degree of matching between the heading direction of the mobile robot and the road segment, the greater the possibility that the mobile robot is located in the road segment. In the indoor environment, the error of the heading direction of the mobile robot not only comes from the accumulation error, but also comes from the interference of various metal materials in the buildings. In general, the error of the heading direction is relatively large and it is difficult to accurately model this error. Therefore, in this paper, Eq. 5 is used to model the heading direction in the observable state.

$$P(\varphi(t)|s_{j,t})$$
$$= P\{\varphi(t)|s_j.\varphi_i, i = 1, 2\} = \begin{cases} 1, if|\varphi(t) - s_j.\varphi_i| < H_{TH}, i = 1, 2 \\ 0, others \end{cases} \quad (5)$$

where, H_{TH} is a constant threshold used to determine whether the heading direction of the mobile robot matches the direction of the road segment or not. In order to avoid that the correct road segment is excluded due to the large error of the heading direction, H_{TH} is set to $59°$ in this paper.

The relative displacement error of the mobile robot mainly comes from the accumulative error caused by the acceleration error in the dead reckoning process. Here we assume that the relative displacement of the mobile robot obeys the Gaussian distribution. On the one hand, intuitively speaking, the closer the relative displacement of the mobile robot and the length of the road segment is, the more likely the mobile robot is located in the road segment; on the other hand, For the road segments whose lengths are much larger than the relative displacement of the mobile robot, all of them should have the same possibility. Combining the above two situations, this paper uses Eq. 6 to model the relative displacement in the observable state.

$$P(dist(t)|s_{j,t})$$
$$= P\{dist(t)|s_j.dist\} = \begin{cases} \frac{1}{\sqrt{2\pi}\sigma_d}e^{-4.5}, dist(t) + 3\sigma_d \le s_j.dist \\ \frac{1}{\sqrt{2\pi}\sigma_d}e^{-\frac{(dist(t)-s_j.dist)^2}{2\sigma_d^2}}, others \end{cases} \quad (6)$$

where $s_j.dist$ is the length of the road segment, which can be derived from the two endpoints of the road segment s_j and σ_d is the standard deviation of the relative displacement of the mobile robot at time t. In order to estimate the value of σ_d, this paper firstly tests the change of the accelerometer's value Δa when the mobile robot is stationary, and estimates the standard deviation of the acceleration σ_a based on the absolute median error (MAD) of the test data [18]. It can be inferred that there is a secondary relationship between σ_d and σ_a according to the principle of the dead reckoning described in Sect. 2.1.

$$\sigma_a = 1.4826 \times median(|\Delta a|) \quad (7)$$

3.4   Initial State Distribution

If the starting point of the mobile robot is already known, then the road segment where the starting point is located is the initial state, and the probability is set to 1; if the starting point of the moving robot is unknown, all candidates can be selected by Eq. 5 based on the initial heading direction information of the mobile robot and the initial probability distribution is a uniform distribution over the candidate road segments.

3.5   Optimal Motion Trajectory Estimation

Based on the above-defined Hidden Markov Model, this paper uses Viterbi algorithm to determine the optimal estimation of the moving trajectory of a mobile robot. For a given observable state sequence $(z_1, z_2, ..., z_k)$, the goal of the Viterbi algorithm is to find the most possible hidden state sequence $(q_1, q_2, ..., q_k)$. Figure 5 briefly illustrates the decoding process of the Viterbi algorithm.

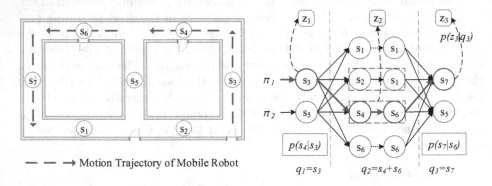

Fig. 5. Illustration of the proposed HMM model Viterbi decoding.

The Viterbi decoder is implemented by the dynamic programming method. First, a Viterbi variable is defined to represent the maximum probability that the Hidden Markov Model will reach the state s_i along a path at time t:

$$\delta_t(i) = \max P\{q_1, q_2, \cdots, q_t = s_i, z_1, z_2, \cdots, z_t | \lambda\} \tag{8}$$

At time $t+1$, the maximum probability reaching the hidden state s_j can be recursively derived from the Viterbi variable at time t by the following equation.

$$\delta_{t+1}(j) = [\max_i(\delta_t(i) \cdot P\{q_{t+1} = s_i | q_t = s_j\})] \cdot P\{z_{t+1} | q_{t+1}\}, 1 \leq t \leq k \tag{9}$$

By recording the backward pointers, at time k, the most likely hidden state sequence, that is, the optimal estimation of the motion trajectory of the mobile robot can be obtained by the path backtracking method.

4   Evaluation

We uses the wheeled mobile robot described in Sect. 2 to complete the experimental analysis. The experimental environment is the fifth floor of a teaching hall on our campus. The experimental area is divided into east and west parts, and the east part is approximately $84.85 * 66.8$ (m^2). The west part is approximately $68.7 * 106.75$ (m^2), the length of connecting corridor between two parts is 46.25 m and the width is 2.4 m. The overall layout is shown in Fig. 6. In order to record the real position of the robot during the movement, this article divides the experimental area into squares of $0.8 * 0.8$ (m^2) and marks every small areas. In the experiment process, another mobile robot with camera is used to move in parallel with the robot to record real-time positions. In the experimental area, the robot moves along the two planned trajectories denoted as T_1 and T_2 in Fig. 6. The length of T_1 is 181.9 m, including 3 posture-related positions. The whole trajectory is divided into 4 sub-trajectories. The length of T_2 is 180.5 m, including 2 posture-related positions, the whole trajectory is divided into 3 sub-trajectories, and the mobile robot repeats 9 times for each trajectories.

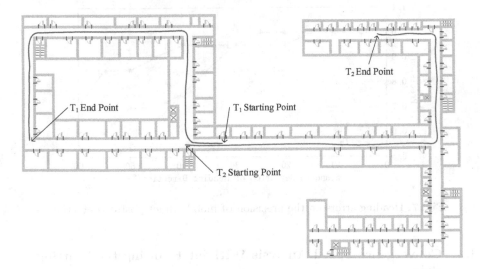

Fig. 6. Indoor floor plan of experimental environment and mobile robot trajectories.

4.1   Influence of Heading Direction Errors

When the starting point is unknown, the convergence performance of the algorithm is closely related to the detection results of position-related postures. In general, after at least correctly detected two consecutive position-related postures, the map matching algorithm based on the posture detection is likely to converge. Facing the position-related posture detection in 2D floor plan, such as left and right turning, the error of the heading direction has a greater impact on the detection results. Therefore, this section first analyzes the influence of heading direction error on the convergence performance of map matching algorithm. Here, we first define the precision of position-related posture detection by Eq. 10.

$$Precison = \frac{Number\ of\ Correctly\ Detected\ Consecutive\ Two\ Postures}{Total\ Number\ of\ Consecutive\ Two\ Postures}$$

(10)

Supposing that the distribution of the heading direction estimation error obeys Gaussian and the average is 0. Based on the raw data of the heading direction, a Gaussian random value is added to simulate different degrees of error. Figure 7 shows the variation of the precision of position-related posture detection under different values of the standard deviation of the heading direction error. It can be seen from Fig. 7 that the precision of position-related posture detection is stable under certain heading direction error conditions, but when the standard deviation of heading direction error reaches a certain level (T_1 is 40° and T_2 is 30°), the precision drops rapidly.

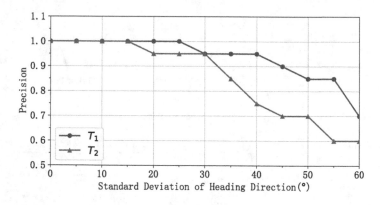

Fig. 7. Heading errors on the precision of mobile robot posture detection.

4.2   Convergence Speed Analysis Without Knowing the Starting Point

If the starting point is unknown, after the mobile robot moves a certain distance, the algorithm can still converge and finally estimate the real-time position of the mobile robot. The distance before convergence of the algorithm represents the convergence performance of the positioning algorithm. In order to evaluate the convergence performance of the proposed map matching algorithm, we compare the proposed map matching algorithm with the *semMatch* algorithm proposed in [18] because *semMatch* has certain similarities with the algorithm presented in this paper. The hidden Markov model is also used to implement map matching operations in *semMatch*, however, the details of the HMM model are slightly different.

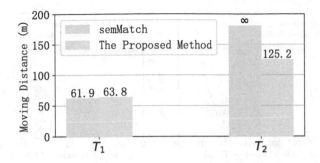

Fig. 8. Distance traveled before convergence for each trajectory.

Using the same decision tree model to detect the position-related postures in the trajectory of mobile robot, Fig. 8 shows the convergence performance of the two algorithms. On the one hand, for T_1, both algorithms reach the convergence state after passing through two posture-relate positions. However, the algorithm proposed in this paper needs to observe the subsequent road segment after detect the corresponding posture, so the convergence performance is slightly worse. When it reaches the convergence state, the mobile robot moves 1.9 m more. On the other hand, for T_2, the algorithm proposed in this paper reaches the convergence state shortly after the correct detection of the first position-related posture, but *semMatch* does not converge due to the symmetry of indoor road network denoted by ∞ in Fig. 8. The main reason is the difference in the HMM model definition of the two map matching algorithms. The hidden state of the map matching algorithm proposed in this paper is the straight road segment in the indoor road network. For T_2, the mobile robot firstly pass a long enough road segment, and the proposed algorithm combines this observable state with the subsequent detection of the first position-related posture to achieve the convergence.

4.3   Online Positioning Performance with Knowing the Starting Point

If the starting point is already known, the proposed algorithm does not need to pass the motion trajectory matching stage to converge. After convergence, the algorithm can track the moving trajectory of the mobile robot in real time. We use the Euler distance between the real position of the mobile robot and the position estimate given by the algorithm to analyze the real-time positioning performance. Figure 9 shows the variation of positioning error of the mobile robots with increasing distances on both T_1 and T_2 trajectories.

When the motion trajectory does not include posture-related positions, the map matching assisted positioning technology proposed in this paper is equivalent to the traditional dead reckoning technology, but after detecting the posture-related positions, the known coordinates of the posture-related positions can be used to calibrate the real-time position estimation of the robot. The real-time

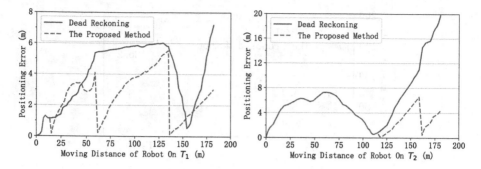

Fig. 9. Online positioning errors for each trajectory.

positioning results of the mobile robot on T_1 and T_2 shown in Fig. 9 verify this trend. For T_1, the average positioning error decreases from 4.0 m to 2.49 m, while for T_2, the average positioning error decreases from 6.58 m to 3.39 m. From the experimental results, it can be deduced that in the actual environment, with the density of posture-related positions increasing, the improvement of positioning performance of the proposed algorithm is more obvious.

5   Conclusion

In order to solve the difficult problem of positioning of autonomous mobile robots in dark complex building corridors, subway tunnels, or underground mines after sudden accident such as a fire, this paper proposes an indoor autonomous mobile robot tracking and positioning algorithm based on a novel hidden Markov Model. In the structured indoor environment, this method uses the detection of position-related postures to match the motion trajectory of mobile robot to the abstraction of indoor floor plan. Compared with the traditional dead reckoning technology, the proposed algorithm can significantly reduce the influence of cumulative errors on the positioning accuracy, and is robust to the heading direction and acceleration value noises within a certain error range. This algorithm does not rely on cameras, and uses only motion sensors installed in autonomous mobile robots and known indoor floor plan to achieve fusion positioning of dead reckoning and map matching techniques, even when the starting point is unknown. This algorithm has the characteristics of simple deployment, low manufacturing cost and easy operation.

Acknowledgment. This work was supported by the National Natural Science Foundation of China (No. 61702288), the Natural Science Foundation of Tianjin in China (No. 16JCQNJC00700) and the Fundamental Research Funds for the Central Universities.

References

1. Garcia, E., Jimenez, M.A., De Santos, P.G., Armada, M.: The evolution of robotics research. Robot. Autom. Mag. IEEE **14**(1), 90–103 (2007)
2. Wu, J., Li, T.M., Tang, X.Q.: Robust trajectory tracking control of a planar parallel mechanism. J. Tsinghua Univ. **5**, 642–646 (2005)
3. Wu, J., Wang, D., Wang, L.: A control strategy of a two degrees-of-freedom heavy duty parallel manipulator. J. Dyn. Syst. Meas. Contr. **137**(6), 061007 (2015)
4. Yang, J., Yang, J., Cai, Z.: An efficient approach to pose tracking based on odometric error modelling for mobile robots. Robotica **33**(6), 1231–1249 (2015)
5. Yuan, X., Wang, D., Yan, Y.: Self-positioning of robot based on dead reckoning and ultrasonic data fusion (in chinese). J. Naval Univ. Eng. **21**(5), 67–72 (2009)
6. Yu, N., Wang, S., Xu, C.: RGB-D based autonomous exploration and mapping of a mobile robot in unknown indoor environment. Robot **39**(6), 860–871 (2017). (in chinese)
7. Bachrach, A., De Winter, A., He, R., Hemann, G.: Range - robust autonomous navigation in GPS-denied environments. In: IEEE International Conference on Robotics and Automation, pp. 1096–1097. IEEE (2011)
8. Bao, H., Wong, W.C.: An indoor dead-reckoning algorithm with map matching. In: 2013 9th International Wireless Communications and Mobile Computing Conference (IWCMC), pp. 1534–1539. IEEE (2013)
9. Tang, H., Chen, W., Wang, J.: Artificial landmark distribution based on multi-ary m-sequence. Robot **36**(1), 29–35 (2014). (in chinese)
10. Lu, Y., Song, D.: Visual navigation using heterogeneous landmarks and unsupervised geometric constraints. IEEE Trans. Robotic. **31**(3), 736–749 (2015)
11. Gao, X., Zhang, T.: Unsupervised learning to detect loops using deep neural networks for visual slam system. Auton. Robots **41**(1), 1–18 (2017)
12. Kim, J.H., Lee, J.C.: Dead-reckoning scheme for wheeled mobile robots moving on curved surfaces. J. Intell. Robotic Syst. **79**(2), 211–220 (2015)
13. Grisetti, G., Stachniss, C., Burgard, W.: Improved techniques for grid mapping with rao-blackwellized particle filters. IEEE Trans. Robotics **23**(1), 34–46 (2007)
14. Cheng, H., Chen, H., Liu, Y.: Topological indoor localization and navigation for autonomous mobile robot. IEEE Trans. Autom. Sci. Eng. **12**(2), 729–738 (2015)
15. de la Puente, P., Rodríguez-Losada, D.: Feature based graph-slam in structured environments. Auton. Robots **37**(3), 243–260 (2014)
16. Havangi, R., Taghirad, H.D., Nekoui, M.A., Teshnehlab, M.: A square root unscented fastslam with improved proposal distribution and resampling. IEEE Trans. Ind. Electron. **61**(5), 2334–2345 (2014)
17. Richter, C., Vega-Brown, W., Roy, N.: Bayesian learning for safe high-speed navigation in unknown environments. In: Bicchi, A., Burgard, W. (eds.) Robotics Research. SPAR, vol. 3, pp. 325–341. Springer, Cham (2018). https://doi.org/10.1007/978-3-319-60916-4_19
18. Aly, H., Youssef, M.: Semmatch: road semantics-based accurate map matching for challenging positioning data. In: The 23rd SIGSPATIAL International Conference on Advances in Geographic Information Systems, p. 5. ACM (2015)

Towards the Independent Spanning Trees in the Line Graphs of Interconnection Networks

Baolei Cheng[1,2,3], Jianxi Fan[1,2(✉)], Xiaoyan Li[1], Guijuan Wang[1],
Jingya Zhou[1], and Yuejuan Han[1]

[1] School of Computer Science and Technology, Soochow University,
Suzhou 215006, China
{chengbaolei,jxfan,jy_zhou,hyj}@suda.edu.cn,
{xyli,20164027004}@stu.suda.edu.cn
[2] Jiangsu High Technology Research Key Laboratory for Wireless Sensor Networks,
Nanjing 21000, Jiangsu, China
[3] Provincial Key Laboratory for Computer Information Processing Technology,
Soochow University, Suzhou, China

Abstract. Node/edge-Independent spanning trees (ISTs) have
attracted a lot of attention in the past twenty years. Many results such
as edge-disjoint Hamilton cycles, traceability, number of spanning trees,
structural properties, topological indices, etc, have been obtained on line
graphs, and researchers have applied the line graphs of some interconnection networks into data center networks, such as SWCube, BCDC,
etc. However, node/edge conjecture is still open for n-node-connected
interconnection network with $n \geq 5$. So far, results have been obtained
on a lot of special interconnection networks, but few results are reported
on the line graphs of them. In this paper, we consider the problem of
constructing node-ISTs in a line graph G of an interconnection network
G'. We first give the construction of node-ISTs in G' based on the edge-
ISTs in G. Then, an algorithm to construct node-ISTs in G based on
the edge-ISTs in G' is presented. At the end, simulation experiments
on the line graphs of hypercubes show that the maximal height of the
constructed node-ISTs on the line graph of n-dimensional hypercube is
$n + 1$ for $n \geq 3$.

Keywords: Independent spanning trees · Internally disjoint paths
Line graph · Interconnection network

1 Introduction

Node/edge-Independent spanning trees (ISTs) can be used in reliable communication protocols [2,20], one-to-all broadcasting [29], multi-node broadcasting [4],
reliable broadcasting, and secure message distribution [3]. Therefore, the problem to construct multiple node/edge-ISTs for a given interconnection network is
becoming an important issue.

© Springer Nature Switzerland AG 2018
J. Vaidya and J. Li (Eds.): ICA3PP 2018, LNCS 11336, pp. 342–354, 2018.
https://doi.org/10.1007/978-3-030-05057-3_27

We focus on the well-known two conjectures on the existence of ISTs in any interconnection network [20,33] as follows:

Conjecture 1. Given an n-node-connected interconnection network G with $n \geq 1$, there exist n node-ISTs rooted at an arbitrary node in G.

Conjecture 2. Given an n-edge-connected interconnection network G with $n \geq 1$, there exist n edge-ISTs rooted at an arbitrary node in G.

Khuller and Schieber gave a proof that if any n-node-connected interconnection network has n node-ISTs, then any n-edge-connected interconnection network has n edge-ISTs [21]. However, Gopalan and Ramasubramanian found a counterexample to disprove Khuller and Schieber's results [12]. Thus, either the node conjecture implies the edge conjecture or vice versa is still an open problem. For any interconnection network with $n \leq 4$, Conjectures 1 and 2 were solved in [9,10,13,16,20,33]. For $n \geq 5$, Conjectures 1 and 2 have been solved for some restricted classes of networks, such as planar networks [17], product networks [26], hypercubes [30,32], locally twisted cubes [25], crossed cubes [5–7], Möbius cubes [8], even networks [22], odd networks [23], Gaussian networks [18], etc.

The line graph has received much attention by researchers in recent years. Results have been reported on edge-disjoint Hamilton cycles [24], traceability [28], number of spanning trees [11], structural properties [14], topological indices [27], treewidth [15], clique-perfectness [1], etc. Line graphs have applications in some data center networks by deploying servers on the edge of the original interconnection networks, such as SWCube [19], BCDC [31], etc. However, few results have been reported on the topic of independent spanning trees on line graphs. In this paper, we first adopt the definition of line graph G of n-edge-connected interconnection network G'. We mainly obtained the following results:

1. If there are n edge-ISTs rooted at an arbitrary node in G', then there are n node-ISTs rooted at an arbitrary node in G.
2. An algorithm to construct n node-ISTs rooted at an arbitrary node in G based on the n edge-ISTs rooted at an arbitrary node in G' is presented.
3. Some simulation results on the line graphs of hypercubes based on Java and JUNG technology are shown.

Finally, we pointed out that the algorithm proposed in this paper can be used to construct node-independent spanning trees on SWCube and BCDC data center networks.

2 Preliminaries

2.1 Graph Terminology and Notation

An interconnection network can be abstracted as a graph $G(V(G), E(G))$, where $V(G)$ denotes the node set and $E(G)$ denotes the edge set. In this paper, graphs and networks are used interchangeably. We can also use the decimal numbers to denote the nodes in G.

Two $\langle x, y \rangle$-paths P and Q started at x and ended with y are *edge-disjoint* if $E(P) \cap E(Q) = \varnothing$. Two $\langle x, y \rangle$-paths P and Q are *internally node-disjoint* if they are edge-disjoint and $V(P) \cap V(Q) = \{x, y\}$. Two spanning trees T_1 and T_2, rooted at the same node u in G, are *edge-independent* if the $\langle u, v \rangle$-path in T_1 and the $\langle u, v \rangle$-path in T_2 are edge-disjoint for each $v \in V(G) \backslash \{u\}$. Two spanning trees T_1 and T_2 rooted at u in network G are *node-independent* if the $\langle u, v \rangle$-path in T_1 and the $\langle u, v \rangle$-path in T_2 are internally node-disjoint for each $v \in V(G) \backslash \{u\}$. Clearly, if two trees T_1 and T_2 are node-independent spanning trees, then they are also edge-independent spanning trees. We can also use path(u, v, T) to denote the $\langle u, v \rangle$-path in a tree T rooted at node u.

A set of spanning trees rooted at the same node in G are edge-independent (resp., node-independent) if they are pairwisely edge-independent (resp., node-independent). We also use node-ISTs (resp., edge-ISTs) for short to represent node-independent spanning trees (resp., edge-independent spanning trees).

2.2   A Class of Networks—Line Graphs

Given a network G', its *line graph* G is a graph such that each vertex of G represents an edge of G' and two vertices of G are adjacent if and only if their corresponding edges share a common endpoint (which are incident) in G'. Now we provide Transformation 1 to demonstrate the construction of a line graph based on an existing network.

Transformation 1. Given a network G', we construct the line graph G by the following steps:

(1) For every edge started from node x and ended at y in $E(G')$, add a node $[x, y]$ to network G, which is referred to as *edge-node*.
(2) For every two adjacent edges (x, y) and (y, z) in G', connect $[x, y]$ with $[y, z]$ in G.

Figure 1 shows the network G' and its line graph G. Network G is derived from network G', where the number of edges in G' equals to the number of nodes in G.

Enlightened by Conjectures 1 and 2, the following interesting problem is naturally proposed.

Problem 1. Given n edge-ISTs in an n edge-connected network G', can we construct n node-ISTs in the line graph of G'?

In the following section, we try to answer this question by providing a general algorithm for any n-edge-connected network and its line graph.

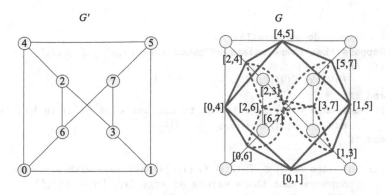

Fig. 1. A network G' and its line graph G.

3   Node-Independent Spanning Trees in Line Graphs

In this section, we first propose an algorithm, called NodeIST, to construct n node-ISTs in its line graph based on the n edge-ISTs in G'. Then, we prove that the n trees obtained by Algorithm NodeIST based on Transformation 1 are n node-ISTs.

3.1   Construction Algorithm of Node-Independent Spanning Trees for Line Graphs

We now present an algorithm, called NodeIST, to construct n node-ISTs T_1, $T_2, \ldots, T_n$ rooted at node $[u, v]$ in the line graph G of G', based on the n edge-ISTs $T_1', T_2', \ldots, T_n'$ rooted at u in n-edge-connected network G' and an edge (u, v). Since (u, v) and (v, u) are the same edge in G', we will let $[u, v]$ and $[v, u]$ denote the same node in G. For simplicity, we will always let an edge started at a smaller node and ended with a bigger node in the examples shown in Fig. 2. In Algorithm NodeIST, Step 1 is called to initialize trees $T_1, T_2, \ldots, T_n$. By Step 2, the edge started at the root node $[u, v]$ in each tree is determined and the edges derived from $T_1', T_2', \ldots, T_n'$ are determined. After executing Step 3, each tree contains all the edges in G.

```
Algorithm NodeIST
Input:  n edge-independent spanning trees T₁', T₂',
..., Tₙ' rooted at u in n-edge-connected network G',
v is an arbitrary adjacent node of u in G', where v > u;
Output: n node-independent spanning trees T₁, T₂, ...,
Tₙ rooted at node [u,v] in the line graph of G', denoted as
G;
Begin
Step 1:
1: V(Tᵢ) = V(G) and E(Tᵢ) = ∅ for i = 1 to n.
```

```
Step 2:
2: for i = 1 to n do in parallel
3:     Suppose that there exists u⁽ⁱ⁾ such that (u, u⁽ⁱ⁾) ∈ E(Tᵢ').
4:     if (u⁽ⁱ⁾) ≠ v)
5:          E(Tᵢ) = E(Tᵢ) ∪ {([u, v], [u, u⁽ⁱ⁾])}.
6:     end if
7:     if any edge (x, y) is adjacent to another edge (w, z) in V(Tᵢ')
8:          E(Tᵢ) = E(Tᵢ) ∪ {([x, y], [w, z])}.
9:     end if
Step 3:
10:    for any edge (x, y) ∈ E(G')\ (E(Tᵢ') ∪ {(u, v)}) with x < y do
11:        Suppose that there exists an edge (x, y⁽ⁱ⁾) ∈ E(Tᵢ').
12:        E(Tᵢ) = E(Tᵢ) ∪ {([x, y], [x, y⁽ⁱ⁾])}.
13:    end for
end
```

Example 1. Take the network G' and its line graph G in Fig. 1 for example. The three trees in Fig. 2(a) are not edge-ISTs in G', because the $\langle 0, 7 \rangle$-path in the second tree and the $\langle 0, 7 \rangle$-path in the third tree have the common edge $(2, 6)$. In Fig. 2(b), the three trees are edge-ISTs rooted at node 0 in G' which are isomorphic to each other. Suppose that the three trees in Fig. 2(b) from left to right are T_1', T_2', and T_3'. We let the three trees and node 1 as the input of Algorithm NodeIST. After the first step, we obtain trees T_1, T_2, and T_3 shown in Fig. 2(c), the edge sets of which are empty and the node sets of which contain all the edge-nodes of G'; after the second step, the three trees are shown in Fig. 2(d); lastly, the constructed node-ISTs are demonstrated in Fig. 2(e). We notice that each node in Fig. 2(b) is denoted by one decimal value, while each node in Fig. 2(c), (d), and (e) are denoted by two decimal values. Now, T_1, T_2, and T_3 are three node-ISTs rooted at $[0, 1]$ in G.

3.2 Correctness of Node-Independent Spanning Trees Obtained by Algorithm NodeIST

By Algorithm NodeIST, every edge of G is contained in T_i for $i = 1, 2, \ldots, n$. Thus, we have the following lemma.

Lemma 1. T_i obtained by Algorithm NodeIST is a spanning tree in G for any integer i with $1 \le i \le n$.

Proof. By Algorithm NodeIST, T_i contains all the nodes in $V(G)$ and it is easy to verify that T_i is a tree for any integer i with $1 \le i \le n$. Thus, the proof is completed.   □

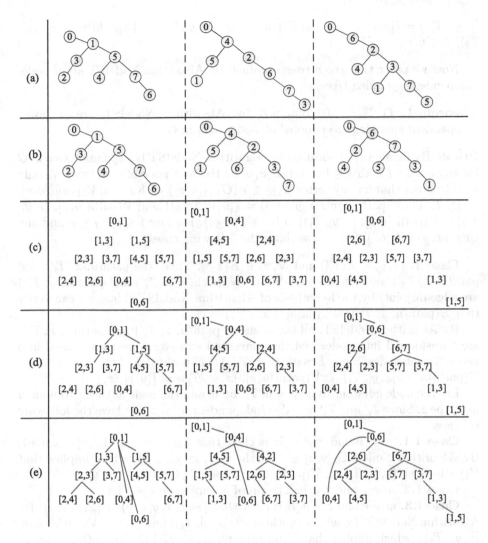

Fig. 2. (a) Wrong edge-ISTs. (b) Correct edge-ISTs. (c) Trees obtained by Step 1 of Algorithm NodeIST. (d) Trees obtained by Step 2 of Algorithm NodeIST. (e) Node-ISTs.

Suppose that T is a tree rooted at node $[u,v]$ and $[x,y]$ is an arbitrary node in the set $V(G)\backslash\{[u,v]\}$. We use path($[u,v]$, $[x,y]$, T) to denote the node set of the path started at $[u,v]$ and ended at $[x,y]$ in T. By the definition of independent spanning trees, we present the following lemma to redefine node-independent.

Lemma 2. Let T_i and T_j be two different spanning trees rooted at node $[u,v]$ in G where $1 \le i < j \le n$. T_i and T_j are node-independent if and only if for every node $[x,y]$ in G, $[x,y] \neq [u,v]$, $V(\text{path}([u,v], [x,y], T_i)) \cap V(\text{path}([u,v],$

$[x, y], T_j)) = \{[u, v], [x, y]\}$ and $V(\text{path}([u, v], [x, y], T_i)) \cup V(\text{path}([u, v], v[x, y], T_j)) \supset \{[u, v], [x, y]\}$.

Now we prove that the n trees obtained by Algorithm NodeIST are n node-independent spanning trees.

Theorem 1. $T_1, T_2, \ldots, T_n$ obtained by Algorithm NodeIST are n node-independent spanning trees rooted at node $[u, v]$ in G.

Proof. By Lemma 1, T_l obtained by Algorithm NodeIST is a spanning tree in G for any integer l with $1 \leq l \leq n$. Let $[u, v]$ be the root node of each tree. We only need to prove that for any vertex $[x, y] \in V(G) \setminus \{[u, v]\}$ with $x < y$, $V(\text{path}([u, v], [x, y], T_i)) \cap V(\text{path}([u, v], [x, y], T_j)) = \{[u, v], [x, y]\}$ and $V(\text{path}([u, v], [x, y], T_i)) \cup V(\text{path}([u, v], [x, y], T_j)) \supset \{[u, v], [x, y]\}$. For any $1 \leq i < j \leq n$ and any edge $(x, y) \in E(G') \setminus \{(u, v)\}$, we have the following cases:

Case 1. $(x, y) \in E(T_i')$ and $(x, y) \in E(T_j')$. Then, the $\text{path}(u, x, T_i')$ and $\text{path}(u, x, T_j')$ are edge-disjoint (Similarly, $\text{path}(u, y, T_i')$ and $\text{path}(u, y, T_j')$ are edge-disjoint) by the hypothesis of Algorithm NodeIST. Thus, we can verify that $E(\text{path}(u, x, T_i')) \cap E(\text{path}(u, x, T_j')) = \varnothing$.

By Algorithm NodeIST, all the edges in $\text{path}(u, x, T_i')$ and $\text{path}(u, x, T_j')$ are transformed into nodes and the connected two edges are transformed into two adjacent nodes. Since $E(\text{path}(u, x, T_i')) \cap E(\text{path}(u, x, T_j')) = \varnothing$, we have $V(\text{path}([u, v], [x, y], T_i)) \cap V(\text{path}([u, v], [x, y], T_j)) = \{[u, v], [x, y]\}$.

Let the node adjacent to node u in T_i' be w and the node adjacent to node u in T_j' be z. Since T_i' and T_j' are edge-independent, $w \neq z$. We have the following subcases.

Case 1.1. $w = v$ and $z \neq v$. It is clear that $\{w, z, x, y, u, v\} \supset \{x, y, u, v\}$. By Algorithm NodeIST, $[u, z] \in V(\text{path}([u, v], [x, y], T_j))$, which implies that $V(\text{path}([u, v], [x, y], T_i)) \cup V(\text{path}([u, v], [x, y], T_j)) \supset \{[u, v], [x, y]\}$.

Case 1.2. $w \neq v$ and $z = v$. The proof is similar to Case 1.1.

Case 1.3. $w \neq v$ and $z \neq v$. It is clear that $\{w, z, x, y, u, v\} \supset \{x, y, u, v\}$. By Algorithm NodeIST, $[u, w] \in V(\text{path}([u, v], [x, y], T_i))$ and $[u, z] \in V(\text{path}([u, v], [x, y], T_j))$, which implies that $V(\text{path}([u, v], [x, y], T_i)) \cup V(\text{path}([u, v], [x, y], T_j)) \supset \{[u, v], [x, y]\}$.

Case 2. $(x, y) \notin E(T_i')$ and $(x, y) \in E(T_j')$. By Algorithm NodeIST, if the node adjacent to node u in T_i' is v, we can verify that $V(\text{path}([u, v], [x, y], T_i))$ equals to the set of edge-nodes transformed from edges in $\text{path}(u, x, T_i')$ plus the set $\{[x, y]\}$. Otherwise, $V(\text{path}([u, v], [x, y], T_i))$ equals to the set of edge-nodes transformed from edges in $\text{path}(u, x, T_i')$ plus the set $\{[u, v], [x, y]\}$. The following proof is similar to Case 1.

Case 3. $(x, y) \in E(T_i')$ and $(x, y) \notin E(T_j')$. The proof is similar to Case 2.

Case 4. $(x, y) \notin E(T_i')$ and $(x, y) \notin E(T_j')$. By Algorithm NodeIST, if the node adjacent to node u in T_i' is v, we can verify that $V(\text{path}([u, v], [x, y], T_i))$ equals to the set of edge-nodes transformed from edges in $\text{path}(u, x, T_i')$ plus the set $\{[x, y]\}$. Otherwise, $V(\text{path}([u, v], [x, y], T_i))$ equals to the set of edge-nodes transformed from edges in $\text{path}(u, x, T_i')$ plus the set $\{[u, v], [x, y]\}$.

If the node adjacent to node u in T_j' is v, we can verify that $V(\text{path}([u, v], [x, y],$ $T_j))$ equals to the set of edge-nodes transformed from edges in $\text{path}(u, x, T_j')$ plus the set $\{[x, y]\}$. Otherwise, $V(\text{path}([u, v], [x, y], T_j))$ equals to the set of edge-nodes transformed from edges in $\text{path}(u, x, T_j')$ plus the set $\{[u, v], [x, y]\}$. Since T_i' and T_j' are edge-independent, the node adjacent to node u in T_i' and T_j' are different. The following proof is similar to Case 1.

By Lemma 2, T_i and T_j are independent.

As a result, the theorem holds.   □

Based on the n edge-independent spanning trees T_1', T_2', ..., T_n' rooted at u in n-edge-connected network G', v is an arbitrary adjacent node of u in G', where $v > u$, the n node-independent spanning trees T_1, T_2, ..., T_n rooted at node $[u, v]$ in G are constructed in parallel, thus we have the following theorem.

Theorem 2. The set of node-independent spanning trees $T_1, T_2, ..., T_n$ obtained by Algorithm NodeIST can be obtained in $O(N)$ time, where N is the number of nodes in G (or the number of edges in G').

Based on the above discussion, we further present the following observations.

Observation 1. Algorithm NodeIST can be improved to obtain optimized node-ISTs. For example, in Fig. 2(e), if we let the node $[1, 5]$ be adjacent to node $[5, 7]$ in the third tree. Then, we can obtain another set of optimized node-ISTs with lower height.

Observation 2. Given n node-independent spanning trees in an n-node-connected network G', we can also construct n node-independent spanning trees in the line graph of G' based on Algorithm NodeIST.

Observation 3. It is also interesting to study another similar algorithm with the reverse direction based on Algorithm NodeIST.

4   Simulation of Node-ISTs on the Line Graphs of Hypercubes

As well-known interconnection networks, hypercubes have received much attention from researchers. In this section, we mainly simulate the construction of node-ISTs on hypercubes based on Java and JUNG technology. The n-dimensional hypercube Q_n, is a graph consisting of 2^n nodes and $n2^{n-1}$ edges. Each node in Q_n is represented by binary strings of length n, and any two nodes in Q_n are adjacent whenever their corresponding strings differ in exactly one place. For example, Fig. 3 shows the four node-ISTs rooted at 0 in Q_4 constructed by the algorithm in [30], the maximal height of which is 5. To simulate the duplicate nodes by JUNG technology, which do not admit the same node in one canvas, here, the prefixes A, B, C, D are only used to distinguish nodes, for example, A0, B0, C0, D0 are used to denote the same node 0.

Since hypercube is node-symmetric, the line graph of hypercube is also node-symmetric. If the nodes in 4-dimensional hypercube are 0, 1, ..., 15, then there

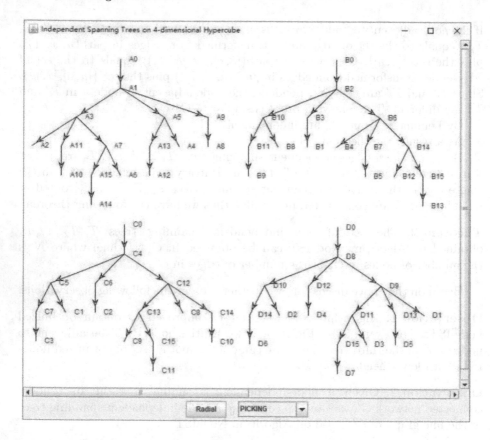

Fig. 3. 4 edge-ISTs rooted at 0 on 4-dimensional hypercube.

are 32 edge-nodes in the line graph of 4-dimensional hypercube. For simplification, we use the numbers 1, 2, ..., 32 to denote the edge-nodes, the corresponding relation is shown in Table 1, which will be used in the simulation program
to show the node-ISTs. Similarly, the prefixes a, b, c, d are only used by the
program to distinguish nodes, for example, a1, b1, c1, d1 are used to denote the
same node 1.

Table 1. Corresponding relations between numbers and edge-nodes.

1→ [0, 1]	2→ [0, 2]	3→ [0, 4]	4→ [0, 8]	5→ [2, 3]	6→ [1, 3]
7→ [1, 5]	8→ [3, 11]	9→ [1, 9]	10→ [2, 6]	11→ [3, 7]	12→ [6, 7]
13→ [4, 6]	14→ [6, 14]	15→ [7, 15]	16→ [5, 7]	17→ [4, 5]	18→ [2, 10]
19→ [4, 12]	20→ [5, 13]	21→ [8, 12]	22→ [12, 14]	23→ [12, 13]	24→ [14, 15]
25→ [13, 15]	26→ [10, 14]	27→ [11, 15]	28→ [9, 13]	29→ [8, 10]	30→ [10, 11]
31→ [9, 11]	32→ [8, 9]				

The node-ISTs rooted at 1 (corresponding to the edge-node $[0, 1]$ in the line graph of 4-dimensional hypercube) in the line graph of 4-dimensional hypercube based on Algorithm NodeIST are shown in Fig. 4, the height of the four trees are 4, 5, 5, 5, respectively. Take the internally node-disjoint paths between 1 and 25, the 4 paths are as follows:

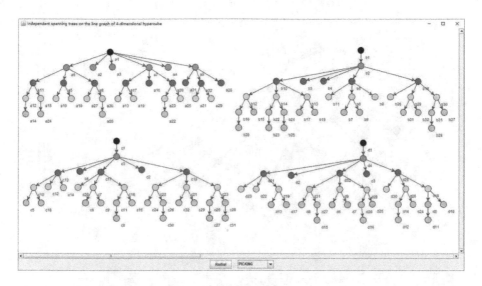

Fig. 4. The node-ISTs on the line graph of 4-dimensional hypercube.

$1\rightarrow 7\rightarrow 20\rightarrow 25$
$1\rightarrow 2\rightarrow 10\rightarrow 14\rightarrow 24\rightarrow 25$
$1\rightarrow 3\rightarrow 19\rightarrow 23\rightarrow 25$
$1\rightarrow 4\rightarrow 32\rightarrow 28\rightarrow 25$
The paths denoted in edge-nodes are as follows:
$[0, 1]\rightarrow [1, 5]\rightarrow [5, 13]\rightarrow [13, 15]$
$[0, 1]\rightarrow [0, 2]\rightarrow [2, 6]\rightarrow [6, 14]\rightarrow [14, 15]\rightarrow [13, 15]$
$[0, 1]\rightarrow [0, 4]\rightarrow [4, 12]\rightarrow [12, 13]\rightarrow [13, 15]$
$[0, 1]\rightarrow [0, 8]\rightarrow [8, 9]\rightarrow [9, 13]\rightarrow [13, 15]$
It is easy to verify that the paths between the edge-node $[0, 1]$ and any other edge-node are also internally node-disjoint.

The radial mode of the node-ISTs rooted at 1 are shown in Fig. 5. Here, the number of nodes deployed in the layers from the inside to the outside are 4, 9, 24, 39, 40, 12, respectively.

Simulation results show that the maximal height of the node-ISTs rooted at any node in the line graph of n-dimensional hypercube is $n+1$. We have the following observation.

Observation 4. The height of ISTs T_1 and T_i in the line graph of n-dimensional hypercube are n and $n + 1$ for $i = 2, 3, \ldots, n$, respectively, where $n \geq 3$.

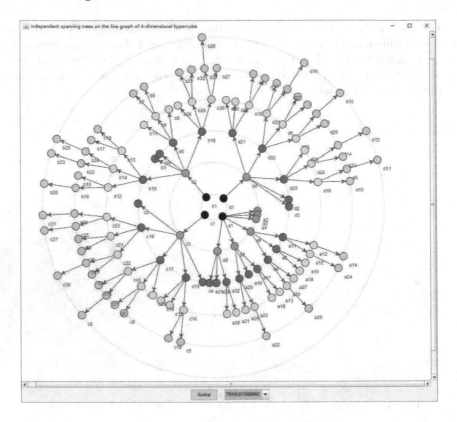

Fig. 5. The radial mode of node-ISTs.

Observing that all the height of the n optimal node-ISTs rooted at any node in n-dimensional hypercube Q_n is $n + 1$ [30] and $L(Q_n)$ contains more nodes than Q_n for $n \geq 3$, the set of node-ISTs rooted at any node in $L(Q_n)$ have advantages in the height with respect to the number of nodes.

If we abstract the interconnection network of severs in SWCube and BCDC, we obtain the line graph of generalized hypercube and crossed cube, respectively. Thus, we only need to construct independent spanning trees in the two networks. Let the input be the set of independent spanning trees from [26] and [31], we can use Algorithm NodeIST to construct independent spanning trees in the line graph of generalized hypercube and crossed cube, respectively.

5   Conclusions

In this paper, we have proved that if there are n edge-independent spanning trees rooted at an arbitrary node in the n-edge-connected network G', then there are n node-independent spanning trees rooted at an arbitrary node in the line graph of G'. An algorithm to construct node-ISTs in G based on the node/edge-ISTs in G' is also presented. Some simulations of independent spanning trees on the line graphs of hypercubes were presented and we also pointed out that the algorithm proposed in this paper can be used to construct independent spanning trees on SWCube and BCDC data center networks. It is still interesting to prove that either the node conjecture implies the edge conjecture, or vice versa.

Acknowledgment. This work is supported by National Natural Science Foundation of China (No. 61572337, No. 61502328, and No. 61602333), China Postdoctoral Science Foundation Funded Project (No. 2015M581858), the Natural Science Foundation of the Jiangsu Higher Education Institutions of China (No. 18KJA520009), the Jiangsu Planned Projects for Postdoctoral Research Funds (No. 1501089B and No. 1701173B), Opening Foundation of Jiangsu High Technology Research Key Laboratory for Wireless Sensor Networks (No. WSNLBKF201701), and Postgraduate Research & Practice Innovation Program of Jiangsu Province (No. KYCX17_2005 and No. KYCX18_2510).

References

1. Bonomom, F., Durán, G., Safe, M.D., Wagler, A.K.: Clique-perfectness of complements of line graphs. Discret. Appl. Math. **186**(1), 19–44 (2015)
2. Bao, F., Funyu, Y., Hamada, Y., Igarashi, Y.: Reliable broadcasting and secure distributing in channel networks. IEICE Trans. Fundam. Electron. Commun. Comput. Sci. **E81–A**, 796–806 (1998)
3. Bao, F., Igarashi, Y., Öhring, S.R.: Reliable broadcasting in product networks. Discret. Appl. Math. **83**(1–3), 3–20 (1998)
4. Chen, Y.-S., Chiang, C.-Y., Chen, C.-Y.: Multi-node broadcasting in all-ported 3-D wormhole-routed torus using an aggregation-then-distribution strategy. J. Syst. Arch. **50**(9), 575–589 (2004)
5. Cheng, B., Fan, J., Jia, X., Zhang, S.: Independent spanning trees in crossed cubes. Inf. Sci. **233**(1), 276–289 (2013)
6. Cheng, B., Fan, J., Jia, X., Wang, J.: Dimension-adjacent trees and parallel construction of independent spanning trees on crossed cubes. J. Parallel Distrib. Comput. **73**, 641–652 (2013)
7. Cheng, B., Fan, J., Lyu, Q., Zhou, J., Liu, Z.: Constructing independent spanning trees with height n on the n-dimensional crossed cube. Futur. Gener. Comput. Syst. **87**, 404–415 (2018)
8. Cheng, B., Fan, J., Jia, X., Jia, J.: Parallel construction of independent spanning trees and an application in diagnosis on Möbius cubes. J. Supercomput. **65**(3), 1279–1301 (2013)
9. Cheriyan, J., Maheshwari, S.N.: Finding nonseparating induced cycles and independent spanning trees in 3-connected graphs. J. Algorithms **9**(4), 507–537 (1988)
10. Curran, S., Lee, O., Yu, X.: Finding four independent trees. SIAM J. Comput. **35**(5), 1023–1058 (2006)
11. Dong, F., Yan, W.: Expression for the number of spanning trees of line graphs of arbitrary connected graphs. J. Graph Theory **85**(1), 74–93 (2017)
12. Gopalan, A., Ramasubramanian, S.: A counterexample for the proof of implication conjecture on independent spanning trees. Inf. Process. Lett. **113**(14–16), 522–526 (2013)
13. Gopalan, A., Ramasubramanian, S.: On constructing three edge independent spanning trees. SIAM J. Comput. (2011, submitted)

14. Hasunuma, T.: Structural properties of subdivided-line graphs. J. Discret. Algorithms **31**, 69–86 (2015)
15. Harvey, D.J., Wood, D.R.: Treewidth of the line graph of a complete graph. J. Graph Theory **79**(1), 48–54 (2015)
16. Hoyer, A., Thomas, R.: Four edge-independent spanning tree. SIAM J. Discret. Math. **32**(1), 233–248 (2018)
17. Huck, A.: Independent trees in planar graphs. Graphs Comb. **15**(1), 29–77 (1999)
18. Hussain, Z., AlBdaiwi, B., Cerny, A.: Node-independent spanning trees in Gaussian networks. J. Parallel Distrib. Comput. **109**, 324–332 (2017)
19. Li, D., Wu, J.: On data center network architectures for interconnecting dual-port servers. IEEE Trans. Comput. **64**(11), 3210–3222 (2015)
20. Itai, A., Rodeh, M.: The multi-tree approach to reliability in distributed networks. Inf. Comput. **79**(1), 43–59 (1988)
21. Khuller, S., Schieber, B.: On independent spanning trees. Inf. Process. Lett. **42**(6), 321–323 (1992)
22. Kim, J.-S., Lee, H.-O., Cheng, E., Lipták, L.: Independent spanning trees on even networks. Inf. Sci. **181**(13), 2892–2905 (2011)
23. Kim, J.-S., Lee, H.-O., Cheng, E., Lipták, L.: Optimal independent spanning trees on odd graphs. J. Supercomput. **56**(2), 212–225 (2011)
24. Li, H., He, W., Yang, W., Bai, Y.: A note on edge-disjoint Hamilton cycles in line graphs. Graphs Comb. **32**, 741–744 (2016)
25. Liu, Y.-J., Chou, W.Y., Lan, J.K., Chen, C.: Constructing independent spanning trees for locally twisted cubes. Theor. Comput. Sci. **412**(22), 2237–2252 (2011)
26. Obokata, K., Iwasaki, Y., Bao, F., Igarashi, Y.: Independent spanning trees of product graphs and their construction. IEICE Trans. Fundam. Electron. Commun. Comput. Sci. **E79–A**(11), 1894–1903 (1996)
27. Su, G., Xu, L.: Topological indices of the line graph of subdivision graphs and their Schur-bounds. Appl. Math. Comput. **253**, 395–401 (2015)
28. Tian, T., Xiong, L.: Traceability on 2-connected line graphs. Appl. Math. Comput. **321**, 1339–1351 (2018)
29. Tseng, Y.-C., Wang, S.-Y., Ho, C.-W.: Efficient broadcasting in wormhole-routed multicomputers: a network-partitioning approach. IEEE Trans. Parallel Distrib. Syst. **10**(1), 44–61 (1999)
30. Tang, S.-M., Wang, Y.-L., Leu, Y.-H.: Optimal independent spanning trees on hypercubes. J. Inf. Sci. Eng. **20**(1), 143–155 (2004)
31. Wang, X., Fan, J., Lin, C.-K., Zhou, J., Liu, Z.: BCDC: a high-performance, server-centric data center network. J. Comput. Sci. Technol. **33**(2), 400–416 (2018)
32. Yang, J.-S., Tang, S.-M., Chang, J.-M., Wang, Y.-L.: Parallel construction of optimal independent spanning trees on hypercubes. Parallel Comput. **33**(1), 73–79 (2007)
33. Zehavi, A., Itai, A.: Three tree-paths. J. Graph Theory **13**(2), 175–188 (1989)

POEM: Pricing Longer for Edge Computing in the Device Cloud

Qiankun Yu, Jigang Wu[✉], and Long Chen

Guangdong University of technology, Guangzhou 510006, China
yuqiankun1992@foxmail.com, asjgwucn@outlook.com, lonchen@mail.ustc.edu.cn

Abstract. Multiple access mobile edge computing has been proposed as a promising technology to bring computation services close to end users, by making good use of edge cloud servers. In mobile device clouds (MDC), idle end devices may act as edge servers to offer computation services for busy end devices. Most existing auction based incentive mechanisms in MDC focus on only one round auction without considering the time correlation. Moreover, although existing single round auctions can also be used for multiple times, users should trade with higher bids to get more resources in the cascading rounds of auctions, then their budgets will run out too early to participate in the next auction, leading to auction failures and the whole benefit may suffer. In this paper, we formulate the computation offloading problem as a social welfare optimization problem with given budgets of mobile devices, and consider pricing longer of mobile devices. This problem is a multiple-choice multi-dimensional 0-1 knapsack problem, which is a NP-hard problem. We propose an auction framework named MAFL for long-term benefits that runs a single round resource auction in each round. Extensive simulation results show that the proposed auction mechanism outperforms the single round by about 55.6% on the revenue on average.

Keywords: Edge computing · Computation offloading · Multiple rounds · Mobile device cloud · Long-term · Auction

1 Introduction

In the past few years, despite the increasing capabilities of mobile devices including smart phones, Internet of Things (IoT) devices, and wearable devices, resource requirements for mobile applications can often transcend the computation of a single device [1–4]. Therefore, mobile cloud computing is proposed to offload tasks to remote cloud for execution [5–9], though it may introduce longer delay and user experience may suffer. Moreover, long distance telecommunication will consume more energy. In recent work, multiple access mobile edge computing has been proposed as a promising technology to bring computation services close to end users, by making good use of edge cloud servers. There are three types of architecture used in edge computing [10]: edge server,

© Springer Nature Switzerland AG 2018
J. Vaidya and J. Li (Eds.): ICA3PP 2018, LNCS 11336, pp. 355–369, 2018.
https://doi.org/10.1007/978-3-030-05057-3_28

coordinator device, and device cloud. This paper uses the third architecture. The computation offloading [11,12] can be performed in Mobile Device Clouds (MDC) [13–16], which use idle resources of nearby mobile devices to execute tasks. However, mobile devices that provide idle resources may also incur extra cost to themselves, which should be monetary compensated.

To encourage more devices sharing their idle resources, several prior works have been done in MDC. Miluzzo et al. [17] proposed an incentive scheme in MDC. However, this scheme ignored the resource requirements of tasks. Song et al. [18] designed a non-competitive pricing mechanism, with a bill backlog threshold. If a device exceeds the threshold, it can reduce its bill backlog by providing services for others. Otherwise it will not be able to get the service. However, they do not consider whether the device has sufficient resources to provide services for others or not. Wang et al. [19] proposed a Stackelberg Game approach for cooperative application execution in mobile cloud computing. However, they do not consider that the mobile device is heterogeneous, different mobile devices may have different processing power levels and energy consumption levels. Therefore, the payment of the tasks should be different. In recent studies, auction has been widely used as one of the most popular incentive schemes in many areas, such as virtual machine allocation [20,21] and wireless spectrum allocation [22,23]. The celebrated VCG mechanism [24] is a well known type of auction. It is essentially the only type of auction that simultaneously guarantees both truthfulness and absolute economic efficiency. Li et al. [25] proposed an online spectrum auction framework. This mechanism can also be used in MDC's resource allocation, but buyer's budget constraints are not considered. Jin et al. [26] designed an incentive compatible auction mechanism for cloudlet resource sharing in mobile cloud computing. However, this mechanism uses a one-to-one match and assumes that the resource requirements are homogeneous. In this work, we consider a seller can serve multiple buyers and the resource requirements of buyers are heterogeneous. Wang et al. [27] designed an efficient auction mechanism to solve the task assignment problem in MDC. However, this auction mechanism assumes that every buyer must be allocated to resources. In this work, we consider that resources are limited and can not ensure that every buyer can be allocated resources. In MDC, existing auction mechanisms only focus on a single-round auction [26,27]. In many cases, we need multiple rounds of auctions. Although existing single round auctions can also be used for multiple times, the user's budget constraints should be considered. The budget is the total amount of money a buyer could pay, it plays a key role in designing periodical auctions.

Despite long-term and budget constraints are considered in crowdsourcing [28], tasks are homogeneous and a task can be allocated to multiple workers. However, authors in [28] as assumed unlimited resources at workers. In a resource limited MDC, idle mobile devices are unlikely to meet the needs of all users at the same time. So the scheme can't be used directly in MDC, which motivates us to design a long-term auction of multiple rounds with budget constraint. To design effective schemes, the following challenges should be property handled: (1) How to prevent the user's budget from running out prematurely by multi-round auction? (2) How to efficiently allocate resources for different bids of different devices? (3) How to attract more sellers to participate in MDC?

To solve the above challenges, in this paper, we consider Pricing lOnger for Edge coMputing in the device cloud (POEM). We aim to design a long-term auction of multiple rounds. The main features are as follows: (1) the mobile tasks are indivisible and the number of resources (CPU, memory, battery etc.) requirements for a task are different. (2) The number of resources requested by each user is not a fixed value in each round, and the amount of resources provided by the nearby mobile device is also not a fixed value in each round. (3) We punish the winning user to reduce the bid according to its remaining budget in the next round of the auction.

The main contributions of this paper are as follows:

- Considering the time correlation of resource allocation, we formulate the task offloading problem as an integer linear programming. And we design an MDC Auction Framework for Long-term (MAFL). The next round of genuine bids will be adjusted according to the results of the previous round.
- We design a Single Round Mobile Resources Auction (SRMRA) algorithm for comparing purposes with the MAFL. And we demonstrate the performance of the algorithm by proofs and extensive experiments.
- We conduct extensive simulation experiments to demonstrate the performance of our mechanism. MAFL is better than the single round auction SRMRA. MAFL outperforms SRMRA by about 12.2% on revenue when the number of users is 40, the 80 round auction is performed. MAFL outperforms SRMRA by about 55.6% on revenue on average when the number of users changed from 10 to 80, the 80 round auction is performed.

The rest of the paper is organized as follows. Section 2 describes the system model and problem formulation. The auction mechanism for single round MDC's resources allocation is designed in Sect. 3. Section 4 proposes an auction framework in the MDC for long-term optimisation. Section 5 presents the simulation results. Finally, we conclude the paper in Sect. 6.

2 Problem Definition

2.1 System Model

We assume that the total time of the whole auction period is T (T is a long time) [21], and divide T into multiple time slots. Perform one round auction at each time slot $l \in \mathcal{L}$, where $\mathcal{L} = \{1, 2, 3, \cdots, L\}$ and L is the total number of auction rounds. There are U users in the MDC, each user $u \in \mathcal{U}$ needs some resources (CPU, memory, battery etc.) to perform its indivisible tasks, where $\mathcal{U} = \{1, 2, 3, \cdots, U\}$. There are M sellers in MDC, each seller $m \in \mathcal{M}$ can share their resources with others, where $\mathcal{M} = \{1, 2, 3, \cdots, M\}$. Let $r_u^{(l)}$ be the amount of resources requested by user u and $R_m^{(l)}$ be the amount of resources provided by the seller in the l-th round. The U users are bidders in the auctions, each user submits its valuation $\mathcal{V}_u^{(l)} = \{v_{u,1}^{(l)}, v_{u,2}^{(l)}, \cdots, V_{u,M}^{(l)}\}$ in round l, where $v_{u,m}^{(l)} \in \mathcal{V}_u^{(l)}$ denotes the valuation of buyer for seller m. Moreover, as each user is also budget constrained, we use B_u to denote the user u's total budget in all rounds. Of course, sellers can not provide unlimited resources. So we use W_m to represent the total number of resources provided by the seller m in all rounds. Specifically, the resource allocation is determined by $\mathcal{Y}_u^{(l)} = \{y_{u,1}^{(l)}, y_{u,2}^{(l)}, \cdots, y_{u,M}^{(l)}\}$, where $y_{u,m}^{(l)} \in \{0,1\}$ is a binary indicator whose value is 1 if user u's tasks is performed on seller m in round l and 0 otherwise. We list basic notations used in this paper in Table 1.

Table 1. Basic notations

Notation	Descriptions
T	The total time of whole auction period
L	The total number of auction rounds
U, M	The total number of users and sellers
$\mathcal{L}$	The set $\{1, 2, 3, \cdots, L\}$
$\mathcal{U}, \mathcal{M}$	The set of users and sellers
$r_u^{(l)}$	The amount of resources requested by user u in the l-th round
$R_m^{(l)}$	The amount of resources provided by the seller m in the l-th round
$\mathcal{V}_u^{(l)}$	The set of u's valuation in the l-th round
$\mathcal{Y}_u^{(l)}$	The set of u's indicator in the l-th round
$v_{u,m}^{(l)}$	The user u's valuation for seller m in the l-th round
$y_{u,m}^{(l)}$	The user u wins the resources provided by the seller m in the l-th round or not
B_u	The user u's total budget
W_m	The total number of resources provided by seller m

2.2 Problem Formulation

The objective of the MDC (mobile device clouds) resource allocation problem is to maximize the user's bids. In the whole auction period, the higher the total price of the user's bids, the more compensation of the device that provided, so the more people will be attracted to share the idle resources in his device. We formalize our objective as follows:

$$\textbf{OPT-1} \quad obj: \max \sum_{l \in \mathcal{L}} \sum_{u \in \mathcal{U}} \sum_{m \in \mathcal{M}} v_{u,m}^{(l)} y_{u,m}^{(l)} \tag{1}$$

subject to:

$$\sum_{m \in \mathcal{M}} y_{u,m}^{(l)} \le 1 \quad \forall u \in \mathcal{U} \; \forall l \in \mathcal{L} \tag{1-1}$$

$$\sum_{u \in \mathcal{U}} r_u^{(l)} y_{u,m}^{(l)} \leq R_m^{(l)} \quad \forall m \in \mathcal{M} \ \forall l \in \mathcal{L} \tag{1-2}$$

$$\sum_{m \in \mathcal{M}} \sum_{l \in \mathcal{L}} v_{u,m}^{(l)} y_{u,m}^{(l)} \leq B_u \quad \forall u \in \mathcal{U} \tag{1-3}$$

$$\sum_{l \in \mathcal{L}} \sum_{u \in \mathcal{U}} r_u^{(l)} y_{u,m}^{(l)} \leq W_m \quad \forall m \in \mathcal{M} \tag{1-4}$$

$$y_{u,m}^{(l)} \in \{0,1\} \quad \forall u \in \mathcal{U} \ \forall m \in \mathcal{M} \ \forall l \in \mathcal{L} \tag{1-5}$$

The constraint (1-1) means that a user's task can only be performed on one device. Constraint (1-2) ensures that the resources of the devices that can be provided is limited in each round, so it is forbidden to exceed the number of resources the device offered. The constraint (1-3) is to make sure that the user's bid can't exceed its budget in the whole auction period of T. The constraint (1-4) indicates that the amount of resources provided by sellers is limited in the whole auction period of T.

Theorem 1. *Social welfare optimization problem (OPT-1) is NP-hard.*

Proof. The multiple-choice multi-dimensional knapsack problem is a NP-hard problem [29]. In OPT-1, the amount of resources that each seller can provide is equivalent to the capacity of the backpack in each round of the auction. The resource requirement of each user is equivalent to the weight of the object. Each user can be allocated to resources or not. So OPT-1 is a special case of the multiple-choice multi-dimensional 0-1 knapsack problem, which is NP-hard.

We ignore the indicator variable constraint (1-5) temporarily, and introduce dual variable vectors α, β, η and χ. We then obtain the dual problem of OPT-1:

OPT-2 $obj : \min \sum_{u \in \mathcal{U}} B_u \alpha_u^{(l)} + \sum_{u \in \mathcal{U}} \sum_{l \in \mathcal{L}} \beta_u^{(l)} + \sum_{m \in \mathcal{M}} \sum_{l \in \mathcal{L}} R_m^{(l)} \eta_m^{(l)} + \sum_{m \in \mathcal{M}} W_m \chi_m^{(l)}$
$$\tag{2}$$

subject to:

$$v_{u,m}^{(l)} \alpha_u + \beta_u^{(l)} + \sum_{m \in \mathcal{M}} r_u^{(l)} \eta_m^{(l)} + r_u^{(l)} \chi_m^{(l)} \geq v_{u,m}^{(l)} \quad \forall u \in \mathcal{U} \ \forall m \in \mathcal{M} \ \forall l \in \mathcal{L} \tag{2-1}$$

$$\alpha_u^{(l)}, \beta_u^{(l)}, \eta_m^{(l)}, \chi_m^{(l)} \in [0,1] \quad \forall u \in \mathcal{U} \ \forall m \in \mathcal{M} \ \forall l \in \mathcal{L} \tag{2-2}$$

Since we do not know all the information in each round auction during the whole auction period of T, i.e. the demand for user resources and the corresponding bids, as well as the amount of resources provided by sellers. The auction mechanism is carried out round after round with time. So we just consider the current bids and resources in each round auction.

To prevent users from running out of budget too early. We adjust the user's bid according to its remaining budget in each round. So we introduce an auxiliary variable $\alpha_u^{(l)}$ for each user $u \in \mathcal{U}$, where $\alpha_u^{(l)} \in [0,1]$. Let $v_{u,m}^{(l)'} = v_{u,m}^{(l)} \left(1 - \alpha_u^{(l-1)}\right)$ denote the real valuation. Now, we give the following formulation.

$$\textbf{OPT-3} \quad obj : \max \sum_{u \in \mathcal{U}} \sum_{m \in \mathcal{M}} v_{u,m}^{(l)'} y_{u,m}^{(l)} \tag{3}$$

subject to:

$$\sum_{m \in \mathcal{M}} y_{u,m}^{(l)} \leq 1 \quad \forall u \in \mathcal{U} \tag{3-1}$$

$$\sum_{u \in \mathcal{U}} r_u^{(l)} y_{u,m}^{(l)} \leq R_m^{(l)} \quad \forall m \in \mathcal{M} \tag{3-2}$$

$$y_{u,m}^{(l)} \in \{0,1\} \quad \forall u \in \mathcal{U} \, \forall m \in \mathcal{M} \tag{3-3}$$

We ignore the indicator variable constraint (3-3) temporarily, and adopt the same dual variables as in the dual of (1). We then obtain the dual problem of OPT-3:

$$\textbf{OPT-4} \quad obj : \min \sum_{u \in \mathcal{U}} \beta_u^{(l)} + \sum_{m \in \mathcal{M}} R_m^{(l)} \eta_m^{(l)} \tag{4}$$

subject to:

$$\beta_u^{(l)} + \sum_{m \in \mathcal{M}} r_u^{(l)} \eta_m^{(l)} \geq w_{u,m}^{(l)} \quad \forall u \in \mathcal{U} \, \forall m \in \mathcal{M} \tag{4-1}$$

$$\beta_u^{(l)}, \eta_m^{(l)} \in [0,1] \quad \forall u \in \mathcal{U} \, \forall m \in \mathcal{M} \tag{4-2}$$

3   Single Round Resources Auction Design in MDC

In this section, we focus on the design of Single Round Mobile Resources Auction (SRMRA), and we prove that SRMRA is truthful, individual rationality.

The detailed description of SRMRA in round l is showed in Algorithm 1. The resources demand information of users and the resources information shared by sellers is collected by the auctioneer. The U users are bidders in auctions, each submits a bid containing M valuations of sellers in round l. We consider that users or sellers may join and leave during the auction period. In this case, the default is 0 in bids. We use Q to denote the set of winners. We choose the user u who has the largest bid density $v_{u,m}^{(l)}/r_u^{(l)}$, i.e. the algorithm chooses each user according to the bid and the amount of requested resources, and always chooses the user with a highest bid on few resources as the winner. However, the resources provided by the seller are limited. Resource allocation cannot exceed the amount of resources shared by the seller in round l (line 13). And the amount of resources provided by sellers in the whole auction period is limited (line 3 and 14). Then, We use the VCG price mechanism. Let $p_u^{(l)}$ denote the price of the user's final payment in round l. Let $S_{-u}^{(l)}$ and $S_u^{(l)}$ denote the social welfare achieved when winner u is excluded and the social welfare achieved when u is not involved in bidding in round l, respectively. The payment of the winner u, $p_u^{(l)} = S_{-u}^{(l)} - S_u^{(l)}$.

Algorithm 1. (SRMRA): Single Round Mobile Resources Auction

1: **for** $m = 1, 2, 3, \cdots, M$ **do**
2:     The amount of shared resources collected from seller m.
3:     **if** $W_m < R_m^{(l)}$ **then**
4:         $R_m^{(l)} = W_m$;
5:     **end if**
6: **end for**
7: **for** $u = 1, 2, 3, \cdots, U$ **do**
8:     Collect bid $\mathcal{V}_u^{(l)} = \{v_{u,1}^{(l)}, v_{u,2}^{(l)}, \cdots, v_{u,M}^{(l)}\}$ and resource requirements quantity $r_u^{(l)}$ from user u.
9: **end for**
10: $Q = \emptyset$;
11: **for all** $u \notin Q$ **do**
12:     $\{u, m\} = \arg\max \left\{ v_{u,m}^{(l)}/r_u^{(l)} \right\}$ $u \in \mathcal{U}$ $m \in \mathcal{M}$;
13:     **if** $r_u^{(l)} \leq R_m^{(l)}$ **then**
14:         $Q = Q \bigcup u$; $R_m^{(l)} = R_m^{(l)} - r_u^{(l)}$; $W_m = W_m - r_u^{(l)}$; (update W_m)
15:     **end if**
16: **end for**
17: **for all** $u \in Q$ **do**
18:     Execution of the 10 to 16 line of the algorithm again with user u excluded.
19:     $p_u^{(l)} = S_{-u}^{(l)} - S_u^{(l)}$;
20: **end for**

Theorem 2. *SRMRA is a truthful auction mechanism.*

Proof. If the allocation algorithm is monotone and exact and the payment scheme calculates critical value for each winner, then the mechanism is truthful [30]. From line 12 of the SRMRA, it is clear that a user can increase its chance of winning by increasing its bid. Therefore, the winner determination algorithm of SRMRA is monotone. Then, a winning bidder u pays the minimum amount it has to bid to get resources, i.e., its critical value. This is done by finding the losing bidder who would win if u would not participate in the auction. User u's minimum bid density has to be at least equal to the bid density of user the losing bidder for winning its resources. Therefore, user u's critical valuation is $v_{u,m}^{(l)}/r_u^{(l)}$, which is the payment calculated by SRMRA. Thus, we conclude that SRMRA is a truthful mechanism.

Theorem 3. *SRMRA is individual rationality.*

Proof. $p_u^{(l)}$ is the critical value for winner u by the analysis in Theorem 2. Thus $p_u^{(l)} \leq v_{u,m}^{(l)'}$. Due to $v_{u,m}^{(l)} \geq v_{u,m}^{(l)'}$, we can conclude that $p_u^{(l)} \leq v_{u,m}^{(l)}$. So, SRMRA is individual rationality.

4   MDC Auction Framework Design for Long-Term

In this section, we propose a MDC Auction Framework for Long-term (MAFL) that runs a Single Round Mobile Resources Auction (SRMRA) in each round. Then, we give the theoretical analysis of approximate ratio of MAFL.

Although existing single round auctions can also be used for multiple times, users should trade with higher bids to get more resources in the cascading rounds of auctions. On the one hand, some users continue to bid a high price, causing other users can not get resources. On the other hand, if a large portion of buyers run out their budget rapidly in short-terms, the users who participate in the competition may be reduced. Therefore, the total revenue may reduce significantly. Our main idea is to design an appropriate long-term auction framework with budget constraint handled elaborately. In MAFL (Algorithm 2), we introduce an auxiliary variable $\alpha_u^{(l)} \in [0,1]$ for each user $u \in \mathcal{U}$. Its initial value is 0, which increases with the decrease of the remaining budget of the user. Then, in each round l, we use $v_{u,m}^{(l)'} = v_{u,m}^{(l)} \left(1 - \alpha_u^{(l-1)}\right)$ as the virtual valuation for user u. After executing SRMRA, Let $\mathcal{Q}$ be set of winning users and adjust $\alpha_u^{(l)}$ for each user $u \in \mathcal{Q}$. The detailed process is displayed in Algorithm 2.

Theorem 4. *When the algorithm MAFL terminates, the constraint condition (1-1) are satisfied in the formulation (1). And each user will not be over budget with a factor of $1 + \varphi$, i.e.* $\sum_{m \in \mathcal{M}} \sum_{l \in \mathcal{L}} v_{u,m}^{(l)} y_{u,m}^{(l)} \leq B_u(1 + \varphi), \forall u \in \mathcal{U}$, *where* $\varphi = max_{u \in \mathcal{U}, m \in \mathcal{M}, l \in \mathcal{L}} \left\{ v_{u,m}^{(l)}/B_u \right\}$.

Proof. $\alpha_u^{(l)}$ is the auxiliary variable we have introduced. When the user u gets the requested resources, the $\alpha_u^{(l)}$ will be increase, where $\alpha_u^{(l)}$ is the budget that has been used at the end of round l in MAFL. Therefore, when the user u runs

Algorithm 2. (MAFL): MDC Auction Framework for Long-term

1: $\alpha_u^{(l)} = 0 \quad \forall u \in \mathcal{U}$;
2: **for** $l = 1, 2, 3, \cdots, L$ **do**
3: $\quad v_{u,m}^{(l)'} = v_{u,m}^{(l)} \left(1 - \alpha_u^{(l-1)}\right)$;
4: $\quad$ Execute SRMRA, Let $\mathcal{Q}$ be set of winning users.
5: $\quad$ **for all** $u \in \mathcal{Q}$ **do**
6: $\quad\quad$ **if** $\alpha_u^{(l-1)} + v_{u,m}^{(l)} / B_u < 1$ **then**
7: $\quad\quad\quad \alpha_u^{(l)} = \alpha_u^{(l-1)} + v_{u,m}^{(l)} / B_u$;
8: $\quad\quad$ **else**
9: $\quad\quad\quad \alpha_u^{(l)} = 1$;
10: $\quad\quad$ **end if**
11: $\quad$ **end for**
12: $\quad$ **for all** $u \notin \mathcal{Q}$ **do**
13: $\quad\quad \alpha_u^{(l)} = \alpha_u^{(l-1)}$;
14: $\quad$ **end for**
15: **end for**
16: $\alpha_u^{(l)} = \alpha_u^{(L)} \quad \forall u \in \mathcal{U}$;

out its budget ($\alpha_u^{(l)} = 1$), it won't get any more resources in the next rounds. We assume $\alpha_u^{(l)} = 1$, when $l = l^*$, then we get:

$$
\sum_{m \in \mathcal{M}} \sum_{l \in \mathcal{L}} v_{u,m}^{(l)} y_{u,m}^{(l)} \leq \sum_{m \in \mathcal{M}} \sum_{1 \leq l \leq l^*} v_{u,m}^{(l)} y_{u,m}^{(l)}
$$
$$
= \sum_{m \in \mathcal{M}} \sum_{1 \leq l < l^*} v_{u,m}^{(l)} y_{u,m}^{(l)} + \sum_{m \in \mathcal{M}} v_{u,m}^{(l^*)} y_{u,m}^{(l^*)} \tag{5}
$$
$$
\leq B_u + v_{u,m}^{(l^*)} \leq B_u (1 + \varphi)
$$

Theorem 5. *The approximation ratio of MAFL is $(1 + \varphi)(1 + \sqrt{M})$ for formulation (1), where $\varphi = max_{u \in \mathcal{U}, m \in \mathcal{M}, l \in \mathcal{L}} \left\{ v_{u,m}^{(l)} / B_u \right\}$. M is the total number of sellers in MDC.*

Proof. Each user's bid can not exceed the budget. Therefore, the social welfare that we can get from user u is at most B_u. In MAFL, the total welfare is:

$$
\sum_{u \in \mathcal{U}} \min\{B_u, \sum_{l \in \mathcal{L}} \sum_{m \in \mathcal{M}} v_{u,m}^{(l)} y_{u,m}^{(l)}\}
$$
$$
\geq \sum_{u \in \mathcal{U}} \sum_{l \in \mathcal{L}} \sum_{m \in \mathcal{M}} v_{u,m}^{(l)} y_{u,m}^{(l)} / (1 + \varphi) \tag{6}
$$
$$
= Z_L / (1 + \varphi).
$$

Where Z_L is the objective value of the formulation (1) when MAFL terminates. Let $\Delta D^{(l)}$ denote a feasible solution for the formulation (2) in round l. $d^{(l)}$ is the objective value for the formulation (4) in round l. We get:

$$
\begin{aligned}
\Delta D^{(l)} &= \sum_{u \in \mathcal{Q}} B_u(\alpha_u^{(l)} - \alpha_u^{(l-1)}) + d^{(l)} \leq \sum_{u \in \mathcal{Q}} v_{u,m}^{(l)} + d^{(l)} \\
&\leq \sum_{u \in \mathcal{Q}} v_{u,m}^{(l)} + \sqrt{M} \sum_{u \in \mathcal{Q}} v_{u,m}^{(l)}(1 - \alpha_u^{(l)}) \\
&\leq (1 + \sqrt{M})\Delta Z^{(l)}.
\end{aligned}
\tag{7}
$$

Where $\Delta Z^{(l)} = Z^{(l)} - Z^{(l-1)}$, $Z^{(l)}$ is the objective value of the formulation (1) at the end of round l. Then, we conclude $D^{(L)} \leq Z^{(L)}(1 + \sqrt{M})$. The total social welfare of MAFL has a lower bound $D^{(L)}/(1 + \varphi)(1 + \sqrt{M})$. Therefore, the approximation ratio of MAFL is $(1 + \varphi)(1 + \sqrt{M})$.

5   Simulation Results

In this section, we conduct simulations to evaluate the performance of SRMRA and MAFL algorithms in MATLAB R2014a [31]. By default, we assume that the number of users is $U = 40$, and the number of sellers is $M = 20$ in the simulation. Similar to [27], each user's bid is randomly generated according to a uniform distribution within $[0, 1]$. The number of resources shared by each seller is generated from the range $[10, 30]$. The amount of resources requested by each user is selected from the range $[10, 20]$. To analyze the performance of MAFL, we vary the number of auction rounds L and the number of users U. Simulation results are the average value of each data after running the program for 1000 times.

5.1   Revenue Comparisons

The revenue is the total payment of winning users. The single round auctions can also be used multiple times, forming multiple rounds of auctions. Therefore, We compare the revenue of SRMRA and MAFL, where SRMRA is executed L rounds. To better illustrate the performance of the MAFL algorithm, in this paper, the contrast experiment of WBD is added, WBD is obtained from reference [27].

We set $U = 40$ and vary the number of auction rounds in Fig. 1. We can see that the revenue increases with the number of rounds L and converges to a constant for all algorithms. The WBD assumes that each buyer must be allocated to resources, so its revenue is lower than that of SRMRA when the condition is relaxed. For the first 60 rounds of the auction, the resources of sellers and budgets of users are abundant. Therefore, the revenue of MAFL is higher than SRMRA. After 60 rounds of auctions, the budget of most users will run out too early to participate in the next round auction in SRMRA, leading to auction failure and the whole benefit will suffer. When $L = 80$, MAFL outperforms

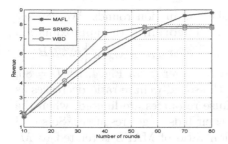

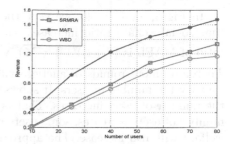

Fig. 1. Revenue under different numbers of rounds L $(U = 40)$

Fig. 2. Revenue under different numbers of users U $(L = 80)$

SRMRA by about 12.2%, MAFL outperforms WBD by about 13.4% in terms of the revenue.

In Fig. 2, we set $L = 80$ and vary the number of users. We can see that the revenue increases with U. That is because the resources are limited, some users could pay high bid to get resources when more users participate in. We can also see in Fig. 2 that the revenue of MAFL is higher when L and U are fixed. That is because MAFL solves the problem that the user's budget is run out too early. On average, MAFL outperforms SRMRA by about 55.6% on the revenue, MAFL outperforms WBD by about 68.6% in terms of the revenue.

5.2 Social-Welfare Ratio

The social-welfare ratio is the ratio of the social welfare of MAFL to the optimal social welfare obtained by solving the formulation (1). We next analyze the social welfare ratio of MAFL. We consider that the optimal solution to the problem (1) is intractable, thus use the solution of its LP-relaxation as an upper bound of (1). The total number of sellers M is set as 10, 20, and 30 for MAFL respectively.

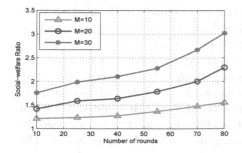

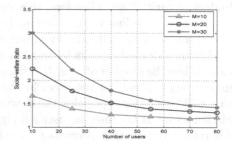

Fig. 3. Social-welfare Ratio under different numbers of rounds L $(U = 40)$

Fig. 4. Social-welfare Ratio under different numbers of users U $(L = 80)$

In Fig. 3, let $U = 40$, we vary the number of auction rounds. We can see that social-welfare ratio increases with L. In **Theorem** 5, the approximation ratio of MAFL is $(1 + \varphi)(1 + \sqrt{M})$, where $\varphi = max_{u \in \mathcal{U}, m \in \mathcal{M}, l \in \mathcal{L}} \left\{ v_{u,m}^{(l)} / B_u \right\}$. Therefore, more rounds of auction will lead to larger φ. In Fig. 4, let $L = 80$, we vary the number of users. It shows that the social-welfare ratio decreases as the number of users increases. That is because resources are limited, when the number of users increases, some users raise their bids to get resources. So social welfare will also increase. The approximation ratio of MAFL is related to M. Therefore, the bigger the M in Figs. 3 and 4, the higher the social-welfare ratio. The experimental results show that the social-welfare ratio is between 1.2 and 3.1, this is better than our theoretical analysis.

5.3   User Satisfaction

Finally, we compare the user satisfaction of MAFL, SRMRA and WBD. The user satisfaction is the average percentage of winning users in each round.

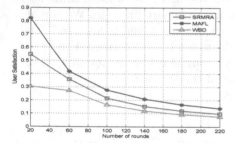

Fig. 5. User Satisfaction under different numbers of rounds L ($U = 40$)

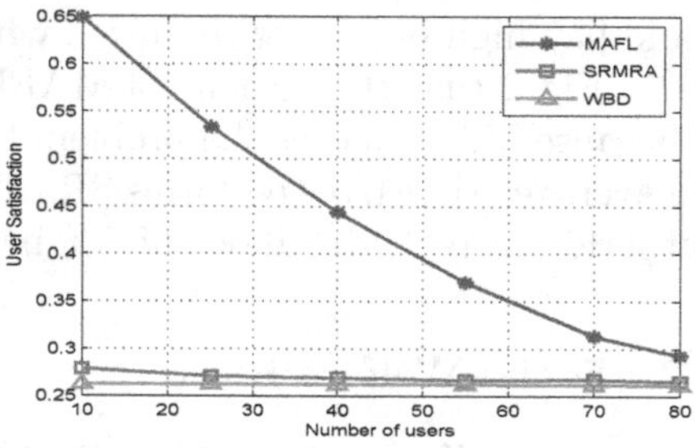

Fig. 6. User Satisfaction under different numbers of users U ($L = 80$)

Figure 5 shows that larger number of rounds will lead to smaller user satisfaction. When the number of rounds L becomes larger, more users run out their budget at early stage. Therefore, they can not get resources in the auction later, resulting in a decline in satisfaction. In Fig. 5, when $U = 40$, we can see that MAFL outperforms SRMRA by about 32.5% on average.

Figure 6 shows that smaller number of users will lead to higher user satisfaction. When the number of users U becomes larger, since the resources are limited, more users can not get resources in the auction. As a result, the user satisfaction will be smaller. Specially, the downward trend of SRMRA and WBD is not obvious, that is because the user's budget is exhausted in the first few rounds. Therefore, the average percentage of winning users in each round is low. The WBD assumes that every buyer must be allocated to resources, so the number of winning users is less than SRMRA when the condition is relaxed. In Fig. 6, when $L = 80$, we can see that MAFL outperforms SRMRA by about 55.2% on average.

In MAFL, we adjust the coefficients (i.e. $\alpha_u^{(l)} \in [0,1]$) for the winning users for rational allocation of resources. We can see in Figs. 5 and 6 that the MAFL has a significant advantage over SRMRA and WBD on user satisfaction.

6 Conclusion

In this paper, we have considered resources auction is time related in MDC. The auction of resources should not be a single round. Although existing single round auctions can also be used multiple times, forming multiple rounds of auction, the problem of user budget must be considered. We have proposed a MDC Auction Framework for Long-term (MAFL) that runs a Single Round Mobile Resources Auction (SRMRA) in each round. And we have adopted the VCG auction to determine the payment of winning user. Both theoretical analysis and simulations show that the proposed auction mechanism achieve a small loss of the approximation ratio. And experimental results verify that MAFL outperforms a single round of multiple auctions significantly on various metrics.

Acknowledgement. This work was supported by the National Natural Science Foundation of China under Grant Nos. 61702115 and 61672171, Natural Science Foundation of Guangdong, China under Grant No. 2018B030311007, and Major R&D Project of Educational Commission of Guangdong under Grant No. 2016KZDXM052. This work was also supported by China Postdoctoral Science Foundation Fund under Grant No. 2017M622632.

References

1. Miettinen, A.P., Nurminen, J.K.: Energy efficiency of mobile clients in cloud computing. In: Usenix Conference on Hot Topics in Cloud Computing, Boston, MA, p. 4. USENIX Association (2010)
2. Burgstahler, D., Richerzhagen, N., Englert, F., et al.: Switching push and pull: an energy efficient notification approach. In: Anchorage, AK, USA, pp. 68–75. IEEE (2014)
3. Ahn, S., Lee, J., et al.: Competitive partial computation offloading for maximizing energy efficiency in mobile cloud computing. IEEE Access **6**, 899–912 (2018)
4. Thanapal, P., Durai, M.A.S.: A framework for computational offloading to extend the energy of mobile devices in mobile cloud computing. Int. J. Embed. Syst. **9**(5), 444 (2017)
5. Chun, B.G., Ihm, S., Maniatis, P., et al.: CloneCloud: elastic execution between mobile device and cloud. In: Salzburg, Austria, pp. 301–314. ACM (2011)
6. Khan, A.U.R., Othman, M., et al.: A survey of mobile cloud computing application models. IEEE Commun. Surv. Tutor. **16**(1), 393–413 (2014)
7. Wu, J., Yuen, C., Cheung, N.M., et al.: Enabling adaptive high-frame-rate video streaming in mobile cloud gaming applications. IEEE Trans. Circuits Syst. Video Technol. **25**(12), 1988–2001 (2015)
8. Chunlin, L.I., Layuan, L.I.: An optimization approach for utilizing cloud services for mobile devices in cloud environment. Informatica **26**(1), 89–110 (2015)

9. Meng, S., Wang, Y., Miao, Z., et al.: Joint optimization of wireless bandwidth and computing resource in cloudlet-based mobile cloud computing environment. Peer-to-Peer Netw. Appl. **11**(3), 462–472 (2017)
10. Tocz, K., Nadjmtehrani, S.: A taxonomy for management and optimization of multiple resources in edge computing. CoRR (2018)
11. Chen, L., Wu, J., Dai, H.N., et al.: BRAINS: joint bandwidth-relay allocation in multi-homing cooperative D2D networks. IEEE Trans. Veh. Technol. **99**(99) (2018)
12. Chen, L., Wu, J., Zhang, X.X., et al.: TARCO: two-stage auction for D2D relay aided computation resource allocation in HetNet. IEEE Trans. Serv. Comput. **PP**(99), 1 (2017)
13. Mtibaa, A., Fahim, A., Harras, K.A., et al.: Towards resource sharing in mobile device clouds: power balancing across mobile devices. In: ACM SIGCOMM Workshop on Mobile Cloud Computing, Hong Kong, China, pp. 51–56. ACM (2013)
14. Mtibaa, A., Harras, K.A., Fahim, A.: Towards computational offloading in mobile device clouds. In: Bristol, UK, pp. 331–338. IEEE (2014)
15. Fahim, A., Mtibaa, A., Harras, K.A.: Making the case for computational offloading in mobile device clouds. In: Networking (ed.), pp. 203–205. ACM, New York (2013)
16. Habak, K., Shi, C., et al.: Elastic mobile device clouds: leveraging mobile devices to provide cloud computing services at the edge. In: Fog for 5G and IoT (2017)
17. Miluzzo, E., Chen, Y.F.: Vision: mClouds - computing on clouds of mobile devices. In: ACM Workshop on Mobile Cloud Computing and Services, Low Wood Bay, Lake District, UK, pp. 9–14. ACM (2012)
18. Song, J., et al.: Energy-traffic tradeoff cooperative offloading for mobile cloud computing. In: Quality of Service, Hong Kong, China, pp. 284–289. IEEE (2014)
19. Wang, X., Chen, X., Wu, W., et al.: Cooperative application execution in mobile cloud computing: a Stackelberg Game approach. IEEE Commun. Lett. **20**(5), 946–949 (2016)
20. Zaman, S., Grosu, D.: Combinatorial auction-based allocation of virtual machine instances in clouds. In: IEEE Second International Conference on Cloud Computing Technology and Science. IEEE Computer Society, Indianapolis, IN, USA, pp. 127–134. IEEE (2010)
21. Shi, W., Zhang, L., Wu, C., et al.: An online auction framework for dynamic resource provisioning in cloud computing. IEEE/ACM Trans. Netw. **24**(4), 2060–2073 (2016)
22. Zhu, Y., Li, B., Li, Z.: Truthful spectrum auction design for secondary networks. In: IEEE INFOCOM, Orlando, FL, USA, pp. 873–881. IEEE (2012)
23. Wang, X., Huang, L., Xu, H., et al.: Social welfare maximization auction for secondary spectrum markets: a long-term perspective. In: IEEE International Conference on Sensing, Communication, and Networking, London, UK, pp. 1–9. IEEE (2016)
24. Vickrey, W.: Counterspeculation, auctions, and competitive sealed tenders. J. Financ. **16**(1), 8–37 (1961)
25. Li, H., Wu, C., Li, Z.: Socially-optimal online spectrum auctions for secondary wireless communication. In: Computer Communications, Kowloon, Hong Kong, pp. 2047–2055. IEEE (2015)
26. Jin, A., Song, W., Zhuang, W.: Auction-based resource allocation for sharing cloudlets in mobile cloud computing. IEEE Trans. Emerg. Top. Comput. **6**(1), 45–57 (2018)
27. Wang, X., Chen, X., Wu, W.: Towards truthful auction mechanisms for task assignment in mobile device clouds. In: IEEE INFOCOM 2017 - IEEE Conference on Computer Communications, Atlanta, GA, USA, pp. 1–9. IEEE (2017)

28. Wang, H., Guo, S., Cao, J., et al.: MELODY: a long-term dynamic quality-aware incentive mechanism for crowdsourcing. IEEE Trans. Parallel Distrib. Syst. **29**(4), 901–914 (2018)

29. Cherfi, N., Hifi, M.: A column generation method for the multiple-choice multidimensional knapsack problem. Comput. Optim. Appl. **46**(1), 51–73 (2010)

30. Briest, P., Krysta, P., Vcking, B.: Approximation techniques for utilitarian mechanism design. In: Thirty-Seventh ACM Symposium on Theory of Computing, Baltimore, MD, USA, pp. 39–48. ACM (2016)

31. MATLAB Homepage. https://www.mathworks.com/academia/student_version. html. Accessed 4 June 2018

Mobility Analysis and Response
for Software-Defined Internet of Things

Zhiyong Zhang, Rui Wang, Xiaojun Cai, and Zhiping Jia[✉]

School of Computer Science and Technology, Shandong University, QingDao, China
{zhangzhiyong,xj_cai,jzp}@sdu.edu.cn, rw@mail.sdu.edu.cn

Abstract. The exponential growth of devices connected to the network has resulted in the development of new IoT applications and services. A large number of IoT devices are application-specific which makes the network difficult to manage and change. The Software Defined Networking (SDN) paradigm brings a new perspective of solving the network rigidity issue. By decoupling the control plane from the data plane, the routing decisions can be conducted in a centralized way, thus simplifying the network configuration and management. However, the behavior of IoT nodes is diverse and some nodes demonstrate the features of high mobility. The high mobility makes the centralized routing protocols perform badly since the Controller cannot maintain the frequently changing topology information in real-time, which produces unnecessary control overheads, even incorrect network policies.

To address the problem, in this paper, we first propose a behavior analysis and modeling method to identify the high mobility nodes in the IoT network. After that, a Mobility-aware Flow Table Reservation (MFTR) mechanism is proposed for the high mobility nodes to realize the local search and collaboration. Finally, we implement a prototype with the proposed techniques on Contiki 2.6 in a real testbed. The experimental results show our scheme outperforms the original SDN-based scheme in terms of packet delivery ratio and energy consumption.

Keywords: Internet of Things · SDN · Behavior analysis
Mobility-aware Flow Table Reservation · Control overhead

1 Introduction

The rapid advancement of information and communication technologies promotes the development of smart devices, such as RFID, Bluetooth devices and embedded systems. These kinds of smart devices automatically record, process and communicate with each other through the network, which leads to the emergence of new services and applications, and makes it possible to create a paradigm of Internet of Things (IoT). At present, a large number of IoT devices use different ways to connect to the Internet. It is estimated the IoT will consist of almost 50 billion objects by 2020 [1]. However, the traditional

© Springer Nature Switzerland AG 2018
J. Vaidya and J. Li (Eds.): ICA3PP 2018, LNCS 11336, pp. 370–384, 2018.
https://doi.org/10.1007/978-3-030-05057-3_29

equipment and network protocols are not designed to support the high level of scalability and large amount of traffic. Moreover, IoT devices are commonly characterized by different requirements depending on the specific application and deployment scenario which results in extremely difficult management. Thus, the current architectures are inefficient and have significant limitations to satisfy the varied IoT requirements.

The Software Defined Networking (SDN) paradigm and OpenFlow [2], which currently is the most popular southbound interface for SDN, provide a new opportunity to solve these problems by separating the *control plane* from the *data plane* and making the control plane programmable. OpenFlow exploits the concept of *flow table* to process the incoming packets. If a *flow* matches the *matching-rule* of an entry, it will be processed according to the *action* of this entry. If the flow table does not contain any entry specifying how to deal a certain packet, the node sends a request to one or more remote *Controllers*. The Controller has a high level abstraction of the network elements, which is based to manage the flow table and decide how packets are routed in the network. In this manner, the Controller completely control over the operation of the datapath and new services and management policies can be introduced by simply modifying the flow table rules.

Different from the wired domain, in which the nodes maintain a relatively stable state, the behavior of IoT nodes is more diverse and complex. The high mobility of some IoT nodes lead to the network topology change frequently, but the Controller cannot be aware of the changes in real-time, which produces unnecessary control overheads, even incorrect flow table entries. In addition, the IoT nodes communicate with the Controller in a multi-hop way instead of a dedicated OpenFlow channel, which further amplifies the impact of mobility since the multi-hop communication not only increases the probability of network topology invalidations, but also increases the risk of control packets (e.g. packet-in and packet-out packets) losses.

In order to reduce the impact of the high mobility nodes, in this paper, we propose a behavior analysis method to model and predict the mobility of IoT nodes. Different from the practise of the previous work [3–5], our method can adapt to more diverse behavior patterns. For the nodes which are predicted to be "high mobility", we propose a Mobility-aware Flow Table Reservation (MFTR) mechanism to realize the local search. The reserved flow table is managed by the Controller and can be modified to implement different distributed protocols, which eliminates the invalid control overheads and avoids the incorrect routing decisions.

We have implemented the behavior analysis method and the mobility-aware flow table reservation mechanism on Contiki 2.6 [6], which is a popular open source operating system for the Internet of things. Extensive experiments have been conducted in a real testbed for various performance indicators. The experimental results show the proposed techniques can effectively improve the network performance and better cope with the high mobility environment, compared with the original SDN-based scheme.

The main contributions of this paper can be summarized as follows:

– We propose a behavior analysis and modeling method to realize the identification and behavior prediction of the high mobility IoT nodes.
– Based on the prediction results, we put forward a mobility-aware flow table reservation mechanism to eliminate the invalid control overheads and avoid the incorrect routing decisions.
– We implement the behavior analysis method and the MFTR mechanism on Contiki 2.6 and extensive experiments are conducted in a real testbed to evaluate the effectiveness of the proposed techniques.

The rest of this paper is organized as follows. Section 2 presents the behavior analysis method for IoT nodes. Section 3 describes the mobility-aware flow table reservation mechanism. Section 4 presents the experimental results and analysis. The previous work is detailed in Sect. 5 and finally, this paper is concluded in Sect. 6.

2   Behavior Analysis Method

In the SDN-based IoT architecture, there is usually a central node to act as the gateway of other IoT nodes and the Controller. The central node uses the same wireless communication technology as the other IoT nodes, such as Bluetooth, RFID, Zigbee, and so on. An IoT node handles the arriving packets as specified in its flow table, which is continuously updated by the configuration of the Controller.

In order to maintain the global view of the network, the Controller needs to continuously collect the topology information of all the IoT nodes. If a node moves in a high speed, it will lead to all the topology information of its neighbours change frequently. Since the multi-hop wireless communication between the Controller and the IoT nodes takes a considerable time, the Controller cannot be aware of the network topology in real-time which makes it incapable of adapting to the high mobility environments. In order to reduce the extra overheads, e.g. expired topology or duplicate packet-in/packet-out packets, caused by the high mobility nodes, we need to carefully analyze the behavior of these nodes.

2.1   Basic Assumption

In this paper, if a node is predicted to be the high mobility state in a period of time with a great probability, it is defined as "high mobility" node. Once a node is identified as a high mobility node, the Controller will process it in a different way from the normal nodes to minimize the control overheads. To this purpose, we need to analyze and model the mobility of the IoT nodes to achieve the behavioural prediction.

However, it is not an easy task to identify whether a node is a high mobility node. Since the hardware resource of different kinds of IoT nodes varies widely, we cannot assume all nodes are equipped with a variety of accessories to detect the mobility activities, such as GPS devices, acceleration sensors, and so on. Instead, we implement the prediction through the behavioral characteristics of the IoT network itself. For example, in the scene of event monitoring, when an IoT node completes the detection of an area, it is likely to move to one of the geographically adjacent areas. Furthermore, even the same IoT node may exhibit different mobility patterns depends on different areas to be detected. Therefore, we need to consider the impacts of all these factors.

In the SDN-based IoT architecture, the Controller obtains the information of each node by the periodic TD (Topology Discovery) packets. In this section, we focus on mining the behavior pattern of the high mobility IoT nodes from these discrete TD packets.

2.2   Selection of the Candidate Nodes

Before performing the behavior analysis, we pre-process the historical topology information to get a candidate set. The nodes in this set are considered as the potential high mobility nodes. When we need to identify whether an IoT node is a high mobility node, we first examine if it is a member of the candidate set. If it doesn't belong to the set, we treat it as a low mobility node without further calculations. Obviously, the candidate set significantly reduces unnecessary calculation overheads.

In the SDN-based IoT network, the periodic topology information collected by the Controller usually contains the neighbour nodes list and the RSSI value of each link. If a node keeps moving during a period of time, the RSSI values of the links associated with it would change frequently. Therefore, the Controller can estimate the mobility of a node based on the degree of volatility of its surrounding RSSI values [7].

Suppose the Controller has already received n TD packets sent by each IoT node. We denote the n-th RSSI of node i to link (i, j) as P_n^{ij}. In order to evaluate the mobility of node j from the view of node i, we calculate the *variance* of the n RSSI values. The mobility evaluation of node j relative to node i can be expressed as follows:

$$Mob(i,j) = \text{var}\{\frac{1}{\sqrt{P_1^{ij}}}, \frac{1}{\sqrt{P_2^{ij}}}, \cdots, \frac{1}{\sqrt{P_n^{ij}}}\} \tag{1}$$

The rationale behind the equation is that a small $Mob(i, j)$ means node j has a lower mobility relative to node i. Furthermore, if all neighbours have lower mobility relative to node i, we treat node i as a "low mobility" node. To this end, we need to calculate all the mobility evaluation values between node i and its neighbours.

Suppose node i has K neighbours. In order to evaluate the mobility of node i, we compute all the K mobility values according to Eq. (1). It is worth noting that a high mobility node will affects all the mobility evaluations of its neighbors. For example, if node j_1 is a high mobility node, even node i keeps still, the mobility evaluation of link (i, j_1) will also be large. To this end, we sort the K mobility values and choose the smallest $0.5K$ values, which are expressed as $Mob(i, j_1), Mob(i, j_2), \cdots, Mob(i, j_{0.5K})$. Finally, we get the mobility of node i by calculating the mean of all the $0.5K$ values.

$$M(i) = \mathrm{E}\{Mob(i, j_1), Mob(i, j_2), \cdots, Mob(i, j_{0.5K})\} \tag{2}$$

According to Eqs. (1) and (2), the Controller can compute the mobility of all the IoT nodes in the same way. We sort the mobility of all the nodes and place the nodes with larger mobility evaluations to the candidate set. To simplify the problem, in this paper, we simply put 50% nodes with the largest mobility evaluations to the candidate set. Since different types of IoT applications exhibit different characteristics, in real environments, the ratio can be set to a more accurate value depending on the specific applications.

2.3   Generation of the History Sequence

The Controller updates the candidate set in real-time, which makes it unnecessary for us to analyze and model all the nodes to determine whether they are high mobility nodes. Moreover, even for the nodes in the candidate set, we do not have to model the behavior for each of them. In this paper, we use an event-driven approach to trigger the behavior analysis of the nodes in candidate set. We define the trigger condition as: if a link on a path specified by the Controller is broken and at least one node of the link belongs to the candidate set, the behavior analysis will be initiated. For this case, we only need to initiate the analysis for the node(s) in the candidate set.

However, although the Controller maintains the real-time and historical topology of all nodes, these topology information cannot visually indicate the node's mobility state, i.e. high mobility or low mobility, at a specific moment in the past. Thus, in order to perform the behavior analysis of a potentially high mobility node, the Controller first transforms the topology information into the corresponding mobility sequence, i.e. a discrete sequence $(s_1, s_2, \cdots, s_n)$ to indicates the mobility state of the node at each moment. If $s_i = 0 (i \in [0, n])$, then the node is in the low mobility state, otherwise, it is in the high mobility state.

To get the mobility sequence of the node to be analyzed, we compare the topology information of the node at time t and $t + 1$. At time $t + 1$, if there are more than half of the neighbours whose rate of change of RSSI is lower than a preset $threshold\%$, we think the node is in the "low mobility" state at time t, otherwise it is in the high mobility state. Doing like this, we get the history mobility sequence of the node to be analyzed, which constitutes the basis of the further behavior modeling. Similarly, the $threshold\%$ also varies depending on the types of IoT applications.

2.4   Behavior Modeling

As we analyzed in the previous section, the behavior of a node is affected by its "network state". In this paper, the "network state" is a broad concept. It can be a specific geographic location or a service currently providing. In the example of event monitoring, when an Iot node moves to one of the geographically adjacent areas, the movement achieves the switches of different "network states". Here, the "network state" refers to the physical areas to be monitored. Similarly, in the scenarios of providing services, the "network state" corresponds to the service being executed.

For a specific application scenario, the number of "network state" are determined. But the switching rules between different "network states" are usually not visible to the Controller. For example, when an IoT node completes the monitoring of an area, it can randomly move to an adjacent area while the Controller can only obtain the transition rules between different "network states" by the way of probability estimation. Here, we assume there are N "network states" for a given IoT network. The transition matrix between different "network states" A is expressed as:

$$A = \left[a_{ij}\right]_{N*N} \tag{3}$$

Where, a_{ij} represents the probability of the node switching from the state i to state j.

In addition, the mobility of a node is inevitably affected by its "network state". For example, when a node is outdoors, it is more likely to maintain the high mobility state than it is indoors. When the "network state" is switched to another, the behavior of the node would be likely different from the previous. Unfortunately, the impacts of the "network state" on the mobility cannot be directly observed. Since we simply divides the mobility into high mobility and low mobility, we use another matrix B to represent the relationship between mobility and its "network state".

$$B = \left[b_i(k)\right]_{N*2}, k = 0, 1 \tag{4}$$

Where, $b_i(1)$ is the probability of the node being high mobility when it is in the "network state" i. Similarly, $b_i(0)$ is the probability of low mobility.

Furthermore, we use $\pi = \left[\pi_i\right]_N$ to represent the probability of a node in each "network state" at the initial time. Obviously, the combination of A, B and π determine the mobility behavior of an IoT node. Our task is to perform maximum likelihood estimation of the parameters of model (A, B, π) with the history mobility sequence obtained in Sect. 2.3.

Here, we use the Baum-Welch algorithm [8] to solve the above problem. Baum-Welch algorithm begins with random initial conditions and adopts the iterative approach to get the parameters until a desired level of convergence, that is:

$$a_{ij}^{(n+1)} = \frac{\sum\limits_{t=1}^{T-1} \xi_t(i,j)}{\sum\limits_{t=1}^{T-1} \gamma_t(i)} \tag{5}$$

$$b_j(k)^{(n+1)} = \frac{\sum\limits_{t=1,m_t=k}^{T} \gamma_t(j)}{\sum\limits_{t=1}^{T} \gamma_t(j)} \tag{6}$$

$$\pi_i^{(n+1)} = \gamma_1(i) \tag{7}$$

Where, T is the length of the history mobility sequence and m_t is the m-th value of the sequence. In addition, $\gamma_t(i)$ is the probability of the node being in state i at time t given the history sequence and the model (A, B, π), while $\xi_t(i, j)$ is the probability of being in state i and j at times t and $t+1$ respectively given the history sequence and the model (A, B, π). They are expressed as follows:

$$\gamma_t(i) = \frac{\alpha_t(j)\beta_t(j)}{\sum\limits_{j=1}^{N} \alpha_t(j)\beta_t(j)} \tag{8}$$

$$\xi_t(i, j) = \frac{\alpha_t(i)a_{ij}b_j(m_{t+1})\beta_{t+1}(j)}{\sum\limits_{i=1}^{N}\sum\limits_{j=1}^{N} \alpha_t(i)a_{ij}b_j(m_{t+1})\beta_{t+1}(j)} \tag{9}$$

Where, $\alpha_t(i)$ is the probability of seeing the mobility sequence $m_1, m_2, \cdots, m_t$ and being in state i at time t, while $\beta_t(i)$ is the probability of the ending partial mobility sequence $m_{t+1}, m_{t+2}, \cdots, m_T$ given starting state i at time t. They can be calculated by the forward-backward algorithm [8].

When the behavior analysis of a node is triggered, the Controller will model the mobility of the node using the above equations. After finish training all the parameters, we get the behavior model of the node. According to the state transition matrix A and the mobility matrix B, the Controller can easily predict the probability of the node being in the high mobility state in a period of time, which is based to make the corresponding decisions.

3 Mobility-Aware Flow Table Reservation Mechanism

As discussed above, the SDN-based IoT architecture cannot adapt to the high mobility environments well. The reason is that the SDN architecture makes the routing decisions in a centralized way. Although this way shows its advantages in terms of network control and management, it is not sufficient in the IoT environment because it cannot quickly react to the rapid topology changes caused by the high mobility nodes. On the contrary, the traditional wireless network architecture can deal with the mobility with varied distributed routing algorithms, but it suffers from the constrains of extreme application-specific and is lack of the programming ability. Thus, in this section, we propose a Mobility-aware Flow Table Reservation (MFTR) mechanism to integrate the on-demand local search of distributed routing protocols to the SDN-based IoT architecture. The

MFTR mechanism achieves the effect of distributed routing algorithms. Meanwhile, it is programmable and can be easily modified by the Controller according to different service requirements.

It is worth noting that in some kinds of IoT networks, such as wireless sensor network and home network, the nodes often have the demands of local collaboration which requires the nodes can quickly response to local events. If each event requires the participation of the Controller, the extra control overheads will result in longer latency, thus affecting the efficiency of collaboration. Although the problem is different from the high mobility problem, it can also be solved by our MFTR mechanism.

3.1 Local Search Activation

To deal with the communication demands of the high mobility (HM) nodes, the Controller maintains a list of all the HM nodes and distributes it to the whole network. The Controller pre-installs flow table entries for the HM nodes. Once a node is identified as an HM node, all the related packets will be processed according to the reserved flow table entries. To make sure the reserved entries can implement the local search, we need to extend the *actions* of the OpenFlow protocol.

To take Fig. 1 as an example, if a source node S wants to communicate with a destination node D, and S or D is in the HM list, even though S does not have a route to D, it will not generate a packet-in message to the Controller because one of the reserved flow table entries can be matched, as shown in the first two entries of Fig. 1(c). In order to find a path to the destination node without the participation of the Controller, the entry specifies node S to *generate* a *local_search* packet with the source_address set to S and the destination_address set to D. Then the *local_search* packet is sent to all the neighbours.

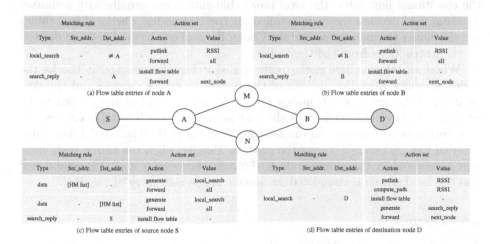

Fig. 1. Schematic diagram of the MFTR mechanism

3.2   Request Transmission

In order to make sure the packet can be transmitted to the destination node, another flow table entry is reserved to match the *local_search* packet, as shown in the first entry of Fig. 1(a) and (b). In addition to the *generate* operation, we also extend a new action, *putlink*. The *putlink* operation inserts the information of the link that the packet has just passed through to the *local_search* packet. The information can be RSSI, time delay or the other characteristic of the link, which can be dynamically specified and modified by the Controller. After that, the packet is broadcasted.

3.3   Local Search Reply

Finally, the *local_search* packet reaches the destination node D. It inserts the information of the last link to the packet. Since the *local_search* packet contains all the links' information it have traversed. The node D selects an optimal path from the *local_search* packets according to the routing metrics specified by the Controller. After that, D generates a *search_reply* packet to response the source node S. The reply packet contains all the nodes on the optimal path, which is based to establish a route from S to D. These operations are shown in Fig. 1(d).

3.4   Flow Table Establishment

In the traditional SDN-based network, the flow table can only be managed by the Controller. But in our architecture, in order to implement the quick response for the HM nodes, we set up a *local flow table* space on each node to support the temporary communications of the HM nodes. Initially, all the local flow tables are empty. When a node receives a *search_reply* message, it installs a local flow table entry according to the content of the message. Compared with the traditional flow table, the local flow table entries are usually with a shorter *Timeout* field because they are installed for the HM nodes. The local flow tables are also under the management of the Controller and can be modified and deleted by the instructions from the Controller.

When an intermediate node receives a *search_reply* message, it checks the nodes sequence from the payload of the packet to get the source and the destination of the path, which makes up the matching field of the entries to be established. After that, it installs the corresponding local flow table entries and then forwards the message to the next node of the path. The second flow table entry of Fig. 1(a) and (b) shows the process. Finally, when the *search_reply* message is received by the source node S, the route between S and D is established and the local search is completed, as shown in the last entry of Fig. 1(c).

3.5   Discussions

As mentioned above, the MFTR mechanism implements the effects of distributed routing algorithms. But it also maintains SDN's programmability. For the MFTR mechanism, the reserved flow table entries can be modified easily by the Controller. Meanwhile, the action set of each entry can also be modified. Even for the extended actions, such as *putlink* and *compute_path*, the Controller can change the *value* field to specify different routing metrics. Thus, the proposed MFTR mechanism enhances the capability of OpenFlow without weakening the programmable characteristics of SDN.

To reduce the overheads of the local search, a TTL field can be set for each *local_search* packet. For the MFTR mechanism, the upper bound of TTL for the HM nodes can be determined. In this paper, we set the TTL filed of all the *local_search* packets to the hops from the source node to the Controller. In addition, for the HM nodes, the rate of the TD packets can be decreased because most of them are expired. Once an HM node is identified as a normal node, the rate can be restored.

4   Experimental Evaluation

4.1   Experimental Setup

We implement a prototype of an SDN-based IoT architecture with the proposed techniques. The data plane is composed of several Texas Instruments CC2530 single chip devices which is an 8051 8-bit controller. Each IoT node is equipped with 8 KB RAM and 256 KB Flash memory. The Controller is running on a desktop computer which contains an Intel Core i5-3470 CPU running at 3.2 GHz and 4 GB memory. We use a TI CC2530 as the central node and gateway to connect to the Controller via USB interface.

We implement the mobility-aware flow table reservation (MFTR) mechanism on Contiki 2.6, which is a popular open source operating system for the Internet of things. Meanwhile, the data plane provides the interface to support the proposed behavior modeling method. We deploy 10 nodes in different rooms and compare our scheme with the original SDN-based scheme to show the advantages of the proposed policies in terms of packet delivery ratio and energy consumption.

4.2   Experimental Results

Packet Delivery Ratio. In order to evaluate the performance of the proposed behavior analysis and the MFTR mechanism, we test the packet delivery ratio of our scheme and the original SDN scheme. We set one node moves randomly in the space with the speed ranging from 1 m/s to 5 m/s. The node randomly sends connection requests once a second. For our scheme, we use the proposed behavior modeling method to maintain an HM list to trigger the MFTR mechanism. However, the number of nodes in the test is limited. To restore the characteristic of huge number of nodes and connections of the real IoT network, once a path is established and the packet is forwarded successfully, the corresponding flow table entry is deleted. Doing like this, we ensure each connection request will

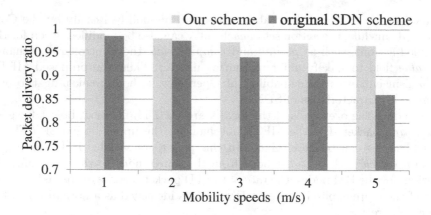

Fig. 2. Packet delivery ratio

generate a path-finding process. We test 10 min for each speed, and the results are shown in Fig. 2.

We can see from the figure, when the node moves slowly, both schemes achieve higher delivery ratio. But under the circumstances of higher speed, our scheme outperforms the original SDN scheme. When the node moves fast, the Controller cannot get the topology information in real-time. The expired topology leads to the Controller make incorrect decisions. As a result, when the node receives the packet-out message, the next hop specified by the Controller may not be reachable. In addition, even the packet-out message itself may also become unreachable. Therefore, the packet delivery ratio of the original SDN scheme decreases as the speed increases. But for our scheme, the delivery ratio remains stable for different situations since our scheme successfully identifies the high mobility node and inserts it to the HM list. Furthermore, the proposed MFTR mechanism treats the high mobility node in a different way with others, i.e. the MFTR mechanism adopts the local search to eliminate the interaction with the Controller. Thus, compared with the original SDN scheme, our scheme has the ability to deal with the high mobility scenes and is more suitable for the complex IoT environment.

Energy Consumption. To further evaluate the impact of the high mobility nodes, we measure the energy consumption under our scheme and the original SDN scheme with varied packets rates. In our experiments, we make 3 nodes move randomly at the speed of 5 m/s. Similarly, for our scheme, we adopt the proposed behavior analysis method to identify the HM nodes and use the MFTR mechanism to process the requests of HM nodes. All the IoT nodes communicate with each other randomly in different packets rate. We use the YOKOGAWA WT310 digital power meter to measure the energy. The output power of each IoT node is set to 1 dBm. We test 10 min for each rate and the results are shown in Fig. 3.

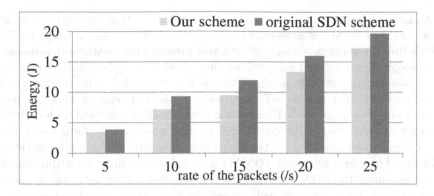

Fig. 3. The energy consumption of two schemes

As shown in Fig. 3, our scheme consumes less energy than the original SDN scheme. The high mobility nodes leads to the network topology change frequently, which generates much more expire control packets. Different from the original SDN scheme, the proposed behavior analysis method has the ability of identifying the high mobility nodes. Once an IoT node is added into the HM list, the rate of its TD packets will be greatly reduced since most of them are expired, which significantly reduces the control overheads. Moreover, under the original SDN scheme, invalid flow table entries generated by the Controller will cause unnecessary energy consumption, such as retransmitted packets, duplicate packet-in messages and potentially incorrect packet-out messages. But for our scheme, we use the MFTR mechanism to trigger the local search without the participation of the Controller, which eliminates unnecessary overheads as much as possible. Therefore, our scheme can effectively enhance the lifetime of the IoT network.

5   Related Work

Recently, the software defined networking has received intensive attentions since it provides a more flexible management architecture than traditional network by decoupling the control plane and data plane. Since SDN enables network control to become programmable and the underlying infrastructure to be abstracted from applications and network services, many solutions have been proposed to extend the SDN and OpenFlow concept to the wireless domain [4,5,9–25], such as wireless mesh networks (WMN) [4,9], wireless sensor networks (WSN) [10–14], wireless personal area networks (WPAN) [15] and wireless local area networks (WLAN) [5]. In [14], the technical challenges in introducing the OpenFlow to wireless sensor network are identified and then the Sensor OpenFlow solution is proposed. In [10], the SDSN approach is described to adapt to various application requirements. In order to fully utilize the computation and communication resources, the SDSN nodes have to be reprogrammed. Although these studies make great contributions, they don't provide enough protocol details for implementation.

A detailed implementation of a stateful SDN solution for wireless sensor networks (SDN-WISE) is presented in [16]. SDN-WISE defines a complete SDN architecture for wireless sensor network and provides the protocol details, such as topology discovery and packet handling. However, SDN-WISE is designed for wireless sensor network, in which the nodes usually have the characteristics of low mobility. But in the IoT environment, the behavior of nodes is more complex and diverse. Some IoT nodes demonstrate the features of high mobility. The high mobility makes the centralized routing protocols perform badly since the Controller cannot maintain the frequently changed topology information in real-time. Therefore, although SDN-WISE provides excellent contributions for the extension of the SDN paradigm to the wireless sensor network, it cannot adapt to the IoT environment well, especially for the high mobility scenarios.

For some regular movement applications, the SDN paradigm and the flow based model can be utilized to offer better management [3]. A mobility application on the mesh routers is presented in [4]. This application is integrated into NOX, which is a popular network operating system, to enable the client mobility to allow to trigger handovers of a station from one Mesh Access Point (MAP) to another. Focusing on the seamless mobility in enterprise WLAN, an Odin based application is implemented in [5]. However, in the IoT field, the behavior of the IoT devices is more complex, but these studies cannot adapt to the irregular and high mobility situations.

In this paper, we propose a set of mobility analysis and response schemes for the Internet of things. Compared with the current works, our architecture shows its advantages in three aspects. First, we propose a modeling method to transform the discrete topology information to a mobility sequence. Meanwhile, we put forward a behavior analysis and predicting method for the potential high mobility IoT nodes. Finally, we present a mobility-aware flow table reservation mechanism for the high mobility nodes to eliminate the invalid control overheads and achieve quick routing decisions.

6   Conclusion

In the SDN-based IoT architecture, the high mobility nodes lead to the network topology change frequently. Since the Controller cannot be aware of the network topology in real-time which makes the SDN-based architecture incapable of adapting to the high mobility environments. To address the problem, in this paper, we propose a behavior analysis and modeling method to identify the high mobility nodes in the IoT network. After that, we put forward a mobility-aware flow table reservation mechanism to deal with the high mobility nodes. We implement a prototype with the proposed techniques on Contiki 2.6 in a real testbed. The experimental results show our scheme effectively improves the network performance and better copes with the high mobility environment, compared with the original SDN scheme.

Acknowledgements. This research is sponsored by the State Key Program of National Natural Science Foundation of China No. 61533011 and the National Key R&D Program of China No. 2017YFB0902602.

References

1. Evans, D.: The Internet of Things: how the next evolution of the internet is changing everything. Cisco (2016)
2. McKeown, N., et al.: OpenFlow: enabling innovation in campus networks. ACM SIGCOMM Comput. Commun. Rev. **38**(2), 69–74 (2008)
3. Valdivieso Caraguay, Á.L., Benito Peral, A., Barona López, L.I., García Villalba, L.J.: SDN: evolution and opportunities in the development IoT applications. Int. J. Distrib. Sens. Netw. (2014)
4. Dely, P., Kassler, A., Bayer, N.: OpenFlow for wireless mesh networks. In: 2011 Proceedings of 20th International Conference on Computer Communications and Networks (ICCCN), pp. 1–6. IEEE (2011)
5. Suresh, L., Schulz-Zander, J., Merz, R., Feldmann, A., Vazao, T.: Towards programmable enterprise WLANS with Odin. In: Proceedings of the First Workshop on Hot Topics in Software Defined Networks, pp. 115–120. ACM (2012)
6. Dunkels, A., Gronvall, B., Voigt, T.: Contiki-a lightweight and flexible operating system for tiny networked sensors. In: 29th Annual IEEE International Conference on Local Computer Networks, pp. 455–462. IEEE (2004)
7. Zhang, Z., Jia, Z., Xia, H.: Link stability evaluation and stability based multicast routing protocol in mobile ad hoc networks. In: 2012 IEEE 11th International Conference on Trust, Security and Privacy in Computing and Communications (TrustCom), pp. 1570–1577. IEEE (2012)
8. Rabiner, L.: First hand: the hidden Markov model. In: IEEE Global History Network, Retrieved 2 October 2013
9. Detti, A., Pisa, C., Salsano, S., Blefari-Melazzi, N.: Wireless mesh software defined networks (wmSDN). In: WiMob, pp. 89–95 (2013)
10. Zeng, D., Miyazaki, T., Guo, S., Tsukahara, T., Kitamichi, J., Hayashi, T.: Evolution of software-defined sensor networks. In: 2013 IEEE Ninth International Conference on Mobile Ad-hoc and Sensor Networks (MSN), pp. 410–413. IEEE (2013)
11. Yuan, A.S., Fang, H.-T., Wu, Q.: OpenFlow based hybrid routing in wireless sensor networks. In: 2014 IEEE Ninth International Conference on Intelligent Sensors, Sensor Networks and Information Processing (ISSNIP), pp. 1–5. IEEE (2014)
12. Mahmud, A., Rahmani, R.: Exploitation of OpenFlow in wireless sensor networks. In: 2011 International Conference on Computer Science and Network Technology (ICCSNT), vol. 1, pp. 594–600. IEEE (2011)
13. Han, Z., Ren, W.: A novel wireless sensor networks structure based on the SDN. Int. J. Distrib. Sens. Netw. (2014)
14. Luo, T., Tan, H.-P., Quek, T.Q.S.: Sensor OpenFlow: enabling software-defined wireless sensor networks. IEEE Commun. Lett. **16**(11), 1896–1899 (2012)
15. Costanzo, S., Galluccio, L., Morabito, G., Palazzo, S.: Software defined wireless networks: unbridling SDNs. In: 2012 European Workshop on Software Defined Networking, pp. 1–6. IEEE (2012)
16. Galluccio, L., Milardo, S., Morabito, G., Palazzo, S.: SDN-WISE: design, prototyping and experimentation of a stateful SDN solution for wireless sensor networks. In: 2015 IEEE Conference on Computer Communications (INFOCOM), pp. 513–521. IEEE (2015)

17. Yap, K.-K., et al.: Blueprint for introducing innovation into wireless mobile networks. In: Proceedings of the Second ACM SIGCOMM Workshop on Virtualized Infrastructure Systems and Architectures, pp. 25–32. ACM (2010)
18. Li, L.E., Mao, Z.M., Rexford, J.: Toward software-defined cellular networks. In: 2012 European Workshop on Software Defined Networking, pp. 7–12. IEEE (2012)
19. Zeng, D., Li, P., Guo, S., Miyazaki, T., Hu, J., Xiang, Y.: Energy minimization in multi-task software-defined sensor networks. IEEE Trans. Comput. 64(11), 3128–3139 (2015)
20. Qin, Z., Denker, G., Giannelli, C., Bellavista, P., Venkatasubramanian, N.: A software defined networking architecture for the Internet-of-Things. In: 2014 IEEE Network Operations and Management Symposium (NOMS), pp. 1–9. IEEE (2014)
21. Zhang, Z., Zhang, Z., Wang, R., Jia, Z., Lei, H., Cai, X.: ESD-WSN: an efficient SDN-based wireless sensor network architecture for iot applications. In: Ibrahim, S., Choo, K.-K.R., Yan, Z., Pedrycz, W. (eds.) ICA3PP 2017. LNCS, vol. 10393, pp. 735–745. Springer, Cham (2017). https://doi.org/10.1007/978-3-319-65482-9_59
22. Wang, K., Wang, Y., Zeng, D., Guo, S.: An SDN-based architecture for next-generation wireless networks. IEEE Wirel. Commun. 24(1), 25–31 (2017)
23. De Gante, A., Aslan, M., Matrawy, A.: Smart wireless sensor network management based on software-defined networking. In: 2014 27th Biennial Symposium on Communications (QBSC), pp. 71–75. IEEE (2014)
24. Jagadeesan, N.A., Krishnamachari, B.: Software-defined networking paradigms in wireless networks: a survey. ACM Comput. Surv. (CSUR) 47(2), 27 (2015)
25. Wang, R., Zhang, Z., Zhang, Z., Jia, Z.: ETMRM: an energy-efficient trust management and routing mechanism for SDWSNs. Comput. Netw. 139, 119–135 (2018)

DStore: A Distributed Cloud Storage System Based on Smart Contracts and Blockchain

Jingting Xue[1(✉)], Chunxiang Xu[1(✉)], Yuan Zhang[1,2], and Lanhua Bai[1]

[1] Center for Cyber Security, School of Computer Science and Engineering,
University of Electronic Science and Technology of China, Chengdu 611731, China
JTXXue@yeah.net, chxxu@uestc.edu.cn

[2] Department of Electrical and Computer Engineering, University of Waterloo,
Waterloo N2L 3G1, Canada

Abstract. In this article, we propose a client-side encrypted distributed cloud storage system named DStore, which is constructed in a peer-to-peer networking environment. DStore allows data owners to rent the local idle disks of other peers to store personal data in a distributed manner without relying on centralized control by trusted third parties. For DStore, we propose a challenge-verification solution based on the Merkle hash tree to periodically audit the integrity of outsourced data. DStore employs smart contracts to generate records and achieve consensus regarding lease relationships. Upon completion of an audit, the smart contract verifies the audit result and automatically performs the payment operation. Finally, we conduct a comprehensive evaluation to ensure that DStore is secure and feasible.

Keywords: Distributed storage · Peer-to-peer networking
Personal data · Smart contract · Blockchain

1 Introduction

Traditional cloud storage [1] relies solely on storage service providers as trusted third parties. This approach has many inherent weaknesses in terms of a trust model. First, traditional cloud storage services can result in data leakage or losses due to technology failures [2]. An example is the Amazon S3 service disruption in Virginia on February 28, 2017 [3]. Additionally, cloud storage service providers currently demand excessive surcharges over their core costs, thereby resulting in a significant increase in storage costs for users [4]. Moreover, traditional clouds face security threats such as online attacks and hacking programs that can expose sensitive private data due to their nonstandard end-to-end encryption [5].

Compared with traditional cloud storage, a decentralized storage model built on peer-to-peer (P2P) networks [6] provides higher data confidentiality and better user control at lower storage costs. Data transmission and storage are distributed among nodes without the need to through a certain centralized link;

© Springer Nature Switzerland AG 2018
J. Vaidya and J. Li (Eds.): ICA3PP 2018, LNCS 11336, pp. 385–401, 2018.
https://doi.org/10.1007/978-3-030-05057-3_30

thus, the possibility of eavesdropping on and leaking privacy user information is greatly reduced. Meanwhile, all the network nodes offer a relay forwarding function, which greatly improves the flexibility and reliability of anonymous communication and can provide better privacy protection for users. However, P2P networks are usually set up in a self-organizing manner that allows nodes to join and leave freely, which can affect user data availability to some extent.

To solve the above issue, paying fees to online and resource-providing nodes is regarded as an effective incentive mechanism. Regarding this mechanism, to ensure the unbiased execution of payment, the potential solution requires a fair and trusted third party to verify whether a network node provides resources. However, choosing trusted third parties is a considerable challenge. Fortunately, a new type of accountability system has emerged. In Ethereum [7], smart contracts are presented in the form of computer programs and published in a blockchain. The Ethereum protocol specifies how nodes in the network extend and maintain the blockchain, thereby ensuring that transactions in smart contracts are performed according to predefined rules without a central regulator.

In this article, we propose a distributed cloud storage scheme called DStore, which is based on Ethereum and completes the node-to-node leasing of idle disks. In DStore, users join the network by registering an Ethereum client. A data owner (represented by a network node that wishes to rent space on idle disks), broadcasts its storage contracts in the network. After multiple rounds of negotiation, the data owner signs storage contracts with certain lessors (network nodes willing to rent their idle disk space) and deploys smart contracts in the blockchain. The storage contracts, which detail the storage terms and payment terms as well as other necessary parameters, are stored locally by both contracting parties. After the outsourced data are delivered to the corresponding lessor, the data owner periodically audits the integrity of the data block by adding salt challenges. Finally, the smart contracts automatically perform a fee transfer based on the audit result. In DStore, the blockchain is an immutable ledger used to record storage contracts. A comprehensive evaluation shows that DStore, constructed on Ethereum, is secure, efficient and inexpensive.

Specifically, the contributions of this work are as follows.

1. We propose the DStore distributed cloud storage scheme, which is based on Ethereum. In DStore, nodes pay for idle disks of others to store their data. The outsourced data are stored in a distributed manner on physically isolated disks of different lessors. This scheme ensures that no one but the data owner can construct readable files from the encrypted blocks scattered across a network.
2. We employ smart contracts to act as trusted third parties that record and store digital summaries of the storage contracts, check the audit results, and pay the storage fee or charge a penalty based on the audit result. The smart contracts stored in the blockchain are public, providing undeniable evidence of the data owner's payment obligations and the lessor's storage obligations.
3. A security analysis and performance evaluation show that DStore is a secure, efficient and low cost. Its execution of encryption and redundancy before data

are delivered can guarantee the confidentiality and recoverability of data. DStore eliminates the need to build and maintain data centers, which significantly reduces the storage fees of data owners. The data blocks formed by the original file segmentation can be transferred, stored and audited in parallel, which is both safer and more efficient.

The remainder of this article is organized as follows. We review related works in Sect. 2, and present preliminaries in Sect. 3. We then describe DStore in Sect. 4. We analyze the security of DStore and evaluate the system's security and performance in Sect. 5. Finally, we draw conclusions and propose directions for future research in Sect. 6.

2   Related Work

DStore spans the following areas of literature.

P2P File System. Since 2000, P2P storage [8], which is based on a distributed hash table (DHT) has received extensive attention. In 2000, Kubitanicz et al. [9] proposed a global-scale persistent storage architecture called OceanStore, which was designed to span the globe and provide continuous access to persistent information. In 2002, Cooper et al. [10] proposed a peer-to-peer document backup system in which users exchange contracts stating that they agree to store copies of other people's files. In recent years, a large number of P2P network storage schemes have been proposed, such as [11–13].

Blockchain Application. Bitcoin [14], the quintessential blockchain example, allows network nodes to securely transfer digital assets using publicly verifiable ledgers without requiring a central regulator. In 2014, Miller et al. [15] proposed using the Bitcoin approach to store public archives, where the archives are copied to the global network with the highest probability of replying to them. That same year, the *Counterparty* launched a decentralized cloud storage network named Storj [16] that uses blockchain technology to create a user community in which users determine the storage-lease relationships by signing storage contracts. However, Storj does not provide a public ledger system to achieve consensus on storage contracts. Additional related studies [17–20] can also be found.

Proof of Storage. In 2007, Juels et al. [21] proposed proofs of retrievability (PORs) for large files. Subsequently, a number of variations have been proposed, including variations with improved efficiency [22], variations that disclose verifiable functionality [23], variations of the POR that can be distributed [24], and variations that support the capabilities of the file system rather than the static-document original approach [25]. As a related concept, the proof of data property (PDP) [26] attempts to prove that most, but not necessarily all, data are stored. Unlike the PDP, PORs support a feature called extraction that allows file recovery via a challenge-response mechanism. Additional related studies include [27,28].

3   Preliminaries

In this section, we define the system model and threat model, present our design goals, and briefly describe the smart contract and P2P networking.

3.1   System Model

The system model of DStore[1] is shown in Fig. 1. It involves four entities: a *data owner*, a *lessor*, many *contract servers* and a *smart contract*.

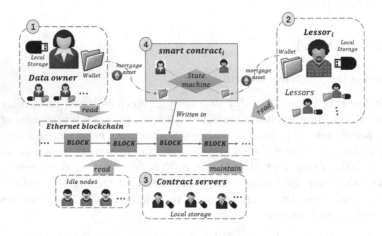

Fig. 1. System model

A *data owner* is a network node that leases idle disks from other nodes to store personal data. The data owner has the ability to complete the original data processing, perform data block transmission and integrity audits, and make payments of storage charges.

A *lessor* is a network node that is willing to lease local idle disks to the data owner. The lessor has idle disks that can be used to store data and sufficient computing power to generate integrity proofs.

Contract servers are network nodes that handle smart contracts, including collecting smart contracts that are broadcast over a period of time, verifying them, and writing the validated smart contracts to the blockchain.

A *smart contract* is a computer program written into the smart contract blockchain that helps the data owner to verify the audit result and automatically transfer digital assets based on that result.

Three additional concepts are noted.

A node that neither participates in idle disk leases nor handles smart contracts is called an *idle node*.

---

[1] Actually, many lessors are involved in DStore, but this article focuses on the data storage process for a data owner and one lessor.

Wallet is an entity in which nodes store digital assets. Before a smart contract is written to the blockchain, the contract servers determine whether each contract signer's wallet balance is greater than the assets to be mortgaged in the smart contract.

Local storage is a local storage server. For example, for the data owner, local storage can be used to save keys, signed storage contracts, pregenerated challenge messages, and some auditing information.

Next, we briefly describe how a data owner stores data in DStore. First, the data owner locally preprocesses the original data to form many data blocks; then, the data owner creates the corresponding storage contracts and broadcasts them. Next, a lessor signs a storage contract and stores the corresponding outsourced data block in local storage. Contract servers then verify and write the smart contracts deployed by the data owner and the lessor to the blockchain. The data owner and the lessor transfer mortgage assets from their wallets to the smart contract address. Finally, the data owner audits the integrity of the data block(s) stored on the lessor, and the smart contract automatically processes the payments or collects fines.

A formal definition of the proposed scheme is provided below.

Definition 1 (DStore). *DStore involves six algorithms: Setup, Genblock, Subscribe, Store, Gencontract and Audit.*

$Setup(1^\lambda) \to ((pk_\mathcal{O}, sk_\mathcal{O}), addr_\mathcal{O}, (pk_\mathcal{L}, sk_\mathcal{L}), addr_\mathcal{L}, s, (K, M), k)$: Based on the input of the security parameter λ, *Setup* generates a key pair $(pk_\mathcal{O}, sk_\mathcal{O})$, an address $addr_\mathcal{O}$, a symmetric key k, a set of random challenge salts s, and a redundant algorithm parameter (K, M) for the data owner $\mathcal{O}$. Meanwhile, *Setup* generates a key pair $(pk_\mathcal{L}, sk_\mathcal{L})$ and an address $addr_\mathcal{L}$ for the lessor $\mathcal{L}$.

$Genblock(F, k, K, M) \to (F_1, F_2, ..., F_n)$: From the input, an original data file F, k and (K, M), *Genblock* generates n data blocks $F_1, F_2, ..., F_n$ for $\mathcal{O}$.

$Subscribe((pk_\mathcal{O}, sk_\mathcal{O}), (pk_\mathcal{L}, sk_\mathcal{L}), F_1, F_2, ..., F_n) \to SSC_{\mathcal{L}\mathcal{O}}$: From the input, $(pk_\mathcal{O}, sk_\mathcal{O})$, $(pk_\mathcal{L}, sk_\mathcal{L})$, and $F_1, F_2, ..., F_n$, *Subscribe* generates a storage contract $SSC_{\mathcal{L}\mathcal{O}}$ for $\mathcal{O}$ and $\mathcal{L}$.

$Store(s, F_1, F_2, ..., F_n) \to Merkle\,hash\,tree$: From the input, $F_1, F_2, ..., F_n$, and s, *Store* generates a *Merkle hash tree* for $\mathcal{O}$, including the *digest*, *nodes* and *leaves*.

$Gencontract(SSC_{\mathcal{L}\mathcal{O}}, (pk_\mathcal{O}, sk_\mathcal{O}), (pk_\mathcal{L}, sk_\mathcal{L})) \to Smart\,contract$: From the input, $SSC_{\mathcal{L}\mathcal{O}}$, $(pk_\mathcal{O}, sk_\mathcal{O})$, and $(pk_\mathcal{L}, sk_\mathcal{L})$, *Gencontract* generates the *Smart contract* for $\mathcal{O}$ and $\mathcal{L}$.

$Audit(s, F_1, F_2, ..., F_n, digest) \to 1/0$: From the input, s, $F_1, F_2, ..., F_n$, and a *digest*, *Audit* generates audit results $1/0$ for $\mathcal{O}$ and $\mathcal{L}$.

3.2   Threat Model

Regarding the threat model, we discuss three adversaries: *malicious data owner*, *semi-trusted lessor* and *online adversary*.

A *malicious data owner* can provide incorrect digest values before the audit results are validated. Thus, even if the lessor integrally stores the corresponding data block, he cannot pass the audit. A *malicious data owner* can also deny the lessor's storage service after auditing, i.e., refuse to pay for the storage.

A *semi-trusted lessor* can destroy the integrity of a data block and then generate a forged digest that attempts to trick the data owner. A *semi-trusted lessor* can also attempt to read the contents of a stored data block.

An *online adversary* can attempt to destroy a data block stored by a lessor or conspire to partially delete a block stored by the lessor.

Here, we do not discuss *malicious contract servers*. Because of the maintenance and extension mechanism of a blockchain, the forging of smart contracts by malicious contract servers is not possible.

3.3 Design Goals

In this article, we focus on distributed storage in a P2P networking environment in relation to the following challenges.

1. Ensuring the reliability of distributed cloud storage. Because nodes can join or leave the network at any time, the availability of the data blocks stored on the lessors cannot be guaranteed. Therefore, an effective mechanism to motivate lessors to remain online should be fully considered.
2. Ensuring node consensus regarding the storage contracts. Without accounting systems, the rights and obligations of both parties to a contract cannot be regulated, which poses a great obstacle to accountability. Therefore, a public accounting measure is essential to the auditability and nonrepudiation of a storage contract.
3. Reducing the cost of audit and verification. A data file is segmented into several data blocks and stored in the local storage of many lessors. To ensure the recoverability of the original data file, a data owner must occasionally audit the integrity of outsourced data blocks. When the number of data blocks is large and audits occur frequently, an efficient audit and verification algorithm must be designed to reduce the computational cost.

To ensure secure and efficient storage in a P2P networking system via the above threat model, DStore should achieve the following goals:

- *Functionality:* A data owner should be able to deliver, audit and download outsourced data blocks and receive compensation for data losses. A lessor should be able to store blocks on local storage, generate proof of data integrity, upload data, and be paid for the integrated data storage. A smart contract can automatically perform transfers based on the audit result.
- *Security:* (a) Confidentiality, i.e., only the data owner should be able to read data; (b) availability, i.e., data blocks stored on different lessors can recover the original data file; (c) anonymity, i.e., the data owner and the lessor are anonymous throughout the interaction; (d) nonrepudiation, i.e., all nodes must agree on the storage contract between the data owner and the lessor.
- *Efficiency:* A data owner should be able to preprocess, transfer and audit data with low overhead. A lessor must be able to generate proof of data integrity and transmit data block(s) with low overhead.

3.4   Smart Contract and P2P Networking

A smart contract [7, 29] is a set of commitments defined in digital form that are automatically executed by computer systems. Structurally, smart contracts based on a blockchain include a transaction-processing and storage mechanism and a complete state machine, as shown in Figs. 2 and 3. Smart contracts enable a complex set of triggered digital commitments to be executed correctly based on the desires of the contract participants. Specifically, upon receiving a new transaction, the resource status is updated, and the smart contract is triggered to judge the state machine. If the trigger conditions indicate that one or several actions have been met, the smart contract automatically executes the transaction according to the preset information and notifies its participants.

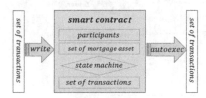

Fig. 2. Smart contract model   **Fig. 3.** Blockchain of smart contract

In P2P networking [6], nodes share some of their hardware resources, such as processing power and storage space. These shared resources are serviced over the network and can be accessed directly by other peer nodes without passing through an intermediate entity. Therefore, the P2P model is more decentralized and has higher scalability and robustness compared with the client/server model. In addition, data is distributed among nodes without first having to pass through a centralized link, which greatly reduces the possibility of eavesdropping and leakage of a user's private information.

4   Proposed Scheme

The data owner registers the Ethereum connection to obtain a key pair and a corresponding address. Then, the data owner encrypts and segments the original data file and broadcasts offer contracts over the Ethereum. An intended node becomes a lessor after signing any offer contract. When the data block is sent to the corresponding lessor, the data owner and the lessor deploy a smart contract[2]. In a subsequent data-integrity audit, the smart contract checks the proof generated by the lessor and automatically processes the transfer.

---

[2] To improve readability, we refer to a storage contract as a smart contract. In practice, to reduce the cost of paying smart contracts, multiple storage contracts among a data owner and multiple lessors are written as one smart contract.

In DStore, employing smart contracts to verify an audit result and perform the transfer operation is both convenient and provides undeniable evidence of the lease relationship between the data owner and the lessor due to the public nature and nontamperability of the smart contract blockchain.

4.1 Construction

A data owner $\mathcal{O}$, a lessor $\mathcal{L}_i$, a smart contract SC_i, and a set of contract servers $\mathcal{S}_1, \mathcal{S}_2, \ldots$ are involved in DStore, as shown in Fig. 4.

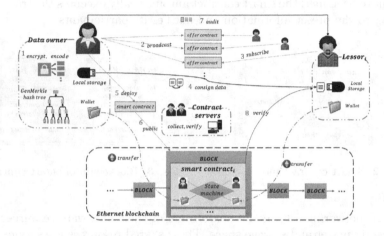

Fig. 4. DStore procedure

Setup.

- $\mathcal{O}$ and $\mathcal{L}_i$ download the Ethereum client and register the client to obtain key pairs $(pk_\mathcal{O}, sk_\mathcal{O})$ and $(pk_{\mathcal{L}_i}, sk_{\mathcal{L}_i})$ and corresponding addresses $addr_\mathcal{O}$ and $addr_{\mathcal{L}_i}$, respectively.
- Given a security parameter λ, *Setup* selects m random challenge salt sets $\{s^{(j)}\}_{j \in [1,m]}$ and the redundancy algorithm parameter (K, M) for $\mathcal{O}$, where m is the number of audits.

Genblock. $\mathcal{O}$ locally encrypts and segments the original data F.

- *Encrypt.* $\mathcal{O}$ encrypts F using the *advanced encryption standard* (AES) to obtain

$$F' = E_k(F), \tag{1}$$

where F' is divided into $F_1, F_2, \ldots, F_K$, and the key k of the AES is stored locally.
- *Erasure code* (K-of-M) is used to obtain

$$F'' = \begin{bmatrix} I_{K \times K} \\ B_{M \times K} \end{bmatrix} \times F'_{K \times 1} = \begin{bmatrix} F'_{K \times 1} \\ C_{(n-K) \times 1} \end{bmatrix}, \tag{2}$$

where $n = K + M$, $F'' = (F_1, F_2, ..., F_K, ..., F_n)$, I denotes a $K \times K$ *identity matrix*, B denotes an $M \times K$ *Vandermonde matrix* and C is a matrix of generated erasure code blocks.

Subscribe. $\mathcal{O}$ and $\mathcal{L}_i$ sign the storage contract SSC_i.

- *Offer contract.* $\mathcal{O}$ creates n offer messages $SSC_{i,void}$ corresponding to $F_1, F_2, ..., F_n$ and broadcasts them over the network, where $i \in [1, n]$.
  Using data block F_i as an example, the $SSC_{i,void}$ is as shown in Fig. 5, where XXX identifies that the item needs to be written.
- *Subscribe contract.* $\mathcal{L}_i$ signs $SSC_{i,void}$ with $sk_{\mathcal{L}_i}$, i.e.,

$$SSC_{i,\mathcal{L}_i} = Sign_{sk_{\mathcal{L}_i}}(SSC_{i,void}), \tag{3}$$

and sends $SSC_{i,\mathcal{L}_i}$ to $\mathcal{O}$, where $SSC_{i,\mathcal{L}_i}$ is as shown in Fig. 6.

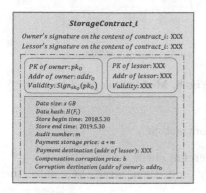

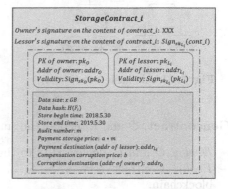

Fig. 5. Storage contract $SSC_{i,void}$ **Fig. 6.** Storage contract $SSC_{i,\mathcal{L}_i}$

Store. $\mathcal{L}_i$ stores F_i, which is consigned by $\mathcal{O}$.

- *Preserve contract.* $\mathcal{O}$ signs $SSC_{i,\mathcal{L}_i}$ with $sk_{\mathcal{O}}$, i.e.,

$$SSC_{i,\mathcal{L}_i\mathcal{O}} = Sign_{sk_{\mathcal{O}}}(SSC_{i,\mathcal{L}_i}), \tag{4}$$

and stores $E_k(SSC_{i,\mathcal{L}_i\mathcal{O}})$ in local storage.
- *GenMerkle.* Based on $\{s^{(j)}\}_{j \in [1,m]}$ and $F_1, F_2, ..., F_n$, $\mathcal{O}$ generates m *Merkle hash trees*, and then stores $\{s^{(j)}\}_{j \in [1,m]}$ corresponding to m sets $\{leaves, nodes, digests\}$ in an audit table, as shown in Table 1.
  For example, when $n = 4$, the *Merkle hash tree* generated by $\mathcal{O}$ for the j-th audit is as shown in Fig. 7.
- *Consign data.* $\mathcal{O}$ sends a consign message i to $\mathcal{L}_i$. The message content includes $SSC_{i,\mathcal{L}_i\mathcal{O}}$, the data block F_i and the corresponding hash $H(F_i)$, i.e.,

$$Consign\, i = SSC_{i,\mathcal{L}_i\mathcal{O}}||F_i||H(F_i). \tag{5}$$

- *Store.* After verifying the validity of $SSC_{i,\mathcal{L}_i\mathcal{O}}$ and the integrity of F_i, $\mathcal{L}_i$ stores F_i and $E_{k'}(SSC_{i,\mathcal{L}_i\mathcal{O}})$ in local storage, where the key k' is stored locally.

Table 1. Audit table

Challenge salts	Leaves	Nodes	Digest
$s^{(1)}$	$\{leaf_1^{(1)},...,leaf_n^{(1)}\}$	$\{node_{12}^{(1)},node_{34}^{(1)},...,node_{1234}^{(1)},...\}$	$digest^{(1)}$
...	...	...	...
$s^{(j)}$	$\{leaf_1^{(j)},...,leaf_n^{(j)}\}$	$\{node_{12}^{(j)},node_{34}^{(j)},...,node_{1234}^{(j)},...\}$	$digest^{(j)}$
...	...	...	...
$s^{(m)}$	$\{leaf_1^{(m)},...,leaf_n^{(m)}\}$	$\{node_{12}^{(m)},node_{34}^{(m)},...,node_{1234}^{(m)},...\}$	$digest^{(m)}$

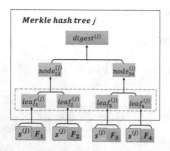

Fig. 7. Merkle hash tree (n = 4)   **Fig. 8.** Merkle hash proof (n = 4)

Gencontract. $\mathcal{O}$ and $\mathcal{L}_i$ deploy the smart contract SC_i.

- *Deploy.* $\mathcal{O}$ and $\mathcal{L}_i$ deploy SC_i[3] to the Ethereum client.
- *Public.* Contract servers $\mathcal{S}_1, \mathcal{S}_2,...$ verify and then write SC_i into the blockchain.
- *Transfer.* $\mathcal{L}_i$ transfers the asset mortgage b to SC_i's address $addr_{SC_i}$. $\mathcal{O}$ transfers the asset mortgage $a * m$ to $addr_{SC_i}$ and then deletes the local data file F, where a is a storage fee, and m is the number of audits agreed by $\mathcal{O}$ and $\mathcal{L}_i$.

Audit. $\mathcal{O}$ audits the integrity of F_i. Taking the j-challenge as an example, the following steps occur.

- *Challenge.* $\mathcal{O}$ sends $s^{(j)}$ and the (necessary, not all) leaves and nodes to $\mathcal{L}_i$. For an audit of F_3 $(n = 4)$ integrity, $\mathcal{O}$ sends $\mathcal{L}_3$ the challenge information

$$chall_j = s^{(j)}||leaf_4^{(j)}||node_{12}^{(j)}. \tag{6}$$

- *Genproof.* After receiving $chall_j$, $\mathcal{L}_i$ generates $leaf_i = H(s^{(j)} + F_i)$ with $s^{(j)}$ and the locally stored F_i; then, it combines the other leaves and nodes to generate the $digest_i^{(j)}$, which it returns to SC_i.
  When $n = 4$ and $i = 3$, the *Merkle hash proof* generation process is as shown in Fig. 8.

---

[3] The specific code of SC_i can be found here.

$$H(s^{(j)} + F_3) = leaf_3^{(j)}, \tag{7}$$

$$H(leaf_3^{(j)} + leaf_4^{(j)}) = node_{34}^{(j)}, \tag{8}$$

$$H(node_{12}^{(j)} + node_{34}^{(j)}) = digest_3^{(j)}. \tag{9}$$

– *Pay/fine.* SC_i reads the $digest_i^{(j)}$ from $\mathcal{L}_i$'s j-th proof. If the $\mathcal{L}_i$-generated $digest_i^{(j)}$ is consistent with the prewritten $H(digest^{(j)})$ in SC_i, i.e.,

$$H(digest^{(j)}) = H(digest_i^{(j)}), \tag{10}$$

then SC_i transfers a, the storage fee, to $\mathcal{L}_i$'s address $addr_{\mathcal{L}_i}$. If the verification fails, SC_i transfers b (the fine amount) and the remaining asset mortgage $a * (m - j + 1)$ to $\mathcal{O}$'s address $addr_{\mathcal{O}}$.

When SC_i expires, $\mathcal{S}_1, \mathcal{S}_2, \ldots$ generates a contract termination record and publishes it to the blockchain. If fewer than M lessors lose data blocks before the corresponding contracts expire, K well-stored data blocks can be downloaded to reconstruct the original data F, and DStore can again be used to store data.

4.2 Remarks

As mentioned in the threat model in Sect. 3.2, if $\mathcal{O}$ writes a false $H(digest)$ into SC_i, then $\mathcal{L}_i$ cannot pass the audit even if it stores the corresponding block in its entirety. SC_i is automatically processed in the event that $\mathcal{L}_i$ loses F_i, which transfers b as a fine to $\mathcal{O}$. To avoid this, $\mathcal{L}_i$ can ask $\mathcal{O}$ to send him a root. This root is the digest of a Merkle hash tree whose leaves are $digest_{(1)}, digest_{(2)}, \ldots, digest_{(m)}$. In this way, $\mathcal{L}_i$ can randomly extract several sets of challenge salts and the corresponding digests for validation when disagreement occurs between the two parties over what is prewritten in SC_i. If the samples of salts and digest are verified, then $\mathcal{L}_i$ can assume that the digests written into SC_i are unbiased. To improve readability, the above idea was not written into DStore, although this strategy is available to address this type of attack.

In addition, after F is encrypted locally, $\mathcal{O}$ can outsource a series of operations, such as redundant processing, Merkle hash tree and challenge salt generation, and challenge information transmission, to reduce the computational cost and communication overhead. Certainly, this reduction requires a series of measures to prevent fraud and collusion. Here, we simply propose this idea but do not provide an in-depth discussion.

5   Security and Performance Evaluation

5.1   Security Analysis

We analyze the security of DStore in terms of the confidentiality and availability of F.

Confidentiality of F. In DStore, the confidentiality of F is provided by encryption and segmentation. As the sole owner of k and (K, M), the data owner is the only one who has the ability to rebuild and decrypt F', even if a single lessor has all the data blocks. In addition, F' is segmented into blocks of data, which are then stored dispersedly on a physically isolated local disk. The uploader of the data block is the only one who knows the destinations of all the pieces. When a lessor receives a segment, it has already been encrypted as part of a larger file. Without all the other fragments and the encryption key, the data blocks that lessors hold are useless.

Availability. Based on the importance of F, the data owner can set different redundancy levels, forming a trade-off between storage costs and data availability. In DStore, the K-of-M redundancy code guarantees that F can be reconstructed as long as the number of missing data blocks does not exceed M. Obviously, a larger ratio of check blocks ensures greater availability of the original data file. However, as the ratio of check blocks increases, the error decoding rate and the erasure decoding rate synchronously decline sharply.

5.2   Performance Evaluation

The Implementation of Genblock. We evaluated the performance of DStore based on the data owner's computational overhead and storage payment as well as a lessor's computational overhead. All the experiments were conducted on an HP desktop made in China running a Windows 7 SP1 64-bit operating system with a 4.4 GHz Intel Core i7-4790K CPU and 16 GB of DDR3 RAM installed. The software implementations were coded in C++ and compiled using Microsoft Visual C++ 2005 SP1. All the experimental results are the averages of 100 experiments.

The computational overhead of the data owner is mainly consumed by *Genblock*, while that of the lessor is mainly consumed by *Genproof*. We implemented *Genblock* and *Genproof* to demonstrate the feasibility of DStore. In *Genblock*, the data owner encrypts F using AES-256 encryption and the erasure code F' using *Reed-Solomon* encoding. To evaluate the feasibility of *Genblock* more intuitively, we implemented the CTR, ECB, CBC, CFB, and OFB modes of AES-256 and presented the *Genblock*-CTR procedure as shown in Fig. 9.

Computational Overhead. Table 2 and Fig. 10 shows the average encryption time (Time) and performance (PERF) of the five AES-256 cipher operation modes when $F = 2000\ MB$. The CTR mode yields the highest performance level and has a satisfactory level of security (confidentiality). Consequently, it can be recommended to ensure a secure data transfer over the network. Although

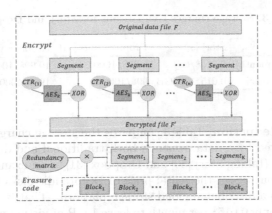

Fig. 9. *Genblock*-CTR procedure

the ECB mode yields the second-highest performance, we do not recommend the use of ECB because it encrypts data blocks into identical ciphertext blocks; therefore, it does not completely hide patterns in the data.

Table 2. AES cipher performance on Intel Core^{TM} i7-4790K

	CTR mode	ECB mode	CBC mode	CFB mode	OFB mode
Time (in Sec)	0.31	0.37	0.38	0.38	0.39
PERF (MB/Sec)	335.11	282.34	274.12	274.61	260.29

In *Genproof*, the *Merkle hash proof* always consists of exactly $log_2 l$ hashes, where l is the number of leaves. That is, the lessor needs to calculate only $log_2 l$ hash values for every audit. Figure 11 shows that with an exponential increase in the number of data blocks, the lessor needs to calculate fewer hashes.

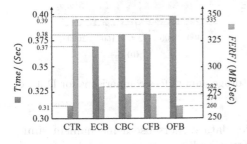

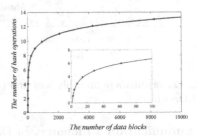

Fig. 10. Performance in AES-256 modes   **Fig. 11.** Computational cost of a lessor

Table 3. Storage charges comparisons for Storj and Dropbox

	Storj [30]	Dropbox plus [31]	Dropbox professional [31]
Storage fees (per month)	0.015$/GB	9.99$/1000 GB	19.99$/1000 GB
Storage fees (per year)	0.015*12$/GB	99$/1000 GB	199$/1000 GB

Storage Cost Reduction. Table 3 compares the storage charges for 1000 GB of disk space rented by a data owner in both traditional and distributed cloud storage platforms (taking Storj [30] and Dropbox [31] as an example). To offer a realistic description, we set the rental price of DStore idle disks to that of Storj [16], which is also a distributed cloud storage platform. That is, with DStore, a data owner pays only 0.015$ per month to lease 1 GB of virtual personal hosting [32] and spends an additional 0.05$ to purchase data search services. However, the monthly fee for a data owner to rent 1000 GB of storage space from Dropbox Plus is 9.99$. Note that even if a data owner does not use that space, he will still charged 9.99$ a month. Notably, when a data owner does not fully use the 1000 GB on the idle disks, he can lease the unused space on DStore to offset some of the overhead.

Figure 12 compares the fees of renting disk space with different sizes and duration on DStore and Dropbox Plus. In the case of renting storage space in months and the outsourced storage data less than 666 GB and 1000 GB to 1332 GB, it is cheaper for data owners to lease storage space on DStore. Similarly, in the case of renting storage space in years, if the outsourced data is less than 550 GB or in the range of 1000 GB to 1100 GB, Dstore is still a better choice.

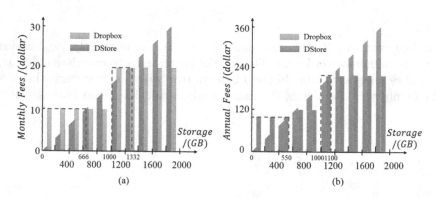

Fig. 12. (a) Storage monthly fees and (b) Storage annual fees comparisons for DStore and Dropbox

Communication Efficiency. In DStore, data owners use a mechanism similar to Bittorrent [33] to download data from multiple lessors instead of from a central server, which greatly speeds up the download process. The geographical distribution of the entire network can effectively guarantee an excellent download speed.

6   Conclusions and Future Work

In this article, we propose the DStore scheme which works in a P2P network environment. DStore can efficiently and securely store and audit data and accurately process payments. To enable DStore, we introduce smart contracts for publishing lease relationships, verifying the correctness of the Merkle proof, and automating transfers. We also conduct a security analysis to demonstrate the feasibility of DStore. In addition, although our approach is designed for data storage and auditing, it can potentially be applied to multiple scenarios that emphasize the automatic execution of digital asset transfers and nonrepudiation.

In the future, we will continue to study the effective combination of data storage and blockchain/smart contract technology to solve new problems. We will then attempt to apply our ideas to other areas where data privacy and digital asset management need to be protected. Cloud storage based on P2P networking has become the infrastructure of the information age. Therefore, exploring P2P networking cloud storage paradigms and applications will have a profound impact on data storage outsourcing. However, ensuring outsourced data security will remain a challenging issue.

Acknowledgments. This work is supported by the National Key R&D Program of China under Grant 2017YFB0802000 and the National Natural Science Foundation of China under Grant 61370203.

References

1. Kamara, S., Lauter, K.: Cryptographic cloud storage. In: Sion, R., et al. (eds.) FC 2010. LNCS, vol. 6054, pp. 136–149. Springer, Heidelberg (2010). https://doi.org/10.1007/978-3-642-14992-4_13
2. Jiang, T., Chen, X.F., Li, J., et al.: Towards secure and reliable cloud storage against data re-outsourcing. Future Gener. Comput. Syst. **52**, 86–94 (2015)
3. Summary of the Amazon S3 Service Disruption in the Northern Virginia (US-EAST-1) Region. https://aws.amazon.com/cn/message/41926/
4. Storj vs Dropbox: Why Decentralized Storage is the Future. http://www.8btc.com/storj-vs-dropbox-why-decentralized-storage-is-the-future
5. Li, J., Yan, Q.B., Chang, V.: Internet of things: security and privacy in a connected world. Future Gener Comput. Syst. **78**(3), 931–932 (2018)
6. Schollmeier, R.: A definition of peer-to-peer networking for the classification of peer-to-peer architectures and applications. In: 1st International Conference on Peer-to-Peer Computing, pp. 101–102. IEEE Press, Linköping (2001)
7. Wood, G.: Ethereum: a secure decentralised generalised transaction ledger. Ethereum Project Yellow Paper **151**, 1–32 (2014)
8. Rowstron, A., Druschel, P.: Storage management and caching in PAST, a large-scale, persistent peer-to-peer storage utility. In: 18th ACM SIGOPS Operating Systems Review, vol. 35, no. 5, pp. 188–201. ACM Press, Banff (2001)
9. Kubiatowicz, J., Bindel, D., Chen, Y.: OceanStore: an architecture for global-scale persistent storage. In: 17th ACM SIGOPS Operating Systems Review, vol. 34, no. 5, pp. 190–201. ACM Press, Cambridge (2000)

10. Cooper, B.F., Garcia-Molina, H.: Peer-to-peer data trading to preserve information. ACM TOIS **20**(2), 133–170 (2002)
11. Hesselink, L., Rizal, D., Bjornson, E.S.: Managed Peer-to-peer Applications, Systems and Methods for Distributed Data Access and Storage. US Patent 9,894,141 (2018)
12. Li, J.: Reliable, Efficient Peer-to-peer Storage. US Patent 9,047,310 (2015)
13. Chen, Y.F., Huang, Y., Rahe, J., et al.: Peer-to-peer Distributed Storage for Internet Protocol Television. US Patent 9,578,288 (2017)
14. Nakamoto, S.: Bitcoin: A Peer-to-peer Electronic Cash System (2008)
15. Miller, A., Juels, A., Shi, E., et al.: Permacoin: repurposing Bitcoin Work for Data Preservation. In: 35th IEEE Symposium on Security and Privacy, pp. 475–490. IEEE Press, Berkeley (2014)
16. Wilkinson, S., Boshevski, T., Brandoff, J., et al.: Storj: A Peer-to-peer Cloud Storage Network (V2). Citeseer Press (2016)
17. Kuo, T.T., Ohno-Machado, L.: ModelChain: Decentralized Privacy-Preserving Healthcare Predictive Modeling Framework on Private Blockchain Networks. arXiv preprint arXiv:1802.01746 (2018)
18. Kang, J.W., Yu, R., Huang, X.M., et al.: Enabling localized peer-to-peer electricity trading among plug-in hybrid electric vehicles using consortium blockchains. IEEE T Ind. Inform. **13**(6), 3154–3164 (2017)
19. Zyskind, G., Nathan, O., et al.: Decentralizing privacy: using blockchain to protect personal data. In: 36th IEEE Symposium on Security and Privacy Workshops, pp. 180–184. IEEE Press, San Jose (2015)
20. Azaria, A., Ekblaw, A., Vieira, T., et al.: MedRec: using blockchain for medical data access and permission management. In: 2nd International Conference on Open and Big Data, pp. 25–30. IEEE Press, Vienna (2016)
21. Juels, A., Kaliski, B.: PORs: proofs of retrievability for large files. In: 14th ACM Conference on Computer and Communications Security, pp. 584–597. ACM Press, Alexandria (2007)
22. Bowers, K.D., Juels, A., Oprea, A.: Proofs of retrievability: theory and implementation. In: 1st ACM Workshop on Cloud Computing Security, pp. 43–54. ACM Press, Chicago (2009)
23. Shacham, H., Waters, B.: Compact proofs of retrievability. J. Cryptol. **26**(3), 442–483 (2013)
24. Bowers, K.D., Juels, A., Oprea, A.: HAIL: a high-availability and integrity layer for cloud storage. In: 16th ACM Conference on Computer and Communications Security, pp. 187–198. ACM Press, Chicago (2009)
25. Shi, E., Stefanov, E., Papamanthou, C.: Practical dynamic proofs of retrievability. In: 20th ACM SIGSAC Conference on Computer and Communications Security, pp. 325–336. ACM Press, Berlin (2013)
26. Ateniese, G., Burns, R., Curtmola, R., et al.: Provable data possession at untrusted stores. In: 14th ACM Conference on Computer and Communications Security, pp. 598–609. ACM Press, Alexandria (2007)
27. Cash, D., Küpçü, A., Wichs, D.: Dynamic proofs of retrievability via oblivious RAM. J. Cryptol. **30**(1), 22–57 (2017)
28. Erway, C.C., Küpçü, A., Papamanthou, C., et al.: Dynamic provable data possession. ACM T Inform. Syst. Secur. **17**(4), 15 (2015)
29. Buterin, V., et al.: A Next-generation Smart Contract and Decentralized Application Platform. White Paper (2014)
30. https://storj.io/

31. https://www.dropbox.com/
32. What is Storj. https://coincentral.com/storj-beginners-guide/
33. Pouwelse, J., Garbacki, P., Epema, D., Sips, H.: The bittorrent P2P file-sharing system: measurements and analysis. In: Castro, M., van Renesse, R. (eds.) IPTPS 2005. LNCS, vol. 3640, pp. 205–216. Springer, Heidelberg (2005). https://doi.org/10.1007/11558989_19

Towards an Efficient and Real-Time Scheduling Platform for Mobile Charging Vehicles

Qi Liu[1], Jinyang Li[1], Xiaoshan Sun[1], Junjie Wang[1], Yang Ning[1], Wei Zheng[2], Jian Li[3], and Hengchang Liu[1(✉)]

[1] University of Science and Technology of China, Hefei, China
{liuqi100,ljyustc,sxs1166,sa516302,ning1992}@mail.ustc.edu.cn,
hcliu@ustc.edu.cn
[2] Comprehend (Suzhou) Information Technology Inc., Suzhou, China
18.weizheng@gmail.com
[3] Evehicle Inc., Shangrao, China
lijian@evehicle.cn

Abstract. With increasing environmental awareness from the society, electric vehicles (EVs) have been taking a steady increasing market share each year. Meanwhile, the development of the infrastructure of the public charging facilities for EVs is much more restricted compared to fossil-fuel vehicles. Moreover, the overall charging demand usually significantly varies in both spatial and time domains. As a result, the availability of public charging facilities usually do not match the exact demand during different hours of the day. In this paper, we introduce a new charging facility – mobile charging vehicles (MCVs), which carry batteries that can be used for charging other EVs. We propose three different scheduling strategies of MCVs and evaluate the performance through a real world EVs charging dataset. Our experiment shows that the addition of MCVs to current charging facilities greatly increases the overall charging efficiency, in both waiting time of EVs and the load rate of stations.

Keywords: Mobile charging vehicle · Electric vehicle
Scheduling strategy

1 Introduction

For environmental considerations, governments around the world are actively promoting EVs. In 2016, 351,000 EVs were sold in China, the largest EV market in the world, accounting for half of the world's total sales [1]. Beijing, the capital of China, is one of the pioneer cities adopting EVs. By the end of July 2017, the number of new EVs in Beijing has reached 141,400. However there are only about 17,500 public charging piles in the city, 8 times less than the number of EVs [2]. The existing charging infrastructure cannot fully meet the charging needs of EVs in the city.

© Springer Nature Switzerland AG 2018
J. Vaidya and J. Li (Eds.): ICA3PP 2018, LNCS 11336, pp. 402–416, 2018.
https://doi.org/10.1007/978-3-030-05057-3_31

Several planning methods have been proposed to facilitate the deployment of charging infrastructure. Most of the studies indirectly estimates the distribution of charging demand based on traffic data, such as parking records, traffic flow, the market share of EVs and GPS trajectories. However, the estimated results may not reflect the real charging demand of EVs since the driving patterns of EVs are different from those of fossil-fuel vehicles and currently EVs only account for a small fraction of the total traffic. Additionally, fine-grained temporal patterns and user preferences have not been fully explored. We found from our real-world charging records that, just like there are morning and evening peaks in traffic, the distribution of charging demand also varies during a day. Consequently, existing planning strategies may result in longer queuing time for charging at peak hours and under-utilization of charging piles at other times due to inaccurate charging demand estimation.

On the other hand, most of these studies focuses on the planning of battery charging or swapping stations. However, the construction of a station is a lengthy and expensive process. Once the station is built, it is difficult to change the location of the station and number of charging piles. So the design of a new charging mechanism with lower cost and better flexibility, which complements existing charging infrastructure to better balance the charging demand and supply, becomes very important.

Fig. 1. Mobile charging vehicles

Fig. 2. Charging pile failure

In this paper, we introduce the MCVs to address this issue. The relationship between charging stations and MCVs is like the relationship between buses and taxis. The former is relatively stable and has a large capacity, but lacks flexibility. The latter's capacity is small, but its scalability and mobility are relatively strong. Therefore, the latter is used to share the pressure with the former during the peak period, as well as to handle some unexpected situations. Compared to the fixed charging stations, MCVs have the following advantages:

- The construction of charging stations are constrained by budget, site size, power grid facilities, and etc, thus there are many places not suitable for building charging stations [3]. However, the MCVs have fewer restrictions for the venue and the ability to relocate to new locations with the charging demand change, and they are not dependent on nearby grid facilities to charge EVs. Figure 1 shows the actual use of MCVs in Beijing.
- MCV are charged at valley period when there is less charging demand, and deployed to the locations to charge EVs during peak period, which reduces the pressure on the grid and charging stations during the peak periods.
- As shown in Fig. 2, while the charging piles are used, there are usually no service staff on duty, so there may be some improper use, which will damage the charging pile. While for MCVs, the whole process is manned, which not only reduces the failure rate, but also improve user's experience.

In this paper, we propose a novel data-driven MCV scheduling method that utilizes real-world charging records and app data and schedules MCVs based on fine-grained temporal patterns and user preferences. The contributions of this paper include:

- We design and implement a novel data-driven MCV scheduling algorithm that estimates the unmet charging demand and optimizes the MCV dispatching. The fine-grained temporal patterns and user preferences in different time periods during a day are considered. The scheduling problem is formulated as an integer programming problem. To the best of our knowledge, this is the first work that addresses the MCV scheduling problem.
- We propose a novel fine-grained unmet charging demand estimation algorithm that utilizes the charging records from 17,500 charging piles in Beijing and usage data (search and navigation records) of a dedicate mobile app.
- We design and evaluate three scheduling strategies on the real-world datasets. The evaluation results show that the waiting time of EVs to be charged in each time period can be significantly reduced by deploying MCVs. We also find that a local greedy algorithm can achieve comparable effect of the global optimization algorithm but is less computationally intensive, which is more suitable for real-time dispatch.

The remainder of the paper is organized as follows. We review previous work in Sect. 2 and describe the estimation algorithm of unmet demand in Sect. 3. In Sect. 4, we describe the three different scheduling strategies for MCVs. We evaluate the scheduling strategies in Sect. 5. Finally, Sect. 6 concludes this paper.

2   Related Work

The user's charging behavior is affected by various factors, such as service price, incentive mechanism, location of the charging station and scale of the charging station, etc. Zhang et al. [5] studied the impact of actual needs of drives and gasoline prices on the choice of gas station. Wang et al. [6] studied the issues related to grid balancing to reduce the load on the power grid and indirectly reduce the price of electricity. Sun et al. [7] proposed an incentive mechanism to motivate smart phone users collecting and uploading sensory data for participatory sensing applications. Xu et al. [8] and Malandrino et al. [9] studied the impact of charging price on the choice of charging station of EV drivers. There have been many researches on the impact of location and size of battery charging/swapping stations:

Battery Charging Stations (BCSs): Li et al. [10] analyzed the drivers' charging behaviors and proposed an Bayesian-inference-based algorithm. Ge et al. [11] considered traffic density and BCS's capacity constraints and determined the location and size of BCSs using a genetic-algorithm-based method. Li et al. [12] developed a data-driven framework to performs optimal BCSs placement and optimal charging point assignment. Liu et al. [13] developed a method which combining the two-step screening method and the modified primal-dual interior point algorithm to solve the optimal planning problem of BCSs. Liu et al. [14] proposed an adaptive particle swarm optimization algorithm to solve the problem of locating and sizing of BCSs. Timpner et al. [15] presented a design of scheduling concepts for a coordinated charging strategy based on V-Charge. Chen et al. [16] determined the best locations for installing a constrained number of BCSs based on parking demand, population densities, trip attributes and so on in different areas.

Battery Swapping Stations (BSSs): McPherson et al. [17] proposed a model for determining the best geographical location of a BSS for Australia by considering four different location models and the behavior of different EV drivers. Zheng et al. [18] proposed a method to find the optimal planning of BSSs in the distribution level of the power system, including locations, sizes, and charging strategies of the BSSs. Mak et al. [19] developed two distributed optimization models for the location of BSSs. Xiong et al. [20] determined the service area of BSSs through Volonoi diagram and then proposed an optimization strategy for the allocation of BSSs based on the improved particle swarm optimization algorithm. Yang et al. [21] proposed a BSS-EV location routing solution to simultaneously determine the location policy of BSSs and the routing strategy of EVs. In addition, Liu et al. [22] and Cao et al. [23] both considered the impact of photovoltaic on BSSs.

What distinguishes our work from existing studies is that we consider the fine-grained temporal charging behaviors and user preferences based on real-world charging records and charging mobile application usage data to give accurate charging demand estimation in different time and space.

3 Demand Estimation

Data Description: In future, when unmanned technology becomes popular and widely used in EVs, users can easily collect integrated datasets including vehicle GPS, battery status, charging records, etc. But in present, we can only integrate the multi-source data such as the location and scale of charging stations, the location of parking lots, the charging records of EVs, and the records

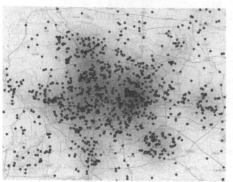

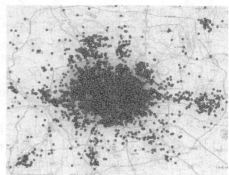

Fig. 3. Distribution of charging stations

Fig. 4. Distribution of parking lots

of using mobile phone APP to achieve the effect of integrated datasets. Currently, the coverage of charging service within the Sixth Ring Road in Beijing is approximately 95% with the service radius of each charging station set to 3 km. OpenStreetMap [4] (OSM) is used to provide road network of the corresponding area, and Tiananmen Square is used as a reference point of the city center. The other datasets are listed as follows:

- **Charging Stations and Piles:** The data include the ID, location, region type (community, market, school, etc) and the number of charging piles of the charging stations. Figure 3 shows the spatial distribution of charging stations in Sixth-Ring Road of Beijing.
- **Parking Lots:** The data include the parking lot ID and location in Beijing. A use case is depicted in Fig. 1. Because both the MCVs and the EVs to be charged need to be parked for charging, so we only consider deploying MCVs to parking lots. Figure 4 shows the distribution of parking lots in Sixth-Ring Road of Beijing.
- **Real-time Charging Status:** The charging record dataset contains the user ID, start and end charging time, the station ID and pile ID, etc. As shown in Fig. 5, most of users, whose average charging interval is less than a week in 2016, finish their charge in 90 min. Figure 6 shows the distance distribution from the charging location to the center of Beijing (Tiananmen Square) in different time periods, where the gray lower bound represents the distance distribution between 5:00–6:00, and the gray upper bound represents the one between 15:00–16:00. A tidal phenomenon can be observed that from 5:00, the distribution gradually moves towards the city center, and then from 15:00, began to move away from the city center.
- **APP Usage:** This dataset contains the usage data of a mobile application for EV charging service developed by the official public platform for EV services of Beijing. Users can use the app to search and navigate to charging stations. The data include the user ID, location of origin and destination (each destination corresponds to a charging station), time, etc. Fig. 7 shows the time

distribution of the start time of charging and the time distribution of app usage in 24 hours. We find that these two distributions are similar, which shows a correlation between app usage and actual charging. We integrate these two data sources to determine locations where the charging demands are generated. Figure 8 shows the distance distribution of user using the app to navigate to the nearby charging station.

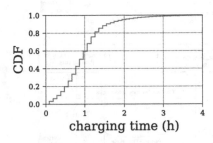

Fig. 5. Charging duration

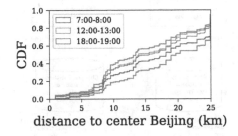

Fig. 6. Charging distance

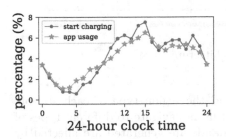

Fig. 7. Temporal distribution during a day

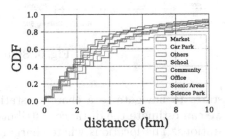

Fig. 8. Navigation distance

Time Division: Three time factors are considered in this paper. The first is the charging time as shown in Fig. 5. The second factor is the travel time that an EV spends on traveling from the demand generation point to the parking lot where MCVs are deployed. The last one is the time that the MCVs need to be scheduled from the current positions to the next parking lots. MCVs' working hours (7:00–22:00) are divided into 3-hour intervals. We assume that an MCV can charge up to 3 EVs at the same time, and the service capacity of one charging station depends on the number of charging piles in the station.

Unmet Demand: If the number of EVs to be charged exceeds the capacity (the number of charging piles) of the charging station, users need to wait in line for charging. This part of the demand in the queue is defined as the unmet demand.

Mapping Method: We divide the urban area of Beijing within Sixth Ring Road into equal-sized grids. Then based on the data of locations when the user

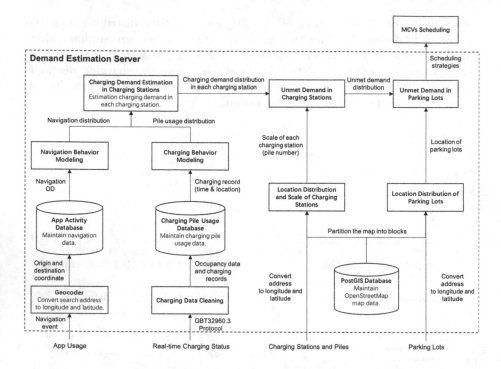

Fig. 9. System Architecture

starts to navigate to a charging station and the region type of each station, we can estimate the distance distribution of users navigate to different types of stations. The locations where charging demands are generated are affected by the tidal phenomenon shown in Fig. 6. For example, a charging is more likely to take place in the fringe of the city during morning peak (7:00–10:00), while it is more likely to take place at inner city during evening peak (16:00–19:00).

The system architecture is shown in Fig. 9. The app usage data includes information of each navigation event. We first convert each target address to longitude and latitude by the geocoder, and then store the origin and destination of each event in the *App Activity Database*. The real-time charging status received by pile complies with the GBT32960.3 [24] standard. After removed some undesired fields and error data caused by device failure, we store the cleaned data in the *Charging Pile Usage Database*. In addition, the *PostGIS Database* maintain the OSM map data. First, we divide the area within the Sixth Ring Road into unified grids, and then map each charging station and parking lot to the OSM map by converting the location address to longitude and latitude.

The charging records and app usage data are fused to estimate the distribution of all charging demands in each time period. A recorded charging has at least one of the following records: (1) navigation event (using the app) and (2) charging event (on charging pile). The two kinds of data are filtered to ensure they are mutually exclusive to avoid redundant calculations. Then, based on the distance distribution in Fig. 8 and the tidal phenomenon in Fig. 6, we mapped the demand generation points corresponding to these navigation and charging events to the map. After that, we can allocate the demand in each grid point to all stations according to the probability $P_d(i, j)$ and then the total demand D_{tj} in station j at the time period t can be calculated by:

$$D_{tj} = \sum_{i=1}^{n} d_{ti} \times P_d(i, j) \tag{1}$$

$$P_d(i, j) = \frac{z_j \exp(-c_{ij})}{\sum_{j=1}^{S} z_j \exp(-c_{ij})} \tag{2}$$

where z_j is the number of charging piles in station j, and there are a total of S existing charging stations, d_{ti} represents the demand of grid point i at time period t, $P_d(i, j)$ and c_{ij} represent the probability of demand shift and distance from the grid point i to the station j. So the unmet demand (UD) r_{tj} in each charging station is:

$$r_{tj} = D_{tj} - z_j \tag{3}$$

Then, we can obtain the amount of UD R_{ti} at each point in different time periods by assigning the UD in each station to all points with $P_r(i, j)$:

$$R_{ti} = \sum_{j=1}^{S} r_{tj} \times P_r(i, j) \tag{4}$$

$$P_r(i, j) = \frac{\exp(-c_{ji})}{\sum_{i=1}^{n} \exp(-c_{ji})} \tag{5}$$

where $P_r(i, j)$ represents the probability of the UD allocated from station j to point i in t time period.

To obtain the distribution of charging demand, we first map each parking lot to the grid, so that we can get the distribution of all the parking lot. We do not need to know how many parking lots at each grid point, but only need to know whether there is a parking lot at that point. Then we allocate the UD to each parking lot according to Eq. (6):

$$E_{tj} = \sum_{i=1}^{n} R_{ti} \times P_R(i, j) \tag{6}$$

$$P_R(i, j) = \frac{\exp(-c_{ij})}{\sum_{j=1}^{U} \exp(-c_{ij})} \tag{7}$$

where E_{tj} is the amount of UD in parking lot j at time period t; U is the number of grid points with at least one parking lot; and $P_R(i, j)$ is the probability that UD shifts from point i to parking lot j. The distribution of charging demand and UD between 19:00 and 22:00 is shown in Fig. 10 as an example.

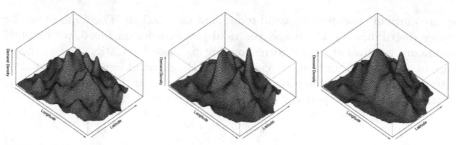

(a) Demand in charging stations

(b) Unmet demand in charging stations

(c) Unmet demand in park-
ing lots

Fig. 10. Estimated distribution of charging demand

4   Scheduling Strategy

After getting the demand in each parking lot at different time periods, we can
schedule the MCVs according to the demand distribution. We have taken three
different scheduling strategies, including the greedy algorithm based on demand
only, greedy algorithm based on demand and scheduling distance, and a global
optimization algorithm based on demand and scheduling distance. Then we compare the results of these three different schedules at the end of this chapter.

Greedy Strategy Based on Demand (GSD): This scheduling strategy only
considers the total amount of UD in each parking lot for the current time period.
Specifically, the MCV which has the most remaining power is scheduled to the
most needed parking lot each time, so that it not only maximizes the number
of served charging demand in the parking lot, but also balances the remaining
power of all MCVs, avoiding excessive fragmentation of the residual power of
some MCVs. The objective function is as follows:

$$max: \sum_{k=1}^{K} \sum_{j=1}^{n} f_{ktj}$$

$$s.t.: f_{ktj} = min[M, y_{kt}, E'_{tj}] > 0 \tag{8}$$

$$y_{kt} = \begin{cases} B, & if\ t = 1 \\ y_{k(t-1)} - f_{k(t-1)j}, & else\ 2 \le t \le 5 \end{cases}$$

where K represents the total number of MCVs, B and M are the battery capacity
and the number of charging guns of each MCV, respectively. We assume that
one MCV can meet the charging demand of 10 EVs and it has 3 charging guns.
We further assume that f_{ktj} is the amount of demand can be satisfied this time
for each MCV dispatched from the current position i to the target parking lot
j and if $f_{ktj} = 0$ the MCV will not be scheduled; y_{kt} is the left power of MCV
k at the start of time period t, by default, one MCV can charge no more than
3 EVs at the same time; E'_{tj} represents the current demand at the grid point

j in the time period t and the initial demand at j is E_{tj}. As shown in Eq. (9), after a MCV k is scheduled to this point during this time period, the demand for satisfaction is f'_{ktj}, and then the distribution of UD in the current time period will be reset.

$$E'_{tj} = E_{tj} - f'_{ktj} \tag{9}$$

GSD and Scheduling Distance (GSDD): This strategy considers both the UD in each parking lot and the scheduling distance of this schedule, because the movement of MCVs will also consume part of the power. For this strategy, the schedule result is the same as that of GSD for $t = 1$, which satisfies the Eq. (8). Starting from the second time period, the objective function is as follows:

$$\max : \sum_{k=1}^{K} \sum_{j=1}^{n} f_{ktj} - \mu_{kt} \times rate$$

$$s.t.: f_{ktj} = \min[M, y_{kt}, E'_{tj}] > 0 \tag{10}$$

$$2 \leq t \leq 5$$

$$0 < rate < 1$$

$$\mu_{kt} \geq 0$$

where μ_{kt} represents the distance traveled by the MCV k in the time period t, and $rate$ is the influence of the distance on each dispatch. When $rate = 0$, this strategy is equivalent to the previous scheduling strategy.

Global Optimization Strategy Based on Demand and Scheduling Distance (GOSDD): Unlike the second scheduling strategy, this strategy considers the possible scheduling situations for all time periods, and then find the optimal solution. We define the penalty cost to represent the sum of the weighted dispatch distance and the UD of all the dispatches in each time period. The specific objective function is as follows:

$$\min : \sum_{j=1}^{n} \delta_{tj} + \sum_{k=1}^{K} \mu_{kt} \times rate$$

$$s.t.: \sum_{k=1}^{K} f_{ktj} + \delta_{tj} = E_{tj} \tag{11}$$

$$\delta_{tj} \geq 0, \ 1 \leq t \leq 5$$

$$0 \leq f_{ktj} \leq y_{kt} \ and \ f_{ktj} \leq M \times x_{ktj}$$

$$x_{ktj} = \{0,1\} \ and \ \sum_{j=1}^{n} x_{ktj} = 1$$

where the $\sum_{k=1}^{K} f_{ktj}$ and δ_{tj} represent the total amount of demand that can and cannot be satisfied by all the MCVs which are scheduled to the grid point j during the time period t respectively. When $x_{ktj} = 1$, MCV k is scheduled to the parking lot j during time period t.

5   Evaluation

Figure 11 shows the impact of different distance weights on the total number of services, where the ordinate is the total number of services in a day. We can see that the curve of $rate = 0.05$ is similar to the one of $rate = 0$, due to the reason that the radius of Sixth Ring Road is about 25 km. In the case of $rate = 0.1$, the total number of services in a day reaches the upper limit when $K = 150$.

Figure 12 shows the service times distribution of different numbers of MCVs in each time period when $rate = 0.1$. It can be seen that affected by demand, for all possible K, the service times is the lowest when $t = 1$, and reaches the maximum at $t = 3$. For $K = 50$, we can see that it has the least amount of service at $t = 5$, which is due to the fact that most MCVs have reached the maximum number of services before the 5th time period. In addition, we can also see in this figure that the distribution of $K = 150$ is similar to that of $K = 200$, which also shows that for $rate = 0.1$, 150 is already the upper limit of K, beyond which the extra MCVs will not bring additional improvements to the service times.

Figure 13 shows the utilization of different numbers of MCVs and the number of EVs they served in one day when $rate = 0.1$. In this figure, the blue and red curves represent the utilization rate of MCVs and the number of service times, respectively. From the blue curve, we can see that when the number of MCVs is less than 75, the utilization of MCVs is more than 95%. It is because the amount of UD is far greater than the services that MCVs can provide, so before the end of the day, most MCVs have already run out of electricity. The number of unserved

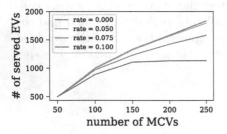

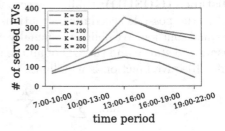

Fig. 11. Scheduling distance weight   **Fig. 12.** MCVs number analysis

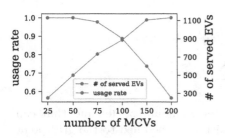

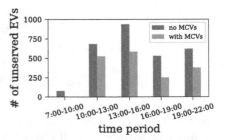

Fig. 13. Usage rate and service times   **Fig. 14.** Number of unmet EVs

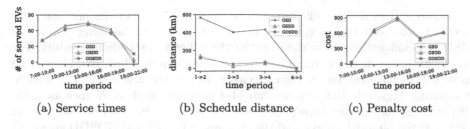

(a) Service times (b) Schedule distance (c) Penalty cost

Fig. 15. Analysis of scheduling results (rate = 0.1, K = 25)

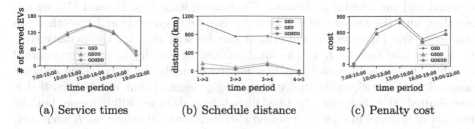

(a) Service times (b) Schedule distance (c) Penalty cost

Fig. 16. Analysis of scheduling results (rate = 0.1, K = 50)

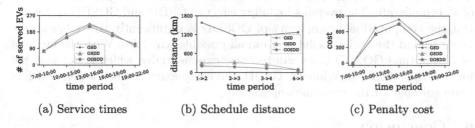

(a) Service times (b) Schedule distance (c) Penalty cost

Fig. 17. Analysis of scheduling results (rate = 0.1, K = 75)

EVs in each time period before and after deploying MCVs when $rate = 0.1$ is shown in Fig. 14. The histograms of blue and orange indicate the number of unserved EVs in each time period when $K = 0$ and $K = 150$, respectively.

We compared the scheduling results of these three different scheduling strategies in Figs. 15, 16 and 17. Figure 15a shows the comparison of the number of services in each time period. It can be seen that before the start of the 5th time period, the demand satisfied by GSD is slightly higher than those of the other two strategies. In the case of $t = 5$, the number of services under each of the three strategies drops sharply, because most of MCVs run out of power before the start of the 5th time period. Comparison between Figs. 16a and 17a shows that as K increases, the number of services in each time period also increases, and the change is the most significant when $t = 5$.

Figure 15b shows the scheduling distance of MCVs from the previous time period to the next time period. It can be seen that the scheduling distance of GSD is significantly greater than that of the other two scheduling results. The total scheduling distance from $t = 4$ to $t = 5$ is about 0, which also shows that most MCVs have run out of their service power at the end of $t = 4$. Similarly, comparing Figs. 16b and 17b, we can also conclude that as K increases, the dispatch distance in each time period will also increase. However, in comparison, GSD has the largest increase, and the changes in GSDD and GOSDD are small.

Figure 15c shows the comparison between the total penalty costs of different scheduling strategies in each time period, that is, the weighted sum of the unmet demand and the scheduling distance. Comparing with Figs. 16c and 17c, we can see that with the increase of K, the difference between GSD and the other two strategies also increases. In addition, it can be seen that for the penalty cost, no matter how big the K is, the total amount of penalty in each time period is about the same, because when K is relatively small, the dispatching distance is small, and consequently the corresponding demand that can be satisfied is also limited. If K is larger, the total dispatching distance will increase, but the number of services in each time period also increases. Of course, as K increases, the average penalty for each MCV will become smaller and smaller.

Through the comparison of Figs. 15, 16 and 17, we can find that the effect of GSD is obviously worse than the other two scheduling strategies when the size of K is moderate. The overall scheduling effect of GSDD and GOSDD is similar. But the computational complexity of GOSDD is significantly larger because it needs to find the optimal solution from all possible schedules. With the increase of K, the time GOSDD takes will increase exponentially, which is not suitable for real-time dispatch. While for GSDD, the complexity is much lower, which is more suitable for the real-time application.

6   Conclusion

MCVs have good mobility and scalability. They can be used not only to alleviate the pressure of charging stations and reduce the waiting time for users, but also to provide guidance for the construction of charging stations in the future. For example, the place where MCVs are often dispatched may be more suitable for building a new charging station. The size of the charging station can also be roughly estimated according to the service times of the MCVs.

From the comparison of the three different scheduling strategies, the scheduling result of GSDD is similar to that of GOSDD. If we consider the computation complexity of the algorithms, GSDD is more applicable to actual scheduling. In the future work, we will consider unexpected events, such as the break down of EVs caused by the depletion of electricity, in order to achieve multi-functional scheduling. One the other hand, we will also consider the impact of different driving paths (especially with traffic jam) on the scheduling of MCVs.

Acknowledgment. This work was partially funded by NSFC-61472384. And we are particularly grateful for the cooperation and support from *echarge*.

References

1. China has methodically built the world's largest market for electric vehicles. http://cn.wsj.com/gb/20171006/biz102359.asp
2. The new parking space in Beijing must be equipped with charging piles. http://www.evehicle.cn/?p=3579
3. Charging pile, why became a "stumbling block" of electric cars? http://society.people.com.cn/n1/2016/0603/c1008-28410174.html
4. OpenStreetMap contributors. https://www.openstreetmap.org
5. Zhang, Q.H., Xiu, N.N., Cheng, G.Q., Wang, Z.: Research on gas station selection support system with given refueling volume. In: Advanced Materials Research, pp. 756–760. Trans Tech Publ (2012)
6. Wang, J., Li, J., Pang, T., Sun, X., Liu, Q., Liu, H.: Towards a holistic and optimized framework for smart grid regulation. In: The 36th IEEE International Performance Computing and Communications Conference (IPCCC). IEEE (2017)
7. Sun, X., Li, J., Zheng, W., Liu, H.: Towards a sustainable incentive mechanism for participatory sensing. In: 2016 IEEE First International Conference on Internet-of-Things Design and Implementation (IoTDI), p. 4960. IEEE (2016)
8. Xu, P., Li, J., Sun, X., Zheng, W., Liu, H.: Dynamic pricing at electric vehicle charging stations for Queueing delay reduction. In: 2017 IEEE 37th International Conference on Distributed Computing Systems (ICDCS), pp. 2565–2566. IEEE (2017)
9. Malandrino, F., Casetti, C., Chiasserini, C.-F.: The role of its in charging opportunities for EVs. In: 2013 16th International IEEE Conference on Intelligent Transportation Systems-(ITSC), pp. 1953–1958 (2013)
10. Li, J., Sun, X., Liu, Q., Zheng, W., Liu, H., Stankovic, J.: Planning electric vehicle charging stations based on user charging behavior. In: The 3rd ACM/IEEE International Conference on Internet-of-Things Design and Implementation (2018)
11. Ge, S., Feng, L., Liu, H.: The planning of electric vehicle charging station based on grid partition method. In: 2011 International Conference on Electrical and Control Engineering (ICECE), pp. 2726–2730 (2011)
12. Li, Y., Luo, J., Chow, C.-Y., Chan, K.-L., Ding, Y., Zhang, F.: Growing the charging station network for electric vehicles with trajectory data analytics. In: 2015 IEEE 31st International Conference on Data Engineering (ICDE), pp. 1376–1387. IEEE (2015)
13. Liu, Z., Wen, F., Ledwich, G.: Optimal planning of electric-vehicle charging stations in distribution systems. IEEE Trans. Power Deliv. **28**, 102–110 (2013)
14. Liu, Z.-F., Zhang, W., Ji, X., Li, K.: Optimal planning of charging station for electric vehicle based on particle swarm optimization. In: Innovative Smart Grid Technologies-Asia (ISGT Asia), pp. 1–5. IEEE (2012)
15. Timpner, J., Wolf, L.: Design and evaluation of charging station scheduling strategies for electric vehicles. IEEE Trans. Intell. Transp. Syst. **15**, 579–588 (2014)
16. Chen, T.D., Kockelman, K.M., Khan, M., et al.: The electric vehicle charging station location problem: a parking-based assignment method for seattle. In: Transportation Research Board 92nd Annual Meeting, pp. 13–1254 (2013)
17. McPherson, C., Richardson, J., McLennan, O., Zippel, G.: Planning an electric vehicle battery-switch network for Australia. In: Australasian Transport Research Forum 2011 Proceedings (2011)
18. Zheng, Y., Dong, Z.Y., Xu, Y., Meng, K., Zhao, J.H., Qiu, J.: Electric vehicle battery charging/swap stations in distribution systems: comparison study and optimal planning. IEEE Trans. Power Syst. **29**, 221–229 (2014)

19. Mak, H.-Y., Rong, Y., Shen, Z.-J.M.: Infrastructure planning for electric vehicles with battery swapping. Manag. Sci. **59**, 1557–1575 (2013)
20. Xiong, H., Xiang, T., Rong, X., Chen, H.: Optimal allocation of electric vehicle battery swap stations. Electr. Power Autom. Equipment, 1–6 (2012)
21. Yang, J., Sun, H.: Battery swap station location-routing problem with capacitated electric vehicles. Comput. Oper. Res. **55**, 217–232 (2015)
22. Liu, N., Chen, Q., Lu, X., Liu, J., Zhang, J.: A charging strategy for PV-based battery switch stations considering service availability and self-consumption of PV energy. IEEE Trans. Ind. Electr. **62**, 4878–4889 (2015)
23. Cao, Y., Miao, Y., Jiang, Q.: Optimal operation of islanded microgrid with battery swap stations. Electr. Power Autom. Equipment, 1–6 (2012)
24. Technical specifications of remote service and management system for electric vehicles - Part 3: Communication protocol and data forma. In: National Technical Committee of Auto Standardization, Tech (2016)

SoProtector: Securing Native C/C++ Libraries for Mobile Applications

Ning Zhang[1], Guangquan Xu[1(✉)], Guozhu Meng[2], and Xi Zheng[3]

[1] Tianjin Key Laboratory of Advanced Networking (TANK), School of Computer Science and Technology, Tianjin University, Tianjin 300350, China
losin@tju.edu.cn
[2] Nanyang Technological University, Singapore, Singapore
[3] Department of Computing, Macquarie University, Sydney, Australia

Abstract. Java code is easy to be decompiled, and third-party SO files are used frequently by developers to improve development efficiency. Therefore, more and more core functions of Android applications are implemented in the native layer. However, there is neither comprehensive security research work nor automated security analysis tools on Android native layer, especially for third-party SO files that are dynamically loaded within the applications. To solve this problem, SoProtector, a novel and effective system is proposed to defend against the privacy leaks, which mainly analyzes the data stream between two levels: application and Native layers. In addition, SoProtector includes a real-time monitor to detect malicious functions in binary code. Our evaluation using 3400 applications has demonstrated that SoProtector can detect more sources, sinks and smudges than most static analysis tools; And it detects and effectively blocks more than 82% of applications that dynamically load malicious third-party SO files with low performance overhead.

Keywords: Mobile security · Mobile privacy · Native C/C++ libraries · Android

1 Introduction

At present, the privacy disclosure is still a serious problem in smartphone applications. Here are a few examples: (1) Facebook leaked the phone number from a mobile device before the user logged into the application [1]; (2) Angry Birds collected user data, which was found to be used by the NSA to profile users [2]; (3) out of 25,976 Android applications, 969 applications leaked location data and 347 recorded audio without the user's permission [3].

Along with privacy concerns there are security concerns as well. Malware constitute the main media for security attacks against mobile devices. It has been recently reported [4] that almost 60 percent of existing malware send stealthy premium rate SMS messages. Also Google Play, the official market for Android apps, has hosted applications which have been found to be malicious [5]. In the past few years, malware have increasingly relied on root exploit. Some of the famous malware families include DroidKungfu [6], GingerMaster [7] and DroidDream [8]. These exploits allow for the

© Springer Nature Switzerland AG 2018
J. Vaidya and J. Li (Eds.): ICA3PP 2018, LNCS 11336, pp. 417–431, 2018.
https://doi.org/10.1007/978-3-030-05057-3_32

escalation of privileges, which bypassed the security measures of the Android operating system. It allows the malware to have unlimited access to the device, resulting in the downloading and running of the payload to get information of users. Mostly important, a new family of malware (Godless [9]) using the root exploit that is stored in a native library, has emerged recently in 2016. The exploit binary contains a series of vulnerability that includes the Towelroot exploit (vulnerability numbers: CVE-2014-3153) and PingPong exploit (vulnerability numbers: CVE-2015-3636). This alarming trend of malware using native library code plays an important motivation for us to create a detection system to identify malware that contains such exploit [9].

For the detection of privacy leak (although there existed some detection frameworks [19–22]), the most important method is stain analysis, including static stain analysis and dynamic stain analysis. The main dynamic stain analysis tools are TainDroid [10] and AppFence [11]. The typical static stain analysis tools include FlowDroid [12] and AndroidLeaks [3]. However, static stain analysis tools cannot effectively handle the Android dynamic loading mechanism and the reflection mechanism, while dynamic stain analysis tools cannot generate data stream graph of the C/C++ programs (which generate SO files) on the native layer. Unfortunately, reference [13] points out that from 2010 to 2014, the proportion of malicious Android applications using dynamic loading and reflection mechanism increased from 43.87% to 78%, non-malicious applications from 55% to 93%. The large number of applications using dynamic loading techniques makes it increasingly difficult for current stain analysis tools to effectively detect privacy leaks in Android applications [14].

Standing on the security's point, SO files (see Fig. 1) are binary code files, reference [15] measured that 1,161 insecure code snippets posted on Stack Overflow were copied and pasted into 1,305,820 Android applications available on Google Play. They demonstrated that the proliferation of insecure code snippets within the Android ecosystem and the reuse rate of insecure code (Java and C/C++ code) are high. Inspired by this situation, given two binary functions such as the malicious function and the unknown function, we could detect whether they are similar [16]. This problem is known as "binary code similarity detection." Reference [17, 18] used a graph matching algorithm to check whether two functions' control flow graph representations are similar to conduct a binary code similarity detection. Genius [19] learns high-level feature representations from the control flow graphs and encodes (i.e., embeds) the graphs into embeddings (i.e., high dimensional numerical vectors). However, the graph matching algorithms are slow, i.e., requiring super-linear runtime in the graph size. Thus such approaches are inevitably inefficient. In recent years, deep learning [20] has been applied to many application domains, including binary analysis [21], and has shown stronger results than other approaches. Reference [22] proposed a deep neural network-based approach to generate embeddings for binary functions for similarity detection. On the other hand, reference [27, 28] presented a method to extract important byte sequences in malware samples by application of convolutional neural network (CNN) to images converted from binary data. However, related work listed above is not in the ARM platform.

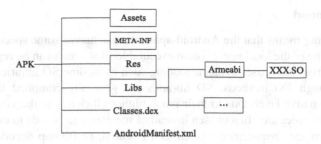

Fig. 1. The SO libraries in Android APK

Contributions. In summary, this paper makes the following contributions.

- Based on FlowDroid, we developed an effective stain analysis tool for the data interaction between native C/C++ libraries and Java API framework by changing Android source code, which is not yet solved by traditional static stain analysis and dynamic stain analysis methods. Through experiments, we also verified its effectiveness.

- For reversible SO files, we designed an automation tool to analyze the combined characteristics of assembly code to detect whether they are malicious. We tested the performance of the automated tools and verified its effectiveness through experiments. For non-reversible SO files, we developed a new method to construct texture maps by combining image processing with machine learning to detect malicious variants.

- For the third-party SO files called by dynamic loading mechanism, we first proposed to establish a real-time monitoring platform by uploading the SO files for online examining, monitoring changes of the third party SO Files. By changing the Android source code and combining with the tools of dynamic stain analysis, the monitoring platform is set up to monitor the third-party SO file loaded in the test APPs in real time. The validity of the method is verified through experiments.

- We have created a malicious native program dataset, including their Android source programs and malicious binary SO files.

Roadmap. The rest of this paper is organized as follows. Section 2 gives the motivation example, and then introduces some background knowledge about Android dynamic loading. Section 3 gives an overview of SoProtector and illustrates the key techniques applied for it. Section 4 describes the approach step by step. Section 5 describes the experiment and gives the evaluation. Section 6 discusses the limitation of SoProtector and concludes this work.

2 Problem Statement

In this section, we investigate challenges in static analysis to analyze the SO files. We also give some background knowledge about some important mechanisms in the Android platform.

2.1 Background

Dynamic loading means that the Android application achieves some specific functions by loading some of the local non-existent executable files which can be replaced at run time; and Android NDK uses dynamic loading such as loading SO libraries and calling functions through JNI methods. SO libraries are generally compiled from C/C++, running in the native layer. Due to their much higher efficiency in the virtual machine layer, the SO libraries are often chosen instead of the native java code to do some work to meet performance requirements (such as T9 search, or Bitmap decoding, etc.). In addition, since the SO library is compiled by C/C++ and decompiled into assembly codes (sometimes they are hard to be understood), the SO library can also be used for other purposes. For instance, a new family of malware (Godless) uses the root exploit method whose code is stored in a native library [9]. In general, we package the SO libraries together inside the apps, but the SO libraries also can be loaded from the external storage files.

2.2 Challenges

SO libraries are binary files which are composed of 0 and 1: if we take security measures like pacify, maybe we are unable to get their assembly codes.

There is no automated tool: we need to manually analyze the data interaction between the native and java layers: no automated tool means less efficient.

In addition, dynamic loading SO libraries from third-party is becoming more and more popular during application development. Third-party so libraries do not need to be packaged directly in the APK (see Fig. 2).

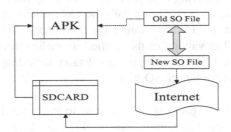

Fig. 2. Third-party SO libraries can be updated from the Internet

With the program is running, the required SO files are loaded into the specified executable private directory. Because the using SO files are not in the application, static analysis cannot effectively analyze the data flows that involve on the native layer. More importantly, since the SO files can be updated at any time after the program is run and no user is required to reinstall the APK, if a malicious APK replaces the benign SO file with a malicious SO file after installing the security check, it will not be monitored and processed by security protection software.

3   System Overview

In this section, we give an overview of the SoProtector framework, which consists of SoDetection and SoPlatform and describe the key techniques applied in our framework.

Figure 3 shows the overall architecture of SoProtector. In order to facilitate the following description, we make the following definitions of terms:

(1) Source method: the method called from native layer, denoted by Sf, as shown in Listing 1 (e.g. *JNITransmit* method).
(2) Source file: the C /C++ file where source method lies, denoted by Sw.
(3) The target method: the native layer function, which calls the Java layer method, denoted by Tf, as shown in Listing 3.
(4) Target class: the class where the target method lies in, denoted by Tc.

JNI interaction method: The method invoked by the caller to implement the reflection mechanism, denoted by Jh, (e.g.*GetMethodID* and *GetSaticMethodID* methods).

SoProtector consists of SoDetection and SoPlatform, SoDetection mainly consists of two parts: the dynamic execution module and the static analysis module. For the convenience of the following description, we abbreviate them as SoDetection-x and SoDetection-y respectively.

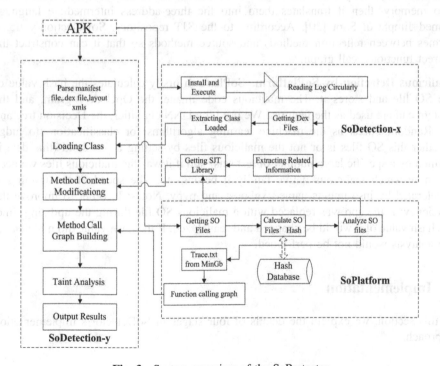

Fig. 3. System overview of the SoProtector

Information Extraction. SoDetection firstly runs the SoDetection-x on the computer, and the tested application is installed onto the Android device. The Android system installed in the Android device is generated after Android source codes are modified and recompiled. The SoDetection-x can record the relevant information like dynamic loading functions that occur in the output of the log. We will illustrate in the next section about some changes made to the Android system source code. After installing the application, SoDetection-x runs the application and reads the log output of the system cyclically to obtain information about application's dynamic loading and reflection invocation. When capturing the application's dynamic loading behavior, SoDetection-x would send the download command by adb to the Android device to download the SO files and.dex files to the local computer. When capturing the reflection calling behavior of the application, SoDetection-x would extract the source method named Sf, the JNI interaction method named Jh, the target method named Tf corresponding to the reflection call from the log and store the information by the form of a triplet <Sf, Jh, Tf> in the local computer's file, which is named SJT repository. The.dex files and the SJT repository will be used for subsequent static analysis, and the downloaded SO files will be used in SoPlatform's work.

Data Analysis. When the dynamic analysis module is finished, SoDetection will run SoDetection-y that is actually an improvement of FlowDroid. We added the dex files and SJT information library into SoDetection-y's static stain analysis process. SoDetection-y firstly loads the required JavaClass files of the APK and the.dex files into memory, then it translates them into the three-address intermediate language named Jimple of Soot [20]. According to the SJT repository, SoDetection-y trans-formes between reflection methods and source methods so that it can construct the correct functions' call graph.

Malicious Detection by SoPlatform. SoPlatform firstly calculates the hash value of the SO file and stores it. The malicious code image, the OpCode n-gram, and the system call are used as the features. We used the DNN classifier, the Decision tree and the Random Forest as the machine learning algorithms for classification (to judge whether this SO files is or not the malicious files by setting a threshold (this data is defined by a specific large number of test sets) and if it was the malicious files we need to know which malicious native family it belongs to. The speed of the training is accelerated by instruments named xgboost and pypy. Notes: In order to improve the efficiency: if the app was replaced with a malicious SO file during the updating time, the hash value of it would be changed and reanalyzed. If the hash value did not change, the analysis would not be performed.

4   Implementation

In this section, we explain the details of four stages in SoDetector's implementation approach.

4.1 Stage 1: Pre-processing

We modified the Android (its version is 4.1.2) source code. The main changes include:

(a) We modified the Android source code so that it can store method parameters to get complete information in the method stack.
(b) We hooked the Runtime Class by recording the mLibPaths so that when the external SO file is loaded, name and address of the SO file is recorded to facilitate SoProtector's next steps.
(c) Hook the GetMethodID and GetstaticMethodID methods.
(d) Hook some invoke methods.
(e) Hook the pNewEntry to get some process information.

4.2 Stage 2: Disposal by SoDetection-X

SoDetection-x will read the phone's log information and extract the uid number as the log records of the tested app. When reading a record of a dynamically loaded dex file, the dex file is downloaded to a designated folder on the local computer according to the file information recorded in the log in order to provide analysis for SoDetection-y. When capturing the output information of GetMethodID, GetstaticMethodID, or the reflection calling information output by some invoke methods, the information of the corresponding source method Sf, JNI interaction method Jh, target method Tf is extracted, and stored as a triplet in the SJT repository in order to provide reflection calling information for SoDetection-y's stain analysis process. Figure 4 describes the extraction principle for this information. Because GetMethodID and GetstaticMethodID method are called by the upper layer function, in order to capture the functions' calling and displaying, there are two ways:

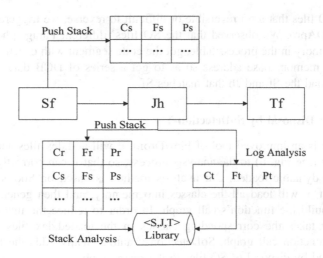

Fig. 4. The way to get the <S, J, T> library

For the SO files that are able to be reversible to the ARM and C code, we need to use four tools: GCC, Addr2line tools, open source tools Pvtrace and Dot (see Fig. 5); we labeled the native functions where lie Tf by GCC detection functions, which generated the trace files named trace.txt; After using Addr2line tools to transform the address of the function into the function name, we could get the function calling graph by the dot and the map can be transformed into the data flow diagram of native layer added in the FlowDroid diagram. By analyzing the calling relationship, we could find Sf and Jh that Tf matches;

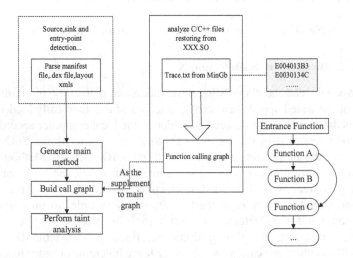

Fig. 5. The way to deal with the reversible SO files

For the SO files that are irreversible or difficult to reverse, we triggered the native function by IDApro. We observed that the SO files' different Paragraph information mapped to memory in the process table, got the code segment with execute permission and found its memory base address so as to get a series of DCB data. DCB data's header string had the Sf and Jh that matches Sf.

4.3   Stage 3: Disposal by SoDetection-Y

SoDetection-y is an improved tool of FlowDroid, it will add.dex files and SJT information library (see Fig. 6) to the analysis process, so that it can correctly handle SO files which is dynamic loaded. Our analysis method is based on Soot's Jimple language. At first, it will load all the classes into memory, and then generate the main method and build the function's call graph. In order to reduce the memory burden, SoDetection-y takes the corresponding classes in the loaded.dex files only. When building the function call graph, SoDetection-y automatically adds the function call graph generated by disposal of SO files to the main graph.

In a word, SoDetection-y deals with the reflection method (in the native layer and application layer) of the source files so as to form the complete control flow graph

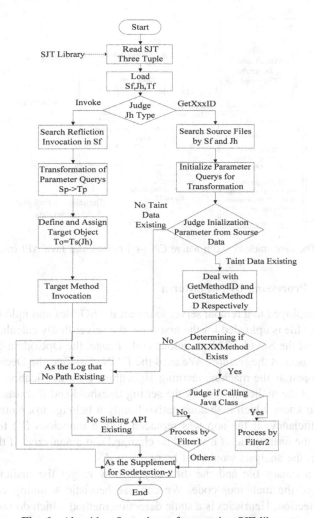

Fig. 6. Algorithm flow chart of processing SJT library

containing the data interaction of the application layer and the native layer. The algorithm flow chart of processing SJT library is shown in Fig. 6. For a SJT mapping, SoDetection-y firstly determines the method is getxxxid or invoke method. Then SoDetection-y converts the target reflection parameter Sp to the target parameter Tp; Then, it determines whether the target reflection object is empty; if it is empty, it will define and assign the target object. For the getxxxid method, it mainly judges initialization parameters from source data as shown in Fig. 6. The taint track between native C/C++ libraries and Java API framework is shown in Fig. 7. Our tool can distinguish the flow of private data between the application and native layers.

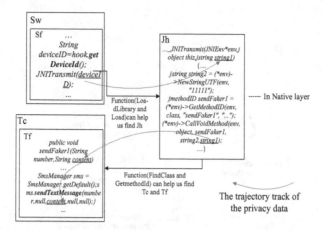

Fig. 7. The taint track between native C/C++ libraries and Java API framework.

4.4   Stage 4: Processing by SoPlatform

SoPlatform is deployed to a remote server to detect the SO files and upload them to the server. If the SO file is uploaded for the first time, the server firstly calculates and stores the hash value of the SO file. The malicious code image, the OpCode n-gram, and the system call are used as the features. We used the DNN classifier, the Decision Tree and the Random Forest as the machine learning algorithms for classification (to judge this SO files is or not the malicious files by the setting threshold and if it was the malicious files we need to know which malicious native family it belongs to). Notes: In order to improve the efficiency: if the app was replaced with a malicious SO file during the updating time, the hash value of it would be changed and reanalyzed. If the hash value did not change, the analysis would not be performed.

SO file is a binary file and the difficulty is how to get the malicious behavior characteristics of the malicious code. We can use heuristic scanning with unknown binary code detection. Heuristics is a static detection method which do not actually run the binary file with the highest efficiency (see the experimental part). Notes: SO files will have different segment information mapped to memory (including the data segment and the code segment, the process table will see a number of SO sub-paragraph), we need to find the code segment with executive SO segment.

Next, we describe the three major features selected in detail:

- **Feature 1: Presenting a binary file as a gray scale image, using the texture features in the image to determine the maliciousness of the binary**

For a binary file, each byte ranges between 00 ~ FF, just corresponding to gray scale 0 ~ 255 (0 is black, 255 is white). Converting a binary file into a matrix (each byte in the matrix element corresponds to the size of the matrix, which can be adjusted according to the actual situation), the matrix can be easily converted into a gray scale. Specific implementation (by python):

(1) We used hexlify function to transform a binary file into a hexadecimal string;
(2) By byte segmentation, we used reshape function to create the rectangle according to the width set;
(3) we used fromarray function to convert this rectangle into an image.

The same family of malicious code images in the texture exists a certain similarity and different malicious code family is different. Using the GIST feature technology of computer vision, Using the GIST feature technology of computer vision, a five-dimensional perception dimension (vector) is used to describe the image. That is, an image is input and the corresponding GIST descriptor is output. After getting these vectors, classification training of machine learning algorithm can be done.

- **Feature 2: Opcode Sequence Frequency of Appearance**

The code of the SO file is reversely obtained by using the ARM instruction set. The opcode sequence is obtained by using the python. The sequence is processed according to the length of the sub-sequence as n (n is 1, 2, 3), and then we calculate the TF result of each opcode sequence. The vector $S = (\Delta_1, \Delta_2,... \Delta_n)$ consisting of the opcode sequence frequency is obtained. We combined two values above to the weighted vector $V = (wtf_1, wtf_2,... wtf_n)$. Also we calculated the vector V1 for the malicious SO files to be tested and the vector V_{m+1} cosine similarity of m different kinds of malicious samples respectively.

- **Feature 3: Sequences of System API calls**

With the use of IDAPro, each file is disassembled into the assembly language and a gdl file that contains the assembly code will be generated. Since IDAPro can disassemble binary files into a basic block of assembly code, the gdl file will capture this valuable information. The system call (see Fig. 8) will be recorded into an output format of text file as an input to feed into a machine learning algorithm. The output files are used to model the behavior of the binary or native code that are in both malware and benign application. Then we will use machine learning algorithm such as random forest tree classifier for classification and detection of malware.

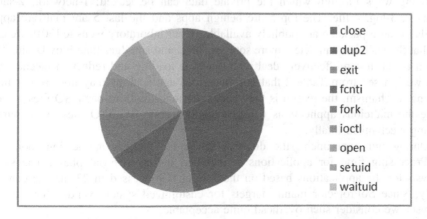

Fig. 8. Statistic of system call for AnserverBot Malware

5   Empirical Study

In this section, we first present our empirical settings and then we present our evaluation results.

5.1   Empirical Settings

Dataset: We crawled 3000 apps from Wandoujia Store [24] (covering its pre-classified 15 categories) and 400 apps with Native layer from VirusShare [25] (with malware spanning from 2013 to 2017), Genome (apps are divided in 49 malware families), Contagio Mobile [26] (we have tested SoProtector against 13 malware families from the Contagio database) and reference [29]. For each category in the Wandoujia store, we downloaded the top 200 apps. Excepting some connection errors occurred in the crawling process, totally we collected 3400 apps as our dataset. This dataset will be used in both model training and evaluation of SoProtector. Notes: the malware native families include: (1) ADRD (2) AnserverBot (3) BaseBridge (4) Geinimi (5) Asroot (6) BeanBot (7) Bgserv (8) DroidKungFu1 (9) DroidKungFu2 (10) DroidKungFu3 (11) DroidKungFu4.

Environment: The main hardware devices for the experiment were a Samsung S6 mobile phone (4-core processor) and an ASUS computer (8-core CPU with 8 GB of memory). We made the modified Android system into a ROM and flushed it into a Samsung mobile phone. All tested APK by SoProtector ran on this Android system. The Dell computer is used to run the main program of SoPlatform.

5.2   Overall Analysis and Performance

From Table 1 (note: the numbers in column "Content of Privacy" represent the following types of the private data that can be leaked: 1-call records, 2-geolocation information, 3-message records, 4-contacts, 5-mobile phone identification, 6-baidu accounts, 7-wifi information, 8-bluetooth information, 9-base station information, 10-browser information. The marks in column "Ways of Privacy Leakage" represent the following ways through which the private data can be leaked: 1-network, 2-short message, 3-log, 4-file. The top 5 are benign apps and the last 5 are malware apps, details of these package are publicly available in our laboratory website [30]), we can see that SoDetection can detect more sources, sinks and smudges than FlowDroid. The reason is that it can effectively deal with dynamic loading and reflection mechanism. And we can see from Table 2 that non-malicious applications may not use dynamic loading mechanism, the reason is they could not load the third-party SO files, meanwhile the malicious applications whose malicious code is in SO files use dynamic loading mechanism totally.

During our experiment, the disposal phase for the per application took 2 s. Pre-Processing time for applications is included in the disposal phase. The static analysis for the applications based on the dataset is processed in 23 threads concurrently. Since SoProtector mainly targets for customized system vendors or security analysts, we consider such overhead quite acceptable.

Table 1. Effectiveness analysis

APK ID	FlowDroid		SoDetection		Content of privacy	Ways of privacy leakage
	Sink number	Taint propogation path number	Sink number	Taint propogation path number		
1	35	0	41	4	{1,2}	{1}
2	24	3	30	7	[3, 5], {3,5}	{1,2}
3	72	12	74	19	[6, 10], {6,10}	[1],{1}
4	44	21	44	26	[1, 2], {1,2}	[1, 3], {1,3,4}
5	86	0	86	0	{7,10}	[1],{1}
6	14	5	17	7	[3, 6], {3,6}	[1, 3], {1,3}
7	29	14	30	15	[2,3], {2,3,4,5}	[1, 2], {1,2}
8	0	0	1	1	{1,3}	{1,2,4}
9	14	5	16	6	[4],{4,9}	[1],{1,2,3}
10	11	4	17	9	[1],{1,7}	[1, 3], {1,3,4}

Table 2. Mechanism analysis

Type	Total	With dynamic loading mechanism		With invoke mechanism	
		App number	Proportion	App number	Proportion
Non-malicious Apps	3000	1637	0.5456	1892	0.6306
Malicious Apps	400	400	1	135	0.3375

5.3 Precision

Based on the total number of TPs, FPs (non-malware apps mistakes as malware apps) and FNs (malware apps mistakes as non-malware apps) (2972, 375, 53), we compute the precision and recall of SoProtector as follows: based on the total number of TPs, FPs and FNs (973, 68, 103), we compute the precision and recall of SoDetection as follows:

$$Precision = \frac{TP}{TP + FP} \qquad Recall = \frac{TP}{TP + FN}$$

Overall, SoProtector precisely identified most of Apps, with 88.79% precision and 98.25% recall.

An important class of tested malware is the DroidKongFu app, which is a type of malware whose core code is in the native layer that became popular in the last years, especially in China, where SoProtector has successfully identified it's malicious in the dataset. In particular, DuanXinGongJiQi is a recent malware (SMS Trojan) known to be able to evade most anti-virus in China. In these cases, SoProtector detected the misbehavior of the outgoing SMS message, typical of SMS Trojan. These results shows how the SoProtector approach is a valid and effective alternative to static stain analysis approaches, which are more accurate against malware whose core functions are in native layer, such as some apps are not detected by FlowDroid.

By the way, in Sect. 4.4, due to the randomness in the random forest training process, each result is not the same. But in general, the accuracy of the combination of the two methods is much higher than each one, where the basic accuracy can reach more than 72%.

6   Discussion

In this section, we discuss the general applicability of SoProtector, as well as limitations and future work.

SoDetection can output the complete path of the application layer and the native layer pollution source to the sinking point, but the defect lies in the prevention of the implementation part of the api kernel in the in-depth linux kernel analysis, which affects the detection effect to a certain extent, which is also going to continue in the future Research work.

SoPlatform needs to set up related servers and has the cost of network transmission, which has affected its efficiency to some extent.

Acknowledgement. This work has been partially sponsored by the National Key R&D Program of China (No. 2017YFE0111900), the National Science Foundation of China (No. 61572355, U1736115), the Tianjin Research Program of Application Foundation and Advanced Technology (No. 15JCYBJC15700), and the Fundamental Research of Xinjiang Corps (No. 2016AC015).

References

1. Symantec index. http://www.symantec.com/connect/blogs/norton-mobile-insight-discovers-facebook-privacyleak
2. Ball index. http://www.theguardian.com/world/2014/jan/27/nsa-gchqsmartphone-app-angry-birds-personal-data
3. Gibler, C., Crussell, J., Erickson, J., Chen, H.: AndroidLeaks: automatically detecting potential privacy leaks in android applications on a large scale. In: Katzenbeisser, S., Weippl, E., Camp, L.Jean, Volkamer, M., Reiter, M., Zhang, X. (eds.) Trust 2012. LNCS, vol. 7344, pp. 291–307. Springer, Heidelberg (2012). https://doi.org/10.1007/978-3-642-30921-2_17
4. Kaspersky index. http://usa.kaspersky.com/about-us/press-center/pressreleases
5. Symantec index. http://www..com/connect/blogs/yet-another-bunchmalicious-apps-found-google-play
6. News index. https://www.csc2.ncsu.edu/faculty/xjiang4/DroidKungFu2/

7. GingerMaster index. https://www.csc2.ncsu.edu/faculty/xjiang4
8. News index. https://blog.lookout.com/blog/2011/03/02/android-malware-droiddream-how-it-works/. Accessed 4 Mar 2017
9. Liu, Z.: Verifiable searchable encryption with aggregate keys for data sharing system. Future Gener. Comput. Syst. **78**, 778–788 (2018)
10. Enck, W.: TaintDroid: an information-flow tracking system for realtime privacy monitoring on smartphones. ACM Trans. Comput. Syst., 2–32 (2014)
11. Hornyack, P.: These aren't the droids you are looking for: retrofitting Android to protect data from imperious applications. In: Proceedings of the 18th ACM Conference on Computer and Communications Security, pp. 639–652 (2011)
12. Arzt, S.: Flowdroid: Precise context, flow, field, object-sensitive and lifecycle-aware taint analysis for Android apps. ACM SIGPLAN Not. **49**, 259–269 (2014)
13. Chen, X.: N-Mobishare: new privacy-perserving location-sharing system for mobile online social networks. Int. J. Comput. Math. **93**, 384–400 (2018)
14. Li, T.: CDFS: a cryptographic data publishing system. J. Comput. Syst. Sci., 80–91 (2018)
15. Fischer, F.: Stack overflow considered harmful? the impact of copy & paste on android application security. In: IEEE Symposium on Security and Privacy (SP), pp. 121–136 (2017)
16. Xu, D.: Cryptographic function detection in obfuscated binaries via bit-precise symbolic loop mapping. In: IEEE Symposium on Security and Privacy (SP), pp. 921–937 (2017)
17. Eschweiler, S.: Efficient cross-architecture identification of bugs in binary code. In: The Network and Distributed System Security Symposium (2016)
18. Pewny, J.: Cross-architecture bug search in binary executables. In: IEEE Symposium on Security and Privacy, pp. 709–724 (2015)
19. Feng, Q.: Scalable graph-based bug search for firmware images. In: ACM SIGSAC Conference on Computer and Communications Security, pp. 480–491 (2016)
20. Geoffrey, H.: Deep learning. Nature **521**, 436–444 (2015)
21. Richard, S.: Recognizing functions in binaries with neural networks. In: USENIX Security, pp. 611–626 (2015)
22. Xiao, J.: Neural network-based graph embedding for cross-platform binary code similarity detection. In: ACM Conference on Computer and Communications Security, pp. 435–446 (2017)
23. Wang, H.: A secure, usable, and transparent middleware for permission managers on Android. In: IEEE Transactions on Dependable and Secure Computing, pp. 350–362 (2017)
24. Wandoujia Store Index. http://www.wandoujia.com/apps
25. VirusShare Index. https://virusshare.com
26. Krupp, B.: SPE: security and privacy enhancement framework for mobile devices. IEEE Trans. Dependable Sec. Comput. **14**, 433–446 (2017)
27. Saracino, A.: MADAM: effective and efficient behavior-based android malware detection and prevention. IEEE Trans. Dependable Sec. Comput. **15**, 83–97 (2018)
28. Tongxin, L.: Unleashing the walking dead: understanding cross-app remote infections on mobile WebViews. In: Proceedings of the 2017 ACM SIGSAC Conference on Computer and Communications Security, pp. 829–844 (2017)
29. Paranthaman, R.: Malware collection and analysis. In: 2017 IEEE International Conference on Information Reuse and Integration, pp. 26–31 (2017)
30. Files Websites index. http://cs.tju.edu.cn/csweb/cyxz

CloudPT: Performance Testing for Identifying and Detecting Bottlenecks in IaaS

Ameen Alkasem[✉] [iD], Hongwei Liu, and Decheng Zuo

School of Computer Science and Technology, Harbin Institute of Technology, Harbin, China
77ameen@ftcl.hit.edu.cn, {liuhw,zdc}@hit.edu.cn

Abstract. This work addresses performance testing for monitoring mass quantities of large-dataset measurements in infrastructure-as-a-Service (IaaS). Physical resources are not virtualized in sharing dynamic clouds; thus, shared resources compete for access to system resources. This competition introduces significant new challenges when assessing the performance of IaaS. A bottleneck may occur if one system resource is critical to IaaS; this may shut down the system and services, which would reduce the workflow performance by a large margin. To protect against bottlenecks, we propose CloudPT, a performance test management framework for IaaS. CloudPT has many advantages: (I) high-efficiency detection; (II) a unified end-to-end feedback loop to collaborate with cloud-ecosystems management; and (III) a troubleshooting performance test. This paper shows that CloudPT efficiently identifies and detects bottlenecks with a minimal false-positive rate (<13%) and it correlates high accuracy using the failure of a host virtual machine (host VM) to start-up with both cloud illustrative batches and transactional workloads such as the Spark, and Kafka framework for a data partitioning and collecting events on an each server. In a framework based on a trace case study, CloudPT diagnosed performance bottlenecks in 20 s with a precision rate of 86%, confirming its real-time efficiency.

Keywords: IaaS · Bottlenecks · Performance testing · VMs · Apache Spark

1 Introduction

Sharing resources and the high dynamism of resources in cloud computing and large data normally cause frequent anomalous behaviors or fault bottlenecks. Thus, companies seek to create Service Level Agreement (SLA) desecrations of the presented services, which is a leading contributor to their total management costs. A new survey revealed that organizations face $26 billion in lost annual revenue when its IT experiences an average of 15 h of downtime [1]. This reflects that the increasing unwillingness in customers to move to cloud computing is because its performance is unpredictable. Moreover, huge amounts of data in cloud services require large-scale analysis and data management technology. Performance issues may also originate from the complex interactions between diverse subsystems that perform in isolation. They are typically caused by a cascading failure when one unsuccessful component causes performance issues in others. For one to have a clear understanding of the resulting issue, tone must

© Springer Nature Switzerland AG 2018
J. Vaidya and J. Li (Eds.): ICA3PP 2018, LNCS 11336, pp. 432–452, 2018.
https://doi.org/10.1007/978-3-030-05057-3_33

disentangle the relationships between the components and identify how they contribute to the performance issues. Bottlenecks can also be complex and connected in unforeseen ways; as such, fixing one bottleneck may simply move it somewhere else in the system. In such cases, an intended fix may fail to improve the overall performance [2]. Performance testing is used to determine the throughput, reliability, responsiveness, and scalability of a system's workload.

Recently-designed Apache Spark is one of the most used engines for processing large datasets. It is a fast, general purpose computing engine that is purpose-built for such processing [3]. Spark has the benefits of Hadoop and MapReduce, but it is different because its jobs' intermediate results can be stored in the memory; this detects the need to read and write Hadoop Distributed File System (HDFS) [3]. As a result, one can apply Spark to the large dataset and machine learning iterative MapReduce algorithms. We used the Spark and Kafka framework to handle the events data. Performance testing does not aim to find errors in the application and systems do not pass or fail the test. Instead, performance testing deals with the important task of setting the application's target and standard [4]. The infrastructure-as-a-service (IaaS) enables handlers to hire merchandise in a pay-as-you-go fashion. Shared dynamic clouds provide application service providers (ASPs) with a more product solution compared with traditional in-house computing. Shared dynamic clouds can be achieved through averting the prerequisite for ASPs to have and to manage an intricate physical computing infrastructure [5]. However, it remains difficult to identify and avert performance irregularities in virtualized cloud computing environments for various reasons. These reasons include:

(I)   The high frequency of performance test failing to detect bottlenecks: Sharing high dynamic resources can lead to various cloud anomalies. We found that the frequency of faulty VM's CPU operation and network overhead are high over time. In such cases, the virtual machine manager (VMM) allocated more assets to VM, leading to the decline of CPU utilization and a network over head failure bottleneck (which became an infinite loop) [6]. Figure 1 shows an example of a high CPU utilization, with quite low load averages in its anomaly behavior system state [7]. This can affect its performance test by more than 15%. Furthermore, we found that approximately 15% of cloud reconfiguration actions can be defective. Thus, testing the performance of a diagnosis failure bottleneck or an anomaly behavior in IaaS requires that one deals with a complex frequency accuracy of detection that is higher than in customary methods.

(II) Dynamic cloud services: A cloud is a dynamic throughout a platform; as such, it responds dynamically to transformations in workload needs. A performance testing system that alerts of a cloud's faulty manual or glitch, such as those virtualized in clouds faults, does not match the dynamic cloud model. To test the performance identification and to remove bottlenecks in a cloud requires taking an entirely dynamic all-through approach for detecting glitch, analysis, classification, and fixing. This is done by integrating it with a big dataset monitor collected in real-time management using a Spark streaming engine.

(III) Troubleshooting performance test: To the best of our knowledge, there is no such framework that currently exists for a shared dynamic cloud. That manages non-virtualized failure bottlenecks linked to the cloud.

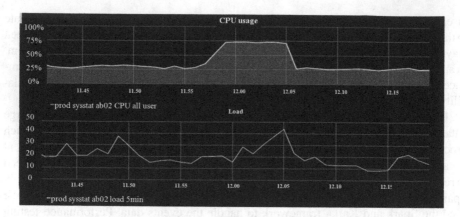

Fig. 1. A sample of anomaly behavior at a system state

Consequently, in this particular paper, we will introduce the new design methodology and apply a comprehensive end-to-end performance testing outline for IaaS based on runtime bottleneck inspection with Apache Spark; this is known as CloudPT. In addition, we will address the issue of troubleshooting performance bottlenecks in IaaS using three construction troubleshooting performance steps: (I) data collection, (II) analysis and classification engines, and (III) decision engine. These are presented in Fig. 2.

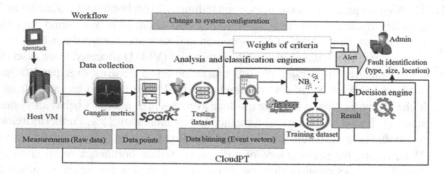

Fig. 2. Three proposed construction troubleshooting and performance testing steps

The objectives of CloudPT are to monitor collections, develop analysis, and classify the attributes of measurements, as opposed to the individual metric thresholds, by extending the diagnosis of fault into troubleshooting. The contribution of this paper is propose performance testing for identifying and detecting failures model, called CloudPT, which acts as a performance test management framework for IaaS. CloudPT has the following advantages: (I) high-efficiency detection; (II) a unified end-to-end feedback loop to collaborate with cloud-ecosystems management; and (III) a troubleshooting performance test. Using the failure of a host virtual machine (host VM) to startup with a cloud representative batch and transactional workloads, like Spark and Hadoop, we show that CloudPT efficiently identifies and detects bottlenecks with a low false-positive rate (<13%) and high accuracy. In a framework trace-based case study, CloudPT diagnosed performance bottlenecks within 20 s with an accuracy of 86%, confirming its real-time efficiency.

We started working on CloudPT after observing that machine learning algorithms, such as a Naïve-Bayes classifier (NBC), multi-valued decision diagram (MDD) and influence diagram (ID), are widely used in flexible industrial control fields and in some intelligence models for decision making [8]. We have thoroughly evaluated CloudPT in a stream process system, where the generated simulation stream data centered on the Apache Spark streaming engine and Hadoop MapReduce. Moreover, the data might be valuable only for a short time (seconds or minutes) after being generated, more details in Sect. 4.3.

The remainder of the paper is organized as follows. Section 2 describes the background and related work. In Sect. 3 focuses on CloudPT architecture. Section 4 explains the implementation details of CloudPT proposed. Section 5 presents the experimental setup, evaluation results and performance testing overheads. Finally, conclusions is presented in Sect. 6.

2   Background

Below, we will outline the work associated with performance testing for identifying and detecting fault bottlenecks; subsequently, we will discuss the manner in which CloudPT merges with a cloud-ecosystem service.

2.1   Related Works

We categorize preceding works based on the approaches used and on the current frameworks for performance testing that they exhibit.

Core performance testing techniques: Performance testing and bottleneck elimination methods can be categorized into a few categories. (I) Efficient Bottleneck Detection: Zhai et al. [9] proposed fuzzy logic based on runtime bottleneck and operator detection approach to improve the scalability of stream processing engines (SPEs) by providing resources within the cloud environment. Fernandez et al. [10] proposed an approach that shows that both overload and failure are managed in the same model, while operation recovery is a distinct case for scale out. (II) Threshold-based technical: Thresholds are put on the application; system performance testing metrics use historical observations of a system or application's behavior along with an alarm [11]. The technical basis of these open source monitoring tools includes Ganglia [12] and Nagios [13]. Nevertheless, this is unsuitable for an environment that has dynamic transformations because it has a tendency to be vulnerable to have high false alarm rates. Moreover, in general, its performance is anticipated to be poor within the dynamic of large-scale shard utility clouds. (III) Methods of statistical machine learning techniques: A simplified approach to establish the determination issues using statistical techniques to develop a system performance approach under standard behavior, while flagging nonconformities as anomalies [14]. Sharma et al. [15] proposed a light-weight, automated, and accurate fault detection and diagnosis system. However, such a technique only recognizes the basic correlations. Cherkasova et al. [16] proposed a new integrated framework of measurement and system modeling techniques to detect the anomaly and to analyze important transformations in application behavior. (IV) Performance testing framework: Kumar et al. [17] developed a MapReduce approach to be used in automatic pattern recognition according to fault analysis; they did so by solving an issue linked to data disparity in a cloud-based manufacturing (CBM) system.

In the context of virtualized environments, all previous works focus on identifying applications or OS-related anomalies. However, none of them concentrates on identifying the irregularities that arise due to cloud activities and virtualization artifacts. These may include issues that cause a failure bottleneck in a host-VM, which is a major aspect of this work. In part, it seeks to fill the gap identified in the literature.

2.2 Performance Testing Model for Cloud System

Autonomic optimization and continuous optimization are two main features of IaaS cloud management systems; they enable systems to familiarize to different workload changes [18]. As future actions in a cloud depend on the results of preceding actions, the approach of cloud management should be aware of any fault bottlenecks or anomalies that have happened as a result of these events. A performance testing model system must, therefore, be autonomic and offer actions to repair faults for bottlenecks linked to cloud or anomaly faults. Cloud ecosystems have two aspects that require attention. First, IaaS cloud services use multi-tenancy to guarantee the efficient utilization of computational resources. Second, hence, there are continual reconfigurations in the cloud. Therefore, cloud performance testing systems (like CloudPT) should link with the infrastructure of cloud management and update any detected fault bottlenecks or anomalous variations in the workflow environment.

Such a program alerts recognizes errors in handle system and application services by notifying administrators; then a cloud ecosystem imposes the need for detecting faults and for high-performance testing. These are important in identifying and detecting fault bottlenecks and other anomalous behavior.

3   CloudPT Architecture

As seen in Fig. 3, the architecture of CloudPT consists of four components: (I) a Monitoring Engine, which monitors the metrics of interest and resources for host VMs based on collecting and processing; (II) an Event Production Engine that quickly identifies symptoms of bottleneck faults and event vector generators; (III) a Performance Testing and Diagnosis Engine that assesses event vectors to define changes in normal behavior. This classifier detects anomaly/fault bottlenecks based on their severity levels and utility values (weights of criteria) [19]; this would be determined by the administrator or service providers with expert knowledge using online training and testing datasets; and (IV) a Decision Engine that performs repair actions on the diagnosed bottlenecks and generates fault notifications so the faults can be identified (type, size, and location). Such notification goes directly to the system administrator or to an applications manager who can easily control or change the system configuration based on the feedback.

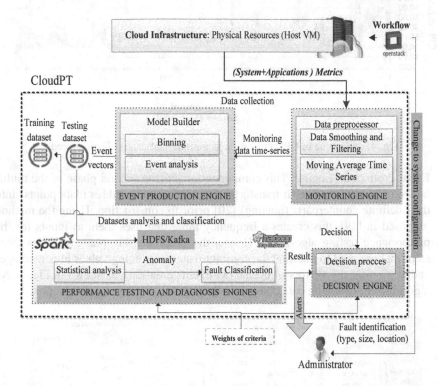

Fig. 3. The architecture of CloudPT

(1) Monitoring Engine: This component was designed to capture, collect, and process the system metrics attached to system and network resources in virtual machines (reported in Table 1). The CPU utilization appears in Fig. 4. All metrics are gathered at periodic intervals; based on Spark streaming technical, a monitoring interval restriction can be configured online to detect a bottleneck.

Table 1. System metrics monitored by CloudPT

System metrics (Bottlenecks)	Description	Measurement level
CPU utilization	% CPU time in user-space/ kernel-space	Host, VM
Memory usage	% of used memory	Host, VM
Network I/O usage	% of Network bandwidth	Host, VM
Storage I/O usage	% of limited storage I/O bandwidth;	Host

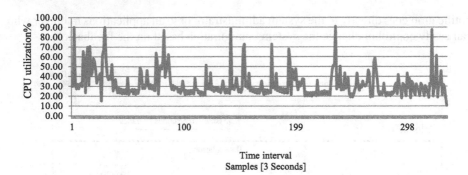

Fig. 4. A sample of CPU utilization as a numerical dataset is monitored

(2) Event Production Engine: This component enacts the second phase of the multi-layered CloudPT outline. It transforms the numerical variables (data points) into their definite counterparts (binning) [20] prior to construction. Using the method proposed in [19], this creates a frequency table that uses them as inputs for the performance testing algorithms. Hence, the preprocessing phase includes three steps that are used to interpret the constant usage of binning values in percentages and to monitor the vectors of events (M-events creation), as shown in Fig. 5. An algorithm for changing data points into data binning vectors is also proposed.

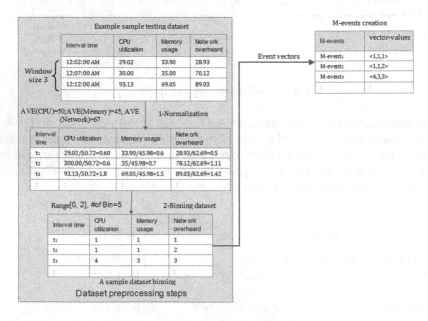

Fig. 5. The process method steps and an illustration of transformed datasets tables and event vectors

The algorithmic approach has a buffer size of n (a look-back window). The purpose measures of n sample were observed (for instance, $n = 3$, range [0, 2] as well as #Bin = 5). Look-back windows are used in different manners and they satisfy multiple needs: (I) when there is a change in the work or the process, it can render earlier data obsolete and inaccurate, (II) it is unrealistic to manage all history data, and (III) it is carried out in a RAM with high speed, which can further enhance detection performance [21].

(3) Performance Testing and Diagnosis Engines: These components use statistical correlations across VMs and use resource metrics to determine the irregularities and failure (a bottleneck). This phase assesses the data further to identify anomalies and errors and generates decision values for each event produced by the component engines of Event Generation. Moreover, these components assign and test datasets to analyze, classify, and categorize potential anomalous or failure bottleneck situations, which have been sensed by the Performance Testing Engine, into one of the fault state classes (yes or no). Finally, expert knowledge of the system is presented in the consistent fault identifiers. A characterization of system irregularities occurs in the areas of illustrative notification; this is an essential step in performance testing and diagnosing. The fault notification catches sets of perversions from the original pattern of performance, both in the attachment values generated by the Performance Testing Engine and in the workflow environment. After detecting anomalous behaviors, the system matches the correlated perversions with the recognized error notification. If there is a match, the module will effectively classify the bottleneck) or it will flag the state as an unusual behavior.

(4) Decision Engine Component: This component receives predefined expert knowledge to classify the potential faults detected by the Performance Testing and Diagnosis Engines. As such, it performs suitable repair actions and creates an XML file for defining the anomaly/bottleneck fault state characteristic notifications that are asserted by the host VM's monitored metrics [22].

Figure 6 presents a professionally-created fault notification for a fault bottleneck (an infinite loop) of a host VM. The system generates these notifications automatically. Allowing CloudPT and experts to categorize new bugs errors will add to the training dataset, which is designed to interact with the anomalous linked to cloud or faults thus far recognized. Application manager services or system administrators receive warnings for fault identification (type, size, and location).

```
1. <?xml version="1.0" encoding="UTF-8" standalone='yes'?>
2. <Performance-test-identify>
3.      <Name?"host VM under-bottleneck"</Name>
4.      <Category>"Fault a bottleneck (an infinite loop)"</Category>
5.      <Fault-category>"Serious"</Fault-category>
6.      <Fault-state>"yes"</Fault-state>
7.      <Description>host VM is sized to very high CPU utilization & low throughput in the
network</Description>
8.      <Identify>
9.            <Host-VM-environment>
10.                 <CPU-utilization>0.80</CPU-utilization>
11.                 <Network-I-O-usage>0.40</Network-I-O-usage>
12.            </Host-VM-environment>
13.      </Identify>
14. </Performance-test-identify>
```

Fig. 6. An example of fault notification for a host VM under-bottleneck

4   Implementation Details

We have implemented CloudPT with a testbed using two virtual machines (VM1 and VM2) designed on a Xen (hypervisor) [23, 24] stage, which is presented on a host VM (Dell blade server) with dual core 3.2 GHz CPUs and 32 GB RAM; it performed tests to identify and resolve the bottlenecks in the IaaS(details in Sect. 5). The architecture of the Apache Spark cluster appears in Fig. 7. For comparison, we have also implemented the same environment using Apache Spark.

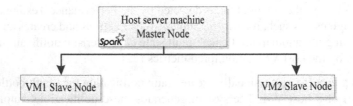

Fig. 7. Architecture of the experiment of Apache Spark's cluster

4.1   Monitoring Engine

Monitoring Engine components gather measurements from a single host. The measurement data (Table 1) has fundamental resource measurements (CPU, memory, network and storage I/O) using Ganglia measurements; they collect the resources of the host VM. The monitored datasets across the host VM and all VMs are gathered and stored in XML formatting at the main host VM's HDFS or Kafka storage platforms. This enables more processing and analyzing in the ensuing stages. The Data Preprocessor component gathers the raw time-series information and uses it to generate data-points. A data-point is a classification that moves average standards over a particular interval of time and generates a simple input unit for the different irregularity/fault bottleneck uncovering algorithms that are used in CloudPT. We used an input parameters window size of 3, a sampling interval of 3 s, and a 15 min interval length. The data points in the 15-minute interval are thereby $(15*60)/(3*3) = 100$. The metrics in the look-back window at each time instance served $(t_1, t_2, ..., t_i, i$ is some of instances) as inputs for the Event Production Engine. These generated the creation m-events $(M_1, M_2, ..., M_i)$, which are the inputs for every component metric of four presented methodology.

4.2 Event Production of Performance Models

We gathered the CPU, Memory, and Network usages in every sample. After collecting and processing sample information points, the numerical data is transformed into a string of bin numbers for every metric type [25, 26], using Eqs. (1), (2), (3) to perform data binning alongside time instance serves $(t_1, t_2, ..., t_i)$ and m-events $(M_1, M_2, ..., M_i)$.

$$\mu = \frac{1}{n} \sum_{i=1}^{n} x_i \tag{1}$$

$$\sigma = \left[\frac{1}{n-1} \sum_{i=1}^{n} (x_i - \mu)^2 \right]^{0.5} \tag{2}$$

$$f(x) = \frac{1}{\sigma\sqrt{2\pi}} e^{\frac{-1}{2}\left(\frac{x-\mu}{2\sigma^2}\right)^2} \tag{3}$$

In the equations above, the population mean is represented by μ, while the population standard deviation is represented by σ; x is from the measurement standards area ($-\infty < x < \infty$) and n represents amount of components or services. A standard probability distribution the parameters of μ and σ. Otherwise, the standard probability density function (PDF) $f(x)$ relies on the constants e (roughly 2.718) and π (roughly 3.142) [26]; with the data in the form of numbers, the values should now be converted into their categories and classes (binning) by Eqs. (4) and (5) (for example, look-back window size = 3, range = [0, 2], quantity of bins = 5) to develop their frequency tables. This can be seen in Fig. 8. These formulas are used to assess the values for binning-value and decision-value:

If $(x > 2)$**Then** binning $-$ value $= 5$, **else** binning $-$ value $=$ TRUNC$(x/0.4)$ \quad (4)

decision $-$ value $=$ MAX(binning $-$ value) \quad (5)

The standardization value for this characteristic is represented by x. In contrast, 0.4 is the statistic recommended by the probability values. Next, one must start categorizing and analyzing the dataset by determining the probability or predictor of the cumulative distribution function (CDF). For a continuously random variable, the CDF equation is:

$$P(X \leq x) = \frac{x-a}{b-a} \tag{6}$$

where a is the lower limit and b is the upper limit, $5:a \leq x \leq b$.

M-events creation	
M-events	**vector-values**
M-event₁	<1,1,1>
M-event₂	<1,1,2>
M-event₃	<4,3,3>
:	:

3-Binning vector values analysis   A sample dataset for analysis

Instances	CPU utilization	Memory usage	Network overhead	Decision value	Fault category	Fault state
inst₁	1	1	1	1	Normal	?
inst₂	1	1	2	2	Minor	?
inst₃	4	3	3	4	Serious	?
:	:	:	:	:	:	:

Fig. 8. The values of the binning data and the decision value for the fault category states before the classifier fault state

4.3   Performance Test and Diagnosis Engine

4.3.1   Performance Test Engine

At this stage, we implemented the hybrid intelligent models MDD and NBC. The MDD acquired the overall severity level of the error and, if needed, it can create an alarm. The MDD processes and assesses m-events and it implements its analysis through pre-processing; it also utilizes I/O pairs to calculate the parameters projected by NBC in the Hadoop MapReduce for massive training or testing datasets. A new CPU utilization probability dataset is illustrated in Fig. 9. There are various changes from the earlier set: the marked vertical lines signify anomaly events, the red lines represent probability effects, and the spikes in those effects show alarms.

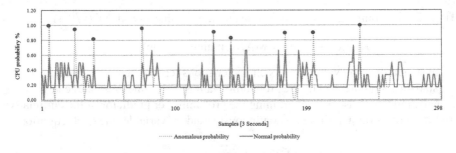

Fig. 9. A sample of CPU utilization probability dataset results

Figure 10 shows the algorithm proposed for faults or anomalies detected and generated in the final fault state, which we name AFBD algorithm. Categorizing component states and system situations is a major step in the workflow; Fig. 11 represents the job sequence of this step. When the actual dataset is in place, a new system model can be developed. Using a decision approach with a look-back window size of 3, one can develop a dataset table in reference to the decision values.

- If (0 = Decision value < 2), then the error class is "Normal," while the node fault state is "no" (working);
- If (2 = Decision value ≤ 3), then the error class is "Minor", while the node fault error state is "no" (working);
- If (Decision value > 3), then the error class is "Serious", while the node fault state is "yes" (fault/abnormal).

Initiation: Let the Pro.$t[i]$, $i = 1, \ldots, k$ be the testing dataset probability table classifier for event vectors instances, Let fault_identify[n] be list of dataset training.

1.	**For** all Pro.t instances **do**
2.	**If** Pro.$t[i]$.*Fault_state*="yes" and Pro.$t[i]$.*Fault_category*="Serious" then
3.	**For** all row$[i]$.*values* **do** // list values of component probability metric
	// deviations from normal behaviors are matched with the known fault identifiers
4.	**If** row$[i]$.*values* in fault_identifiers.*getvalues()* **then**
5.	fault_state ="fault bottleneck"
6.	else
7.	fault_state=" Anomaly behavior"
8.	**end if**
9.	**end for**
10.	**end if**
11.	**end for**

Fig. 10. AFBD Algorithm proposed for fault bottlenecks/anomalies behavior detected

4.3.2 Diagnosis Engine Stage

In this stage, we proposed then implemented algorithms that combined the test data with the exercising dataset model to generate an intermediate table and classify the job. This allowed us to concurrently compute the probability of every component in the three classes via the java and Scala language coding programs and for the algorithms, this is displayed in Appendix A.1, Fig. 16. Our simple dataset outlines a probability model based on the state predicted component usage. Here, the measurement level differs wildly from 0–100%. We observed the percentage component utilization at discrete times $t_1, \ldots, t_n$. The component usage utilized CPU∈{0–25%, 26–75%, 76–100%} as thresholds [27].

The new dataset held outcomes on the model classifier by combining the test and training datasets; it evolves when using the proposed algorithm, as shown in Fig. 17 in Appendix A.1. In the process, we initially defined our task to categorize the three states utilizing the new model. When one component is faulty, the system cannot work. We employed 0, 1, and 2 to embody the system and the component situations. In this case, 0 represented good status (standard working situations), 1 signified a minor error, and

M-events creation		
M-events	**vector-values**	
M-event₁	<1,1,1>	
M-event₂	<1,1,2>	
M-event₃	<4,3,3>	
:	:	

3-Binning vector values analysis ↓ A sample dataset for analysis

Instances	CPU utilization	Memory usage	Network overhead	Decision value	Fault category	Fault state
inst₁	1	1	1	1	Normal	?
inst₂	1	1	2	2	Minor	?
inst₃	4	3	3	4	Serious	?
:	:	:	:	:	:	:

4- means of a CDF values ↓ A sample dataset probability for NBC classifier

Probability.Inst	CPU utilization	Memory usage	Network overhead	Fault category	Fault state
Pro.t₁	0.20	0.20	0.20	Normal	no
Pro.t₂	0.20	0.20	0.40	Minor	no
Pro.t₃	0.80	0.60	0.60	Serious	yes
:	:	:	:		

Dataset classification and analysis steps

Fig. 11. A classification of a probability dataset with final result fault states (no or yes)

2 symbolized a server error. For instance, the CPU, memory and network signify 3 simple modules while host state server signifies the system state (Fig. 12). The results represent only three classes (normal, minor, and serious) for the component state and two (yes, no) for the system fault state. To ease the problem, we chose the same amount of normal, minor, and serious measures for all the models (see Fig. 13(A)–(B)) [27].

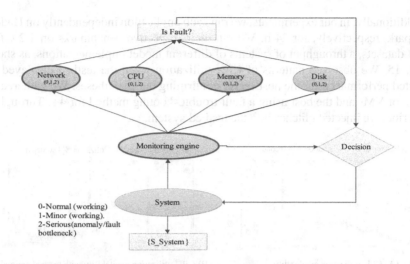

Fig. 12. An NBC Model predicting the components utilization for a host VM system

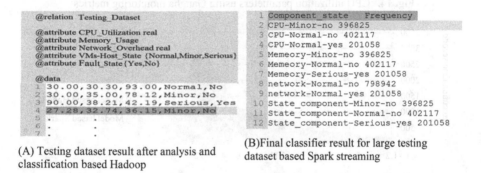

(A) Testing dataset result after analysis and classification based Hadoop

(B)Final classifier result for large testing dataset based Spark streaming

Fig. 13. Results of the algorithms proposed

5   Experimental and Evaluation Results

5.1   OpenStack

OpenStack [28] is open source software that can control massive amounts of storage, computing, and network resources at a datacenter. Typically, one manages it on a dashboard or on an OpenStack API. We introduced 40 irregularities into the OpenStack online service of the host server [29], which resulted in faults/anomalies for global resource consumption (see Fig. 14(A)–(B)). These 40 irregularities represent the extreme failure source issues one can identify within online services [21].

Additionally, in our experiments, we ran each application independently on Hadoop and Spark, respectively, for 24 h. We ran their respective benchmarks on 1.2 GB to 12 GB datasets, a throughput of systems of different model implementations, as shown in Fig. 15. We observed patterns of CPU utilization when the testbed displayed the projected performance for the host server confirming our hypotheses. We gathered the metrics of VMs and the host using a fault troubleshooting method for 4 s. Throughout this period, we injected glitches into the testbed system.

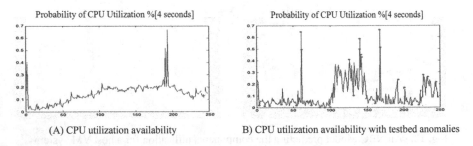

(A) CPU utilization availability   B) CPU utilization availability with testbed anomalies

Fig. 14. CPU utilization parameters using Ganglia monitoring metrics

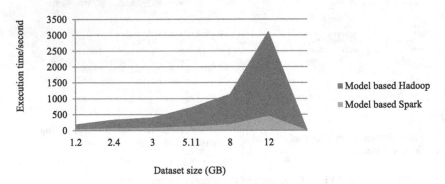

Fig. 15. System throughput of experiments using Hadoop and Spark

5.2 Evaluation and Experiment Results

The statistical measures, recall, precision, and accuracy, along with exactness were used to assess whether the fault diagnosis was effective using Apache Spark and NBC for the massive dataset problem. As displayed in Table 2, we utilized four statistical measures [26, 30] to evaluate CloudPT's effectiveness in identifying and eradicating bottlenecks. A successful anomaly/fault bottleneck recognition was defined by the program diagnosing the irregularity carefully utilizing the fault type identification (type, size, location) and conferring to the affected host VM and metrics. CloudPT is the first end-to-end performance testing management framework that can troubleshoot, analyze, classify and suggest repair actions for virtualized cloud based fault bottlenecks and anomalisms.

Table 2. Four statistical measures

Precision	Recall	Accuracy	False-alarm rate (FAR)
$\dfrac{successful detections}{of total alarms}$	$\dfrac{successful detections}{of total anomalies}$	$\dfrac{2 * precision * recall}{precision + recall}$	$1 - presision$

Overall, the all-around feedback loop performance effectiveness of the CloudPT diagnosed performance bottlenecks in 20 s. The results showed an 86% improvement in the Accuracy (F1) score compared with the theoretical method, with a standard false alarm rate of <=13% (Table 3).

Table 3. Comparing the CloudPT, the threshold-method and CloudPD

Models	Description	Alarms	Successful detections	Recall	Precision	Accuracy (F1)	FAR
CloudPT	A troubleshooti ng performance testing	40	35	0.87	0.87	**0.86**	**0.13**
Threshold-based method	Static Thresholds: 5% > Static thresholds > 90%	25	16	0.40	0.64	0.48	0.36
CloudPD	Problem definition in sharing dynamic cloud	44	32	0.80	0.72	0.76	0.28

5.3 Performance Testing Overheads

CloudPT uses non-virtualization cloud assets to test the performance of bottlenecks and behavior anomalies. We quantified the overhead of CloudPT according to CPU, memory and network overhead utilization. For our experiments, we made bottlenecks and considered the failure of a host VM to startup. We used the virtualization's resources averaged across VMs and over the 24-hour experiment duration; this is represented in Table 3. It is evident that CloudPT presents minimal overhead on the system. Hence, our experimental study confirms the effectiveness of CloudPT's accuracy and frequency in detecting bottlenecks and anomaly faults in accumulation to having a low cloud system overhead.

6 Conclusion

We proposed an Apache Spark-based bottleneck troubleshooting performance framework, called CloudPT for IaaS. The proposed framework includes three construction troubleshooting measures: (I) data collection, (II) analysis and classification engine implementation, and (III) decision engine implementation. The objectives of CloudPT are to monitor collections, develop analysis, and classify the attributes of measurements, as opposed to the individual metric thresholds, by extending the detect of faults into troubleshooting. In general, the framework focuses on monitoring the shared virtualized resource measurements to address the problems that lead to failure bottlenecks. More specifically, CloudPT troubleshoots all apparent bottlenecks or anomalies by using pre-computed fault notifications. Through this framework, we also measured and modelled CPU utilization, memory usage, and the network overhead. CloudPT troubleshoots all apparent bottlenecks or anomalies using pre-computed fault notifications. Simultaneously, it allows recovery to occur in an automated model that is integrated into cloud management services. We conducted a comprehensive assessment of CloudPT on two representative cloud workloads: Hadoop and Spark. Shortly thereafter, we also conducted a host VM startup failure case study. The outcomes of all the experiments demonstrate that CloudPT attains significant accuracy with a low occurrence of false alarms; in short, it efficiently identifies and eradicates bottlenecks and behavior anomalies. One area of future work will mainly cover the development of additional features for the CloudPT, such as recovering and self-healing.

Acknowledgments. We are also thankful to anonymous reviewers for their valuable feedback and comments for improving the quality of the manuscript.

Appendix A

A.1. A Proposed Algorithms

Input: *value*←Training dataset.//XML format

Output: Result. //a new dataset result saves in HDFS

```
1-   Begin
2-     Map(Object key, Text value, Context context)
3-       component_name ←"";
4-       Row[] ← value.toString().split(",");
5-       if(row.length>= 5)
6-         state_component←row[3];
7-         for col=0 to col<=3 do  // filtering datasets
8-           component_name ← "State_component"
9-           elseif (row[col]>=0&&row[col] <=25)
10-             state_component="Normal";
11-           elseif (row[col]>=26&&row[col] <=74)
12-             state_component="Minor";
13-           elseif (row[col]>=75&&row[col] <=100)
14-             state_component="Serious";
15-           if (col==0) component_name="CPU";
16-           elseif (col==1) component_name="Memory";
17-           elseif (col==2) component_name=" Network"
18-     word.set(component_name+"-"+state_component+"-"+row[4]);
19-             context.write(word, one);
20-         End for
21-       End if
22-     End Map
23-     Reduce(Text key, Iterable<IntWritable>values, Context context)
24-       Sum←0;
25-         for (Int Writableval:values) do
26-           sum += val.get();
27-         End for
28-         result.set(sum);
29-         context.write(key, result);
30-     End reduce
31-   Result←result;// save in hdfs://localhost:9000/result
32-   Call DataStream.main();
33- End
34- object DataStream // Scala streaming dataset program
35-   Begin
36-     def main(args: Array[String]) {
37-       val ssc←new StreamingContext("local[4]","DataStream",
                        Seconds(3))
38-       val test_dataset ←ssc.textFileStream
                      ("hdfs://localhost:9000/result")
39-       val instances←test_dataset.flatMap(_.split(" "))
40-       val pairs←instances.map(word => (word, 1))
41-         val instancesCounts← pairs.reduceByKey(_ + _)
42-         instancesCounts.print()
43-           ssc.start()
44-             ssc.awaitTermination()
45- End
```

Fig. 16. Algorithm for training, filtering and streaming dataset based on Hadoop and Spark

Input: Training and testing datasets //XML format
Output: A new-dataset-result.XML, F.Measure, Precision and Recall.

```
1-   Begin
2-   Classify(Dataset-train, Dataset-test) //Datasets with XML format
3-      BufferedReader breader←null;
4-        Breader← new BufferedReader(new FileReader(Dataset-train));
5-        Instances train←new Instances(breader);
6-        train.setClassIndex(train.numAttributes()-1);
7-         Breader←new BufferedReader(newFileReader(Dataset-test));
8-         Instances test←new Instances (breader);
9-           test.setClassIndex(train.numAttributes()-1);
10-          breader.close();
11-          J48 tree←new J48();
12-           tree.buildClassifier(train); //build classifier
13-           Instances labeled← new Instances(test);//label instances
14-          for i=0 to i<test.numInstances()do
15-            clsLabel←tree.classifyInstance(test.instance(i));
16-            labeled.instance(i).setClassValue(clsLabel);
17-          End for
18-          BufferedWriter writer←new BufferedWriter(new FileWriter("Anew-dataset-result.XML"));
19-             writer.write(labeled.toString());
20-             writer.close();   Call-Produce StartNBC("A new-dataset-result.XML");
21-   End //classify
22-   StartNBC (Dataset)// evaluation results
23-     BufferedReader breader ←null;
24-     breader ←new BufferedReader(new FileReader(Dataset));
25-     Instances train←new Instances (breader);
26-        train.setClassIndex(train.numAttributes()-1);
27-        breader.close();
28-        NaiveBayesnB←new NaiveBayes();
29-        nB.buildClassifier(train);
30-        Evaluation eval←new Evaluation(train);
31-         eval.crossValidateModel(nB, train, 20, new Random(1));
32-         The F.Measure← eval.fMeasure(1);
33-         The Precision← eval.precision(1);
34-         The Recall← eval.recall(1);
35-   End
```

Fig. 17. Algorithm for combining the testing and training datasets classification and evaluation results

References

1. Malli, S.S., Soundararajan, V., Venkataraman, B.: Real Time Big Data Analytics to Derive Actionable Intelligence in Enterprise Applications, Internet of Things and Big Data Analytics Toward Next-Generation Intelligence, pp. 99–121. Springer, Cham (2018)
2. Gregg, B. Systems Performance: Enterprise and The Cloud. Pearson Education, New Jersey
3. Alsheikh, M.A., Niyato, D., Lin, S., Tan, H.P., Han, Z.: Mobile big data analytics using deep learning and apache spark. IEEE Network **30**(3), 22–29 (2016)
4. Performance-testing   (2017).   http://www.softwaretestinghelp.com/what-is-performance-testing-load-testing-stress-testing/
5. Zhang, Q., Cheng, L., Boutaba, R.: Cloud computing: state-of-the-art and research challenges. J. Internet Serv. Appl. **1**(1), 7–18 (2010)

6. Alkasem, A., Liu, H., Decheng, Z., et al.: AFDI: A Virtualization-based Accelerated Fault Diagnosis Innovation for High Availability Computing, arXiv preprint arXiv:1507.08036 (2015)

7. High CPU utilization but low load average (2017). https://serverfault.com/questions/667078/high-cpu-utilization-but-low-load-average/667089

8. Alkasem, A., Liu, H., Zuo, D.: Utility cloud: a novel approach for diagnosis and self-healing based on the uncertainty in anomalous metrics. In: Proceedings of the 2017 International Conference on Management Engineering, Software Engineering and Service Sciences, pp. 99–107. ACM (2017)

9. Zhai, Y., Xu, W.: March. efficient bottleneck detection in stream process system using fuzzy logic model. In: Euromicro International Conference on Parallel, Distributed and Network-based Processing (PDP), pp. 438–445. IEEE (2017)

10. Castro Fernandez, R., Migliavacca, M., Kalyvianaki, E., Pietzuch, P.: Integrating scale out and fault tolerance in stream processing using operator state management. In: Proceedings of the 2013 ACM SIGMOD International Conference on Management of Data. ACM (2013)

11. Garcia-Teodoro, P., Diaz-Verdejo, J., Maciá-Fernández, G., et al.: Anomaly-based network intrusion detection: techniques, systems and challenges. Comput. Secur. **28**(1), 18–28 (2009)

12. Massie, M., et al.: Monitoring with Ganglia: Tracking Dynamic Host and Application Metrics at Scale. O'Reilly Media, Inc., Massachusetts (2012)

13. Barth, W.N.: System and Network Monitoring. No Starch Press, San Francisco (2008)

14. Witten, I.H., Frank, E., Hall, M.A., Pal, C.J.: Data Mining: Practical Machine Learning Tools and Techniques. Morgan Kaufmann, Massachusetts (2016)

15. Sharma, B., Praveen, A., Chita, R.D.: Problem determination and diagnosis in shared dynamic clouds. In: 43rd Annual IEEE/IFIP International Conference on Dependable Systems and Networks (DSN). IEEE (2013)

16. Cherkasova, L., Ozonat, K., Mi, N., Symons, J., Smirni, E.: Automated anomaly detection and performance modeling of enterprise applications. ACM Trans. Comput. Syst. (TOCS) **27**(3), 1–32 (2009)

17. Kumar, A., Shankar, R., Choudhary, A., Thakur, L.S.: A big data MapReduce framework for fault diagnosis in cloud-based manufacturing. Int. J. Prod. Res. **54**(23), 7060–7073 (2016)

18. Li, J., Qiu, M., Ming, Z., Quan, G., Qin, X., Gu, Z.: Online optimization for scheduling preemptable tasks on IaaS cloud systems. J. Parallel Distrib. Comput. **72**(5), 666–677 (2012)

19. Alkasem, A., Liu, H., Shafiq, M., Zuo, D.: A new theoretical approach: a model construct for fault troubleshooting in cloud computing. Mobile Inf. Syst. **2017**, 16 (2017). https://doi.org/10.1155/2017/9038634. Article ID 9038634

20. SivaSelvan, N., Haider, M.Y., Selvan, N.S., Hegde, G.: Design and Development of Performance Management System (2016)

21. Wang, C., Talwar, V., Schwan, K., Ranganathan, P.: Online detection of utility cloud anomalies using metric distributions. In: Network Operations and Management Symposium (NOMS). IEEE (2010)

22. Bertino, Elisa, Catania, Barbara: Integrating XML and databases. IEEE Internet Comput. **5**(4), 84–88 (2001)

23. Barham, P., Boris, D., Keir, F., Steven, H., et al.: Xen and the art of virtualization. In: ACM SIGOPS Operating Systems Review, vol. 37, no. 5, pp. 164–177. ACM (2003)

24. Riddle, A.R., Soon, M.C.: A survey on the security of hypervisors in cloud computing. In: 2015 IEEE 35th International Conference on Distributed Computing Systems Workshops (ICDCSW), pp. 100–104. IEEE (2015)

25. Gelman, A., John, B.C., Hal, S.S., Donald, B.R.: Bayesian Data Analysis, vol. 2. Chapman & Hall/CRC, Boca Raton (2014)

26. Doane, D.P., Lori, E.S.: Applied Statistics in Business and Economics. Irwin, New York (2005)
27. Alkasem, A., Liu, H., Zuo, D., Algarash, B.: Cloud computing: a model construct of real-time monitoring for big dataset analytics using apache spark. J. Phys: Conf. Ser. **933**(1), 012018 (2018)
28. Jackson, K.: OpenStack Cloud Computing Cookbook. Packt Publishing Ltd, Birmingham (2012)
29. Kumar, V., Karsten, S.S., Yuan, C., Akhil, S.: A state-space approach to SLA based management. In: Network Operations and Management Symposium NOMS 2008 IEEE, pp. 192–199. IEEE (2008)
30. Alkasem, A., Liu, H.: A survey of fault-tolerance in cloud computing: concepts and practice. Res. J. Appl. Sci. Eng. Technol. **11**(12), 1365–1377 (2015)

Smart Grid Power Trading
Based on Consortium Blockchain
in Internet of Things

Dong Zheng[1,2]([✉]), Kaixin Deng[1], Yinghui Zhang[1,2]([✉]), Jiangfan Zhao[1],
Xiaokun Zheng[3], and Xinwei Ma[1]

[1] National Engineering Laboratory for Wireless Security, Xi'an University of Posts
and Telecommunications, Xi'an 710121, People's Republic of China
zhengdong@xupt.edu.cn, dkx523121943@163.com, yhzhaang@163.com,
zjf2914957910163.com, xwellma@163.com
[2] Westone Cryptologic Research Center, Beijing 100070, China
[3] School of Computer Science and Technology, Xi'an University of Posts and
Telecommunications, Xi'an 710121, People's Republic of China
xiaokzheng@163.com

Abstract. Internet of Things (IoT) technologies have attracted enormous attention from academics and industries, and one of the most representative application is the smart grid. Most smart grid system models have to rely on trusted third-parties, but there are no trusted third-parties in practice. Blockchain technologies show a lot of advantages in IoT due to its unique characteristics. In this paper, to enable reliability, efficiency, flexibility and security in smart grid trading, we combine blockchain technologies, *proof of stake* consensus mechanisms and cryptography tools to build a novel smart grid power trading system. Our security analysis shows that the proposed system can protect users' data privacy.

Keywords: Smart grid · Blockchain · Smart contracts
Internet of Things · Energy market

1 Introduction

In future smart grid designs, users can use renewable energy such as solar energy and wind energy to convert them into storable electricity to reduce power companies' dependence on fossil fuels [9]. Users can complete trading with companies or other users through gateways [20]. It is easy to cause privacy disclosure while

Supported by National Key R&D Program of China (No. 2017YFB0802000), National Natural Science Foundation of China (No. 61772418, 61472472, 61402366), Natural Science Basic Research Plan in Shaanxi Province of China (No. 2018JZ6001, 2015JQ6236). Yinghui Zhang is supported by New Star Team of Xi'an University of Posts and Telecommunications (No. 2016-02).

© Springer Nature Switzerland AG 2018
J. Vaidya and J. Li (Eds.): ICA3PP 2018, LNCS 11336, pp. 453–459, 2018.
https://doi.org/10.1007/978-3-030-05057-3_34

the information is not be encrypted. In recent years, many technologies were used to protect Internet of Things (IoT) security [6,8,12,15]. Electric power companies as trusted third-parties are vulnerable to suffer attacks, and there still exists some security issues [1,12]. In view of these security threats, it is urgent to design a safe and reliable decentralized system to ensure that the interests of users and companies are not violated.

Blockchain is defined as a distributed database that records transactions of value using a cryptographic signature that is inherently resistant to modifiction [11]. It allows to have a distributed peer-to-peer network where non-trusting members can interact with each other without a trusted intermediary [2]. Famous WannaCry blackmail virus used bitcoin as the payment currency [3], which makes more and more people aware of the uniqueness of the blockchain. With the development of cloud computing [16,19] and wireless network technologies [13,14], blockchain technologies have been used in outsourcing services for payment [18] and keyword search [17] in cloud computing and intelligent control in energy market [4,10], and consortium blockchain has high potential to establish decentralized electricity trading system with moderate cost [7]. However, most of existing schemes adopt *proof of work* (PoW) consensus mechanisms or private chains, where PoW is wasteful and private chains are not decentralize in essence.

In the future smart grid systems, using blockchain technology, constructing a decentralized peer-to-peer network system can bring the system more security and flexibility. This paper presents a smart grid power trading system. The main contributions of this paper are two-fold.

- For one thing, we adopt the *proof of stake* (PoS) consensus mechanism instead of PoW to present a new architecture of smart grid power trading system. Our architecture overcomes the shortcomings of the 51% attack, which is the most common attack method in the blockchain.
- For another, for the security problems of users' uploading data to the authorized nodes, we use cryptography to encrypt data collected by the sensors.

Organization. The remaining of this paper is organized as follows. In Sect. 2, we describe the proposed system in detail together with the proposed system architecture. In Sect. 3, we give the security analysis of the proposed system. We draw our conclusions in Sect. 4.

2   Smart Grid Power Trading System

2.1   System Architecture

Figure 1 presents an overview of the model, which uses blockchain as the protocol layer, rely on the Ethereum to run the smart contract, and uses the PoS consensus mechanism, completes power trading with the help of market. The system has these following levels:

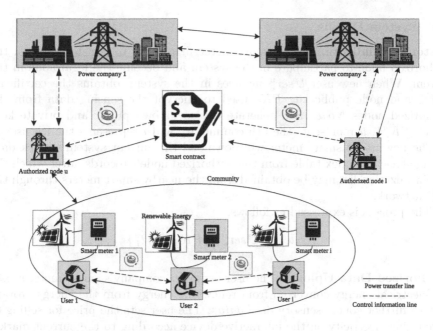

Fig. 1. System model

(1) *User layer.* Users register in the system through smart meters [5] with true identity, system returns his public key and certificate, the certificate can be used to uniquely identify the user node through binding registration information of the user. Then users generate their public key and private key by their own. Users can price electrical energy through interactive devices, set the expected sales price and electricity waiting for smart contract processing.

(2) *Authorized nodes layer.* The system establishes authorized nodes based on the users' geographical distribution for the user to participate in the system. A consensus reached between authorized nodes according to user needs. When the user's transaction requirements are satisfied, the smart contract is automatically executed.

(3) *Power company layer.* In system, power companies play the role of power balance energy storage. Performing big data analysis and forecasting according to the regional electricity situation, and complete the estimation of the current regional peak time, sending request information through contract during low electricity period for low-cost electricity purchase. Power companies are also important power carriers to transmit power over long distances.

(4) *PoS consensus mechanism.* We use PoS mechanism instead of PoW, it is based on the energy converted from renewable energy and the time it is stored for interest release and block generation. If a region is rich in electricity resources, due to PoS mechanism will have interest compensation for emptying more power areas, the authorized node will charge a part of the commission by agreement, then distribute most of the interest to users. Users will be more willing to sell the electricity at a lower price than the market price.

2.2   System Details

System Initialization. The smart meter first needs to register through the authorized node to participate in the system and become the legal node in the system. When new user $User_i^u$ involves in the system, obtains the certificate $Cert_i^u$ and node public key PK_u used to encrypt the sensing data from the authorized nodes $Node_u$ and generate the user's own public and private keys $\{PK_i^u, SK_i^u\}$. u represents the uth community and i represents the ith user in u. The new user's smart meter will download the current system's block data storage location index table from the authorized node's records, after which the synchronization list may be obtained from the nearby smart meters through the P2P network.

The process is expressed as follows:

$$Node_u \rightarrow User_i^u : \{PK_u, Cert_i^u\} \tag{1}$$

Authorized Data Upload. The user or power company's smart meter senses the electrical energy converted from renewable energy from the energy storage unit to further collect sensory data $data_i^u$; The user sets the price for selling or purchasing electricity on the interactive device according to the current market price p_i^u, then set up to sell or buy electricity x_i^u, the smart meter packages the data and encrypts the signature, which is passed to the authorized node. Upload data using pseudonyms and digital signatures to ensure the integrity and authenticity of data.

The process is expressed as follows:

$$User_i^u \rightarrow Node_u : data_{px}^i = Enc_{PK_u}(data_i^u||Cert_i^u||Sig_i^u||timestamp) \tag{2}$$

Among them:

$$data_i^u = Enc_{PK_i^u}\{data||p_i^u||x_i^u\} \tag{3}$$

Authorized Node Validation. When the $Node_u$ receives the data, it uses SK_i^u to decrypt $data_{px}^i$ for verifying user's identity. If the information is valid, it can be saved in the data record pool for the next processing; If the information is not secure or invalid, the data is ignored.

PoS Consensus Mechanism Operation. The PoS consensus mechanism has a unique concept: coindays, the currency multiplied by the number of holding days. The authorized node is responsible for running smart contract and the generation of blocks. Total electricity used to generate coindays for block generation, as long as the node holding electricity, no matter how many can be dug to data blocks, without using any mineral pools it will not cause computing power concentration. At the same time, it reduces the resource consumption because of the use of coindays to generate blocks instead of computing power. If a new PoS block is discovered by the authorized node, it will clear the coindays to gain pay to compensate users and the authorized node.

If a authorized node $Node_u$ consumes coindays and generated a new block $data\_block$, the node integrates the data sets $data_t^u$ received from other nodes during the integration, and attach the signature Sig_u and the hash value of the new data blocks, broadcast to other authorized nodes.

The process is expressed as follows:

$$data_t^u = \{data_{px1}^u || data_{px2}^u || \cdots || data_{pxn}^u || timestamp\} \tag{4}$$

$$Node_u \rightarrow All\_Node : (data_t^u || data\_hash || Cert_u || Sig_u || timestamp) \tag{5}$$

Among them:

$$data\_hash = Hash(data_t^u || timestamp) \tag{6}$$

Reply. After the other authorized nodes receive the node's broadcast, they verify the legitimacy and correctness of the data block through the block hash and digital signature, and broadcast the audit $result$ to other authorized node $Node_l$ with their signatures. After the $Node_u$ receives and summarizes all the audit results, it signs and sends a reply to the master node.

$$Node_l \rightarrow Node_u : reply = Enc_{PK_u}(result\_sets || Cert_l || Sig_l || timestamp) \tag{7}$$

Among them:

$$result\_sets = \{result_1 || result_2 || \cdots || result_l\} \tag{8}$$

Writing in the Chain. The authorized node $Node_u$ can decrypt the replies with its own private key SK_u after receiving the $reply$ from other authorized nodes. If the audit results of other nodes pass, then the $Node_u$ will put the audit result into the data block and write it into the main chain, so as to get the system reward.

Contract Operation. There is a virtual trading market in our model. Authorized node packaged power sales and quotes are broadcast on the entire network, smart contracts will be automatically executed according to the needs of users and power companies by running scripts, such as searching electricity prices from low to high, according to the user's estimated price for intelligent sales, buy electricity at a lower price; power companies can buy electricity in the low valley period and sell electricity in the peak period according to the smart contract.

Power Transfer. When the smart contract is completed, the smart meter will conduct electricity dispatching according to the data broadcasted by the authorized nodes, and obtain or pay the corresponding digital currency.

3 Security Analysis

The system proposed in this paper utilizes asymmetric encryption technology and has good resistance to traditional security attacks. Through the cryptographic authentication mechanism, the attacker cannot crack the encrypted information within the effective time; by adding a time stamp to the data information, attackers cannot launch the replay attack; by using the digital signature technology in the data information, it can prevent attackers from forging fake data or tampering with data.

In blockchain security, our system does not require a reliable third-party. The data is backed up at each authorized node. A small number of nodes that are attacked cannot affect the collapse of the entire system. System uses pseudonyms to ensure the privacy of the user's personal information so that nodes cannot obtain the true identity. This article uses smart contracts to share data, restricts data access rights, and makes transactions transparent.

The PoS mechanism will submit its consumed coindays to each block in order to increase the score of the block. The block with the highest depletion coindays will be selected as the main chain. In PoW mechanism, if someone has more than 50% of the computing power, he can mine the block faster than others, so he actually has the absolute right to the block, such as undo the payment transactions. Our design reduces the worries of the 51% attack, because in the PoS consensus mechanism, the 51% attack need to be controlled in a large number of coins, the cost may be higher than the 51% computing power, so it increases the cost of the attack.

4   Conclusion

With the rapid development of smart grid systems, centralized data storage methods are increasingly difficult to deal with attacks. Turning data centered storage into distributed storage is the future trend. This paper proposes a smart grid trading system based on the consortium blockchain, relies on smart contracts and PoS consensus mechanism, enables users and operators who maintain the nodes to form a win-win situation. In order to further improve the security of the system, we consider improving the consensus algorithm based on the PoS consensus to ensure that the verifier of the highest-value deposit in each block can operate the blockchain in the best profit model.

References

1. Aitzhan, N.Z., Svetinovic, D.: Security and privacy in decentralized energy trading through multi-signatures, blockchain and anonymous messaging streams. IEEE Trans. Dependable Sec. Comput. (2016). https://doi.org/10.1109/TDSC.2016.2616861
2. Christidis, K., Devetsikiotis, M.: Blockchains and smart contracts for the internet of things. IEEE Access 4, 2292–2303 (2016)
3. Crowe, J.: Wannacry ransomware statistics: the numbers behind the outbreak. https://blog.barkly.com/wannacry-ransomeware-statistics-2017/
4. Etemad, R.H., Lahouti, F.: Resilient decentralized consensus-based state estimation for smart grid in presence of false data. In: IEEE International Conference on Acoustics, Speech and Signal Processing (ICASSP), pp. 3466–3470. IEEE (2016)

5. Han, Q., Zhang, Y., Chen, X., Li, H., Quan, J.: Efficient and robust identity-based handoff authentication in wireless networks. In: Xu, L., Bertino, E., Mu, Y. (eds.) NSS 2012. LNCS, vol. 7645, pp. 180–191. Springer, Heidelberg (2012). https://doi.org/10.1007/978-3-642-34601-9_14

6. Li, J., Zhang, Y., Chen, X., Xiang, Y.: Secure attribute-based data sharing for resource-limited users in cloud computing. Comput. Secur. **72**, 1–12 (2018)

7. Li, Z., Kang, J., Yu, R., Ye, D., Deng, Q., Zhang, Y.: Consortium blockchain for secure energy trading in industrial internet of things. IEEE Trans. Ind. Inform. (2017). https://doi.org/10.1109/TII.2017.2786307

8. Liu, Y., Zhang, Y., Ling, J., Liu, Z.: Secure and fine-grained access control on e-healthcare records in mobile cloud computing. Future Gener. Comput. Syst. **78**, 1020–1026 (2018)

9. Mahmoud, M.M., Saputro, N., Akula, P.K., Akkaya, K.: Privacy-preserving power injection over a hybrid AMI/LTE smart grid network. IEEE Internet Things J. **4**(4), 870–880 (2017)

10. Mannaro, K., Pinna, A., Marchesi, M.: Crypto-trading: Blockchain-oriented energy market. In: AEIT International Annual Conference, pp. 1–5. IEEE (2017)

11. Mylrea, M., Gourisetti, S.N.G.: Blockchain for smart grid resilience: exchanging distributed energy at speed, scale and security. In: Resilience Week (RWS), pp. 18–23 (2017)

12. Zhang, Y., Zheng, D., Deng, R.H.: Security and privacy in smart health: efficient policy-hiding attribute-based access control. IEEE Internet Things J. **5**(3), 2130–2145 (2018)

13. Zhang, Y., Chen, X., Li, H., Cao, J.: Identity-based construction for secure and efficient handoff authentication schemes in wireless networks. Secur. Commun. Netw. **5**(10), 1121–1130 (2012)

14. Zhang, Y., Chen, X., Li, J., Li, H.: Generic construction for secure and efficient handoff authentication schemes in EAP-based wireless networks. Comput. Netw. **75**, 192–211 (2014)

15. Zhang, Y., Chen, X., Li, J., Li, H., Li, F.: FDR-ABE: attribute-based encryption with flexible and direct revocation. In: International Conference on Intelligent Networking and Collaborative Systems (INCoS), pp. 38–45. IEEE (2013)

16. Zhang, Y., Chen, X., Li, J., Wong, D.S., Li, H.: Anonymous attribute-based encryption supporting efficient decryption test. In: Proceedings of the 8th ACM SIGSAC Symposium on Information, Computer and Communications Security, pp. 511–516. ACM (2013)

17. Zhang, Y., Deng, R.H., Jiangang, S., Kan, Y., Dong, Z.: TKSE: trustworthy keyword search over encrypted data with two-side verifiability via blockchain. IEEE Access **6**, 31077–31087 (2018)

18. Zhang, Y., Deng, R.H., Ximeng, L., Dong, Z.: Blockchain based efficient and robust fair payment for outsourcing services in cloud computing. Inf. Sci. **462**, 262–277 (2018)

19. Zhang, Y., Li, J., Chen, X., Li, H.: Anonymous attribute-based proxy re-encryption for access control in cloud computing. Secur. Commun. Netw. **9**(14), 2397–2411 (2016)

20. Zhang, Y., Zhao, J., Zheng, D.: Efficient and privacy-aware power injection over AMI and smart grid slice in future 5G networks. Mob. Inf. Syst. **2017**, 1–11 (2017)

Energy-Efficient Offloading in Mobile Edge Computing with Edge-Cloud Collaboration

Xin Long[iD], Jigang Wu[(⊠)][iD], and Long Chen[iD]

School of Computer Science and Technology,
Guangdong University of Technology, Guangzhou, China
longyiyuan@outlook.com, asjgwucn@outlook.com, lonchen@mail.ustc.edu.cn

Abstract. Multiple access mobile edge computing is an emerging technique to bring computation resources close to end mobile users. By deploying edge servers at WiFi access points or cellular base stations, the computation capabilities of mobile users can be extended. Existing works mostly assume the remote cloud server can be viewed as a special edge server or the edge servers are willing to cooperate, which is not practical. In this work, we propose an edge-cloud cooperative architecture where edge servers can rent for the remote cloud servers to expedite the computation of tasks from mobile users. With this architecture, the computation offloading problem is modeled as a mixed integer programming with delay constraints, which is NP-hard. The objective is to minimize the total energy consumption of mobile devices. We propose a greedy algorithm with approximation radio of $(1 + \varepsilon)$ as well as a simulated annealing algorithm to effectively solve the problem. Extensive simulation results demonstrate that, the proposed greedy algorithm can achieve the same application completing time budget performance of the Brute Force optional algorithm with only 31% extra energy cost.

Keywords: Mobile edge computing · Cooperate · Greedy algorithm
Remote cloud · Task dependency

1 Introduction

The recent tremendous growth of various wireless devices and diverse applications has brought the challenge in wireless systems. Since the proliferation of smart mobile devices and wearable sensors, mobile traffic and computation tasks have increased dramatically. Therefore, cloud computing [2] as well as 5G communication [5,9] has been proposed to deal with this challenge in the big data era. Despite the potential in data storage and analysis, cloud computing cannot fulfill the growing application requirements such as low latency and context awareness. Multiple-access mobile Edge Computing (MEC) [13] that serves as a complement for cloud computing can potentially overcome the weakness of

© Springer Nature Switzerland AG 2018
J. Vaidya and J. Li (Eds.): ICA3PP 2018, LNCS 11336, pp. 460–475, 2018.
https://doi.org/10.1007/978-3-030-05057-3_35

mobile cloud computing by offloading computation intensive tasks at the edge of wireless networks.

Task allocation and computation resource assignment are crucial to MEC, especially in the presence of an application with a large number of delay sensensitive subtasks. For example, on-line gaming for recreation or face recognition for security purposes. Those tasks should be handled in time taking the finite bandwidth and limited computation resources into consideration. The offloading problem that taking into consideration the above factors jointly are usually mixed integer programming problems which are non-convex and NP-hard [7,8]. Among the task allocation and resource assignment schemes, energy optimization is one of the key factors that affect the performance of the computation resource limited mobile devices. That's because the energy consumption of mobile devices would exponentially grow when there are multiple complex tasks on the devices.

Earlier works on energy optimization for MEC, such as [3,17], assumed unlimited energy supply of edge servers. Bi et al. [3] addressed the computation rate maximization problem in wireless powered MEC networks. Mobile devices can harvest energy from the cellular base station that with an MEC server. The original problem was non-convex and a decoupled optimization with coordinate descent method was proposed to solve the proposed problem. Lyu et al. in [17] studied the total energy consumption of multiple devices with latency constraints. The problem was modeled as a mixed-integer programming, followed by a dynamic programming algorithm based on Bellman equation. More recent researches [4,14] have been focused on delay minimization with energy or budget constraints of edge servers. Chen et al. [4] carried out with a novel multi-cell MEC architecture where edge devices such as base stations can cooperate with remote server on task execution. Considering the ON/OFF nature of edge servers, they used Lyapunov optimization technique to obtain optimal decisions on task offloading. Considering task dependency, Kao et al. [14] presented Hermes, aiming at minimizing total execution time of tasks with user budget constraints (Table 1).

Based on the literature reviews, task dependency was not properly investigated by [3,4,17], which is important for real deployment. Although task dependency was used in the model by [14], authors in [14] merely neglected the influence of remote cloud servers. Moreover, all the above works assume the remote cloud server can be viewed as a special edge server or the edge servers are willing

Table 1. Comparison between existing works and this work.

Existing works	[3]	[4]	Hermes [14]	[17]	This work
Task dependency	No	No	Yes	No	Yes
Edge-cloud collaboration	No	No	No	No	Yes
Energy constraint of users	No	Yes	Yes	No	Yes
Server utility constraint	No	No	No	No	Yes
Objective	Computation rate	Delay	Delay	Energy	Energy

to cooperate. In real scenarios, the remote cloud server has higher computation capability than the edge server and the transmission delay between edge cloud and remote server cannot be neglected when designing proper offloading schemes. Take face recognition as an example. The feature extraction tasks for face images obtained by individual mobile devices can be offloaded to edge servers while the machine learning and face recognition, i.e., image matching tasks can be executed on the remote cloud servers. Therefore, with edge-cloud cooperation, the target faces can be detected with certain bounded delay for distributed mobile devices.

In this work, we investigate computation offloading decision and resource allocation problem with given delay requirements of mobile applications. The objective is to minimize sum energy consumption of mobile devices. Different from above works, we take edge-cloud cooperation into account, which being new challenges for the energy optimization problem. Since there are heterogeneous network resources, it is necessary to determine which the computation tasks should be done at remote clouds, processed at edge servers or local mobile devices. From the perspective of edge and remote cloud servers, their service for mobile devices should be compensated for the cost of execution and their profits should be guaranteed. Since the tasks of one application is delay bounded, how to handle edge-cloud cooperation with user budget constraints should be carefully designed.

The main contributions of this paper can be summarized as follows:

- A novel edge-cloud cooperation architecture is proposed in wireless heterogeneous network with edge servers deployed at small-cell base stations and remote cloud servers connected to the macro-cell base station. The edge server can hire remote edge servers to process some of the tasks originated from mobile devices.
- The offloading problem is modeled as a mixed integer non-linear programming, which is NP-hard. We then propose a greedy algorithm as well as a simulated annealing algorithm to effectively solve the problem.
- To provide incentive for edge servers, we propose a pricing scheme with virtual currency from mobile users to edge servers and remote cloud servers for the dedication of servers serving mobile users.

The remainder paper is organized as follows. System model and computation model are presented in Sect. 2. Section 3 presents the problem formulation. The proposed algorithms is described in Sect. 4. Section 5 presents the performance evaluation. Section 6 concludes this paper with future remarks.

2 System Model and Computation Model

This section firstly describes the system model and formulates the offloading problem for energy saving with local computing, edge computing and the collaboration between edge and cloud servers.

Fig. 1. System architecture

2.1 System Model

As shown in Fig. 1, each edge server is located at the access point (AP) [6] which is also being attached by multiple mobile devices. The edge server is deployed at the AP and is linked to the remote cloud via high speed fiber links. Let U be the set of mobile devices, We assume that there are M mobile devices. Therefore, we have $U = \{u_1, u_2, u_3, \cdots, u_M\}$, where $M \geq 1$. Meanwhile, there is a set T_m subtasks on the m-th mobile device, which cloud be denoted as $T_m = \{\tau_{m,1}, \tau_{m,2}, \tau_{m,3}, \cdots, \tau_{m,N}\}$, where $N \geq 0$.

Next, we will introduce the communication and computation models for mobile devices, edge servers and remote cloud in detail.

2.2 Communication Model

Transmission between Mobile Devices and Edge. Let $X_{m,n}^m \in \{0,1\}$, $X_{m,n}^f \in \{0,1\}$ and $X_{m,n}^c \in \{0,1\}$ each represents the computation offloading policy made by the m-th mobile device. Particularly, $X_{m,n}^m = 1$ denotes that the subtask n on mobile device m is executed locally while $X_{m,n}^f = 1$ denotes that the subtask n of mobile device m is executed on the edge server. Similarly, $X_{m,n}^c = 1$ denotes that the subtask n on mobile device m is executed on the remote cloud. We can compute the uplink data rate for wireless transmission between mobile device and edge server as [5]:

$$R_{m,n} = W log_2 \left(1 + \frac{P_{m,n}^m G_{m,n}}{\sigma_m^2 + \sum_{i \neq m, j \neq m} P_{i,j}^m G_{i,j}} \right), \quad (1)$$

where $P_{m,n}^m$ is the transmission power of mobile device m to upload the subtask n to the edge server via AP, $G_{m,n}$ is the channel gain between the mth mobile device and the corresponding AP when transmitting subtask n. $G_{m,n} = (dis_{m,p}^{-\eta}) |h_{m,p}|^2$ where $dis_{m,p}$ denotes the Euclidean distance between mobile device and edge server, $h_{m,p}$ is the corresponding Rayleigh fading channel coefficient that obeys the distribution of $N(0,1)$ [20]. The surrounding noise power at the receiver, i.e. the AP, is σ_m^2 [20].

It should be noted that, for the benefit of presentation, the downlink transmission rate is represented by the corresponding uplink rate. In the following expressions, we also utilize the expression of uplink transmission delay to represent the downlink transmission delay. That's because the downlink transmission rate is usually a few times larger than the uplink transmission rate due to the channel allocation result of network operator. With this change, we can reduce the complexity of delay and energy cost expressions, which will be described in detail in following paragraphs (Table 2).

Table 2. Basic notations

Notation	Descriptions
M	Number of mobile devices
N	Number of subtasks
$D_{m,n}$	Data size of subtask n on mobile device m
$W_{m,n}$	Workload of subtask n on mobile device m
$R_{m,n}$	Uplink data rate for subtask n of mobile device m
$t_{m,n}^t$	Time spent when sending subtask n of device m to edge server
$t_{m,n}^r$	Time spent when sending subtask n of device m from edge server to remote cloud
$E_{m,n}^t$	Energy cost during transmission between mobile device and edge server for subtask n of device m
$E_{m,n}^r$	Energy cost during transmission between edge and cloud for subtask n of mobile device m
$t_{m,n}^l$	The delay when executing subtask n locally
$E_{m,n}^l$	Energy consumption when executing subtask n of device m
$TF_{m,n}^l$	Completing time of subtask n on mobile device m that executed locally
$EF_{m,n}^l$	Energy cost during the completing time of subtask n on device with local computing
$Budget_m$	Budget or allowed delay threshold for subtasks on device m
E_m	Total energy cost for all subtasks of device m
TF_m	Total time consumed for all subtasks of mobile device m
U_p^f	Profit of the edge server
$X_{m,n}^l$	Offloading policy for subtask n of device m on local computing
$X_{m,n}^f$	Offloading policy for subtask n of device m on edge computing
$X_{m,n}^c$	Offloading policy for subtask n of device m on remote execution

The transmission delay of subtask n between mobile device m and the corresponding edge server thus can be [11]

$$t^t_{m,n} = \frac{D_{m,n}}{R_{m,n}}, \tag{2}$$

where $t^t_{m,n}$ represents the time spent on sending the subtask n on mobile device m to the edge server, while $D_{m,n}$ is the data size of the subtask n of device m. Based on the above equations, we can obtain the energy consumption when transmitting subtask n of mobile device m to the edge server as

$$E^t_{m,n} = P^m_{m,n} t^t_{m,n}, \tag{3}$$

where $P^{tx}_{m,n}$ is the power of mobile device m when sending subtask n.

Transmission between Edge and Cloud. Due to fact that the edge server links the remote cloud via wired connection, the delay of data transmission from edge server to the cloud thus is

$$t^r_{m,n} = \frac{D_{m,n}}{\omega}, \tag{4}$$

where $t^r_{m,n}$ denotes the transmission delay for subtask n of mobile device m from edge server to the cloud. ω denotes the upstream bandwidth. Given the transmission delaybetween edge and remote cloud $t^r_{m,n}$ and the transmission power P_0, $E^r_{m,n}$ can be expressed as

$$E^r_{m,n} = P_0 t^r_{m,n}, \tag{5}$$

where $E^r_{m,n}$ is the energy consumed when sending the subtask n of mobile device m from edge to the cloud.

2.3   Computation Model

Computation on Local Device. Let f^l_m be the CPU clock speed of mobile device m and $W_{m,n}$ be the workload of subtask n of mobile device m, if the subtask n on mobile device m is executed locally, then the subtask's execution time is

$$t^l_{m,n} = \frac{W_{m,n}}{f^l_m}. \tag{6}$$

Given the computation time $t^l_{m,n}$, the energy consumed for subtask n of mobile device m for local computing is

$$E^l_{m,n} = k W_{m,n} f^l_m{}^2. \tag{7}$$

By default, k is set as 10^{-11} following [12].

Computation on Edge. Let f^f be the CPU frequency of edge server, if the subtask n of mobile device m is executed on the edge server, the computation time of the edge server can be

$$t^f_{m,n} = \frac{W_{m,n}}{f^f}, \tag{8}$$

and the energy cost of edge server can be expressed as:

$$E^f_{m,n} = \left(\alpha_f \left(f^f\right)^\sigma + \beta_f\right) t^f_{m,n}. \tag{9}$$

According to [19], α_f and β_f are the positive constants which can be obtained by offline power fitting and σ ranges from 2.5 to 3. If subtask n of mobile device m is executed on the cloud, the computation delay and energy cost of remote cloud are as follows:

$$t^c_{m,n} = \frac{W_{m,n}}{f^c}, \tag{10}$$

and

$$E^c_{m,n} = (\alpha_c (f^c)^\sigma + \beta_c) t^c_{m,n}. \tag{11}$$

2.4   Dependency Constraints

Definition 1. *Subtask's completing time: subtask n of mobile device m can only start when all its predecessor subtasks has been completed. The completion time for the nth subtask of mobile device m is consisted of two parts: the time spent to obtain the results of all its predecessor tasks and the time spent for its own computation.*

Definition 2. *Energy cost to accomplish one subtask: it is also consisted of two parts: the energy spent getting the result of predecessor tasks and the energy spent for its own execution.*

Base on the above definitions, if subtask n of mobile device m is assigned to be executed locally, its completion time can be expressed as:

$$TF^l_{m,n} = max_{k \in pre(n)} \left\{ X^f_{m,k} t^t_{m,n} + X^c_{m,k} \left(t^t_{m,n} + t^r_{m,n}\right) \right\} + t^l_{m,n}, \tag{12}$$

and the energy cost for local completion is

$$EF^l_{m,n} = \sum_{k \in pre(n)} \left[X^f_{m,k} E^t_{m,n} + X^c_{m,k} \left(E^t_{m,n} + E^r_{m,n}\right) \right] + E^l_{m,n}. \tag{13}$$

In (12) and (13), $X^f_{m,k} X^c_{m,k} = 0$. The notation $pre(n)$ in (12) means all the predecessor subtasks of the nth subtask. In (12), the term $X^f_{m,k} t^t_{m,n}$ is the delay to obtain the predecessor subtask's result of the nth subtask, if the predecessor subtask of n is executed on the edge server. Similarly, the term $X^c_{m,k} \left(t^t_{m,n} + t^r_{m,n}\right)$

is the delay to obtain the result if the predecessor subtask of n is accomplished on the cloud server.

If subtask n of mobile device m is assigned to be executed on the edge server, the completion time of subtask n can be defined as:

$$TF_{m,n}^f = max_{k \in pre(n)} \left\{ X_{m,k}^m t_{m,n}^t + X_{m,k}^c t_{m,n}^r \right\} + t_{m,n}^f, \tag{14}$$

where $X_{m,k}^m$ is predecessor subtask's assignment strategy on mobile device. $X_{m,k}^m = 1$ means the kth subtask is computed on the local mobile device, while $X_{m,k}^m = 0$, otherwise. The term $X_{m,k}^m t_{m,n}^t$ is the delay to transmit the result of predecessor task from mobile device to the edge server while $X_{m,k}^c t_{m,n}^r$ is the delay to send the prior result from the remote cloud to the edge server.

Let $EF_{m,n}^f$ be the energy cost for subtask n of device m executed on the edge server, similarly as (13), it can be defined as

$$EF_{m,n}^f = \sum_{k \in pre(n)} \left[X_{m,k}^m E_{m,n}^t + X_{m,k}^c E_{m,n}^r \right] + E_{m,n}^f. \tag{15}$$

Similarly as (12) and (14), if subtask n of mobile device m is assigned to be executed in the remote cloud, its completion time can be expressed as

$$TF_{m,n}^c = max_{k \in pre(n)} \left\{ X_{m,k}^m \left(t_{m,n}^t + t_{m,n}^r \right) + X_{m,k}^f t_{m,n}^r \right\} + t_{m,n}^c, \tag{16}$$

and the corresponding energy cost to complete the subtask on the remote cloud, $EF_{m,n}^c$ is

$$EF_{m,n}^c = \sum_{k \in pre(n)} \left[X_{m,k}^m \left(E_{m,n}^t + E_{m,n}^r \right) + X_{m,k}^f E_{m,n}^f \right] + E_{m,n}^c. \tag{17}$$

2.5 Utility Constraints

Next, we drive the utility constraints of edge server and the time budget for the completion time. The utility of edge server is

$$U_p^f = \sum_{m=1}^{M} \sum_{n=0}^{N} \left(P^f X_{m,n}^f - E_{m,n}^r X_{m,n}^c \right), \tag{18}$$

where U_p^f is the utility of the edge server, P^f is service price of edge server.

3 Problem Formulation

In this section, we will present the problem formulation with constraint of time budget and utility constraint U_p^f. Firstly, the completion time of all tasks on mobile device m can be defined as

$$TF_m = \sum_{n=0}^{N} \left[X_{m,n}^m TF_{m,n}^l + X_{m,n}^f TF_{m,n}^f + X_{m,n}^c TF_{m,n}^c \right], \tag{19}$$

where $TF_{m,n}^l$ is the task completion time of subtask n if it is executed locally, $TF_{m,n}^f$ is the task completion time of subtask n if it is executed on the edge server and $TF_{m,n}^c$ is the task completion time of subtask n if it is executed on the remote cloud.

The total energy consumption of one application, which is denoted as E_m is

$$E_m = \sum_{n=0}^{N} \left[EF_{m,n}^l X_{m,n}^l + EF_{m,n}^f X_{m,n}^f + EF_{m,n}^c X_{m,n}^c \right], \tag{20}$$

where $EF_{m,n}^l$ is the energy consumption of subtask n if it is executed on the mobile device, $EF_{m,n}^f$ is the energy cost of subtask n if it is executed on edge server and $EF_{m,n}^c$ is the energy cost of subtask n if it is executed on the remote cloud.

In this work, the goal is to minimize the total energy consumption of tasks while meeting the completion time constraint. Meanwhile, the utility of the edge server U_p^f is guaranteed. The energy consumption minimization problem thus can be defined as:

$$\mathbf{OPT-1} \quad obj : \min E_m$$

$$C1 : U_p^f > 0,$$

$$C2 : TF_m < Budget_m,$$

$$C3 : X_{m,n}^m \in \{0,1\}, X_{m,n}^f \in \{0,1\}, X_{m,n}^c \in \{0,1\}, n \in [0,N], m \in [1,M],$$

$$C4 : X_{m,n}^m + X_{m,n}^f + X_{m,n}^c = 1, n \in [0,N], m \in [1,M].$$

Where constraint $C1$ is the utility constraint which guarantees the positive utility of the edge server. $C2$ is the task completion time budget, i.e., the delay constraint. $C3$ lists binary constraints and $C4$ is the unique solution constraint, which means that one subtask can only be executed at one place.

Theorem 1. *The sum task completion energy minimization problem for computation offloading in this study is NP-hard.*

Proof. We transform the oriental problem depicted in $OPT-1$ and consider a special case that the mobile device, edge server and remote cloud server are with the same configurations, which result in the same energy costs and executing time when executing tasks. Regarding each subtask as a goods with value and weight, then the value corresponds to the execution time while the weight corresponds to the energy cost. Then we ignore the task dependency constraint between subtasks as well as the constraint $C1$. $C2$ can then be viewed as the knapsack's value constraint. Therefore, the relaxed problem of $OPT-1$ has changed into a knapsack problem [15] which is NP-hard. Therefore, the original problem $OPT-1$ is also NP-hard, which concludes this proof.

4   Algorithms

4.1   Gain Method

Based on the above models and analysis, first of all, we design a greedy method named Gain to minimize the energy consumption of mobile device m when finish executing tasks. To acquire the minimum energy cost of all subtasks in an application on mobile device m, the minimum energy cost of subtask n is selected from $EF_{m,n}^l, EF_{m,n}^f, EF_{m,n}^c$. This subtask-procedure is shown between Lines 1 to 11 of Algorithm 1.

Then, we iteratively adjust the initial offloading policy to fit for the constraint of U_p^f and the completion time budget $Budget_m$. If the offloading policy does not satisfy the constraint of U_p^f, which means that the number of subtask executed on remote cloud is too much to make the edge server get profits when serving mobile users. To fit the constraint of U_p^f, we must offload some subtasks from the remote cloud to mobile device or to the edge servers.

Then the algorithm chooses subtask considering which subtask will be offloaded. To obtain the minimum energy cost, we take the changing energy cost as the criteria to set the priority. The smaller the changing energy cost is, the higher the priority will be.

To fit for the constraint of completion time budget, we compute the changing completion time and the changing energy cost in each offloading choice. We choose the corresponding offloading strategy in the choice, which decreases the changing completion time and guarantees the minimum changing of energy cost. Due to the constraint of utility U_p^f, the choosing of offloading site for subtasks should be very careful. If subtask n is assigned to be executed on mobile device, the offloading choice must be from mobile device to the edge server. If subtask n is assigned to be executed on edge server, the offloading choice must be from edge server to mobile device. If subtask n is assigned to be executed on remote cloud, the offloading choice can either be from the remote cloud to edge serve or from the remote cloud to mobile device. The detail of the Gain algorithm is depicted in Algorithm 1.

Theorem 2. *The time complexity of the Gain algorithm is $O(N)$.*

Proof. In Algorithm 1, the time complexity of subprocess from line 1 to 12 is $O(N)$ and the time complexity of subprocess from line 14 to 31 is $O(N)$ for the reason that the adjust time of time won't be more than N. So the time complexity of the Gain algorithm is $O(N)$.

Theorem 3. *the approximation ratio is $(1 + \varepsilon)$.*

Proof. Due to limited space, omitted

5   Performance Evaluation

5.1   Simulation Setup

To study the performance of proposed algorithms, We implement the algorithms on a high performance work station with an Intel I7 processor at frequency 3.9

Algorithm 1. Gain method for mobile device m

Input:
    $tasks$: a sequence of N subtask-tasks mobile device
    m, the execute order of subtasks;
    W: the workload size of subtasks;
    D: the data size of subtasks;
    $Budget_m$: the completion time budget for subtasks;
    pre: 2-D array for each subtask's predecessor's task;
Output:
    X^m: the policy of subtask executed on mobile device locally; X^f: the policy of
    subtask executed on edge server; X^c: the policy of subtask executed on remote
    cloud;
1: **for** n in $tasks$ **do**
2:     computer $EF^l_{m,n}$, $EF^f_{m,n}$, $EF^c_{m,n}$ by Equation (13), (15), (17)
3:     **if** $min\left(EF^l_{m,n}, EF^f_{m,n}, EF^c_{m,n}\right) = EF^l_{m,n}$ **then**
4:         $X^l_{m,n} \leftarrow 1, X^f_{m,n} \leftarrow 0, X^c_{m,n} \leftarrow 0$
5:     **end if**
6:     **if** $min\left(EF^l_{m,n}, EF^f_{m,n}, EF^c_{m,n}\right) = EF^f_{m,n}$ **then**
7:         $X^l_{m,n} \leftarrow 0, X^f_{m,n} \leftarrow 1, X^c_{m,n} \leftarrow 0$
8:     **end if**
9:     **if** $min\left(EF^l_{m,n}, EF^f_{m,n}, EF^c_{m,n}\right) = EF^c_{m,n}$ **then**
10:       $X^l_{m,n} \leftarrow 0, X^f_{m,n} \leftarrow 0, X^c_{m,n} \leftarrow 1$
11:     **end if**
12: **end for**
13: compute U^f_p and TF_m
14: **while** $U^f_p \leq 0 \parallel TF_m \geq Budget_m$ **do**
15:     **if** $U^f_p \leq 0$ **then**
16:         choose the subtask that bings about minimum changing energy consumption
            when offloading the subtask from the remote cloud to the edge server, or from
            the remote cloud to mobile device.
17:     **end if**
18:     **if** $TF_m \geq Budget_m$ **then**
19:         **for** $n = 0 \rightarrow N$ **do**
20:             **if** $X^m_{m,n} = 1$ **then**
21:                 compute the changing energy cost when offloading the subtask from
                mobile device to the edge server.
22:             **end if**
23:             **if** $X^f_{m,n} = 1$ **then**
24:                 compute the changing energy cost when offloading the subtask from the
                edge server to mobile device
25:             **end if**
26:             **if** $X^c_{m,n} = 1$ **then**
27:                 compute the changing energy cost when offloading the subtask from
                remote cloud to mobile device or from remote cloud to edge server.
28:             **end if**
29:             choose the offloading policy with the minimum changing energy cost and
            decrease changing completing time
30:         **end for**
31:     **end if**
32: **end while**

GHz and has a 8G RAM. We use Python 3.6 [1] to simulate the offloading of subtasks and evaluate the algorithms in terms of running time, application completion time and energy cost with 100 repeated trials.

In order to simulate real-world tasks, we use a typical task graph as shown in Fig. 2. In Fig. 2, dependency constraints exists between subtasks, which determine the execution order. Based on the task graph, one possible execution sequence for subtasks is $[0, 1, 2, 3, 4, 5, 6, 7]$.

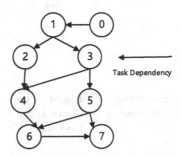

Fig. 2. The task graph.

We set 8 subtasks in an application with evenly distributed workload and evenly distributed data size. The signal noise between the edge server and mobile device is set as $\sigma^2 = 1$, the wireless bandwidth of upload is set as $W = 2$ Mbps and the wireless bandwidth of download is set as $W = 10$ Mbps [10]. The bandwidth between edge server and remote cloud of upload is $W = 1024$ Mbps and the bandwidth between edge server and remote cloud of download is $W = 8192$ Mbps [10]. The CPU frequency of mobile device is $f^m = 5 \times 10^6$ Hz, while the CPU frequency of edge server is $f^f = 2 \times 10^9$ Hz [18]. The CPU frequency of remote cloud is set as $f^c = 4 \times 10^9$ Hz [18]. System parameters $\alpha_f = 0.1, \beta_f = 0.1, \alpha_c = 0.2, \beta_c = 0.2$ [18]. The communication chip power of mobile device is 0.1 watt [16]. The communication chip power of edge server is 1watt [16] and the communication chip power of remote cloud is 3 watt [16].

5.2 Simulation Result

Figure 3 shows the comparisons of Gain, Brute Force and SA in terms of running time with different workload sizes. From Fig. 3, we observe that, the running time of Brute Force ranges from 7.54 s to 7.68 s and the running time of Gain is less than 0.02 s. That is because the Brute Force tries to exhaustively search all solutions and the solution space of the problem is N^3, where N denotes the number of subtasks. From Fig. 3, we can observe that, the running time of three algorithms stay almost no fluctuations, which indicates the robustness of algorithms. For example, in Brute Force, the maximum running time is 7.66 s, while the minimum running time is 7.547 s, the difference value between the maximum running time and the minimum running time is only 0.12 s. In Gain, the maximum running time is 0.0015 s and the minimum running time is 0.001 s.

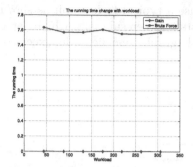

Fig. 3. The comparisons of three algorithms' executing time with different workload size.

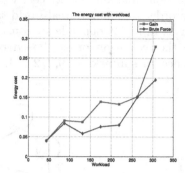

Fig. 4. The energy cost of Gain and Brute Force with the change of workload size.

Figure 4 show the comparisons of Gain, Brute Force on energy cost with different workload sizes. In Fig. 4, The Brute Force always obtains the minimum energy cost compared with the other algorithm. From the comparison between Brute Force and Gain, we observe that Gain can optimally achieve the same completion time budget performance of optimal result with only 31% extra energy cost averagely. The energy cost of Gain approximates the optimal result, especially for case when the workload sizes are 87.5 M and 262.5 M. In Fig. 4, when the workload size grows from 43.75 to 87.5 M, the energy cost also increases by 0.06 KJ but the energy cost falls by 0.04 KJ when the workload size grows from 87.5 M to 131.25 M due to the constraint of task dependency. From Fig. 4, the change of curve in energy consumption of Gain is almost the same as the changes of curves in energy consumption of Brute Force.

Figure 5 shows the comparisons of application completion time of Gain, Brute Force. The completion time budget $Budget$ can be represent as (21) and W denotes the workload matrix, N denotes the number of subtask of the mobile device m, which is,

$$Budget = 0.5 \times \sum_{n=0}^{N} W_{m,n}. \tag{21}$$

From Fig. 5, we observe that the completion time of Gain and Brute Force are always lower than that of the completion time budget. Therefore Gain and Brute Force always obtain efficient solutions which satisfy the completion budget. When the workload size increases from 43.7 M to 206.25 M, the completion time of Gain also increases from 1.05 s to 6.22 s, because the greater the workload is, the longer time the Gain will be. In Fig. 6, we can see the completion time of Gain occupies 40% to 80% of the completion time budget. While the completion time of Brute Force occupies 22% to 80% of the completion time budget, which is optimal.

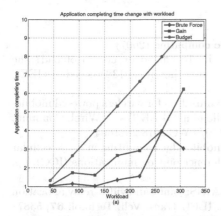

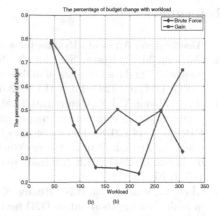

Fig. 5. The comparisons of application completion time of Gain, Brute Force and Budget on different workload size.

Fig. 6. The comparisons of application completion time as a percentage of Budget.

6   Conclusions

This paper has addressed novel computation offloading schemes with device, edge server and remote cloud collaboration. We have formulated the offloading problem as an energy cost minimization problem with application completion time budget and edge server profit's constraint. The problem is NP-hard. We have designed a Gain algorithm aimed to minimize the energy cost, which also follows the constraints of completion time, utility and task dependency. After extensive simulation, we can obtain following finding. Firstly, the implementation shows that in a three-tier structure such as mobile, edge server and remote cloud, edge server plays a very important role in reducing the energy consumption during task execution. Secondly, the proposed greedy algorithm can achieve the same application completion time performance of the Brute Force optimal algorithm with only 31% extra energy cost on average.

In the future, we will devise online algorithms by modifying the initialization process of each algorithms and explore the energy cost minimization problem with completion time constraint of each subtask.

Acknowledgment. This work was supported by the National Natural Science Foundation of China under Grant Nos. 61702115 and 61672171, Natural Science Foundation of Guangdong, China under Grant No. 2018B030311007, and Major R&D Project of Educational Commission of Guangdong under Grant No. 2016KZDXM052. This work was also supported by China Postdoctoral Science Foundation Fund under Grant No. 2017M622632. The corresponding author is Jigang Wu (asjgwucn@outlook.com).

References

1. Aksimentiev, A., et al.: Python for scientific computing (2007)
2. Barbera, M.V., Kosta, S., Mei, A., Stefa, J.: To offload or not to offload? the bandwidth and energy costs of mobile cloud computing. In: 2013 Proceedings IEEE INFOCOM, pp. 1285–1293. IEEE (2013)
3. Bi, S., Zhang, Y.J.A.: Computation rate maximization for wireless powered mobile-edge computing with binary computation offloading. IEEE Trans. Wirel. Commun. **PP**(99), 1–14 (2018). https://doi.org/10.1109/TWC.2018.2821664
4. Chen, L., Zhou, S., Xu, J.: Energy efficient mobile edge computing in dense cellular networks. In: 2017 IEEE International Conference on Communications (ICC), pp. 1–6. IEEE (2017)
5. Chen, L., Wu, J., Dai, H.N., Huang, X.: BRAINS: joint bandwidth-relay allocation in multi-homing cooperative D2D networks. IEEE Trans. Veh. Technol. **67**, 5387–5398 (2018). https://doi.org/10.1109/TVT.2018.2799970
6. Chen, L., Wu, J., Zhou, G., Ma, L.: QUICK: QoS-guaranteed efficient cloudlet placement in wireless metropolitan area networks. J. Supercomput. **74**, 1–23 (2018). https://doi.org/10.1007/s11227-018-2412-8
7. Chen, M.H., Dong, M., Liang, B.: Joint offloading decision and resource allocation for mobile cloud with computing access point. In: IEEE International Conference on Acoustics, Speech and Signal Processing, pp. 3516–3520 (2016)
8. Chen, M.H., Liang, B., Dong, M.: Joint offloading and resource allocation for computation and communication in mobile cloud with computing access point. In: INFOCOM 2017 IEEE Conference on Computer Communications, pp. 1–9. IEEE (2017)
9. Dhillon, H.S., Ganti, R.K., Baccelli, F., Andrews, J.G.: Modeling and analysis of K-Tier downlink heterogeneous cellular networks. IEEE J. Sel. Areas Commun. **30**(3), 550–560 (2012)
10. Ding, L., Melodia, T., Batalama, S.N., Matyjas, J.D.: Distributed routing, relay selection, and spectrum allocation in cognitive and cooperative ad hoc networks. In: Sensor Mesh and Ad Hoc Communications and Networks, pp. 1–9 (2010)
11. Dinh, T.Q., Tang, J., La, Q.D., Quek, T.Q.S.: Offloading in mobile edge computing: task allocation and computational frequency scaling. IEEE Trans. Commun. **65**(8), 3571–3584 (2017)
12. Guo, S., Xiao, B., Yang, Y., Yang, Y.: Energy-efficient dynamic offloading and resource scheduling in mobile cloud computing. In: IEEE INFOCOM 2016 the IEEE International Conference on Computer Communications, pp. 1–9 (2016)
13. Hu, Y.C., Patel, M., Sabella, D., Sprecher, N., Young, V.: Mobile edge computing. A key technology towards 5G. ETSI White Paper **11**(11), 1–16 (2015)
14. Kao, Y.H., Krishnamachari, B., Ra, M.R., Fan, B.: Hermes: Latency optimal task assignment for resource-constrained mobile computing. In: IEEE Conference on Computer Communications (ICC), pp. 1894–1902 (2015)
15. Kellerer, H., Pferschy, U., Pisinger, D.: Knapsack Problems. Springer, Heidelberg (2004)
16. Liu, P.J., Lo, Y.K., Chiu, H.J., Chen, Y.J.E.: Dual-current pump module for transient improvement of step-down DC-DC converters. IEEE Trans. Power Electr. **24**(4), 985–990 (2009)
17. Lyu, X., Tian, H., Ni, W., Zhang, Y., Zhang, P., Liu, R.P.: Energy-efficient admission of delay-sensitive tasks for mobile edge computing. IEEE Trans. Commun. **66**, 2603–2616 (2018). https://doi.org/10.1109/TCOMM.2018.2799937

18. Park, C.B., Park, B.S., Uhm, H.J., Choi, H., Kim, H.S.: IEEE 802.15.4 based service configuration mechanism for smartphone. IEEE Trans. Consum. Electr. **56**(3), 2004–2010 (2010). https://doi.org/10.1109/TCE.2010.5606358
19. Rao, L., Liu, X., Ilic, M.D., Liu, J.: Distributed coordination of internet data centers under multiregional electricity markets. Proc. IEEE **100**(1, SI), 269–282 (2012). https://doi.org/10.1109/JPROC.2011.2161236
20. Zhang, L., et al.: Primary channel gain estimation for spectrum sharing in cognitive radio networks. IEEE Trans. Commun. **PP**(99), 1 (2016)

Quantitatively Investigating Multihop Localization Errors in Regular 2-D Sensor Networks

Bing Jia[1,2], Baoqi Huang[1,2(✉)], Tao Zhou[1,2], and Wuyungerile Li[1,2]

[1] Inner Mongolia A.R. Key Laboratory of Wireless Networking and Mobile Computing, Hohhot 010021, China
cshbq@imu.edu.cn
[2] College of Computer Science, Inner Mongolia University, Hohhot 010021, China

Abstract. In practice, a wireless sensor network normally includes a small portion of nodes with known locations, termed anchors, and the other nodes with unknown locations, termed sensors, have to be localized through dedicated algorithms. Since not every sensor is directly neighboring with anchors, sensor locations are determined in a multi-hop localization manner, and therein, localization errors of sensors display to rise up with their minimal hop count to anchors, which is termed error propagation. Grasping the rule of error propagation is critical to design and develop both localization algorithms as well as various applications. In this paper, we focus on quantitatively measuring how the localization errors vary across different sensors. To do so, regular 2-dimensional wireless sensor networks are taken into consideration, and formulae with respect to different sensors and different anchor placement are obtained. Simulation results are conducted to validate these formulae and analyze the characteristics of error propagation.

Keywords: Localization errors · Wireless sensor network · Multihop
Error propagation

1 Introduction

In wireless sensor networks (WSNs), sensor locations are key prerequisite for many applications and techniques, such as reporting the geographic origin of events, assisting in target tracking, and achieving geographic aware routing. Therefore, considerable effort has been invested in the development of localization systems [1–6]. Range-based sensor localization [7] is the problem of identifying the locations of sensor nodes, or simply sensors, given estimates of the

Supported by the National Natural Science Foundation of China under Grants 41761086, 41401519, 61461037, 61761035 and 61661041, the National Science and Technology Major Project of the Ministry of Science and Technology of China under Grant No. 2016YFB0502102, the Natural Science Foundation of Inner Mongolia Autonomous Region of China under Grant 2017JQ09, and the Grassland Elite Project of the Inner Mongolia Autonomous Region under Grant CYYC5016.

J. Vaidya and J. Li (Eds.): ICA3PP 2018, LNCS 11336, pp. 476–488, 2018.
https://doi.org/10.1007/978-3-030-05057-3_36

distances between them, known as range measurements. The basic range-based localization algorithms include trilateration which in 2-dimensional (2-D) space employs at least three range measurements from non-collinear nodes at known locations, termed anchors, to localize a sensor. Due to the existence of noises in range measurements, only location estimates as opposed to exact positions can be derived. If not every sensor can measure its distances to sufficient anchors, already localized sensors must be used as pseudo-anchors to help their neighboring sensors become localized; this process is called multihop sensor localization. As a result, localization errors of pseudo-anchors propagate into localization results of later localized sensors, a phenomenon which is called error propagation.

In the literature, discussions in [8,9] have raised series concerns about error propagation. In particular, error propagation in regular 1-dimensional WSNs was examined by obtaining the closed-form Cramér-Rao Lower Bound (CRLB) in [10,11], and some key conclusions were drawn on how fast the error is propagated and how anchor placement affects error propagation have been reported. Moreover, error propagation in 2-D random WSNs was studied through a semi-quantitative approach in [9], in the sense that the influences of the sensor density and the hop count from a sensor to anchors have been investigated based on certain approximations. As such, it is still challenging to precisely measure how localization errors are propagated in 2-D WSNs. As a preliminary study, we shall investigate the phenomenon of error propagation through exact formulation of localization errors in regular 2-D WSNs.

To be specific, we firstly discuss the error propagation in a specific bilateration WSN, in which nodes with odd labels and nodes with even labels are regularly deployed with equal spaces in two parallel and horizontal straight lines, and obtain the formulae for localization errors through a linearized Maximum Likelihood Estimator (MLE); then, we generalize this specific bilateration WSN to a new bilateration WSN by integrally moving one horizontal line towards one horizontal direction, and extend the error formulae as well. These formulae accurately describe how the localization errors in the considered bilateration WSNs increase with the corresponding hop count to anchors increasing, and also demonstrate that different anchor placement will result in dramatically different localization performance. Finally, we explore the error propagation of a regular 2-D sensor network consisting of multiple bilateration networks, and formulate localization errors through CRLB which essentially equals to perturbed Toeplitz block matrices [12]. Simulation results are presented to validate the formulae obtained in this paper and illustrate the characteristics of error propagation in regular 2-D WSNs.

The remainder of this paper is organized as follows. Section 2 establishes the problem model of a specific bilateration network WSN (SBWSN) and give the solving process of multihop localization errors. Section 3 presents the solving process of multihop localization errors in general bilateration WSN (GBWSN) with both the two anchors and the four anchors. Section 4 discusses the rate of error propagation of a regular 2-D WSN and Sect. 5 concludes the paper.

2   The Specific Bilateration WSN

2.1   The SBWSN with Anchors on One Side

The SBWSN with anchors on one side is illustrated in Fig. 1. As can be seen, nodes with odd labels are located in the same horizontal straight line and so are nodes with even labels; nodes 1, 2 are in the same vertical straight line, so on and so forth; the left-most two nodes are anchors, and all the others are sensors, edges denote range measurement between two nodes. Define the following notations.

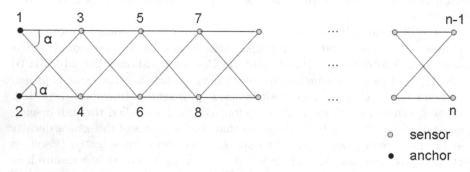

Fig. 1. A bilateration WSN with two anchors on one side.

- n is obviously an even integer;
- Nodes are labeled from 1 to n in order;
- Noise in range measurements is additive independent Gaussian with mean zero and standard deviation 1, denoted by e_i $(0 < i < 2n + 1)$;
- The true location for node i is (x_i, y_i) and the uncertainty or error in node i's estimated location is $U_i (u_{x_i} \ u_{y_i})^T$ where superscript T denotes transposition. Specifically, $U_1 = U_2 = 0$.
- *The covariance matrix for coordinates of nodes $2i+1$ and $2i+2$ $(0 < i < n/2)$ is a 4×4 matrix, denoted by Q_i.*

$$Q_i = Cov \begin{pmatrix} U_{2i+1} \\ U_{2i+2} \end{pmatrix}$$

At first, according to the structure of SBWSN, we can define

- Two 2×2 matrices J_1 and J_2:

$$J_1 = \begin{pmatrix} 1 & 0 \\ \cos\alpha & \sin\alpha \end{pmatrix}$$

$$J_2 = \begin{pmatrix} \cos\alpha & -\sin\alpha \\ 1 & 0 \end{pmatrix}$$

– Two 2×4 matrices K_1 and K_2:

$$K_1 = \begin{pmatrix} 1 & 0 & 0 & 0 \\ 0 & 0 & \cos\alpha & \sin\alpha \end{pmatrix}$$

$$K_2 = \begin{pmatrix} \cos\alpha & -\sin\alpha & 0 & 0 \\ 0 & 0 & 1 & 0 \end{pmatrix}$$

Based on the linearized MLE adopted in [9], the localization errors in node $2i - 1$ and $2i$ are

$$U_{2i-1} = (J_1^T J_1)^{-1} J_1^T \begin{pmatrix} e_{4i-3} \\ e_{4i-2} \end{pmatrix} + (J_1^T J_1)^{-1} J_1^T K_1 \begin{pmatrix} U_{2i-3} \\ U_{2i-2} \end{pmatrix} \tag{1}$$

$$U_{2i} = (J_2^T J_2)^{-1} J_2^T \begin{pmatrix} e_{4i-1} \\ e_{4i} \end{pmatrix} + (J_2^T J_2)^{-1} J_2^T K_2 \begin{pmatrix} U_{2i-3} \\ U_{2i-2} \end{pmatrix} \tag{2}$$

Furthermore, they can be simplified as

$$U_{2i-1} = J_1^{-1} \begin{pmatrix} e_{4i-3} \\ e_{4i-2} \end{pmatrix} + J_1^{-1} K_1 \begin{pmatrix} U_{2i-3} \\ U_{2i-2} \end{pmatrix} \tag{3}$$

$$U_{2i} = J_2^{-1} \begin{pmatrix} e_{4i-1} \\ e_{4i} \end{pmatrix} + J_2^{-1} K_2 \begin{pmatrix} U_{2i-3} \\ U_{2i-2} \end{pmatrix} \tag{4}$$

Then, the covariance matrix is

$$Q_i = \begin{pmatrix} (J_1^T J_1)^{-1} & 0 \\ 0 & (J_2^T J_2)^{-1} \end{pmatrix} + \begin{pmatrix} J_1^{-1} K_1 \\ J_2^{-1} K_2 \end{pmatrix} Q_{i-1} \begin{pmatrix} J_1^{-1} K_1 \\ J_2^{-1} K_2 \end{pmatrix}^T \tag{5}$$

$$= AA^T + BQ_{i-1}B^T \tag{6}$$

$$= \sum_{j=0}^{i-1} B^j AA^T (B^j)^T \tag{7}$$

$$= Q_{i-1} + B^{i-1} AA^T (B^{i-1})^T \tag{8}$$

where $Q_0 = 0$, B^0 is an identity matrix, and

$$- A = \begin{pmatrix} J_1^{-1} & 0 \\ 0 & J_2^{-1} \end{pmatrix}$$

$$- B = \begin{pmatrix} J_1^{-1} K_1 \\ J_2^{-1} K_2 \end{pmatrix}$$

Regarding the matrices A and B, we can obtain following equations ($i \geq 0$):

$$B^{2i+1} = \begin{pmatrix} 1 & 0 & 0 & 0 \\ -(2i+1)\cot\alpha & 0 & (2i+1)\cot\alpha & 1 \\ 0 & 0 & 1 & 0 \\ -(2i+1)\cot\alpha & 1 & (2i+1)\cot\alpha & 0 \end{pmatrix} \tag{9}$$

$$B^{2i} = \begin{pmatrix} 1 & 0 & 0 & 0 \\ -2i\cot\alpha & 1 & 2i\cot\alpha & 0 \\ 0 & 0 & 1 & 0 \\ -2i\cot\alpha & 0 & 2i\cot\alpha & 1 \end{pmatrix} \tag{10}$$

$$B^{2i+1}AA^T(B^{2i+1})^T = \begin{pmatrix} 1 & -(2i+1)\cot\alpha \\ -(2i+1)\cot\alpha & (5+12i+8i^2)\cot^2\alpha + \csc^2\alpha \\ 0 & 2(i+1)\cot\alpha \\ -2(i+1)\cot\alpha & 4(i+1)(2i+1)\cot^2\alpha \end{pmatrix.$$

$$\left. \begin{matrix} 0 & -2(i+1)\cot\alpha \\ 2(i+1)\cot\alpha & 4(i+1)(2i+1)\cot^2\alpha \\ 1 & (2i+1)\cot\alpha \\ (2i+1)\cot\alpha & (5+12i+8i^2)\cot^2\alpha + \csc^2\alpha \end{matrix} \right) \tag{11}$$

$$B^{2i}AA^T(B^{2i})^T = \begin{pmatrix} 1 & -(2i+1)\cot\alpha \\ -(2i+1)\cot\alpha & (1+4i+8i^2)\cot^2\alpha + \csc^2\alpha \\ 0 & 2i\cot\alpha \\ -2i\cot\alpha & 4i(2i+1)\cot^2\alpha \end{pmatrix.$$

$$\left. \begin{matrix} 0 & -2i\cot\alpha \\ 2i\cot\alpha & 4i(2i+1)\cot^2\alpha \\ 1 & (2i+1)\cot\alpha \\ (2i+1)\cot\alpha & (1+4i+8i^2)\cot^2\alpha + \csc^2\alpha \end{matrix} \right) \tag{12}$$

Since we are interested in the diagonal entries in Q_i, we only investigate the diagonal entries in above resulting matrices. To differ even and odd cases, we consider Q_{2i} and Q_{2i+1} respectively.

$$(Q_{2i})_{11} = (Q_{2i})_{33} = 2i$$
$$(Q_{2i})_{22} = (Q_{2i})_{44} = (\frac{16}{3}i^3 + \frac{2}{3}i)\cot^2\alpha + 2i\csc^2\alpha$$
$$(Q_{2i+1})_{11} = (Q_{2i+1})_{33} = 2i+1$$
$$(Q_{2i+1})_{22} = (Q_{2i+1})_{44} = (\frac{16}{3}i^3 + 8i^2 + \frac{14}{3}i + 1)\cot^2\alpha + (2i+1)\csc^2\alpha$$

The formulae can be unified as

$$(Q_i)_{11} = (Q_i)_{33} = i$$
$$(Q_i)_{22} = (Q_i)_{44} = (\frac{2}{3}i^3 + \frac{4}{3}i)\cot^2\alpha + i$$

where $0 \leq i < n/2$. As such, the Mean Squared Error (MSE) can be formulated as

$$MSE(U_i) = (\frac{2}{3}i^3 + \frac{4}{3}i)\cot^2\alpha + 2i \tag{13}$$

Evidently, the localization error measured by MSE is propagated at the speed of $\Theta(i^3)$ where i denotes the hop count from a sensor to the anchors in this regular scenario.

2.2   Placing Anchors on both Sides of the SBWSN

Suppose that another pair of anchors are placed at the right-most side of the bilateration WSN as shown in Fig. 2. However, the localization procedure becomes complicated in comparison with the aforementioned SBWSN with the anchors only at the left-most side. It is straightforward that a centralized localization algorithm will be preferred because the information can be sufficiently used, but the centralized implementation suffers from communication overheads and time delay, especially in large-scale wireless sensor networks. Therefore, we adopt a simple approach by independently performing two localization procedures at first, each of which is initialized by the pair of anchors at one side of the bilateration network and then fuse the two location estimates at each sensor through the weighted average algorithm to produce the final location estimate.

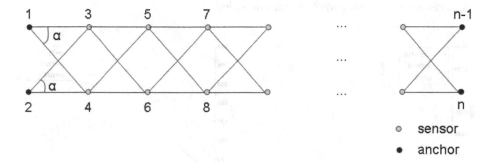

Fig. 2. A SBWSN with four anchors.

Specifically, given node i with i being odd, its location estimate from the localization procedure initialized by the left-most anchors is U_i, and evidently, the location estimate by the right-most anchors equals to U_{n-i} (U_{n+2-i} provided i is even). Then, the final location estimate can be formulated as

$$V_i = w_i U_i + (1 - w_i) U_{n-i} \tag{14}$$

where w_i is the weight. Then, the MSE is

$$MSE(V_i) = w_i^2 MSE(U_i) + (1 - w_i)^2 MSE(U_{n-i}) \tag{15}$$

It is noticeable that different weights will result in dramatically different error characteristics. In order to efficiently fuse two location estimates, the more accurate is a candidate location estimate, the larger is its weight. Therefore, we let w_i be $MSE(U_{n-i})/(MSE(U_i) + MSE(U_{n-i}))$, and then

$$MSE(V_i) = \frac{MSE(U_i)MSE(U_{n-i})}{MSE(U_i) + MSE(U_{n-i})} = \frac{MSE(U_i)}{1 + \frac{MSE(U_i)}{MSE(U_{n-i})}} \tag{16}$$

Obviously, the MSE of the fusion location estimate is smaller than those of both separate location estimates. Consequently, the speed of error propagation will decrease as well.

2.3 Simulation Results

We conduct simulations to validate the results about the error propagation with respect to different hop counts using two anchors and four anchors in the bilateration WSN respectively, with α being one of $\frac{5\pi}{16}$, $\frac{3\pi}{8}$ and $\frac{\pi}{4}$. The simulation results are plotted in Fig. 3.

As can be seen, the angle α has series impact on error propagation in both cases, and the smaller is the angle, the faster is the error propagated. Moreover, placing anchors on both sides dramatically reduces localization errors in comparison with placing anchors on one side.

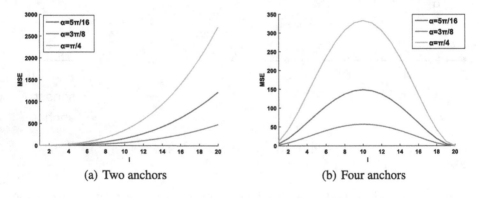

(a) Two anchors   (b) Four anchors

Fig. 3. The MSE with respect to different hops in the SBWSN.

3 A General Bilateration WSN

3.1 Placing Anchors on One Side of the GBWSN

More generally, we generalize the angles by appointing α and β in the bilateration WSN as a GBWSN, which is illustrated in Fig. 4. The left-most two nodes are anchors, and all others are sensors and edges denote range measurement between two nodes. In the network, nodes with odd labels are located in the same horizontal straight line and so are nodes with even labels; nodes 1, 2 are

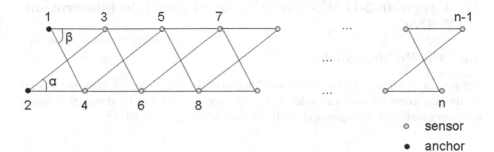

Fig. 4. A GBWSN with two anchors.

not required in the same vertical straight line and so forth, with different angles α and β.

The localization errors can be formulated as

$$(Q_i)_{11} = (Q_i)_{33} = i$$
$$(Q_i)_{22} + (Q_i)_{44} = (\frac{1}{3}i^3 - \frac{1}{3}i)(\cot \alpha + \cot \beta)^2 + 2i(1 + \cot^2 \alpha + \cot^2 \beta).$$

3.2   Simulation Results

We conduct an experiment to analyze the location error with respect to different hops using two anchors and four anchors in the general bilateration network respectively, when α and β are set as $(\frac{5\pi}{16}, \frac{\pi}{4})$, $(\frac{3\pi}{8}$ and $\frac{\pi}{4})$, and $(\frac{3\pi}{8}, \frac{5\pi}{16})$. The result is shown in Fig. 5

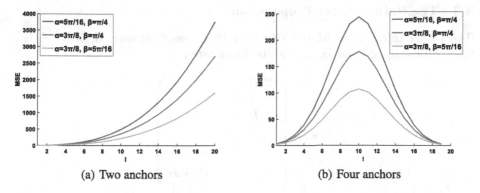

(a) Two anchors   (b) Four anchors

Fig. 5. The MSE with respect to different hops in the GBWSN.

4 A regular 2-D WSN consisting of multiple bilateration WSNs

4.1 The Problem Model

Supposing a regular 2-D network as illustrated in Fig. 6, mn nodes are placed at its mn corners, and the edge between any pair of nodes denotes a range measurement with independent additive Gaussian noise, $N(0, \sigma^2)$.

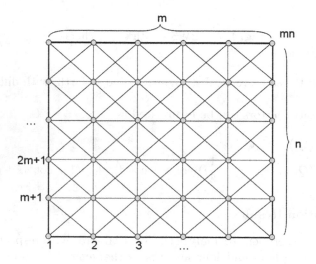

Fig. 6. A grid.

4.2 The Rate of Error Propagation

The Fisher Information Matrix (FIM) of this sensor network, denoted J, is a $2mn \times 2mn$ square matrix and can be formulated as

$$
J = \frac{1}{\sigma^2}
\begin{pmatrix}
A' & B & 0 & & & \\
B & A & B & & & \\
0 & B & A & & & \\
& & & \ddots & & \\
& & & A & B & 0 \\
& & & B & A & B \\
& & & 0 & B & A'
\end{pmatrix}
$$

where A, B, A' are $2\,\mathrm{m} \times 2\,\mathrm{m}$ matrices:

$$A = \begin{pmatrix} 1 & 0 & -1 & 0 & 0 & 0 & & & & & & \\ 0 & 2 & 0 & 0 & 0 & 0 & & & & & & \\ -1 & 0 & 2 & 0 & -1 & 0 & & & & & & \\ 0 & 0 & 0 & 2 & 0 & 0 & & & & & & \\ 0 & 0 & -1 & 0 & 2 & 0 & & & & & & \\ 0 & 0 & 0 & 0 & 0 & 2 & & & & & & \\ & & & & & & \ddots & & & & & \\ & & & & & & & 2 & 0 & -1 & 0 \\ & & & & & & & 0 & 2 & 0 & 0 \\ & & & & & & & -1 & 0 & 1 & 0 \\ & & & & & & & 0 & 0 & 0 & 2 \end{pmatrix}$$

$$A' = \begin{pmatrix} 1 & 0 & -1 & 0 & 0 & 0 & & & & & & \\ 0 & 1 & 0 & 0 & 0 & 0 & & & & & & \\ -1 & 0 & 2 & 0 & -1 & 0 & & & & & & \\ 0 & 0 & 0 & 1 & 0 & 0 & & & & & & \\ 0 & 0 & -1 & 0 & 2 & 0 & & & & & & \\ 0 & 0 & 0 & 0 & 0 & 1 & & & & & & \\ & & & & & & \ddots & & & & & \\ & & & & & & & 2 & 0 & -1 & 0 \\ & & & & & & & 0 & 1 & 0 & 0 \\ & & & & & & & -1 & 0 & 1 & 0 \\ & & & & & & & 0 & 0 & 0 & 1 \end{pmatrix}$$

$$B = \begin{pmatrix} 0 & 0 & 0 & 0 & 0 & 0 & & & \\ 0 & -1 & 0 & 0 & 0 & 0 & & & \\ 0 & 0 & 0 & 0 & 0 & 0 & & & \\ 0 & 0 & 0 & -1 & 0 & 0 & & & \\ 0 & 0 & 0 & 0 & 0 & 0 & & & \\ 0 & 0 & 0 & 0 & 0 & -1 & & & \\ & & & & & & \ddots & & \\ & & & & & & & 0 & 0 \\ & & & & & & & 0 & -1 \end{pmatrix}$$

Obviously, J is an $n \times n$ symmetric tridiagonal block matrix with block size $2m \times 2m$. Each block matrix is associated with one row in the network. Moreover, A and A' are also symmetric tridiagonal block matrices with block size 2×2; while B is a diagonal matrix.

In J, each node is relevant to two adjacent rows and columns. If we want some nodes to be anchors, we just need to eliminate columns and rows associated with these nodes. For example, if all of the bottom and top rows are anchors, we obtain:

$$J' = \frac{1}{\sigma^2} \begin{pmatrix} A & B^T & 0 & & & \\ B & A & B^T & & & \\ 0 & B & A & & & \\ & & & \ddots & & \\ & & & & A & B^T \\ & & & & B & A \end{pmatrix}$$

4.3   Simulation Results

As J is a tridiagonal block Toeplitz matrix, a bunch of papers have been available in the literature, e.g. [12,13]. To obtain the inverse of J, we need at first invert A because A' will be frequently used in inverting J. Due to the simple structure of A, it is not hard to computing A'; however, computing J' will be a difficult problem. For simplicity, we let $p = m - 2$ and $q = n - 2$ and moreover let $\sigma = 1$. Figure 7 shows the inverse of J (i.e. the CRLB) for the case of $p = 10$ and $q = 10$.

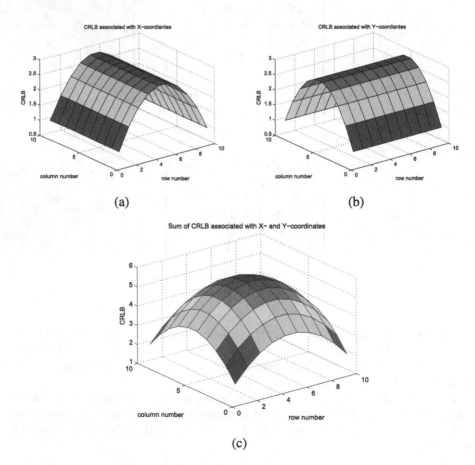

Fig. 7. The CRLB for a 10×10 regular 2-D WSN.

As can be seen from Fig. 7(a), with respect to the different column number, the CRLB has the same tendency with the different row number, and in Fig. 7(b), the with respect to the different row number, the CRLB has the same tendency with the different column number similarly. Therefore, a subgraph when $n = 2$ (or $m = 2$), say bilateration networks, can reflect the error propagation significantly in a regular 2-D WSN.

5 Conclusion

Since in the WSN, sensor locations are determined in a multi-hop localization manner generally, we investigate the error propagation problem in 2-D regular WSNs through quantitatively measuring how the localization errors vary across different sensors in this paper. Furthermore, formulae with respect to different angles, number of hops and different anchor placement are obtained. Simulation results are conducted to validate these formulae and analyze the characteristics of error propagation.

References

1. Albowicz, J., Chen, A., Zhang, L.: Recursive position estimation in sensor networks. In: 2001 Ninth International Conference on Network Protocols, pp. 35–41. IEEE (2001)
2. Huang, B., Yu, C., Anderson, B., Mao, G.: Estimating distances via connectivity in wireless sensor networks. Wirel. Commun. Mob. Comput. 14(5), 541–556 (2014)
3. Liu, Z., Luo, D., Li, J., Chen, X., Jia, C.: N-mobishare: new privacy-preserving location-sharing system for mobile online social networks. Int. J. Comput. Math. 93(2), 384–400 (2013)
4. Han, G., Jiang, J., Zhang, C., Duong, T.Q., Guizani, M., Karagiannidis, G.K.: A survey on mobile anchor node assisted localization in wireless sensor networks. IEEE Commun. Surv. Tutor. 18(3), 2220–2243 (2016)
5. Huang, Y., Li, B., Liang, S., Ma, H., Liu, Z.: Generalized format-preserving encryption for character data. J. Netw. 7(8), 1239–1244 (2016)
6. Liu, Z., Li, T., Li, P., Jia, C., Li, J.: Verifiable searchable encryption with aggregate keys for data sharing system. Futur. Gener. Comput. Syst. 78, 778–788 (2017)
7. Dil, B., Dulman, S., Havinga, P.: Range-based localization in mobile sensor networks. In: Römer, K., Karl, H., Mattern, F. (eds.) EWSN 2006. LNCS, vol. 3868, pp. 164–179. Springer, Heidelberg (2006). https://doi.org/10.1007/11669463_14
8. Liu, J., Zhang, Y., Zhao, F.: Robust distributed node localization with error management. In: Proceedings of the 7th ACM International Symposium on Mobile Ad Hoc Networking and Computing, pp. 250–261. ACM (2006)
9. Huang, B., Yu, C., Anderson, B.: Understanding error propagation in multi-hop sensor network localization. IEEE Trans. Ind. Electron. 60(12), 5811–5819 (2013)
10. Huang, B., Yu, C., Anderson, B.D.: Error propagation in sensor network localization with regular topologies. In: Global Telecommunications Conference, GLOBECOM 2009, pp. 1–6. IEEE (2009)

11. Huang, B., Yu, C., Anderson, B.D.: Analyzing error propagation in range-based multihop sensor localization. In: Proceedings of the 48th IEEE Conference on Decision and Control, 2009 held jointly with the 2009 28th Chinese Control Conference, CDC/CCC 2009, pp. 865–870. IEEE (2009)
12. Akaike, H.: Block toeplitz matrix inversion. SIAM J. Appl. Math. **24**(2), 234–241 (1973)
13. Meurant, G.: A review on the inverse of symmetric tridiagonal and block tridiagonal matrices. SIAM J. Matrix Anal. Appl. **13**(3), 707–728 (1992)

Optimizing WiFi AP Placement for Both Localization and Coverage

Yu Tian[1,2], Baoqi Huang[1,2(✉)], Bing Jia[1,2], and Long Zhao[3]

[1] Inner Mongolia A.R. Key Laboratory of Wireless Networking and Mobile
Computing, Hohhot 010021, China
cshbq@imu.edu.cn
[2] College of Computer Science, Inner Mongolia University, Hohhot 010021, China
[3] School of Automation Science and Electrical Engineering, Beihang University,
Beijing 100191, China

Abstract. Nowadays, WiFi infrastructures and WiFi-enabled mobile
devices have been ubiquitous in our daily lives, and are promising to
provide both network services and indoor positioning and navigation
services due to its simplicity and low costs. But, it is evident that AP
placement is critical to both localization and network coverage, so that
it is helpful to find the optimal AP placement scheme in terms of both
localization and coverage. This paper tackles this problem by leveraging
the widely used Cramer-Rao lower bound (CRLB) and heuristic genetic
algorithm to develop an efficient AP optimization method. To be specific,
the CRLB is used as the metric for localization and a multiple degree
criterion is defined as the metric for coverage, which is incorporated into
the fitness function in the genetic algorithm. Furthermore, instead of
using the idea log distance path loss (LDPL) model, the more practical Motley-keenan model is adopted to reflect the influences of obstacles
which are widespread in indoor environments. Finally, extensive simulations are conducted, and comparisons between the proposed method and
the other three popular methods confirm the efficiency and effectiveness
of the proposed method.

Keywords: WiFi AP · Localization · Coverage · Genetic algorithm
Cramer-Rao lower bound

1 Introduction

Recently, with the development of wireless networks and popularity of mobile
intelligent devices, wireless indoor localization has attained much attention in

Supported by the National Natural Science Foundation of China under Grants
61461037, 41761086 and 61761035, the National Science and Technology Major Project
of the Ministry of Science and Technology of China under Grant No. 2016YFB0502102,
the Natural Science Foundation of Inner Mongolia Autonomous Region of China under
Grant 2017JQ09, and the Grassland Elite Project of the Inner Mongolia Autonomous
Region under Grant CYYC5016.

J. Vaidya and J. Li (Eds.): ICA3PP 2018, LNCS 11336, pp. 489–503, 2018.
https://doi.org/10.1007/978-3-030-05057-3_37

both academia and industries, with the result that various indoor localization techniques and other related research such as location-aware services and location privacy protection have been reported [1–5]. Therein, WiFi based localization is most promising due to its low-cost and existing infrastructures and ubiquitous client devices. In particular, due to its simplicity and tolerance to pervasive multipath effects in indoor environments, WiFi fingerprint-based localization has been widely studied [6,7].

WiFi fingerprint-based localization involves two steps, namely offline site survey and online localization. In the offline site survey, a radio map is constructed by collecting received signal strength (RSS) measurements from surrounding APs at different locations as fingerprints [8]. In the online localization, the RSS measurement collected in real time is compared with the fingerprints in the radio map to select one or several most probable fingerprints, such that the final location estimate can be returned [9,10]. It has been shown that the radio map plays a vital role in both localization accuracy and efficiency, so that many studies have been carried out to improve the construction of radio maps [11–13].

An important and effective approach is developed by optimizing AP placement to improve localization accuracy [14,15], and many efforts have been imposed on this area [16–21]. Most existing studies typically involve the following key aspects: (1) establish a proper objective function for judging the quality of an AP placement scheme; (2) choose a search algorithm for searching the optimal placement scheme from the candidates; (3) determine a signal propagation model for generating RSS measurements given the AP placement and an arbitrary location.

As to the objective function, various localization performance criteria have been reported. In [16,17,20,21], the variation of RSS measurements induced by different AP placement schemes was used as the objective function; in [18], the geometric dilution of precision (GDOP) was utilized to evaluate localization performance; in [19], the total number of similar fingerprints over each pair of fingerprints in the radio map was employed. As to the search algorithm, since the problem of finding the optimal AP placement scheme is essentially NP-complete, different heuristic algorithms have been adopted to improve the time efficiency, but only suboptimal solution is obtained. For instance, the simulated annealing algorithm was used in [17,19], the genetic algorithm was used in [16,18,21], and the differential evolution algorithm was used in [20]. As to the wireless signal propagation model, the simply log distance path loss (LDPL) model was adopted in most studies [16,18,20,21], whereas the more practical Motley-Keenan model and the ray tracing propagation model were used in [17] and [19] respectively.

Intuitively, the WiFi AP placement not only affects localization accuracy, but also determines the coverage of the WiFi network. Therefore, it is critical to tackle the problem of AP placement by taking into consideration both localization and coverage. But, most existing studies ignore the coverage problem, except that the simple one-degree coverage is guaranteed in [17,18].

In this paper, a novel method is proposed to optimize AP placement by satisfying the multiple degree of coverage. To be specific, the widely used mathematical tool for localization performance analysis, i.e. the Cramer-Rao lower bound

(CRLB), is employed to measure the resulting localization error given different AP placement schemes; in order to address the issue that the optimization problem is NP-complete, the heuristic genetic algorithm is leveraged by establishing the fitness function that incorporates both localization and coverage. Besides, to advance the practicability of the proposed method, the Motley-Keenan model is adopted to reflect the characteristics of wireless signal propagation in indoor environments as much as possible. Extensive simulations are conducted and show that the proposed method is advantageous in both time efficiency and localization accuracy, in comparison with two exhaustive methods based on the CRLB or the Fisher information matrix (FIM) and the method in [17].

2 The Metric for WiFi Localization

In this section, we shall introduce some preliminaries on evaluating WiFi localization performance. Firstly, a generic localization model is reported. After that, two critical issues in relation to the metric are addressed.

2.1 A Generic Localization Model

As was commonly assumed [22], the RSS measurements of the signals propagated from n APs to a receiver at a position $\mathbf{x}$, denoted $\mathbf{y} = [y_1, y_2, \cdots, y_n]^T$, are independent and identically distributed random variables, namely

$$\mathbf{y} \sim N(\mathbf{m}(\mathbf{x}), \sigma^2 \mathbf{I}_n), \tag{1}$$

where $\mathbf{m}(\mathbf{x}) = [m_1(\mathbf{x}), m_2(\mathbf{x}), \cdots, m_n(\mathbf{x})]^T$ is a vector function of mean RSS measurements at the position $\mathbf{x} = [x_1, x_2]^T$ from the n APs, and $\mathbf{I}_n$ denotes the identity matrix of order n.

The localization problem aims to infer the unknown position $\mathbf{x}$ given a sample of the RSS measurements $\mathbf{y}$. By suppose that the RSS measurement model in (1) is known, the localization problem can be solved through, e.g. the maximum likelihood estimator (MLE). Define gradients $\mathbf{r}_i = \frac{\partial m_i(\mathbf{x})}{\mathbf{x}} = [r_{i1}, r_{i2}]$ and formulate $\mathbf{r} = [\mathbf{r}_1^T, \mathbf{r}_2^T, \cdots, \mathbf{r}_n^T]^T$. Then, the likelihood function can be formulated as

$$L(\mathbf{y}; \mathbf{x}) = \log p(\mathbf{y}|\mathbf{x}), \tag{2}$$

and the Fisher information matrix (FIM) is

$$\mathbf{F}(\mathbf{x}) = -\mathrm{E}\left(\frac{\partial^2 L(\mathbf{y}; \mathbf{x})}{\partial \mathbf{x}^2}\right) = \frac{1}{\sigma^2} \mathbf{r}^T \mathbf{r}. \tag{3}$$

The Cramer-Rao lower bound (CRLB), which equals to the inverse of the FIM, can be formulated as

$$\mathbf{F}^{-1}(\mathbf{x}) = \sigma^2 \left[\sum_{i=1}^{n} \begin{pmatrix} r_{i1}^2 & r_{i1} r_{i2} \\ r_{i1} r_{i2} & r_{i2}^2 \end{pmatrix}\right]^{-1}, \tag{4}$$

and generally, its trace is utilized to denote the lower bound on the mean squared error (MSE) of any unbiased localization algorithm, namely

$$\text{Tr}(\mathbf{F}^{-1}(\mathbf{x})) = \frac{2\sigma^2 \sum_{i=1}^{n} \mathbf{r}_i\|^2}{\sum_{i=1}^{n} \sum_{j=1}^{n} (\|\mathbf{r}_i\|\|\mathbf{r}_j\| \sin \theta_{ij})^2}, \tag{5}$$

where θ_{ij} denotes the angle subtended by $\mathbf{r}_i$ and $\mathbf{r}_j$ (Fig. 1).

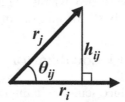

Fig. 1. The illustration of h_{ij} associated with $\mathbf{r}_i$ and $\mathbf{r}_j$.

It is evident that the MSE based on the CRLB, or simply the CRLB, can be applied as a metric to evaluate the localization accuracy given different AP placement, such that it is acceptable to optimize AP placement in terms of localization performance through the CRLB.

It is noticeable that the CRLB essentially involves two aspects of RSS measurements. One is the gradients of RSS measurements, which actually reflect the differences between RSS measurements at nearby locations and have been utilized in several existing studies for evaluating AP deployment [17]. The other one is the angles subtended by gradients, which are usually ignored by these studies but will be considered in the propose method.

2.2   Gradient Approximations

In order to calculate the gradients $\mathbf{r}_i$ with $i = 1, \cdots, n$ which are prerequisite for calculating the CRLB, one must have the formulation of $\mathbf{m}(\mathbf{x})$, which is hard and even impossible due to the following two aspects. Firstly, from the perspective of statistics, the accurate formulation of the mean functions associated with a set of unknown random variables can only be asymptotically approached by their sample means. Secondly, the RSS measurements available for further processing are just collected at a certain number of spatially discrete reference points, which cannot produce accurate gradients. As such, the conditions for precisely calculating the gradients cannot be satisfied.

To address this issue, bivariate polynomial regression is adopted to generate an approximate vector function of $\mathbf{m}(\mathbf{x})$ by making use of the average RSS measurements around any given reference point. Specifically, given any reference point and an arbitrary AP, define a (second-order) bivariate polynomial function, e.g. $f(\mathbf{x}) = \mathbf{x}^T \mathbf{A}\mathbf{x} + \mathbf{b}^T \mathbf{x} + c$. By using the average RSS measurements at nearby reference points, $f(\mathbf{x})$ can be fitted and further, its first derivatives with respect to the considered reference point can be used to approximate the requested gradients at this reference point from the given AP.

2.3   The Motley-Keenan Propagation Model

Another key issue arising in evaluating the CRLB lies in collecting sufficient RSS measurements at a set of reference points to regress the vector function of $\mathbf{m}(\mathbf{x})$, which is often infeasible for the problem of optimizing AP placement due to the fact that the optimization of AP placement should be conducted prior to deploying APs in practice. Therefore, the common approach adopted in the literature is to select an appropriate signal propagation model for predicting RSS measurements at any reference point.

The most commonly adopted model is the LDPL model [23], but cannot embody the attenuation caused by obstacles occurring between an AP and a receiver, like walls, furniture, and etc. As such, the Motley-Keenan model [24] is used in this paper to characterize indoor propagations of WiFi signals, namely

$$\mathrm{PL}(d) = \mathrm{PL}(d_0) + 10\alpha \log\left(\frac{d}{d_0}\right) + \sum_{i=1}^{m} k_i L w_i \tag{6}$$

where $\mathrm{PL}(d)$ is the mean path loss at a distance of d from the AP, $\mathrm{PL}(d_0)$ is the mean path loss at a reference distance d_0 from the AP, α is the path loss exponent, k_i is the number of the i-th type obstacle (there totally exist m types) between the current pair of AP and receiver, and Lw_i is the penetration loss by the i-th type obstacle. Table 1 lists typical attenuation values with respect to different types of materials.

Table 1. The attenuations caused by different materials.

No.	Materials	Typical attenuation (dB)
1	Brick Wall	10
2	Concrete Wall	15
3	Elevator Shaft	10
4	Door	2
5	Window	1

3   The Metric for WiFi Coverage

In this section, we shall introduce the metric for evaluating WiFi coverage. Similar to the approach adopted in evaluating localization performance, although the target deployment region is continuous, only a set of discrete reference points is selected for use.

A reference point satisfies c-degree coverage if and only if the receiver at this reference point is able to receive valid signals with RSS measurements above a threshold from at least c APs. Likewise, an AP placement scheme satisfies c-degree coverage if and only if all the reference points satisfy c-degree coverage. In order to measure the coverage of a AP placement scheme, denoted I, define the coverage ratio as the percentage of the reference points which satisfy c-degree coverage, namely

$$f_C(I, c) = \frac{\sum_{i=1}^{m} C(I, c, i)}{m} \tag{7}$$

where m is the number of reference points, and

$$C(I, c, i) = \begin{cases} 1 & \text{if the } i\text{-th reference point satisfies } c\text{-degree coverage} \\ 0 & \text{otherwise} \end{cases} \tag{8}$$

4   The Proposed Algorithm

In this section, we shall detailed introduce the proposed genetic algorithm which finds the optimal placement of given n APs in terms of both localization accuracy and coverage.

4.1   Analyzing the Computational Complexity of Optimizing AP Placement

Strictly speaking, finding the optimal AP placement requires to search all possible candidate AP placement, but since the area for deploying APs is usually continuous, it will cost infinite time to conduct the search.

Alternatively, such kind of problems is often simplified and thus approximately solved by searching over a set of finite and discrete points. Specifically, the area can be replaced by a lattice of points (i.e. reference points), such that the aim becomes to find the optimal AP placement over this lattice of points, namely that APs can only be placed on these reference points so as to maximize the localization and coverage in relation to these reference points.

However, the performance of the alternative approach remarkably relies on the granularity of the lattice, in the sense that a small granularity benefits the performance but induces severe computation complexities. For instance, given p reference points and n APs, the search space is as large as C_p^n, which exponentially scales with p and n. Therefore, in order to find nearly optimal AP placement as fast as possible, the genetic algorithm is adopted and will be elaborated in the following subsection.

4.2   GA-CRLB

The genetic algorithm is a heuristic search algorithm that evolves from the evolutionary rules of biology. It maintains excellent genes and promotes group evolution through selection, crossover, and mutation operations to obtain the global optimal solution. In this paper, we develop GA-CRLB based on the genetic algorithm and CRLB to search for the optimal AP placement that maximizes localization accuracy and coverage simultaneously.

The specific steps of the GA-CRLB algorithm are described as follows.

1. Initial population.

   Before initializing population, it is necessary determine the coding method. By using the AP coordinates as gene codes, the gene sequence can be coded as $G_i = [x_i, y_i]$ where x_i and y_i denote the coordinates of the i-th AP. Let $P = (I_1, I_2, ..., I_k)$ denotes the population, where $I_i = (G_1, G_2, ..., G_n)$ denotes the i-th individual, n is the number of genes and k is the number of individuals. As a result, $k \times n$ APs are randomly generated to form the initial population. It is noticeable that, each individual corresponds to a AP placement scheme, and the coordinates of these APs are uniformly and randomly generated within the set of reference points.

2. Individual evaluation.

   Calculate the fitness of each individual in the population by using the following fitness function:

$$f_F(I_i) = \begin{cases} \frac{1}{f_L(I_i)} & f_C(I_i, c) \geq F_C \\ 0 & \text{otherwise} \end{cases} \tag{9}$$

   where I_i is the i-th individual in the population, F_C is the coverage ratio threshold, and $f_L(I_i)$ is the average localization error at all reference points, i.e.

$$f_L(I_i) = \frac{\sum_{j=1}^{p} \mathrm{Tr}(\mathbf{F}^{-1}(\mathbf{x}_j))}{p}, \tag{10}$$

   where p is the number of reference points, and $\mathbf{x}_j$ is the coordinate of the j-th reference point.

3. Selection operation.

   The selection operation aims to select some optimal individuals from the parent generation to the next generation based on the evaluation of individual fitness, or generate new individuals in the next generation through the following crossover and mutation operations. The roulette selection model is adopted by evaluating the selection probability based on the fitness as follows:

$$p_i = \frac{f_F(I_i)}{\sum_{j=1}^{k} f_F(I_j)} \tag{11}$$

   where p_i is the selection probability of the i-th individual, i.e. I_i. Consequently, the individual with a high fitness value has a high probability of being selected.

4. Crossover operation.

   Crossover actually determines the global search ability by exchanging parts of genes associated with two individuals and creating new individuals. If a random number between 0 to 1 is less than the crossover probability p_c, we randomly select n cross positions to exchange genes of two individuals.

5. Mutation operation.
   The mutation operation avoids the genetic algorithm falling into a local optimum by changing genetic values in individuals. If a random number 0 to 1 is less than the mutation probability p_m, we randomly select genes in individuals and change the corresponding coordinates x_i and y_i.
6. Termination.
   After the population is initialized, the steps from 2 to 5 will be repeated to produce the next generation population. If the iteration number is greater than the threshold T, GA-CRLB will be terminated and the individual with the maximum fitness among the current population is returned as the optimal solution.

In summary, GA-CRLB leverages CRLB to comprehensively evaluate the influences of APs on localization by satisfying a predefined coverage threshold, and more importantly, is able to quickly return sub optimal solutions in comparison with the approaches relying on searching the huge solution space.

5   Simulations

Extensive simulations are carried out in this section to validate the effectiveness and efficiency of the proposed GA-CRLB.

5.1   Tool Introduction

In order to conveniently validate the proposed algorithm, we develop a Java Application tool, as shown in Fig. 2. It supports the following functions in relation to AP placement optimization:

– load and display floor plans in the shp format;

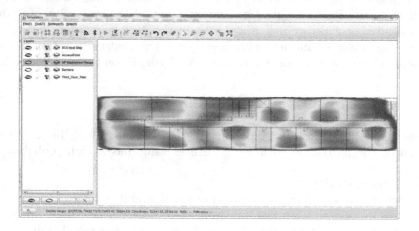

Fig. 2. The GUI of the simulation tool.

- RSS simulations based on different signal propagation models with configurable parameters, e.g. the LDPL model, the Motley-Keenan model, and
  etc.;
- optimize AP placement with different methods, which will be introduced in
  the following subsection;
- evaluate the CRLB based localization errors given different AP placement
  schemes;

5.2 Setup

Two scenarios with different sizes are taken into consideration in the simulations.
The large scenario is the third floor in the Building of College of Computer
Science, Inner Mongolia University, and has the size of 81 m × 14 m, as shown
in Fig. 3(a). The small scenario is part of the large scenario, and has the size of
29 m × 14 m, as shown in Fig. 3(b).

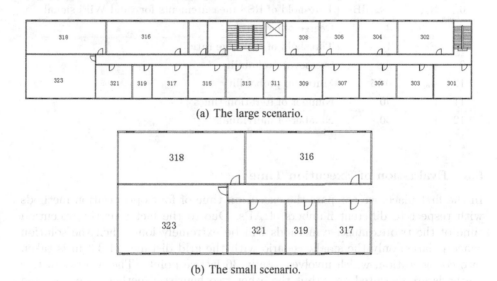

(a) The large scenario.

(b) The small scenario.

Fig. 3. Two scenarios considered in the simulations.

In order to validate the proposed method, the coverage-FD method [17] and
two exhaustive methods are realized for comparison. Specifically, the coverage-
FD adopts the difference between the RSS measurements at nearby reference
points as an optimality metric for localization and uses the simulated annealing algorithm to search for the optimal AP placement; the exhaustive methods
include exhaustion-CRLB and exhaustion-FIM which search the whole solution
space with either CRLB or the determinant of FIM as an optimality metric for
localization. Note that for fair comparison, the coverage-FD method does not

work to find the minimum number of APs for localization, but directly searches for the optimal AP placement given a fixed number of APs.

During the simulations, besides the parameters listed in Table 2, the influences of several critical parameters, including the number of APs, the lattice granularity, and etc., are investigated. The simulation tool is run on a Lenovo PC with core i7 CPU and 8 GB of RAM.

Table 2. The values of different parameters in the simulations.

No.	Name	Value	Usage
1	P_T	20 dBm	AP transmission power
2	d_0	1 m	Reference distance
3	$PL(d_0)$	30	Path loss at the reference distance
4	α	3	Path loss exponent
5	σ	4 dBm	Standard deviation of RSS measurements in dBm
6	R_{min}	−85 dBm	Threshold of RSS measurements for valid WiFi signals
7	c	3	Degree of coverage
8	F_C	1	Threshold of coverage ratio
9	p_c	0.8	Crossover probability
10	p_m	0.15	Mutation probability
11	t	40	Number of iteration times
12	k	30	Number of individuals

5.3   Evaluation of Execution Time

In the first place, we compare the execution time of four optimization methods with respect to different numbers of APs. Due to the fact that the execution time of the two exhaustive methods will be extremely long when the solution space is large, only the small scenario with the grid distance of 3.3 m is taken into consideration, which involves totally 36 lattice points. The two exhaustive methods are executed once, but the other two heuristic methods are executed 10 times and the average execution time is evaluated.

The execution time is plotted in log scale in Fig. 4 with respect to the number of APs rising from 3 to 7. As can be seen, the execution time of the exhaustion-CRLB method increases from 10 s to 4.8 h, and that of the exhaustion-FIM method from 0.02 s to 2.65 min; however, the execution time of both the other two methods increases slowly with increasing the number of APs, and is less than around 5 s regardless of the number of APs. Therefore, it can be concluded that the two heuristic methods are extremely time-efficient in comparison with the two exhaustive methods. Note that the proposed GA-CRLB is slower than the coverage-FD method because computing the CRLB involves matrix inversion and thus spends more time than computing the difference of RSS measurements used in the coverage-FD method.

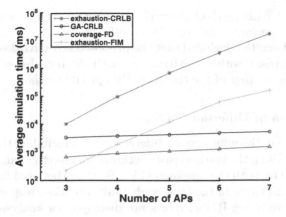

Fig. 4. Execution time vs. the number of APs with respect to the four methods.

In addition, we also compare the resulting localization errors given the optimal AP placement schemes returned by the four methods by evaluating the root mean squared error (RMSE) based on CRLB, namely

$$RMSE = \sqrt{f_L(I)} \tag{12}$$

where I is an optimal AP placement scheme obtained by one of the four methods, and $f_L(I)$ is the average localization error among all reference points using (10).

The RMSE values associated with four methods are plotted in Fig. 5 with respect to different numbers of APs. As can be seen, among all the four methods, the exhaustion-CRLB method unsurprisingly performs best since it returns the theoretically optimal AP placement scheme, but the exhaustion-FIM methods performs worst, which is attributable to the different optimality criterion adopted; moreover, the proposed GA-CRLB performs almost the same as the

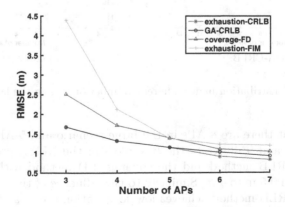

Fig. 5. RMSE vs. number of APs in case of the four algorithms.

best exhaustion-CRLB method when the number of APs is between 3 and 5, and evidently outperforms the other two methods.

To sum up, it can be concluded that the proposed GA-CRLB is not only time-efficient in comparison with the exhaustive methods, but also achieves superior performance close to that of the theoretically optimal method.

5.4   Evaluation of Different Factors

In the second place, the influences of different factors including the grid distance and number of APs on the two heuristic methods are investigated. To do so, given every configuration, both the proposed GA-CRLB method and the coverage-FD method are run 10 times in the large and small scenarios, respectively, and the box plots of the resulting RMSE values are displayed for analysis purposes.

Provided that the grid distance is 1 m in both the large and small scenarios, Figs. 6 and 7 illustrate the box plots of the RMSE produced by the proposed GA-CRLB method and the coverage-FD method with respect to different numbers of APs, respectively. As can be seen, the magnitudes of the RMSE values obtained by both methods in both scenarios reduce with the AP number increasing, and the proposed GA-CRLB method significantly outperforms the coverage-FD method in terms of both the median RMSE and the stability, which verifies the advantage of the proposed GA-CRLB method. In particular, when the AP number is relatively large, the resulting RMSE values appear to be quite concentrated, which is a key merit for practical applications.

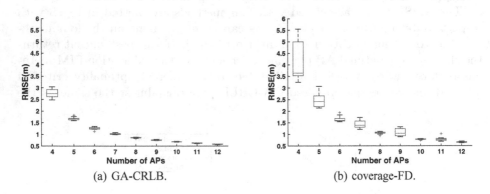

(a) GA-CRLB.   (b) coverage-FD.

Fig. 6. RMSE distribution under different number of APs in the large scenario.

Provided that there are 8 APs in the large scenario and 5 APs in the small scenario, Figs. 8 and 9 illustrate the box plots of the RMSE produced by the proposed GA-CRLB method and the coverage-FD method with the grid distance rising from 0.5 m to 4 m. Similarly to the influence of the AP number, the proposed GA-CRLB method achieves low localization errors and high stability in comparison with the coverage-FD method in all the circumstances considered. However, even though it is shown that the RMSE decreases with the grid

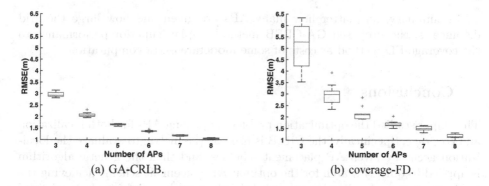

Fig. 7. RMSE distribution under different number of APs in the small scenario.

distance increasing in most cases, this should be attributable to the fact that a large grid distance results in less reference points, which induces large errors in approximating the localization errors in continuous region; that is to say, the significance of the simulations is limited as the grid distance is large.

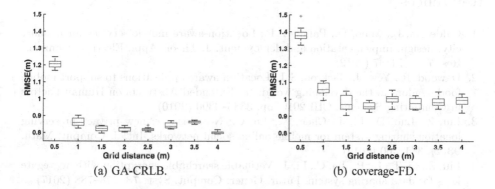

Fig. 8. RMSE distribution under different grid distances in the large scenario.

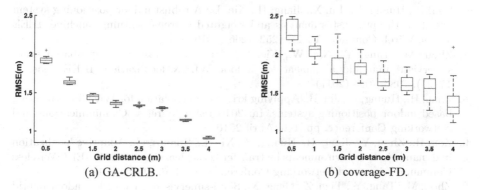

Fig. 9. RMSE distribution under different grid distances in the small scenario.

In summary, no matter how many APs are given and how large the grid distance is, the proposed GA-CRLB method display superior performance to the coverage-FD method at costs of some moderate extra computations.

6   Conclusions

This paper studied the optimization problem of placing APs for both localization and coverage. Specifically, the CRLB is used as the metric to evaluate the localization accuracy given AP placement schemes, and then the genetic algorithm is applied to quickly search for the optimal AP placement scheme achieving the minimum average localization error and simultaneously satisfying the predefined coverage requirement. Simulation results show that the proposed algorithm is not only time-efficient in comparison with the exhaustive methods, but also derives nearly optimal performance that the exhaustive method can derive and significantly outperforms the other popular heuristic method based on the fingerprint difference and the simulated annealing algorithm.

References

1. Calderoni, L., Maio, D., Palmieri, P.: Location-aware mobile services for a smart city: design, implementation and deployment. J. Theor. Appl. Electron. Commer. Res. **7**(3), 74–87 (2012)
2. Dawood, R., Yew, J., Jackson, S.J.: Location aware applications to support mobile food vendors in the developing world. In: Extended Abstracts on Human Factors in Computing Systems, CHI 2010, pp. 3385–3390 (2010)
3. Liu, Z., Luo, D., Li, J., Chen, X., Jia, C.: N-mobishare: new privacy-preserving location-sharing system for mobile online social networks. Int. J. Comput. Math. **93**(2), 384–400 (2013)
4. Liu, Z., Li, T., Li, P., Jia, C., Li, J.: Verifiable searchable encryption with aggregate keys for data sharing system. Futur. Gener. Comput. Syst. **78**, 778–788 (2017)
5. Li, M., Liu, Z., Li, J., Jia, C.: Format-preserving encryption for character data. J. Netw. **7**, 1239–1244 (2012)
6. Zou, H., Huang, B., Lu, X., Jiang, H., Xie, L.: A robust indoor positioning system based on the procrustes analysis and weighted extreme learning machine. IEEE Trans. Wirel. Commun. **15**(2), 1252–1266 (2016)
7. Zhou, M., Tang, Y., Nie, W., Xie, L., Yang, X.: Grassma: graph-based semi-supervised manifold alignment for indoor WLAN localization. IEEE Sens. J. **17**(21), 7086–7095 (2017)
8. Zhao, H., Huang, B., Jia, B.: Applying kriging interpolation for WiFi fingerprinting based indoor positioning systems. In: 2016 IEEE Wireless Communications and Networking Conference, pp. 1–6, April 2016
9. Zou, H., Zhou, Y., Jiang, H., Huang, B., Xie, L., Spanos, C.: Adaptive localization in dynamic indoor environments by transfer kernel learning. In: 2017 IEEE Wireless Communications and Networking Conference, pp. 1–6, March 2017
10. Zhou, M., Tang, Y., Tian, Z., Geng, X.: Semi-supervised learning for indoor hybrid fingerprint database calibration with low effort. IEEE Access **5**, 4388–4400 (2017)

11. Fang, S.H., Lin, T.N., Lin, P.C.: Location fingerprinting in a decorrelated space. IEEE Trans. Knowl. Data Eng. **20**(5), 685–691 (2008)
12. Jia, B., Huang, B., Gao, H., Li, W.: On the dimension reduction of radio maps with a supervised approach. In: 2017 IEEE 42nd Conference on Local Computer Networks (LCN), pp. 199–202, October 2017
13. Jia, B., Huang, B., Gao, H., Li, W.: Dimension reduction in radio maps based on the supervised kernel principal component analysis. Soft Comput. **22**, 1–7 (2018)
14. Baala, O., Zheng, Y., Caminada, A.: The impact of AP placement in WLAN-based indoor positioning system. In: 2009 Eighth International Conference on Networks, pp. 12–17, March 2009
15. Huang, B., Liu, M., Xu, Z., Jia, B.: On the performance analysis of WiFi based localization. In: 2018 IEEE Conference on International Conference on Acoustics, Speech and Signal Processing (ICASSP), pp. 1–5. IEEE (2018)
16. Alsmady, A., Awad, F.: Optimal Wi-Fi access point placement for RSSI-based indoor localization using genetic algorithm. In: 2017 8th International Conference on Information and Communication Systems (ICICS), pp. 287–291, April 2017
17. Chen, Q., Wang, B., Deng, X., Mo, Y., Yang, L.T.: Placement of access points for indoor wireless coverage and fingerprint-based localization. In: 2013 IEEE 10th International Conference on High Performance Computing and Communications, 2013 IEEE International Conference on Embedded and Ubiquitous Computing, pp. 2253–2257, November 2013
18. Zirazi, S., Canalda, P., Mabed, H., Spies, F.: Wi-Fi access point placement within stand-alone, hybrid and combined wireless positioning systems. In: 2012 Fourth International Conference on Communications and Electronics (ICCE), pp. 279–284, August 2012
19. Sharma, C., Wong, Y.F., Soh, W.S., Wong, W.C.: Access point placement for fingerprint-based localization. In: 2010 IEEE International Conference on Communication Systems, pp. 238–243, November 2010
20. Zhao, Y., Zhou, H., Li, M.: Indoor access points location optimization using differential evolution. In: 2008 International Conference on Computer Science and Software Engineering, vol. 1, pp. 382–385, December 2008
21. He, Y., Meng, W., Ma, L., Deng, Z.: Rapid deployment of APS in WLAN indoor positioning system. In: 2011 6th International ICST Conference on Communications and Networking in China (CHINACOM), pp. 268–273, August 2011
22. Wen, Y., Tian, X., Wang, X., Lu, S.: Fundamental limits of RSS fingerprinting based indoor localization. In: 2015 IEEE Conference on Computer Communications (INFOCOM), pp. 2479–2487. IEEE (2015)
23. Rappaport, T.: Wireless Communications: Principles and Practice, 2nd edn. Prentice Hall PTR, Upper Saddle River (2001)
24. Keenan, J., Motley, A.: Radio coverage in buildings. Br. Telecom Technol. J. **8**, 19–24 (1990)

PLZMA: A Parallel Data Compression Method for Cloud Computing

Xin Wang[1,3], Lin Gan[1,3,5(✉)], Jingheng Xu[1,3], Jinzhe Yang[3,4], Maocai Xia[1,3], Haohuan Fu[2,3,5], Xiaomeng Huang[2,3,5], and Guangwen Yang[1,2,3,5]

[1] Department of Computer Science and Technology, Tsinghua University, Beijing, China
lingan@tsinghua.edu.cn
[2] Ministry of Education Key Lab. for Earth System Modeling, and Department of Earth System Science, Tsinghua University, Beijing, China
[3] National Supercomputing Center, Wuxi, China
[4] Department of Computing, Imperial College London, London, UK
[5] Lab. for Regional Oceanography and Numerical Modeling, Qingdao National Lab. for Marine Science and Technology, Qingdao, China

Abstract. Recent decades have seen the rapid development of cloud computing, resulting in a huge breakthrough for people to handle the data produced every second and everywhere. Meanwhile, data compression is becoming increasingly important, due to its great potential in benefiting both the network transportation and the storage. Based on the urgent demand in high-efficient compression method with balanced performance in both merits of compression time and ratio, this paper presents PLZMA, a parallel design of LZMA. Process-level and thread-level parallelisms are implemented according to the algorithm of LZMA, which have gained great improvement in compression time, while ensuring a fair compression ratio. Experimental results on real-world application showed that PLZMA is able to achieve more balanced performance over other famous methods. The parallel design is able to achieve a performance speedup of 8× over the serial baseline, using 12 threads.

Keywords: Data compression · Parallel computing · LZMA

1 Introduction

In the past few decades, the society, or the way of people's life, is completely changed due to a revolutionary development of technology, and the world is now entering a new era, when data containing sufficient useful information, via various of networks, which exits everywhere and are easy to access in no time. Among different technical breakthroughs that contribute to the new era, cloud storage is undoubtedly one of the most essential and efficient approaches. Unlike traditional storage method that mainly relies on local systems, cloud storage is able to provide more secure, simple, and convenient way of accommodating

J. Vaidya and J. Li (Eds.): ICA3PP 2018, LNCS 11336, pp. 504–518, 2018.
https://doi.org/10.1007/978-3-030-05057-3_38

data, thanks to these technical innovations in areas such as parallel computing, virtualization, and data center infrastructure.

In the meantime, the data surge continues, and has increased to an extraordinarily huge level. For example, the amount of data that Google needs to process every day is already over 20PB [1], while the amount of image storage for Facebook already exceeding 540 TB, with 100 million images to upload per week, and 475,000 image requests to respond per second. In return, the surge of data for processing and storage is greatly challenging the network systems. Scientists and researchers are eager to seeing more efficient approaches to appera, so that data convey over the network is able to be further accelerated.

To be capable of decreasing both the bandwidth of data communication and the space of data storage, data compression is undoubtedly one of the most efficient solutions. Currently, data compression has been widely applied in many key applications, including telecommunication [2], and multi-media technology [3], as well as in some high performance computing areas such as geophysics exploration [4,5]. Data compression plays important role to provide high performance in data communication and accommodation. Particular in the field of cloud storage, with the demand on storing larger amounts of data on the cloud, the popularity of virtualization and cloud technologies, the establishment of worldwide ultra-large-scale data centers worldwide, traditional data storage technologies that focusing on data storage effectiveness, such as Data Deduplication and Thin Provisioning, are no longer enough to ensure the efficiency of frequent cloud services. Therefore data compression, becomes necessary to provide further contributions in cloud-related applications. Many compression algorithms, such as BWT [6], Deflate algorithm [7], and LZ77/78 [8], have been applied in cloud computing system.

On the other hand, even though data compression is able to decrease the demand for both the network bandwidth, and the system storage for cloud storage, extra modules for data compression and decompression, within the cloud system, will bring overhead, and might slow down the overall performance. Therefore, the performance of the selected data compression method, also matters in a cloud storage system, to achieve the best overall performance. However, most compression algorithms used in cloud storage are still largely based on serial algorithm, and are only able to guarantee a fair compression ratio, instead of the compression speed that should have been considered as well.

Up to now, parallel data compression method with balanced performance in both compression ratio and speed is still less to be seen. For example, Pigz [9] is a parallel compression software based on the Deflate algorithm. It greatly improved the compression time but has resulted in poor performance in compression ratio due to the use of parallel methods that have destroyed the integrity of the files.

As good performance in both the compression ratio and speed is required, this work mainly focuses on designing an efficient parallel compression method that is qualified for a high efficient cloud storage system. Among different data compression methods available, the popular LZMA algorithm is selected as the baseline, and is carefully parallelized and optimized based on traditional multi-core parallel system. The reason for selecting LZMA is that LZMA has a good compression ratio when processing binary files, and consumes a small amount of memory at the same time. Therefore, parallelization of LZMA can achieve relatively good results, so as to make up for the lack of compression time.

To summarize, this paper designs PLZMA, a parallel data compression method. The major compression modules of the LZMA algorithm are fully scaled onto parallel systems, with fine grained tuning efforts such as task overlapping, to customize into a parallel framework that fits well with the parallel system.

2   Related Work

2.1   Traditional Compression Algorithm

Prediction by partial matching (PPM) [10], which is considered to be one of the best lossless compression algorithms for text data compression, is a typical statistic-based compression algorithm. Based on the context modeling, PPM model uses the previous symbol-patterns in the uncompressed text stream to predict the upcoming symbol. To make the prediction more effective, each context model used in the algorithm is updated based on statistical information. Compared with other compression algorithms, PPM can achieve a very high compression rate for text files. However, the compression speed of PPM is very limited, mainly due to the huge amount of computation.

Deflate algorithm [7], which is widely used in HTTP protocol [11], PPP compression control protocol [12], PNG and MNG file formats [13], zlib compression library [14], etc., is a combination of LZ77 algorithm and Huffman code. It is a general-used compression algorithm whose memory consumption is independent of the size of the compressed-file, thus the Deflate algorithm is more suitable for servers with limited memory capacity.

Based on the successful experience of Deflate, the Lempel-Ziv-Markov chain algorithm (LZMA)[15] is a further improvement to the LZ77 algorithm. The LZMA algorithm offers two longest matching choices for users: Fast mode (find patterns based on the hash array of index lists) and normal mode (find patterns based on the hash array of binary tree). The purpose of the LZMA algorithm is to increase the compression rate by using a large dictionary, so as to reduce both the compression time and the memory usage during decompression. Compared with other compression method, LZ77 is applicable when user wants to achieve real-time decompression but the compression speed is not emphasized.

The BurrowsWheeler transform (BWT) [16] is also a widely used compression algorithm which rearranges a character string into runs of similar characters. Compared with other algorithm, the biggest advantage of BWT is that it can obtain a large compression throughput rate.

In general, traditional compression algorithms can achieve very good performance in compression ratio or compression throughput, but it is difficult to achieve good performance in both aspects at the same time.

In the meantime, some customised toolkits or libraries have also been developed to facilitate the usage of data compression, such as Snappy [17], LZMA SDK [18], QuickLZ [19], and LZO [20].

2.2 Parallel Compression Algorithm

Compared with traditional compression method based on serial algorithm, the parallel compression algorithm can effectively reduce the compression time, and thereby achieve a very high compression efficiency.

A good example is the Pigz compression algorithm, a parallel version of the zlib compression library [9]. During the pigz compression process, the input is decomposed into blocks of 128 KB, and the data in each block is compressed/decompressed in parallel. At the same time, the check point is introduced to ensure accuracy, and it is also calculated in parallel. The compressed data will be written to the output sequentially, and the check values obtained by each processor will be combined into a valid system check value.

Pbzip compression method [21], which could be regarded as the parallel version of BWT, is another famous parallel compression method. As the separated blocks in BWT method are independent for each other, we could run the computation simultaneously. That is the basic principle of Pbzip algorithm.

However, though remarkable compression speed improvement could be achieved by adopting both of the two compression methods, the compression ratio of such technique is affected due to the overhead of implementing parallelisms. With the surge of the data size in current applications such as cloud computing, novel compression technique which could achieve balanced performance in both the compression speed and the compression ratio is becoming an urgent demand.

3 Design Overview

3.1 Baseline Algorithm: LZMA

This work aims at a novel compression approach with good performance in both the compression speed and the compression ratio, and is suitable to be applied in cloud computing system to provide better overall efficiency.

The LZMA (Lempel-Ziv-Markov chain-Algorithm) [15] algorithm is an improved version based on the Deflate algorithm [7], and is considered as one of the most popular compression methods. LZMA was developed by Igor Pavlov and used in his own 7-ZIP [22] product which was designed for a high compression ratio, a rapid decompression/compression, and a low memory consumption when decompressing. Essentially, users can set two modes for finding the longest match string, which is a key step during the compression procedure. The fast search mode uses the hash array of the index list for searching, while the general search mode uses the hash array of the binary decision tree for searching. Both the index list and the binary decision tree are parallelised in this work.

An important reason to select LZMA method as the baseline compression method is that LZMA has a very high compression ratio to resist the overhead brought by parallelisation. The compression speed can be well increased while the compression ratio is still good. Therefore, LZMA is of great potential to achieve the balanced performance in both merits.

3.2   Overview of the Parallel Design

In this part we first show the overview of the PLZMA library proposed in this work. In general, PZLMA contains three steps, with two different levels of parallelisms, as is demonstrated in Fig. 1.

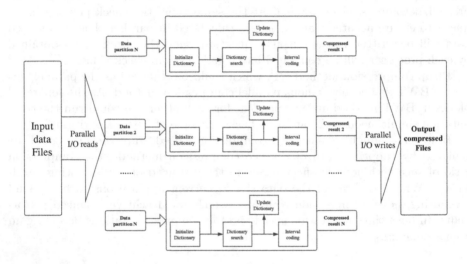

Fig. 1. Overview of the PLZMA method

***Step 1*: Data Partition.** According to the number of the computing processes available of the selected parallel computing platform, the original files are first divided into several data partitions. The principle is to ensure that the sizes of different data partitions are as close as possible, so as to ensure the load balance after parallelization.

***Step 2*: Two-Level Parallel Data Compression.** For each data partition, compression method can be applied in parallel and independently. Compressing each data partition generally contains two parts. One is a dictionary-based compression process. First, the dictionary is initialized, and then the dictionary is queried and the dictionary is updated based on the new data that is continuously entered. The other part is the operation of interval encoding. After the input data is compressed by the dictionary, it is converted to the matching position, the length of the match, and the triplet composition of the next character.

In this part, we will use interval coding to further compress the data. Step 2 is the essential procedure during the PLZMA process, and this work will use two levels of parallelism to achieve better performance. The first level (**Process Level**) is data parallelism in the upper level. Each data partition is compressed by the computing processes independently and simultaneously. The second level (**Thread Level**) is in the dictionary compression part. A finer-grained parallelization on the thread level is applied to further improve the performance.

***Step 3*: Data Combination.** After each data segment has been compressed, the final result file is written in parallel according to the length of the resulting compressed data.

In our parallel design of the PLZMA, *Step 1* and *Step 3* are implemented using the parallel I/O library (e.g., MPIO). The **Process Level** compression in *Step 2* is implemented using MPI directly. So the essential part of this work is the **Thread Level** parallelism, which will be explained in detail in the following section.

4   Thread-Level Parallel Design

In this part we present a parallelized dictionary compression algorithm based on the multi-thread resources, which could full take advantage of the hardware units of modern multi-core CPU processor.

4.1   Algorithm and Workflow

The algorithm description of the dictionary compression part of PLZMA is shown in Algorithm 1. First, we should build basic data structure and hyper-parameters, such as the data structure of hash table, and size of the dictionary. Secondly, while there are still some data needing to be compressed in current position, the algorithm will calculate the hash value of the first-batch-of-characters at the current position. Thirdly, if the hash value can be found in the hash table, that means pairing successfully, then we could do the query and update task according to our demand. On the contrary, if the corresponding value can not be found, then the pairing failed and the algorithm directly jump to line 8.

When we do the update task (line 5), firstly we should update the current item to the data structure of the hash table. We should notice that the procedure is various according to the data structure of the hash table. Secondly, a parallel matching search should be performed on the possible matching positions in the hash table entry so as to obtain the maximum matching position in the dictionary that could be matched with the current position.

From the above description, we could find out that the basic idea is similar to the algorithm of the LZ77, and the data is matched and compression-encoded by maintaining the sliding window. Compared with the previous dictionary compression algorithm, the biggest progress of PLZMA is to adopt the fast-search data structures (such as the hash table and corresponding data structures such as link, binary-tree) so as to accelerate the speed of search procedure. In the

---

Algorithm 1. The Parallel Dictionary Compression Algorithm

1: Dictionary compression initialization
2: While (there are still some data need to be compressed in current position)
3:     Calculate the hash value of the first batch
4:     if (the hash value can be found in the hash table) {
5:         Update the value into hash table
6:         Encode the value as (offset, len, c) according to the current position
7:     } else {
8:         Encode the value as (0, 0, c) according to the current position
9:     }
10: End While

---

following part of this section, we will focus on the implementation of update and query of the PLAMA algorithm.

4.2   The Search Entry of Parallel Dictionary

The main compression method we use in PLZMA is also based on the concept of a sliding window. As shown in Fig. 2, in the compression process, we will maintain a fixed size dictionary window. The content of the window is the data that has been compressed before the current position. Behind the current position is the data to be compressed. The basic principle of compression processing is to look for the longest string that can match the current data to be compressed in the dictionary window (as shown in the green block in Fig. 2), and then convert the matching data to a triple (offset, len, c). Among them, offset is the offset from the current position to the matching position in the dictionary window, len is the length of the match, and c is the next character after the matched data. After finding a match, the dictionary window moves back after the current position moving to the matching data. If the current data cannot find a match, a triplet (0, 0, c) is output, where c is the first character in the data to be compressed and then the current position is shifted back by one.

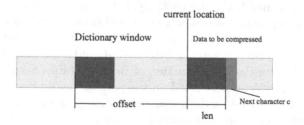

Fig. 2. Sliding window matching schematic (Color figure online)

Most of the early dictionary compression algorithms only support smaller dictionaries (32 KB). In the PLZMA algorithm, depending on the size of the input file, we will support dictionaries of several MB or even tens of MB. By using a large-capacity dictionary, we can store more data patterns that have appeared in the file, so that we can achieve more content matching and higher compression ratios in the compression process. However, the large-capacity dictionary will also bring another problem, i.e., the time-consuming query of the dictionary. To solve this problem, we use a hash table in the dictionary so as to reduce the query time. The hash function is calculated based on the first few (generally one to three) characters of the compressed data to obtain the matching position in the dictionary.

Due to the large dictionary capacity, the hash value of the first few characters may have multiple corresponding positions in the dictionary, and in such case, which position has the longest matching distance with the current data is unknown. Therefore, in order to achieve the best compression effect, we will store multiple possible matching positions in each hash table entry. Compared with other dictionary compression algorithms, the hash table entries in PLZMA can be stored in binary trees, linked lists, and static arrays. Among these choices, the storage form of the static array can support simultaneous access to different matching positions, thereby providing better support for parallel dictionary queries. Thus, we should use this kind of data structure whenever possible.

4.3 Dictionary Update and Maintenance

The introduction of the hash table can greatly speed up the pattern matching speed, but it also brings certain overhead to the updating and maintenance of the dictionary. While moving the window forward, the corresponding structure in the hash table needs to be updated accordingly. As described above, in the PLZMA algorithm, there are three kinds of possible data structures to store the hash table entry: linked list, binary tree, or static array.

1. Store the hash table by linked list

In this mode, elements within the hash table will point to values stored in a linked list, while the starting node of the corresponding linked list stores in the hash table. Since there is no limit to the length of the list itself, in order to avoid the algorithm spending too much time searching for a specific match, PLZMA will provide a settable parameter to specify the maximum length of the search in the linked list. At the same time, the latest matching data will be added to the beginning of the linked list in the hash table entry, thus to ensure that the matching is performed from the most recent position each time.

As indicated above, PLZMA uses sliding window technology. As the window slides forward, the hash table updates accordingly. Since adopting the dynamic allocation of memory to maintain the list would bring a huge memory management overhead, PLZMA uses static arrays and cyclic buffer technology to avoid frequent allocation and release of memory operations. The structure of such cyclic buffer is shown in Fig. 3.

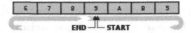

Fig. 3. Basic structure of the cyclic buffer

As demonstrated in Fig. 3, cyclic buffer is essentially an array one byte more than the sliding window size (window plus the current encoded byte), but it maintains a logical ring. When the window slides forward, we only need to change the values of start and end accordingly. Each byte in the cyclic buffer corresponds to each byte in the sliding window, as shown in Fig. 4.

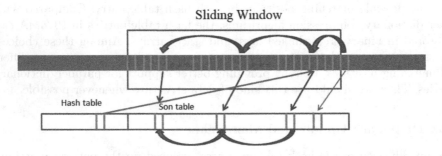

Fig. 4. Cyclic buffer before coding

As shown in Fig. 4, when encoding the current byte, the index in the hash table is obtained by the hash function. With this index, the algorithm can get the absolute position of the previous byte with the same hash value. Through the current encoding byte position and the offset of the position, the corresponding position can be found in the son table (namely the cyclic buffer). Since the cyclic table is a linked list, we can find all the matching positions in the current dictionary accordingly.

After coding, PLZMA makes corresponding changes to the hash table and son table, as shown in Fig. 5. Comparing the above two figures, we can see that the hash table and its son table slide forward with the window and keep changing. In this process, there is no memory redistribution and release operation, which greatly enhances the speed.

2. Store the hash table by binary tree

As indicated above, in some cases we could also employ binary tree to store the hash table entry so as to achieve satisfying search performance. Similar to the linked list, in the binary tree mode, the hash table entry points to a binary search tree which is empty at the first. With point reading and encoding of data, trees are continuously created or grown. Each data unit will have a corresponding node on the binary tree. For instance, if we hash each two bytes of a work, then every two consecutive bytes will correspond to a node on the binary tree, and the

Sliding Window

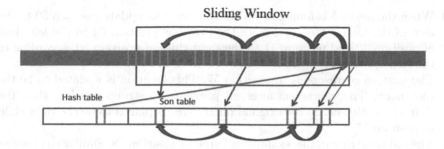

Fig. 5. Cyclic buffer after coding

word 'good' will be split into three nodes: 'go', 'oo', and 'od', which are assigned to the corresponding binary tree.

Below we will use a detailed example to illustrate the specific process of binary tree establishment and maintenance. Suppose we are going to compress a long string that contains five ab-starting data items in different locations. These content and location are (*abm, abcd2, abcx, abcd1, aby*) and (11, 24, 30, 57, 78) respectively.

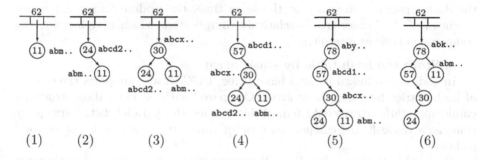

Fig. 6. Binary Tree Establishment and Maintenance

(1) Suppose that *ab* has a hash value of 62. When the first scan obtains the position of *ab* as 11, the binary tree is empty. Thus, a binary tree is created in position 62 in the hash table. At this moment, the binary tree only have one root node storing the value 11. Since no match was formed, the character *a* was directly output and then the encoder started processing the next string *bm*.

(2) When the compression algorithm processes position 24 to the next occurrence of ab, 62 is pop-up by calculating the hash value of *ab*, thereby starting the search in the binary tree that belongs to position 62 in the hash table. First of all, the encoder updates the new location 24 to the root of the binary tree. Then, position 11 is connected as the right child of position 24, since the character *c* of the string *abcd2* is smaller than the character *m* of string *abm*.

(3) When the next *ab* is found at position 30, we first update position 30 to the root of the binary tree, and place the previous position 24 to the left child of position 30 and position 11 to the right child of position 30, according to the character order.

(4) The next *ab* corresponds to position 57. This location is updated to be the root node. The characters after all previous ab-strings are less than the characters after *ab*. So the original binary tree is placed to be the right child of position 57.

(5) The last ab-string in this example is found at position 78. Similar to previous ones, such value is updated to the root node of the binary tree. Since the characters of all previous positions after *ab* are smaller than the character *y* of position 78 after ab, in the previous binary tree is placed as the left child of the root node.

As demonstrated the above example, the binary search tree used by PLZMA will ensure that the most recent pattern must be presented at the root place of the binary tree. At the same time, the internal nodes of the binary tree will be arranged in accordance with the character sequence, so as to achieve an effective search during the matching process. Benefit from these two features, the compression ratio is able to further improved by using the binary tree as the data structure. However, at the same time, the update and maintenance overhead of the binary tree is relatively complicated, which may increase the compression time as a result.

3. Store the hash table by static array

In addition to linked list and binary tree, PLZMA also supports the storage of hash entries by using static array. Compared with previous data structure, employing static array could remarkably reduce the parallel dictionary query time, as a tradeoff, the comparison ratio of such data structure is not as good as before.

To simplify the narrative, Fig. 7 demonstrates the basic ideas of static-array based hash table. In order to maintain and update each hash table entry, we store two variables for each hash table entry's corresponding array. The first variable is the number of valid positions in the array. At the beginning, the variable is initialized to 0, and then increases as the match pattern gradually

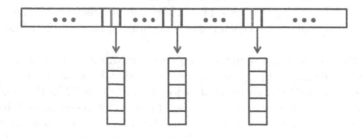

Fig. 7. Static array

added, up to the upper limit of the array size, and then no longer changes. The other variable is the index corresponding to the latest matching position in the array. By using this variable, we can guarantee that the searching will start at the nearest matching position every time when we make a query. When the static array elements are used up, the most recent match will be updated into the hash table entry to replace the longest match before.

4.4   Parallel Dictionary Query

As indicated in previous sections, to achieve optimal compression performance, a multi-level parallelism should be adopted in the PLZMA algorithm. Besides the parallel data compression discussed earlier, the parallel dictionary query is also one of the most important parts of the algorithm design.

As the data structure of hash table entry changes, implementation of the parallel dictionary query should also be different so as to achieve the optimal performance. (1) For the hash table using the linked list, for each query we can directly traverse along the list and perform matching search on the position that corresponds to each linked list entry, and thread management techniques such as thread-pool could be adopted in this case. (2) For the hash table using binary tree, the implementation of the parallel dictionary query is relatively difficult, because the parallel search and update of the binary tree are not easy. In this case, we can allocate multiple threads to the task, using one thread to perform the longest matching search in the binary tree, and then come up with another thread to update and maintain the binary tree. (3) For the hash table with static array, parallel dictionary queries are more straightforward. Since the possible matching positions corresponding to the same hash value have been sequentially stored in the array, we can initiate multiple threads directly through OpenMP or pthread to process different positions in parallel.

5   Performance Results on Telecommunication Dataset

5.1   Selected Platform and Dataset

Table 1 shows the hardware configuration of the selected platform. As for the dataset for testing the performance of the PLZMA, we choose different types of data, including 10 files in text format (ranging from 1.8 MB to 1 GB), and some other files including video, audio, and ppt format.

5.2   Performance Result

For all test case, we first validate the parallel program by comparing between the original data with the decompressed data, and guarantee that the data is identical. So the program is validated. Figure 8 shows the performance speedups of PLZMA over different threads. With the increase of the threads number, the performance improves. Using 12 threads is able to achieve a speedup of 8× over the serial LZMA.

Table 1. Hardware configuration

Hardware	Configuration
CPU	Intel(R) Xeon(R), E5645, 6 cores, 2.40 GHz
CPU number	12
Cache	1 MB
Memory	36 GB
Disk	4 TB
OS	Red Hat Enterprise 5.5
Compiler	Intel Compiler ICC 12.0
MPI	Intel MPI Library 4.0

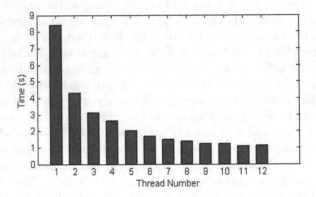

Fig. 8. Speedups over different thread

Figure 9 shows the compression time of PLZMA as well as some other famous compression methods, while Fig. 10 shows the compression ratio of these different methods. From the two figures concerning compression time and ratio, we can see that PLZMA is able to gain more balanced performance in both merits.

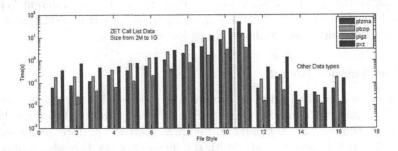

Fig. 9. Compression time over other parallel compression method

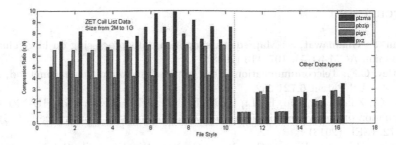

Fig. 10. Compression ratio over other parallel compression method

5.3 Analysis

Based on the experimental result we can figure out that, compared with other compression methods, our PLZMA method is more balanced in both the time-to-solution and the compression ratio. Pigz is based on zlib, and performs worse in the compression ratio. Pbzip2 is based on bzip2, and performs worse in the compression time. Both Pxz and PLZMA are based on LZMA, but the former performs worse in scalability. Therefore, PLZMA outperforms other methods, and have already been applied in industry now for compressing the real data in cloud computing system.

6   Conclusion

This work presents PLZMA, a parallel data compression method for high performance solutions in cloud computing system. Based on two different levels of parallelisms, every fine-grained step of the original LZMA method is well tuned, and obtained better performance in the merits of time and ratio.

Acknowledgement. L. Gan, and J. Xu are supported by the National Natural Science Foundation of China (grant no. 61702297); and the China Postdoctoral Science Foundation (grant no. 2016M601031).

H. Fu, and X. Wang are supported by the National Key Research & Development Plan of China (grant no. 2017YFA0604500), the National Natural Science Foundation of China (grant no. 91530323, 41661134014, 41504040 and 61361120098); and the Tsinghua University Initiative Scientific Research Program (grant no. 20131089356).

G. Yang, and J. Yang are supported by the National Key Research & Development Plan of China (grant no. 2016YFA0602200).

X. Huang is supported by a grant from the State's Key Project of Research and Development Plan (2016YFB0201100) and the National Natural Science Foundation of China (41375102).

References

1. Dean, J., Ghemawat, S.: Mapreduce: simplified data processing on large clusters. Commun. ACM **51**(1), 107–113 (2008)
2. Motley, C.F.: Telecommunication data compression apparatus and method, April 13 2004. US Patent 6,721,282
3. Yan, C., Zhang, Y., Dai, F., Li, L.: Highly parallel framework for HEVC motion estimation on many-core platform. In: Data Compression Conference (DCC), pp. 63–72. IEEE (2013)
4. Gan, L., Haohuan, F., Luk, W., Yang, C., Xue, W., Yang, G.: Solving mesoscale atmospheric dynamics using a reconfigurable dataflow architecture. IEEE Micro **37**(4), 40–50 (2017)
5. Gan, L., Fu, H., Mencer, O., Luk, W., Yang, G.: Data flow computing in geoscience applications. Adv. Comput. **104**, 125–158 (2017)
6. Burrows, M., Wheeler, D.J.: A block-sorting lossless data compression algorithm (1994)
7. Deutsch, P.L.: Deflate compressed data format specification version 1, 3 (1996)
8. Ziv, J., Lempel, A.: A universal algorithm for sequential data compression. IEEE Trans. Inf. Theory **23**(3), 337–343 (1977)
9. Gristwood, T., Fineran, P.C., Everson, L., Salmond, G.P.C.: PigZ, a TetR/AcrR family repressor, modulates secondary metabolism via the expression of a putative four-component resistance-nodulation-cell-division efflux pump, zrpadbc, in serratia sp. atcc 39006. Mol. Microbiol. **69**(2), 418–435 (2008)
10. Adiego, J., Fuente, P.D.L.: Merging prediction by partial matching with structural contexts model, p. 522 (2004)
11. Berners-Lee, T., Fielding, R., Frystyk, H.: Hypertext transfer protocol-http/1.0. Technical report (1996)
12. Woods, J.: PPP deflate protocol (1996)
13. Boutell, T.: PNG (portable network graphics) specification version 1.0. (1997)
14. Deutsch, P., Gailly, J.-L.: Zlib compressed data format specification version 3.3. Technical report (1996)
15. Zhu, W., Xu, J., Ding, W., Shi, Y.: Adaptive LZMA-based coding for screen content. In: Picture Coding Symposium, pp. 373–376 (2013)
16. Kärkkäinen, J.: Fast BWT in small space by blockwise suffix sorting. Elsevier Science Publishers Ltd. (2007)
17. Culler, M., Dunfield, N.M., Weeks, J.R.: Snappy, a computer program for studying the geometry and topology of 3-manifolds (2017)
18. Pavlov, I.: Lzma sdk (software development kit) (2007)
19. Reinhold, L.M.: Quicklz website
20. Oberhumer, M.F.X.J.: Lzo-a real-time data compression library (2008). http://www.oberhumer.com/opensource/lzo/
21. Varsaki, A., Afendra, A.S., Vartholomatos, G., Tegos, G., Drainas, C.: Production of ice nuclei from two recombinant zymomonas mobilis strains employing the inaZ gene of pseudomonas syringae. Biotechnol. Lett. **20**(7), 647–651 (1998)
22. Lembayung, W.: Comparative analysis on the izarc compression process and 7-zip (2011)

A Caching-Based Parallel FP-Growth in Apache Spark

Zhicheng Cai[✉], Xingyu Zhu, Yuehui Zheng, Duan Liu, and Lei Xu

School of Computer Science and Engineering, Nanjing University of Science and
Technology, Nanjing, China
caizhicheng@njust.edu.cn

Abstract. The association-rule-based recommendation is widespread in
many big data applications which need quick response to improve user
experience. Spark is a widely used distributed computing platform, which
accelerates the processing of large-scale distributed data. Developing
appropriate distributed algorithm for Spark is essential to decrease the
processing time of distributed recommendation. The existing FP-Growth
in Spark is a popular parallel recommendation method but getting the
best performance only when the memory of machines can accommodate
all immediate Resilient Distributed DataSets (RDDs). However, memory of many practice data centers is still not large enough for large data
sets. Therefore, in this paper, a caching-based parallel FP-Growth is proposed which consists of an integer-based sorting and an RDD-caching
strategy to improve the efficiency. Experimental results show that the
proposal decreases the execution time by 32.37% on average compared
with the existing parallel FP-Growth in Spark. Furthermore, impacts of
some important parameters upon the performance of the proposal are
analyzed by numerous realistic experiments in Spark.

Keywords: Spark · Parallel FP-Growth · Caching strategy

1 Introduction

The main objective of recommendation systems is to recommend appropriate
items such as products, movies and the like to consumers [15,19]. Association
rule mining is one of the widespread methods for recommendation systems [3,13]
which has been adopted in diverse fields. Mining of frequent itemsets is essential
for generating association rules from training data. Contemporarily, there are
many single-machine based association-rule mining algorithms such as Apriori [2]
and FPGrowth [8,27]. The FPGrowth is a widely used frequent-itemset mining
algorithm, which requires a tremendous amount of memory when a transaction
consists of quite a few items. In some occasions, the data size is so large that the
FPTree cannot be accommodated in the memory of a single machine which is
likely to result in failure events. Moreover, single-machine-based methods cannot
fulfill the requirement of timely response when they confront a large amount of
data.

© Springer Nature Switzerland AG 2018
J. Vaidya and J. Li (Eds.): ICA3PP 2018, LNCS 11336, pp. 519–533, 2018.
https://doi.org/10.1007/978-3-030-05057-3_39

Parallel algorithms have been developed to reduce memory usage and computation times of frequent itemset mining algorithms. MapReduce, which has been widely used in many fields, is a much more flexible programming model compared with multiprocessing systems [6]. MapReduce-based parallel versions of the FP-Growth [25] and the Apriori [10] algorithms have been proposed to accelerate the process distributed data. Although the MapReduce programming model provides a parallel computing environment, the intermediate results of MapReduce are stored to disks, which inevitably leads to many time-consuming I/O operations. Apache Spark [1,23] compensates for this defect by storing the intermediate data in memory. Therefore, Spark versions of parallel FPGrowth (PFPGrowth) [7] and Apriori [12,16] have been developed.

Existing works about frequent itemset mining in Spark mainly focus on the parallelism itself without considering the impact of caching strategies and the influences of Spark parameters upon the performance. The PFPGrowth divides the data into different partitions, generating one separate FPTree for each partition. Then frequent itemsets are generated by mining each FPTree, which will be collected to recommend items. The traditional parallel FP-Growth in Spark assumes that intermediate Resilient Distributed DataSets (RDD) are not released from memory whenever they are needed. However, the mining of FPTree is very memory consuming. Therefore, following tasks mining new FPTrees will occupy the memory used to store intermediate RDDs generated during the mining of previous FPTrees which leads to recomputing of these intermediate RDDs.

In this paper, a caching strategy is proposed to avoid the recomputing of critical intermediate RDDs. For example, the RDD of transactions of training data and the RDD of frequent itemsets, which will be used multiple times, are cached in disk or memory. In the original PFPGrowth, single items are sorted according to their frequencies based on String formats and transformed to integer formats after the sorting, which is memory consuming. Therefore, in this paper, the String-to-Integer transformation is adjusted to be done before the sorting, which will reduce the memory consuming significantly. Moreover, less attention has been paid on the influence of data partition numbers on the performance. Therefore, experiments have been done to evaluate the performance of processing the same amount of data under different data partition numbers. The main contributions of this paper are as follows:

i. A caching strategy is developed to cache appropriate RDDs to eliminate the recomputing of them to reduce the execution time.
ii. Extensive experiments were carried out to analyze the impact of dividing the same size of input data into different data partitions on the Spark performance which is used to guide the selection of the number of data partitions.

The rest of the paper is organized as follows. Related works are presented in Sect. 2. Section 3 describes the problem followed by the introduction in Sect. 4. Sections 5 and 6 present the proposed recommendation methods and experimental results respectively. The paper is concluded in Sect. 7.

2   Related Works

There are many recommendation algorithms such as Apriori [2], FPGrowth [8] and other collaborative filtering-based algorithms [14]. Traditional single-machine based recommendation algorithm cannot process distributed data efficiently. It is vital to develop distributed algorithms to process distributed data [5]. For high-performance computing systems such as multiprocessing systems, a parallel Apriori algorithm was investigated by Ye et al. [21] to increase the capacity of single-machine algorithms. A message-passing-interface based parallel FPGrowth algorithm was developed by Yu et al. [22] in which the data set is divided by evaluating the width and depth of the FPTrees to balance the size of generated FPTrees. The MapReduce-based programming model is more flexible and scalable compared with many other parallel and distributed computing platforms [26]. Therefore, different MapReduce-based recommendation algorithms have been developed in the literature. A MapReduce-based parallel version of the FP-Growth algorithm was proposed by Zhang et al. [25]. Xun et al. [20] investigated a parallel FP-Growth on MapReduce clusters, which places similar transactions into the same partition to reduce excessive redundant conditional pattern bases. Lin et al. [10] developed an Apriori-based parallel algorithm on MapReduce. A MapReduce-based collaborative filtering recommendation algorithm is proposed by Li et al. [9]. However, the MapReduce model stores results to disks which is time-consuming and is not suitable for multi-step or iterative computing.

Apache Spark is a new distributed computing platform [1,23], which stores intermediate data in memory to avoid frequent disk I/O. Many recommendation algorithms have been converted to parallel version and deployed to Spark. For instance, Qiu et al. [12] investigated a parallel Apriori on Spark which outperforms the MapReduce method around 25 times. A hybrid parallel Apriori in Spark is proposed by Sethi et al. [16] which avoids scanning the complete dataset each iteration. A distributed Apriori-like frequent-itemset-mining algorithm on spark was developed by Zhang et al. [26] which reduces the number of candidate sets by applying a matrix-based pruning approach. Winlaw et al. [19] proposed a method to accelerate the collaborative filtering optimization method on Spark which consists of an efficient line search technique, requiring only one pass over distributed data. Gassama et al. [7] developed a parallel version of FPGrowth which scales flexibly and process distributed data efficiently. Most of the existing work about parallel FPGrowth and Apriori focus on the converting from single-machine algorithms. However, caching strategies are very crucial to parallel algorithms in Spark, which have been ignored by existing work.

Spark parameters exert a tremendous influence upon the algorithm performance, which can be tuned by users according to characteristics of specific applications to optimize the performance. A case in point is that the execution time is different when the same amount of data is divided into different numbers of data partitions for the same algorithm [24]. Wang et al. [18] present a method to predict the performance of different applications on the Spark by running a small fraction of the original data. Petridis et al. [11] investigates the impact of the most important of the tunable Spark parameters on the application performance. A machine-learning-based method is proposed by Wang et al. [17] to set the configuration the Spark automatically. However, the impact of dividing the same size of input data into different numbers of partitions on the Spark performance has not been investigated.

Therefore, in this paper, caching strategies have been developed to appropriately use limited memory to improve the performance of parallel FPGrowth on Spark. Moreover, the influence of the number of data partitions on the execution time and memory usage has been analyzed by extensive experiments.

3   Problem Description

Let $I = \{i_1, i_2, ..., i_n\}$ be the set of distinct items where i_k is the k-th item and n is the number of items. $T = \{t_1, t_2, ...t_m\}$ represents the set of transactions in which t_w is the w-th transaction and the subset of I, and m is the number of transactions. A set of items is called an itemset. The ratio of the number of transactions containing an itemset X in T to m is referred to as the frequency (support) of X and labeled as $support(X)$. An association rule is a pair of itemsets in the form of $X \Rightarrow Y$, where X is called antecedent and Y is the consequent of X. $X \Rightarrow Y$ means that the appearance of X usually leads to the appearance of Y. The confidence of an association rule is equal to the ratio $support(X \cup Y)/support(X)$.

To fulfill the requirement of quick response, it is vital to accelerate the speed of the existing parallel FP-growth. The current parallel FP-growth in Spark assumes that there is enough memory to support the computation which cannot adapt to data clusters composed of computers with low memories. When the same RDD need to be used multiple times, it will be recomputed at the second time because it is released after the first use which is time-consuming. Consequently, the objective of this paper is to develop appropriate cache strategies to accelerate the execution speed.

4   Existing Parallel FP-Growth in Spark

The traditional FP-growth is composed of two steps [27]. In the first step, the data is scanned for the first time to calculate the frequency of each item, and items are sorted in descending order of frequencies. Then, the data is scanned secondly to eliminate items of which the frequencies are smaller than a threshold and to sort each transaction according to frequencies. In the second step, an FP-Tree is constructed based on sorted transactions and mined recursively to generate the frequent-item set. The existing Parallel FP-growth [1,7] in Spark is composed of following steps:

S1: *Single frequent item generating and sorting.* As shown in Stage 0 and 1 in Fig. 1, data is first divided into p partitions and stored in distributed storage system like HDFS. Each partition contains many transactions each of which is split into an array of items and then flatted into (item, 1) pairs. Next, such pairs on different partition are reduced by items to calculate the frequency of each item and the results are stored in (item, frequency) pairs. Items with frequencies (*support*) lower than a threshold *minSup* are eliminated. Finally, items are sorted in descending order of frequencies and the sorted results are stored in SortList. Meanwhile, a map from the original item to the rank in the SortList is generated.

S2: *Conditional-pattern-base generating.* According to a given partition function, items are divided into p groups each of which has a unique group-id (p is the number of data partitions). For each data partition, each transaction is converted into multiple conditional pattern bases. Items of each transaction are scanned from the last to the first. Whenever an item belongs to a new group (the conditional pattern base for the current transaction has not been generated for this group), a new conditional pattern base consisting of the first item to the current item is generated for this group. Finally, one conditional pattern base will be generated for each group. Generated conditional pattern bases are stored in *ConditionTransRDD[Map(group id, conditional pattern bases)]* as shown in Stage 2 of Fig. 1.

S3: *Frequent-itemset based association rule generating.* Conditional pattern bases are reduced by the group-id into different data partitions, each of which consists of bases with the same group-id. A FP-tree is first generated for each group and stored in *FPTreeRDD[groupid, FPTree]* as shown in Stage 3 of Fig. 1. Then, each FPtree is mined to generate frequent items *FrequentItemRDD[FreqItemset]*, where *FreqItemset* is a class which stores a frequent itemset and its *support*. Next, based on *FrequentItemRDD*, association rules *AssociationRDD[(antecedent, (consequent, union-frequency))]* are obtained by splitting each frequent itemset where antecedent and consequent are itemsets, and union-frequency is equal to *support(antecedent ∪ consequent)*. To calculate the confidence of each association rule, *support(antecedent)* is needed. It has been proved that all antecedents are contained in the original *FrequentItemRDD*. Therefore, *FrequentItemRDD* is transformed into a new join-available *PairFrequentItemRDD[(frequent-itemset, frequency = support(frequent − itemset))]* by unfolding attributes of the class *FreqItemset*. Details can be found in Stage 3 and 4 of Fig. 1.

S4: *Computing confidences of association rules.* Stage 5 of Fig. 1 shows that *PairFrequentItemRDD* and *AssociationRDD* are first joined and reduced according to the key *frequent-itemset* and *antecedent*. Reduced results are stored in *AssociationConfRDD[(antecedent, (consequent, union-frequency), frequency)]*. Next confidence degrees of association rules are calculated by mapping *AssociationConfRDD* to *AssociationConfDoubleRDD [(antecedent, consequent, conf]* in which *conf* is equal to *union-frequency/frequency*. If *conf* of an association rule is smaller than *minConf*, the rule is eliminated.

5 Proposed Caching Based Recommendation

For one thing, transactions of input data are usually stored in String formats. Although the original parallel FP-growth algorithm has a map from items in String formats to rank values of integer in Stage 2, it is still very memory-consuming in Stage 0 and 1 to operate on String data directly. Therefore, a storage type transforming method is proposed first to preprocess the original data. For another one, as shown in Stage 3 of Fig. 1, in the original algorithm, FPTreeRDD is first constructed and used to generate the FrequentItemRDD. Then, FrequentItemRDD is used to generate PairFrequentItemRDD. Next, AssociationRDD is generated from the same FrequentItemRDD which forms a Stage 4. If tasks of Stage 3 is scheduled and executed first, all the previous three RDDs are computed one by one. When the memory is not large enough, the memory cannot accommodate all the intermediate RDDs including the FrequentItemRDD which will be released to support the calculation of following tasks. When tasks of Stage 4 are scheduled later and want to use the intermediate FrequentItemRDD to generate the AssociationRDD, the FrequentItemRDD has been removed from memory and needs to be recomputed. The recomputing of FrequentItemRDD involves

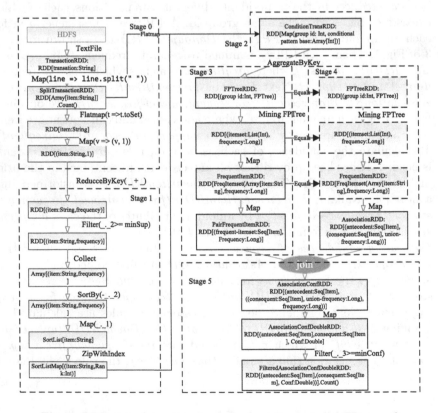

Fig. 1. RDD transformation process of existing parallel FP-growth

the recomputing of many previous RDDs even the RDDs in previous Stages like the ConditionTransRDD, which is time-consuming. RDDs in Spark can be cached (including persisting) into memory or disk to reuse some important RDDs and avoid unnecessary recomputing. However, caching consumes additional time, and it is not sensible to cache all RDDs. Therefore, appropriate caching strategies are essential to Spark applications. In this paper, a caching strategy is developed to accelerate the processing speed of the parallel FP-Growth algorithm. At last, a set-matching based recommendation method is proposed to recommend based on user data. Details of the proposal are as follows.

5.1   Integer Based Sorting

The main objective of Stage 0 and 1 of the parallel FP-Growth is to read transactions, calculate frequencies of single items and sort them. The original training data is stored in String formats which make the following computation memory-consuming. For example, when the original input data in HDFS is 1.5 GB, the total memory consumption of split transactions in *SplitTransactionRDD* is about 13 GB. Although the input training data is in String formats, each item is a number. Therefore, when *TransactionRDD* is mapped to *SplitTransactionRDD* by splitting each String to an Array of String, each String value is transformed to an integer value, i.e., each transaction is stored by an Array of integers. The new integer-based *SplitTransactionRDD* only consumes 1 GB approximately. In Spark, execution and storage share the total memory, reducing the memory consumption of *SplitTransactionRDD* is helpful to accelerate later sorting.

5.2   Proposed Caching Strategy

As shown in Fig. 1, *SplitTransactionRDD* are used to sort items first in Stage 1, and to generate conditional FPtrees in Stage 2. In Spark, when the memory is not large enough, intermediate RDDs will be replaced to accommodate later RDDs if these intermediate RDDs are not cached. Consequently, if *SplitTransactionRDD* is not cached after it is first obtained, *SplitTransactionRDD* will be removed from memory in later steps. When it is needed again in Stage 2, *SplitTransactionRDD* needs to be recomputed. In this paper, *SplitTransactionRDD* can be cached (The cache operation includes cache and persist operations in Spark) by two different ways: *Memory-and-Disk* based caching and *Disk* based caching when it is first generated. The *Memory-and-Disk* caching uses memory as much as possible to cache RDDs while the *Disk* only use the disk.

In Fig. 1, the FPTree constructing and frequent-itemset mining are two most time-consuming steps. The obtained frequent itemsets are stored in the intermediate *FrequentItemRDD*. Then, the intermediate *FrequentItemRDD* will be used twice to generate the *PairFrequentItemRDD* and the *AssociationRDD* in Stage 3 and 4 respectively. Because the computing of *PairFrequentItemRDD* and the *AssociationRDD* belong to different Stages, they cannot be computed together. After *FrequentItemRDD* is used in Stage 3, it will be removed from memory for later computation when there is not enough memory to hold all intermediate

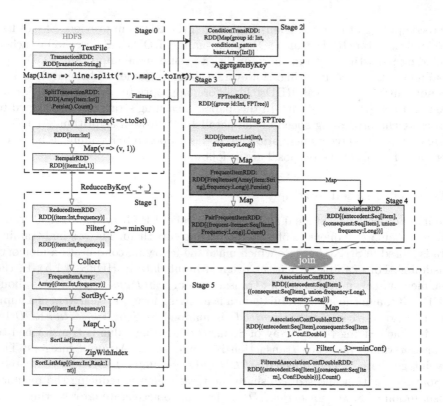

Fig. 2. RDD transformation process of proposed caching-based parallel FP-growth

RDDs. Therefore, in this paper, *FrequentItemRDD* is cached when it is first generated. Moreover, the number of frequent itemsets is counted which trigger the computation of Stage 3 first in a separate Spark job. At last, in Stage 4, association rules are generated from the cached *FrequentItemRDD* without recomputing of *FrequentItemRDD* which speeds up the execution. Transformation of RDDs of caching-based parallel FPGrowth are shown in Fig. 2 in detail.

5.3 Set-Matching-Based Recommendation

The existing parallel FP-growth does not consist of recommendation method. Therefore, a set-matching based recommendation method is developed in this paper. As shown in Fig. 3, the user data is first read from distributed storage system like HDFS. Each user transaction is split and transformed into an integer-value-based array which is stored in *UserTransactionRDD[Array[item:Int]]*. To match user transaction with antecedents of association rules quickly, each user transaction is mapped to a set of integer, generating *UserSetRDD[Set[item:Int]]*. Then, if an user transaction is the subset of the antecedent of a rule in *CombinedRulesRDD[(antecedent, List[(consequent, Confidence)])]*, a new recommendation result *(user-transaction, List[(consequent, Confidence)])* is generated.

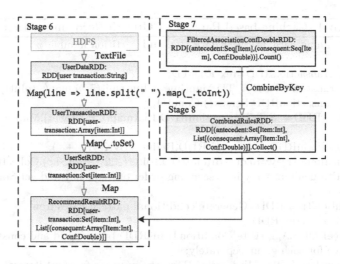

Fig. 3. Set-matching-based recommendation

5.4   Description of the Proposal

The caching-based parallel FPGrowth (CPFPGrowth) is described in Algorithm 1. First, from Step 2 to 8 frequencies of items are counted, and items are sorted in the order of frequency. Then conditional pattern bases are generated in Step 9 and FPTree is constructed for each group at Step 10. FPTrees are mined to generate frequent itemsets and association rules from Step 11 to 14. Next, from Step 15 to 19, frequencies of itemsets and association rules are joined to compute confidence degrees of association rules. Finally, recommendations are generated for user data. The CPFPGrowth with *Memory-and-Disk* and *Disk* based caching strategies are referred as CPFPGrowth-MD and CPFPGrowth-D respectively.

6   Performance Evaluation

Experiments are performed to compare the execution times of the caching-based parallel FPGrowth with the traditional PFPGrowth of which the source codes are available in public Spark website. Source codes of the proposed caching-based parallel FPGrowth is available on the website [4]. Two sets of data are used to evaluate the proposal which includes a training set TD and a test set UD. TD is composed of 169208 records (transactions) and there are 526765 items in total. Each line of TD and UD is a transaction which consists of multiple items. To evaluate the effectiveness of our methods, a private Spark cluster is built on three physical machines in which each node has two cores and 5 GB Memory. Meanwhile, a cluster with six nodes is established on virtual machines rented from public clouds with the configuration of 4 cores and 62 GB memory. Spark 2.3.0 and Hadoop 2.7.5 are installed on each node.

Algorithm 1. Caching-based Parallel FPGrowth Recommendation

Input: Training data TD, user data UD, and partition number p

1 **begin**
2 | Read TransactionRDD=textFile(TD, p);
3 | SplitTransactionRDD = TD.Map(line⇒ line.split(" ").map(_.toInt));
4 | SplitTransactionRDD.Persist().Count();
5 | ItempairRDD = SplitTransactionRDD.Flatmap(t ⇒t.toSet).Map(v ⇒ (v, 1));
6 | ReducedItemRDD = ItempairRDD.ReducceByKey(_ + _);
7 | FrequenitemArray=ReducedItemRDD.Filter(_._2≥ $minSup$).Collect();
8 | Sort FrequenitemArray in descending order of frequency and get SortList of items;
9 | ConditionTransRDD=Generate conditional pattern bases from SplitTransactionRDD;
10 | FPTreeRDD=Aggregate ConditionTransRDD by group id and construct FPTree for each group separately;
11 | FrequentItemRDD=Mine each FPTree to generate frequent itemsets;
12 | PairFrequentItemRDD= FrequentItemRDD to join-available pairs;
13 | PairFrequentItemRDD.Count();
14 | AssociationRDD=Generate association rules from FrequentItemRDD;
15 | AssociationConfRDD=Join and Reduce AssociationRDD and PairFrequentItemRDD;
16 | AssociationConfDoubleRDD=Divide the union-frequency by the frequency to calculate the confidence of each rule;
17 | AssociationConfDoubleRDD.Filter(_._3≥ $minConf$).Count();
18 | CombinedRulesRDD=Combine rules with the same antecedent;
19 | RuleList=CombinedRulesRDD.Collect();
20 | Read UserDataRDD=textFile(UD, p);
21 | UserTransactionRDD= UserDataRDD.Map(line⇒ line.split(" ").map(_.toInt));
22 | UserSetRDD=UserTransactionRDD.Map(_.toSet);
23 | RecommendResultRDD=Recommend items for UserSetRDD by comparing whether user transaction is the subset of antecedent of association rules;
24 | **return** *RecommendResultRDD*

6.1 Results Under Different minSups

Execution times of different algorithms on different *minSup*s are shown in Table 1 which shows that the proposed CPFPGrowth-MD and CPFPGrowth-D is faster than the traditional PFPGrowth. Moreover, as the *minSup* decreases, the proposals save much more execution times. The reason is that more items with frequencies (*support*) higher than the *minSup* are kept for later analysis as *minSup* decreases. For instance, Fig. 4 shows the size of shuffle data in Stage 2 of Fig. 2, which demonstrates that the size of shuffle data increases as the *minSup* decreases. Furthermore, Table 1 also illustrates that CPFPGrowth-D has shorter times than CPFPGrowth-MD. The cause is that CPFPGrowth-MD uses more memory space to cache intermediate RDDs, leaving less memory to computation which makes the *Memory-and-Disk* based strategy consume more time than the *Disk* based caching. Therefore, caching RDDs in memory to accelerate and using the memory to computing should be balanced according to the characteristics of applications. For example, for CPFPGrowth algorithms, the constructing and mining of FPTrees are very memory-consuming. If the memory cannot accommodate all intermediate RDDs, it is beneficial to use the *Disk*-based strategy to cache RDDs which will be used multiple times.

Table 1. Average execution times under different *minSups* (Min)

Algorithm/*minSup*	0.3	0.25	0.20	0.15	0.10
PFPGrowth	1.2	1.3	4.6	15	49
CPFPGrowth-D	0.7	1.1	3.3	11	35
CPFPGrowth-MD	1.3	1.1	3.6	11	48

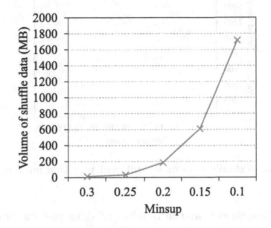

Fig. 4. Size of shuffle data generated by CPFPGrowth (MB)

6.2 Results Under Different Partition Numbers

For a given size of input data, dividing the data into different numbers of partitions is crucial to the performance. Computation times of compared algorithms under different partition numbers p are shown in Fig. 5 which demonstrates that the proposed CPFPGrowth-MD and CPFPGrowth-D have shorter times than the original PFPGrowth. The average execution time is decreased by 32.37% through caching essential RDDs appropriately. The reason lies in the fact that essential intermediate RDDs are cached to avoid recomputing them when the memory is not large enough to hold all intermediate RDDs. Therefore, the proposed caching-based methods are more suitable for the execution on data centers without enough memory to accommodate all RDDs.

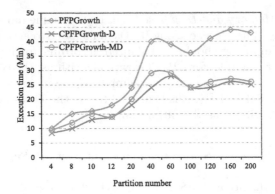

Fig. 5. Execution times under different partition numbers (Min)

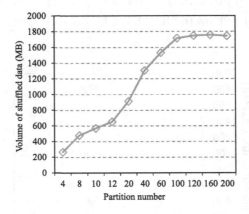

Fig. 6. Size of shuffle data under different partition numbers (MB)

Figure 5 also illustrates that the number of data partitions exerts an enormous influence upon the execution time. The reason is that more conditional pattern bases are generated when the number of partitions increases. For each transaction, items are scanned from the last to the first. Whenever an item belongs to a new partition, a new conditional pattern base consisting of the first item to the current item is generated. Consequently, a larger partition number means more conditional pattern bases which lead to more shuffle data as shown in Fig. 6. Processing more data usually consumes a much longer time if tasks cannot be processed in parallel. Only when the number of data partition is smaller than the number of executors, increasing the number of data partition can decrease the total execution time by executing tasks simultaneously. However, the test data center only consists of 6 executors. Increasing the number of data partition only leads to long execution times. Therefore, the number of data partition should be as small as possible but larger than the number of executors.

On the contrary, the number of data partitions cannot be too small either. A smaller number of partitions means there is a larger FPTree to process in

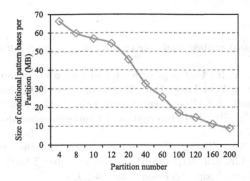

Fig. 7. Size of pattern bases per partition under different partition numbers (MB)

each partition. For instance, Fig. 7 shows the size of conditional pattern bases per partition, which indicates that more conditional pattern bases are used to construct an FPTree in each partition given smaller partition numbers. Because constructing and mining FPTrees are very memory-consuming, a failure event will occur when the memory is not large enough to handle the processing of a large FPTree. Therefore, the number of data partition should be determined considering the size of FPtrees, the size of shuffle data and the number of executors together. Consequently, the number of partition should be as small as possible but larger than the number of executors and large enough to decrease the size of FPTrees to be available for the memory of the cluster.

7 Conclusion

FPTree constructing and mining in traditional parallel FP-Growths are very time consuming, which makes the parallel FP-Growth in Spark only get the best performance in data centers with large enough memory to accommodate all intermediate RDDs. However, there are many data centers without sufficient large memory. In this paper, the traditional parallel FP-Growth is improved to fit such data centers by adding appropriate caching strategies. Experimental results show that the proposed caching-based PFPGrowth decreases the execution time by 32.37% on average. Moreover, influences of the minimum support degree and the number of data partitions upon the performance of the proposal is evaluated by extensive experiments. The principle about determining the number of data partition is concluded from experiments. Since the proposal fails when the memory cannot accommodate an FPTree, decreasing the memory consumption of FPTree constructing is a promising future work.

Acknowledgments. Zhicheng Cai is supported by the National Natural Science Foundation of China (Grant No. 61602243) and the Natural Science Foundation of Jiangsu Province (Grant No. BK20160846). Lei Xu is supported by the National Natural Science Foundation of China (No. 61671244). Duan Liu is supported by Postgraduate Research & Practice Innovation Program of Jiangsu Province.

References

1. Spark: Lightning-fast unified analytics engine. http://spark.apache.org/. Accessed 14 June 2018
2. Agrawal, R., Srikant, R.: Fast algorithms for mining association rules. In: International Conference on Very Large Data Bases, pp. 487–499 (1994)
3. Agrawal, R., Swami, A.: Mining association rules between sets of items in large databases. In: ACM SIGMOD International Conference on Management of Data, pp. 207–216 (1993)
4. Cai, Z., Zhu, X., Zheng, Y.: Source codes of the proposed caching-based parallel FP-Growth. https://github.com/czcnjust/ElasticSim/blob/master/cachingbasedFPGrowth.zip. Accessed June 14 2018
5. Chung, H., Nah, Y.: Performance comparison of distributed processing of large volume of data on top of Xen and Docker-based virtual clusters. In: Candan, S., Chen, L., Pedersen, T.B., Chang, L., Hua, W. (eds.) DASFAA 2017. LNCS, vol. 10177, pp. 103–113. Springer, Cham (2017). https://doi.org/10.1007/978-3-319-55753-3_7
6. Dean, J., Ghemawat, S.: Mapreduce: a flexible data processing tool. Commun. ACM **53**(1), 72–77 (2010)
7. Gassama, A.D.D., Camara, F., Ndiaye, S.: S-FPG: a parallel version of FP-growth algorithm under apache spark. In: IEEE International Conference on Cloud Computing and Big Data Analysis, pp. 98–101 (2017)
8. Han, J., Pei, J., Yin, Y.: Mining frequent patterns without candidate generation. In: ACM SIGMOD International Conference on Management of Data, pp. 1–12 (2000)
9. Li, C., He, K.: CBMR: an optimized mapreduce for item based collaborative filtering recommendation algorithm with empirical analysis. Concurr. Comput. Pract. Exp. **29**(10), 1–7 (2017)
10. Lin, M.Y., Lee, P.Y., Hsueh, S.C.: Apriori-based frequent itemset mining algorithms on mapreduce. In: ICUIMC 2012, pp. 76:1–76:8. ACM, New York (2012)
11. Petridis, P., Gounaris, A., Torres, J.: Spark parameter tuning via trial-and-error. In: Angelov, P., Manolopoulos, Y., Iliadis, L., Roy, A., Vellasco, M. (eds.) INNS 2016. AISC, vol. 529, pp. 226–237. Springer, Cham (2017). https://doi.org/10.1007/978-3-319-47898-2_24
12. Qiu, H., Gu, R., Yuan, C., Huang, Y.: Yafim: a parallel frequent itemset mining algorithm with spark. In: Parallel and Distributed Processing Symposium Workshops, pp. 1664–1671 (2014)
13. Rathee, S., Kashyap, A.: Adaptive-miner: an efficient distributed association rule mining algorithm on spark. J. Big Data **5**(1), 6 (2018)
14. Sarwar, B., Karypis, G., Konstan, J., Riedl, J.: Item-based collaborative filtering recommendation algorithms. In: International Conference on World Wide Web, pp. 285–295 (2001)
15. Schafer, J.B., Konstan, J., Riedl, J.: Recommender systems in e-commerce. In: ACM Conference on Electronic Commerce, pp. 158–166 (1999)
16. Sethi, K.K., Ramesh, D.: HFIM: a spark-based hybrid frequent itemset mining algorithm for big data processing. J. Supercomput. **73**, 1–17 (2017)
17. Wang, G., Xu, J., He, B.: A novel method for tuning configuration parameters of spark based on machine learning. In: IEEE International Conference on High PERFORMANCE Computing and Communications; IEEE International Conference on Smart City; IEEE International Conference on Data Science and Systems, pp. 586–593 (2017)

18. Wang, K., Khan, M.M.H.: Performance prediction for apache spark platform. In: IEEE International Conference on High PERFORMANCE Computing and Communications, 2015 IEEE International Symposium on Cyberspace Safety and Security, and 2015 IEEE International Conference on Embedded Software and Systems, pp. 166–173 (2015)
19. Winlaw, M., Hynes, M.B., Caterini, A., Sterck, H.D.: Algorithmic acceleration of parallel ALS for collaborative filtering: speeding up distributed big data recommendation in spark. In: IEEE International Conference on Parallel and Distributed Systems, pp. 682–691 (2016)
20. Xun, Y., Zhang, J., Qin, X., Zhao, X.: Fidoop-dp: data partitioning in frequent itemset mining on hadoop clusters. IEEE Trans. Parallel Distrib. Syst. **28**, 101–114 (2017)
21. Ye, Y., Chiang, C.C.: A parallel apriori algorithm for frequent itemsets mining. In: International Conference on Software Engineering Research, Management and Applications, pp. 87–94 (2006)
22. Yu, K.-M., Zhou, J., Hsiao, W.C.: Load balancing approach parallel algorithm for frequent pattern mining. In: Malyshkin, V. (ed.) PaCT 2007. LNCS, vol. 4671, pp. 623–631. Springer, Heidelberg (2007). https://doi.org/10.1007/978-3-540-73940-1_63
23. Zaharia, M., Chowdhury, M., Franklin, M.J., Shenker, S., Stoica, I.: Spark: cluster computing with working sets. In: Usenix Conference on Hot Topics in Cloud Computing, p. 10 (2010)
24. Zaharia, M., et al.: Apache spark: a unified engine for big data processing. Commun. ACM **59**(11), 56–65 (2016)
25. Zhang, D., Zhang, D., Zhang, D., Zhang, M., Chang, E.Y.: PFP: parallel FP-growth for query recommendation. In: ACM Conference on Recommender Systems, pp. 107–114 (2008)
26. Zhang, F., Liu, M., Gui, F., Shen, W., Shami, A., Ma, Y.: A distributed frequent itemset mining algorithm using spark for big data analytics. Cluster Comput. **18**(4), 1493–1501 (2015)
27. Zhou, L., Wang, X.: Research of the FP-growth algorithm based on cloud environments. J. Softw. **9**(3), 676 (2014)

Contextual-Field Supported Iterative Representation for Face Hallucination

Kangli Zeng[1], Tao Lu[1](✉) (iD), Xiaolin Li[1](✉), Yanduo Zhang[1], Li Peng[2], and Shenming Qu[3]

[1] Hubei Key Laboratory of Intelligent Robot, School of Computer Science and Engineering, Wuhan Institute of Technology, Wuhan 430205, China
lutxyl@gmail.com, 932233986@qq.com
[2] School of Computer Science and Technology,
Huazhong University of Science and Technology, Wuhan 430074, China
[3] School of Software, He'nan University, Kaifeng 475004, China

Abstract. Face hallucination is a special super-resolution (SR) algorithm that enhances the resolution and quality of low-resolution (LR) facial image. For reconstructing finer high frequency information which are missing in image degradation, learning-based face SR methods rely on accurate prior information from training samples. In this paper, we propose a contextual-field supported iterative representation algorithm for face hallucination to discovery accurate prior. Different from traditional local-patch based methods, we use contextual-field supported sampling to replace local receptive field patch sampling for enriching prior information. Then, two weighted matrices are introduced to constrain reconstruction-errors term and representation-coefficients term simultaneously, one matrix ameliorates the heteroscedasticity of real data and the other one improves the stability of solution. Finally, we use iterative representation learning to iteratively update the supported dictionary pairs and their representation-coefficients to refine accurate high-frequency information. The experimental results show that the proposed approach outperforms some state-of-the-art face hallucination methods over FERET and CMU-MIT face databases using both subjective and objective evaluation indexes.

Keywords: Face hallucination · Iterative representation
Contextual information · Dictionary learning

This work is supported by the National Natural Science Foundation of China (61502354, 61501413, 61671332, 41501505, U1404618), the Natural Science Foundation of Hubei Province of China (2018ZYYD059, 2015CFB451, 2014CFA130, 2012FFA099, 2012FFA134, 2013CF125), the Science and Technique Development Program of He'nan (172102210186), Scientific Research Foundation of Wuhan Institute of Technology (K201713), Graduate Education Innovation Foundation of Wuhan Institute of Technology (CX2017069, CX2017070).

J. Vaidya and J. Li (Eds.): ICA3PP 2018, LNCS 11336, pp. 534–546, 2018.
https://doi.org/10.1007/978-3-030-05057-3_40

1   Introduction

In scenario of video surveillance, face images are often in LR and poor image quality. Accurate recognition tasks with those LR face images are very challenge, there is an urgent need to improve the resolution and quality of LR face images. Face hallucination is a special kind of SR algorithm to reconstruct high-resolution (HR) images from one or multiple LR images, which has important applications in security monitoring, computer vision and other fields.

Recently, learning-based face SR which mainly learns the mapping relationship between HR and LR from training samples [9], which has attracted more and more attention from scholars. Because they showed strong advantages by generating details that can not be found in LR input from training samples. Considering the special characteristics of face images, Baker and Kanade [1] first proposed a learning-based face SR approach for reconstructing HR face images, which learned a prior on the distribution of image gradients from local patch level. Chang et al. used neighbourhood embedding method [2] to explore the accurate local prior by linear combination. Yang et al. first introduced sparse coding scheme [23] into SR algorithm to avoid the over-fitting problem. Assuming that the position patches share the similar geometry structure in the LR and HR spaces, Ma et al. [12] used position-patch to get accurate prior, which represent and reconstruct image patch position-by-position. Obviously, specific position-patch represents certain face semantic information, i.e., facial configuration. Jiang et al. [5] proposed a locality-constrained representation (LCR) scheme for face hallucination, which applied locality regularization to the least squares inversion problem and achieved sparsity and locality. Moreover, in order to improve the performance of accurate position-patch, they used an iterative version of LCR [6], which matched the interpolated LR image in HR space and achieved good results. Considering the accuracy of prior from patch, Zhang et al. [25,26] proposed an iterative collaborative representation SR algorithm, which iteratively improved the visual results by multi-layer scheme. Timofte et al. [19,20] employed regression-based methods for transforming the input LR patches into HR ones. Shi et al. [18] proposed two novel regularization models to deal with LR face hallucination problem in high-resolution feature space. Then, weighted representations [21,24], context-patch [7], low-rank constraints [10,11] have made impressive results.

On the other hand, deep learning based approaches has been proposed for SR [3,4,8]. Cui et al. [3] proposed a deep network cascaded (DNC) enhancement to the perform SR tasks. Dong et al. [4] first used convolution neural network (SRCNN) to learn the mapping functions from LR to HR by an end-to-end manner. Kim et al. [8] further increased network depth by residual network. Although above mentioned deep-learning based approaches providers new paradigms for image SR task. The end-to-end "black box" mapping model and stochastic gradient optimization cannot provide a clear physical interpretation of SR process which limit their further improvement.

Although above algorithms achieve excellent SR performance, for the sake of accuracy prior, iterative scheme always brings refining function of solution which benefits better reconstruction performance [16]. From this point, we propose a simple but effective contextual-field supported iterative representation for face hallucination in this paper. We interpolate LR images into the same size as the HR ones. Then contextual patch is sampled to enrich prior with a larger contextual-field. Reconstruction-errors and representation-coefficients terms are weighted simultaneously for precise prior. Thus we use the iterative framework to refine the high-frequency details of the reconstructed HR output. Here, the output of upper layer are treated as the input of the next layer. Finally, the residual learning algorithm is used to stitch the final image. The proposed method has obtained excellent subjective and objective SR performance.

For accurate prior information, some contributions are proposed through the following aspects. **First**, we use contextual-field to support a prior for contextual-patch which enriches its representation ability. **Second**, reconstruction-errors and representation-coefficients terms are simultaneously weighted to achieve the purpose of eliminating the heteroskedasticity of the original data and obtaining a more stable solution. **Third**, iterative representation learning is used to iteratively update the reconstructed residual patches to recover the missing high-frequency information for better visual effects.

2   Related Work

2.1   Notations

Let us define $\{A_i\}_{i=1}^N \in \Re^{p \times q}$ and $\{B_i\}_{i=1}^N \in \Re^{pt \times qt}$ as the LR and HR training face images, where t is the scale factor and N is the number of training sample. We assume that $Y \in \Re^{p \times q}$ is a LR input, and $y_i \in \Re^{d \times 1}$ (the patch size is $\sqrt{d} \times \sqrt{d}$ and they are represented by column vectors) is a LR patch. Therefore, the corresponding reconstructed HR image is $X \in \Re^{pt \times qt}$, and the HR image patch is $x_i \in \Re^{(d \times t^2) \times 1}$.

2.2   Face Hallucination Based on Least Squares

Assuming we have already learned the HR and LR dictionary pairs D_i^H and D_i^L, y_i represents one patch in a LR image, the optimal weight can be solved by the following constrained least square fitting problem [13]:

$$\alpha_i^* = \arg\min_{\alpha_i} \left\{ \|y_i - D_i^L \alpha_i\|_2^2 \right\}. \tag{1}$$

Because Eq. (1) is a convex optimization function, it has an analytical solution:

$$\alpha_i^* = \left((D_i^L)^T D_i^L \right)^{-1} (D_i^L)^T y_i. \tag{2}$$

In the image super-resolution scene, according to the manifold consistency assumption, the corresponding HR patch and LR patch have the same representation coefficients. Therefore, the weighted coefficients of the LR patches can be mapped onto the HR patch dictionary and the reconstructed HR patch can be obtained:

$$x_i = D_i^H \alpha_i^*. \tag{3}$$

After each input LR patch is rebuilt, the final HR image X can be generated from x_i by averaging pixel values of overlapped regions according to the original position.

3 Contextual-Field Supported Iterative Representation (CSIR)

3.1 Context Dictionary Learning

Different from traditional position-based patch methods, we use context-patch [15] to get the priori of the image representation. An illustration is shown in Fig. 1. We take the i−th position patch of the same image, and the context increases the local receptive field through its local area to enrich the context information. The position-based patch method only takes its fixed position patch, ignoring the prior information provided by the local area. As shown in Fig. 1 that the local receptive field of context-patch is much larger than that of position-based patch method.

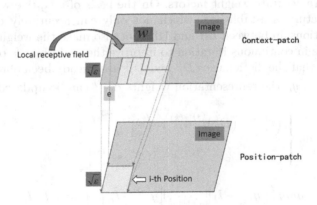

Fig. 1. Comparison of local receptive fields provided by position-patch and context-patch. Contextual-field supports more receptive areas than position-patch.

Let us define context window size is $w \times w$, patch size is $\sqrt{d} \times \sqrt{d}$. In this larger window (window size greater than or equal to patch size), we use the step length e to sample multiple patches, the number of context patches c can be obtained by:

$$c = \begin{cases} \left(1 + \dfrac{w - \sqrt{d}}{e}\right)^2 &, w > \sqrt{d} \text{ (context - patch)} \\ \\ 1 &, w = \sqrt{d} \text{ (position - patch)} \end{cases} \tag{4}$$

From the upper form, we can see that as the size of the window size w increases, the number of patches will increase exponentially. Therefore, these patches provide more contextual information.

After taking the patches from the context, we can get the HR and LR contextual dictionary pool $C_i^H = [c_1^H, c_2^H, \cdots, c_{c\times N}^H] \in \Re^{(d\times t^2)\times(c\times N)}$ and $C_i^L = [c_1^L, c_2^L, \cdots, c_{c\times N}^L] \in \Re^{(d\times t^2)\times(c\times N)}$ corresponding to i−th patch (LR is used for representation and HR is used for reconstruction). Here, we interpolate LR into the same size as HR.

Since LR and HR images have the same information to a large extent, the modeling and analysis of their residual images is helpful for the reconstruction task, because it shows the differences between the HR and the LR. Therefore, Therefore, we not only use contextual information but also use residual learning to perform better. The contextual information residual dictionary is $R_i = C_i^H - C_i^L$. Therefore, C_i^L and R_i are used as a representation dictionary and a reconstruction dictionary, respectively.

3.2   Face Hallucination via CSIR

Inspired by deep learning, we develop a method of contextual-field supported iterative representation for face hallucination. The model of we propose is mainly to obtain more accurate weight factors. On the basis of adaptive weighting, an iterative structure is established, which not only can accurately describe the mapping relationship between LR and HR, but also make the weight coefficient more accurate in continuous iteration to improve the performance of the CSIR.

Assuming that the dictionaries D_i^L and D_i^H has already been obtained, given the input patch y_i, the representation weights $\alpha_i^{*(s)}$ can be updated by:

$$
\alpha_i^{*(s)} = \arg\min_{\alpha_i^{(s)}} \left\{ \begin{array}{c} \left(y_i^{(s)} - (D_i^L)^{(s)} \alpha_i^{(s)} \right)^T \left(\Phi_i^{(s)} \right)^{-1} \left(y_i^{(s)} - (D_i^L)^{(s)} \alpha_i^{(s)} \right) \\ + \lambda \left\| \Omega_i^{(s)} \bullet \alpha_i^{(s)} \right\|_2^2 \end{array} \right\}, \quad (5)
$$

where $\Omega_i^{(s)} = diag\left(\left\| y_i^{(s)} - l_1 \right\|_2, \cdots, \left\| y_i^{(s)} - l_K \right\|_2 \right)$ and $l_1, l_2, \cdots, l_K$ is the atom in $(D_i^L)^{(s)}$. And we define the reconstruction error as $\sigma_i = y_i - D_i^L \alpha_i$, and their variance $var\left(\sigma_i \middle| D_i^L \right) = \Phi_i$. And Φ_i are independent variables that determines the particular heteroskedasticity and $\Phi_i = diag\left(\left\| \sigma_i \right\| \right)$.

Given a LR image, after interpolation, get the i−th position patch. We find K nearest neighbor patches from C_i^L using $K - NN$ clustering. The $K - NN$ index of the y_i is defined as:

$$
C_K(y_i) = \sup port(dist|_K), \quad (6)
$$

where the $dist|_K$ denotes the smallest K entries of $dist$ and $dist_i = \|y_i - l_j\|_2$. Here $dist$ is a distance metric between y_i and the k−th dictionary atom l_j from LR patch pool C_i^L, we use Euclidean distance in this paper. When the K nearest neighbor patches in the LR dictionary D_i^L is ready, we use index to learn the corresponding residual dictionary D_i^H from R_i.

According to the following formulate, we can obtain the iterative weight coefficient,

$$\alpha_i^{*(s)} = \left\{ \left[\left(D_i^L\right)^{(s)} \right]^T \left(\Phi_i^{(s)}\right)^{-1} \left(D_i^L\right)^{(s)} + \lambda \left(\Omega_i^{(s)}\right)^T \Omega_i^{(s)} \right\} \left[\left(D_i^L\right)^{(s)} \right]^T \left(\Phi_i^{(s)}\right)^{-1} y_i^{(s)}. \tag{7}$$

In our model, the main idea is to get the exact weight coefficient, so the SR problem can be effectively solved and improved in an iterative way. We set the initial input to the interpolated version of the test LR patch. Then, we use the following steps to solve iteratively:

Updating $\left(D_i^L\right)^{(s)}$, $\left(D_i^H\right)^{(s)}$, $\Phi_i^{(s)}$ and $\Omega_i^{(s)}$: we find the K neighborhood patches cluster $\left(D_i^L\right)^{(s)}$ and $\left(D_i^H\right)^{(s)}$ from C_i^L and R_i. And calculating $\Phi_i^{(s)}$ and $\Omega_i^{(s)}$ by,

$$\Phi_i^{(s)} = diag(\left\| \sigma_i^{(s-1)} \right\|), \text{ s.t } \sigma_i^{(s-1)} = y_i^{(s-1)} - \left(D_i^L\right)^{(s-1)} \alpha_i^{(s-1)}, \tag{8}$$

$$\Omega_i^{(s)} = diag \left(\left\| y_i^{(s-1)} - l_1 \right\|_2, \cdots, \left\| y_i^{(s-1)} - l_K \right\|_2 \right). \tag{9}$$

Updating $\alpha_i^{*(s)}$: calculate $\alpha_i^{*(s)}$ according to the following formula,

$$\alpha_i^{*(s)} = \left\{ \left[\left(D_i^L\right)^{(s-1)} \right]^T \left(\Phi_i^{(s-1)}\right)^{-1} \left(D_i^L\right)^{(s-1)} + \lambda \left(\Omega_i^{(s-1)}\right)^T \Omega_i^{(s-1)} \right\} \\ \left[\left(D_i^L\right)^{(s-1)} \right]^T \left(\Phi_i^{(s-1)}\right)^{-1} y_i^{(s-1)}. \tag{10}$$

Updating $x_i^{*(s)}$: the residual patch $x_i^{*(s)}$ is reconstructed with $\left(D_i^H\right)^{(s)}$ and $\alpha_i^{*(s)}$ and $x_i^{*(s)} = y_i^{(s+1)}$,

$$x_i^{*(s)} = R_i^{(s)} \alpha_i^{(s)}. \tag{11}$$

Therefore, we use the following formula to find the reconstructed HR image:

$$X = \sum_{i=1}^{M} \left\{ R_i^{(s)} \alpha_i^{(s)} + y_i^* \right\}, \tag{12}$$

where y_i^* is the interpolated version of the tested LR y_i.

4   Experimental Results

4.1   Database

The experiments are conducted on the FERET face databases [14] for demonstrating the performance of the proposed method. The FERET database contains 1400 images from 200 subjects and each subject has seven different images,

including a frontal image, two left sides, two right sides and two expressive images
(Fig. 2). In this experiment, 400 images were randomly selected, and two subjects were selected from all subjects. The size of the sample face image is 80 × 80
pixels. All of the 400 images, we randomly selected 360 images (including 180
subjects) as training samples and the remaining 40 as test images. So all test
images are not in the training sample. The LR image is formed by smoothing
(by a 4 × 4 size average filter) and down sampling (by a factor of 4) from a corresponding HR image. In this paper, we interpolate all LR images to the same
size as HR.

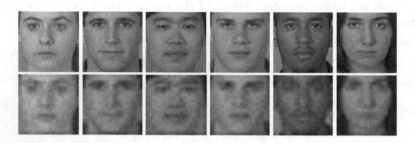

Fig. 2. Some training faces in FERET face database (The first row is the HR image,
and the second row is the LR image.).

4.2   Parameter Settings

In this experiment, we adjusted all parameters of the proposed method to obtain
better results. We set the patch size of the HR image to 12 × 12 pixels, and the
overlap between adjacent patches is 4 pixels, then the patch size in the LR image
is 3 × 3 pixels and the overlap is 1 pixel (the down-sampling factor is 4). For the
window size w of the context information patch and the number of iterations m
will be discussed and analyzed as follows:

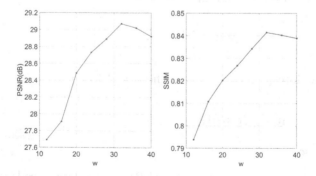

Fig. 3. Performance of face reconstruction with different values of window size (w) on
the FERET dataset.

The Window Size w of the Context Information Patch: We select the window size w of different context information patches to test the performance of our method, which controls the amount of priori information provided. As shown in Fig. 3, we can clearly see that with the increase of w, more benefits can be obtained. This means that context information is important for image reconstruction. Because it can provide more prior knowledge than position patches. However, as can be seen from Fig. 3, setting w too large will degrade the performance of the algorithm. Therefore, choosing the appropriate context window $w = 32$, the proposed algorithm can achieve better results.

The Number of Iterations s: Moreover, in order to test the effect of the number of iterations s, we give the performance of CSIR with different iterations s. As shown in Fig. 4, we plot the average PSNR and SSIM [22] for all test images. We found: (i) as the number of iterations s increases, the gain of the proposed method is significantly increased, which means that increasing the high frequency information by iteration is very important for improving the performance of the algorithm; (ii) The proposed method needs to iterate several times to achieve convergence, i.e. the number of iterations for our experiments is set to 30, which means there is a lot of room for improvement in obtaining more a priori information.

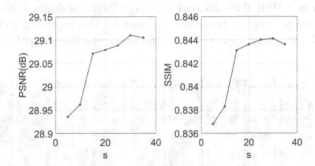

Fig. 4. The influence of different the number of iterations s on the proposed CSIR method.

4.3   Analysis of Proposed Models

In this section, our approach will be compared with several typical face hallucination method, including LSR [13], WASR [21], LLE [2], LCR [5], CLNE [6], RMHF [18], TLCR [7], SRCNN [4] and VDSR [8]. All of the comparison methods are set to the best performance. PSNR and SSIM are used to evaluate the qualitatively of facia image hallucination. The higher the value of PSNR and SSIM, the better the performance of the reconstruction.

As shown in Table 1, we compare PSNR and SSIM of different face hallucination methods. Both LCR and CLNE use position-patch method. Compared with our method, the PSNR of our method is higher than LCR and CLNE 0.94 dB

Table 1. Comparison of PSNR and SSIM for different face hallucination methods.

| Method | LSR | WSR | LLE | LCR | CLNE | RMHF | TLCR | CSIR | Remove border | | |
									SRCNN	VDSR	CSIR
PSNR	26.88	27.77	27.92	28.17	28.38	28.57	28.85	29.11	29.04	29.25	29.45
SSIM	0.7485	0.7933	0.8019	0.8156	0.8217	0.8273	0.8351	0.8441	0.8401	0.8465	0.8479

and 0.73 dB, SSIM is higher than LCR and CLNE 0.0285 and 0.0224, respectively. This fully shows that context information patches can provide more useful prior information. Moreover, CLNE and CSIR both use the iterative structure to improve the performance of the algorithm by continuously updating the representation coefficients. Due to the establishment of regularization models in different spaces, CSIR performs better than RMHF in reconstruction performance. Although TLCR and CSIR both use context information patches, CSIR combines contextual information and residual learning to make prior knowledge more accurate than TLCR. In order to be able to make fair comparison, we have also done the remove edge processing when compared with the deep learning method. Compared with VDSR, CSIR has many similarities with it, such as residual learning and deep structure. However, our deep structure and deep learning structure are different. And the PSNR and SSIM of our algorithm are still higher than VDSR 0.20 dB and 0.0014. CSIR combines context residual learning with deep iterative structure to improve the representation ability of the image and effectively improve the performance of the algorithm.

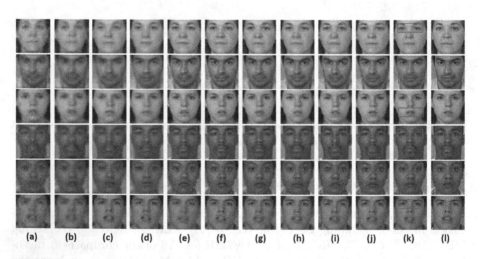

Fig. 5. Some visualized hallucination with different methods on FERET database. From left to right: (a) input, (b) LSR [13], (c) WASR [21], (d) LLE [2], (e) LCR [5], (f) CLNE [6], (g) RMHF [18], (h) TLCR [7], (i) SRCNN [4], (j) VDSR [8], (k) ours and (l) Original HR image.

Some visualized hallucination are shown in Fig. 5. It can be clearly seen that LSR and WSR has obvious fuzziness in the details of the face. CLNE, LCR and other position-based super-resolution methods have many noises in the eyes, nose, mouth and other parts, so that the face contour is not clear. CSIR can overcome the problem of alignment before using the position-patch, and the facial contour is clearer than the position-based method. Because CSIR introduces residual learning to better recover high-frequency information, it performs better than TLCR. Compared to the deep learning method (SRCNN, VDSR), although there is little difference between PSNR and SSIM, it can be seen from the results of the reconstruction that the methods we propose are clearer in the eyes, nose and other parts. The eleventh column is the hallucination HR face image we proposed, and we can see that CSIR is superior to all comparison methods and produces reasonable results with more facial details.

4.4 Experiments on the Real-World Images

In this section, we tested our proposed method on CMU-MIT face database [17] and use FERET database as training set. As shown in Fig. 6, we have selected the test images on the CMU-MIT database. For face images in real scenes, the image degradation process can not be simply obtained by adding fuzzy and down sampling to the corresponding HR images. Since the FERET database only contains face images and don't have other background patterns, we need to preprocess the CMU-MIT database. We manually tailor face images to the actual scene images and adjust them to 80 × 80 pixels. Figure 7 shows the results of super-resolution reconstruction of different methods. It can be clearly seen that CSIR not only can produce reasonable results of the face hallucination, but also handle the noise well, which fully demonstrates the effectiveness of our method.

Fig. 6. These images used for testing in the CMU-MIT database.

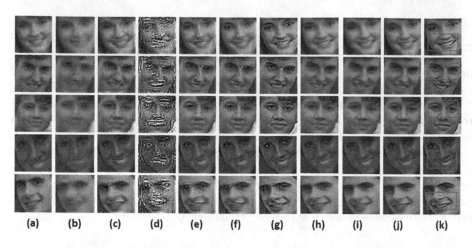

(a)   (b)   (c)   (d)   (e)   (f)   (g)   (h)   (i)   (j)   (k)

Fig. 7. The hallucination results of different methods are in CMU-MIT. From left to right: (a) input, (b) LSR [13], (c) WASR [21], (d) LLE [2], (e) LCR [5], (f) CLNE [6], (g) RMHF [18], (h) TLCR [7], (i) SRCNN [4], (j) VDSR [8] and (k) ours.

5 Conclusion

In this paper, we propose a new face hallucination via contextual-field supported iterative representation. For better image representation, we not only increase the local perception area through the context in order to obtain the useful prior information, but also weight the reconstruction error and use the weighted Tikhonov regularization constraint. Furthermore, we update reconstructed HR images iteratively so as to obtain a more accurate weight coefficient matrix and improve the performance of the algorithm. At the same time, residual dictionary learning is used to obtain high frequency information and achieve fast convergence. The results show that the proposed algorithm not only can effectively study the mapping relationship between HR and LR, but also overcome most of the noise and have robustness.

References

1. Baker, S., Kanade, T.: Hallucinating faces. In: Proceedings of IEEE International Conference on Automatic Face and Gesture Recognition 2000, p. 83 (2002)
2. Chang, H., Yeung, D., Xiong, Y.: Super-resolution through neighbor embedding. Proc. Comput. Vis. Pattern Recogn. **1**, I-275–I-282 (2004)
3. Cui, Z., Chang, H., Shan, S., Zhong, B., Chen, X.: Deep network cascade for image super-resolution. In: Fleet, D., Pajdla, T., Schiele, B., Tuytelaars, T. (eds.) ECCV 2014. LNCS, vol. 8693, pp. 49–64. Springer, Cham (2014). https://doi.org/10.1007/978-3-319-10602-1_4
4. Dong, C., Chen, C.L., He, K., Tang, X.: Image super-resolution using deep convolutional networks. IEEE Trans. Pattern Anal. Mach. Intell. **38**(2), 295–307 (2016)

5. Jiang, J., Hu, R., Han, Z., Lu, T., Huang, K.: Position-patch based face hallucination via locality-constrained representation. In: IEEE International Conference on Multimedia and Expo, pp. 212–217 (2012)
6. Jiang, J., Hu, R., Wang, Z., Han, Z., Ma, J.: Facial image hallucination through coupled-layer neighbor embedding. IEEE Trans. Circuits Syst. Video Technol. **26**(9), 1674–1684 (2016)
7. Jiang, J., Yu, Y., Tang, S., Ma, J., Qi, G.J., Aizawa, A.: Context-patch based face hallucination via thresholding locality-constrained representation and reproducing learning. In: IEEE International Conference on Multimedia and Expo, pp. 469–474 (2017)
8. Kim, J., Lee, J.K., Lee, K.M.: Accurate image super-resolution using very deep convolutional networks, pp. 1646–1654 (2015)
9. Liu, C., Shum, H.Y., Freeman, W.T.: Face Hallucination: Theory and Practice. Kluwer Academic Publishers, Dordrecht (2007)
10. Lu, T., Guan, Y., Chen, D., Xiong, Z., He, W.: Low-rank constrained collaborative representation for robust face recognition. In: IEEE International Workshop on Multimedia Signal Processing, pp. 1–7 (2017)
11. Lu, T., Xiong, Z., Zhang, Y., Wang, B., Lu, T.: Robust face super-resolution via locality-constrained low-rank representation. IEEE Access **5**(99), 13103–13117 (2017)
12. Ma, X., Huang, H., Wang, S., Qi, C.: A simple approach to multiview face hallucination. IEEE Signal Process. Lett. **17**(6), 579–582 (2010)
13. Ma, X., Zhang, J., Qi, C.: Hallucinating face by position-patch. Pattern Recogn. **43**(6), 2224–2236 (2010)
14. Phillips, P., Moon, H., Rizvi, S., Rauss, P.: The feret evaluation methodology for face-recognition algorithms. IEEE Trans. Pattern Anal. Mach. Intell. **22**(10), 1090–1104 (2000)
15. Romano, Y., Elad, M.: Con-patch: when a patch meets its context. IEEE Trans. Image Process. Publ. IEEE Signal Process. Soc. **25**(9), 3967–3978 (2016)
16. Romano, Y., Isidoro, J., Milanfar, P.: RAISR: rapid and accurate image super resolution. IEEE Trans. Comput. Imaging **3**(1), 110–125 (2017). https://doi.org/10.1109/TCI.2016.2629284
17. Rowleys, H.: Neural network-based face detection. IEEE Trans. Pattern Anal. Mach. Intell. **20**(1), 23–38 (1998)
18. Shi, J., Liu, X., Zong, Y., Qi, C., Zhao, G.: Hallucinating face image by regularization models in high-resolution feature space. IEEE Trans. Image Process. **PP**(99), 1 (2018)
19. Timofte, R., De, V., Gool, L.V.: Anchored neighborhood regression for fast example-based super-resolution. In: IEEE International Conference on Computer Vision, pp. 1920–1927 (2013)
20. Timofte, R., De Smet, V., Van Gool, L.: A+: adjusted anchored neighborhood regression for fast super-resolution. In: Cremers, D., Reid, I., Saito, H., Yang, M.-H. (eds.) ACCV 2014. LNCS, vol. 9006, pp. 111–126. Springer, Cham (2015). https://doi.org/10.1007/978-3-319-16817-3_8
21. Wang, Z., Hu, R., Wang, S., Jiang, J.: Face hallucination via weighted adaptive sparse regularization. IEEE Trans. Circuits Syst. Video Technol. **24**(5), 802–813 (2014)
22. Wang, Z., Bovik, A., Sheikh, H., Simoncelli, E.: Image quality assessment: from error visibility to structural similarity. IEEE Trans. Image Process **13**(4), 600–612 (2004)

23. Yang, J., Wright, J., Huang, T.S., Ma, Y.: Image super-resolution via sparse representation. IEEE Trans. Image Process. **19**(11), 2861–2873 (2010)
24. Yang, Z., He, P.: Non-local diffusion weighted image super-resolution using collaborative joint information. Exp. Ther. Med. **15**(1), 217–225 (2018)
25. Zhang, Y., et al.: Collaborative representation cascade for single-image super-resolution. IEEE Trans. Syst. Man Cybern. Syst. **PP**(99), 1–16 (2017)
26. Zhang, Y., Zhang, Y., Zhang, J., Wang, H., Dai, Q.: Single image super-resolution via iterative collaborative representation. In: Ho, Y.-S., Sang, J., Ro, Y.M., Kim, J., Wu, F. (eds.) PCM 2015. LNCS, vol. 9315, pp. 63–73. Springer, Cham (2015). https://doi.org/10.1007/978-3-319-24078-7_7

A Cancelable Multi-Biometric Template Generation Algorithm Based on Bloom Filter

Lin You[✉] and Xun Li

College of Communication Engineering, Hangzhou Dianzi University,
Hangzhou 310018, China
mryoulin@gmail.com

Abstract. For the security issue of multiple biometric templates in current multi-biometric systems, this paper proposes a cancelable multi-biometric template generation algorithm based on Bloom filter. Our algorithm uses the XOR operation to fuse the grouped fingerprint binary features and the face binary features into one template at the feature level, then transforms the fusion template based on the irreversibility of the Bloom filter. The cancelability and diversity of the fusion template can be achieved by updating the random matrix. Finally, a traversal matching method is used to calculate the matching score in the encryption domain. The experimental results show that our algorithm can ensure the reliability of the identity authentication and improve the security of the multi-biometric template.

Keywords: Bloom filter · Fingerprint feature · Face feature
Template protection

1 Introduction

Multi-biometric recognition technology can bring a more secure and reliable identity authentication [1]. However, there always exist some security risks in biometric-based identification systems. Due to the uniqueness and invariability of human biometrics, once the biometric template is exposed, it is compromised forever. Another problem is that cross-matching across different applications can easily covertly track the user in biometric systems. Especially for the multi-biometric recognition system that stores multiple biometric template information of the same user, the loss of the templates is more harmful to the user's privacy.

To improve the security of biometric templates, Ratha et al. [2] indicated that the ideal biometric template protection scheme should have diversity, cancelability, and irreversibility besides the accuracy of the authentication. Since

This research is partially supported by the National Science Foundation of China (No. 61772166, 61272045) and the Key Program of the Nature Science Foundation of Zhejiang province of China (No. LZ17F020002).

ⓒ Springer Nature Switzerland AG 2018
J. Vaidya and J. Li (Eds.): ICA3PP 2018, LNCS 11336, pp. 547–559, 2018.
https://doi.org/10.1007/978-3-030-05057-3_41

then, more and more biometric template protection schemes have been proposed. However, most of the existed biometric protection schemes are proposed for single biometric template. Such schemes can be used to protect multi-biometric template separately in multi-biometric systems, but the security of these solutions is worse than the security of fusing multiple biometric templates into one encrypted template [3]. In addition, the cancelability of multi-biometric template is also a major challenge. How to effectively protect multi-biometric template and achieve cancelable multi-biometric template is an urgent problem in multi-biometric recognition systems.

In this work, we employ the Bloom filter in biometric templates protection and propose a cancelable multi-biometric template generation algorithm. We design a grouping combination method and use an XOR operation to fuse both the binary fingerprint features and the binary face features into one template at the feature level. The fusion template is transformed by using Bloom filter. Using our feature level fusion method can make the entire multi-biometric template cancelable by updating the random matrix, and the irreversibility of the Bloom filter mapping in our algorithm will ensure the security of the multi-biometric template.

The rest of this paper is organized as following: Sect. 2 reviews some related work on biometric template protection based on Bloom filter. Section 3 describes our proposed algorithm in detail. Section 4 describes the experimental results. Section 5 analyzes the security of our algorithm. Finally, concluding remarks are drawn in Sect. 6.

2   Related Work

The Bloom filter was first applied by Rathgeb et al. [4] in biometric template protection. The authors proposed an alignment-free cancelable iris biometric templates scheme which adapted a standard Bloom filter to an adaptive Bloom filter. Additionally, they combined and implemented the Bloom filter's idea of protecting biometric templates with iris features from both eyes of a single subject, which ensured the diversity of multi-biometric template to some extent [5]. Subsequently, the authors summed up the previous work and proposed a generic framework for the protection of multi-biometric template [6], which can fuse different biometric features at the feature level. They used the face and iris as a case to implement the framework, but this framework did not indicate how the final fusion template can be cancelable and updated.

Based on the work of the Rathgeb et al., Gomez-Barrero et al. [7] used Bloom filter to encrypt and compress face binary features. Li et al. [8] proposed a fingerprint protection scheme based on Bloom filter and achieved cancelability. But their scheme required to select appropriate reference minutiae, while the change of the reference minutiae position may cause the associated errors which can degrade the recognition performance. Stokkennes et al. [9] proposed a multi-biometric template protection scheme based on Bloom filter at the mobile terminal which fused face features and the eyes periocular regions features by using weighted score level fusion. Sadhya et al. [10] made XOY on the biometrics transformed by the Bloom filter with a *Key* (a random (0,1) matrix) to ensure the cancelability of the templates. But this scheme heavily relied on the *Key*. Once the *Key* is compromised, the original biometrics encrypted by the Bloom filter will be exposed and the unlinkability between the templates cannot be effectively ensured.

3   Proposed Algorithm

3.1   Binary Feature Extraction

Fingerprint Binary Feature Extraction. To obtain the fingerprint binary features, we adopt a general method named the array mapping [11–13], which can map the relative distance and direction difference of the minutiae on the 2D array. The specific implementation method is as follows:

Extract the minutiae $M = \{m_i = (x_i, y_i, \theta_i) | i = 1, \ldots, N_M\}$ from the fingerprint image. Here, x_i, y_i, and θ_i respectively represent the x-coordinate value, the y-coordinate value, and the direction of the i-th minutiae m_i. And N_M is the number of minutiae. Use Eqs. (1) and (2) to calculate the relative distance d_{rk} and the direction difference θ_{rk} between m_r and m_k ($m_k \in M \backslash \{m_r\}, k = 1, \ldots, N_M - 1$). Repeat the above method for $k = 1$ to $N_M - 1$, we can obtain a new set of features (d_{rk}, θ_{rk}) of reference minutiae m_r.

$$d_{rk} = \sqrt{(x_r - x_k)^2 + (y_r - y_k)^2} \tag{1}$$

$$\theta_{rk} = |\theta_r - \theta_k| \tag{2}$$

Create a 2D array to map the new features. The 2D array model is shown in Fig. 1, where C_X^M and C_Y^M are the length and width of cell, respectively. M_X and M_Y are the length and width of the 2D array, respectively. The new features (d_{rk}, θ_{rk}) can be mapped on the 2D array using Eq. (3), where $\lceil . \rceil$ represents the ceil function. x_{rk}^T and y_{rk}^T are the cell index of the k-th new feature on the horizontal axis M_X and the vertical axis M_Y, respectively. To fix the number of the new features (d_{rk}, θ_{rk}) mapped on the 2D array each time, the extracted (d_{rk}, θ_{rk}) are sorted by d_{rk} from the largest to the smallest. Only the first a new features can be mapped on the 2D array. The specific method is as follows:

$$\begin{pmatrix} x_{rk}^T \\ y_{rk}^T \end{pmatrix} = \begin{pmatrix} \lceil d_{rk}/C_X^M \rceil \\ \lceil \theta_{rk}/C_Y^M \rceil \end{pmatrix} \tag{3}$$

If there are points in the cell, set the value of the cell to 1; otherwise, set the value of the cell to 0. Read the 2D array from left to right and form top to bottom to obtain a set of binary features f_r^M of m_r, where f_r^M is a binary sequence of length N_T. N_T is equal to the total number of the cells in the 2D array and it can be divided by t, where t is an integer not equal to 0.

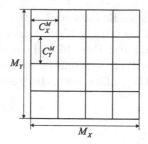

Fig. 1. The 2D array model

Let the minutiae in the set $M\backslash\{m_r\}$ be used as reference minutiae one after another, and repeat the same method as m_r to obtain the binary features $F^M = \{f_i^M | i = 1, \ldots, N_M\}$ of the fingerprint image, where f_i^M is the binary features of m_i. According to the above processing method, the binary features size of the fingerprint image is $N_M \times N_T$.

Face Binary Features Extraction. The basic idea of BioHashing [14] is to product the user's biometric vector $X \in \mathbb{R}^\Gamma$ and the random matrix $R \in \mathbb{R}^{\Gamma' \times \Gamma}$ in the user's identity token, that is to calculate $X' = RX$ to obtain $X' = \{x_n | n = 1, \ldots, \Gamma'\}$, where Γ is the biometric dimension and $\Gamma' \leq \Gamma$.

$$x_n' = \begin{cases} 0 , & x_n \leq \tau \\ 1 , & x_n > \tau \end{cases} \quad n = 1, \ldots, \Gamma' \tag{4}$$

Quantize the elements in X' to obtain a binary value x_n' using the preset threshold τ and Eq. (4). Finally, the purpose of the identity authentication is achieved by comparing the binary sequences. Applying this method to the face image, we can obtain the face binary features F^P. The specific method is as follows:

Extract the first N_P dimension PCA features $P = \{p_j | j = 1, \ldots, N_P\}$ of the face image, where $N_P = N_T/t$. Generate a random matrix $R \in \mathbb{R}^{N_P \times N_P}$. Where R obeys the standard normal distribution, namely, $R \sim N(0,1)$. By using BioHashing algorithm, we can obtain the cancelable binary features $F^P = \{f_j^P | j = 1, \ldots, N_P\}$ of the face images. Where $f_j^P \in \{0,1\}$ and the binary features size of the face image is $1 \times N_P$.

3.2 Feature Level Fusion Method

Divide the processed fingerprint binary features f_i^M into t groups, each group is denoted as v_{iz}, $z = 1, \ldots, t$. For $z = 1$ to t, do XOY operation as follows:

$$g_{iz} = v_{iz} \oplus F^P \tag{5}$$

where v_{iz} is of length N_P and "$\oplus$" is a bitwise XOR operation. The meaning of Eq. (5) is to perform the XOR operation between each group of fingerprint binary features and face binary features, so as to obtain the fusion features g_{iz} of the z-th group binary features of the i-th fingerprint minutiae and the face binary features, where g_{iz} is a binary sequence of length N_P. The fusion features of the binary features of the i-th fingerprint minutiae and the face features can be denoted as $f_i^U = \{g_{iz}|z = 1,\ldots,t\}$.

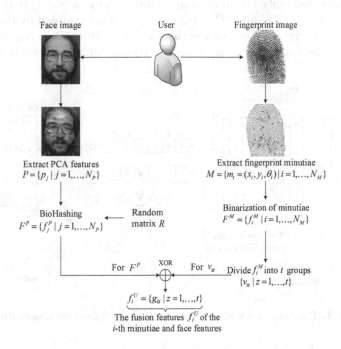

Fig. 2. The fusion framework of fingerprint and face features

The fusion feature template $F^U = \{f_i^U|i = 1,\ldots,N_M\}$ of the fingerprint image and the face image can be obtained by repeating the above method for the binary features of the remaining fingerprint minutiae. The size of F^U is $N_M \times N_P \times t = N_M \times N_T$, and it is the same size as that of the fingerprint binary features. The above described is the entire process of fusing fingerprint features and face features at the feature level. The framework is shown in Fig. 2.

3.3   Feature Mapping Based on Bloom Filter

A Bloom filter is a bit array of length N_B, where all bits are initially set to 0. The fusion features of fingerprint features and face features can be irreversibly mapped based on the Bloom filter. The detail procedures are as follows:

Transform f_i^U from top to bottom and left to right into a binary matrix FT_i of size $w \times l$, where $2^w \geq l$. Then, each column is transformed by Eq. (6), where

$$h(x) = \sum_{\lambda=0}^{w-1} x_\lambda 2^\lambda \tag{6}$$

x_λ is the λ-th element of the column, and the $h(x)$ means transforming each column of FT_i into a decimal. Set an initial Bloom filter b_i of length $N_B = 2^w$ with an index range of $[0, 2^{w-1}]$. According to the calculation result of Eq. (6), let $b_i[h(x)] = 1$. Namely, after each column is transformed into a decimal, its value on the corresponding index is set to 1 on b_i. The index values can be mapped multiple times, but only the first mapped index value is valid. Hence, we can obtain the cancelable template $B = \{b_i | i = 1, \ldots, N_M\}$ mapped by Bloom filter, where b_i is a binary sequence of length N_B. The size of B is $N_M \times N_B$. The framework of the feature mapping based on Bloom filter is shown in Fig. 3.

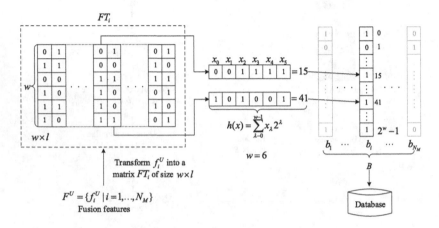

Fig. 3. The framework of the feature mapping based on Bloom filter

3.4   The Matching Method

Assume that for the user's registered fingerprint M^E, registered face P^E, query fingerprint M^Q and query face P^E, we use the same random matrix R to generate the registration fusion template $B^E = \{b_i^E | i = 1, \ldots, N_E\}$ and the query fusion template $B^Q = \{b_i^Q | i = 1, \ldots, N_Q\}$, respectively. Where N_E and N_Q are the number of the minutiae for the registered fingerprint and the query fingerprint, respectively. For the reason that the number of the extracted fingerprint minutiae is not fixed, the elements in B^Q required to be matched with the elements in B^E one by one. The matching method [11] is shown in Fig. 4, and their similar score $Score(B^E, B^Q)$ can be computed as follows:

Step 1: Calculate the distance score $dis(b_i^E, b_j^Q)$ and the similarity $SI(b_i^E, b_j^Q)$ between b_i^E and b_j^Q.

$$dis(b_i^E, b_j^Q) = \frac{||b_i^E - b_j^Q||_2}{||b_i^E||_2 + ||b_j^Q||_2} \tag{7}$$

$$SI(b_i^E, b_j^Q) = 1 - dis(b_i^E, b_j^Q) = 1 - \frac{||b_i^E - b_j^Q||_2}{||b_i^E||_2 + ||b_j^Q||_2} \tag{8}$$

where $||.||_2$ is a 2-norm and the range of $SI(b_i^E, b_j^Q)$ is $[0, 1]$.

Step 2: The similarity matrix $\overline{S} = \{SI_{ij}\}$ of B^E and B^Q can be obtained from Step 1, where $SI_{ij} = SI(b_i^E, b_j^Q)$. Take the maximum value of each row in the matrix $\overline{S}$ to obtain the maximum similarity set $SImax$.

$$SImax(j) = \max_i\{SI_{ij}\} \tag{9}$$

Calculate the mean $SImean$ of all elements in $SImax$.

$$SImean = \frac{\sum\limits_{j=1}^{N_Q} SImax(j)}{N_Q} \tag{10}$$

Step 3: Calculate the mean of all elements greater than $SImean$ in $SImax$ to obtain a matching score $Score(B^E, B^Q)$ for B^Q and B^E.

$$Score(B^E, B^Q) = \frac{\sum\limits_{\mu=1}^{N_S} S_\mu}{N_S} \tag{11}$$

where S_μ is an element in $SImax$ such that $S_\mu > SImean$ and N_S is the number of S_μ. If $Score(B^E, B^Q) \geq Th$, the authentication succeeds; otherwise, it fails. Where Th is the preset threshold.

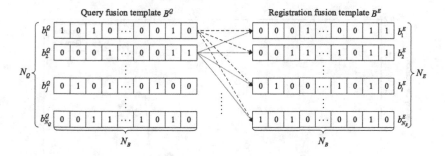

Fig. 4. The matching method

4   Experiments

To evaluate the performance of our algorithm, the simulation experiments will use the ORL face database and FVC2002-DB1 fingerprint database (DB1). Since the PCA feature extraction requires training images, we divide the image of each face sample in the ORL face database into two parts. The first 5 are training images and the last 5 are test images. We select the first 40 samples in DB1 to combine with the ORL to create a multi-biometric database DB1-ORL. There are 40 samples in the DB1-ORL multi-biometric database. Each sample has 5 fingerprint images, 5 face images, and a face image corresponds to a fingerprint image. The number of the images in the DB1-ORL is 400.

4.1   Performance Evaluation

Three performance indices are used for performance evaluation: GAR (Genuine Accept Rate), FAR (False Accept Rate), and EER (Equal Error Rate). In the experiment process, the first group of images in each sample of DB1-ORL is selected to generate registration fusion template, and the latter four groups of images are respectively generated query fusion templates. The number of the genuine attempts is 160 (40×4), and the number of the imposter attempts is 1560 (40×39).

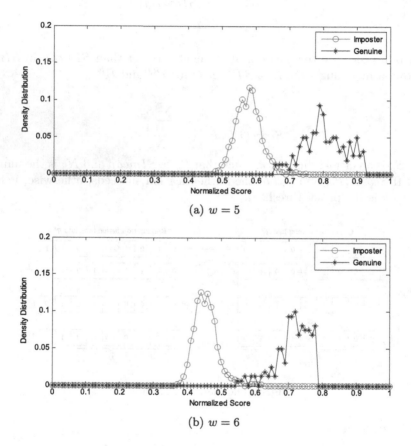

(a) $w = 5$

(b) $w = 6$

Fig. 5. Genuine and imposter distributions.

We extract the face features and the fingerprint features in the DB1-ORL database. The range of the fingerprint minutiae number N_M is $21 \sim 34$, the range of the relative distance d_{ik} is $0 \sim 300$, and the range of the direction difference θ_{ik} is $0 \sim 2\pi$. Hence, the first $a = 20$ (the largest integer less than 21) new features are selected to map on the 2D array with size $M_X \times M_Y = 300 \times 360$. Our experimental results will be more ideal when the cell size $C_X^M \times C_Y^M = 30 \times 30$, the threshold $\tau = 200$, the face features length $N_P = 60$ and the fingerprint grouping number $t = 2$. Hence, these parameters will be used in the following experiments. Figure 5 shows the genuine and imposter distributions when the fusion feature f_i^U is transformed into the binary matrix FT_i with the $w = 5$ or $w = 6$, respectively.

Table 1. Experimental results (GARs are obtained at FAR = 0%)

Parameter	Fusion template (bits)	GAR (%)	EER (%)
Without Bloom filter	$N_M \times 120$	96.25	0.39
$w = 6$	$N_M \times 64$	94.37	0.79
$w = 5$	$N_M \times 32$	81.25	1.27

Table 1 shows the experimental results of EER, GAR (FAR = 0%) and fusion template size in the case of $w = 5$, $w = 6$ and without Bloom filter mapping. For our algorithm performance, compared to the no Bloom filter mapping, the GAR at $w = 5$ is reduced by 15%. The reason for this decrease in performance is that the Bloom filter map loses some part of effective information. But the GAR of the fusion template mapped by the Bloom filter only decreases by 1.88% at $w = 6$, it shows that our algorithm still maintains a high recognition rate. For the size of the final template, it shows that after the Bloom filter mapping, the size of the fusion template is compressed. For the security of the final template, the irreversibility of the Bloom filter mapping improves the security of multi-biometric template while losing some part of effective information. For the overall performance of our algorithm, the EERs in the three cases are all less than 1.5%. It shows that our algorithm has good overall performance. Figure 6 shows the ROC curves of our algorithm at $w = 5$, $w = 6$ and without Bloom filter, respectively.

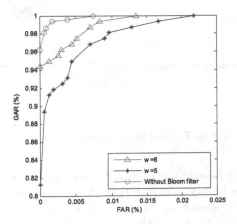

Fig. 6. ROC curves of our algorithm at $w = 5$, $w = 6$ and without Bloom filter

4.2   Cancelability of the Fusion Template

To measure the diversity and cancelability of the fusion template in our algorithm, we set up the experiment in this section: Generate 10 different random matrices $R_1, \ldots, R_{10}$. Each set of images for each sample in the DB1-ORL is represented by T, and T is combined with $R_1, \ldots, R_{10}$ to generate a corresponding fusion template $TR_1, \ldots, TR_{10}$, respectively. Set TR_1 is used as registration fusion template and $TR_2, \ldots, TR_{10}$ are used as query fusion template. Calculate the matching scores of $TR_2, \ldots, TR_{10}$ with TR_1 respectively, the experimental results are denoted as false imposter matches, the number of the false imposter attempts is 1800 (200×9).

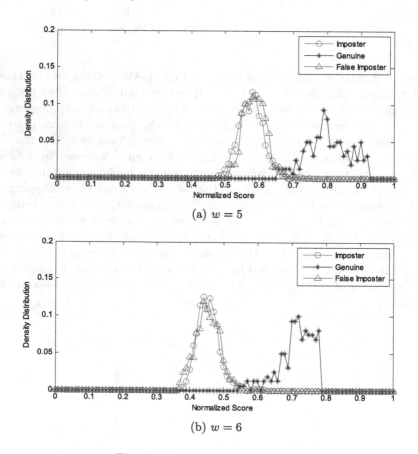

(a) $w = 5$

(b) $w = 6$

Fig. 7. False imposter distribution.

Figure 7 shows the false imposter distributions when the fusion feature f_i^U is transformed into the binary matrix FT_i with the row height $w = 5$ or $w = 6$, respectively. It can be seen that the normalized score distribution of the false imposter is very similar to that of the imposter. Hence, our algorithm can generate a new fusion template by updating the random matrix R when the user's fusion template is compromised. The template stolen by the attacker will no longer be able to impersonate the user's authentication through the system, and so our algorithm can ensure the reliability of the identity authentication and the security of the multi-biometric template.

4.3 Algorithm Performance Comparison

Table 2 shows the performance comparison between our algorithm and the existing multi-biometric template protection methods based on Bloom filter. The experimental results are the optimized data. Stokkenes et al. [9] extracted face features and the periocular regions features, and the weighted comparison score level fusion was applied to increase recognition accuracy in their work. Our algorithm extracts the fingerprint features and the face features, and fuses these two biometric features into one template at the feature level. As shown in Table 2, whether a Bloom filter mapping was applied or not, our algorithm is more accurate.

Table 2. Performance comparison with existing multi-biometric template protection based on Bloom filter

Algorithm	With Bloom filter	GAR (%)	FAR (%)	EER (%)
Stokkenes et al. [9]	No	95.95	0.01	1.12
	Yes	91.61	0.01	1.38
Proposed	No	96.25	0	0.39
	Yes	94.37	0	0.79

5   Security Analysis

Our algorithm proposes a grouping combination method and uses an XOR operation to fuse the binary fingerprint features and the binary face features into one template at the feature level. According to Eq. (5), if F^P is changed, then g_{iz} will be changed. In addition, F_P is required to be performed a bit-by-bit XOR operation with each group v_{iz} of each f_i^M to obtain g_{iz} in the feature fusion. When the user updates the random matrix R, F^P will be changed, and so that the entire fusion template will be updated. The advantages of the above biometric processing methods are as follows:

Diversity: When users register multiple accounts for different applications (PC or mobile) using the same biometrics, they can update R to obtain multiple multi-biometric templates and it ensures that the templates are unlinkable.

Cancelability: Once the user's multi-biometric template is found to be compromised, a new template can be generated immediately by updating R, and the compromised template can be immediately invalidated.

Irreversibility: According to our algorithm, we assume that there is a fusion template $F^U = \{f_i^U | i = 1, \ldots, N_M\}$ of fingerprint features and face features without Bloom filter mapping. Firstly, f_i^U is transformed into a binary matrix FT_i of size $w \times l$, then FT_i is mapped to b_i based on Bloom filter. The irreversibility of our algorithm lies in following:

On the one hand, FT_i transformed by f_i^U whose original position of each column will be hidden. In other words, it is hard to infer from the position of 1 on b_i that it is obtained by mapping which column of FT_i. Moreover, the high correlation between the biometric features strengthens the difficulty of this inverse operation. If the attacker can't invert the complete arrangement of FT_i, the original fusion features cannot be recovered. On the other hand, FT_i transformed by f_i^U may have multiple columns mapped to the same position. The Bloom filter is a many-to-one mapping, it is hard to infer from the position of 1 on b_i that which columns of FT_i are mapped in the same position. The irreversibility of the Bloom filter mapping had been proven by Rathgeb et al. [5].

6   Conclusion

In this work, we propose a cancelable multi-biometric template generation algorithm based on Bloom filter. In the proposed algorithm, the fingerprint features and the face features are binarized respectively, which makes that the fingerprint features do not need to be pre-aligned and the face binary features have cancelability. Then, using the XOR operation to fuse the grouped fingerprint binary features and the face binary features into one template at the feature level, and the irreversibly transform is made on the fusion template using Bloom filter. This method of feature fusion transformation can makes the entire multi-biometric template cancelable by updating the random matrix (can be stored in the user's identity token) for the binarization of face features. Finally, the traversal matching method is used to calculate the matching score between different templates so that the entire matching process can be completed in the encryption domain. The experimental results show that the EER without Bloom filter mapping is 0.39%, while the optimal EER with Bloom filter mapping is 0.79%. Hence, the proposed algorithm ensures the reliability of identity authentication and improves the security of multi-biometric template.

On the other hand, our algorithm implements the cancelability and diversity of multi-biometric template, but for this purpose we use the method of random projection in BioHashing. In fact, Biohashing have the disadvantage that EER will rise when the random matrix is stolen. Therefore, in the feature work, we will consider the effect of random matrix loss on the performance of our algorithm, and use some improved methods (such as Zheng's novel BioHashing [15]) instead of the BioHashing used in our algorithm to further improve the reliability of our algorithm.

References

1. Chen, Y., Yang, J., Wang, C., Liu, N.: Multimodal biometrics recognition based on local fusion visual features and variational Bayesian extreme learning machine. Expert Syst. Appl. **64**, 93–103 (2016)
2. Ratha, N.K., Chikkerur, S., Connell, J.H., Bolle, R.M.: Generating cancelable fingerprint templates. IEEE Trans. Pattern Anal. Mach. Intell. **29**(4), 561–572 (2007)
3. Lim, M., Verma, S., Mai, G., Yuen, P.C.: Learning discriminability-preserving histogram representation from unordered features for multibiometric feature-fused-template protection. Pattern Recognit. **60**, 706–719 (2016)
4. Rathgeb, C., Breitinger, F., Busch, C.: Alignment-free cancelable iris biometric templates based on adaptive bloom filters. In: International Conference on Biometrics, Madrid, pp. 1–8. IEEE (2013)
5. Rathgeb, C., Busch, C.: Cancelable multi-biometrics: mixing iris-codes based on adaptive bloom filters. Comput. Secur. **42**(4), 1–12 (2014)
6. Rathgeb, C., Gomez-Barrero, M., Busch, C., Galbally, J., Fierrez, J.: Towards cancelable multi-biometrics based on bloom filters: a case study on feature level fusion of face and iris. In: International Workshop on Biometrics and Forensics, Gjovik, pp. 1–6. IEEE(2015)
7. Gomez-Barrero, M., Rathgeb, C., Galbally, J., Fierrez, J.: Protected facial biometric templates based on local gabor patterns and adaptive bloom filters. In: International Conference on Pattern Recognition, Stockholm, pp. 4483–4488. IEEE (2014)
8. Li, G., Yang, B., Rathgeb, C., Busch, C.: Towards generating protected fingerprint templates based on bloom filters. In: International Workshop on Biometrics and Forensics, Gjovik, pp. 1–6. IEEE (2015)
9. Stokkenes, M., Ramachandra, R., Sigaard, M.K., Raja, K., Gomez-Barrero, M., Busch, C.: Multi-biometric template protection – a security analysis of binarized statistical features for bloom filters on smartphones. In: 2016 Sixth International Conference on Image Processing Theory, Tools and Applications, Oulu, pp. 1–6. IEEE (2016)
10. Sadhya, D., Singh, S.K.: Providing robust security measures to Bloom filter based biometric template protection schemes. Comput. Secur. **67**, 59–72 (2017)
11. Lee, C., Kim, J.: Cancelable fingerprint templates using minutiae-based bit-strings. J. Netw. Comput. Appl. **33**(3), 236–246 (2010)
12. Yang, W., Hu, J., Wang, S., Stojmenovic, M.: An alignment-free fingerprint biocryptosystem based on modified Voronoi neighbor structures. Pattern Recognit. **47**(3), 1309–1320 (2014)
13. Sandhya, M., Prasad, M.V.N.K.: k-Nearest Neighborhood Structure (k-NNS) based alignment-free method for fingerprint template protection. In: International Conference on Biometrics, Phuket, pp. 386–393. IEEE (2015)
14. Teoh, A.B.J., Goh, A., Ngo, D.C.L.: Random multispace quantization as an analytic mechanism for biohashing of biometric and random identity inputs. IEEE Trans. Pattern Anal. Mach. Intell. **28**(12), 1892–1901 (2006)
15. Zheng, Y., Cao, Y., Chang, C.H.: Facial biohashing based user-device physical unclonable function for bring your own device security. In: 2018 IEEE International Conference on Consumer Electronics, Las Vegas, pp. 1–6. IEEE (2018)

Streaming ETL in Polystore Era

Nabila Berkani[1] and Ladjel Bellatreche[2(✉)]

[1] Ecole Nationale Supérieure d'Informatique,
BP 68M, 16309 Oued-Smar, Alger, Algeria
n_berkani@esi.dz
[2] LIAS/ISAE-ENSMA, Futuruscope, Poitiers, France
bellatreche@ensma.fr

Abstract. In today's digital environment, businesses have to access, store and analyze in a real time fashion vast amounts of data issued from streaming graph-structure data sources. To meet these requirements, companies owning the data warehouse ($\mathcal{DW}$) technology have to combine hardware and software solutions to reduce the time latency between a $\mathcal{DW}$ and its data sources. The explosion of advanced hardware deployment platforms such as polystore represents an opportunity as pointed in recent studies. But, deploying a graph-structure $\mathcal{DW}$ over a polystore is not a simple task, since it requires two important phases which are data partitioning and allocation. We claim that these phases have to be connected to the ETL (Extract, Transform, Load) phase, especially its loading process. This connection questions the initial schedule of ETL and deployment processes. In this paper, we present a new approach that connects ETL and deployment processes and challenges their traditional scheduling to meet real time analysis requirements.

Keywords: RDF · Fragmentation · Allocation · ETL · Polystore

1 Introduction

With the arrival of Big Data Era, several voices have been raised in the demise of $\mathcal{DW}$, in the same way as relational DBMSs after the appearance of NoSQL. The risk of such a campaign puts aside several interesting research issues that are not well studied and solved. The change of name of several thematic conferences such as DaWaK and DOLAP by removing $\mathcal{DW}$ and substituting it by Big Data is an example of the discussed risk. We claim that the Big Data era is a chance for the renaissance of the $\mathcal{DW}$. This is because it brings several interesting dimensions that have to be exploited in the $\mathcal{DW}$ design. Some recent research efforts have been made in this direction such as: the incremental incorporation of its V's in the $\mathcal{DW}$ design (e.g., Variety [1], Value [2]), the embedding learning techniques and tools inside DBMSs hosting $\mathcal{DW}$ [20]), etc. Linked Open Data (an important element of the Big Data Landscape) offer additional stream RDF graph sources feeding $\mathcal{DW}$ [2].

© Springer Nature Switzerland AG 2018
J. Vaidya and J. Li (Eds.): ICA3PP 2018, LNCS 11336, pp. 560–574, 2018.
https://doi.org/10.1007/978-3-030-05057-3_42

The proliferation of graph-structure data streams fueled the demand for real-time data analytics [18]. To satisfy this requirement, hardware and software solutions have to be combined in order to reduce latency time between data sources and target $\mathcal{DW}$. From a software perspective, the traditional ETL (Extract, Transform, Load) phase has to be revisited to handle two main issues: (i) the new variety brought by graph-structure of data and (ii) streaming nature of data sources. The first issue has been addressed in [2], where a meta-model describing graph sources has been proposed. It has been also used as a support to redefine the traditional ETL operations identified in [25]. A couple of studies have been proposed to deal with the second issue that covers two main aspects: (i) rescheduling the processes of ETL in the context of traditional $\mathcal{DW}$. In [28], ETL has been turned into ELT. In this scenario, data are loaded into the $\mathcal{DW}$. Transformation primitives are then transformed inside DBMS hosting the $\mathcal{DW}$ via SQL queries. To speed up these queries, materialized views are selected incrementally as new data arrives. (ii) optimizations of ETL processes performed outside the DBMS which requires main memory (caching) and processes management [3,13].

From hardware perspective, the usage of advanced platforms such as polystores to deploy $\mathcal{DW}$ represents an interesting direction. Polystores have been launched based on the M. Stonebraker principle of "one size does not fit all", where platforms with a variety of storage engines, where each one designed for a specialized use case have been developed. Several polystores exist: BigIntegrator [31], BigDAWG [7], etc. Setting up a polystore in our context of $\mathcal{DW}$ necessitates the resolution of graph data partitioning[1] and allocation problems which are formalized as follows: given a $\mathcal{DW}$, a Sparql workload, a polystore with l stores $\{S_1, \ldots, S_l\}$ and a set of constraints related to each site such as storage cost. These problems consist in partitioning the $\mathcal{DW}$ into N fragments $\{F_1, \ldots, F_N\}$, and in allocating the obtained fragments over sites. The selected partitioning and the allocation schemes have to optimize the workload and respect the set of constraints. Due to the high interaction of Sparql queries [16], any partitioning algorithm has to consider this interaction.

Usually, ETL and deployment (denoted by D) phases are treated in an isolated way, except the recent work presented in CIDR'2017 [19] that largely discussed the issue of associating streaming ETL to polystore in Internet of Things to reduce the data latency. With combining software and hardware solutions in mind to reduce the latency matters, the used processes have to be well-scheduled and algorithms optimized with appropriate data structures. We have identified three possible schedules: (1) $[(ET||D) \longrightarrow L]$: the extraction and transformation processes of ETL and the deployment (partitioning and allocation) are first executed in parallel and then the loading process populates the deployed $\mathcal{DW}$. (2) $[ET \longrightarrow DL]$: extraction and transformation processes are executed first, then the deployment and loading processes. (3) $[D \longrightarrow ETL]$: a deployment schema of the $\mathcal{DW}$ is obtained by executing our partitioning and allocation algorithms,

---

[1] In this paper, we use fragmentation and partitioning interchangeably.

then the whole ETL processes are executed. These schedules with their corresponding optimizations are detailed in this paper.

The paper is organized as follows: Sect. 2 overviews the main existing studies on real time ETL processes and graph-structure data partitioning and allocation. Section 3 details our proposal by presenting all software and hardware solutions dedicated to ETL and deployment processes and including scheduling and optimizations. Section 4 presents our experimental studies. Section 5 concludes the paper.

2   Related Work

This section overviews the main important studies tackling real time ETL process and RDF data partitioning and allocation.

Real Time ETL Process. The main existing studies on real-time ETL are mainly focused on optimization aspects of the processes in the context of traditional $\mathcal{DW}$. These optimizations cover three mains points: (i) change data capture (CDC), (ii) join operations and (iii) scheduling ETL flows. CDC consists in identifying, capturing and delivering data as it is being inserted, updated, or deleted from data sources. In [11,12], the traditional loading processes are transformed to incremental loadings. [32] proposes an approach implementing a real-time $\mathcal{DW}$ by the means of Web services that ensure the CDC using XML Language. During ETL, join operations are widely used. [5] focused on the speed arrival of stream data and the management of disk and main memory accesses to perform these joins. Therefore, they proposed a MESH join operation in transformation phase of ETL. For the same purpose, the authors in [24] have proposed an algorithm that uses Semi-Streaming Index Join. Regarding scheduling of ETL jobs, the authors in [14] used a queue network in which an Active Data Staging Area is built between the sources and the target $\mathcal{DW}$. This area allows managing different jobs associated to ETL processes.

RDF Partitioning and Allocation did not get the same attention as traditional data [21]. The existing studies on RDF data partitioning were mainly concentrated on the partitioning modes, where two types exist: *hash-based* partitioning and *oriented-graph*. Trinity.RDF [30] is a distributed in-memory RDF engine that uses hash partitioning mode to fragment RDF data represented in its native graph form and stored in a key-value store system. SHAPE [17] is based on a semantic hash partitioning approach for RDF data. It starts by a simple hash partitioning and then employs the k-hop strategy proposed in [10]. To ensure the scalability of RDF data partitioning methods, several studies proposed algorithms based on graph theory. [10] uses METIS in order to partition RDF graphs into several fragments. [29] proposed an end-to-end path partitioning scheme, which considers all possible directed paths in the RDF graph. These paths are merged in bottom-up fashion. A few studies related to the processes of RDF data partitioning and allocation exists, where workload-driven approaches were proposed and implemented in the systems WARP [9] and Partout [8]. The authors in [22] propose a methodology that considers the processes of partitioning a RDF graph database and allocating its fragments over various sites. This work is totally inspired from traditional distributed databases [21].

3 Our Proposal

Before detailing our proposal, let us present some concepts and definitions related to the inputs of our problem and processes of deployment phase.

RDF[2] is a set of 4-tuple $< s, o, p, g >$, where its subject s has the property p, and the value of that property is the object o, and the graph label IRI g. Note that the graph label g can be omitted, in which case the triples are considered part of the default graph. N-Quads is a line-based, plain text format for encoding an RDF dataset. It defines an RDF dataset composed of RDF graphs. Sparql[3] is the standard query language for RDF.

Definition 1. *RDF Graph* G *is a finite set of RDF N-Quads in which every 4-tuple describes a directed edge labeled with p from the node labeled with s to the node labeled with o belonging to G. Subjects s can be URIs or blank nodes, properties p are URIs, while objects o can be URIs, blank nodes, or literals.*

Definition 2. *Sparql Query Graph* *is a finite set of RDF triple patterns; some nodes in a pattern are variables which may appear in multiple patterns.*

The global architecture of our proposal, presented in Fig. 1, takes as input various graph-structure data sources (e.g. semantic and graph databases, knowledge graph, etc.) and integrates them into the $\mathcal{DW}$ deployed on a Polystore system. It is composed of three main components: (i) *CDC component* that extracts and retrieves updated data from integrated sources, (2) *In-memory store management component* is responsible for partitioning phase and the required transformations of ETL process using pipeline strategy and (3) *Graph Distributed Management component* is responsible of the allocation of graphs over the polystore and their loading in each site store.

3.1 Partitioning and Allocation

In this section, we present the different steps of the fragmentation and allocation strategies. We consider a Sparql workload, given in the form of Sparql query patterns $Q = \{q_1, q_2, \ldots, q_n\}$. Our goal is to define the strategy to partition an RDF data-sets represented by an RDF graph G into RDF fragments (sub-graphs). Each RDF fragment will be allocated to the target site. Figure 3 illustrates the strategy applied.

---

[2] https://www.w3.org/RDF/.
[3] www.w3.org/TR/rdf-SPARQL-query/.

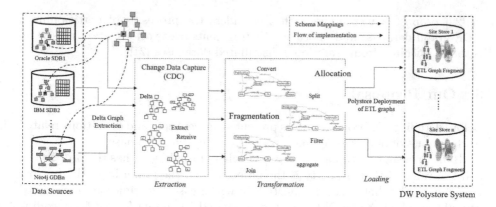

Fig. 1. A general architecture of our proposal.

Hypergraph Partitioning. As already stated, Sparql queries are naturally represented via graphs. Moreover, the volume of the RDF data becomes increasingly large, Sparql queries also reference a high number of quads and would therefore generate a huge number of connections between patterns giving rise to the problem of Multi-Query Optimization [16]. Managing a scenario with large number of complex queries with high interaction requires an adequate graph representation for Sparql queries. In this perspective, we propose to use the *hypergraph* structure, for representing Sparql queries, which are massively used to design and test integrated circuits [15]. Hypergraphs have the characteristic that their hyperedges are an arbitrary sets of vertices (nodes), and can therefore connect several vertices. From that, we project sparql queries to an hypergraph structure. We map the vertices of the hypergraph to quad patterns, and hyperedges to connect quad patterns when a transaction accesses quads pattern in queries. Figure 2 describe an example of query interactions applied to the 14 LUBM[4] queries.

Partitioning of graphs is a well-studied problem in computer science, and we therefore can leverage previously existing strategies to do the fragmentation of our query workload represented by an hypergraph. The following are the different steps applied to the workload Q:

– **Step 1:** parses the Sparql query workload Q in order to identify the vertices (nodes) and hyperedges. Each sparql query quad pattern is represented by a vertex and each operation in the query (join, ...) that connects quad patterns is defined by an hyperedge in the form (subject/object, operation, subject/object).

   For instance, for these two patterns: $t_1 = $ *(?x yago:wasBornIn yago: Cyprus)* and $t_2 = $ *(?y yago:isLocatedIn ?z)*, (t_1,t_2) are the vertices and $e_1 = $ *(yago:Cyprus, join, ?y)* is the hyperedge connecting both vertices using a join operation. The result of this step is an hypergraph HG, having a set of vertices

---

[4] http://swat.cse.lehigh.edu/projects/lubm/.

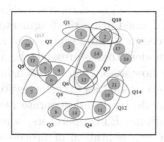
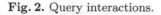

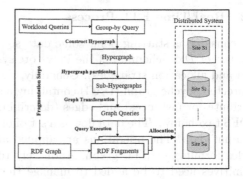

Fig. 2. Query interactions.   **Fig. 3.** Fragmentation and allocation strategies.

V and a set of hyperedges E. Each vertex $v_i \in V$ represents a Sparql query pattern and each hyperedge $e_i \in E$ connecting vertices v_i represents the operation linking query patterns (such as join and filter).

- **Step 2:** In this step, we use the hypergraph partitioning algorithm derived from graph theory. We choose hMETIS[5], a hypergraph partitioning program [15] that divides a hypergraph into k partitions representing sub-hypergraphs having disjoint vertices. We input the Sparql workload Q as a hypergraph to hMETIS Algorithm, and we specify the desired number of partitions which corresponds to the number of Polystore sites k. Then, hMETIS outputs the partitions of components. Each component represents a sub-hypergraph.
- **Step 3:** Here, we have partitioned the workload Q into k sub-hypergraphs. We need to transform each sub-hypergraph into a labeled graph that represents a Sparql query graph, whose its nodes are triple patterns and edges the connection between triple patterns. We adapted the algorithm proposed in SLEMAS [6].

Once the labeled sub-graphs are generated, we use them as Sparql sub-queries to construct RDF fragments. We run each Sparql sub-query on the RDF graph G. The result of each sub-query is an RDF fragment that needs to be allocated over the stores of our polystore in a *round-robin* mode.

To evaluate the cost of data partitioning and allocation, we develop mathematical cost models. Let $Cost_F$ and $Cost_A$ be these respective costs defined as follows: $Cost_F = Cost_{hmetis} + Cost_{HypgraphToGraph}$, where $Cost_{hmetis}$ and $Cost_{HypgraphToGraph}$ represent respectively, the time spent by HMETIS and the process of translating of a hypergraph to a graph; and $Cost_A = m \times Cost_{A_i}$, where $Cost_{A_i}$ is the time taken to allocate the fragment F_i over the Polystore.

---

[5] http://glaros.dtc.umn.edu/gkhome/metis/metis/overview.

3.2   Real Time ETL Process

We consider as starting point some data sources having a graph representation and target $\mathcal{DW}$ schemata of the Polystore system (defined using the fragmentation and allocation strategies). Generally, ETL process is usually represented as a directed acyclic graph (DAG) containing a set of nodes (that represent schema attributes or instances) and edges (describing data flow among the nodes using RDFS taxonomy). The data flow is a set of operations needed for transformation of input data. The operations are applied at the node level and generate new nodes forming an ETL graph. Additively to traditional ETL operators, some primitives need to be added to manage the graph representation of processed data:

- $AddNode(G_T, V_j, E_j, L_j)$: adds node V_j, edge E_j, label L_j required to G_T.
- $UpdateNode(G_T, V_j, E_j, L_j)$: updates node V_j, edge E_j, label L_j in G_T.
- $RenameNode(G_T, V_j, E_j, L_j)$: renames node V_j, edge E_j, label L_j in G_T.
- $DeleteNode(G_T, V_j, E_j, L_j)$: deletes node V_j, edge E_j, label L_j from G_T.
- $SortGraph(G_T, V_j, CS)$: sorts nodes of G_T based on some criteria CS to improve search performance.

Our objective is to facilitate, manage and optimize the design of the ETL process, deployment phase and during the continuous evolution of the $\mathcal{DW}$. For that, we enrich the existing ETL operators with *split*, *context* and *Link* operators elevating the clean-up and deployment of ETL process at the conceptual level.

- $Split(G, G_i, G_j, CS)$: splits G into two sub-graphs G_i and G_j based on CS.
- $Link(G_T, V_i, V_j, CS)$: links two nodes V_i and V_j using the rule CS.
- $Context(G, G_T, CS)$: extracts from the graph G a sub-graph G_T that satisfies the context defined by restrictions CS using axioms.

After having described the representation of ETL operators, we will detail the various components of our solution, that the process is depicted in Fig. 4:

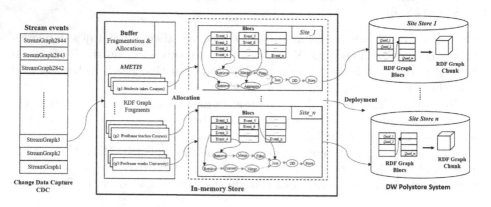

Fig. 4. Real time ETL process components

Change Data Capture (CDC) Component. In order to process the updated stream data from sources, we use the CDC technique *trigger-based capture* [23], that identifies the deltas of data sources using triggers implemented in each source participating in the integration. Processed data are usually freely accessible over sparql endpoints. Triggers have been implemented using Sparql query language to discover the necessary information itself.

The extracted data (graphs) are sent to the *In-memory Store Management* and are considered as events that trigger the process of transformation. Each event correspond to a unit of graph. Figure 4 in the left side illustrates this mechanism.

In-Memory Store Management Component. This component is dedicated to handle the ETL transformations and the distribution of the resulting ETL graphs to the Polystore System. These two operations are performed according our three scenarios: $[(ET||D) \longrightarrow L]$, $[ET \longrightarrow DL]$ and $[D \longrightarrow ETL]$.

The *In-memory Store* area contains the following zones: (1) $B_{F\&A}$: buffer dedicated to the execution of the fragmentation and allocation operations and (2) memory server$_i$ $(1 \leq i \leq n)$: a memory area dedicated to the ETL transformations according to the target n schemata of the Polystore. Note that the strategy of fragmentation and allocation defined in the previous section, produces as a result a fragmentation and allocation schemes saved at the DBMS catalog level. These schemes are used during the transformation and loading steps of the ETL process. For example, Oracle graph database offers the MDSYS schema that allows keeping this information and using it during the ETL process.

The real time ETL process starts when an incoming event from CDC component triggers it. These events are sent to the appropriate memory zone ($server_i$). The memory zones are organized as blocks and are handled depending on incoming events generating a data flow. Each event involves the execution of an ETL operator according to the transformation required by the fragmentation schema. As these events continue to show up in the stream, the corresponding blocks will stay in the memory and keep updating the ETL flow. After each event has been passed, the block will be crushed by new events. Note that the life cycle of any block, which means the period between a last update and the eviction from the cache is less than the real-time window (for example 2 min). Figure 4 illustrates this process.

Further, ETL operations are executed in a pipelining order [27], to ensure an efficient parallelism treatment. The ETL process is divided into various subprocesses that can work simultaneously using the *split* operator. ETL flows are processed concurrently with a data stream from the consumer operator to the producer. During the implementation, different delta batches are executed at the same time while still guaranteeing the consistency of the system. Some physical operations are required such as: multi-threading, callbacks, cancel, pause, resume. Figure 5 describes and example of our pipeline strategy for monthly_publication process. Suppose the monthly_publication fact table (having the schema <dateKey, pubKey, conferenceTotal, journalsTotal>) records the total publications in conferences and journals. The ETL flow can be flushed by three delta batches where two sub-processes (triggered by two different events) can be executed in concurrency giving rise to pipelining of delta batches. The final operation is the union of the resulting sub-processes, which can not starts until it makes sure that both have been finalized. Data pipelining is introduced here to increase the throughput of the ETL flow.

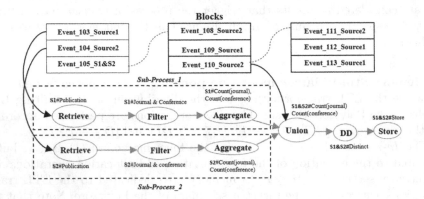

Fig. 5. Example of pipelined execution of ETL flow.

One of the main challenge is to ensure the fault-tolerance of the solution. This can be done by maintaining the memory zones recovery. To do so, the cache based system is designed by appending all stream events (blocks) to their corresponding files on the disk. This strategy can be implemented by almost DBMS. For instance, Oracle implements the redo logfiles to store the logs generated during processing, it allows a redo write-ahead log for the memory operations. When the system restarts, the DBMS reads all persisted files and reconstruct the in-memory zones.

Graph Distributed Management Component. This step comes at the end of ETL transformations and is responsible of the allocation of resulting data (graphs) to the Polystore system. Here, the allocation scheme (according to the allocation strategy described in the previous section) is needed to distribute data (each partitioned and transformed graph) to the appropriate site.

Once the graphs have been allocated, the loading phase is executed on the Polystore system. This latter, repeatedly merges the generated sub-graphs from the ETL flow into a single graph that we call *chunk* (a fixed number of sub-graphs is merged). Each chunk has a unique id assigned which is mostly used for locating chunks. The creation of chunks happens whenever blocks of ETL events have been completely processed and evicted from the in-memory store. Converting multiple small sub-graphs to a single graph chunk depends on storage layout of the target Polystore system. For instance, Oracle database stores RDF graphs using N-Quads format based on a data model store (RDF_MODELS, RDF_NODES, RDF_LINKS, RDF_VALUES, ...) where sub-graphs can be merged using union operations on the table RDF_NODES.

3.3 Polystore Deployment: REST-Based ETL Process

The deployment of our solution is carried out based on Loosely-Coupled Polystore System [4] which is a reminiscent of a multidatabase system. We believe that this approach is the most appropriate for our integration solution using partitioning and allocation strategies. To achieve our goal, we have implemented a service-based solution: ETL as a Service (ETLaaS) and Polystore as a Service (PaaS). The solution takes as inputs: (i) a set of stream data sources referencing a shared ontology or knowledge base and (ii) a set of mappings defined between these sources and target DW. It outputs a DW distributed storage system (Fig. 6).

Each component is implemented as a web service. Since we deal with RDF data coming from the web (ontologies, knowledge bases, ...), we choose the protocol REST and have implemented our solution using RESTFul API. For data exchange we opted for the JavaScript Object Notation (JSON) format. The communication between data sources and target DW is done using JSON objects with a unique identifier through the RESTful HTTP API. Our solution is implemented as a service oriented architecture (SOA). SOA offers the loose coupling of the web services defined below, and interaction among them which is more appropriate to the loosely-coupled Polystore systems. It allows the integration of new web services without affecting the existing one. This provides the flexibility of the physical deployments of DW.

4 Experiments

In this section we conduct an experimental study to analyze the effectiveness of our proposal. We start by describing the environment of test and the evaluated scenarios, then we present the results obtained by discussing the advantages and disadvantages of the scenarios.

Settings. We used Oracle Semantic Database 12c release 2 as the database backend for each store. RDF data are stored in Quad tables, using a distinct integer for each distinct URI or literal value. B-tree indexes are created on each Quad table on s, p, o, g columns, and all two and three columns combinations for performance issues. Moreover, some PL/SQL APIs are invoked after the integration of each data source (load of instances). The memory SGA and PGA are also increased to 8 GB. The ontology of LUBM benchmark[6] related to the university domain is used to generate the schemes of data sources. It offers fourteen extensional queries representing a variety of properties. We used a real world data set from YAGO KB, version 3.0.2, having an architecture classified

---

[6] http://swat.cse.lehigh.edu/projects/lubm/.

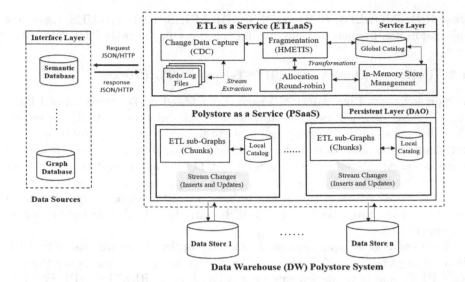

Fig. 6. Polystore deployment of the ETL process.

on themes. Each theme is a set of facts. A fact is a RDF graph. YAGO has defined the context relation between individuals [26] which we used to extract the set of themes related to our context study (e-learning domain). The resulting contextual YAGO $\mathcal{DW}$ contains around 562M Quads. From this contextual set, we have generated five data-sets with respectively 120, 280, 420, 720 and 950 universities, representing data sources. The five data sources and the $\mathcal{DW}$ stores schemata have been deployed using Oracle DBMS. Oracle offers different format for data loading such as: RDF/XML, N-TRIPLES, N-QUADS, TriG and Turtle. We choose N-QUADS format to load instances using Oracle SQL*Loader into the data sources and site stores of the $\mathcal{DW}$. Our evaluations were performed on a laptop computer (HP Elite-Book 840 G3) with an Intel(R) CoreTM i76th Gen, 3.4 GHZ and 8 GB of RAM and 1 T hard disk. We use Windows10 64bits. We use Oracle Database 12c release 2 that offers RDF Semantic Graph features of Oracle Spatial and Graph. Cytoscape[7] is used for visualization.

We conduct several experiments to evaluate our proposal. In the first experiment, we evaluate the response time of our proposal compared to our previous work [2] that does not use partitioning strategy and memory cache. Note that a memory cache is allocated for the stream processing of the integration process. Figure 7 illustrates our finding that fragmentation strategy greatly improve the response time of ETL process. The use of the in-memory cache as well.

In the second experiment, we try to evaluate the performance of the $\mathcal{DW}$ construction according to life cycle phases. To do so, we use a random workload of LUBM queries.

---

[7] http://www.cytoscape.org/.

Figure 8 illustrates the time spent to deploy the $\mathcal{DW}$ and run the ETL process according to the different scenarios descried above. The deployment and ETL process time basically consists on the fragmentation and allocation time, the execution time of the ETL process in order to populates the $\mathcal{DW}$ site stores. We notice that the $[(ET\|D) \longrightarrow L]$ scenario is the optimal one. We can conclude that the parallel execution of the deployment and ETL phases considerably improves the response time. In addition, the graph partitioning using hMETIS algorithm and our round-robin allocation of fragments are performed in a reasonable time depending on the size of data sources.

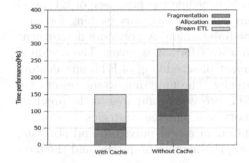
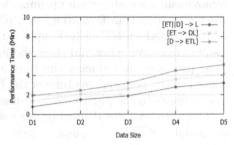

Fig. 7. ETL performance time.   **Fig. 8.** Data loading time.

In the third experiment, we compare our partitioning proposal with two approaches: H-RDF-3X a graph based partitioning [10] and Partout a workload based partitioning [8] on 14 LUBM benchmark queries. Figure 9 shows the query performance of the different approaches. Generally speaking, we find out that our method outperforms the state-of-art techniques in most cases. This is because that hMETIS algorithm takes in account the interaction among queries during the partitioning process. Hence, each site stores the fragments that are semantically linked.

Finally, we evaluate the scalability of our partitioning approach by varying RDF data-set sizes. The results are shown in Fig. 10. Generally, the result shows that the duration of partitioning remain reasonable vs the size of the data-set increases which shows the partitioning scalability.

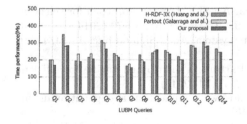
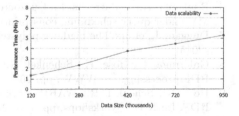

Fig. 9. Performance of queries.   **Fig. 10.** Scalability

5   Conclusion

In this paper, we couple hardware and software solutions to design streaming ETL involving graph-structure data sources to reduce the latency time between a $\mathcal{DW}$ and its sources. We propose the usage of polystore systems as a hardware solution for deploying the target $\mathcal{DW}$ and ETL software techniques to achieve the fixed objective. This coupling has to be well-mastered, since ETL and deployment processes are cumbersome and strongly interact. We first proposed a scalable partitioning algorithm of graph-structure $\mathcal{DW}$ that exploits the interaction among Sparql queries. It is based on a hypergraph data structure. Then, three scenarios are identified to schedule the processes of ETL and deployment associated with optimizations such as in-memory caching for handling streaming transformations in a pipe-line fashion. A polystore deployment solution based on REST technique with JSON format is given. The obtained results are encouraging and show the impact of scheduling of ETL and deployment processes on reducing the time latency. The most important results are related to the performance time of the ETL processes compared to the previous work, thanks to the partitioning, in-memory and pipeline strategies.

Currently, we are deploying our solution in a real polystore and studying the scalability of our proposal in increasing the number of queries and the data volume.

References

1. Berkani, N., Bellatreche, L.: A variety-sensitive ETL processes. In: Benslimane, D., Damiani, E., Grosky, W.I., Hameurlain, A., Sheth, A., Wagner, R.R. (eds.) DEXA 2017. LNCS, vol. 10439, pp. 201–216. Springer, Cham (2017). https://doi.org/10.1007/978-3-319-64471-4_17
2. Berkani, N., Bellatreche, L., Benatallah, B.: A value-added approach to design BI applications. In: Madria, S., Hara, T. (eds.) DaWaK 2016. LNCS, vol. 9829, pp. 361–375. Springer, Cham (2016). https://doi.org/10.1007/978-3-319-43946-4_24
3. Berkani, N., Bellatreche, L., Ordonez, C.: ETL-aware materialized view selection in semantic data streamwarehouses. In: RCIS. IEEE (2018)
4. Bondiombouy, C., Valduriez, P.: Query processing in multistore systems: an overview. IJCC **5**(4), 309–346 (2016)
5. Bornea, M.A., Deligiannakis, A., Kotidis, Y., Vassalos, V.: Semi-streamed index join for near-real time execution of ETL transformations. In: ICDE, pp. 159–170 (2011)
6. Boukorca, A., Bellatreche, L., Cuzzocrea, A.: SLEMAS: an approach for selecting MV under query scheduling constraints. In: COMAD, pp. 66–73 (2014)
7. Duggan, J., et al.: The bigdawg polystore system. ACM Sigmod Rec. **44**(2), 11–16 (2015)
8. Galárraga, L., Hose, K., Schenkel, R.: Partout: a distributed engine for efficient RDF processing. In: WWW, pp. 267–268. ACM (2014)
9. Hose, K., Schenkel, R.: WARP: workload-aware replication and partitioning for RDF. In: ICDE Workshops, pp. 1–6 (2013)
10. Huang, J., Abadi, D.J., Ren, K.: Scalable SPARQL querying of large RDF graphs. PVLDB **4**(11), 1123–1134 (2011)

11. Jörg, T., Deßloch, S.: Towards generating ETL processes for incremental loading. In: IDEAS, pp. 101–110 (2008)

12. Jörg, T., Dessloch, S.: Formalizing ETL jobs for incremental loading of data warehouses. In: BTW, pp. 327–346 (2009)

13. Jörg, T., Dessloch, S.: Near real-time data warehousing using state-of-the-art ETL tools. In: Castellanos, M., Dayal, U., Miller, R.J. (eds.) BIRTE 2009. LNBIP, vol. 41, pp. 100–117. Springer, Heidelberg (2010). https://doi.org/10.1007/978-3-642-14559-9_7

14. Karakasidis, A., Vassiliadis, P., Pitoura, E.: ETL queues for active data warehousing. In: IQIS, pp. 28–39 (2005)

15. Karypis, G., Kumar, V.: Multilevel k-way hypergraph partitioning. In: DAC, pp. 343–348 (1999)

16. Le, W., Kementsietsidis, A., Duan, S., Li, F.: Scalable multi-query optimization for SPARQL. In: ICDE, pp. 666–677 (2012)

17. Lee, K., Liu, L.: Scaling queries over big RDF graphs with semantic hash partitioning. Proc. VLDB Endow. 6(14), 1894–1905 (2013)

18. Mayer, R., Mayer, C., Tariq, M.A., Rothermel, K.: Graphcep: real-time data analytics using parallel complex event and graph processing. In: DEBS, pp. 309–316 (2016)

19. Meehan, J., Aslantas, C., Zdonik, S., Tatbul, N., Du, J.: Data ingestion for the connected world. In: CIDR (2017)

20. Ordonez, C., Johnson, T., Urbanek, S., Shkapenyuk, V., Srivastava, D.: Integrating the R language runtime system with a data stream warehouse. In: Benslimane, D., Damiani, E., Grosky, W.I., Hameurlain, A., Sheth, A., Wagner, R.R. (eds.) DEXA 2017. LNCS, vol. 10439, pp. 217–231. Springer, Cham (2017). https://doi.org/10.1007/978-3-319-64471-4_18

21. Ozsu, M.T., Valduriez, P.: Principles of Distributed Database Systems, 3rd edn. Springer, Heidelberg (2011). https://doi.org/10.1007/978-1-4419-8834-8

22. Peng, P., Zou, L., Chen, L., Zhao, D.: Query workload-based RDF graph fragmentation and allocation. In: EDBT, pp. 377–388 (2016)

23. Ram, P., Do, L.: Extracting delta for incremental data warehouse maintenance. In: ICDE, pp. 220–229 (2000)

24. Simitsis, A., Wilkinson, K., Dayal, U., Castellanos, M.: Optimizing ETL workflows for fault-tolerance. In: ICDE, pp. 385–396 (2010)

25. Skoutas, D., Simitsis, A.: Ontology-based conceptual design of ETL processes for both structured and semi-structured data. Seman. Web 3(4), 1–24 (2007)

26. Suchanek, F.M., Kasneci, G., Weikum, G.: Yago: a core of semantic knowledge. In: WWW, pp. 697–706 (2007)

27. Vassiliadis, P., Simitsis, A.: Near real time ETL. In: Vassiliadis, P., Simitsis, A., et al. (eds.) New Trends in Data Warehousing and Data Analysis, pp. 1–31. Springer, Heidelberg (2009). https://doi.org/10.1007/978-0-387-87431-9

28. Waas, F., Wrembel, R., Freudenreich, T., Thiele, M., Koncilia, C., Furtado, P.: On-demand ELT architecture for right-time BI: extending the vision. IJDWM 9(2), 21–38 (2013)

29. Wu, B., Zhou, Y., Yuan, P., Liu, L., Jin, H.: Scalable SPARQL querying using path partitioning. In: ICDE, pp. 795–806 (2015)

30. Zeng, K., Yang, J., Wang, H., Shao, B., Wang, Z.: A distributed graph engine for web scale RDF data. PVLDB **6**(4), 265–276 (2013)
31. Zhu, M., Risch, T.: Querying combined cloud-based and relational databases. In: Cloud and Service Computing (CSC), pp. 330–335. IEEE (2011)
32. Zhu, Y., An, L., Liu, S.: Data updating and query in real-time data warehouse system. In: CSSE, vol. 5, pp. 1295–1297 (2008)

Communication-Aware Prediction-Based Online Scheduling in High-Performance Real-Time Embedded Systems

Baptiste Goupille-Lescar[1,2](✉), Eric Lenormand[1], Nikos Parlavantzas[2,3], and Christine Morin[2]

[1] Thales Research and Technology, 1 av. Augustin Fresnel, 91120 Palaiseau, France
{baptiste.goupillelescar,eric.lenormand}@thalesgroup.com
[2] Inria, IRISA, 263 av. General Leclerc, 35042 Rennes, France
christine.morin@inria.fr
[3] INSA Rennes, IRISA, 263 av. General Leclerc, 35042 Rennes, France
nikos.parlavantzas@irisa.fr
https://www.thalesgroup.com/en
https://www.inria.fr/en/

Abstract. Current high-end, data-intensive real-time embedded sensor applications (e.g., radar, optronics) require very specific computing platforms. The nature of such applications and the environment in which they are deployed impose numerous constraints, including real-time constraints, and computing throughput and latency needs. Static application placement is traditionally used to deal with these constraints. However, this approach fails to provide adaptation capabilities in an environment in constant evolution. Through the study of an industrial radar use-case, our work aims at mitigating the aforementioned limitations by proposing a low-latency online resource manager derived from techniques used in large-scale systems, such as cloud and grid environments. The resource manager introduced in this paper is able to dynamically allocate resources to fulfill requests coming from several sensors, making the most of the computing platform while providing guaranties on non-functional properties and Quality of Service (QoS) levels. Thanks to the load prediction implemented in the manager, we are able to achieve a 83% load increase before overloading the platform while managing to reduce ten times the incurred QoS penalty. Further methods to reduce the impact of the overload are as well as possible future improvements are proposed and discussed.

Keywords: Embedded systems · Real-time · Scheduling
Dynamic resource management

1 Introduction

Nowadays, with the increasing demand for high-performance computing and smart sensing, high-end embedded system designers are facing an increasing

© Springer Nature Switzerland AG 2018
J. Vaidya and J. Li (Eds.): ICA3PP 2018, LNCS 11336, pp. 575–592, 2018.
https://doi.org/10.1007/978-3-030-05057-3_43

number of challenges. Indeed, the targeted platforms must respect a great number of non-functional constraints, such as Size, Weight and Power (SWaP), real-time computing and cost constraints. Currently, most embedded systems meet these constraints by the use of dedicated components and static resource allocation approaches based on worst-case scenarios. This method, coupled with the emergence of workloads integrating hard, soft real-time and best-effort applications and the increase of their variability, results in massive over-provisioning and under-utilization of resources. Moreover, while this method allows the design of efficient and reliable systems, it nearly eliminates their adaptation and evolution capabilities by preventing the deployment of highly variable or opportunistic applications for smart sensing. To address these limitations, this paper proposes a smart resource management system, able to fulfill low-latency runtime requests for application execution while providing non-functional guarantees. Timing properties are considered in this paper, while other properties such as heat dissipation, will be addressed in future work. To achieve high performance gains while guaranteeing timing properties, our contribution is inspired by large-scale resource managers found in cloud or grid infrastructures, making the most of application profiling to enable high-level predictability, low mapping latency as well as high resource utilization. This work is supported by several industrial use-cases, including an Active Electronically Scanned Array (AESA) radar use-case, which is detailed in this paper. To fit the targeted context, a complete simulation framework has been implemented. The results obtained through simulations show that our mapping method results in improvements in both performance and predictability of the system.

This paper is organized as follows: Sect. 2 provides a quick description of the motivating use-case context. In Sect. 3, related research from both the embedded and large-scale systems communities are presented. Section 4 describes the models and methods used in our approach. In Sect. 5 the simulation framework created is explained and simulation results are analyzed. Section 6 introduces future work and discusses several open questions. Finally, Sect. 7 draws some conclusions and perspectives.

2   Use-Case Specific Context

Our use-case deals with optimizing the computing resource utilization of a multi-function electronically-steered surface radar and has been characterized with the support of domain experts. This equipment can typically be installed on the ground vehicles or on some surface ships such as frigates, with the mission of detecting, tracking and identifying objects of interest. This is done by illuminating narrow angular sectors by one or more sequences of known signals (waveforms) and processing the returned echoes captured on a large number of receivers. Such an observation is commonly referred as "dwell". Dwells can be of several types, depending on their objective (e.g., scanning an unknown sector, tracking a known target) and make use of different waveforms, each with its known duration. The radar antenna is constantly kept busy and scans the whole radar angular range by successively sending signals with the appropriate wave-forms. The processing of received echoes is traditionally split into two distinct phases:

- A front-end one that applies fixed filtering functions on the digitized received channels. It processes a massive bandwidth of input data, and selects a limited set of points of interest by using appropriate detection thresholds. This phase is highly computation-intensive and computing times are deterministic.
- A back-end phase whose goal is to extract operational information (e.g., position, speed, trajectory, nature of target) from the detection results. Among functions executed in the back-end are the extraction, which delivers so-called "plots" that characterize one or more targets in precise directions of space, and tracking, which consolidates plots issued by extraction and builds trajectories of targets.

Considering the regularity of the front-end workload, a near-optimal mapping (i.e., resource allocation) can be found at design-time and used during run-time processing. Thus, front-end tasks are not targeted by this study as their high predictability limits the potential performance gain from the integration of dynamic elements. On the contrary, static design-time mapping methods loose efficiency when applied to functions with data-dependent complexities, which is the case for most back-end applications. Functions like extraction have a largely variable computational cost, depending on the type of dwell as well as the number and configurations of targets that must be discriminated from the front-end detection. The actual run-time of each extraction is only known at the end of its execution. However, this cost is bounded by known minimum/maximum values related to each dwell type.

The computing platform used for back-end processing must fit within a specific SWaP budget. In our case, the targeted computing platform consists of 4 racks each one hosting several boards with several processing elements and a shared memory. All these elements are linked together by an Ethernet network using a star topology with one central router connected with the routers present in each rack. In addition to SWaP constraints, processing latencies matter, as observing and tracking targets needs to be kept in pace with their kinematics. The combination of variable computation times (and data transfer), constrained platform and real-time computing renders design-time mapping policies inefficient and drives the need for agile methods. Another goal of the introduction of online resource management in traditionally static systems is to serve

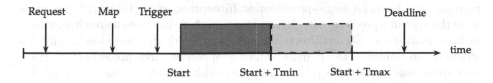

Fig. 1. Application execution timeline

as an enabler for the implementation of new applications with varying resource demand or unknown completion time.

To add adaptation capabilities to the system, we experiment with a resource management functionality that receives sporadic sequences of requests, each corresponding to a dwell that will be input to one of the 4 radar antennas. The *trigger* (see Fig. 1) represents the moment at which the data will be available for the back-end (e.g. extraction) applications, after waveform emission/reception and front-end processing. The resource manager allocates the different back-end computation and communication activities of the dwell application onto the platform resources so that they can be executed before their deadline. For reasons discussed later, this placement decision *Map* is taken just before the trigger reception. After having been placed, an application's execution effectively starts only when all its dependencies are met and the targeted processing elements are free, which ideally happens at $T = trigger$. It then executes for a time depending on the data content before sending the results and freeing the occupied computing and communication resources. Furthermore, note that the processing of separate dwells (addressing different regions in space) can be done independently from each other.

Their execution is mandatory, every request must be fulfilled, and is non-preemptive. As of now, the resource management system is only seen as an executant and does not have the opportunity to reject or terminate an application. Once a request has been received, the associated application is executed in its entirety.

3   Related Work

As we are addressing high-performance computing problems in an embedded environment, the following related work is divided into two parts: studies targeting embedded systems with SWaP and timing constraints and studies addressing the placement of similar application models on large-scale systems.

3.1   Embedded Systems

We first take a look at works that consider similar computing platforms with timing constraints. In our study, as in numerous embedded systems design problems, the real-time execution of applications is a major concern. A great number of published works aim at providing timing guaranties for hard real-time applications. Works aiming at aeronautic or automotive certification reject dynamic methods and focus on single-processor architectures, as in [15] or [19], to maximize the system's predictability. In recent years, there has been a growing interest in both multi-processor architectures and mixed-criticality workloads. This led to numerous publications [3] and several European research projects [1,2]. However these studies, such as [11] or [22], only address design-time schedulability analysis.

In [21], run-time adaptation consists in mapping long-lasting jobs onto a multi-processor system-on-chip architecture by making use of configurations elaborated at design-time. However, in our case the run-time management system operates in a non-periodic context by taking very frequent mapping decisions for computing jobs with a very limited duration. Similarly, the authors of [9] use design-time exploration results to dynamically adapt the application run-time setting depending on the context. While both these works show promising results, our workload's temporal behavior makes it impossible to adapt the resource allocated to an application once it started. The fact that all applications of our use-case are short-lived and must meet their deadline makes it impossible to modify the set of resources they are deployed on after the applications have started their execution.

3.2   Large-Scale Systems

While studies in the embedded community essentially focus on real-time control workloads or signal/video processing applications, our use-case's workload is much closer to workflows encountered in large-scale systems, such as cloud computing. With the democratization of cloud computing and an increasing need for efficient scientific simulations, more and more works address the scheduling of workflows in HPC systems [16]. These workflows are often materialized as Directed Acyclic Graphs (DAGs) for which computing and communication resources are allocated until their completion. Among the numerous publications, two main categories of resource management systems can be identified:

- Purely dynamic approaches with close to no prior knowledge of the applications and relying on cloud elasticity to compensate for QoS run-time variation by allocating/releasing and/or migrating Virtual Machines (VMs) [7,27].
- Static methods relying on exhaustive or evolutionary algorithms to find an optimal placement before executing the application. Commonly used methods include genetic, ant colony and Min-Min algorithm variations [4,6,14,23,25].

While both of these approaches have merits and can achieve great results in cloud or grid computing, none are directly applicable to our use-case for several reasons. First, due to the arrival rate of requests, a placement solution must be found in a few milliseconds, which prevents us from using, for example, genetic or particle swarm algorithms. Furthermore, while some methods using online model derivation, such as [8] can show great results, they are only applicable to long-lasting applications. Then, the use-case's applications being non-preemptive and the resources not being virtual makes it impossible to rely on migration or virtual machine re-dimension mechanisms.

A fair number of studies try to incorporate predictability via the use of priorities or isolation mechanisms, as in [13,17]. Unfortunately, due to the ever-changing nature of cloud environments, most "real-time" cloud resource managers react to deadline misses and do not prevent them. Thus, while no management system is actually able to provide hard real-time guaranties, there exist few satisfying solutions able to accurately provide soft real-time guaranties when targeting data streaming. However, while it is manageable to obtain these timing properties *inside* a cloud environment, it is noticeably more difficult to do so when considering communications with users as data have to go through heavy software stacks as well as non-deterministic communication protocols [10]. In [5], while the authors use similar workload and resource reservation mechanisms to ours, they only target bag of tasks applications, for which they have control over the parallelism level, do not consider SWaP constraints and can potentially reserve an infinite number of VMs.

Finally, while the problem has already been addressed for single processor systems [18], only few works actually target non-preemptive resource allocation for stochastic workloads on multi-processor platforms [12,24]. Moreover, they are purely mathematical approaches and totally abstract the computing platform by considering a set of identical unrelated machines.

To conclude, while a significant number of works seem to address a similar problem, the specificity of the considered use-case applications and the computing platform makes it impossible to simply adapt existing solutions.

4   Our Approach

In this section we first describe the overall functioning of our resource manager, consisting of the *mapper* and *predictor* components. Afterwards, this section describes the proposed mapping heuristic. Our final objective being to maximize the QoS provided to the radar's operator, a QoS-aware extension of our method is finally introduced.

4.1   Mapping Process

The overall mapping process is shown Fig. 2 which serves as a guideline for this section. As explained in Sect. 2, the resource manager receives requests from the radar every few milliseconds (*1* in Fig. 2). Each of these requests contains the type of application to execute, its identifier, its priority, the input and output memories and the time at which the data will be available in the input memory. The application's type defines its structure (i.e., directed acyclic graph) and profiling data, such as computing time and input and output data volume for which only minimal and maximal values are known. Note that priorities are only partially correlated to the application's type because they are dynamically attributed depending on the context (e.g., threat level of a target).

It is necessary to find a valid mapping solution for these requests before the data is available to reduce latency as well as to avoid congestion in the input memory. Furthermore, only probabilistic execution times of each computation and communication activity are known when evaluating placement possibilities. Thus, unlike numerous approaches present in the literature, it is necessary to take a decision based not on the current state of resources but on an estimation of their future availability. To this extend, the *Mapper* interacts with the load *Predictor*

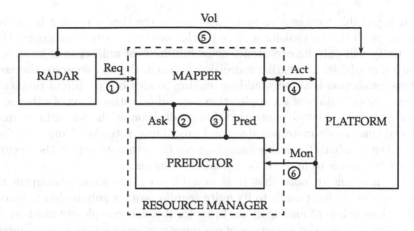

Fig. 2. Simplified model view

$(2)(3)$ to find a suitable placement for both communication and computation activities of the application (i.e., nodes of the DAG). Once a decision has been made, the application's activities are sent to their respective hosts (4). They are executed on the platform using data from the radar (5) to determine their actual execution timings. Finally, monitoring signals from the platform (6) are then exploited to update the load prediction model.

4.2 Prediction Model

Computing time predictions are handled by our *Predictor* module. Its role consists in keeping an up-to-date simplified overview of the platform's processors, links and memories state as well as queued activities to provide the *Mapper* with execution time predictions. Keeping in mind that a valid mapping solution must be found in a few milliseconds, the simulation of the actual computing platform in its entirety is far too computationally intensive to consider in detail while looking for a run-time solution. Indeed, since the platform comprises multiple shared resources (memories, communication links), estimating the impact of the deployment of an application on all the applications already running (or queued) represents a significant amount of computation, impossible to terminate in a few milliseconds on an embedded platform. Thus, the *Predictor* maintains a simplified model of the real architecture containing every resource (processors, memories, links) as well as the activities queued for execution in each of these resources. The execution time predictions are made without taking into account some of the resource access conflicts happening in the actual platform. The architecture model inside the predictor is kept up-to-date using both the *Mapper*'s placement decisions in addition to the platform's monitoring signals. The interactions between *Mapper*, *Platform* and *Predictor* can be seen as a MAPE (Monitoring, Analysis, Planning and Execution) control loop often found in large-scale systems management systems. Some adjustments are necessary to this loop as, while it is possible to take a mapping decision at the time a request is received, it may be profitable to wait for a more precise prediction since the application's first activity will only be executed tens or hundreds of milliseconds later, when the data is available. The earlier a decision is taken, the less accurate the execution time prediction is as we would be making predictions on top of predictions since execution timings of an application depend on estimations of other applications' end times. On the contrary, taking a decision at the last minute means a reduced time to evaluate possible solutions. Thus, a trade-off must be found between the number of possible mappings we can evaluate versus the accuracy of these evaluations to find the best possible solution.

It is important to note that it is possible to make some assumptions on the system's evolution thanks to its quite regular request submission pattern; it would be impossible to anticipate its behavior if it was completely random. The system receives aperiodic sequences of mapping requests with an average interval between them in the range of a few milliseconds. Indeed, the rate at which the mapper receives requests is correlated with the radar antennas emission rate and, in practical use-cases, the antennas operate close to their maximum capabilities at all times. As mentioned before, their execution times can greatly vary depending on the data to process which can not be known before execution. In summary, we are faced with a system whose dynamic behavior enables short term predictions ranging from a few milliseconds to tens of milliseconds.

4.3   Proposed Mapping Heuristics

The considered application model is as follows: Each application is seen as a directed acyclic graph $APP = (A, D, prio, trigger, dl, input, output)$ having a priority $prio$, a memory $input$ at which necessary data will be available at $t = trigger$ and the memory $output$ in which the results have to be stored before the deadline dl. A represents a set of computing activities linked by execution order constraints, or dependencies D. An Activity $A_n = (vol_{comp_{max}}, vol_{comp_{min}}, vol_{in_{max}}, vol_{in_{min}}, vol_{out_{max}}, vol_{out_{min}}, \alpha)$ has minimum/maximum values of the number of instructions to execute (vol_{comp}), the data input vol_{in} and output vol_{out} volumes as well as a memory access ratio α. The memory access ratio α of a computing node determines the minimum memory bandwidth needed by a target processor to perform the computation of this activity at maximum speed. For an application to be schedulable, we assume that $\forall APP, T_{max} < (deadline - trigger)$, T_{max} being the sum of maximum computation times of the activities part of the critical path of APP. In other words, applications have *slack*, meaning most of them can be slightly delayed and still respect their timing constraints.

Concerning the architecture, reasoning is made on the architecture model maintained by the predictor and defined as follows. The platform $PF = (P, M, L)$ is seen as a set of processors P, memories M and links L. Each processor P_n possess a computing capacity expressed in instructions per second in addition to its type, each memory M_n a maximum bandwidth and each link L_n

a maximum throughput expressed in Bytes per second. At run-time the architecture runs several applications. Processors (resp. communication links) can
only serve one computation (resp. communication) at a time. Memories on the
contrary potentially share their bandwidth between different computations and
communications, which may result in slowing down some of them in case of
excessive demands.

Static Mapping. This mapping strategy is used as a reference for comparison
with dynamic strategies shown below. In this context, processors are allocated
to successive requests in each rack on a systematic round-robin basis, without
considering the computing cost or priority of each requested activity.

Prediction-Based Load Balancing. This dynamic strategy consists in allocating at run-time the best communication path and computing elements in the
machine, by taking account of an estimated load status of the different resources
of the architecture. Its objective is to minimize the end time of the next request
to be executed. This is done by investigating all sets of processors $SP_n \subset P$ able
to host the different computation activities to execute. For each of them, since
an application request carries information on input and output memories, it is
possible to identify and generate an adequate set of communication activities to
transfer data from the input memory to computing activities hosts' memories
and, finally, to the output memory. From this set of activity sets, the mapper
then estimates for each of them the worst-case completion times of the application request according to the architecture resources used and their estimated
current workload. The predictor is used there, providing for each resource an
estimation of the completion time of its last queued activity, or the indication
that it has no activity still running. This is then used to evaluate the completion time of the new candidate activity request, and elect the hosting processor
and associated communication path that achieves the earliest predicted completion time. To estimate the worst-case execution time of a computing activity
on a processor, this processor's frequency and the maximum possible number of
instructions for this type of activity are used. Concerning communication time
predictions, it is necessary to take the maximum availability of links on the path
in addition to the input and output memories bandwidths. Then, an estimated
worst-case communication time is computed using the maximum data volume
for this activity and the lowest available bandwidth on the path. Note that in
our test bench, the possibility is left to choose to off-load a request of a busy rack
to a less busy neighbour rack, when the additional cost of moving data to and
from the receiving rack compensates advantageously for long potential delays in
the original rack.

QoS-Aware Load Balancing. This strategy is an extension of the previous
prediction-based load balancing whose goal was the reduction of application
latencies. While the latter allocates the earliest finishing resources to individual

requests, this strategy now aims at optimizing a QoS indicator based on the global cost of exceeding deadlines. As mentioned before, the activity requests are of different types with different priorities, and thus a variable degree of flexibility can be left to miss deadlines. This is an alternative to the hard deadline model. This alternative fits better our radar context, which runs activities at variable computing costs and variable requirements on reactivity; as an example, activities related to tracking targets are expected to complete soon enough to avoid loosing the target, while others operate in a human time scale.

Each type of activity has a penalty factor proportional to the extent of the deadline miss, and null if the deadline is met. The goal is now to keep the accumulated penalty as low as possible while executing the same workload on the same computing platform. Then the QoS-based strategy now considers a sequence of n activity requests of potentially different types (and priorities), sorted in trigger time order. We call R_0 the request in the queue with the earliest trigger time and R_n the nth requests in the queue. While the execution order (i.e. trigger time) isn't impacted, the objective is now to determine if the best mapping found should be used for the next request R_0 or a later, more critical one.

- selects the best host processor P_0 for R_0 and estimates its potential deadline miss and resulting penalty Q_{R_0/P_0}
- $\forall 0 < i <= n$ select the best host processor P_i for R_i with P_0 removed from the list of candidate processors and estimates the potential deadline miss of R_i and resulting penalty Q_{R_i/P_i}
- if $Q_{R_i/P_i} + Q_{R_0/P_0} > Q_{R_i/P_0} + Q_{R_0/P_i}$ and if R_i has a larger priority than R_0, processor P_i is allocated to R_0, leaving P_0 free
- else processor P_0 is allocated to R_0

This resource allocation strategy can be seen as an extension of the first load-balancing method as its behaviour will deviate from the non QoS-aware one only when predicting significant penalty overheads.

5   Evaluation

To evaluate the proposed mapping heuristics a simulation framework has been created mostly because the objective is to evaluate the resource management policies themselves, which would be too time consuming if one had to develop and integrate real-time software for each candidate computing platforms. A modular approach has been adopted, allowing us to calibrate the simulation with actual data while having some freedom in the testing done. This section first describes the created simulation environment before discussing some interesting results.

5.1   Simulation Framework

The simulation environment, realized for this study using the Ptolemy II Framework [20], is divided into three main components:

- a request generation module
- the resource management system
- a computing platform simulator

Request Generation. A request generation module has been developed to reproduce representative radar scenarios. It emulates the radar management system request submission pattern and generated requests possess properties close to actual ones. As such, it generates dwell requests as if feeding 4 antennas. The type of dwells and the request released dates are randomized to a certain extend, but in a reproducible way. The generator also includes parameters allowing us to represent the complexity of the environment observed by each antenna by manipulating the probability distribution of actual instruction and communication data volumes of dwells treated by this antenna. These volumes are sent directly to the simulator (see *Vol* Fig. 2) and aren't known by the resource manager which has only knowledge of the request type, min/max volume values, trigger time, deadline and priority.

Resource Manager. The resource manager represents the core of our work and encompasses both the mapper and predictor module. It contains the implementation of the proposed mapping algorithms and, for comparison purposes, the implementation of a standard static round-robin placement algorithm in addition to the proposed dynamic methods. Moreover, it keeps track of every missed deadline and assigns a penalty to each application execution calculated as follow: $penalty_n = prio_n * (end\_time_n - deadline_n)$ if $end\_time_n > deadline_n$ or 0 otherwise. The applications' priorities being correlated to the operational interest of a dwell, the sum of suffered penalties during a run represents a relevant estimation of a mapping strategy's impact on the QoS provided to the user while running a scenario.

Platform Simulator. To both implement the full MAPE loop and evaluate the proposed methods, an execution environment was required. In order to have more control over it and flexibility on testing parameters, a computing platform simulator has been designed. However, to retain meaningful evaluation results and feedback to the predictor, this simulator has been modeled on an actual platform. Moreover, to accurately simulate the activities' execution, their memory access volume as well as interference (i.e. resource access conflicts) with other running activities are represented. Both the platform simulator and the interference model have been validated by domain experts.

To obtain the following results, the considered platform contains 4 racks linked via an Ethernet switch, each one hosting 6 dual-processor boards with one shared memory per board. Inside a rack, all boards communicate also via an Ethernet switch. Note that each rack receives input data from the front-end of one antenna which is stored in an input memory and must send results to a fixed output memory.

5.2   Results Analysis

We now compare the performance of different mapping methods in several operational scenarios as well as the influence of anticipation delay (i.e. the time between the decision taking process and the application deployment) on the quality of results produced. We first identify the four operational scenarios used in the following experiments:

- *SCE 1* where all antennas share an equal, average load.
- *SCE 2* representing a classic shore surveillance scenario with one antenna (pointing towards the coastline) illuminating a high-complexity environment with a very high number of detections, its 2 neighbors harboring average load and the last antenna treating only few detections.
- *SCE 3* where 2 antennas face numerous detections and the other 2 an average amount.
- *SCE 4*, where all antennas have to treat an important quantity of detections.

While *SCE 1* and *SCE 4* are mostly used as reference points, the second scenario *SCE 2* presents a real operational interest as it represents a traditionally problematic case.

Each result presented below comes from the average of 10 simulation runs with different random seed values. During each run 2000 requests are generated, each request containing 1 computing activity and 1 to 2 communication activities, which translates in an average of 5000 activities mapped per run.

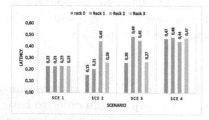

Fig. 3. Latency using static mapping

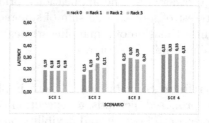

Fig. 4. Latency using dynamic load balancing

Figure 3 shows the average observed latencies of deployed applications while using a standard round-robin static mapping method. As it is clearly visible in *SCE 2* and *SCE 3*, using a pre-determined mapping prevents online resource sharing and can cause a great load unbalance between computing racks. On the other hand, when using the dynamic load-balancing approach described in 4.3.2 (see Fig. 4) we can see that resource sharing has been efficiently carried out, narrowing the gap between computing racks load in both *SCE 2* and *SCE 3*. Moreover, we can observe a global latency reduction anywhere between 18% and 32% across all scenarios. This is due to the fact that our mapping method avoids random latency spikes that can happen while using a static mapping method. These spikes can be caused by the execution of a heavy activity on a pre-determined processor which is possibly already busy executing another expensive activity, effectively leading to an increased queuing time. Additionally,

the execution time gains provided by the proposed predictive mapping system
are only partly due to the resource sharing between racks as, when preventing
the inter-rack migration of activities 10 to 20% execution time reduction was
still observed.

Table 1. QoS results.

		Static Mapping	Load-Balancing
SCE 1	penalty	3.21	0
	nb miss	23	0
SCE 2	penalty	69.67	0.17
	nb miss	136.6	3.6
SCE 3	penalty	172.36	2.37
	nb miss	284	28.2
SCE 4	penalty	342.06	31.8
	nb miss	507.4	175

While looking at the QoS provided by both static and predictive methods in
Table 1, one can notice an even greater difference in terms of perceived QoS. In
the *Static Mapping* column we can observe that, even in a average load scenario
(*SCE 1*), a few latency spikes cause some deadline misses, generating some QoS
penalties. While the *Load-Balancing* method consistently maintains 0 deadline
misses.

In *SCE 2* and *SCE 3* massive differences can be seen in provided QoS with
the load balancing method, only missing 3.6 to 28.2 deadlines and the static
method between 136.6 and 284 on average. This represent a more than ten
times average QoS improvement under the most realistic operational scenarios.

Finally, in *SCE 4* where all racks are overloaded, around one fourth of the
deadlines are missed with the static mapping and one eleventh with the dynamic
method. Note that these show as well that the use of an efficient load-balancing
helps mitigating the effects of an overload. While the load prediction method
misses only three times fewer deadlines, it receives only less than 10% the amount
of QoS penalty suffered by the static mapping.

Figure 5 shows the impact of computing load of applications on the amount
of QoS penalty received for different mapping methods on one computing rack.
The computation load is normalized on the computation volume at which the
first deadline misses (due to latency spikes) are observed while using the static
method. It is possible to observe a steep increase in penalty for all mapping methods around at around three times this load. At this point we reach the maximum
capacity of the computing platform and enter a global overload state. As every
application must be executed, numerous computing activities will accumulate
inside processors' execution queue and be executed well after their deadlines,
generating high penalty.

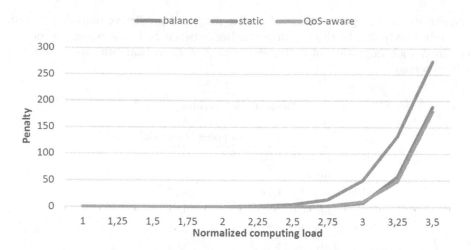

Fig. 5. Impact of computation load on the quality of result

However, when using a dynamic load-balancing technique, the computing volume at which an overload state is entered differs vastly from the one at which the static method overloads. Even when not taking into account random latency spikes happening for volumes from 1 to 1.5, a constant increase in observed penalty can be noticed for the static mapping from 1.5 onward. On the other hand, when using load-balancing or QoS-aware mapping methods, the first deadline misses and received penalty only appear at the 2.75 mark. This is a straight 83% increase in the computation volume that the platform can absorb before encountering any QoS issue. The QoS-aware mapping method introduced in 4.3.3 shows results close to the first load balancing mapping with an average penalty reduction close to 10%. Moreover, both the QoS-aware and the load-balancing methods tend to mitigate the QoS impact of an overload as they consistently suffer a lower QoS penalty than the static round-robin technique.

As discussed before, the moment at which an application placement decision is taken can greatly influence the quality of load prediction used to take this decision and, thus, impact the quality of produced mapping. This is especially true when operating close to the platform's maximal load. For example, when using a 2.5 volume in *SCE 3*, the average number of missed deadlines can vary from 0 to 38 depending on the anticipation with which the decision is taken. An ideal anticipation of 0 means that the mapping decision is taken instantly at trigger time and yields perfect results when not in an overload state. On the contrary, placing an application as soon as its execution request is received (between 100 to 300 ms before its execution) often yields noticeably inferior results due to more approximate predictions on the platform's future state. The results presented above were obtained using a 10ms anticipation time which provides near optimal results while being a realistic mapping decision delay.

6 Discussion

The results presented in the previous section are encouraging and prove the potential gains of QoS-aware dynamic resource manager for the specialized and demanding systems that are multi-function radars. However, while this work's context seems very specific, the presented predictive load balancing mechanism could be adapted to other domains with similar needs such as high-performance automotive computing platforms. For example, for high performance sensors, this technique could be used to dynamically select the proper algorithms variant that fits best the current observed situation, while maintaining real-time objectives. Moreover, while they operate at completely different scales, cloud environment processing business workflows share some of our use-case constraints [28] and could benefit from an online predictive mapping method.

In addition, this approach opens important opportunities of improvement. First of all, the realized resource management system currently stands in a passive position due to its lack of control over incoming requests and its obligation to execute each of them. Thus, it can only increase the computing load supported by the computing platform before reaching an overload state, with no means to prevent it. Two solutions can be envisaged to address this issue. The first one is the implementation of an admission control unit discarding low priority applications to make room for high priority ones when anticipating an overload. The other envisaged solution is a second control loop between the resource manager and the radar manager. This loop would receive regular updates of the platform state to help determine which type of waveform it could process efficiently as well as to exploit free computing opportunities by launching context-aware useful functions and, thus, enhance the QoS provided to the operator.

While the results of the QoS-aware mapping method are encouraging, one anticipates that its efficiency will largely depend on the relevant weighting of priorities and deadline penalty factors. These parameters being characterized by the radar management system, future work will include the investigation of the influence of these factors when using real-life workloads. Moreover, the computing time prediction algorithms used in the predictor are limited by the worst-case approach used. We are currently exploring a mixed-critical stochastic approach aiming at providing an even better trade-off between QoS provided and predictability of the systems.

To explore these ideas, the simulator presented in this paper is being extended by adding support for heterogeneous processing elements as well as the generation of more complex and diverse workloads. This will allow us to finely tune the prediction model to improve the QoS-aware mapping method presented above as well as to profile the mapping algorithms on the target platform. These profiling data are crucial as they will determine the computing volume limit of the envisaged mapping heuristics. This will directly influence the size and complexity of application graphs that can be considered for further tests. In addition to that, several other QoS metrics, both radar specific (false alarm rate) and generic (processor slack time minimization), are investigated to further improve the mapping results' quality.

Finally, as a centralized resource manager is currently in use, the computing platform's scaling might be an issue. As a fully distributed resources management system is hardly conceivable in the studied use-case, a hierarchical manager composed of both a central unit and locally distributed manager will be considered. Such systems have already been successfully implemented in dynamic large-scale environments such as clouds [26].

7 Conclusion

In this paper we presented a dynamic mapping method for real-time application execution on a heavily-constrained embedded architecture. This method was tested on an AESA radar use-case using a custom simulator. We showed that this approach allows us to obtain lower execution latencies than current mapping solutions while maintaining high predictability and allowing gradual performance degradation in overload scenarios.

Acknowledgments. This work was made possible thanks to the support of the Surface Radar Business Line of Thales.

References

1. http://www.uni-siegen.de/dreams/home/
2. http://www.certainty-project.eu/
3. Baruah, S., Li, H., Stougie, L.: Towards the design of certifiable mixed-criticality systems. In: 2010 16th IEEE Real-Time and Embedded Technology and Applications Symposium (RTAS), pp. 13–22. IEEE (2010)
4. Braun, T.D., et al.: A comparison of eleven static heuristics for mapping a class of independent tasks onto heterogeneous distributed computing systems. J. Parallel Distrib. Comput. **61**(6), 810–837 (2001)
5. Cai, Z., Li, X., Ruiz, R., Li, Q.: A delay-based dynamic scheduling algorithm for bag-of-task workflows with stochastic task execution times in clouds. Futur. Gener. Comput. Syst. **71**, 57–72 (2017)
6. Chen, H., Wang, F., Helian, N., Akanmu, G.: User-priority guided min-min scheduling algorithm for load balancing in cloud computing. In: 2013 National Conference on Parallel computing technologies (PARCOMPTECH), pp. 1–8. IEEE (2013)
7. Costache, S., Parlavantzas, N., Morin, C., Kortas, S.: Merkat: a market-based SLO-driven cloud platform. In: 2013 IEEE 5th International Conference on Cloud Computing Technology and Science (CloudCom). vol. 1, pp. 403–410, December 2013. https://doi.org/10.1109/CloudCom.2013.59
8. De Sensi, D., Torquati, M., Danelutto, M.: A reconfiguration algorithm for power-aware parallel applications. ACM Trans. Archit. Code Optim. **13**(4), 43:1–43:25 (2016). https://doi.org/10.1145/3004054, https://doi.org/10.1145/3004054
9. Gadioli, D., Palermo, G., Silvano, C.: Application autotuning to support runtime adaptivity in multicore architectures. In: 2015 International Conference on Embedded Computer Systems: Architectures, Modeling, and Simulation (SAMOS), pp. 173–180. IEEE (2015)

10. García-Valls, M., Cucinotta, T., Lu, C.: Challenges in real-time virtualization and predictable cloud computing. J. Syst. Arch. **60**(9), 726–740 (2014). https://doi.org/10.1016/j.sysarc.2014.07.004, http://www.sciencedirect.com/science/article/pii/S1383762114001015
11. Giannopoulou, G., Stoimenov, N., Huang, P., Thiele, L.: Scheduling of mixed-criticality applications on resource-sharing multicore systems. In: 2013 Proceedings of the International Conference on Embedded Software (EMSOFT), pp. 1–15, September 2013. https://doi.org/10.1109/EMSOFT.2013.6658595
12. Gupta, A., Kumar, A., Nagarajan, V., Shen, X.: Stochastic load balancing on unrelated machines. In: Proceedings of the Twenty-Ninth Annual ACM-SIAM Symposium on Discrete Algorithms, pp. 1274–1285. SIAM (2018)
13. Khemka, B., et al.: Utility maximizing dynamic resource management in an oversubscribed energy-constrained heterogeneous computing system. Sustain. Comput. Inform. Syst. **5**, 14–30 (2015). https://doi.org/10.1016/j.suscom.2014.08.001, http://www.sciencedirect.com/science/article/pii/S2210537914000420
14. Kousalya, G., Balakrishnan, P., Pethuru Raj, C.: Workflow scheduling algorithms and approaches. In: Automated Workflow Scheduling in Self-Adaptive Clouds. CCN, pp. 65–83. Springer, Cham (2017). https://doi.org/10.1007/978-3-319-56982-6_4
15. Li, H., Baruah, S.: An algorithm for scheduling certifiable mixed-criticality sporadic task systems. In: 2010 IEEE 31st Real-Time Systems Symposium (RTSS), pp. 183–192, November 2010. https://doi.org/10.1109/RTSS.2010.18
16. Liu, J., Pacitti, E., Valduriez, P., Mattoso, M.: A survey of data-intensive scientific workflow management. J. Grid Comput. **13**(4), 457–493 (2015)
17. Lucier, B., Menache, I., Naor, J.S., Yaniv, J.: Efficient online scheduling for deadline-sensitive jobs. In: Proceedings of the Twenty-Fifth Annual ACM Symposium on Parallelism in Algorithms and Architectures, pp. 305–314. ACM (2013)
18. Megow, N., Uetz, M., Vredeveld, T.: Models and algorithms for stochastic online scheduling. Math. Oper. Res. **31**(3), 513–525 (2006)
19. Nasri, M., Brandenburg, B.B.: Offline equivalence: a non-preemptive scheduling technique for resource-constrained embedded real-time systems (outstanding paper). In: 2017 IEEE Real-Time and Embedded Technology and Applications Symposium (RTAS), pp. 75–86. IEEE (2017)
20. Ptolemaeus, C. (ed.): System Design, Modeling, and Simulation using Ptolemy II. Ptolemy.org (2014). http://ptolemy.org/books/Systems
21. Quan, W., Pimentel, A.D.: A hierarchical run-time adaptive resource allocation framework for large-scale mpsoc systems. Des. Autom. Embed. Syst. **20**(4), 311–339 (2016)
22. Ren, J., Phan, L.T.X.: Mixed-criticality scheduling on multiprocessors using task grouping. In: 2015 27th Euromicro Conference on Real-Time Systems (ECRTS), pp. 25–34. IEEE (2015)
23. Rodriguez, M.A., Buyya, R.: Deadline based resource provisioningand scheduling algorithm for scientific workflows on clouds. IEEE Trans. Cloud Comput. **2**(2), 222–235 (2014)
24. Skutella, M., Sviridenko, M., Uetz, M.: Unrelated machine scheduling with stochastic processing times. Math. Oper. Res. **41**(3), 851–864 (2016)
25. Tang, X., Li, X., Fu, Z.: Budget-constraint stochastic task scheduling on heterogeneous cloud systems. Concurr. Comput. Pract. Exp. **29**(19), e4210 (2017)
26. Wang, Z., Su, X.: Dynamically hierarchical resource-allocation algorithm in cloud computing environment. J. Supercomput. **71**(7), 2748–2766 (2015). https://doi.org/10.1007/s11227-015-1416-x, https://doi.org/10.1007/s11227-015-1416-x

27. Warneke, D., Kao, O.: Exploiting dynamic resource allocation for efficient parallel data processing in the cloud. IEEE Trans. Parallel Distrib. Syst. **22**(6), 985–997 (2011). https://doi.org/10.1109/TPDS.2011.65
28. Xu, R., Wang, Y., Huang, W., Yuan, D., Xie, Y., Yang, Y.: Near-optimal dynamic priority scheduling strategy for instance-intensive business workflows in cloud computing. Concurr. Comput. Pract. Exp. **29**(18), e4167 (2017)

Predicting SDC Vulnerability of Instructions Based on Random Forests Algorithm

LiPing Liu$^{(\boxtimes)}$, LinLin Ci , and Wei Liu

Computer Department, Beijing Institute of Technology, Beijing, China
llp19860623@163.com, cilinlin_bit@126.com,
Liuwei_bit@126.com

Abstract. Silent Data Corruptions (SDCs) is a serious reliability issue in many domains of computer system. Selectively protecting of the program instructions that have a higher SDC vulnerability is one of the research hot spots in computer reliability field at present. A number of algorithms have already been presented to tackle this problem. However, many of them require tens of thousands of fault injection experiments, which are highly time and resource intensive. This paper proposes SDCPredictor, a novel solution that identify the SDC-vulnerable instructions based on random forests algorithm. SDCPredictor are based on static and dynamic features of the program alone, and do not require fault injections to be performed. SDCPredictor selectively protects the most SDC-vulnerable instructions in the program subject to a given performance overhead bound. Our experimental results show that SDCPredictor can obtain higher SDC detection efficiency than previous similar techniques.

Keywords: Fault tolerance · Error detection · Reliability · SDC vulnerability Random forests

1 Introduction

SEU-induced soft errors have been known as one of the major threats to functionality and reliability of space-borne computers and their host spacecrafts. Soft errors may be explicit bit flips in latches or memories, or glitches in combinational logics that can propagate and be captured in latches [1]. SEU could result in silent data corruption (SDC), which means wrong outcomes of a program without any crash detected. When an SDC occurs, the program will fail without any indication of the failure. This can lead to the error propagating in the system and causing catastrophic effects. Thus, with the increase in the number of transistors on a chip and the reduction of chip sizes, the transient fault rate of software will grow with Moore's Law [2]. Therefore, it is necessary to protect these devices against SDC errors.

Conventional hardware only solutions such as guard banding and hardware redundancy are challenging to apply due to power constraints. As a result, researchers have explored software-based techniques to tolerate hardware faults [3]. Software-based techniques do not require any modification in the hardware of the microprocessor. In fact, some of these approaches have already been used in mission critical systems for satellites and space missions [4].

© Springer Nature Switzerland AG 2018
J. Vaidya and J. Li (Eds.): ICA3PP 2018, LNCS 11336, pp. 593–607, 2018.
https://doi.org/10.1007/978-3-030-05057-3_44

Although software-based approaches such as full duplication are more cost-effective than the hardware-based ones, they provoke a non-negligible overhead to the programs in terms of execution time and code size. In many cases, this is the main difficulty for the software-based techniques feasibility. In order to reduce these overheads and to offer more exibility to designers, recent works have proposed the selective hardening based on software [5–7].

Studies have shown that SDCs are caused by errors in a relatively small proportion of programs' data variables [8, 9], and by selectively protecting these SDC-prone variables, one can achieve high coverage against SDCs. However, most prior work has identified SDC-prone variables using fault injection experiments, which are expensive for large applications.

Various efforts have been made to refine the injection framework. CriticalFault [10] applied vulnerability analysis to avoid the injections that result in mask. Since SFI was applied by Relyzer and CriticalFault, the weaknesses of SFI cannot be avoided. Relyzer [11] ran fault injections for the selected dynamic instruction sequences called "pilots". SymPLIFIED [12] identified SDC-causing instructions by symbolic execution, which covers all SDCs in real executions. However, it was even more time-consuming than fault injection. Shoestring [13] assumed that instructions, which impact global memory or produce arguments passed to function calls, can incur SDCs. Although the time cost was reduced, it brought a large number of false positives.

The work [16] proposes a configurable protection technique for SDC-causing errors that allows users to trade-off performance for reliability. Two models, namely SDCTune and SDCAuto, are built to predict the SDC proneness of a program's data. SDCAuto is built automatically using a machine learning approach known as the Classification and Regression Tree (CART) algorithm. Compared with fault injection based method, SDCAuto can obtain a relative accurate predicting of the SDC rate of an application and save a lot of time. However, one disadvantage of CART algorithm is that the tree may grow to be biased if some classes of data dominate. Besides, SDCAuto does not consider the data deviation of program output, which is important for some soft computing applications. For example, multimedia applications can tolerate blurry decoded images, and machine learning applications can tolerate noise. Such applications can tolerate most hardware errors as long as the erroneous outputs do not deviate significantly from error-free outcomes. Even instructions in the same application with the same SDC rate may cause different data deviation. It's obvious that the instruction causing more serious data deviation should give priority to be protected.

We propose a new configurable protection approach, SDCPredictor, to predict the SDC vulnerability of program instructions. Our goal is to find the subset of instructions which are the most SDC-vulnerable against SDC errors for a given performance cost budget. SDCPredictor predicts SDC vulnerability of program instructions based on random forest algorithm. Random forest has an effective method for estimating missing data, and has some mechanisms to deal with unbalanced data sets. SDCPredictor predicts the SDC vulnerability of program instructions by analyzing the features of an instruction, without requiring any fault injections to be performed, thus achieving significant time-saving. Because the parameters of the prediction model is optimized, SDCPredictor has a better prediction speed and accurate than previous methods. The contributions of this work are as follows:

We develop an intelligent prediction model, SDCPredictor, based on random forests algorithm, which can predict the SDC vulnerability of program instructions precisely. To the best of our knowledge, we are the first to predict the SDC vulnerability of program instructions using random forests.

SDCPredictor not only concerns about the probability that a fault in instruction will lead to SDC, but also the severity of SDC.

When building the individual tree of random forests, we evaluate its quality to determine whether the tree should be retained or discarded. This screening process improve the predictive power of SDCPredictor.

We evaluate the SDC vulnerability prediction accuracy and fault coverage of SDCPredictor on a set of benchmark programs. The experimental results demonstrate that SDCPredictor can obtain higher SDC detection efficiency than previous similar techniques.

The remainder of the paper is organized as follows. In Sect. 2 the related works on identifying SDC-Causing instructions are reviewed. In Sect. 3 we describe the proposed approach in detail. Section 4 reports the experimental results we gathered and finally in Sect. 5 draws some conclusions.

2   Related Works

A variety of efforts have been made to identify and protect SDC-causing instructions. To ensure system robustness, prior work has used statistical fault injection (SFI) to model the soft error rate (SER) of targeted systems.

CriticalFault [10] proposes a biased injection framework that employs vulnerability analysis to map out relevant faults for stress testing. However, the remaining faults are still too many to be simulated for accurate SDC rate analysis. Relyzer [11] systematically analyzes all fault injection sites in an application for transient faults, and employs fault pruning techniques that prune faults that need detailed study by either predicting their outcomes or showing them equivalent to other faults. SmartInjector [12] firstly lists all possible faults in an application, and then exploits the fault pruning techniques to remove most faults from injections by performing program analysis. SmartInjector also exploits a fault outcome prediction technique to determine the outcome of a simulation before it runs to completion.

Although SFI has proven to be effective for identifying SDC-causing instructions, it is extremely time-consuming and not unacceptable for large applications.

Another SDC identifying method is statistical vulnerability analysis. Shoestring [13] uses a static analysis approach to identify the instructions which are likely to result in SDCs, and employs instruction duplication to protect these instructions. Shoestring only considers the instructions in the backward slices of the instructions which update global variables or the arguments of library calls as the SDC-inducing instructions. The remaining instructions in a program are left unprotected. Although Shoestring only incurs an average performance overhead of 15.8%, the simple heuristic it uses only covers 33.9% of SDCs. SymPLIFIED [14] identifies SDC-causing instructions by symbolic execution, which covers all SDCs in real executions. However, it is even more time-consuming than fault injection.

The work [15] proposes a software-based method to identify and harden the most vulnerable blocks of a program. Using the genetic algorithm (GA), the proposed method takes the dynamic behavior of the programs into consideration to identify the most vulnerable blocks of a program. However, not all the instructions of vulnerable blocks are SDC-causing instructions and should be protected, as they incur high performance overhead when protected.

In recent years, machine learning based methods are introduced to identify the SDC-causing instructions. The work [16] proposes a machine learning algorithm based model, namely SDCAuto, to predict the SDC proneness of a program's data. SDCAuto builds the model automatically through a machine learning algorithm, thus requiring little to no effort on the part of the developer. It performs configurable protection against SDC-causing errors in general purpose applications without using fault injections.

3 Proposed Method

In this Section we will describe the proposed approach in detail. We first define some terms used in this paper, some of which are drawn from work [16].

Dynamic Dependency Graph: A Dynamic Dependency Graph (DDG) is a directed acyclic graph (V, E) that captures the dynamic dependencies among the values produced in the course of program execution, where V is the set of vertexes and E is the set of edges. In a DDG, a vertex v can be a register, a memory address or even a constant value. An edge e records the instruction (i.e., an operation) and links source operand(s) to destination operand(s). **Data propagation distance:** This is the maximum dynamic distance between the def and use of a value. This is denoted as $Dis(v)$. **Fanout:** The fanout of a node is the set of all immediate successors of the node in the DDG. In terms of values, it is the set of uses of the value represented by the node. The fanout of a node indicates how many nodes are directly impacted by an error in that node. **Cover:** The cover of a node is the number of nodes from which an error can propagate to a given node before causing a crash. **Basic Block:** A Basic Block (BB) is a maximal set of ordered non-branching instructions (except in the last instruction) or branch destinations (except in the first instruction) in which the execution always enters at the first instruction and leaves via the last instruction. **SDC coverage:** The SDC coverage is defined as the fraction of SDC causing errors detected by error detection technology. **SDC proneness per instruction:** This is the probability that a fault in instruction I leads to an SDC. This is denoted as $P(SDC)$. **SDC vulnerability per instruction:** This is the SDC vulnerability of instruction I. SDC vulnerability not only concerns about the SDC proneness, but also the data deviation of program output. This is denoted as $V(SDC)$. **Dynamic count ratio:** This is the ratio of the number of dynamic instances of instruction executed to the total number of dynamic instructions in the program. This is denoted as $D(I)$. **SDC impact:** The SDC impact is defined as the rate of the number of incorrect program outcome caused by SDC over the total number fault-free program outcome during the execution.

In this section, we first extract program features of instructions that correlate with highly SDC vulnerability. We then implement fault injection experiments on a small set of benchmark programs to generate training data set for training purposes. Finally, we use training data set to build our models and generate protected code. Figure 1 shows the block diagram of the proposed method. Details of each component are given below.

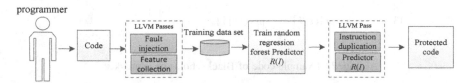

Fig. 1. Block diagram of the proposed method

3.1 Feature Extraction

Recent studies show hardware faults are often derated or masked. A hardware-error is said to be derated if it is inherently masked in the system. Different instructions of a program have different error-derating rate [15]. In other words, different instructions of a program have different SDC vulnerability.

Fault propagation can be stopped by an instruction either masking the fault, or by crashing the program. Both masking and crashing decrease the probability of an SDC resulting from the instruction that propagates its data to the other crashing/masking instruction, as a result of which its SDC proneness is lower. Our fault injection experiments show that the masking of an error at an instruction I can occur due to the following factors: (1) The error at instruction I may be masked by I itself. (2) The error at instruction I may be masked due to the successor instruction in path p. Faults that occur in the higher bit positions of operands of memory address calculation instructions are more likely to cause the program to crash. Shift instructions, comparison instructions and logical operation instructions can decrease the SDC proneness of the source operands by a certain extent. We call these instructions as SDC-masked instructions.

Our fault injection experiments show that the SDC proneness of instruction is not equal to its SDC vulnerability. Figure 2 shows an example code based on Blackscholes benchmark from PARSEC benchmarks. In Fig. 2, the integer variable named numOptions determine the loop time of the two for loops. A fault corrupted the value of variable numOptions in the line 1 cause SDC of six variables; while a fault corrupted the value of variable numOptions in line 11 only cause SDC of one variable. It is obvious that the assignment instruction in line 1 has a higher SDC vulnerability than the assignment instruction in line 11. However, the SDC proneness of the assignment instruction in line 1 is equal to the assignment instruction in line 14. Therefore, the severity of SDC should be consideration in determining the SDC vulnerability of instruction.

```
1   for (i=0; i<numOptions; i++)
2   {
3           otype[i]      = (data[i].OptionType == 'P') ? 1 : 0;
4           sptprice[i]   = data[i].s;
5           strike[i]     = data[i].strike;
6           rate[i]       = data[i].r;
7           volatility[i] = data[i].v;
8           otime[i]      = data[i].t;
9   }
10  ...
11  for (i=0; i<numOptions; i++)
12  {
13          sptprice[i]   = prices[i];
14  }
```

Fig. 2. Example code of Blackscholes benchmark

Features are extracted according to the above analysis and also based on prior work [12, 13, 16–18]. In total, 62 features are extracted. We categorize these features of instructions into nine categories shown in Table 1. (1) Data dependency related features. An error occurred in one variable can propagate to multiple variables by data dependencies among the instructions. Variables with a long data propagation distance or large fanout usually have a higher SDC vulnerability. (2) Type of end points of data dependency chains related features. The SDC proneness of a variable depends on (1) the fault propagation in its data dependency chain, and (2) the SDC proneness of the end point of that chain. (3) Memory address calculation related features. Memory address calculation instructions are usually used for pointer dereferences and are likely to cause SDCs and segmentation faults which crash the application. (4) Sub-word operations related features. Sub-word operations only utilize a fraction of the bits in the incoming values. Thus, fault occurred in the not utilized bits will be masked and SDC proneness of the source operands will decrease by a certain extent. (5) Logical operations related features. Logical operations derate errors that occur in AND operations when the corresponding bit in the other operand is 0, as well as OR operations when the corresponding bit in the other operand is 1. (6) Successor instruction related features. If SDC-masked instructions exist in the successor instruction of an instruction *I*, the SDC proneness of *I* will be derated. (7) Code structure related features. SDC causing code tends to be on the hot paths of the application. BBs with a higher in-degree or within a loop usually tend to be on the hot paths. (8) Data width related features. Data width is the number of bits in values, and is a major feature affecting the SDC proneness. (9) Execution time related features. Generally speaking, the instructions with a higher dynamic count ratio (DCR) have a higher SDC proneness. Our experimental results show that those instructions on the long path of DDG usually have a higher SDC vulnerability.

Table 1. Some features extracted for model building.

Feature group	Feature	Description
Data dependency related features	destination_operand_fanout	the fanout of destination operand
	destination_operand_cover	the cover of destination operand
Type of end points of data dependency chains related features	is_stroe	whether the operation is used to write to memory
	is_function_call	whether the operation is a function-call operation
	is_cmp	whether the comparison is made between primitive data
Memory access and addressing related features	is_load	whether the operation is used to read from memory
	is_memory_addressing	whether the operation is a memory addressing operation
Sub-word operations related features	is_shl	whether the operation is a shift left operation
	is_lshr	whether the operation is a logicalshift right operation
	is_ashr	whether the operation is a arithmetic shift right operation
Logical operations related features	is_and	whether the operation is a logic "and" operation
	is_or	whether the operation is a logic "or" operation
Successor instruction related features	shl_instructions_count	the number of left shift instructions contained in successor instruction
	shr_instructions_count	the number of right shift instructions contained in successor instruction
Code structure related features	number_of_pred _BBs	number of predecessor BBs
	number_of_suc _BBs	number of successor BBs
	is_within_loop	basic blocks is within a loop
	is_loop_terminator	whether the result can break a loop execution
	is_accumulative_computation	whether the operation is a accumulative-computation operation
Data width related features	data_width_Source _operand	the data width of source operand
	data_width_destination_operand	the data width of destination operand
Execution time related features	dynamic_count_ratio	dynamic count ratio

3.2 Fault Injection and Training Data Generation

The goal of fault injection is to create a training set for the machine learning regression mode. The fault injection experiment is conducted using LLFI, a program level fault injection tool, which has been shown to be accurate for measuring SDCs in programs [19]. LLFI works at the LLVM compiler's intermediate code level [9], and allows fault injections to be performed at specific program points, and into specific data types. It also enables tracing the propagation of the fault in the program by instrumenting the program at selected points. LLFI is closely integrated with the LLVM compiler, and can hence support a wide variety of programs.

We selected a set of 12 benchmarks which are drawn from SPEC benchmarks [20], Stanford benchmarks [21], Parboil benchmarks [22] and PARSEC benchmarks [23]. We divide the 15 applications into two groups; one group for training and the other for testing.

We choose these benchmarks to represent a wide range of commodity and scientific applications. Tables 2 and 3 illustrate the characteristics of the benchmarks. These benchmarks are compiled by LLVM compiler with standard optimization level (−O2). We compile the IR file and feed the produced executable file to LLFI after linking.

Table 2. Characteristics of the training benchmarks

Program	Description	Benchmark suite
Bzip2	File compression and decompression program	SPEC benchmarks
Perlbench	SPEC benchmark for perl interpreter	SPEC benchmarks
Blackscholes	Financial Analysis	PARSEC benchmarks
Swaptions	Price portfolio of swaptions	PARSEC benchmarks
TSP	Solving the classic TSP problem	Stanford benchmarks
Qsort	Sorting the a list of random numbers by quick-sort	Stanford benchmarks
BFS	Breadth-First Search	Parboil benchmarks
LBM	Fluid dynamics	Parboil benchmarks

Table 3. Characteristics of the testing benchmarks

Program	Description	Benchmark suite
Gzip	Compression	SPEC benchmarks
Ferret	Similarity Search	PARSEC benchmarks
Queens	Solving the classic n-queens problem	Stanford benchmarks
MM	Dense Matrix-Matrix Multiply	Parboil benchmarks

The experiments are carried out on an Intel core i7 based machine, with 8 GB of RAM and 400 GB Hard drive. The machine is running Debian Linux Version 6.0.

The previous research results show that SDC proneness is highly influenced by data dependencies among the instructions and a considerable number of program instructions have no effect on the program results. In this paper, we use the static-slicing technique [24] to transform a program to an identical but smaller and simpler executable version. The executable slice of a program is a subset of program instructions that can be executed.

First, we run LLFI on each executable slice of program, and select specific instructions as fault injection targets.

Second, we use statistical fault injection to implement fault injection. We corrupt the instruction's source register by flipping a single bit in it and each bit flips one time. In each run, a fault, i.e., a single bit flip, is injected into the source register of exactly one dynamic instance of an instruction, and the outcome of the fault is classified by comparing the final output with the fault free outcome. The fault-free or baseline outcome is obtained by running the original executable with the same input, but without any injected faults. We classify the outcome into four categories: (1) Crash, meaning that the program threw an exception, (2) SDC, which means the program's output deviated from the fault-free outcome, (3) Hang, which means the program took significantly longer to execute than a fault-free run, and (4) Benign, which means the program completed successfully and its output matched the fault-free outcome. The above outcomes are mutually exclusive and exhaustive.

Third, the SDC proneness $P(SDC)$ of each instruction is gathered and computed by Eq. (1):

$$P(SDC) = \frac{N_{SDC}}{N_{fault}} \times D(I) \tag{1}$$

where N_{SDC} is the SDC count caused by instruction I, N_{fault} is the total number of initial faults attributed to the instruction I, $D(I)$ is the dynamic count ratio of the instruction I. Meanwhile, we gather and compute the average SDC impact of each instruction by Eq. (2):

$$Impact(I) = \frac{1}{N_{SDC}} (\sum_{i=1}^{N_{SDC}} \frac{CIO_i}{CO}) \tag{2}$$

where CIO_i is the number of incorrect program caused by i-th SDC, CO is the total number of program output during the execution. In this paper, we treat the store operation as program output.

Finally, we obtain the SDC vulnerability of instruction I by equation $Vulnerability(I) = P(SDC) \times Impact(I)$. Thus, training data set $\{F, C\}$ is generated, where F is the extracted features vector, and C is the annotated class labels (i.e., SDC vulnerability).

3.3   Regression Model Training

Training Random Regression Forests
We train the models from a set of training instructions with the above features. The SDC vulnerability of these instructions depends on the extracted features. The full

training samples have 8146 training instructions. Based on the 8146 training instructions, a random regression forest is constructed. The random forest is an ensemble learner consisting of a collection of tree-structured base learners. Each base learner is a classification and regression tree (CART), and for regression, each tree individually predicts the target response while the forest predicts the target as the average of the individual tree predictions. Let $F=\{f_i \in R | i = 1, 2,\dots, N\}$ denote the extracted features, and let $C = \{c_1, c_2,\dots, c_N\}$ denote the annotated class labels of the training samples (i.e., SDC vulnerability). We build the trees following the random forest framework [25]. For each tree in the random forest, a subset of samples is randomly chosen by bootstrap from the training samples, while the remaining is used to test the prediction accuracy of the random forest. The random selection of features is done at each node split for building the tree. Typically this setting is $\sqrt{n}$, where n is the number of features. In our method the number of features is 8.

Furthermore, once a tree is built, we evaluate its quality to determine whether the tree should be retained or discarded. Only the trees which have sufficiently high accuracy will be kept. As mentioned above, the bootstrap method is used to randomly choose a subset of samples from the given training samples to construct a tree. These chosen samples are called in-of-bag (IOB) data, while the remainder is called out-of-bag (OOB) data. The OOB data are utilized to evaluate the tree constructed based on the IOB data. Given a tree regressor $h_k(x)$ built from the kth training data subset, we define the mean square error (denoted by MSE) of the tree $h_k(x)$ as

$$MSE = \frac{\sum_{i=1}^{N-N_s} (h_k(x_i) - C_i)^2}{N - N_s} \tag{3}$$

where x_i is a sample in the OOB data and C_i is the class label of the sample x_i. It is obvious that the tree with low MSE has high accuracy. Hence, we accept a tree whose MSE on the OOB data is below the prespecified threshold. In this way, the trees constructed in the forest are all with lower MSE, and a better random forest can be obtained.

Choose the Instructions to Protect and Design Detector

After predicting the SDC vulnerability for each instruction, we then choose instructions to minimize the SDC impact subject to a given performance overhead, using a standard dynamic programming algorithm [27]. Once we identify a set of instructions to protect, the next step is to insert error detectors at these instructions. Our detectors are based on duplicating the backward slices of the instructions to protect, similar to prior work [16]. We insert a check immediately after the instructions to be protected, which compares the original value computed by the instruction with the value computed by the duplicated instructions. Any difference in these values is deemed to be error detection and the program is stopped.

4   Experimental Evaluation

SDC vulnerability accuracy, SDC coverage, SDC detection efficiency and SDC impact are imperative parameters for evaluating our approach. So all of these parameters are measured and reported.

4.1   SDC Vulnerability Accuracy

There are primarily 3 parameters which can be tuned to improve the predictive power of the random regression forests model: (1) maximum number of features in individual tree, and (2) number of trees, and (3) minimum sample leaf size of an individual tree. We set the value of first parameter as $\sqrt{n}$, where n is the total number of features. As for the number of trees, we gradually increased it from 150 with a step-size 5 until the prediction accuracy becomes stable or decreasing. Finally, this value is determined to be 285. There are primarily 3 parameters which can be tuned to improve the predictive power of the random regression forests model: (1) maximum number of features in individual tree, and (2) number of trees, and (3) minimum sample leaf size of an individual tree. We set the value of first parameter as $\sqrt{n}$, where n is the total number of features. As for the number of trees, we gradually increased it from 150 with a step-size 5 until the prediction accuracy becomes stable or decreasing. Finally, this value is determined to be 285.

In order to avoid over-fitting problem, we set the third parameter as 50. To evaluate the predicting results of SDC vulnerability for each instruction, we calculate the average squared errors for testing dataset and the accuracy (the percentage of the samples whose SDC vulnerability estimation error is less than 10%) of SDC vulnerability estimation.

Table 4 shows the accuracy and MSE of SDC vulnerability on the four testing benchmarks. It can be observed that our models are highly accurate in predicting the SDCs vulnerability. The high accuracy benefits from that we strengthen the generalization error of a tree by choosing features according to their weights when building the tree of random forests. Besides, the SDC vulnerability of testing programs is closely to real probability because we use statistical fault injection method to implement fault injection. In addition, we optimize the parameters of the random forests which improve the prediction accuracy.

Thus, it can guide detector placement to obtain high coverage at low performance overheads.

Table 4. The MSE and accuracy of the testing programs

Program	MSE	Accuracy
Gzip	0.00549	88.76%
Ferret	0.00247	94.56%
Queens	0.00178	95.28%
MM	0.00428	90.13%

4.2 SDC Impact

The SDC impact is defined as the rate of the number of incorrect program outcome caused by SDC over the total number fault-free program outcome during the execution. We apply our approach to predict the SDC vulnerability for different instructions to satisfy the performance overhead bounds provided by the user.

Figure 3 shows the SDC impact obtained by our approach (SCDPredictor) and SDCAuto for each benchmark under three different performance overhead bounds: 20%, 40% and 60%. As it can be seen in Fig. 3, the averages SDC impact for SCDPredictor and SDCAuto are 74.70% and 79.31% respectively for the 20% performance overhead bound, the corresponding averages SDC impact are 59.20% and 66.30% for the 40% performance overhead bound, and 39.81% and 42.50% for the 60% performance overhead bound. It is obvious that the SCDPredictor obtains lower SDC impact at the same performance overhead bound than SDCAuto. The reason is that SCDPredictor is SDC impact sensitive. It not only concerns about the SDC proneness, but also the SDC impact of program instructions. SCDPredictor protects instructions with high SDC proneness and high SDC impact. While SDCAuto only concerns about the SDC proneness and ignore the SDC severity of instructions. Besides, the prediction model of SDCAuto is built using CART. It is well known that the tree of CART is easy to be biased. It is hard to keep robust and stable prediction accuracy for CART. Unlike SDCAuto, the prediction model of SCDPredictor is built using random forests, which hardly cause over-fitting and are less sensitive to noisy due to it constructs a series of tree-based learners. Thus, SCDPredictor can offer more stable and accurate prediction performance than SDCAuto.

4.3 SDC Coverage and Detection Efficiency

The SDC coverage is defined as the fraction of SDC causing errors detected by our detectors. Figure 4 shows the SDC coverage obtained by our approach and SDCAuto for each benchmark under three different performance overhead bounds: 20%, 40% and 60%. As it can be seen in Fig. 4, the averages SDC coverage for SCDPredictor and SDCAuto are 33.08% and 38.10% respectively for the 20% performance overhead bound, the corresponding averages SDC coverage are 50.30% and 51.90% for the 40% performance overhead bound, and 66.10% and 65.76% for the 60% performance overhead bound. As mentioned before, SDC coverage, SDC detection efficiency and SDC impact are imperative parameters for evaluating our approach. In literature [16], the SDC detection efficiency (DE) is defined as the ratio between SDC coverage and performance overhead. However, the SDC impact is not taken into account. We redefined the SDC detection efficiency; the new definition of SDC detection efficiency is showed in Eq. 4.

$$SDC\ detection\ efficiency = \frac{SDC\ coverage \times\ (1 - SDC\ impact)}{performance\ overhead} \qquad (4)$$

The averages SDC detection efficiency for SCDPredictor and SDCAuto are 0.418 and 0.394 respectively for the 20% performance overhead bound, the corresponding

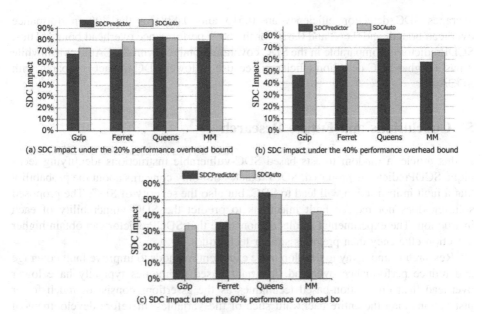

Fig. 3. The comparison of SDC impact under different performance overhead bounds: 20%, 40% and 60%

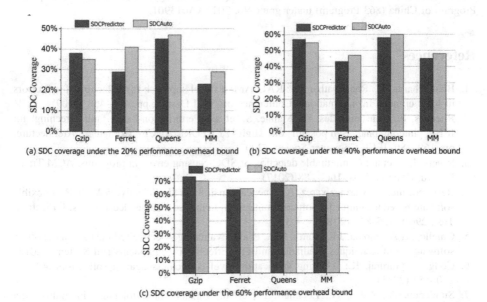

Fig. 4. The comparison of SDC coverage under different performance overhead bounds: 20%, 40% and 60%

averages SDC detection efficiency are 0.513 and 0.438 for the 40% performance overhead bound, and 0.663 and 0.630 for the 60% performance overhead bound. Thus, SCDPredictor is comparable in the SDC coverage obtained with SDCAuto. Meanwhile it has a higher SDC detection efficiency because of lower SDC impact compared with SDCAuto.

5   Conclusions and Future Research

In this article, a random forests based SDC-vulnerable instructions identifying technique SCDPredictor is proposed. SDCPredictor not only concerns about the probability that a fault in instruction will lead to SDC, but also the severity of SDC. The proposed solution does not require fault injections to predict the SDC vulnerability of each instruction. The experimental results demonstrate that SDCPredictor can obtain higher detection efficiency than previous similar techniques.

Research is underway to develop more excellent methods to improve fault coverage and reduce performance overhead. Invariant based techniques typically have lower overhead than duplication-based techniques as the assertions consist of much fewer instructions than the entire backward slice of the variables; therefore development of invariant based techniques is the new research topic for our research group.

Acknowledgment. This research was supported by the National Natural Science Foundation of China under grant No. 61370134, the National High Technology Research and Development Program of China (863 Program) under grant No. 2013AA013901.

References

1. Bhattacharya, K., Ranganathan, N.: RADJAM: a novel approach for reduction of soft errors in logic circuits. In: International Conference on VlSI Design, pp. 453–458 (2009)
2. Racunas, P., Constantinides, K., Manne, S., et al.: Perturbation-based fault screening. In: IEEE, International Symposium on High PERFORMANCE Computer Architecture, pp. 169–180. IEEE Computer Society (2007)
3. Rivers, J.A., et al.: Configurable detection of SDC-causing errors in programs. ACM Trans. Embed. Comput. Syst. **16**(3), 88 (2017)
4. Restrepocalle, F., Martnezlvarez, A., Cuencaasensi, S., et al.: Selective SWIFT-R: a flexible software-based technique for soft error mitigation in low-cost embedded systems. J. Electron. Test. **29**(6), 825–838 (2013)
5. Chielle, E., Azambuja, J.R., Barth, R.S., et al.: Evaluating selective redundancy in data-flow software-based techniques. Radiation and ITS Effects on Components and Systems (2012)
6. Cong, J., Gururaj, K.: Assuring application-level correctness against soft errors, **47**(10), 150–157 (2011)
7. Sundaram, A., Aakel, A., Lockhart, D., et al.: Efficient fault tolerance in multi-media applications through selective instruction replication. In: The Workshop on Radiation Effects and Fault Tolerance in Nanometer Technologies, pp. 339–346. ACM (2008)
8. Hari, S.K.S., Adve, S.V., Naeimi, H.: Low-cost program-level detectors for reducing silent data corruptions. In: IEEE/IFIP International Conference on Dependable Systems and Networks, pp. 1–12. IEEE (2012)

9. Thomas, A., Pattabiraman, K.: Error detector placement for soft computation. In: IEEE/IFIP International Conference on Dependable Systems and Networks, pp. 1–12. IEEE Computer Society (2013)

10. IEEE: Understanding soft error propagation using efficient vulnerability-driven fault injection. In: IEEE/IFIP International Conference on Dependable Systems and Networks, pp. 1–12. IEEE Computer Society (2012)

11. Hari, S.K.S., Adve, S.V., Naeimi, H., et al.: Relyzer: application resiliency analyzer for transient faults. IEEE Micro 33(3), 58–66 (2013)

12. Li, J., Tan, Q.: SmartInjector: exploiting intelligent fault injection for SDC rate analysis. In: IEEE International Symposium on Defect and Fault Tolerance in VLSI and Nanotechnology Systems, pp. 236–242. IEEE (2013)

13. Feng, S., Gupta, S., Ansari, A., et al.: Shoestring: probabilistic soft error reliability on the cheap. In: Fifteenth Edition of ASPLOS on Architectural Support for Programming Languages and Operating Systems, pp. 385–396. ACM (2010)

14. Pattabiraman, K., Nakka, N.M., Kalbarczyk, Z.T., et al.: SymPLFIED: symbolic program-level fault injection and error detection framework. IEEE Trans. Comput. 62(11), 2292–2307 (2013)

15. Arasteh, B., Bouyer, A., Pirahesh, S.: An efficient vulnerability-driven method for hardening a program against soft-error using genetic algorithm. Comput. Electr. Eng. 48, 25–43 (2015)

16. Rivers, J.A., Rivers, J.A., Rivers, J.A., et al.: Configurable detection of SDC-causing errors in programs. ACM Trans. Embed. Comput. Syst. 16(3), 88 (2017)

17. Cook, J.J., Zilles, C.: A characterization of instruction-level error derating and its implications for error detection, pp. 482–491 (2008)

18. Laguna, I., Schulz, M., Richards, D.F., et al.: IPAS: intelligent protection against silent output corruption in scientific applications. In: IEEE/ACM International Symposium on Code Generation and Optimization, pp. 227–238. IEEE (2016)

19. Wei, J., Thomas, A., Li, G., et al.: Quantifying the accuracy of high-level fault injection techniques for hardware faults. In: IEEE/IFIP International Conference on Dependable Systems and Networks, pp. 375–382. IEEE Computer Society (2014)

20. Henning, J.L.: SPEC CPU2006 benchmark descriptions. ACM SIGARCH Comput. Archit. News 34(4), 1–17 (2006)

21. Hsueh, M.C., Tsai, T.K., Iyer, R.K.: Fault injection techniques and tools. Computer 30(4), 75–82 (1997)

22. Stratton, J.A., Rodrigues, C., Sung, I.J., et al.: Parboil: a revised benchmark suite for scientific and commercial throughput computing (2012)

23. Bienia, C., Kumar, S., Singh, J.P., et al.: The PARSEC benchmark suite: characterization and architectural implications. In: International Conference on Parallel Architectures and Compilation Techniques, pp. 72–81. IEEE (2017)

24. Weiser, M.: Program slicing. IEEE Trans. Software Eng. SE-10(4), 352–357 (1984)

25. Breiman, L.: Random forests. Mach. Learn. 45(1), 5–32 (2001)

26. Ye, Y., Li, H., Deng, X., et al.: Feature weighting random forest for detection of hidden web search interfaces. J. Comput. Linguist. Chin. Lang. Process. 13(4), 387–404 (2008)

27. Martello, S., Toth, P.: Knapsack problems. Accessed Nov 1990

Hybrid Cloud Architecture for Cross-Platform Interoperability in Smart Homes

Ming Tao[1]($\boxtimes$)(iD), Chao Qu[1](iD), Wenhong Wei[1](iD), Bin Zhou[1](iD), and Shuqiang Huang[2](iD)

[1] School of Computer Science and Network Security,
Dongguan University of Technology, Dongguan 523808, People's Republic of China
`ming.tao@mail.scut.edu.cn`, {`quc,weiwh,zhoub`}`@dgut.edu.cn`
[2] Department of Optoelectronic Engineering, Jinan University,
Guangzhou 510632, People's Republic of China
`hsq@jnu.edu.cn`

Abstract. With the development and application of Internet of Things (IoT) technology, many home device maker and/or vendors are interested in developing available solutions of smart home. These heterogeneous systems need to be fully interoperable to support the joint and harmonized execution of household operations. However, the heterogeneity of devices, services and communication protocols involved in most of the available solutions developed by different vendors, still remains a challenge issue of interoperability, and is adversely affecting the widespread application. Hence, it needs to be reasonably solved to operate the heterogeneous systems in IoT-enabled smart homes in an optimal fashion. To address this issue of cross-platform interoperability, a hybrid cloud architecture for IoT-enabled smart homes is proposed in this paper, which presents a solid solution to achieve the effective and efficient interoperability of the heterogeneous services and devices from different vendors. The conducted experiments have been shown to demonstrate the performance.

Keywords: Cloud · IoT · Interoperability · Smart home

1 Introduction

Promoted by the advances in emerging Internet of Things (IoT) technology, an ever-growing amount of various information sources in the smart home scenario has been fostered, which are structured in multiple sensing and control platforms/applications connected through several wireless and wireline communication facilities, whereas the fundamental challenge consists in collecting, integrating, aggregating and processing the huge amount of data originated by these sources in order to transform them in the manner of knowledge needed by smart services provided in the modern home [1,2]. This may imply managing many heterogeneous devices and protocols/technologies as well as performing

© Springer Nature Switzerland AG 2018
J. Vaidya and J. Li (Eds.): ICA3PP 2018, LNCS 11336, pp. 608–617, 2018.
https://doi.org/10.1007/978-3-030-05057-3_45

cross-platform harmonization of their produced data, which becomes really feasible only by relying on the virtually unlimited storage and computing resources provided by cloud infrastructures [3]. Furthermore, the virtualization facilities provided by clouds can significantly boost the limited computing capacity of hardware-constrained sensing or actuator devices making them be able to handle the complex processing tasks needed by modern smart home applications [4].

Currently, from various considerations, the vendors of home devices prefer to develop proprietary smart home platforms reflecting their own interests. These platforms often bring their own solutions and service interfaces, such that different communication protocols and standards are typically deployed within each solution. Hence, interconnecting heterogeneous services and devices from different vendors, and providing interoperability across the available platforms remain the main challenges [5]. Although there are many proposals focusing on heterogeneous systems management and interoperability issues, the heterogeneity of, i.e., devices, services, communication protocols, standards and data formats, etc., involved in most of the available solutions developed by different vendors, still remains a challenge issue of interoperability.

To address this issue, a hybrid cloud architecture for IoT-enabled smart homes is developed in this paper to enable effective, efficiency and seamless interoperations on heterogeneous devices/services provided by different vendors. In this context, a public cloud based platform providing virtualization of the involved objects and their interfaces, and allowing their orchestration into generalized on-demand smart home services is built. In each private cloud platform, the communication and access protocols and standards, as well as the device registration, authentication, the used management and manipulation methods, are individuated by the vendor. When the home user wants to manipulate a home device, the operating processes are discussed in two scenarios. Finally, the elaborately designed experiments are conducted to demonstrate the effectiveness and efficiency of the proposed hybrid cloud architecture.

The rest of this paper is organized as follows. In Sect. 2, a brief review of the related achievements in the existing proposals are discussed. In Sect. 3, a hybrid cloud architectural model for cross-platform interoperability in IoT-enabled smart home is firstly developed, and then, the operating processes of home device in two scenarios are discussed. In Sect. 4, the experimental setup and the analysis results of effectiveness and efficiency are addressed. In Sect. 5, this paper is summarized and concluded.

2   Related Work

Recently, with the emerging IoT and Cloud computing technologies, there are many proposals focusing on the smart home design, heterogeneous systems management and interoperability issues. In [4], Soliman et al. presented a smart home approach which consists of embedding intelligence into sensors and actuators by using the Arduino platform, and networking smart things by using ZigBee technology. Ghayvat et al. [6] presented a universal IoT-based smart home model, in which, all the home devices and appliances are connected together and the home network is the integration of different wireless technologies. Seo et al. [7] proposed a platform architecture named HePA (Hexagonal Platform Architecture), that is extremely scalable while maintaining required performance and reflecting requirements of the complex IoT environment. By integrating IoT and service component technologies, Li et al. [8] presented a smart home system architecture which has considered the heterogeneous data fusion in IoT, and Tao et al. [9] proposed a ontology-based scheme to address the problem of managing large volumes of heterogeneous data generated by home entities.

To address the heterogeneous systems management and interoperability issues, using the SOA (Service Oriented Architecture) and web services to integrate various home services and applications as a promising option has been investigated to a much extent. In [10], Wu et al. used SOA and mobile-agent (MA) technology to support the interactions between system components, and designed a smart home architecture that is a peer-to-peer (P2P) model based on multiple Open Services Gateway Initiative (OSGi) platforms. Also OSGi-based, Cheng et al. [11] proposed an extensible architecture for heterogeneous smart home systems enabling dynamic integrations of devices, services and protocols. In [12], Hamza et al. proposed an architecture which uses open source SOA and Smart-M3 framework to provide the core technologies enabling interoperability and extendibility, and designed ontology to enable semantic middleware for integration. By taking into account of the distributed nature of the home environment with heterogeneous devices, Perumal et al. [13] presented an integrated approach using the SOAP/XML protocol for implementing effective web-service-enabled smart home management systems.

New architectures and platforms for smart home management, such as the cloud- and IoT-based should be provably scalable, efficient, reliable and secure before starting their large-scale deployment. Existing mechanisms and approaches, however, are not yet fully satisfactory in meeting all these requirements at the same time. There are still some serious challenges described as follows.

Since there are a number of stakeholders such as device and service vendors involved in smart home clouds, and there are complex dependencies among these stakeholders as well, it necessitates global standards to refrain from incompatibilities and conflicts between private platforms and solutions. However, establishing global standards to push the complexity into smaller and make smart home clouds more compatible and effective, remains a challenge. Further and more efforts on standardization should be conducted to coordinate various kinds of resources for achieving more effective smart home clouds and reducing the number of adaptations and mediation stages.

The utility of smart home clouds mainly relies on their scalability in handling a dynamically and time-varying growing amount of homes. Apart from handling regular operations of home devices, smart home clouds must be able to face the ever-growing demands for home entertainment and some other applications. They also need to provide the interoperability among the heterogeneous devices and services from different vendors, such that further and more advanced developments aimed at optimizing the utilizations of computing, storage and network resources are needed. Meanwhile, the realization of optimization algorithms that coordinate the private platforms/clouds with the public one to achieve real-time cross-layer data synchronization and minimize the traffic load between layers is necessary as well. In addition, with the launch of new home devices and technologies, designing and developing cost-effective IoT middleware supporting the integration of these newly launched devices and technologies with the existing ones will be challenging.

3   Hybrid Cloud Architecture for Cross-Platform Interoperability

Building a public cloud based platform providing virtualization of the involved objects and their interfaces, and allowing their orchestration into generalized on-demand smart home services, may be an effective strategy for facing the above challenges and avoiding conflicts between the different private platforms characterizing the legacy vendor solutions.

The layered scheme of our proposed hybrid cloud architectural model for IoT-enabled smart home is shown in Fig. 1. Generally, the defined layers have different functions and the lower layers provide foundational supports for the upper layers. By integrating under a common cloud-based platform, various devices fit into the broader concept of IoT, e.g., household sensors, actuators, controllers, smart home appliances, smart phones, and other Internet accessed home appliances, interconnect by using the available wireless communications technologies (e.g., Bluetooth, RFID, ZigBee, Wi-Fi, 3/4G, LTE, etc.). Such architecture enables data collection and exchange among all the home devices in order to provide cheap, secure, real-time and on-demand home services. It also allows the seamless interworking of the legacy platforms (typically private clouds) provided by different smart home service vendors through the aforementioned public cloud layer, by generalizing the scope of each individual service, represented by using an Internet-like structure, and integrating it into a common IoT service fabric for sharing and reusing in multiple operating household contexts. SOA here will also be employed to integrate various kinds of information and connect multiple devices from different vendors seamlessly through the smart home cloud. SOA allows the developers of smart home applications to organize, aggregate and package relevant applications into newly advanced and emerging home services. Additionally, a specific middleware stratum can be employed to hide the concrete details of implementing the underlining technologies and to provide support for integrating the specific applications implemented on the smart home cloud. By leveraging such SOA and IoT enabled smart home clouds, more and more innovative home services can be developed by device vendors, third-party service providers and government agencies.

In each private cloud platform, the communication and access protocols and standards, as well as the device registration, authentication, management and manipulation methods used, are individuated by the vendor [14]. In the public

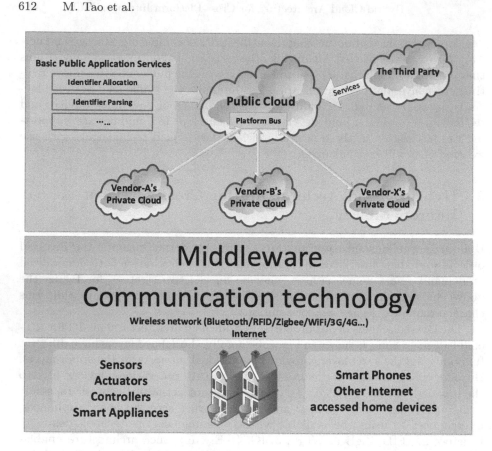

Fig. 1. Multi-layer architecture for IoT-enabled smart home data clouds.

cloud, some basic public application services are provided, e.g., global identifier allocation and parsing for the registered home devices, access admission and management for the service platforms of other industries; additionally, providing the virtualized service and device/object interfaces for the third party access to home services and devices, the platform bus implements protocol conversion and addressing operations for all the devices (with their IDs) registered in the platform [15].

In the developed hybrid cloud platform for IoT-enabled smart home, when the home user wants to manipulate a home device, the operating process should consider the following two scenarios.

In the first scenario where the target device is managed by the associated private cloud, the diagram of operation process is shown in Fig. 2, and the crucial procedures are simply described as follows.

I. The certified home user uses the vendor-specific companion App installed on the smart phone to send a corresponding operation command to the associated private platform directly.

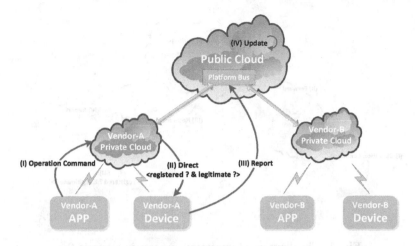

Fig. 2. The diagram of operation process in scenario 1.

II. The ID of the target device will be checked at first locally in such (presumably private cloud) infrastructure. If the target device is registered in the associated private platform, and the legitimacy of the operation command is positive once verified, the operation command would be forwarded to the target device associated to the private platform.

III. After accomplishing the requested manipulation, the target device reports the relevant parameters about its current operating status to the associated private platform which then forwards them to the platform bus in the public cloud.

IV. Subsequently, the platform bus synchronizes the device status with all the other associated private platforms.

In the second scenario where the target device is not managed by the associated private cloud, the diagram of operation process is shown in Fig. 3, and the crucial procedures are simply described as follows.

I. The certified home user uses the vendor-specific companion App installed on the smart phone to send a corresponding operation command to the associated private platform directly.

II. The ID of the target device will be at first checked locally in such infrastructure. If the device is not registered in the associated private cloud, the operation command would be forwarded to the platform bus in the public cloud.

III. The platform bus then redirects the operation command to the corresponding private platform by performing the addressing operation with the ID, and the operation legality would be verified in the associated private platform as well. If the legitimacy of the operation command is positive, the operation command would be forwarded to the target device associated to the private platform.

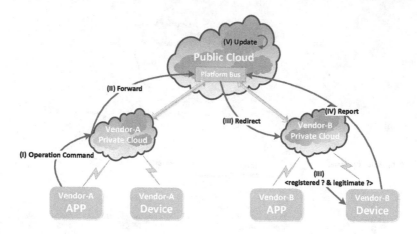

Fig. 3. The diagram of operation process in scenario 2.

IV. After accomplishing the requested manipulation, the target device reports the relevant parameters about its current operating status to the associated private platform which then forwards them to the platform bus in the public cloud.

V. Finally, the platform bus synchronizes the updated device status in the whole hybrid cloud platform just as specified above.

4   Experiments and Analysis

To qualitatively analyze and evaluate the performance of the proposed hybrid cloud architecture addressing the issue of effective and efficient interoperability, we design a prototype consisted of a Amazon EC2 based public cloud, a private smart home cloud platform built in Dongguan University of Technology (DGUT), and a private smart home cloud platform authorized by Canbo CO., LTD, China. As shown in Table 1, the two private cloud platforms employ entirely different architectures. The former is built using some open-source solutions, i.e., virtualization software (KVM), and management software (Open-Stack). The latter is built using VMware solutions, i.e., Virtualization software (VMware vSphere), and management software (VMware vCenter). Additionally, the deployed home devices in the former are provided by different vendors and use different network access technologies. The deployed kitchen and bathroom devices in the latter are the independent productions of Canbo CO., LTD, but the other kinds of deployed home devices are provided by different vendors and use different network access technologies. The consumer located in DGUT connected to the former private cloud platform by campus wireless network connectivity with 10 Mbps ~50 Mbps data transfer rate. To evaluate the interoperability in the same associated platform or across the heterogeneous platforms in smart home environments, the response time defined as the maximum execution time taken by systems tasks is used as the evaluation metric of effectiveness and efficiency.

Table 1. Configurations of the two private cloud platforms.

	DGUT	Canbo
CPU	Intel Xeon E3-1231v3	Intel Xeon E7-4850v3
RAM	16 GB	128 GB
Storage	1 TB	15 TB
OS	Ubuntu Server 12.04 LTS	Ubuntu Server 16.04 LTS

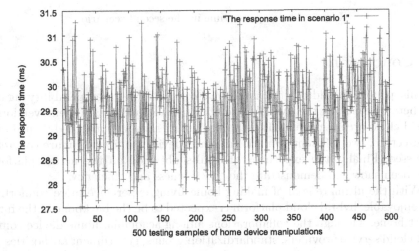

Fig. 4. The response time in the first scenario.

In the two scenarios discussed in Sect. 3, total of 500 testing samples of home device manipulations are performed respectively, and the experimental results are shown in Figs. 4 and 5. In the first scenario that the consumers and the target home devices are associated to the same private platform, the average response time is 29.38 ms and the sample standard deviation is 0.826 ms. In the second scenario that the consumers and the target devices are associated to different private platforms, because the manipulation commands should transmit through the Internet, the average response time is 59.38 ms and the sample standard deviation is 2.023 ms. From the experimental results, we can clearly see that, within the proposed hybrid cloud architecture, the test results of the response time are justified for the requirements of home device manipulation applications. Especially, the test results are acceptable for the interoperations across heterogeneous platforms as well.

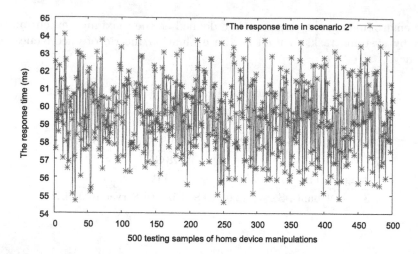

Fig. 5. The response time in the second scenario.

5 Conclusion

In this paper, to address the issue of cross-platform interoperability against the heterogeneity of the available solutions developed by different vendors, a hybrid cloud architecture for IoT-enabled smart homes is proposed. Within this architecture, two different scenarios of home device manipulation are concretely discussed. Finally, the experimental results obtained on the actual platforms have been shown to demonstrate the effectiveness and efficiency.

With the ultimate goal of making home living experience more comfortable and enjoyable, hybrid cloud platform is expected to be the backbone of the future smart home. Through the collaborations among academia, home device companies, cloud service providers, standardization groups, government authorities and law enforcement organizations, as well as various systematic approaches in engineering new architectures and operating schemes, hybrid-cloud enabled solutions can provide promising opportunities for promoting the technology innovations in the smart home industry and other industrial business with tremendous benefits to society.

Acknowledgments. This work was supported in part by the Natural Science Foundation of Guangdong Province, China (Grant No. 2018A030313014); Guangdong University Scientific Innovation Project (Grant No. 2017KTSCX178); the outstanding young teacher training program of the Education Department of Guangdong Province (Grant No. YQ2015158); Guangdong Provincial Science & Technology Plan Projects (Grant Nos. 2016A010101035 & 2016A010101034); and National Natural Science Fund, China (Grant Nos. 61300198 & 61772233).

References

1. Li, M., Lin, H.J.: Design and implementation of smart home control systems based on wireless sensor networks and power line communications. IEEE Trans Ind. Electron. **62**(7), 4430–4442 (2015)
2. Tao, M., Zuo, J., Liu, Z., Castiglione, A., Palmieri, F.: Multi-layer cloud architectural model and ontology-based security service framework for IoT-based smart homes. Futur. Gener. Comput. Syst. **78**, 1040–1051 (2018)
3. Li, J., Li, Y., Chen, X., Lee, P., Lou, W.: A hybrid cloud approach for secure authorized deduplication. IEEE Trans. Parallel Distrib. Syst. **26**(5), 1206–1216 (2015)
4. Soliman, M., Abiodun, T., Hamouda, T., et al.: Smart home: integrating internet of things with web services and cloud computing. In: Diamond, S., Wainwright, N. (eds.) IEEE 5th International Conference on Cloud Computing Technology and Science (CloudCom), pp. 317–320. IEEE, Bristol (2013). https://doi.org/10.1109/CloudCom.2013.155
5. Rossi, L., Belli, A., Santis, A.D., et al.: Interoperability issues among smart home technological frameworks. In: Gao, Y., Zingaretti, P., Koo, J.C., Frontoni, E. (eds.) IEEE/ASME 10th International Conference on Mechatronic and Embedded Systems and Applications (MESA), pp. 1–7. IEEE, Senigallia (2014). https://doi.org/10.1109/MESA.2014.6935626
6. Ghayvat, H., Mukhopadhyay, S., Gui, X., et al.: WSN- and IOT-based smart homes and their extension to smart buildings. Sensors **15**(5), 10350–10379 (2015)
7. Seo, S., Kim, J., Yun, S., et al.: HePA: Hexagonal platform architecture for smart home things. In: Kotagiri, R., Zomaya, A. (eds.) IEEE 21st International Conference on Parallel and Distributed Systems (ICPADS), pp. 181–189. IEEE, Melbourne (2015) https://doi.org/10.1109/ICPADS.2015.31
8. Li, B., Yu, J.: Research and application on the smart home based on component technologies and internet of things. Procedia Eng. **15**, 2087–2092 (2011)
9. Tao, M., Ota, K., Dong, M.: Ontology-based data semantic management and application in IoT-and cloud-enabled smart homes. Futur. Gener. Comput. Syst. **76**, 528–539 (2017)
10. Wu, C.L., Liao, C.F., Fu, L.C.: Service-oriented smart-home architecture based on OSGi and mobile-agent technology. IEEE Trans. Syst. Man Cybern. Part C **37**(2), 193–205 (2007)
11. Cheng, S.T., Wang, C.H., Horng, G.J.: OSGi-based smart home architecture for heterogeneous network. Expert. Syst. Appl. **39**(16), 12418–12429 (2012)
12. Hamza, H.S., Ashraf, E., Nabih, A.K., et al.: Design and implementation of an interaopreable and extednable smart home semantic architecture using smart-M3 and SOA. In: Westphall, C.B., et al. (eds.) The 10th International Conference on Networking and Services (ICNS), pp. 48–53. IARIA, Chamonix, (2014)
13. Perumal, T., Sulaiman, M.N., Sharif, K.Y., et al.: Development of an embedded smart home management scheme. Int. J. Smart Home **7**(2), 15–26 (2013)
14. Li, J., Chen, X., Li, M., Li, J., Lee, P., Lou, W.: Secure deduplication with efficient and reliable convergent key management. IEEE Trans. Parallel Distrib. Syst. **25**(6), 1615–1625 (2014)
15. Qu, C., Tao, M., Zhang, J., et al.: Blockchain Based credibility verification method for IoT entities. Secur. Commun. Netw. **2018**, 1–11 (2018). Article ID 7817614

Conflict-Free Block-with-Stride Access of 2D Storage Structure

Rui Song, Guozhao Zeng, Sheng Liu[✉], and Haiyan Chen

College of Computer, National University of Defense Technology,
Changsha 410073, Hunan, China
liusheng83@nudt.edu.cn

Abstract. Parallel memory modules can be used to increase memory bandwidth and feed a processor with the required access patterns of data. The parallel storage mechanism organized and managed by multiple storage modules can suit applications of images and videos. Previous investigation into data storage schemes can be used to achieve continuous conflict free access by rows, columns or blocks, however it is not only satisfied with some sliding window applications in video and image processing algorithms (including convolutional neural networks, sub-pixel difference, 2D filtering, etc.) which need non-conflicting access by steps in computation, but also there is a different demand for horizontal and vertical strides in computing sub-processes. This paper presents a storage scheme that support for row access without collision alignment, and non-aligned block-with-stride access storage modes beginning at any address. Theoretical proofs and experiments verify the correct ness of the module address (module number to which the address is mapped). And in hardware design, it was found that in the typical case there was no path violation and with less area overhead. It suitable for application of CNN to improve performance in algorithm in convolutional.

Keywords: Main memory architectures · 2D memory conflicts
Parallel storage scheme

1 Introduction

The pros and cons of storage system design is an important factor that restricts the performance of vector SIMD processors. Because processor speeds are substantially higher than memory speeds, it has been necessary to develop architectural features to support parallelism in the memory subsystems. Parallel memory modules can be used to provide special data patterns and feed the processors with only algorithm specific data. In specific data patterns [1, 2], accessed data elements are separated by a distance called stride. Many applications in the fields of digital signal processing and telecommunications benefit from the use of strides. Vector/matrix computation, Fast

This paper is supported by the National Nature Science Foundation of China (No. 61602493, Name Researches on Efficient Parallel Memory Techniques for Wide Vector DSPs).

© Springer Nature Switzerland AG 2018
J. Vaidya and J. Li (Eds.): ICA3PP 2018, LNCS 11336, pp. 618–629, 2018.
https://doi.org/10.1007/978-3-030-05057-3_46

Fourier Transform (FFT), and Viterbi algorithm are some examples [3, 4]. But this is only taking into account the horizontal stride problem. As the latest application needs, we should consider both horizontal stride and vertical stride, so that Two-dimensional (2D) storage is more suitable.

The research of parallel memory systems has been studied by many previous investigators. The key of the storage scheme of the system is the mapping between addresses and physical storage locations in the memory. The initial storage scheme is a low-order interleaved (also referred to simply as interleaved) scheme which maps address a into memory module a mod N, where N is the number of memory modules in the system. And the classic linear mapping method proposed by Bunik and Kuck [5] is to skew the storage scheme of the system. Subsequent studies are based on this and often only consider one-dimensional dynamic storage mechanisms, or two-dimensional dynamic storage that does not take vertical stride into account. Through the existing 2D storage mechanism can be used to achieve continuous conflict-free access by rows, columns or blocks.

Previous investigation proposed a classic memory storage scheme is Park [6–8]. It can support row, column, block, and diagonal access starting anywhere. The Park does not address part of the memory space, thereby avoiding the address calculation circuit caused by the prime memory module being too complicated and causing chip area waste. In addition, the presence of prime memory modules makes it difficult to implement circular addressing. Therefore, the Park scheme is limited. Based on Park, a new scheme was proposed to call Hong et al. [9]. This scheme eliminates the defects of Park but requires more memory and brings a large area overhead.

Another famous storage called Bilinear Skewed Parallel Memory (BilisPM). BilisPM [10] can ensure that it can simultaneously support conflict-free row, column, block and other access modes, and supports circular addressing in both horizontal and vertical directions, and the memory cell area overhead is relatively small. Above solutions do not seem to adapt to the latest needs. Because they all do not consider the problem of stride in storage.

Through the existing 2D storage mechanism can be used to achieve continuous conflict-free access by rows, columns or blocks, some sliding window applications in video and image processing algorithms (including convolutional neural networks, sub-pixel difference, 2D filtering, etc.) which is a need for non-conflicting access by strides in computation, and there is a different demand for horizontal and vertical strides in computing sub-processes. In addition, on the basis of the above requirements, it is a prerequisite for high-bandwidth data loading and result reading to ensure that basic row-based access conflict-free is required. The existing famous 2D memory scheme is that mapping functions proposed by Liu et al. [11].

In this paper, we consider all kinds of horizontal stride, vertical stride, the number of strides, the relationship between the number of banks and so on. We designed a unified address mapping scheme and devices to ensure that each visit to the data required in different storage body, in order to achieve from any address of the conflict-free block-with-stride access and aligned row access. Figure 1 is one of cases shown aligned row access and unaligned block-with-stride.

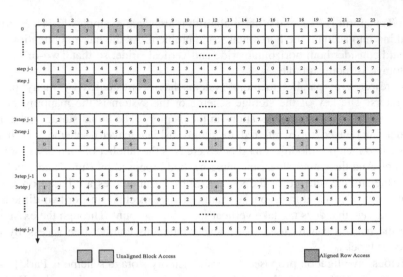

Fig. 1. Aligned row access and unaligned block-with-stride.

2 Storage Space Mapping Schemes

In a memory bank which space is $X_m \times Y_n$ (X_m or Y_n is an integer power of 2), each element can be represented by coordinates (i, j). Let M and N denote the number if elements contained in the data block in both the horizontal and vertical directions when accessed block-with-stride, both M and N are integer power of 2, and $M > =N . M * N$ is the same as the SIMD width and the total number of banks of the processor. The s and h represent the step of horizontal and vertical directions, respectively, when striding by block. Furthermore, let $n = log_2(M * N)$, let s be denoted by the form of $s = \sigma * 2^{s'}$, where s and 2 are relatively prime. Then the number f(w) of the element which coordinate is mapped to the storage module is:

$$f(w) = \begin{cases} (w + (w/(M*N))\%2^{s'})\%(M*N), & s' \le n \\ \left(w + \dfrac{w/(M*N)}{2^{s'-n}}\right)\%(M*N), & s' > n \end{cases} \tag{1}$$

and the w is:

$$w = i + ((j/h) + (j\%2) * (i/(M*2^{s'}))\%2 * (N/4)*2) * M * 2^{s'} \tag{2}$$

Where "/" indicates the quotient operation, "%" indicates the remainder operation.

It can be further determined that the element with the coordinate (i, j) in the bank internal address is:

$$g(i,j) = i/(M*N) + j*(X_m/(2*M*N)) + i*(X_m*Y_m/(2*M*N)) \tag{3}$$

In order to verify the mapping method proposed in this paper, using the following method to proof its correctness. Because of the large number of variables, there is multiple situations. So here gives certification of $M = 4$, $N = 2$.

The module number which was mapped with position (i, j) is:

$$f(w) = (w + (w/8)\%s')\%8 \tag{4}$$

and the w is:

$$w = i + ((j/h)\%2) * 4s' \tag{5}$$

According to (1), Table 1 shows the values of horizontal step and s' which was divided into several groups.

Table 1. Corresponding's values for different strides(s)

Groups	s (1 <= s <= n)	s'
1	1,3, 5, 7...2n + 1	0
2	2, 6...2(2n + 1)	1
...	...	...
n	n(2n + 1)	n − 1

According to the difference of the value of s', prove (4) separately. When the block is $4 * 2$, set these 8 elements' coordinate are:

Line 1: $(i_0, j_0), (i_0 + s, j_0), (i_1 + 2s, j_0), (i_1 + 3s, j_0)$

Line 2: $(i_0, j_0 + h), (i_0 + s, j_0 + h), (i_0 + 2s, j_0 + h), (i_0 + 3s, j_0 + h)$

Case1: when $s' = 1, s = 1, 3, 5, 7, 9, 11, 13, 15$

$$f(i_0, j_0) = (w + (w/8)\%s')\%8 = w\%8 = (i_0 + ((j_0/h)\%2) * 4)\%8 \tag{6}$$

$$f(i_0, j_0 + h) = (w + (w/8)\%s')\%8 = w\%8 = (i_0 + ((j_0/h + 1)\%2) * 4)\%8 \tag{7}$$

Assume $((j/h)\%2) = 0$, then $((j/h + 1)\%2) = 1$, on the contrary, the proof is the same

$$f(i_0, j_0) = i_0\%8 \tag{8}$$

$$f(i_0, j_0 + h) = (i_0 + 4)\%8 \tag{9}$$

Set $i_0\%8 = B_0$, then $i_0 = 8A + B_0$

$$B(m, c) = (i_0 + m * s + 4 * c)\%8 = (8A + B_0 + m * s + 4 * c)\%8$$
$$= (B_0 + m * s + 4 * c)\%8, c = 0, 1. \, m = 1, 2, \cdots 4 \tag{10}$$

Assume $B(k, c_k) = B(l, c_l)$, $k \neq lk, l = 1, 2, \ldots 4$. $c_k = c_l = 0, 1$

$$(B_0 + k * s + 4 * c_k)\%8 = (B_0 + l * s + 4 * c_l)\%8$$
$$k * s + 4 * c_k - (l * s + 4 * c_l) = (k - l) * s + 4 * (c_k - c_l) = 8 * N, \quad N \in Z \quad (11)$$

But $s = 2n + 1, n = 0, 1, \ldots, 7$. So

$$(k - l) = \frac{8 * N - 4 * (c_k - c_l)}{s} = \frac{8 * N - 4 * (c_k - c_l)}{2n + 1} = \frac{4(2 * N - (c_k - c_l))}{2n + 1} \quad (12)$$

The numerator and denominator are relatively prime, so the hypothesis is not true. $B(k) \neq B(l)$.

Case2: when $s' = 2$, $s = 2, 6, 10, 14$

$$f(i_0, j_0) = (w + (w/8)\%s')\%8 = (i_0 + (((j_0/h)\%2) + i_0/8)\%2)\%8 \quad (13)$$

$$f(i_0, j_0 + h) = (i_0 + ((j_0/h + 1)\%2) * 8 + (((j_0/h + 1)\%2) + i_0/8)\%2)\%8 \quad (14)$$

Assume $((j/h)\%2) = 0$, then$((j/h + 1)\%2) = 1$, on the contrary, the proof is the same. Same as (8) (9) after simplification.

Reference case 1 conclusion $s = 2n$, $n = 1, 3, 5, 7$.

$$B(m, c) = (B_0 + m * s + c)\%8, c = 0, 1. m = 1, 2, \cdots 4 \quad (15)$$

assume $B(k, c_k) = B(l, c_l), k \neq lk, l = 1, 2, \ldots 4$. $c_k = c_l = 0, 1$.

$$(k - l) = \frac{8 * N - (c_k - c_l)}{s} = \frac{8 * N - (c_k - c_l)}{2n} \quad (16)$$

if $C_k = C_l,$

$$(k - l) == \frac{8 * N}{2n} = \frac{4 * N}{n} \quad (17)$$

due to n = 1,3,5,7. molecular denominator
    if $C_k = C_l,$

$$(k - l) = \frac{8 * N - (c_k - c_l)}{s} = \frac{8 * N - (c_k - c_l)}{2n} \quad (18)$$

Obviously, in (18) the numerator is odd, the denominator is even, and the numerator and denominator are relatively prime. In summary, the assumption does not hold, $B(k) \neq B(l)$.

Case3: when $s' = 2$, $s = 4$, 12 simplified (1):

$$f(i,j) = (w + (w/8)\%s')\%8 = (i + (((j/h)\%4) * 2 + i/8)\%4)\%8 \qquad (19)$$

$$f(i,j+h) = (i + (((j/h+1)\%4) * 2 + i/8)\%4)\%8 \qquad (20)$$

When a is odd:

$$f(i,j) = (i + i/8)\%8 \qquad (21)$$

$$f(i,j+h) = (i + (2 + i/8)\%4)\%8 \qquad (22)$$

When a is even:

$$f(i,j) = (i + (2 + i/8)\%4)\%8 \qquad (23)$$

$$f(i,j+h) = (i + i/8)\%8 \qquad (24)$$

Assume $(i_0 + i_0/8)\%8 = B_0$, $i_0 + i_0/8 = 8A + B_0$, due to $s = 4*n$, $n = 1,3$, then

$$B(m, c) = (i0 + m * s + (2 * c + (i0 + m * s)/8)\%4)\%8 \quad m = 1,2,3,4, c = 0,1 \qquad (25)$$

Assume B(k, c_k) = B(l, c_l), $k \neq l$ k, l = 1,2, ... 4. c_k, c_1 = 0,1, then

$$B(l, c_l) = (i0 + l * s + (2 * c_l + (i0 + l * s)/8)\%4)\%8 \qquad (26)$$

$$B(k, c_k) = (i0 + k * s + (2 * c_k + (i0 + k * s)/8)\%4)\%8 \qquad (27)$$

Set $(2 * c_k + (i0 + k * s)/8)\%4 = a$, $a \in \{0,1,2,3\}$, $(2 * c_l + (i0 + l * s)/8)$
$\%4 = b$, $b \in \{0,1,2,3\}$

$$(i0 + k * s + a)\%8 = (i0 + k * s + b)\%8$$

$$(a - b) = 8 * N - (k - l) * 4n = 4(2N - (k - l) * n)$$

Because of $(a - b) \in \{-3, -2, -1, 0, 1, 2, 3\}$, the assumption does not hold, $B(k) \neq B(l)$.

Case4: when $s' = 8$, $s = 8$

$$f(i,j) = (w + (w/8)\%s')\%8 = (i + ((j/h)\%8) * 4 + i/8)\%8 \qquad (28)$$

$$f(i,j+h) = (i + ((j/h+1)\%8) * 4 + i/8)\%8 \qquad (29)$$

Here is similar to the post processing of case 3, so there will not be repeated.

In summary, using the memory addressing scheme of (1) and fetching data in the form of $M*N$ blocks, it does not conflict. Here only gives one of the forms to proof, it does not impose any restrictions on (1). In fact, we already verify (1) by software means. Through matlab simulation, it traverses all possible conditions under the limited conditions, verifies its correctness and versatility.

3   Hardware Implementation of 2D Proposed Memory

3.1   Proposed Parallel Memory Architecture

This paper proposes a mapping scheme that supports the 2D structure that block-with-stride and conflict-free access. Figure 2 shows the overall structure of this memory bank. It consists of the following elements: Shift Information Calculation Logic, Bank Internal Address Sort Logic, Shift Information Calculation Logic, Bank Logic, and Busy Signal Generation Logic. The first element bank number calculation logic calculates the first element mapped to the bank number using (1) according to the user provided 2D coordinates and horizontal stride. The shift information calculation logic uses the first element bank number and horizontal stride to obtain the data shift information. The 2D coordinates are calculated according to (2) to get the offsets of these elements within each bank. The position of the original data is selected according to the shift_inf. The Busy generating circuit generates the Busy signal by detecting whether the buffer status and the fetch address are in conflict with each other.

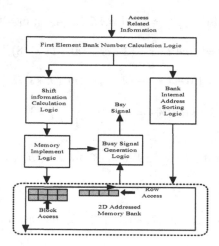

Fig. 2. Hardware design structure.

Figure 3 shows the first element bank number calculation logic. First, according to the type of access based on the horizontal stride, so that determine the value in (2). There designs the modulo circuit to perform the modulo operation. Finally, the bank number corresponding to the first element of this visit is obtained.

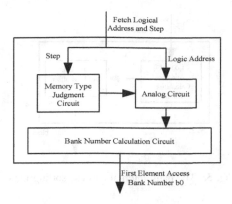

Fig. 3. The first element bank number calculation logic.

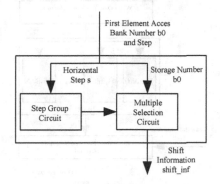

Fig. 4. The shift information calculation logic.

The shift information is used to write data buffer and the sequence of read data. The shift information calculation logic is shown in Fig. 4. The calculation of the read shift information is more complicated. First, stepping is divided into different groups according to horizontal steps, and then the combination memory element number of the first element is determined by the data selector to determine the shift information shift_inf under different steps. By comparison, the operation of writing shift information is simpler. The ordinates in the 2D coordinates of the first element are modeled and selected based on the vertical stride.

Figure 5 is the bank internal address sorting logic. Firstly, the 2D coordinates of the elements needed this time are calculated based on the two-dimensional coordinates of the first element and horizontal stride, and then the offset of these elements within each memory is calculated according to (1).

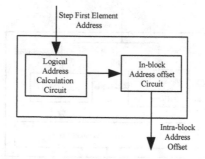

Fig. 5. The bank internal address sorting logic.

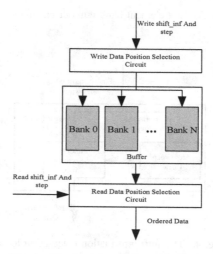

Fig. 6. The fetch implementation logic.

The fetch implementation logic is divided into two parts which is shown in Fig. 6. If it is a write request, since the data to be written by the user is continuous, the actual write to the memory bank is not continuous. Here, the shift_inf and the original data need to be written.

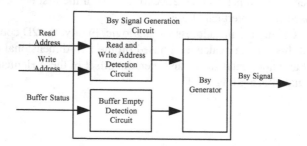

Fig. 7. The Bsy signal generation circuit.

Figure 7 shows the Bsy signal generation circuit. The Bsy signal generation circuit consists of three parts, a read and write address detection circuit, a buffer empty fullness judgment circuit, and a Bsy generator. The read and write address detection circuit is used to detect whether the read request and the write request access the same memory bank. If accessing the same memory bank, a memory access conflict occurs. In this case, it is necessary to stop sending the memory access request, otherwise the data may be lost. Here, the buffer follows the principle of reading before writing. The buffer full detect circuit can detect the empty full state of the buffer.

3.2   Performance Comparison

This paper uses Synopsys' Design Complier tool to synthesize this memory module under the TSMC 40 nm process. At the time of synthesis, the memory bank delay was scaled by 70% and the target period was set to 700 ps. It was found that in the typical case there was no path violation. According to general experience, the design circuit can work at 1 GHz.

The parallel storage mechanism designed in this paper employs 2D addressing, which not only supports aligned row access but also supports block-with-stride access from an arbitrary address and supports double-buffered ping pong access. Compared to the traditional row access scheme, block-with-stride accesses only increase the length of the stride-processing logic because it does not add too much area overhead, as shown in Table 2, increased area is negligible.

Table 2.   Area overhead.

	Area (μm^2)
In_buf	23.996
In_buf add	23.912

Compare the implementation of several parallel storage schemes in Table 3. The earlier proposal only had 1D access without conflict conditions. In the 2D access mode, the scheme of Park and C. Liu provide more access modes. The important access modes they can provide at the same time are row, column, and block access. In addition, there are other access modes (such as Corner line access, interval access by block), but they need to be resolved by reconfiguration and so on. BilisPM can only support conflict-free access by row, column, or block for the same batch of data. This paper provided a storage scheme can simultaneously support continuous row access and block-with stride access in 2D parallel storage scheme. This paper mainly for the image and video processing algorithm contains the sliding window application of the operation, this type of application in the operation of block-with-step access to the need for conflict-free access, and the horizontal and vertical stepping requirements are different. For example, in the convolution operation, assuming that the convolution kernel size is 3*3, the convolution of M*N output image pixels in parallel needs to acquire M*N image data from the buffer in one beat, and the convolution kernel data beat must be captured only once. So, 9 beats can calculate the result of 8 output image pixels.

Table 3. Typical storage mechanism support types

	Park	C. Liu	BilisPM	This work
Support type	row, column, block (without stride), Corner line access	row, column, block (without stride), Corner line access	row, column, block	row, block-with-stride

In order to avoid collisions with memory access, it must be ensured that these data are distributed in different memory banks. Buffers must be addressed specifically. The solution proposed in this paper exactly meets this kind of access requirements of CNN.

4 Conclusion

The results presented in this paper are applicable to a typical type of video and image processing application with a very large amount of motion. Such applications have a large amount of calculations and the access is not regular. With the new addressing method, a dynamic storage scheme was designed to achieve the goal of not only supporting aligned row access but also nonaligned block-with-stride access.

The previous survey storage scheme was to determine a single model, but it could not guarantee that the addresses could be freely switched between one-dimensional and two-dimensional. This synthesizes a storage scheme that allows access to these modes without conflict. The biggest difference between the dynamic storage scheme described in this article and the previous method is its extensiveness, which allows any required valid data to be accessed without conflict.

In terms of hardware design, the first element memory bank number calculation logic, shift information calculation logic, memory bank internal address sort logic, memory access implementation logic, and Bsy signal generation logic module is designed according to requirements, and verified by software and hardware cooperation. Its correctness, and hardware overhead.

Because this dynamic storage scheme has flexibility and low hardware cost, it is suitable for many current applications such as CNN, sub-pixel difference, 2D filtering, and the like. So, in the field of parallel computing, this is a good solution to the existing storage problems.

References

1. Chen, S., Postula, A., Jozwiak, L.: Synthesis of XOR storage schemes with different cost for minimization of memory contention. In: 1999 Proceedings of the Euromicro Conference, vol. 1, pp. 170–177. IEEE (1999)
2. Hartenstein, R.W., Becker, J., Herz, M., Nageldinger, U.: An embedded accelerator for real world computing. In: Reis, R., Claesen, L. (eds.) VLSI: Integrated Systems on Silicon. ITIFIP, pp. 215–226. Springer, Boston (1997). https://doi.org/10.1007/978-0-387-35311-1_18
3. Aho, E., Vanne, J., Kuusilinna, K., et al.: Address computation in configurable parallel memory architecture. IEICE Trans. Inf. Syst. **87-D(7)**, 1674–1681 (2004)

4. Takala, J., Jarvinen, T.: Stride permutation access in interleaved memory systems (2003)
5. Budnik, P., Kuck, D.J.: The organization and use of parallel memories. IEEE Trans. Comput. **20**(12), 1566–1569 (1971)
6. Park, J.W.: An efficient buffer memory system for subarray access. IEEE Trans. Parallel Distrib. Syst. **12**(3), 316–335 (2002)
7. Park, J.W.: Multiaccess memory system for attached SIMD computer. IEEE Trans. Comput. **53**(4), 439–452 (2004)
8. Park, J.W.: Conflict-free memory system and method of address calculation and data routing by using the same. US 6845423 B2[P], US (2005)
9. Hong, Y., Choi, B., Lee, K., et al.: Conflict management considering a smooth transition of aircraft into adjacent airspace. IEEE Trans. Intell. Transp. Syst. **17**(9), 2490–2501 (2016)
10. Liu, C., Yan, X., Qin, X.: An optimized linear skewing interleave scheme for on-chip multi-access memory systems. In: ACM Great Lakes Symposium on VLSI, pp. 8–13. ACM (2007)
11. Liu, S., Chen, S., Chen, H., et al.: A novel parallel memory organization supporting multiple access types with matched memory modules. IEICE Electron Express **9**(6), 602–608 (2012)

Graph-Based Indoor Localization with the Fusion of PDR and RFID Technologies

Jie Wu[1], Minghua Zhu[1(✉)], Bo Xiao[1], and Yunzhou Qiu[2]

[1] MOE Research Center for Software/Hardware Co-Design Engineering and Application, East China Normal University, Shanghai 200062, China
mhzhu@sei.ecnu.edu.cn
[2] Shanghai Internet of Things Co., Ltd., Shanghai 200051, China

Abstract. A text map based indoor localization is proposed with the fusion of radio frequency identification (RFID) and inertial measurement unit (IMU) in the narrow corridor space. The floor plan in narrow corridor is abstracted to a text map which uses the form of characters to represent indoor physical map. Then the indoor localization would be changed in the process of text processing and matching. When tag carrier is walking in the positioning area, the character string would be constructed with pedestrian dead reckoning (PDR) technology according to the path information. We search the character string in the text map and get the corresponding candidate locations, and then received signal strength (RSS) based fingerprint matching method is used to obtain the accurate location from candidate locations. The experiment is conducted to show that proposed method can reduce the mean positioning error to around 1.2 m without initial location specification.

Keywords: Indoor localization · Pedestrian dead reckoning
Received signal strength · Inertial measurement unit · Text map

1 Introduction

The indoor localization technology has inspired recently due to their potential applications in a wide range of indoor localization-based services (ILBS). A lot of technology is used for the indoor localization applications, such as Wi-Fi, Bluetooth, radio frequency identification (RFID), pedestrian dead reckoning (PDR), light, magnetic matching, etc.

The received signal strength (RSS) is the base information of positioning for RFID [1, 2]. There are mainly three methods for the indoor localization with RFID: The first method uses the relationship model of RSS and distance between tag and readers [3, 4]. Through the distance gotten from the model, the position of tags would be calculated with the trilateration localization method; The second method is to use RSS fingerprint matching [5–7]. In the positioning process, the RSSs are compared with the RSS fingerprint database to get the location of tags; The third method is to use the fusion of the RSS and inertial sensors to achieve the indoor localization (motion-assisted localization). He and Chan propose a method that fused the step counter and wireless

© Springer Nature Switzerland AG 2018
J. Vaidya and J. Li (Eds.): ICA3PP 2018, LNCS 11336, pp. 630–639, 2018.
https://doi.org/10.1007/978-3-030-05057-3_47

fingerprints for the indoor localization [8]. Because of the complexity of the surrounding environment, the RSS would be affected by multipath and signal reflection, which would result into a big positioning bias [9–13]. PDR based positioning method includes three critical procedures: step detection, step length estimation, heading estimation [14, 15]. It can be used as an assisted technology for its insensitive to the environment. The method provides a more accurate relative position solution with fewer integration calculations [16]. However, it is inevitable for motion sensor to introduce the accumulated error, which would result in positioning bias.

The paper puts forward a tag positioning method with the fusion of RSS and PDR technology through the construction of a text map in the narrow corridor. The physical indoor positioning problem is changed into a process of the text matching and then several alternative locations are obtained. Then we used the RSS fingerprint to assist the further location matching to get the most Optimal tag position. The method is insensitive to the changing of the environment and is less depended on the RSS, so the method can achieve a high accuracy.

The rest of the paper is organized as follows. The next Section describes the state-of-art of related works. The preliminaries of the paper are listed in Sect. 3. The proposed algorithm is detailed in Sect. 4. In Sect. 5, the experiment was conducted and the comparison between the proposed method and the other two methods was made. The discussion and conclusion are made in the last section.

2   Related Works

In this section, an overview of the state-of-art technology in indoor localization with fusion of PDR and RSS technologies is provided. The methods [17–20] provide a more accurate relative position solution with fewer integration calculations and no additional infrastructure. However, the introduced accumulative error is inevitable for the method that can result in a big positioning bias over time. The RSS can be easily obtained for the RFID. The absolute tag location is also can be derived with RSS. But RSS is easily influenced by the surrounding environment. The graph-based, low-complexity sensor fusion approach is proposed for ubiquitous pedestrian indoor positioning using RSS and PDR [18] to reduce the errors in wireless localization. The Zee method is proposed to conduct the zero effort crowdsourcing based indoor localization with the RSS and IMU based device [19]. An IMU-aided dead-reckoning navigation structure and signal processing algorithms is proposed in the advanced integration of RSS and inertial navigation system to mitigate the positioning errors for indoor localization [20]. However, how to conduct fusion is challenging and interesting question, especially in the complex environment.

3   Preliminaries

To make a clear description about the algorithm, we use a simplified and classic example site to describe the proposed method in this paper. As shown in Fig. 1, the floor plan covers an area of 16 m × 20 m, which includes ten vertices in total.

Four active readers are distributed uniformly on the site. The numbers in the circle of topology refer to the characters in the example of site. The numbers on the line of topology refer to the weight of the graph. We assume that the width of the corridor has little influence to the positioning error.

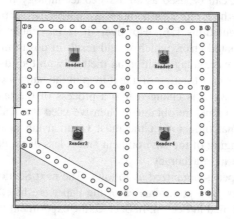

Fig. 1. The example of experiment site. There are ten corners which are represented by five different kinds of letters and four readers on the floor.

The classic path propagation model (1) is adopted to describe the relationship between RSS and distance from the readers to unknown tags.

$$P_m = P_0 - 10\eta \log_{10} d_m/d_0 + \xi(t) \tag{1}$$

where P_m refers to the received power by the m_{th} reader in the d_m distance, and the dBm is denoted as the unit of received power. The number m refers to the reader that receives tag data. P_0 denotes the received power by the m_{th} reader in the d_0 distance. d_m refers to the distance between m_{th} reader and unknown tag. η refers to the path loss coefficient. $\xi(t)$ denotes the environment noise, where t refers to that noise changes with measured time.

4   Materials and Methods

The proposed method is divided into two stages: the offline stage followed by the online stage. At the offline stage, the map of the floor plan is surged to change the physical information to the logical information in the positioning area. We will abstract the positioning area into a weighted undirected connected graph, and then we get the text map through depth-first traversal. Also, the RSS at the vertexes are collected to form the fingerprint database with the RFID technology. At the online stage, the walking length and walking direction are obtained with the PDR technology when the tags carriers are walking in the area of interest. Then, the walk path is changed into the character string according to the text map construction rule. The generated character string is compared with the text map to find the less than three most similarity sequence in the text map. In the last step, we use the RSS fingerprint match method to determine the most suitable string.

4.1   The Offline Stage

Text Map Generation. In the narrow corridor space, the path information is classified as six kinds of basic elements: go straight, 45 degrees-turn, left-turn, right-turn, 180 degrees-turn, and 135 degrees-turn. As shown in Fig. 2, six basic elements which are denoted respectively as A, B, C, D, E and F.

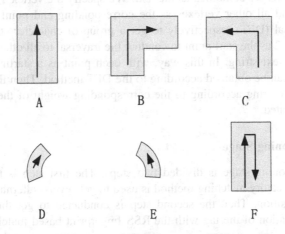

Fig. 2. The six kinds of basic elements which refer to the different motion action respectively.

In this work, some complex paths are considered to be the combination of basic elements. As shown in Fig. 3, three kinds of complex elements are composed of different basic elements and we define them as compound elements. There would be a number of compound elements in practical usage.

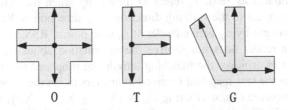

Fig. 3. Three kinds of compound elements which refer to the combination of basic elements.

The weight of the graph is measured by the physical distance (meters) of two vertices. For example, if the physical distance between two vertices is five meters, the weight between two vertices is five. It also shows that five characters 'A' are needed to fill between the two vertices. In this way, physical path information is abstracted into an undirected weighted graph. The graph data objects are denoted by:

$$G = (V, E) \tag{2}$$

where V refers to the set of vertexes and $V \in \{b, c, d, e, f, o, t\}$, E denotes the set of graph sides and $E \in \{n * a | n \in Z\}$. The data relationship is $VR = \{<v, w > | v, w \in V)\}$, $<v, w >$ represents the arc that is from v to w.

Each path in the location area is defined as a character string. All the character strings from the same start vertexes to the same end vertexes are grouped as a section. Then all the sections are combined as the text. We specify the vertex 1 in the graph as the start point, and all other vertexes as the corresponding end point to conduct the depth-first traversal (DFT) respectively to get a group of character strings. Then we specify the vertex 2 as the start point to conduct the traversal to all other vertices to get another group of text string. In this way, with each point as a starting point, the all character strings can be obtained according to the DFT method. Then the character 'A' is inserted in each string according to the corresponding weight of the graph and the text map is generated.

4.2   The Positioning Stage

The online positioning stage is divided two steps. The first step is text map based matching. The trajectory matching method is used to get several alternative choices for the actual tag position. Then the second step is conducted to get the most optimal option for the location of the tag with the RSS fingerprint based matching method.

Text Map Based Location Matching. The data of motion sensor (including data of accelerator and gyroscope) are collected when the tag carrier is walking in the positioning area. The data are sent to the readers through active RFID. The sampling rate of the accelerator is different from the RSS received rate. Therefore, we synchronize the two rates to a lower RSS received rate. The i_{th} element of collected data Q_i is denoted as $\{ID_i, Tu_i, Ts_i, ax_i, ay_i, az_i, Angle_i, RSS_{i,1}, RSS_{i,2}, ..., RSS_{i,n}\}$, where ax_i, ay_i and az_i refer to the 3-axis collected data at ith time points. T_u refers to the send information sign and T_u is initialed as zero. T_s refers to timestamp when the information is collected. The $Angle_i$ refers to the walking direction at i_{th} time points. $RSS_{i,n}$ refer to the received signal strength by n_{th} active reader at i_{th} time points. $RSS_{i, n}$ equals 255 when the corresponding reader does not receive the information about the tag. When the number of characters achieves the matching length, the proposed method would make the match between the text map and received characters to get the most similar places. We denoted the received character string Z_N as $\{X_1, X_2, X_3, ..., X_N\}$, and the N refers to the string length. The N is set as a fixed value firstly. We denote the alternate location as L_M, and M means the number of alternate options. If there are more than three matched strings, it means too many alternate options. The matching length N would be increased and the match would be made again. If there are no more than three alternative choices, the RSS-aided location selection would be used in the next step for the space matching.

RSS Based Optimal Location Selection. In the process of text map matching, there could be several alternative tag locations with the same sequence in the map. Then, the transmission model (1) is introduced as the judgment of the most suitable position. With the received signal strength for every active reader, the transmission model can be used to convert the RSSs to the distance between tag and readers. Among all readers which receive tag signal, every three readers are used to conduct the trilateral positioning method to get the alternative location of tag carrier.

In j_{th} location for tag carriers, the $RL^{(j)} = \left\{ RL_1^{(j)}, RL_2^{(j)}, \ldots, RL_{nj}^{(j)} \right\}$ refers to all n alternative locations, where $RL_{nj}^{(j)}$ refers to the coordinate of the location and is denoted as ($x_{nj}^{(j)}$, $y_{nj}^{(j)}$). nj refers to the number of different calculated location. The ($\hat{x}^{(j)}, \hat{y}^{(j)}$) refers to the j_{th} estimated location that is denoted by the Eq. 3.

$$\begin{cases} \hat{x}^{(j)} = (\sum_{i=1}^{n} x_i^{(j)})/n \\ \hat{y}^{(j)} = (\sum_{i=1}^{n} y_i^{(j)})/n \end{cases} \tag{3}$$

The RFID is at active state and the tag sends the information to readers at the frequency of 3 Hz. When the tag carrier is walking in the area of interest, the tag collects the sensor information and transmits them to the readers, which send the data to the terminal. The send data is denoted as $D_s = \{T_u, T_s, a_x, a_y, a_z\}$, T_u refers to the send information sign and T_u is initialed as zero. T_s refers to timestamp when the information is collected. When tag carrier takes a turn, the IMU collects the corresponding motion. The T_u in D_s is changed from zero to one. Then the turning information is transformed to the terminal via readers. The terminal gets the information of time point when the tag carrier takes a turning movement. The absolute position where the tag carrier takes a turning is calculated with the received signal strength. With a sequence of the turning positions is collected, the corresponding trajectory is obtained by RSS. We denote the obtained trajectory as L_s. The distance between alternative locations in L_s and alternative location obtained by strings match L_m is compared to get the optimal trajectory. Then we can get the real-time location of the tag carrier as (4).

$$S_k = \sum_{i=1}^{N} \frac{(L_{ki} - L_{si})^2}{\sum_{i=1}^{N} (L_{ki} - L_{si})^2} \tag{4}$$

where i refers to i_{th} location in the alternative location. k refers to k_{th} alternative string. S_k refers to the similarity of L_s and k_{th} alternative string. L_{si} refers to the location obtained by received signal strength in the location of i_{th} vertex. L_{ki} refers to the i_{th} vertex of Z_N at physical location. The similarity is calculated according to the least square scheme. Through similarity matching calculation between L_M and L_s, we can get the optimal location of similarity S.

$$S = \max_{k \in M}\{S_k\} \tag{5}$$

where S_k refers to the similarity between L_s and k_{th} alternate string. M means the number of alternate options after the matching of text map.

5 Experiments

5.1 Experiment Setup

In order to verify the effectiveness of the proposed method, the experiment is conducted in the PuDong research center of the Third Research Institute of Ministry of Public Security in Shanghai. As shown in Fig. 4, five readers were deployed in the area of interest in the fourth floor. The reader 1, reader 4 were deployed in hall and reader 2 was deployed in room A. The reader 3 was deployed in room B. The reader 5 was deployed in room C. The volunteer carrying tag walked from the hall to room A and room B. Then tags carriers returned back to the hall. The NRF52832 is used as the chip of active RFID tag and RFID reader. The MPU6050 is used as IMU as the 6-axis chip of accelerometer and gyroscope.

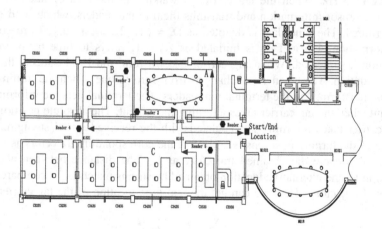

Fig. 4. The experiment site and the trajectory of tag carriers. The red arrow lines refer to the walking trajectory of volunteers and the arrows refer to the walking directions. The black polygons refer to the active readers and the black square refers to the start and end location. (Color figure online)

The experiment lasts 4 h by four volunteers. The volunteers walked through area of interests with the tags on their thighs near the knees. The acceleration data and gyroscope data are collected about three times per second. The RFID sent the data on the frequency of 3 Hz. Then we recorded the location and relevant information. Totally four users traces along with 86,044 sensor data records are collected.

5.2   Test and Result

We compared the cumulative distribution functions of the proposed method for the positioning error with the method in [21] where we use the RFID instead of Wi-Fi technology and the method in [22] where tightly coupling based IMU and RFID fusion technology is proposed.

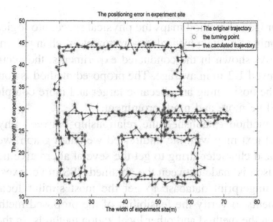

Fig. 5. The positioning error in experiment site. The original trajectory and the calculated trajectory with the proposed method is depicted in the figure. The red circles refer to the turning point which the volunteers take. (Color figure online)

As shown in Fig. 5, we depicted the original trajectory and the calculated trajectory with the proposed method. The positioning error is reduced largely in turning points. Because we used the IMU aided RSS filtering method, the position error is also reduced to about one meter in the trajectory.

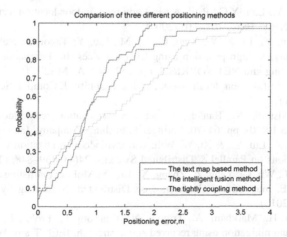

Fig. 6. The cumulative distribution functions of three different positioning methods.

As shown in Fig. 6, the accuracy of the proposed algorithm is higher than the other two methods in literatures and it can achieve about 1.2 m in average. The positioning errors are mostly introduced by the width of the corridors which are not expressed with characters.

6 Discussions and Conclusions

In this paper, the proposed method maps the physical space into logical text map. Then the indoor positioning in the physical environment is changed in the logical text matching process. As shown in the conducted experiments, the accuracy of proposed algorithm has achieved 1.2 m in average. The proposed method is conducted in a small floor plan. When the positioning area became larger and more complex, the advantage of this method will be more and more prominent.

The proposed method established the relationship between physical positioning area and the logical text map with the undirected weighted graph. we make the match with the text map and character string to get the several alternative tag locations. Then the further comparison is made between the obtained RSS in vertexes of alternative tag locations and the fingerprint database to get the most similar location. Finally, we conducted experiments to verify the feasibility of the proposed method and make the comparison between the method and other localization methods. In the future study, we will lay emphasis on symbol expression and text matching accuracy to achieve better effect in complex and 2D environment.

Acknowledgment. This work has been supported by Science and Technology Commission of Shanghai Municipality [Grant No.17511106902 and 15DZ1100400].

References

1. Ni, L.M., Liu, Y., Lau, Y.C., Patil, A.: P: Landmarc: indoor location sensing using active rfid. Wireless Netw. **10**(6), 701–710 (2004)
2. Yang, L., Chen, Y., Li, X. Y., Xiao, C., Li, M., Liu, Y: Tagoram: real-time tracking of mobile RFID tags to high precision using COTS devices. In: International Conference on Mobile Computing and NETWORKING, pp. 237–248. ACM (2014)
3. Liu, Y., Yang, Z.: Location, localization, and localizability. J. Comput. Sci. Technol. **25**(2), 274–297 (2011)
4. Gentile, C., Alsindi, N., Raulefs, R., et al.: Geolocation techniques: principles and applications, 45:10(10), pp. 64–70. Springer Publishing Company, Incorporated (2012)
5. Wu, C., Yang, Z., Liu, Y., & Xi, W: Will: wireless indoor localization without site survey. IEEE Transactions on Parallel & Distributed Systems, 24(4), 839–848. (2013)
6. Sun, W., Liu, J., Wu, C., Yang, Z., Zhang, X., Liu, Y: MoLoc: on distinguishing fingerprint twins. In: IEEE, International Conference on Distributed Computing Systems, vol. 7973, pp. 226–235 (2013)
7. Xiao, Z., Wen, H., Markham, A., Trigoni, N., Blunsom, P., Frolik, J.: Non-line-of-sight identification and mitigation using received signal strength. IEEE Trans. Wireless Commun. **14**(3), 1689–1702 (2015)

8. He, S., Chan, S.H.G., Yu, L., Liu, N: Calibration-free fusion of step counter and wireless fingerprints for indoor localization. In: ACM International Joint Conference, pp. 897–908 (2015)
9. Wang, J., Katabi, D.: Dude, where's my card?: RFID positioning that works with multipath and non-line of sight. In: ACM SIGCOMM 2013 Conference on SIGCOMM, vol. 43, pp. 51–62 (2013)
10. Chen, P. C A: Non-line-of-sight error mitigation algorithm in location estimation. In: Proceedings of IEEE Wireless Communications NETWORKING Conference, vol. 1, pp. 316–320 (1999)
11. Li, X.: An iterative NLOS mitigation algorithm for location estimation in sensor networks. In: Proceedings of 15th IST Mobile Wireless Communication Summit, Miconos, Greece, pp. 1–5. (2006)
12. Guvenc, I., Chong, C.C., Watanabe, F.: NLOS identification and mitigation for UWB localization systems, pp. 1571–1576 (2007)
13. Nawaz, S., Trigoni, N.: Convex programming based robust localization in NLOS prone cluttered environments. In: Proceedings of 10th International Conference IPSN, Chicago, IL, USA, pp. 318–329 (2011)
14. Hilsenbeck, S., Bobkov, D., Schroth, G., Huitl, R., Steinbach, E: Graph-based data fusion of pedometer and WiFi measurements for mobile indoor positioning. In: ACM International Joint Conference on Pervasive and Ubiquitous Computing, pp. 147–158 (2014)
15. Yang, Z., Feng, X., Zhang, Q.: Adometer: push the limit of pedestrian indoor localization through crowdsourcing. IEEE Trans. Mob. Comput. 13(11), 2473–2483 (2014)
16. Xiao, Z., Wen H., Markham, A., Trigoni, N.: Lightweight map matching for indoor localization using conditional random fields. In: Proceedings of ACM/IEEE IPSN, pp. 131–142 (2014)
17. Jiménez, A.R., Seco, F., Prieto, J.C., Guevara, J.: Indoor pedestrian navigation using an INS/EKF framework for yaw drift reduction and a foot-mounted IMU. In: The Workshop on Positioning Navigation & Communication, pp. 135–143 (2010)
18. Chen, L.H., Wu, H.K., Jin, M.H., et al.: Intelligent fusion of Wi-Fi and inertial sensor-based positioning systems for indoor pedestrian navigation. Sensors J. IEEE 14(11), 4034–4042 (2014)
19. Rai, A., Chintalapudi, K.K., Padmanabhan, V.N., et al.: Zee: zero-effort crowdsourcing for indoor localization, pp. 293–304 (2012)
20. Evennou, F., Marx, F.: Advanced integration of WIFI and inertial navigation systems for indoor mobile positioning. Hindawi Limited, pp. 1–11 (2006)
21. Chen, L.H., Wu, H.K., Jin, M.H., et al.: Intelligent fusion of Wi-Fi and inertial sensor-based positioning systems for indoor pedestrian navigation. Sensors J. IEEE 14(11), 4034–4042 (2014)
22. Ruiz, A.R.J., Granja, F.S., Honorato, J.C.P., Rosas, J.I.: G.: Accurate pedestrian indoor navigation by tightly coupling foot-mounted IMU and RFID measurements. IEEE Trans. Instrum. Measur. 61(1), 178–189 (2011)

UAV 3D Mobility Model Oriented to Dynamic and Uncertain Environment

Na Wang[1], Nan Di[2(✉)], Fei Dai[1(✉)], and Fangxin Liu[3]

[1] Army Engineering University of PLA, Nanjing 210007, China
daifei08@163.com
[2] Institute of China Electronic System Engineering Company, Beijing 100039, China
dinan2018@163.com
[3] Shanghai Branch, Coordination Center of China, National Computer Network Emergency Response Technical Team, Shanghai 201315, China

Abstract. Currently, unmanned aerial vehicle (UAV) swarm has been widely used for emergency rescue in disaster areas. In dynamic and uncertain environments, the uneven distribution of events and obstacles seriously affect the efficiency of UAVs' missions and the safety of airborne operations. The traditional UAV mobility models pay more attention to the UAV's own moving rules, so as to make the UAV' flight pattern meet real conditions as much as possible, while ignoring the requirements of UAVs' mission and uncertainties of environment. Based on the 3D Visit-Density Gauss-Semi-Markov Mobility (3D-VDGMM) model, this paper proposes a 3D Mobility Model oriented to Dynamic and Uncertain environment (3D-DUMM). The 3D-DUMM has made improvements to emergency rescue missions while fully considering the dynamic distributed, dense and irregular obstacles in the rescue area. Simulation experiments show that 3D-DUMM can well captured uncertain events and can safely deal with dynamic and complex rescue environments.

Keywords: Three-Dimensional mobility model · Dynamic uncertainty Emergency rescue

1 Introduction

In recent years, serious natural disasters have occurred frequently. The natural disasters such as earthquakes, mudslides, and ice and snow, have the characteristics of strong sudden, high speed of destruction and wide influence. Therefore, it becomes an urgent problem to discover and locate the disasters quickly and transmit the disaster information in real time efficiently. With the development of UAV technology, UAV swarms have gradually been used to solve the problems that many traditional methods cannot effectively solve, and have played a crucial role in target monitoring and tracking, airspace situational awareness interaction, unmanned aerial vehicle automatic collision avoidance, air-to-sea-land coordinated operation and other areas [1]. UAVs have the advantages of flexibility, low cost, small size, high flying altitude, and can adapt to more

© Springer Nature Switzerland AG 2018
J. Vaidya and J. Li (Eds.): ICA3PP 2018, LNCS 11336, pp. 640–650, 2018.
https://doi.org/10.1007/978-3-030-05057-3_48

complex, dynamic and uncertain environments. Therefore, the drone technology has been widely used in the emergency rescue.

A reliable, efficient, and real-time UAV swarm depends on a scientific and flexible mobility model to meet the challenges of events capturing, frequent link changes, and complex and dynamic environments. UAV individuals or UAV swarm usually aim at a specific task and a specific area, and then take corresponding actions around specific tasks and specific areas. Therefore, when designing the UAV mobility model, we must consider the UAV's own motion characteristics, on the one hand. On the other hand, we must fully consider the UAVs' tasks and the dynamics of the regional environment. The traditional UAV mobility models pay more attention to the UAV's own movement law, so as to make the UAV' flight pattern meet real conditions as much as possible, while ignoring the requirements of UAVs' mission and the challenges of the dynamic and uncertain environment. In this paper, aiming at the scene of emergency rescue, the 3D-VDGMM model is improved by introducing the characteristics of tasks and environmental factors to the Gaussian model, and a UAV three-dimensional mobility model oriented to a dynamic uncertain environment (3D-DUMM) is proposed. The detailed contributions of this article are summarized as follows:

(1) Task-oriented UAV mobility modeling is implemented. The mobility model designed in this paper fits the practical scene, and the UAV can dynamically and efficiently capture the target events according to the characteristics of the rescue mission.

(2) Overcoming the uncertainties in the environment. This mobility model greatly enhances the maneuverability of drones in the moving process, and can autonomously adjust its state with environmental changes. This dynamic model can expand the application of the UAVs to more fields.

2 Related Works

Currently, researchers have conducted a series of studies on UAVs mobility models in view of the particularity of high speed motion of UAVs. The quality of the mobility model has a direct impact on the routing algorithm and network topology. After analyzing the main factors affecting the quality of mobility model and their relationship, evaluation index system of mobility model and the quantitative evaluation method based on the analytic hierarchy process (AHP) are proposed in [4]. Then, the validity of the evaluation method is validated by taking the classic random mobility model (random Gauss-Markov (GM), random waypoint model (RWP), random walk model (RW), random direction model (RD)) as an example. For the UAVs own motion control, Broyles designed and implemented the three-dimensional airborne network Gauss Markov mobility model (3D-GMM) based on the high dynamic performance of the airborne network in [5]. The model increases the pitch angle parameter for airborne nodes, enable nodes to be more flexible in the processing of aerial maneuvering. Rohrer increased the effectiveness of the assessment on the basis of the 3D-GMM in [6], through emphasizing the adaptability of the node mobility and the diversity of the movement state. Zheng proposed the three-dimensional Gauss smoothing semi Markov mobility model in [7], taking the actual environment noise and other factors into account, and increased the Gaussian dis-turbaned in the model, but lacking the dealing with the node moving at boundary conditions. Kuiper [8] based on ant colony algorithm and artificial potential energy method, added pheromone and exclusion logic in the UAVs. Effectively solve the problem that network coverage and connectivity cannot optimize at the same time. He inspired by fish and analyzed the way of transforming between nodes in different state, and designed 3D_NMM (3D semi-random node mobility model) in [9], which achieved the effective coverage of regional monitoring target event. The above model only starts from the UAVs' own movement. During the operation, it needs to provide the specific track point or the direction of flight for UAVs, to guide UAVs to move. Otherwise, these models don't consider the dynamic change of the environment.

Considering the influence of large obstacles in the flying environment on the UAVs motion mode, Regis [10] extended the three movement models (random walk, random direction and Gauss-Markov) to accommodate large obstacles. For the static obstacles encountered in UAV flight, the collision avoidance cone method is designed in [11], to achieve the avoidance of obstacles. A local path planning algorithm based on improved morphine search tree is proposed in [12], which is used to avoid "sudden" obstacles. In [13], the method called the velocity obstacle method can provide the necessary situational awareness for UAVs in a dynamic environment, and can help to generate a conflicting maneuver.

In modern emergency rescue work, UAVs need to complete multiple tasks such as rapid response, data collection, relay communication, situation tracking and disaster reconstruction. The complexity of the environment and the tedious tasks make flight routes impossible to design in advance. The 3D Visit-Density Gauss-Semi-Markov Mobility (3D-VDGMM) [14] was designed to solve this problem in the early stage of our research group. However, many uncertainties, such as static and dynamic obstacles in the environment, pose challenges for the flight safety of UAVs. Existing mobility models don't work well for this type of scenario. For this reason, this paper designs the 3D Mobility Model for Dynamic and Uncertainty environment (3D-DUMM) based on 3D-VDGMM, which ensures the safety of UAVs while performing the capture of uncertain events.

3   Overview of 3D-VDGMM

To simulate the UAV network scenario requires accurate analysis of the transmission among wireless signals, which demands accurate knowledge of geographical location of mobility nodes. Due to the fact that the field test is uppity, dangerous and irreproducible while the verification of new applications and protocols is mainly completed with simulation technology, a UAV mobility model is in need to simulate the actual UAV movement. In [14], we have proposed a three-dimensional Gaussian semi-Markov mobility model based on visit density (3D-VDGMM). It first uses the access density to measure the access needs of unmanned people in different spatial locations, thus affecting the flight direction of UAV. For any square $S_{i,j,k}$, the event density ρ_e is equal to the total number of events at the current moment in the square, the drone density ρ_u is equal to the number of UAVs in the square at the current time. The visit density is:

$$\rho_v = \rho_e/(1 + \rho_u) \qquad (1)$$

After introducing the access density, the three-dimensional velocity vector of the UAV in 3D-VDGMM is represented as:

$$
\begin{cases}
x_n = \alpha x_{n-1} + (1 - \alpha)\bar{x} + \sqrt{(1 - \alpha^2)}(-1)^{\beta_x} \left| x_{n-1}, \gamma_x \right| \\
y_n = \alpha y_{n-1} + (1 - \alpha)\bar{y} + \sqrt{(1 - \alpha^2)}(-1)^{\beta_y} \left| y_{n-1}, \gamma_y \right| \\
z_n = \alpha z_{n-1} + (1 - \alpha)\bar{z} + \sqrt{(1 - \alpha^2)}(-1)^{\beta_z} \left| z_{n-1}, \gamma_z \right|
\end{cases} \qquad (2)
$$

$$
\begin{cases}
\beta_{x,y,z} = \begin{cases} 0, & \rho_{x+,y+,z+} \geq \rho_{x-,y-,z-} \\ 1, & \rho_{x-,y-,z-} > \rho_{x+,y+,z+} \end{cases} \\
\gamma_{x,y,z} = \log \left[\dfrac{max(\rho_{x-,y-,z-}, \rho_{x+,y+,z+})}{min(\rho_{x-,y-,z-}, \rho_{x+,y+,z+})} \right] \\
\rho_{x-,y-,z-} = \sum_i^{i \in Square_{negative}} \rho_{x_i, y_i, z_i} \\
\rho_{x+,y+,z+} = \sum_i^{i \in Square_{positive}} \rho_{x_j, y_j, z_j}
\end{cases} \qquad (3)
$$

where $\beta_{x,y,z}$ and $\gamma_{x,y,z}$ represent the parameters of the mobility model in the dimensions of X, Y, Z, respectively, $\beta_{x,y,z}$ directly affects the movement direction of node with a probability of 1, $\gamma_{x,y,z}$ indirectly influences the movement distance of node by affecting the probability of the node's movement distance. They both work in the process of the node moving to a new position. $log(\cdot)$ is used to determine the magnitude of two numbers; $\lfloor \cdot \rfloor$ indicates rounding down; $\rho_{x+,y+,z+}$ and $\rho_{x-,y-,z-}$ respectively represent the sum of the grid density of the front and rear sides of the node in the dimensions of X, Y, and Z. The front is the positive direction of the X, Y, and Z axes, while the rear is the negative direction. As is shown in Fig. 1, $\rho_{x+,y+,z+}$ is the sum of the 9 grid densities of the cube surface where the red arrow is directed.

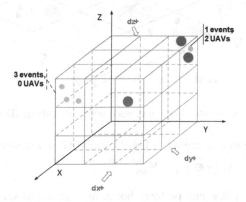

Fig. 1. Monitor areas of UAV in 3D-VDGMM.

4 Problem Description and Model Design

4.1 Problem Description and Conditional Assumptions

In the emergency rescue scenario, the main task of UAV is the disaster monitoring and information transmission. Therefore, the disaster information and the terminal that needs to transmit information can be defined as an event. Due to the different levels of disasters and the number of terminals, the quantity of incidents generated in different regions at different times varies from each other. UAVs need to complete the capture of events as much as possible, while avoiding collisions with uncertain obstacles during the movement. Different from the general scenario of 3D-VDGMM, in the emergency rescue scene, events are mainly distributed in the two-dimensional plane of the ground. Therefore, this paper first abstracts the task area into network G, and makes the following definitions and assumptions:

Definition 1: $U = \{u_1, u_2, \ldots, u_n\}$, indicates the UAV set existing in the network, where n is the number of UAVs.

Definition 2: $T = \{t_1, t_2, \ldots, t_k\}$, indicates the set of events that exist in the network, where k is the total number of random occurrences of the event.

Assumption 1: Divide the network G into small squares. The monitoring range of each node is 9 squares. UAVs are vertically projected to the center position (Fig. 2).

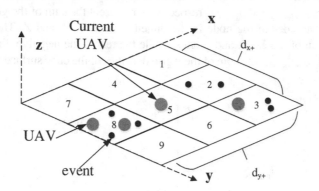

Fig. 2. Schematic diagram of node access density in 2D plane.

Assumption 2: Due to constraints of UAV capability and mission, the UAV node's flying speed v must satisfy $v \in [V_{min}, V_{max}]$.

Assumption 3: The UAV can perform horizontal all-round sensing and can sense events and obstacles as well as the distance to obstacles.

Assumption 4: The horizontal cross section of all obstacles in the dynamic uncertain environment is circular.

Assumption 5: No failure occurs during the task execution of UAVs.

4.2 Task-Based UAV Movement Model

Because the events in the emergency rescue scene are mainly distributed on the ground and the UAV nodes only need to follow the natural Gauss Markov motion in the vertical direction, the 3D-VDGMM is firstly improved to a two-dimensional plane movement model. At this moment, the area that each UAV node needs to directly perceive and calculate is the nine squares centered on the vertical projection point of the UAV on the ground (Fig. 2). The positive forward direction of the UAV node in the two-dimensional plane is the sum of the three grid densities pointed by ρ_{x+} and ρ_{y+} in Fig. 2, and the opposite direction is pointed by ρ_{x-} and ρ_{y-}. Therefore, Formula (2) and Formula (3) can be rewritten as:

$$
\begin{cases}
x_n = \alpha x_{n-1} + (1-\alpha)\bar{x} + \sqrt{(1-\alpha^2)}(-1)^{\beta_x}\left|x_{x_{n-1},\gamma_x}\right| \\
y_n = \alpha y_{n-1} + (1-\alpha)\bar{y} + \sqrt{(1-\alpha^2)}(-1)^{\beta_y}\left|y_{x_{n-1},\gamma_y}\right| \\
z_n = \alpha z_{n-1} + (1-\alpha)\bar{z} + \sqrt{(1-\alpha^2)}z_{x_{n-1}}
\end{cases}
\tag{4}
$$

$$
\begin{cases}
\beta_x = \begin{cases} 0, & \rho_{x+} \geq \rho_{x-} \\ 1, & \rho_{x-} > \rho_{x+} \end{cases} \\[2mm]
\beta_y = \begin{cases} 0, & \rho_{y+} \geq \rho_{y-} \\ 1, & \rho_{y-} > \rho_{y+} \end{cases} \\[2mm]
\gamma_x = \log\left|\dfrac{max(\rho_{x-}, \rho_{x+})}{min(\rho_{x-}, \rho_{x+})}\right| \\[3mm]
\gamma_y = \log\left|\dfrac{max(\rho_{y-}, \rho_{y+})}{min(\rho_{y-}, \rho_{y+})}\right| \\[3mm]
\rho_{x+} = \rho_1 + \rho_2 + \rho_3 \\
\rho_{x-} = \rho_7 + \rho_8 + \rho_9 \\
\rho_{y+} = \rho_3 + \rho_6 + \rho_9 \\
\rho_{y-} = \rho_1 + \rho_4 + \rho_7
\end{cases}
\tag{5}
$$

The definitions of β and γ are the same as formula (2) and (3). β determines the direction in which the UAV should fly, and γ determines the speed (distance) at which the UAV should fly. The specific motion of the UAV node is as follows:

(1) Calculate the access density d_v of 9 squares in the monitoring area according to formula (1);

(2) Compare the access density of 9 squares in the monitoring area. If its vertical projection corresponds to the largest grid density, the node will not perform any

operation, end the current movement, maintain hovering state at the original grid position, and carry out more detailed monitoring activities;

(3) If the density of its own projection grid is not the largest, the next move position of the node will be calculated according to Formula (4) and (5).

4.3   3D-DUMM Model

Section 4.2 improves the 3D-VDGMM model into a two-dimensional planar mobility model for emergency rescue scenarios, solving the problem of how the mobility model is task-oriented and improves event capture efficiency. However, in the emergency rescue scenario, the dynamic uncertainty of the environment directly affects the flight safety of the UAV swarm, so the mobility model must take it into consideration. The dynamic uncertainty environment referred to in this paper is mainly the obstacle affecting flight safety that exist in the rescue area, i.e. those obstacles whose height exceeds the UHV minimum flight height H_{min}. In the 3D-VDGMM, a moving influence, is added as a Gaussian factor to the UAV's original Gauss-Markov movement model, and the influence of the visit density on the UAV is positive, which means it will attract UAVs to be close to the location with high access density. Similarly, when considering obstacles in a dynamic uncertain environment, obstacles can also be added to the Gauss-Markov model in a certain form to make them play a negative role for UAVs, which guides UAVs to be far away from the obstacles.

Firstly, we expand Formula (4) to:

$$
\begin{cases}
x_n = \alpha x_{n-1} + (1 - \alpha)\bar{x} + \mu_x \rho(\beta_x, \gamma_x) + (1 - \mu_x) d(d_x) \\
y_n = \alpha y_{n-1} + (1 - \alpha)\bar{y} + \mu_y \rho(\beta_y, \gamma_y) + (1 - \mu_y) d(d_y) \\
\quad z_n = \alpha z_{n-1} + (1 - \alpha)\bar{z} + \sqrt{(1 - \alpha^2)} z_{x_{n-1}}
\end{cases}
\tag{6}
$$

$$
\begin{cases}
\rho(\beta_x, \gamma_x) = \sqrt{(1 - \alpha^2)}(-1)^{\beta_x} \left| x_{x_{n-1}, \gamma_x} \right| \\
\rho(\beta_y, \gamma_y) = \sqrt{(1 - \alpha^2)}(-1)^{\beta_y} \left| y_{x_{n-1}, \gamma_y} \right|
\end{cases}
\tag{7}
$$

Where $\rho(\beta_x, \gamma_x)$ and $\rho(\beta_y, \gamma_y)$ are the Gaussian influence factors of the access density applied to the UAV nodes in the x and y directions respectively, $d(d_x)$ and $d(d_y)$ are the influence factors applied to the UAV nodes in the x and y direction for obstacles, d_x and d_y are coordinates relative to the obstacle, μ_x and μ_y are priority factors in the x and y directions, and they satisfy:

$$
\mu =
\begin{cases}
1, & d > d_{max} \\
\delta, & d_{min} \le d \le d_{max} \\
0, & d < d_{min}
\end{cases}
\tag{8}
$$

That is, when the distance between the UAV and the obstacle in the x or y direction is less than d_{min}, the UAV enters the mode of obstacle avoidance priority. At this time, the mobility model only considers the influence of the obstacle regardless of the access density; when this distance is greater than d_{max}, the UAV enters the access priority mode. At this time, the mobility model only considers the impact of the access density in this direction regardless of the obstacle. When this distance is between d_{min} and d_{max}, UAV enters the hybrid mode where the mobility model considers the impact of access density and obstacles simultaneously.

Considering Formula (6), (7) and (8) comprehensively, we can find that the problem turns into how to set the function $d(d_x)$ or $d(d_y)$ and how to select the parameter δ. Since d_x and d_y are coordinates of UAV nodes with respect to obstacle respectively, that is $(d_x, d_y) = (x_{n-1} - o_x, y_{n-1} - o_y)$, the direction of d_x and d_y is the direction in which the obstacle is applied to the UAV. With reference to the artificial potential field model, it is clear that the closer the UAV is to the obstacle, the greater the force is to distance it exerts. Therefore, taking the x direction as an example, the $d(d_x)$ can be defined in combination with the away direction:

$$d(d_x) = \sqrt{(1-\alpha^2)}\frac{d_x}{|d_x|}\left|x\Big|_{x_{n-1}}, \frac{1}{d_x^2}\right| \tag{9}$$

In the formula, $\dfrac{d_x}{|d_x|}$ determines the direction in which the UAV should fly, while $\dfrac{1}{d_x^2}$ determines the speed (distance) at which the UAV should fly.

In conclusion, each UAV in the swarm updates the moving position according to Formula (6), (7), (8) and (9), which means it can realize a UAV three-dimensional mobility model oriented to a dynamic uncertain environment.

5   Simulation Results and Analysis

The experimental area is set to three-dimensional in which the length, width and height are 10 km respectively, and the side length of each square is 100 m, The initial speed of the node is a uniform random variable between 50 m/s and 100 m/s with a maximum speed of 100 m/s. Nodes update their mobile status every 1 s time interval.

First, the 3D-DUMM model was simulated in the task-oriented efficiency. The experiments were performed using one, two, and three UAVs, respectively, and the UAV flight time was 300 s. There are 100 events randomly distributed in the experimental area. The maximum number of event captures per unit time for each UAV is 1 and the event disappears when the event is captured by a UAV. The experimental results are shown in Figs. 3 and 4(a).

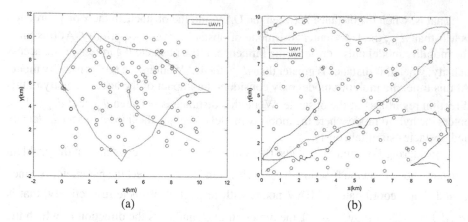

Fig. 3. Trajectory of 1 and 2 UAV in accordance with the 3D-DUMM model.

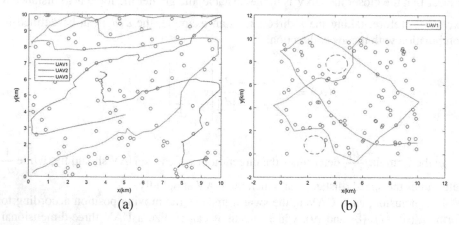

Fig. 4. (a) Trajectory of 3 UAV in accordance with the 3D-DUMM model, (b) Trajectory of the UAV under dynamical and uncertain environment.

Figures 3(a), (b) and 4(a) show traces of event capture by 1 UAV, 2 UAVs, and 3 UAVs in a 3D-DUMM model, respectively. From the above three figures, it can be found that based on the mobility model proposed in this paper, the trajectories of UAVs are basically the same as the event's distribution. As a result, it can achieve a higher event capturing rate during the task. During the flying process of UAVs, there are few phenomena such as sharp turns (except boundary conditions), and the trajectory is relatively smooth, which is closed to the actual movement law of UAV.

In order to verify the ability to adapt to the dynamic and uncertain environment through 3D-DUMM, we further added obstacles under the same experimental conditions. The experimental results are shown in Fig. 4(b).

Figure 4(b) shows the trajectory of 1 UAV according to the 3D-DUMM model with random events and obstacles in the experimental area. From Fig. 4(b), it can be found that, on the one hand, UAVs are highly sensitive to events and can pass through the areas with more events during the task. On the other hand, when UAVs encounter obstacles, they can make reasonable decisions between obstacles and events, and choose to capture more events on the basis of avoiding collisions with obstacles.

In order to quantitatively analyze the efficiency of 3D-DUMM in task execution, the comparisons on event capturing efficiency for 3D-DUMM, 3D-VDGMM, and 3D-GMM are shown in Fig. 5.

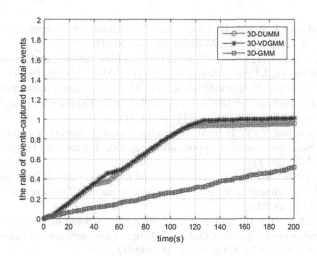

Fig. 5. Relationship between event capturing rate and running time under three different models.

Figure 5 shows the relationship between event capturing rate and running time when UAVs perform tasks under three different mobility models. From Fig. 5, it can be found that in 3D-DUMM and 3D-VDGMM, the event capturing rate is higher relative to 3D-GMM. And they can capture 80% of total events in about 100 s, while 3D-GMM can only captures 50% of events during 200 s. This is because both 3D-DUMM and 3D-VDGMM have added event traction to the model and have a high sensitivity to events. However, 3D-GMM only considers the law of UAV movement and has no sensitivity to events, so the process of capturing events is relatively random.

6   Conclusion

In order to effectively complete the rescue mission, the UAVs must be able to safely deal with complex environments first. Based on the 3D-VDGMM proposed in the earlier part of our research group, this paper fully considers the requirements of the rescue mission and the uncertainty of the environment, and designs 3D-DUMM in the further. Comprehensively combining the Gaussian factors of visit density and obstacles, the next direction of UAV can be calculated. Which ensures that UAVs can effectively capture target events while safely flying. The results of simulation show the validity and rationality of the model, and provide supports to evaluating the performance of three-dimensional environment UAV network. Next, detailed research on the data dissemination of UAV network based on 3D-DUMM will be conducted.

References

1. Erturk, M., Haque, J., Arslan, H.: Challenges of aeronautical data networks. In: Proceedings of IEEE Aerospace Conference, Montana, pp. 1–7, March 2010
2. Bujari, A., Calafate, C.T., Cano, J.C., et al.: Flying ad-hoc network application scenarios and mobility models. Int. J. Distrib. Sens. Netw. 13(10), 155014771773819 (2017)
3. Zaouche, L., Natalizio, E., Bouabdallah, A.: ETTAF: efficient target tracking and filming with a flying ad hoc network. In: International Workshop on Experiences with the Design and Implementation of Smart Objects, pp. 49–54. ACM (2015)
4. Sheng, Z., Ming-hui, Y., Yi, H., et al.: An exploration of evaluation of mobility model based on analytic hierarchy process in opportunistic network. J. Nanchang Hangkong Univ. Nat. Sci. 31(3), 15–22 (2017)
5. Broyles, D., Jabbar, A., Sterbenz, D.: Design and analysis of a 3-D Gauss Markov mobility model for highly-dynamic airborne networks. In: International Telemetering Conference, Las Vegas, NV, October 2009
6. Rohrer, J.P.: AeroRP performance in highly-dynamic airborne networks using 3D Gauss-Markov mobility model. In: MILCOM 2011 Military Communications Conference, pp. 834–841 (2011). ISSN 2155-7578, ISBN 9781467300797
7. Zheng, B., Zhang, H.Y., Huang, G.C., et al.: Design and implemention of a 3-D smooth mobility mode. J. Xidian Univ. 38(6), 179–184 (2011)
8. Kuiper, E., Nadjm-Tehrani, S.: Mobility models for UAV group reconnaissance applications. In: International Conference on Wireless and Mobile Communications, p. 33. IEEE (2006)
9. He, M., Chen, Q.L., Chen, X.L., et al.: Fish swarm inspired Ad hoc networks node random mobility optimization model in 3D environment. Chin. J. Sci. Instrum. 35(12), 2826–2834 (2014)
10. Regis, P.A., Bhunia, S., Sengupta, S.: Implementation of 3D obstacle compliant mobility models for UAV networks in ns-3, pp. 124–131 (2016)
11. Belkhouche, F., Bendjilali, B.: Reactive path planning for 3-D autonomous vehicles. IEEE Trans. Control Syst. Technol. 20(1), 249–256 (2012)
12. Yi, Z., Fan-yu, D., Yuan, L.: A local path planning algorithm based on improved morphin search tree. Electr. Opt. Control 23(7), 15–19 (2016)
13. Jenie, Y.I., Van Kampen, E.J., De Visser, C.C., et al.: Three-dimensional velocity obstacle method for UAV deconicting maneuvers. In: AIAA Guidance, Navigation and Control Conference, AIAA 2015-0592. AIAA Kissimmee (2015)
14. Zhang, G.M., Wang, N., Wang, R., et al.: UAV 3D mobility model based on visit density. J. Beijing Univ. Posts Telecommun. 40(s1), 112–116 (2017)

Acquiring Hidden Space via Modifying Block Bitmap for Android Devices

Wang Lianfang[1], Huang Hong[2], Li Yuanzhang[1], and Zhang Li[3($\boxtimes$)]

[1] School of Computer Science and Technology, Beijing Institute of Technology,
Beijing 100081, China
457361448@qq.com

[2] Troops 61516 of Chinese People's Liberation Army, Beijing 100094, China

[3] School of Computer and Information Technology,
Nanyang Normal University, Nanyang 473061, China
nythhsg@sina.com

Abstract. Mobile devices are widely used to process sensitive data. In certain situations, the sensitive data must be hidden rather than be encrypted. The existing approaches of setting up hidden space are not suitable for advanced Ext4 file system because they may require external storage device. To address the issue, we propose a novel method to establish the hidden space in Ext4 via artificially modifying the block bitmaps. To further improve usefulness of our method, we modify the multiply bits of the block bitmaps one time by creating a "host file" rather than by bit. This method is lightweight and does not require modifying the linux kernel and has no effect on the normal operations of the operating system. To validate the method performance, distributions of hidden spaces under different storage capacity are conducted. The results show that our method is effective and reliable.

Keywords: Hidden space · Ext4 · Block bitmap

1 Introduction

With the popularity of smartphones and other mobile computing devices, the amount of personal data stored in mobile devices has increased. According to a CNNIC report [10], the number of Internet users in China reached 772 million as of Dec. 2017, and the proportion of mobile Internet users were as high as 97.5%. At the same time, the majority of the people would like to share the information and data by Internet; it also brings security issues such as privacy leaks. People are accustomed to store personal data (photos, videos, documents, passwords, etc.) in mobile devices. These sensitive data may become the targets of attacks.

Encryption [2] can be utilized for protecting those sensitive data. However, with the development of forensic technology, encrypted data can be easily found by forensic tools, and it is difficult to prevent encrypted data from being cracked or being modified. Data hiding technology can store data in the redundant area of the storage medium. It makes hidden data difficult to find and ensures data security compared with encryption technology.

© Springer Nature Switzerland AG 2018
J. Vaidya and J. Li (Eds.): ICA3PP 2018, LNCS 11336, pp. 651–660, 2018.
https://doi.org/10.1007/978-3-030-05057-3_49

Data hiding may be implemented in different abstraction layers [3], such as hardware layer, operating system layer, and application layer [4–6]. This paper focuses on data hiding in OS layer. With the wide use of the Android operating system on mobile devices, the huge security threats and data leakage risks become more serious. It is necessary to study how to hide data in the Ext4 file system because Ext4 has now become the default file system for most Android systems.

The traditional hidden data acquisition methods read data from the file and directory slack space [7], preserved areas [8], and the file system timestamps [9] in the Ext4 file system. These methods have a common drawback: the obtained hidden space is too small. They cannot be applied in some real-world scenarios. For example, human rights worker takes the large amounts of video in conflicts areas and stores these data in hidden spaces of file system [10].

Knut et al. proposed a method to hide large amounts of data in journaling file system [11], but the method isn't applied to the ext4 file system; PANG et al. implemented the StegFS system based on Linux kernel 2.4, but the system can only be used in ext2 [12]; Adam Skillen et al. designed the Mobiflage system [13] to hide encrypted volumes, but it requires an external storage space and is not applicable to some mobile models.

In order to ensure the security and the feasibility of data hiding [14, 15], this paper proposes a new method of acquiring large-capacity hidden data in on the Ext4 file system. This method can modify the corresponding block bitmaps to acquire hidden space without affecting the normal operation of the operating system, when a large "host file" is created in the data partition.

Our contributions in this paper include:

1. We analyze the characteristics of the Ext4 file system, and explore the mapping relationship and structural association between metadata and data blocks such as block bitmap and inode.
2. We propose a new method to acquiring a hidden space via modifying block bitmap.

The rest of the paper is organized as follows. Section 2 presents the background. In Sect. 3, we explore methods for acquiring hidden spaces and describe the system design. In Sect. 4, we discuss the implementation for Android. Section 5 presents the results of functional evaluation and performance evaluation. Section 6 is the conclusion and future work.

2   Background

2.1   Overview of the Ext4 File System

A storage device is divided into an array of logical blocks in Ext4 with the default block size of 4 K. These blocks are organized into block groups and each block group consists of metadata blocks and data blocks as displayed in Fig. 1 [16]. An inode contains the metadata of a file, such as timestamps, user and group permissions, as well as pointers to data blocks [17]. A superblock contains metadata of file system and a group descriptor stores metadata of a particular block group. In addition, each block group has a data block bitmap, which records the allocation of data blocks in this group.

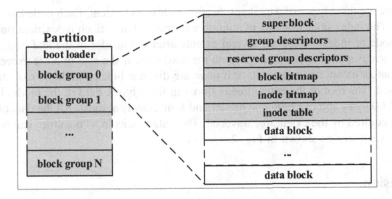

Fig. 1. Ext4 file system structure.

Ext4 uses an extended extent tree to store the file's logical location on disk, rather than the triple indirect pointer used in previous versions. After obtaining the inode number of the file, the logical location of the file can be found according to the extent tree.

2.2 Extent Tree

The extent tree has two types of node, including index node and leaf node. Each node stores a number of 12-byte data items.

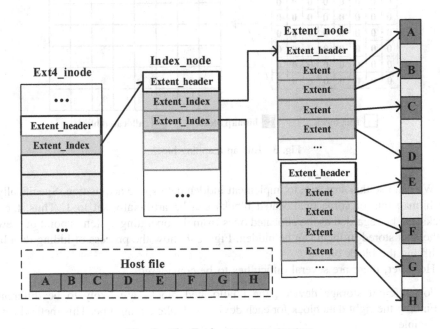

Fig. 2. The Ext4 extent tree structure.

There are three types of data items: header, index, and extent. Each node has a fixed header. The index node consists of a number of index items. Each index item points to a leaf node or index. There are several extents after the header in the leaf node. Each extent locates a continuous data space on the hard disk. If the size of a file exceeds the value that an extent can represent, or if there are discrete blocks, multiple extents need to be used. The root of the extent tree is stored in the i_block field of the inode. It is an array of 60 bytes and can hold one header and four extents at most. All the data of a file can be acquired by the extent tree traversal. The data blocks in a "host file" can be cited by the extent tree as shown in Fig. 2.

3 Design

3.1 Block Bitmap

A partition is divided into standard-sized blocks and then the block bitmap is used to record each block usage. That is to say, if the block has already been allocated, the corresponding bitmap bit is set to 1, otherwise it is set to 0 (see Fig. 3).

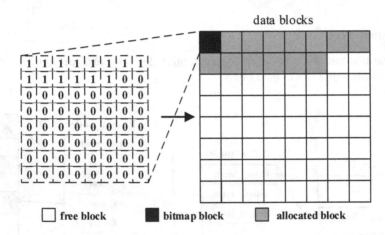

Fig. 3. Bitmap mapping block.

We can use this structure to implement hidden data space acquisition. Specifically, the bitmap bits of some unallocated blocks can be artificially set to 1. Thus, these blocks can be regarded as the allocated ones from the operating system's point of view, so the data stored in them can be hidden. Figure 4 show the process of hiding data by modifying the block bitmap.

However, there are several difficulties to be considered:

1. For different storage devices, the unallocated blocks are likely to be different. Finding the right data block for each device will take a long time. This method isn't flexible.

2. In order to set up a large hidden space, such as 4G, 1048576 bitmap bits need to be modified and it is easy to make mistakes.
3. To ensure the security of the hidden spaces, they should be scattered in the storage device rather than a continuous area. This is a huge challenge for directly modifying the bitmap information.

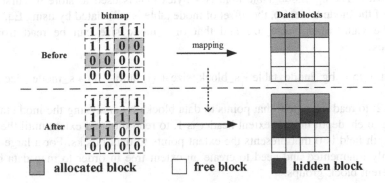

Fig. 4. Acquiring hidden space.

However, the storage characteristic of Ext4 file system can help us to solve the above problems. In the Ext4 file system, each file is stored in a series of data blocks. For a file larger than one block, its data is scattered in the storage area. Based on this fact, this paper proposes an effective method to create "host file" as a hidden data space. When a file is created, enough data blocks are allocated to store the file data. At the same time, their block bitmap bits are all set to 1, indicating that these blocks have already been allocated. As long as the file always exists, these blocks will be reallocated no longer. Thus, we can store hidden data in these areas. The rest of this section shows how to find these hidden spaces by the file name of the "host file".

3.2 Hidden Space Calculation

The method proposed in this paper focuses on setting up hidden space by creating a "host file" that serve as data carriers.

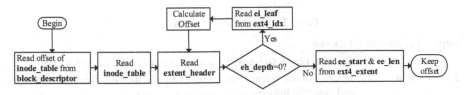

Fig. 5. The process of hidden space calculation.

When a "host file" is created, Ext4 checks the block bitmap and allocates free blocks to the file, as well as modifying block bitmaps. We need to calculate the addresses of these data blocks and their lengths and record them as offsets of hidden spaces. The calculation process is designed as the following Fig. 5.

Step 1: the offset of inode table is read from the block group descriptor. The block group descriptor table is stored in the first logical block. Each block group descriptor has 32 bytes. The bg_inode_table field is 4 bytes that is used to store the first block number of the inode table. So, the offset of inode table is calculated by using Eq. (1), in which the value of s_block_size and that of s_inode_size can be read from the superblock.

$$offset\_i\_tb = bg\_inode\_table * s\_block\_size + (i\_num - 1) * s\_inode\_size \quad (1)$$

Step 2: to read the extent that points to data blocks by analyzing the inode table. If the value of eh_depth field in extent header is 1, to read the next extent until the value of eh_depth field is 0 that presents the extent points to data blocks. For a large file, it was highly fragmented and need to create an extent tree in order to map data blocks into different block groups.

Step 3: we generate a two-dimensional array that stores the value of ee_start field and the value of (ee_start-ee_len) field. Based on the array, the hidden spaces can be set up. The following Fig. 6 shows an example of the array that stores the offsets of the hidden spaces.

Address	12288	4096	1640448	1644544	1738752	1742848	1800192	1808384	1837056
Length	2048	8192	2048	6144	2048	2048	26624	30720	30720

Fig. 6. Array that stores offsets of the hidden space.

4 Implementation

In this article, the process of setting up hidden space can be divided into three steps. First, we create an empty file in the ext4 file system as a "host file"; second, we calculate the addresses of the blocks occupied by the file, and save them in a two-dimensional array; finally, we delete the inode of the file to hide the "host file".

Table 1. The functions of process.

Step	Parameter	Function
1	−n a	Create a file of size a (GB) on/data directory, named hidden.txt
2	−fi_n	Display all the extent trees occupied by the file with inode number i_n, and save the information of extent trees into array
3	−di_n	Conceal the "Host file"
	−w n	Write hidden blocks with number n
	−b N	Display all contents of the Nth block in hexadecimal

We write a JNI program named blc with different parameters (see Table 1), which is compiled and run on a mobile device. In addition, another two programs have been written to evaluate the performance of blc.

Ext4 is a journal file system, so user operations are recorded in the log file. To prevent hidden space from being overwritten, we run the JNI program in recovery mode.

4.1 Create "Host File"

The user enters the command blc -n a and then the program will run, in which the linux shell command dd if =/dev/zero of =/data/text.txt bs = 1G count = a is executed to create a "host file" with aG size. This way makes the method of setting up hidden space more efficient and flexible, because the input parameter a can be changed. The user can set up a large-capacity hidden space when the value of a is large.

4.2 Save Hidden Space

The user changes the work directory into/data directory and enters the command ls -i to get the inode number of the text.txt file named i_n. Then the position of inode table will be calculated. The extent header is read to judge the type of this extent node after the command blc -f i_n is executed. If the node is an index, it need to continue to read the next extent in the extent tree, otherwise the starting block number and the length of data block are stored in the array.

4.3 Conceal "Host File"

The command ls -lt is used to display the basic information of the "host file" named text.txt in current directory (Fig. 7). However, the file should be hidden for reasons of safety. To achieve the goal, we need to deletes the inode of the file rather than the file itself, so as to keep its data blocks invisible. The command blc -d i_n is executed and the directory of text.txt will be located. Then the i_nth index node can be found and the file name stored in it needs to be clear. Thus, the "host file" will disappear from someone else's point of view.

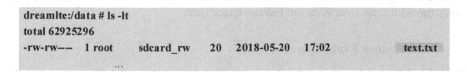

```
dreamlte:/data # ls -lt
total 62925296
-rw-rw---  1 root    sdcard_rw   20   2018-05-20   17:02             text.txt
             ...
```

Fig. 7. Basic information of the "host file" in the directory.

5   Evaluation

In this section the effectiveness and performance of the hidden space approach will be evaluated. A Samsung S8 development mobile phone (Android 7.0, Kernel 4.4.13, Internal storage: 64 G) is used as the test environment.

5.1   Functional Evaluation

In order to allow the user to manage the hidden space based on the operating system, there are two necessary assumptions: one is to acquire the root privilege of operating system, and the other is to close the SELinux security system.

Theoretically, the operating system will not cover the artificial hidden data in normal day-to-day use, because the bitmap bits of these hidden spaces remain 1. We will test whether the hidden data spaces may be overwritten during the normal operations. The experimental steps are as the followings and the result is shown in Fig. 8.

```
dreamlte:/data/local/tmp # ./blc -b 594124
[0000] ee ee ee ee ee ee ee ee ee ee ee ee ee ee ee ee |
[0016] ee ee ee ee ee ee ee ee ee ee ee ee ee ee ee ee |
[0032] ee ee ee ee ee ee ee ee ee ee ee ee ee ee ee ee |
[0048] ee ee ee ee ee ee ee ee ee ee ee ee ee ee ee ee |
```

Fig. 8.   Data read from the hidden spaces.

1. To set up the hidden space by our proposed the method.
2. To execute the command *blc -w 238* to fill the blocks in the hidden spaces with the number 238 (0xee) and to restart the system.
3. To repeat the command *cp/storage/fill.mp4/data/i.mp4* to write a media file with 1G size into the storage device until the file system is full of data. Restart the system.
4. To execute the command *blc –b N* (*N* is an arbitrary block number in the hidden spaces) to read data from the hidden spaces and then to compare it with the written data.

The result shows that the user's normal operations (including restarting the system many times) do not overwrite the hidden space data.

5.2   Performance Evaluation

The size of the hidden spaces depends on the total capacity of the file system and the number of free blocks. In order to know about the distribution of hidden spaces, we write the test data into the file system with a total capacity of 54 G in 5 groups and generate the available space sizes 40 G, 30 G, 20 G, 10 G, and 5 G respectively. By examining the super block, we can see that the total number of blocks in file system is 14296059 and that they are divided into 437 block groups. After that, we set up a 4 G hidden space by using our method 5 times.

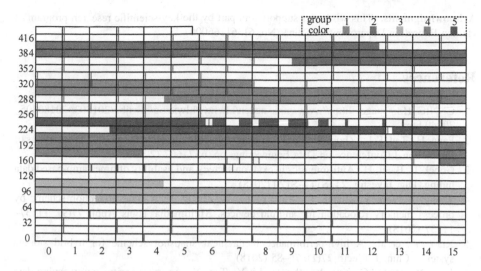

Fig. 9. The distribution of the hidden space.

Figure 9 shows the distribution of the hidden spaces on the storage device, in which the block group numbers increase from left to right and bottom to top.

To reduce the performance loss of file system due to fragmentation, the block allocator tries to keep all the blocks of each file within the same group, thus it can reduce the seek times. From the Fig. 9, we can see that the consecutive block group numbers for a large file are allocated as much as possible. Once the available storage space is limited, the large file is divided into multiple discrete areas.

6 Conclusion and Future Work

In this paper, we analyze the characteristics of the ext4 file system and then propose a flexible method to set up a large-capacity hidden space based on its file allocation mechanism. This method does not require modification of the linux kernel and has little effect on the normal operations of the operating system. After that, a JNI program is developed to implement this method. At last, the experiment results show that the hidden spaces would not be rewritten by the operating system, nor would it lose data after the mobile phone was restarted.

Of course, our proposed method still has several limitations that make it impossible to apply to the actual scene:

1. The established hidden spaces are not easy to be deleted in the user level.
2. The "host file" is still easy to be detected by file system check software, although it has been concealed.

In the future, we will try to solve the above limitations and then apply the established hidden space to the actual scene. At the same time, we will consider setting up multiple host files to increase security.

Acknowledgments. This work was supported in part by the key scientific research program of He'nan Education Department of China (No. 61361166006).

References

1. CNNIC Homepage. http://www.cnnic.net.cn/hlwfzyj/hlwxzbg/hlwtjbg/201803/t20180305_70249.htm
2. Pang, H., Tan, K.L., Zhou, X.: StegFS: a steganographic file system. In: 2003 Proceedings of International Conference on Data Engineering, pp. 657–667 (2003)
3. Göbel, T., Baier, H.: Anti-forensics in ext4: on secrecy and usability of timestamp-based data hiding. Dig. Investig. **24**, S111–S120 (2018)
4. Zhang, X., Tan, Y., Zhang, C., Xue, Y., Li, Y., Zheng, J.: A code protection scheme by process memory relocation for android devices. Multimedia Tools Appl. **77**(9), 11137–11157 (2018)
5. Xiao, Y., et al.: A high-performance hierarchical snapshot scheme for hybrid storage systems. Chin. J. Electr. **27**(1), 76–85 (2018)
6. Xiao, Y., Zhang, C., Xue, Y., Zhu, H., Li, Y., Tan, Y.: An extra-parity energy saving data layout for video surveillance. Multimedia Tools Appl. **77**, 4563–4583 (2018)
7. Skillen, A., Mannan, M.: On implementing deniable storage encryption for mobile devices (2013)
8. Carrier, B.: File System Forensic Analysis. Addison-Wesley Professional, Boston (2005)
9. Piper, S., Davis, M., Manes, G., Shenoi, S.: Detecting hidden data in Ext2/Ext3 file systems. In: Pollitt, M., Shenoi, S. (eds.) DigitalForensics 2005. ITIFIP, vol. 194, pp. 245–256. Springer, Boston, MA (2006). https://doi.org/10.1007/0-387-31163-7_20
10. Sun, Z., Zhang, Q., Li, Y., Tan, Y.: DPPDL: a dynamic partial-parallel data layout for green video surveillance storage. IEEE Trans. Circ. Syst. Video Technol. **28**(1), 193–205 (2018)
11. Eckstein, K., Jahnke, M.: Data hiding in journaling file systems. In: Refereed Proceedings of the Digital Forensic Research Workshop, DFRWS 2005, Astor Crowne Plaza, New Orleans, Louisiana, USA, pp. 595–599, August 2005
12. Wong, D.J.: Ext4 Disk Layout - Ext4 Wiki (2016). https://ext4.wiki.kernel.org/index.php/Ext4_Disk_Layout. Accessed 1 Oct 2017
13. Forensic Research Workshop, DFRWS 2005, Astor Crowne Plaza, New Orleans, Louisiana, USA, pp. 595–599, August 2005
14. Xue, Y., Tan, Y., Liang, C., Zhang, C., Zheng, J.: An optimized data hiding scheme for deflate codes. Soft. Comput. **22**(13), 4445–4455 (2018)
15. Yu, X., Tan, Y., Sun, Z., Liu, J., Liang, C., Zhang, Q.: A fault-tolerant and energy-efficient continuous data protection system. J. Ambient Intell. Humanized Comput. (2018). http://dx.doi.org/10.1007/s12652-018-0726-2
16. Neuner, S., Voyiatzis, A.G., Schmiedecker, M., et al.: Time is on my side: steganography in filesystem metadata. Dig. Investig. **18**, S76–S86 (2016)
17. Fairbanks, K.D.: An analysis of Ext4 for digital forensics. Dig. Investig. **9**, S118–S130 (2012)

Interest Relevance-Based Caching Design in Content-Centric Networking

Guozhi Zhang[1,2] , Jiqiang Liu[1] , Xiaolin Chang[1(✉)] ,
and Yang Yang[1]

[1] Beijing Key Laboratory of Security and Privacy in Intelligent Transportation,
Beijing Jiaotong University, Beijing 100044, China
{zhangguozhi, jqliu, xlchang, 16112082}@bjtu.edu.cn
[2] The School of Computer and Engineering, Northwest Normal University,
Lanzhou 730070, China

Abstract. Among the existing Content Center Networking (CCN) caching
schemes, the most important category is popularity-based schemes which perform better than non-popularity-based in terms of cache-hits. However, these
existing popularity-based caching schemes assumed that they provide services
for a single type of applications and assumed that content requests (interest)
conform to Zipf-like distribution. Although Zipf-like request distribution was
validated in many network applications, this distribution may not exist at the
node level in CCN when there exist multiple types of upper-level applications in
the network. Once the traffic feature of Zipf-like distribution becomes less
obvious, the existing popularity-based caching schemes could not work well.
Therefore, how to predict the content request (interest) for each node becomes a
key problem of caching design.

In this paper, we use the application-level relevance of interest to assist the
caching design, rather than just relying on names. We propose a scheme (named
as ICDCS) based on interest/content tag analyzing in which multiple types of
upper-level applications produced contents/interests and tags is added as a part
of name, then a measuring mechanism is designed to count and predict the trend
of interest. Our scheme can be well combined with existed approaches and
improve their caching performance. Simulations over various system parameters
are done to validate the effectiveness and efficiency of ICDCS.

Keywords: Tagging system · Content centric networking
Cache allocation strategy · Naming design

1 Introduction

One of the fascinating features of Content-Centric Networking (CCN) [1] is *in-network
caching*, which uses router/node cache to exchange communication overheads. The key
idea of *in-network caching* is to predict the demand of consumers correctly, and then
take the "best" way to cache the content to the location where users are interested.

Among the existing CCN caching schemes, popularity-based schemes perform
better than non-popularity-based in terms of *cache-hits*. The popularity-based schemes
work well only for the scenario where the more popular the content, the more

© Springer Nature Switzerland AG 2018
J. Vaidya and J. Li (Eds.): ICA3PP 2018, LNCS 11336, pp. 661–671, 2018.
https://doi.org/10.1007/978-3-030-05057-3_50

frequently the content is requested in the time dimension [2]. There are two major problems with these existing popularity-based caching schemes:

(1) They assumed that request (named interest) arrivals for a content in a region (e.g., AS) follow Zipf distribution [3] at the file level. In addition, they assumed that the Zipf-like traffic pattern still exists in CCN. The latter assumption is reasonable only when there is a single type of applications in the network. When multiple types of applications co-exist in the network, the latter assumption is not correct even content request arrivals of each application still conform to Zipf-like distribution at the file level. The traffic mix at the chunk level makes the CCN traffic distribution more flat and complex [4]. Namely, it is hard, if not impossible, to analyze CCN traffic patterns in the scenario where there are multiple types of applications.

(2) They measured the popularity of a content by applying the CCN naming design. Some schemes applied the flat naming design, in which different interest packages are considered the same if and only if their request prefixes are the same. However, there may exist the potential relationship between contents with different names. Some other existing schemes applied the hierarchical naming design [5]. In this design, if different interest packages are considered the same, the nodes need to be able to parse the name structure, even the semantic relations between names. However, this hierarchical naming design faces design difficulties in terms of efficiency and effectiveness.

These discussions suggest that existing popularity-based caching strategy may not work effectively and efficiently in CCN. This is also validated by our later simulations in which the traffic of various flows is mixed and chunked. This paper considers the scenario where types of upper-level applications co-exist [4]. Therefore, the knowledge of upper-level applications' traffic characteristics at the node level will help caching decision. The analysis in the previous paragraphs suggest the weakness of the naming system in obtaining traffic characteristics at the node level. Thus, a new method for marking traffic features should be explored.

All the above analysis forms the motivation of the work in this paper. We propose a tag-based caching allocation scheme (named as ICDCS, Interest Characterize-tags Distribution based Cache-decision Scheme), which exploits tag information to achieve the content request prediction. Tag information in traffic is generated at consumers or producers according to the pre-defined tags. Simulations over various system parameters are done to validate the effectiveness and efficiency of ICDCS.

We summarize the major contributions as follows.

(1) We design ICDCS caching scheme, which consists of three components: (i) a counting bloom filter-based tag counting component which aims to reduce the popularity calculation overheads, (ii) fitness quantifier which uses cosine distance to quantify the suitability of content, and (iii) piggyback and path collaboration which aim to reduce communication overheads. Each component works in linear time, therefore, ICDCS has less overheads.

(2) We explore a tagging system to assist caching decision in ICDCS. Tag information in traffic helps the prediction of the trend of interests and help nodes to evaluate whether the content is suitable to be cached. To the best of our knowledge, we are the first to introduce a tagging system into CCN caching design. Note that exploiting a tagging system can alleviate the contradiction between caching design and naming design, and it also brings a new perspective to the other mechanism designs such as CCN routing and retrieval.

Note that this paper applies a well-developed collaborative tagging system [6] to generate appropriate tags for content. This tagging system is a powerful tool with which users could tag content while they upload the file. It is widely deployed in Web and Online Social Networks (OSNs) for content recommendation, classification and prediction with very low overheads. In our latter simulations, 20 tags are randomly selected and assigned to each topic. When a consumer/provider requests the content, he/she selects 4–7 tags uniformly from the pre-defined 20 tags.

The rest of paper is organized as follows. Section 2 gives the background and related work. Section 3 describes ICDCS scheme. Section 4 presents the simulation results. Section 5 concludes the paper.

2 Background and Related Work

Because content requests (interests) have temporal and spatial features (such as following the Zip-like distributions), many studies (see [7]) have attempted to exploit these features to design caching strategies. This also makes popularity-based strategies become the most important type of caching strategy. In these strategies, it is assumed that all interests usually follow the Zipf distribution which is defined as $P(x) = C/\gamma^\alpha$, where α reflects the concentration of the distribution.

Table 1. The distribution assumption in some researches

Reference	Distribution assumption
Wang et al. [8]	Zipf with $\alpha \approx 1$
Pacifici et al. [9]	Zipf with $\alpha = 1$
Duan et al. [10]	Zipf with $\alpha = *$
Wang, et al. [11]	Zipf with $\alpha = *$

*: The value cannot be obtained from the paper.

The in-network caching is designed as the fundamental function of the router in CCN. Each node receives content request (named interest) and forwards them, and they process returned contents and determine whether to cache them. Based on the studies of traditional networks [12–14], the popularity-based caching design has also become one of the important ways in CCN [3]. The common feature of studies is to draw on the popularity of traditional network model and try to cache the popular content on path node, and their difference is the use of different factors and popularity measurement methods.

In all these popularity-based caching design, there exist a strong assumption: *the popular patterns used in traditional networks still exist in CCN*. As can be seen in Table 1, some premise and their parameters used in the cache model scene are listed. These studies assumed that the request conforms to Zipf-like distribution but with different exponential parameter. However, we need to be aware that when the rationality of this assumption is problematic, the basis for the design of these strategies will be shaken.

3   ICDCS Caching Scheme

This section presents the details of ICDCS. For convenience, we give some symbols and notation in Table 2 that may is used in later.

Table 2. Symbols and notations

Notation	Description
G	Graph of topology
E	The edge set of G
V	The node set of G
i	The prefix i of content/interest
I_i	The interest with prefix i
C_i	The content with prefix i
$|C_i|$	The volume of content C_i
$P_{x \to y}$	The path from x to y
$|P_{x \to y}|$	The length of $P_{x \to y}^{V(i)}$

3.1   Core Idea of ICDCS

Content requests are closely related to each other at the application and social level, that is, when consumers request certain content in the area within a certain period, other relevant content may also be required. Mainly because these contents belong to the TOPIC, that is, they have similar content characteristics or social attributes because they are closely related to the events that generate these contents.

Is there a way for us to find and count the implicit relevance between requests rather than rely solely on name statistics? In this work we have designed a simpler method based on tag vector distance to calculate the caching fitness of the content in the node. Figure 1 shows the working process of a router/node deploying ICDCS. The core of ICDCS includes: (i) When a node receives an interest/content, it counts tags and establishes its own *Tags Counting Component (TCC)*; and (ii) In caching decision step, router x decides whether to cache the content according to its *TCC*. The details of the three key components in ICDCS are given in the following.

3.2   Tag Counting Component Based on Counting Bloom Filter

To count the tags carried by interests and calculate the content fitness effectively, it is necessary to design an efficient and low-cost tag counting component. Counting Bloom Filter (CBF) is an efficient data structure with a low probability of false positives. Based on CBF, we implement TCC to achieve tag recording, retrieving and counting. Described as in Fig. 2, CBF is the core of TCC. The counting ability of TCC depends on the size of CBF. In our simulation, TCC can count more than 10,000 tags, each with a total of 2^{32} counts over a period. Note that Fitness Quantifier discussed below also depends on CBF.

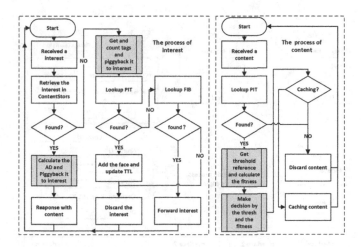

Fig. 1. The working process of a node

3.3   Fitness Quantifier

ICDCS uses the distance between content C_i received on node x and all tags of interests received by this node in the past period to measure the similarity between C_i and the received interest. Cosine distance is used to compute the similarity (also named as fitness degree) between the content and the received interest. Cosine distance is the distinction of the direction but insensitive to the absolute value. Therefore, it can adjust the errors, which are generated due to the non-uniformity of the measurement criteria.

Before explaining how to calculate fitness degree $D_x(C_i)$ of C_i on node x, some denotations are first presented. $TS^x = \{t_1^x, \ldots, t_K^x\}$ denotes the tag space on node x. Here t_i^x is a tag and K denotes the size of tag space. Let $T(C_i) = \{t_1^i, \ldots, t_n^i\} \subset TS^x$ as the tag set of content C_i, here n is the number of tags of C_i. $TCT^x = \{\langle t_1^x, tc_1^x \rangle, \cdots, \langle t_K^x, tc_K^x \rangle\}$ denotes the interest tags counting table of node x. Here, tc_i^x is the counting value of tag t_i^x, and this value is also considered to be the weight of tag t_i^x. Therefore, $T(C_i) = \{t_1^i, \ldots, t_n^i\}$ can be represented as $TCT(C_i) = \{\langle t_1^i, 1 \rangle, \cdots, \langle t_n^i, 1 \rangle\}$ because the tags carried by the content cannot be repeated. With these definitions, we define $D_x(C_i)$ as:

$$D_x(C_i) = \cos(TCT^x, TCT(C_i))$$

$$= \sum_{t^i \in TS^x \cap T(C_i)} tc^i \Bigg/ \sqrt{n \times \sum_{t^i \in TS^x \cap T(C_i)} (tc^i)^2} \tag{1}$$

The greater $D_x(C_i)$, the more likely C_i to be requested. Note that $D_x(C_i)$ can have different meanings, depending on the meanings of tags. For instance, in OSN-like applications, tags can be used to represent the social relations or semantics of content. In geographic-related applications, it can be used to reflect the geographic location of content. In video sharing applications, it can be used to reflect the description of content.

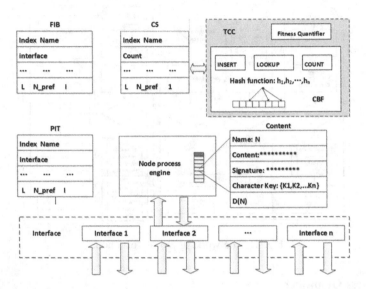

Fig. 2. The node structures

3.4 Piggybacking of Decision Information

$D_x(C_i)$ is computed along the path from providers to consumers. This value suffices for making decision since the caching scope is only limited to the path. This process includes two steps:

(i) The node gets the cumulative fitness $\sum D_w(C_i)$ that is carried by the received interest. The node perceives the interest of all downstream nodes along the path when it receives an interest. $MD_x(C_i) = \sum D_w(C_i) \Big/ \left| P_{x \to y}^V(i) \right|$ denotes the average fitness of C_i along the path $P_{x \to y}^V(i)$. Here, $\left| P_{x \to y}^V(i) \right|$ is the length of $P_{x \to y}^V(i)$, w is a node on $P_{x \to y}^V(i)$, and $D_w(C_i)$ is the fitness of C_i at w. When node x receives C_i, it first calculates $D_x(C_i)$ and $MD_x(C_i)$. Then, $D_x(C_i)$ and $MD_x(C_i)$ are compared to decide whether to cache the content.

(ii) Once a node receives interest and the response conditions are met, it will return the content in which the decision information can be carried. Then the downstream node will decide whether to cache the content according to the threshold. l denotes the length of $P^V_{x \to y}(i)$. $\{v|D_v(C_i) \geq \beta \times MD_x(C_i)\}$ denotes the node set of duplicates of C_i, where β is a parameter used to balance the quantity and the cost of duplicates. To increase the randomness and improve the effectiveness of the algorithm, if a node belongs to $\{v|D_v(C_i) \geq \beta \times MD_x(C_i)\}$, the content will be cached with probability $P = l/L$, where L is the network diameter being evaluated.

ICDCS produces some communication and computation overheads while it brings a series of advantages. But the overheads are small. In our later simulation, we select 4-7 tags as the set of characteristics, and each tag occupies 8 bytes. Then, the maximum cost of tags of each content will be 56 bytes.

4 Simulation and Performance Evaluation

This section aims for evaluating the capability of ICDCS, by comparison with IFDD [2], LCE and POPULAR on ndnSIM [15]. LCE is the default non-popularity-based caching scheme in ndnSIM. POPULAR is a simple popularity-based mechanism proposed in this paper. In POPULAR, each node counts the received interest prefix for a period, and then sorts these prefixes in descending order. When a content is received and its prefix is in the highest range, it is cached. Otherwise it is discarded or cached with a certain probability.

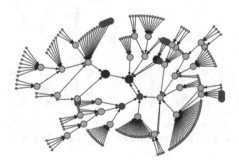

Fig. 3. The topology of simulations

We first build a traffic model to emulate OSN-like applications [16]. Two OSN-like features are embodied in this model. (i) Burst requests for all contents of a certain topic. We use a set of tags (named a topic) to describe a group of contents. The topic popularity varies over time, resulting in changes of request frequency for contents related to this topic. Contents belonging to the same topic are generated by different producers, but their requests are related by the tags. Contents belonging to the same topic have clustered requesting characteristics over time. In this way, traffic generated by different applications is related to each other due to the topic. To make a reasonable comparison of these four schemes, content requests for the same topic follow the Zipf distribution. (ii) User preferences for contents of different topic. It is achieved by setting the different request probabilities to the same topic for users in different regions.

Consumers and producers apply this traffic model and collaborative tagging system to generate traffic and add tags. Figure 3 shows the topology used in our simulations. Consumers and producers are on the edge of the network, and routers are on the network core. Each node is configured to produce 500 contents. Figures 4, 5 and 6 show the results in scatter plots to intuitively reflect the distribution of *cache-hits*. Each point in the figures represents *cache-hits* in the router cache during the content request.

4.1   Impact of Popularity Distribution on Cache-Hits

This sub-section compares *cache-hits* of ICDCS, IFDD [2], LCE, and POPULAR by varying request popularity distribution in terms of *interest dispersion* in traditional scenario and our scenario, respectively. Here, interest dispersion refers to the exponential parameter of Zipf-like distribution. By traditional scenario, we mean that there is only one content producer, and all content requests conform to Zipf distribution. By our scenario, we mean that there are many producers (here, this value is 20 in Fig. 3) and the requests for the same producer follow the Zipf distribution. In addition, all content traffic is mixed at the chunk level.

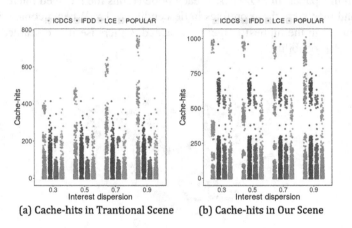

(a) Cache-hits in Trantional Scene   (b) Cache-hits in Our Scene

Fig. 4. Popularity distribution vs. *Cache-hits*

Figure 4(a) and (b) show *cache-hits* differences in the traditional scenario and in our scenario, respectively. We observed that ICDCS has the best *cache-hits* than IFDD, LCE and POPYULAR in both two types of scenarios. The change of traffic of our scenario causes a significant drop in *cache-hits* for all strategies, but ICDCS could still perform best. When interest dispersion is increased, the improvement in ICDCS *cache-hit* performance is more obvious than the other three. ICDCS is more sensitive to interest dispersion. The main reason is that the increase in the popularity of a single type of content is decentralized throughout the network under our assumption, but ICDCS can exploit the inherent relation of these contents rather than just names.

4.2   Impact of Cache Capacity on Cache-Hits

This sub-section investigates the impact of cache capacity on *cache-hits*. As we known, a good caching strategy design should have an exquisite sensitivity to capacity. That is, caching performance could be improved simply by increasing the cache capacity. The results in Fig. 5. Cache Capacity vs. *Cache-hits* indicate that with the increasing cache capacity, *cache-hits* of ICDCS increases more.

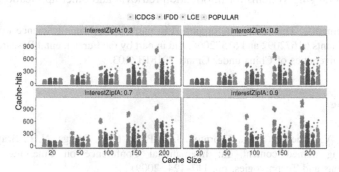

Fig. 5. Cache capacity vs. *Cache-hits*

4.3   Performance of Caching Schemes at Different Decision Thresholds

In the previous description, the content will be cached at $\{v|D_v(C_i) \geq \beta \times MD_x(C_i)\}$, where β is the threshold of decision. Figure 6 presents the results by varying β from 1 to 10, suggesting that β is a decisive factor to *cache-hits*. When β is increased but below the certain value, *cache-hits* does not drop significantly, or even increases. When β reaches a certain value (this value is 5 in Fig. 6. Cache Decision Threshold vs. *Cache-hits*), *cache-hits* decreases rapidly. That is, controlling the number of replicas at a reasonable number will greatly improve network performance. The investigation of the reason behind this is left for our future work.

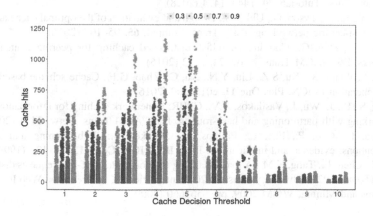

Fig. 6. Cache decision threshold vs. *Cache-hits*

5   Conclusion and Future Work

This paper explores the CCN traffic features at the mixed chunk level. Then a simplified traffic model is built, in which the popularity-based caching strategy could not perform well. We further use the content social attributes to design a cache allocation scheme based on a tagging system. The simulation results show that the proposed scheme performs better than the existing caching schemes. Future work includes the usefulness of tagging systems for information retrieval and other application functions.

Acknowledgements. This work was supported in part by the Natural Science Foundation of China under Grants 61672092 and 61572066, and in part by the Fundamental Research Funds for the Central Universities of China under Grants 2018JBZ103.

References

1. Jacobson, V., Smetters, D.K., Thornton, J.D., Plass, M.F., Briggs, N.H., Braynard, R.L.: Networking named content. In: International Conference on Emerging Networking Experiments and Technologies, pp. 117–124 (2009)
2. Zhang, G., Liu, J., Chang, X., Chen, Z.: Combining popularity and locality to enhance in-network caching performance and mitigate pollution attacks in content-centric networking. IEEE Access **5**, 19012–19022 (2017)
3. Ioannou, A., Weber, S.: A survey of caching policies and forwarding mechanisms in information-centric networking. IEEE Commun. Surv. Tutorials **18**, 2847–2886 (2016)
4. Fricker, C., Robert, P., Roberts, J., Sbihi, N.: Impact of traffic mix on caching performance in a content-centric network. In: 2012 IEEE Conference on Computer Communications Workshops (INFOCOM WKSHPS), pp. 310–315. IEEE (2012)
5. Quan, W., Xu, C., Guan, J., Zhang, H.: Scalable name lookup with adaptive prefix bloom filter for named data networking. IEEE Commun. Lett. **18**, 102–105 (2014)
6. Herlocker, J.L., Konstan, J.A., Terveen, L.G., Riedl, J.T.: Evaluating collaborative filtering recommender systems. ACM Trans. Inf. Syst. (TOIS) **22**, 5–53 (2004)
7. Din, I.U., Hassan, S., Khan, M.K., Guizani, M., Ghazali, O., Habbal, A.: Caching in information-centric networking: strategies, challenges, and future research directions. IEEE Commun. Surv. Tutorials **20**, 1443–1474 (2018)
8. Wang, Y., Li, Z., Tyson, G., Uhlig, S.: Design and evaluation of the optimal cache allocation for content-centric networking. IEEE Trans. Comput. **65**, 95–107 (2016)
9. Pacifici, V., Dán, G.: Coordinated selfish distributed caching for peering content-centric networks. IEEE/ACM Trans. Netw. **24**, 1–12 (2016)
10. Duan, J., Wang, X., Xu, S.Z., Liu, Y.N., Xu, C., Zhao, G.F.: Cache scheme based on pre-fetch operation in ICN. Plos One **11**, e0158260 (2016)
11. Wang, S., Bi, J., Wu, J., Vasilakos, A.V.: CPHR: in-network caching for information-centric networking with partitioning and hash-routing. IEEE/ACM Trans. Netw. **24**, 1 (2015)
12. Breslau, L., Cao, P., Fan, L., Phillips, G., Shenker, S.: Web caching and Zipf-like distributions: evidence and implications. Proc. IEEE INFOCOM **1**, 126–134 (1999)
13. Gu, Y., Chen, L., Tang, K.M.: A load balancing method under zipf-like requests distribution in DHT-based P2P network systems. In: 2009 International Conference on Web Information Systems and Mining, WISM 2009, pp. 656–660 (2009)

14. Mangili, M., Martignon, F., Capone, A.: Performance analysis of content-centric and content-delivery networks with evolving object popularity. Comput. Netw. **94**, 80–98 (2015)
15. Afanasyev, A., Moiseenko, I., Zhang, L.: ndnSIM: NDN simulator for NS-3. University of California, Los Angeles, Technical report 4 (2012)
16. networking Index, C.V.: Forecast and methodology, 2016–2021, White Paper. San Jose, CA, USA 1 (2016)

Author Index

Printed in the United States
By Bookmasters